GREY FRIARS IN OXFORD

THE
GREY FRIARS IN OXFORD

PART I

A HISTORY OF THE CONVENT

PART II

BIOGRAPHICAL NOTICES OF THE FRIARS

TOGETHER WITH

APPENDICES OF ORIGINAL DOCUMENTS

BY

ANDREW G. LITTLE, M.A.

BALLIOL COLLEGE, OXFORD

WIPF & STOCK · Eugene, Oregon

Wipf and Stock Publishers
199 W 8th Ave, Suite 3
Eugene, OR 97401

The Friars in Oxford
Part I: A History of the Convent
Part II: Biographical Notices of the Friars,
 Together with Appendices of Original Documents
By Little, Andrew G.
ISBN 13: 978-1-62032-866-8
Publication date 1/4/2013
Previously published by Clarendon Press, 1892

PREFACE.

THE object of this work is to give an account of the outward life of the Franciscans. This might be fairly taken to include the whole activity of the friars with the exception of their contribution to scholastic philosophy; for that clearly forms a subject by itself. But even with this limitation the account here given of the Franciscans' work does not pretend to be complete. The documents which remain to us do not by any means cover the whole of the active life of the Franciscans. While for the thirteenth century and the Dissolution the records are fairly numerous, the materials for the intervening period are very scanty. Thus any attempt at a chronological narrative was out of the question. And the almost total absence of all Franciscan records (properly so called) in England, has proved an effectual bar to any completeness of treatment at all. The arrangement here adopted, both in the choice of subjects and in the relative prominence given to each of them, is due simply to the exigencies of the available materials relating to the Oxford Convent. The topographical information derived from records and other sources has been neither full enough nor accurate enough to enable me to supply a map or plan of the property and buildings of the Grey Friars.

A few words will be necessary to explain the plan pursued in Part II. An endeavour has been made to collect the names of all the Grey Friars who lived in the Convent at Oxford or who studied in the University: the list, if complete, would have included all the names which were, or ought to have been, entered in the 'Buttery-books' or 'Admission-books' of the house. To show how far short of this aim the result falls, it is only necessary to point out that the names of friars actually included in Part II number little more than three hundred: and the connexion of some of these with Oxford is doubtful. The bibliographies, appended to the biographical notices, are intended to include all the extant works of each friar, but not all the MSS. nor all the editions of each work. Occasionally works are added which have not been identified, but of whose previous existence there is sufficient evidence. For this part of the book I have used, besides the well-known mediaeval bibliographies, a number of catalogues of manuscripts; a list of these is given below, with the object of showing not so much what has been done, as what has been left undone.

Among unpublished sources, the most valuable have been various collections in the Public Record Office, especially the Patent, Close, and Liberate Rolls; the Registers of Congregation (Reg. Aa, G 6, H 7, I 8), the records of the Chancellor's Court (Acta Curiae Cancellarii Ꝙ, Ꝗ, EEE, or Ᏸ), and Brian Twyne's collections, in the Oxford University Archives. Further, I have had occasion to consult the Oxford City Archives, some of the old registers of wills at Somerset House, and various manuscripts in the British Museum, Lambeth Palace, and Gray's Inn; the Bodleian and several College libraries at Oxford; the University (or Public) Library and several College libraries at Cambridge; the library of Sir Thomas Phillipps at Thirlestaine House, Cheltenham; the National Library at Paris, and the Municipal Library at Assisi. I have had no opportunity of examining the episcopal registers of the diocese of Lincoln, extracts from which, however, are contained in Twyne's transcripts.

The Index, so far as it deals with the names of persons and places, will, I hope, be found complete, with the following limitations. The authorities quoted, either in the text or in the notes, the places where the manuscripts cited were written, or were formerly or are now kept, or where the editions referred to were printed, are not mentioned in the Index, unless there is some particular reason for including them. So far as it deals with subjects, the Index is meant to be supplementary to the Table of Contents. The writings of the friars are not classified in the Index, except those which come under the headings *Aristotle*, *Bible*, *Evangelical Poverty* and *Sentences*.

Finally, I wish to express my thanks to those who have given me aid, namely, to the Rev. W. G. D. Fletcher, Vicar of St. Michael's, Shrewsbury, author of 'The Black Friars in Oxford,' who generously placed a valuable collection of references at my disposal; to Mr. Falconer Madan for assistance and advice; to the Keeper of the University Archives and the Town Clerk of Oxford for allowing me free and repeated access to the documents under their respective charges; and to the authorities in the various offices and libraries in which I have worked, for their unfailing courtesy.

ANDREW G. LITTLE.

30 *November*, 1891.

CATALOGUES OF MANUSCRIPTS CONSULTED.

For the compilation of the bibliographies in Part II the following catalogues of manuscripts have been consulted [1]:—

Bernard de Montfaucon, Bibliotheca Bibliothecarum Manuscriptorum; Paris, 1739, 2 vols. fol.

Haenel, Catalogi Librorum Manuscriptorum qui in Bibliothecis Galliae, Helvetiae, Belgii, Britanniae M., Hispaniae, Lusitaniae, asservantur; Lipsiae, 1830.

Edward Bernard, Catalogi Librorum Manuscriptorum Angliae et Hiberniae in unum collecti; Oxon., 1697, 2 vols., fol. Vol. I, Bodleian; Oxford Colleges; Cambridge Colleges and Public (University) Library. Vol. II, Cathedral and other libraries in England; Irish libraries.

Catalogues of the following collections in the British Museum:—Royal MSS. 1734, 4to (Casley); Sloane and Birch, 1782, 2 vols. 4to (Ayscough); Cotton, 1802, fol.; Harley, 1808-1812, 4 vols., fol.; Lansdowne, 2 parts, 1819, fol.; Arundel and Burney, 1834-40, fol.; Additional MSS. from A.D. 1783-1887.

A Catalogue of the Archiepiscopal MSS. in the Library at Lambeth Palace, by H. J. Todd; 1812, fol.

Ancient MSS. in Gray's Inn Library, 1869.

Catalogues of the following collections in the Bodleian:—Laudian MSS., 1858-1885; Canonician MSS., 1854; Tanner MSS., 1860; Rawlinson, 1862-1878; Digby, 1883; Catalogue of the Ashmolean MSS., 1845-1866.

Catalogus Codicum Manuscriptorum qui in Collegiis Aulisque Oxoniensibus hodie adservantur (Coxe); Oxon., 1852, 2 vols., 4to.

A Catalogue of the Manuscripts preserved in the Library of the University of Cambridge, edited for the Syndics of the University Press; Cambridge, 1856, &c., 6 vols., 8vo.

Nasmith, Catalogue of the Parker MSS. in Corpus Christi College, Cambridge; 1787, 4to.

Catalogue of MSS. in the library of Gonville and Caius, by J. J. Smith; 1849, 4to.

Catalogus Manuscriptorum Bibliothecae Regiae Parisiensis; Paris, 1739—1744, 4 vols., fol.

---

[1] A few others have been used occasionally, such as the Phillipps catalogue (1837), and Ulysse Robert's *Inventaire sommaire.*

CATALOGUES OF MANUSCRIPTS CONSULTED.

Inventaire des Manuscrits conservés à la Bibliothèque Impériale sous les Nos. 8823-18613, du Fonds Latin et faisant suite à la série dont le Catalogue a été publié en 1744 par Léopold Delisle; Paris, 1863, &c., 8vo.

Inventaire des MSS. de la Bibliothèque Nationale, Fonds de Cluni, par L. Delisle.

Catalogue général des Manuscrits des Bibliothèques Publiques des Départements; Paris, 1849-1885, 7 vols., 4to.

Catalogue général des Manuscrits des Bibliothèques Publiques de France; (a) Paris: (1) Bibliothèque Mazarine, by A. Molinier, 3 vols. 8vo.; (2) Bibliothèque de l'Arsenal, by H. Martin, 1885, &c. (vols. 1 and 2 contain the Latin MSS.). (β) Départements, vols. 1-12, 1886-1889.

Catalogue des Manuscrits de la Bibliothèque Publique de Bruges (P. J. Laude), Bruges, 1859, 8vo.

Catalogus Codicum Manuscriptorum Bibliothecae Regiae Monacensis, Cod. Lat. vols. 1 and 2[1]; Monachii 1868-1874.

Katalog der Handschriften der königl. öffentlichen Bibliothek zu Dresden; Leipzig, 1882-3, 2 vols., 8vo.

Tabulae Codicum Manuscriptorum praeter Graecos et Orientales in Bibliotheca Palatina Vindobonensi asservatorum; Vienna, 1864-1875, 7 vols., 8vo. (Codices 1-14,000).

Catalogus Codicum Latinorum Bibliothecae Mediceae Laurentianae (Bandini), 1774, 5 vols., folio.

Bibliotheca Leopoldina Laurentiana (Bandini); Florence, 1791, 3 vols., folio.

Bibliotheca Manuscripta ad S. Marci Venetiarum (Valentinelli); Venet. 1868-1873, 6 vols., 8vo.

Bibliotheca Apostolica Vaticana, Codices Palatini Latini, tom. I, codices 1-921; 1886.

Bibliothecae Patavinae Manuscriptae publicae et privatae opera Jacobi Philippi Tomasini; Utini, 1639, 4to. (Tomasin).

Bibliothecae Venetae Manuscriptae publicae et privatae opera Jacobi Philippi Tomasini; Utini, 1650, 4to. (Tomasin).

[1] I have not seen Part 3 of Vol. 2 (Codices 15029-21405), which is missing in the British Museum.

ABBREVIATIONS AND EDITIONS USED.

Anal. Franc. = Analacta Franciscana, sive chronica aliaque varia documenta ad historiam Fratrum Minorum spectantia, edita a Patribus Collegii S. Bonaventurae, Quaracchi, 1885-7, 2 vols.
Archiv f. L. u. K. Gesch. = Archiv für Literatur- und Kirchengeschichte des Mittelalters, herausgegeben von H. Denifle und F. Ehrle.
Bale, Script. = Illustrium Majoris Britanniae Scriptorum ... Summarium, 1559, 2 vols.
B. of Pisa = Bartholomew of Pisa, Liber Conformitatum, ed. Milan, 1510.
Bernard = Catalogi Librorum MSS. Angliae et Hiberniae, Oxon., 1697.
Burnet, Reformation = History of the Reformation of the Church of England, Oxford, 1829.
Foxe = The Acts and Monuments of John Foxe, edited by Cattley, 1841.
Hist. Litt. = Histoire Littéraire de la France (by the Benedictines of St. Maur, and the Members of the Institute), 1733-1873.
Lyte = Maxwell Lyte, History of the University of Oxford, 1886.
Montfaucon = B. Montfaucon, Bibliotheca Bibliothecarum MSS., &c.
P. C. C. = Prerogative Court of Canterbury, Wills proved in the, now at Somerset House.
Q. R. Misc. = Queen's Remembrancer, Miscellaneous Accounts, now in the Public Record Office.
Q. R. Wardrobe = Queen's Remembrancer, Wardrobe Accounts, now in the Public Record Office.
R. O. = Public Record Office.
R. S. = Rolls Series, or Chronicles and Memorials of Great Britain and Ireland during the Middle Ages, published under the direction of the Master of the Rolls.
Tomasin = Bibliotheca Patavinae MSS., and Bibliothecae Venetae MSS. &c. (see above).
Wadding = L. Wadding, Annales Minorum, Romae, 1731, &c.
Wadding, Script. = L. Wadding, Scriptores Ordinis Minorum, Romae, 1806.
Wadding, Sup. ad Script. = Supplementum et castigatio ad Scriptores trium Ordinum S. Francisci a Waddingo aliisve descriptos... opus posthumum Fr. Jo. Hyacinthi Sbaraleae, Romae, 1806.
Wood-Clark = Survey of the Antiquities of the City of Oxford, by Anthony Wood, edited by Andrew Clark, 1889-1890. [The MS. from which this edition is printed is often referred to in the following pages, namely 'Wood MS. F. 29 a' in the Bodleian.]

TABLE OF CONTENTS.

PART I.

HISTORY OF THE CONVENT.

CHAPTER I.

EARLY YEARS.

	PAGE
Arrival and first settlement of the Franciscan Friars at Oxford	1
Their early poverty and cheerfulness	3
Oxford Friars as peacemakers and Crusaders	7
Relations to the University and to the earliest Colleges	8
Their strict observance of the Rule	10

CHAPTER II.

PROPERTY AND BUILDINGS.

	PAGE
First settlement of the Friars was within the City Wall	12
They acquire the houses of William, son of Richard de Wileford (1229), and Robert, son of Robert Oen	13
Increase of the *area* in 1244–1245	14
Grants from the King, Thomas de Valeynes, and others	15
The island in the Thames, 1245	16
Messuage of Laurence Wych, Mayor of Oxford, 1246	17
Friars of the Sack settle in Oxford	17
Their property granted to the Minorites by Boniface VIII, Clement V, and Edward II, 1310	18
Grants from various persons, 1310	19
Inquisitiones ad quod Damnum, concerning properties belonging to Richard Cary and John Culvard, 1319	19
Grants by Walter Morton (1321) and John de Grey de Rotherfield (1337)	20
To what classes did the donors belong?	20
Buildings of the Grey Friars, absence of information about	21
Original houses and chapel	21
School built by Agnellus	21
The stricter Friars oppose the tendency to build	22
Building of the new Church of St. Francis	22
Its site and appearance	23

xii   *TABLE OF CONTENTS.*

	PAGE
William of Worcester's description of it	24
Monuments and tombs in the Church	24
Grave of Roger Bacon	26
Cloisters, Chapter-house, Refectory, and other buildings	27
Conduit and Gates	28

CHAPTER III.
FRANCISCAN SCHOOLS AT OXFORD.

Learning necessary to the Friars	29
The first readers or lectors to the Franciscans at Oxford	30
Nature of the office of lector, as understood by Grostete and Adam Marsh	31
The lector and his *socius*	33
Later lectors were ordinary Regent Masters in Theology	34
Appointment to the office of lector	34
Special regulations concerning the lectors	36
System of instruction in theology recommended by Grostete	36
Lectures by the Friars	37
Controversy with the University about theological degrees in 1253	38
Controversy between the University and the Dominicans	39
Study of Arts (philosophy) before Theology, insisted on by the University	41
Roger Bacon on the need for some preliminary training for the Friars	42
Extortion of graces by external influence; 'wax-doctors'	42
Career of a student Minorite	43
On the numbers of Friars sent to Oxford	43
Course of study before 'opposition'	44
'Opposition' and 'Responsion'	45
The degree of Bachelor of Divinity	46
Exercises before 'Inception'	47
'Vesperies' and Inception	48
Questions disputed on these occasions in the thirteenth century	49
How far were the statutable requirements as to the period of study really carried out?	49
Expenses at Inception	50
Necessary Regency	52
Conditions on which dispensations were granted	52
Maintenance of Franciscan students at the University	53
What proportion took degrees	54
Relative numbers of the various Religious Orders at Oxford	54

CHAPTER IV.
BOOKS AND LIBRARIES.

Absence of privacy in a Franciscan Friary	55
Books of individual Friars	56
The two libraries, and their contents	57
Grostete's bequest of books	57

TABLE OF CONTENTS.

	PAGE
Extant MSS. formerly in the Franciscan Convent	59
Alleged illegal detention of books by the Friars in 1330	60
Richard Fitz-ralph's statements	60
Richard of Bury, on the libraries of Mendicant Friars	61
Dispersion of the books of the Oxford Franciscans	61
Leland's description of the library in his time	62

CHAPTER V.

PLACE OF OXFORD IN THE FRANCISCAN ORGANIZATION.

Learned Friars as practical workers among the people	63
Their Sermons	64
Educational organization throughout the country	64
Relations of the Franciscan School at Oxford to the other Franciscan Schools of Europe	66
English Franciscans teach in foreign Universities	67
Oxford as the head convent of a *custodia*	68
Provincial Chapters held at Oxford	69

CHAPTER VI.

RIVALRY BETWEEN THE ORDERS: ATTACKS ON THE FRIARS.

Rivalry between the Friars Preachers and Minors: proselytism	71
Politics and Philosophy	72
Peckham and the Oxford Friars	73
Evangelical Poverty	75
Contrast between theory and practice	78
Attack on the Friars by Richard Fitz-ralph	79
Charge of stealing children	79
Wiclif's early relations to the Friars	81
His attack on them in his later years	82
Charges of gross immorality made not by Wiclif, but by his followers	83
The University and the Friars; summary of events in 1382	84
Unpopularity of the Friars in the fifteenth century	85
Foreign Minorites expelled from Oxford	86
Conspiracies against Henry IV; part taken by the Oxford Franciscans	87
Relations between the Conventual and Observant Franciscans	87

CHAPTER VII.

ILLUSTRATIONS OF THE FRIARS' MANNER OF LIFE AND MEANS OF LIVELIHOOD: BENEFACTORS.

On the loss of Franciscan Records	89
Mendicancy as a means of livelihood	91
Procurators and limitors	92
Career of Friar Brian Sandon, legal *syndicus* of the Oxford Friary in the sixteenth century	93

xiv   *TABLE OF CONTENTS.*

	PAGE
Charges of immorality against the Friars	94
Their worldly manner of life before the Dissolution	96
Poverty of the Convent	97
Sources of income	97
Annual grants from the King and others	97
Frequency of bequests to the Friars	100
List of benefactors	102
Some other sources of income	110
Classes from which the Friars were drawn	111
Motives which led men to enter the Order	111

CHAPTER VIII.

The Dissolution.

Attitude of the Grey Friars towards the Reformation in its intellectual, religious, and political aspects	112
The Royal Divorce	114
Visitation of Oxford University in 1535	116
Suppression of the Friaries in 1538	116
Condition of the Grey Friary	117
Expulsion of the Friars; their subsequent history; Simon Ludford	119
Houses and site of the Grey Friars	120
Dr. London tries to secure the land for the town	121
Lease and sale of the property	121
Notes on its subsequent history	123
Total destruction of the buildings	124

PART II.

Biographical and Bibliographical Notices of Individual Friars.

CHAPTER I.

Custodians and Wardens 125–133

CHAPTER II.

Lectors or Regent Masters of the Franciscans 134–175

CHAPTER III.

Franciscans who studied in the Convent at Oxford, or had some other connexion with the Town or the University 176–294

APPENDICES OF ORIGINAL DOCUMENTS.

A. Documents relating to the acquisition of land property by the Grey Friars.

		PAGE
1.	Grant of a house by William, son of Richard de Wileford	295
2.	Grant of a house by Robert, son of Robert Oen, 1236	296
3.	Royal license to enclose their possessions and throw down part of the old City Wall, 1244	296
4.	Island in the Thames acquired by Henry III, 1245	297
5.	Grant of the same island to the Friars, 1245	297
6.	Grant of two messuages by Thomas de Valeynes, 1245	298
7.	Grant of a messuage by Laurence Wych, Mayor of Oxford, 1246	299
8.	License to enclose their new possessions; the City Wall to be repaired, 1248	299
9.	Royal grants to the Friars of the Sack, 1262, 1265	300
10.	Grants to the Friars Minors from various persons, 1310	301
11.	Property of the Friars of the Sack conferred on the Friars Minors, 1310	301
12.	Re-grant of the same property to them, 1319	302
13.	Inquiry held at Oxford in 1319 as to the advisability of allowing John Culvard to grant a parcel of ground to the Friars Minors	303
14.	Grant of a parcel of ground by John de Grey de Rotherfield	305

B. Miscellaneous Documents.

1.	Food for the Friars Minors and others, 1244	307
2.	Adam Marsh as royal *nuncius*, 1247	307
3.	For the same, 1257	308
4.	The Church of the Minorites used as a Sanctuary, 1284–5	308
5.	Royal grant of 50 marcs, 1289	308
6.	Decree of the General Chapter at Paris, 1292	309
7.	Royal grant of 50 marcs, 1323	309
8.	'Receptor Denariorum' of the Grey Friars, 1341	310
9.	Goods and chattels of Friar John Welle, S.T.P., 1378	311
10.	Expulsion of foreign Minorites, 1388	312
11.	William Woodford; confirmation of his privileges by Boniface IX, 1396	312
12.	Appointment of a lecturer to the Convent at Hereford, c. 1400	313
13.	Decree of the General Chapter at Florence, 1467	314
14.	Recovery of debt from a Sheriff, 1488	315
15.	Documents relating to the lease of a garden at the Grey Friars to Richard Leke, 1513–1514	316
16.	Extracts from the Will of Richard Leke, 1526	318
17.	An ex-warden called to account, 1529	318

C. Controversy between the Friars Preachers and Friars Minors at Oxford, 1269 320

D. Supplications and Graces from the Registers of Congregation.

John David, $145\frac{0}{1}$, $145\frac{4}{5}$ 336
John Sunday, $145\frac{3}{4}$ 336
Richard Ednam, 1462, 1463 336
Walter Goodfeld, 1506–1510 337
John Thornall, 1525 338
Thomas Kirkham, 1527 338

INDEX 341

CORRIGENDA.

P. 6, *n.* 5, *for* tempora, *read* temporalem.

P. 33. There was no house of Grey Friars at Evesham. Simon de Montfort was buried by the monks of Evesham (*see* Rishanger). The *Miracula Symonis de Montfort*, however, bears evident traces of Franciscan influence.

P. 49, *n.* 3, *for* Church, Quarterly Review, *read* Church Quarterly Review.

P. 54, *l.* 11, *for* because, *read* became.

P. 56, *n.* 5 *for* quos, *read* quas.

THE GREY FRIARS IN OXFORD.

PART I.

HISTORY OF THE CONVENT, A.D. 1224–1538.

CHAPTER I.

EARLY YEARS.

Arrival of the Franciscans at Oxford.—Their early Poverty, and Cheerfulness.—Oxford Friars as Peacemakers, and Crusaders.—Relations to the University, and to the first Colleges.—Their strict observance of the Rule.

THE Franciscans first arrived in England in 1224[1]. On Tuesday, the 10th of September in that year (to follow the account of Friar Thomas Eccleston, the earliest historian of the Order in this country),

---

[1] Chronicle of Thomas Eccleston, 'De Adventu Minorum,' Mon. Francisc. I, p. 5: 'A.D. MCCXXIV . . . feria tertia post festum nativitatis Beatae Virginis.' This date has been disputed. Wadding (Annales Minorum, I, 303, 362) places the arrival in 1219. The arguments in favour of this view are, (1) that St. Francis appointed Agnellus minister of England in 1219; (2) the statement of Matthew Paris *sub anno* 1243, that the friars 'built their first houses in England scarcely twenty-four years ago' (Chron. Majora, IV, 279). But the evidence in favour of (1) is not conclusive; the letter of St. Francis to Agnellus (Wadding. I, 303; Collectanea Anglo-Minoritica, pp. 5–6) is undated. The contention however seems to be supported by a passage in Eccleston (Mon. Franc. I, 10), identifying the 32nd year after the settlement of the friars in England with the second year of the ministry of Peter of Tewkesbury, who according to the received chronology became minister in 1250 (more probably 1251). From this one might conjecture that the establishment of the English province was officially dated from 1219. But the fragment in Mon. Franc. II, and another MS. of Eccleston in the Phillipps Library at Thirlestaine House, No. 3119, fol. 71–80 (a MS. unknown to either of the editors of the Monumenta Franciscana), read here (fol. 73) '*quinto anno administrationis Fratris Petri*,' instead of '*secundo anno*,' and this is probably the correct version. As to argument (2), Paris probably wrote his account (of 1243) a few years later than 1243, and dated accordingly; again the passage refers to Dominicans as well as Franciscans. The evidence in favour of the later date is much stronger. Besides Eccleston, the best authority, we have the statement of the author of the Lanercost Chronicle, himself a Friar Minor: '*Quo et anno (1224) post festum natalis Virginis gloriosae applicuerunt fratres Minorum in An-*

a company of nine friars, four of them clerks and five laymen, landed at Dover, under the leadership of Agnellus of Pisa, the first Provincial Minister. After staying two days at Canterbury, four of them proceeded to London; and at the end of the month, two of these, Friar Richard of Ingeworth and Friar Richard of Devon, set out for Oxford. It is perhaps to this place that the well-known story told by Bartholomew of Pisa properly belongs[1]. As they neared Oxford they were stopped by the floods, and finding themselves at nightfall 'in a vast wood which lies between Bath and Oxford,' they sought refuge ' for the love of God' at a grange belonging to the monks of Abingdon, ' lest they should perish from hunger or the wild beasts in the forest.' The prior, judging them to be jesters[2], had them turned out; but a young monk, when the rest had gone to bed, put them into a hayloft and brought them bread and beer. That night he had a dream. The prior and his brethren were summoned before the judgment-seat of Christ; and

' there came a certain poor man, humble and despised, in the habit of those poor friars, and he cried with a loud voice: "O most impartial Judge, the blood of my brethren, which hath been shed this night, crieth unto Thee. The guardians of this place have refused them meat and lodging, although they have left all for Thy sake, and were now coming here to seek those souls which Thou hast redeemed with Thy blood; they would not, in fact, have refused as much to jesters and mummers." . . . . Then the Judge commanded them to be hanged on the elm that stood in that cloister.'

In the morning the young monk found his companions dead, and became an early convert to the order of St. Francis.

On their arrival at Oxford, the two friars were received with great kindness by the Dominicans.

'They ate in their refectory, and slept in their dormitory, like conventuals for eight days[3].'

They then hired a house in the parish of St. Ebbe from Robert le Mercer[4]. Alms sufficient for the purpose were probably already forth-

gliam' (p. 30). This may be derived from Eccleston, but on the next page is a statement which is certainly independent of him: 'Eodem anno (1224) venerunt primo fratres Minores in Angliam, in festo beati Bartholomaei apostoli' (Aug. 24). Cf. 'Annals of Worcester,' *sub anno* 1224 (Ann. Monast. IV, 416).

[1] If so, Bartholomew's narrative is inaccurate; according to him the adventure happened to Agnellus and his four companions (among whom was Albert of Pisa) on their way from Canterbury to Oxford. But Bartholomew is not remarkable for accuracy. Liber Conformitatum, fol. 79 (ed. Milan, 1510).

[2] 'Joculatores et non dei servos.' Wood's version of the story differs in several points from that of Bartholomew of Pisa, from whom it is professedly derived. (MS. F 29a, f. 175 a, quoted in Dugdale, VI, pt. 3, p. 1524.)

[3] Eccleston, Mon. Franc. I, p. 9.

[4] Ibid. p. 17.

EARLY YEARS.

coming, as the new Order did not have to wait long for recognition. Though they only occupied this house till the following summer[1], they were there joined by 'many honest bachelors and many eminent men'[2]; and it may have been owing to this increase in their numbers that they left their first abode in 1225 and hired a house with ground attached from Richard the Miller[3]. It is significant of the rapid growth of opinion in their favour that Richard

'within a year conferred the land and house on the community of the town for the use of the Friars Minors.'

Enthusiasm and self-sacrifice were the powerful agents which ensured success and favour to the early Franciscans, and many are the stories of their primitive poverty and its effects; and if the convent at Oxford was not especially distinguished like that at Cambridge by '*paucilitas pecuniae*,' or like that at York by '*zelus paupertatis*[4],' the Oxford Minorites, during the time of Agnellus at least, departed but little from the ideal of their founder[5], and lived the life of the poor among whom they ministered. The pangs of hunger were not unknown in the convent; and on one occasion the friars were in debt to the amount of ten marks for food[6]. Their first houses were mean and small—too small for the numbers who flocked to their Order[7]; and the infirmary was

'so low that the height of the walls did not much exceed the height of a man[8].'

When at length they built their church, the brethren worked with their own hands, and a bishop and an abbat who had assumed the coarse habit of the friars are said to have 'carried water and sand and stones for the building of the place[9].'

---

[1] Eccleston, Mon. Franc. I, p. 9.
[2] Ibid. p. 17: 'In qua intraverunt ordinem multi probi baccalaurei et multi nobiles.' Cf. ib. p. 61.
[3] Ibid. Denifle ('Die Universitäten des Mittelalters,' I, 245) puts the arrival of the Franciscans at Oxford in the year 1225, the hiring of their first house in 1226, of their second 'at the beginning of the thirties,' on the authority of Eccleston.
[4] Mon. Franc. I, p. 27.
[5] See, e.g., Wadding, Ann. Minorum, I, 10, 302, &c.; Mon. Franc. I, 567 seq., &c.
[6] Lanercost Chron. 130: 'Tenemur creditoribus in urbe decem marcarum solutionem.' The whole account of the circumstances is very curious, but too long to quote here. The date is about 1280.
[7] Mon. Franc. I, p. 17: 'Fuit autem area ipsa brevis et arcta nimis'; p. 34, 'Usque ad tempus Fratris Alberti domus ipsa diversorio careret.' Wiclif attributed the great plague in a large measure to the friars herding together in cities; Trialogus, IV, cap. 32 (p. 370).
[8] Mon. Franc. I, 34.
[9] Barth. of Pisa, Liber Conform. f. 79 b: cf. Mon. Franc. I, 16, 542. The prelates referred to are Ralph Maidstone and John Reading.

The appearance of the Minorites was no less humble than their buildings. Their habits of coarse gray or brown cloth[1], tied round the waist with a cord, often worn and patched, as Grostete loved to see them, hardly[2] distinguished them from 'simple rustics[3].' In the convent at Oxford, pillows were forbidden, and the use of shoes was permitted only to the infirm or old, and that by special licence[4]. We hear of two of the brethren returning from a chapter held at Oxford at Christmas time singing as they

'picked their way along the rugged path over the frozen mud and rigid snow, whilst the blood lay in the track of their naked feet, without their being conscious of it[5].'

Even from the robbers and murderers who infested the woods near Oxford the Barefoot Friars were safe[6].

'Three things,' said Friar Albert, Minister General, ' tended to the exaltation of the Order,—bare feet, coarse garments, and the rejecting of money[7]'; and the Oxford Franciscans were as zealous in the last respect as in the other two. The Archdeacon of Northampton sent a bag of money to Friar Adam Marsh, and when the latter refused it, the messenger threw it down in the cell and left it:—

'Wherefore,' writes Adam to the Archdeacon, ' the bearer of these presents has at the instance of the brethren taken the said money, just as it was, sealed with your seal, to your lordship, to dispose of according to your pleasure[8].'

The evidence of the Public Records, containing scattered notices of grants from the Crown, is striking on this point, and the poverty of these early Franciscans can hardly be better illustrated than by the

---

[1] Liberate Roll, 23 Hen. III, m. 6: 'ccc ulnas panni grisei' for Minorites; and m. 3: 'Lij ulnas Russetti ad tunicas faciendas ad opus xiij fratrum Minorum de Rading', scilicet ulnam de precio xi denariorum ad plus.' Four ells went to make a habit. The quality was not the best, the ordinary price for russet—i.e. undyed cloth of black wool —was 1s. 4d. an ell; Rogers, 'Hist. of Prices,' II, 536-7. At the end of the fourteenth century Friar W. Woodford says that the friars were better clothed in England than elsewhere owing to the abundance of wool in this country; Twyne, MS. XXI, 501.

[2] Mon. Franc. I, 66: cf. ibid. 55.

[3] Or 'idiots,' as Brewer translates (Mon. Franc. I, 631) the original ' omnes fatui nativi,' Lanerc. Chron. 30. Cf. Mon. Franc. I, 564 (Testament of St. Francis): 'We were content to be taken as ideotis and foolys of euery man.'

[4] Mon. Franc. I, 28; other convents were less scrupulous; see Liberate Roll, 23 Hen. III, m. 6—an order to buy 'ccc paria sotularium' at the Winchester fair for the Friars Minors there.

[5] Lanerc. Chron. 31.

[6] Eccleston, p. 38.

[7] Ibid. p. 52.

[8] Mon. Franc. I, p. 195; the date of the letter is probably about 1250. On the other hand, Adam seems to have accepted 'small coins' (quatrinos) by way of alms from a friend; ibid. p. 229.

means taken to relieve it. During the long reign of Henry III, the Patent, Close, and Liberate Rolls contain only three grants of money to the house of the Minorites at Oxford, and all of them are due to exceptional circumstances. They are, ten marks for the support of a provincial chapter in 1238, 60s. for their houses in 1245 in lieu of six oaks which the king had before given them, and three marks for the fabric of their church in 1246[1]. The alms to the house at Oxford are almost wholly in kind, and consist chiefly of supplies of firewood from the royal forests round Oxford. The earliest recorded instance of royal bounty was a grant of thirteen oaks in 'Brehull' (Brill) forest for fuel on the 9th Jan. 1231[2]. A few years later they received fifteen cartloads of brushwood from Shotover forest[3], and in 1237 fifteen oaks in Wychwood Forest 'to make charcoal[4].' Similar notices occur almost every year—sometimes twice a year—throughout the reign of Henry III[5]. In 1240 the keepers of the wines at Southampton were ordered to deliver one cask of Gascon wine, of the king's bounty, to the Friars Minors at Oxford 'to celebrate masses[6].' In 1248 the Sheriff of Oxford received orders to

'give to the Friars Minors of Oxford one cask of wine of the six casks which he took into the king's hand of the wine of those who lately killed a clerk in the town of Oxford[7].'

But a fortnight later the king repented of his generosity and assigned the same cask to one of his numerous relatives[8]. Of more interest, as showing that the friars were really classed with the poor of the town, is a royal brief of the 12th of Dec. 1244 to the bailiffs of Oxford, bidding them

'give of the ferm of their town to Friar Roger, King's Almoner, on

---

[1] Liberate Rolls, 22 Hen. III, m. 15; 29 Hen. III, m. 5; 30 Hen. III, m. 17. In making this statement, I have relied on the MS. Calendar of the Patent Rolls for Hen. III (3 vols. folio, containing some 4000 pages), the MS. Cal. of the Close Rolls from the 12th year of Hen. III to the end of his reign (10 vols. folio), both in the Public Record Office; the Liberate Rolls of the same reign, for which no Calendar exists, I have gone through; after Hen. III these latter become less full and interesting.

[2] Close, 15 Hen. III, m. 11.
[3] Ibid. 20 Hen. III, m. 11.
[4] Ibid. 21 Hen. III, m. 1.
[5] See *Close Rolls* for the following years of Hen. III: 15 (m. 2), 17 (m. 15, and 10), 18 (m. 28, and 18), 19 (pt. 1, m. 8), 20 (m. 6), 22 (m. 16), 26 (m. 4), 30 (m. 17, and 2), 36 (m. 24), 39 (m. 15), 40 (m. 8), 41 (m. 10), 42 (m. 6), 43 (m. 9), 45 (m. 21), 47 (m. 8), 48 (m. 6), 50 (m. 3), 51 (m. 4), 54 (m. 8), 55 (m. 1). *Liberate Rolls*, 17 (m. 6), 22 (m. 9), 23 (m. 10), 24 (m. 13), 26 (m. 5), 30 (m. 16), 32 (m. 4), 36 (m. 14).

[6] Close, 24 Hen. III, m. 11 (*Custodibus vinorum Suhant*) and Liberate, 24 Hen. III, m. 12 (*Custodibus vinorum R. Oxon*).

[7] Close, 32 Hen. III, m. 9; cf. Lyte, p. 43.

[8] Ibid. m. 8.

Wednesday the morrow of the feast of St. Lucy the Virgin, ten marks, to feed a thousand paupers and the Friars Preachers and Minors of Oxford, for the soul of the Lady Empress sister of the King, on the day of her anniversary[1].'

With all their poverty and holiness they were singularly free from that form of piety which consists in wearing a sad countenance and appearing unto men to fast. We hear indeed of strict silence, of constant prayer, of vigils that lasted the whole night[2].

'Yet,' continues Eccleston[3], 'the brethren were so full of fun among themselves, that a mute could hardly refrain from laughter at the sight. So when the young friars of Oxford laughed too frequently, it was enjoined on one that as often as he laughed he should be punished. Now it happened that, when he had received no punishments in one day, and yet could not restrain himself from laughing, he had a vision one night, that the whole convent stood as usual in the choir, and the friars were beginning to laugh as usual, and behold the crucifix which stood at the door of the choir turned towards them as though alive, and said: "They are the sons of Corah who in the hour of chanting laugh and sleep." . . . . On hearing this dream, the friars were frightened and behaved without very noticeable laughter[4].'

Grostete said to a Friar Preacher, 'Three things are necessary to temporal health—to eat, sleep, and be merry[5].' Excessive austerity was discountenanced by the authorities of the Oxford convent. Friar Albert of Pisa, who was himself 'always cheerful and merry in the society of the brethren[6],' compelled Friar Eustace de Merc, contrary to custom, to eat fish, saying that the Order lost many good persons through their indiscretion[7]. Grostete again

'commanded a melancholy friar to drink a cup full of the best wine as a penance, and when he had drunk it up, though most unwillingly, he said to him, "Dear brother, if you often performed a penance like that, you would have a better ordered conscience[8]."'

The friars lovingly treasured up the great bishop's puns and jokes and

---

[1] Liberate, 29 Hen. III, m. 14. Isabella, sister of Henry III, married Frederick II in 1235, and died Dec. 1, 1241.

[2] Mon. Franc. I, p. 19.

[3] Ibid. p. 20.

[4] Barth. of Pisa has changed this story from a dream into a reality and added miraculous incidents: 'Crux lignea . . . fragore stupendo se vertit ad fratres; . . . et plures eorum mortui sunt in brevi.' Liber Conform. f. 80.

[5] 'Tria sunt necessaria ad salutem tempora, cibus, somnus et jocus.' Mon. Franc. I, 64.

[6] Ibid. p. 56.

[7] Ibid. p. 58; he added, that, 'when he was with St. Francis, the saint compelled him to double every day what he had been accustomed to eat.' Cf. Mrs. Oliphant's 'Francis of Assisi,' p. 85.

[8] Mon. Franc. I. 64-5.

EARLY YEARS.

wise sayings[1], and were always ready to tell or appreciate a good story. From first to last they had the reputation of being excellent company[2], and were welcome at the tables of the rich or well-to-do[3]. They were allowed by the rule to

'eat of all manner of meats which be set before them[4],'

a practice which occasionally caused some scandal[5]; and Friar Albert of Pisa ordered them to keep silence in the house of hosts, except among the preachers and friars of other provinces[6]. Like St. Francis himself, the Oxford friars often possessed the courtesy and charm of manner which is born of sympathy[7]; and it was perhaps to this quality that their employment as diplomatic agents is to be attributed. Thus Agnellus was chosen in 1233 to negotiate with the rebellious Earl Marshall and try to bring him back to his allegiance[8]. Adam Marsh was on more than one occasion sent beyond the sea as royal emissary[9], and Edward I sent Oxford Minorites to treat for peace with his enemies[10]. But to the mediaeval mind, there was a cause more sacred than that of peace or good government; and the Franciscans would not have had their great influence—would not have become leaders of men throughout the world—had they not shared the one ideal, which still even in the thirteenth century appealed to every class in every country of Europe. The Crusades attracted the scholastic philosopher no less than the baron with his sins to expiate, or the serf with his liberty to win. It was partly to increase his influence as a missionary[11] that Adam of Oxford, one of the first 'masters' who joined the Order[12], took the vows of St. Francis;

---

[1] Mon. Franc. pp. 64-66.
[2] Bishop Gardiner's description of a Cambridge Augustinian, quoted by Dixon,'Church of England,' II, p.253,n.: he 'was of a merry scoffing wit, friarlike; and as a good fellow in company was beloved of many.'
[3] In 1398, e.g. 'On Sunday came two Friars Minors to dine with the fellows (of New College), also the farmer of Heyford.' Boase, Oxford, p. 78.
[4] Mon. Franc. II, 68. St. Francis used to sprinkle sumptuous fare with ashes; Oliphant, p. 86.
[5] See story of the warden who on the day that he preached to the people cracked jokes with a monk after dinner in the presence of a secular; Mon. Franc. I, 53. 'Oxoniæ' in the same paragraph should be 'Exoniæ': Serlo was Dean of Exeter, 1225-1231, Le Neve, Fasti.
[6] Mon. Franc. I, p. 55.
[7] Cf. ibid. p. 6, W. of Esseby; and p. 23, Haymo of Faversham; 'fuit enim ita gratiosus et eloquens, ut etiam adversantibus Ordini gratus et acceptus existeret.'
[8] Ibid. 52; M. Paris, Chron. Majora, IV, p. 257. Cf. ibid. p. 251; Annals of Tewkesbury (Ann. Monast. I, 92).
[9] Liberate Rolls, 31 Hen. III, m. 4, 42 Hen. III, m. 3.
[10] See Part II, W. of Gainsborough, H. of Hertepol.
[11] Grosseteste, Epistolæ, p. 21.
[12] Mon. Franc. I, p. 15.

against the wishes of his brethren in England, who hoped to keep among them so famous and learned a convert, and who indeed feared lest he should come under heretical influences[1], he went to Gregory IX, and at his own prayer was sent by the Pope to preach to the Saracens[2]. When Prince Edward went to the Holy Land in 1270, he took with him as preacher Friar William de Hedley, the lecturer and regent master of the Friars Minors at Oxford[3]. Hedley died before the army reached Acre; but these learned friars did not flinch when summoned to meet a sterner fate. In 1289 Tripoli was captured by the Saracens: an English friar led the last charge of the despairing Christians, carrying aloft the cross till his arms were hewn off;

'the above-mentioned friar,' continues the chronicler, 'who by his example provoked very many to martyrdom, had been no small space of time warden of the Oxford Convent[4].'

The friars of both Orders soon took a leading part in the affairs of the University. As Bishop of Lincoln[5], Grostete continued to exercise a kind of paternal authority over the University[6], and his high character and long connexion with Oxford gave him an influence which was denied to his successors. It was natural that this influence should be reflected on the Franciscans, whom he had taken under his especial care and among whom was his 'true friend and faithful counsellor[7]' Adam Marsh. The latter was specially summoned to the congregation to hear and advise on the answer sent by Grostete to some petitions of the University[8], and we find him interceding with the Bishop on behalf of the Chancellor, Radulph of Sempringham[9]. One of the most important stages in the constitutional development of the University is marked by the charter of Henry III in 1244, which constituted a special tribunal for the scholars, and formed the basis of the Chancellor's jurisdiction. On the 11th of May of the same year, a deed of acknowledgment was executed at Reading and signed and sealed on behalf of the University by the Prior of the Friars Preachers, the Minister of the Friars Minors,

---

[1] Grosseteste, Ep. p. 21, 'nec moveat aliquem,' &c. : a striking illustration of the fascination of Eastern heresies at the time.
[2] Ibid. and Mon. Franc. p. 16.
[3] Lanerc. Chron. p. 81.
[4] Ibid. p. 128. His name is not given.
[5] It will of course be remembered that in the early thirteenth century the Chancellor of the University was in fact as in legal theory the delegate of the bishop of the diocese.
[6] Lyte, p. 38.
[7] Grosseteste, Ep. Letter XX.
[8] Mon. Franc. I, p. 99.
[9] Ibid. p. 100–101.

the Chancellor of the University, the Archdeacons of Lincoln and Cornwall, and Friar Robert Bacon[1]. Edward I in 1275[2] appointed 'Friars John de Pecham and Oliver de Encourt' royal commissioners to decide a suit between Master Robert de Flemengvill[3] and a Jewess named Countess, the wife of Isaac Pulet, which had long been pending in the Chancellor's court; this however was not to be treated as a precedent to the prejudice of the Chancellor's jurisdiction.

It is probable that the example afforded by the houses of student friars was not lost on the founders of the early colleges. We know that Walter de Merton was a friend of Adam Marsh[4], and a benefactor of the friars, but it would be dangerous to attempt to trace any direct Franciscan influence in the statutes of his college[5]. There is however no doubt about the connexion of the Franciscans with the foundation of Balliol College. Sir John de Balliol died in 1269 without having established his house for poor scholars on a permanent footing. His widow Devorguila first gave them a definite organisation in 1282. According to an old tradition[6], she was induced to take this step by her Franciscan confessor, Friar Richard de Slikeburne. It is clear that the latter was her most trusted and energetic agent in carrying out the plan. Devorguila urges him by all means in his power to promote the perpetuation of 'our house of Balliol[7],' and the executors of Sir John de Balliol assigned certain moneys to the scholars of the house

'with the consent of Devorguila and at the advice of Friar Richard de Slikeburne[8].'

Nor was the connexion merely a transitory one. The statutes of

[1] Pat. 28 Hen. III, m. 7 *in dorso*. Mr. M. Lyte (p. 42, note 3) makes the date of the king's writ May 10, 1246, of the deed of acknowledgment, May 11, 28 Hen. III (i. e. 1244); and adds to the confusion about the Bacons by reading John instead of Robert.

[2] Close, 3 Edward I, m. 18 *in dorso*, writ to the Chancellor. Oliver was Prior of the Dominicans about this time, Wood–Clark, II, 337.

[3] fflemēguiłł.

[4] Mon. Franc. I, 405.

[5] The *Wardens* of the college and of the convent were liable to be deposed on the petition of the members of their respective houses, and the system of 'exhibitions' for scholars must have resembled that in vogue among the friars at the University. But the year of probation, the observance of silence, the 'scrutinies' or chapters, were common to all monastic institutions.

[6] Twyne, MS. XXII, 103 c; Cap. 32 of Woodford's *Defensorium*: 'It is manifest that one friar minor confessor to a venerable Lady moved her to make that Hall at Oxford which is called the Hall of Balliol.'

[7] Letter of Devorguila to Friar R. de Slikeburne, dated 1284, in College Archives: Hist. MSS. Com. Rep. IV, p. 442.

[8] Ibid. pp. 442, 444, four deeds from 1285 to 1287.

1282[1] are addressed to Friar Hugh de Hertilpoll and Master William de Menyl, who are evidently the two 'proctors' mentioned in the document. To the proctors (who did not belong to the house but were in the position of permanent visitors) was entrusted the institution of the principal after his election by the scholars, together with a general supervision over the economy of the college. They alone could expel a refractory scholar, and they were constituted the special guardians of the poorer students[2]. Nothing remains to show how long the first proctors held their office, or how their successors were appointed. It is probable however that the office was intended to be a perpetual one[3]—not a temporary expedient to be called into existence from time to time,—and further that one of the proctors was always a Franciscan. Two other documents bearing on the subject are known to exist. In 1325 a doubt had arisen whether the members of the college might study any science except the liberal arts; it was declared to be unlawful to do so and contrary to the mind of the founder, and was consequently forbidden

'by Masters Robert of Leicester, of the Order of Friars Minors, S.T.P., and Nicholas de Tyngewick, M.D. and S.T.B., then *Magistri Extranei* of the said House[4].'

The second document[5] is a letter dated 1433 addressed to the Bishop of London by

'Richard Roderham, S.T.P., and John Feckyngtone of the order of Minorites in Oxford, Rectors of Balliol College.'

The Rectors having, 'according to the exigency of the office which we discharge upon the rule of the said college and the observance of the statutes thereof,' inquired into the working of the first statute, decided, with the consent of the majority of the house, that it was prejudicial to the college, and asked the Bishop to consent to the modification of it[6].

It will be readily admitted that in the thirteenth century the Oxford Franciscans deserved their high reputation. It is true, that frequent

---

[1] Preserved in the College Archives: printed in Savage's *Balliofergus*, p. 15 seq.

[2] The care taken of the poorer students, of their feelings no less than of their purses, is particularly interesting in connexion with the Franciscans.

[3] Cf. the Statutes of 1282, which are to be observed 'in the time of all proctors whatsoever;' the Statutes of Sir Philip Somerville (1340) mention ' *duo Magistri extrinseci*' (Statutes of the Oxford Colleges, Vol. I, Balliol, p. x).

[4] History MSS. Com. *ut supra*.

[5] Ibid. (abstract).

[6] The clause to which objection was made was, that if the Master obtained a benefice of the annual value of £10, '*ipso facto noverit (ab officio) se amotum.*' Statutes of the Oxford Colleges, Vol. I, Balliol, p. xx.

complaints are heard of the decline of the Order[1]—that many relaxations had been introduced into the Rule. But these were not demanded by the English province. When Haymo was General, orders were issued by the Chapter that friars should be elected in each province to note any points in the Rule which seemed to require revision, and send them to the Minister General. Eccleston[2] gives the names of three friars elected for this purpose in England—Adam Marsh, the foremost of the Oxford friars; Peter of Tewkesbury, Custodian of Oxford; and Henry de Burford.

'Having marked some articles, the said friars sent them to the General, in a schedule without a seal, beseeching him, by the sprinkling of the blood of Jesus Christ, to let the Rule stand, as it was handed down by St. Francis, at the dictation of the Holy Spirit[3].'

[1] E. g. in 1257, Bonaventura investigates the causes '*cur splendor nostri Ordinis quodammodo obscuratur.*' Wadding, IV, 58; cf. M. Paris, Chron. Majora, IV, 279–8; Mon. Franc. I, 361–3, 408, &c.

[2] Mon. Franc. I, 48.

[3] Ibid. 48. Friar Albert of Pisa, who, as Minister of seven provinces and General of the Order, had no lack of experience, 'died commending the English above all nations in zeal for their Order' (ibid.). Cf. ibid. p. 68, John of Parma, General, frequently exclaimed when in England: 'Would that such a province had been set in the midst of the world to be for an example to all the churches!'

CHAPTER II.

PROPERTY AND BUILDINGS.

First Settlement inside the City Wall.—Acquisition of the houses of W. de Wileford (1229) and Robert Oen (1236).—Increase of the *area* in 1244-1245.—Grants from the King, Thomas Valeynes, and others.—Island in the Thames, 1245.—Messuage of Laurence Wych, 1247.—Friars of the Penitence of Jesus Christ.—Their property in Oxford granted to the Minorites by Clement V, and by Edward II, 1310.—Grants from various persons, 1310.—Richard Cary and John Culvard, 1319.—Walter Morton, 1321.—To what classes did the donors belong?

Absence of information about the buildings at the Grey Friars.—Original houses and chapel.—School built by Agnellus.—The stricter friars oppose the tendency to build, without success.—Building of the new church, 1246, &c.—Its site and appearance.—William of Worcester's description of it.—Richard Plantagenet, Earl of Cornwall, buried there, 1272.—Other tombs in the church, especially that of Agnellus.—Grave of Roger Bacon.—Cloisters, Chapter House, Refectory, and other conventual buildings.—Conduit and Gates.

For about a hundred years from the date of their settlement in Oxford, the Friars Minors were gradually acquiring property. We have seen that after a short sojourn in the house of Robert le Mercer, the house of Richard le Muliner became their first permanent abode. The position of the former cannot be at all definitely ascertained; it was in the parish of St. Ebbe's[1], probably near the church and within the city walls[2]. Wood places it between the church and the Watergate. But he is certainly wrong in the position he ascribes to the second house, namely,

'without the towne wall, and about a stone's cast from their first hired house[3].'

---

[1] Eccleston, p. 9.

[2] An entry in 'Placita Corone 25 Hen. III, Oxon. M. ⁴⁄₅} 2, m. 1 b,' may lead to the identification of the site; it is an agreement between Robert, Master of the Hospital of St. John, outside the East Gate, and Roger Noyf, 'de escambio unius messuagii cum pertinenciis in Oxonia ... videlicet quod idem Rogerus dedit et concessit predicto magistro in escambium predicti messuagii magnam domum ipsius Rogeri lapideam, que est ante ecclesiam Sce Abbe cum pertinenciis. Et quod situm est inter terram Roberti le Mercer et terram quam tenet de Abbate de Abendon.'

[3] Wood–Clark, II, 358.

The house of Richard the Miller was undoubtedly between the wall and Freren Street (Church Street). In 1244 Henry III allowed the friars to throw down the wall of the town in order to 'connect their new place with the old one[1].' Even apart from the fact that the Mercer's house did not at this time belong to them, it is obvious that the houses which they acquired in 1224 and 1225 would not in 1244 be distinguished as the 'old place' and the 'new place' respectively. The 'new place' refers to lands which came into their possession about the time of this grant, and of which Wood knew nothing, while the Miller's house formed part of the 'old place.'

In fact, several years elapsed before the friars obtained property outside the city wall, their first efforts being directed to secure the land between the wall and Freren Street. It was not long before their cramped area was enlarged. In the Mayoralty of John Pady[2] the citizens of Oxford subscribed[3] forty-three marks sterling to buy from William, son of Richard de Wileford, his house in St. Ebbe's, with all its appurtenances, 'to house the Friars Minors for ever,' the said good men of Oxford giving to William one pound of cummin annually in lieu of all service[4]. The next grant of which we find mention seems also to have been an act of municipal, rather than of private, charity. In 1236[5] Robert, son of Robert Oen, had given them a house adjoining their land, on condition that he,

'having been a free tenant of the prior and brethren of St. John of Jerusalem in England in the aforesaid place,'

should have the same privilege attaching to his new house in the parish of St. Michael at the North Gate. This house of Robert Oen's in St. Ebbe's was one of the 'mural mansions,' on the occupiers of which the duty of repairing the city wall fell[6]. The obligation, however, was now, when the house came into the hands of the friars, willingly undertaken with the King's assent by the Mayor and good men of Oxford.

Under the ministry of Agnellus any tendency to accumulate property was rigorously suppressed[7], nor does his successor Albert

---

[1] Pat. 29 Hen. III, m. 9; cf. Pat. 32 Hen. III, m. 10; both printed in Mon. Franc. I, 616-7, and in Appx. A.

[2] Mayor in 1227, 1228, 1229, Wood-Peshall, 'City of Oxford,' p. 355.

[3] 'Ex elemosyna collecta.'

[4] The original of this grant is in the Oxford City Archives, marked '17.' See Appx. A. 1.

[5] Close Roll, 20 Henry III, m. 9: printed in Appx. A. 2.

[6] Parker, 'Early History of Oxford,' p. 342: extracts from Domesday Book.

[7] Eccleston, Mon. Franc. I, p. 34: 'Tantus erat zelator paupertatis, ut vix permitteret vel ampliari areas vel domos aedificari, nisi secundum quod exigit inevitabilis necessitas.'

appear to have been more lenient [1]. But under Haymo of Faversham (1238-9) and William of Nottingham (1239-51) a different spirit began to prevail, and one far less in accordance with the original idea of the Order. Haymo

'preferred that the friars should have ample areas and should cultivate them, that they might have the fruits of the earth at home, rather than beg them from others [2].'

And under William of Nottingham the Oxford house gained a large increase of territory [3].

It was in 1245 that this took place, and a remarkably full series of records relating to the event is still extant. By a deed dated 22nd December, 1244 [4], the King gave the Friars Minors permission,

'for the greater quiet and security of their habitation, to inclose the street which extends under the wall of Oxford, from the gate which is called Watergate [5] in the parish of St. Ebbe, up to the postern in the same wall towards the Castle; so that a crenellated wall like the rest of the wall of the same town be made round the foresaid dwelling, beginning from the west side of Watergate, and reaching southwards as far as the bank of the Thames, and extending along the bank westwards as far as the fee of the Abbat of Bec in the parish of St. Bodhoc, and then turning again northwards till it joins the old wall of the foresaid borough on the east side of the small postern;'

and they were further allowed to throw down the old wall which stretched across their habitation. But in 1248 [6] this grant, as far as it related to the wall, was cancelled; the old wall was to be repaired, and the proposed new wall was not mentioned.

There can be little doubt that in December, 1244, the friars did not possess the land which they were then allowed to enclose; it is indeed very doubtful whether they had any property south of the wall. Possibly they may have acquired already the place which they held in 1278,

'of the gift of Agnes widow of Guydo [7], which the said Agnes had by

---

[1] Mon. Franc. I, p. 55.

[2] Ibid. pp. 34-5.

[3] 'Sufficienter ampliatus,' Eccleston, p. 35 : cf. Wykes, Ann. Monast. IV, 93 (1245): 'The Friars Minors at Oxford, hitherto confined to narrow limits, began to widen their boundaries and build new houses.'

[4] Pat. 29 Hen. III, m. 9; Appx. A. 3.

[5] i. e. Littlegate, not South Gate (as Boase, p. 68), which was in St. Aldate's parish.

[6] Pat. 32 Hen. III, m. 10; Appx. A. 8; Mon. Franc. I, p. 617. It was this grant of 1248 that remained in force: see confirmation of it in Pat. 18 Edw. III, m. 19.

[7] It is uncertain who this Guydo was: a 'Guido filius Roberti' was Sheriff of Oxfordshire in 1249: Liberate, 33 Hen. III, m. 9; and two sons of Guydo had a lawsuit in 13 Ed. I: Placita Corone, Oxon. M. $\frac{5}{2}$} 1, m. 5 d, &c.

descent from her predecessors, and they pay thence to Walter Goldsmith one pound of cummin [1].'

The value was then unknown, nor is the position specified [2]. It was, however, no doubt situated in the suburb of St. Ebbe's parish. Two other plots of ground are mentioned in the same document as belonging to the Friars: of one of these (that granted by Thomas Walonges) we have accurate information, and shall mention it in its due place. Of the other nothing further is known than that they held it by grant from Master Richard de Mepham. But the grant was probably of later date than 1244. Richard was Archdeacon of Oxford in 1263, became Dean of Lincoln in 1273, and probably died in 1274 at the council of Lyons [3].

But the royal grant in the Patent Roll of 29 Henry III is explained by the fact that the Franciscans, or rather their benefactors, were already negotiating for the transfer of a large part of the property there described, if not of the whole of it.

In February, 1245, Thomas Valeynes, or Valoignes (or Walonges as he is called in the Inquisition of 6 & 7 Edward I), carried into effect a plan for the benefit of the Friars Minors which it must have taken long to bring to a successful conclusion [4]. It consisted in begging or buying out a number of holders of property in the south-west 'suburb of Oxford,' and granting in one case at least tenements in another part of the town as compensation. Thus, in exchange for two messuages with their appurtenances on the south-west of the town, Symon son of Benedict and Leticia

---

[1] Brian Twyne, MS. XXII, 131: 'Ex Rotulo general, Inquis. com. et villáe Oxon. per hundred capta A° 6° et 7° Ed¹ I¹ per sacramentum inhabitantium.' Wood (MS. F 29 a, f. 176 a) copies this from B. Twyne: Peshall and Stevens, copying carelessly from Wood, speak of it as an 'Inquisition taken in the year 1221.'

[2] Wood (MS. F 29 a, f. 176) after quoting this Inquisition, goes on : ' besides wch they had another large piece of ground of ye said Agnes since knowne (as now tis) as part of paradise garden;' and he adds in the margin: 'another piece of land they had wch was Tho. Fullonis or Alice Foliot ut in Carta 66 ex lib. S. frid. v. AV. p. 19,' i. e. Wood MS. C 2, p. 19 in Bodleian—a charter from Stephen to St. Frideswide's, confirming the property of the Priory in and outside Oxford : among the tenants is Tho. Fullo, who pays 5s. for land in St. Ebbe's; the charter is No. 66 in the Corpus Copy of St. Frideswide's Chartulary, and dates in its present form from c. 33 Hen. III. (I am indebted to Rev. S. R. Wigram for this reference.) This tenement of Tho. Fullo was very likely near St. Budhoc's, where William and Rad. Fullo had land. See B. Twyne, MS. III, 8–9, Charter of R. de Hokenorton, in 'libro Osneyensi;' and XXII, 286.

[3] Le Neve, Fasti.

[4] Feet of Fines, Oxon., 29 Hen. III, m. 40–44, and 46. For first grant see Appx. A. 6.

his wife, received one messuage outside the North Gate, together with a building then held by Hugh Marshall,

'which same messuage and building were formerly held by Benedictus le Mercer father of the foresaid Symon.'

One messuage with appurtenances was acquired from John Costard and Margery his wife, two from Warin of Dorchester and Juliana his wife, one from William 'le Barbeur' and Alice his wife, one from Henry 'le Teler' and Alice his wife, and a little later[1] one curtilage 'in the suburb of Oxford in the parish of St. Budoc,' from John Aylmer and Christiana his wife. All these eight tenements Thomas de Valeynes, 'at the petition' of the former owners, assigned

'to the increase of the area in which the Friars Minors dwelling at Oxford are lodged in pure and perpetual alms free and quit of all secular service and exaction for ever;'

and we may reasonably conclude that they filled the space from the City Wall on the north to Trill Mill Stream on the south, and from Littlegate Street on the east to a line drawn from the 'fee of the Abbat of Bec in the parish of St. Bodhoc's' to the West Gate on the west[2].

Shortly after this, namely, on the 22nd of April, 1245[3], Henry III gave the Friars, to enlarge their new area,

'our island in the Thames, which we have bought from Henry son of Henry Simeon,'

with permission to make a bridge over the arm of the river dividing it from their houses, and to enclose it with a wall, or in any other way which would insure 'the security of their houses and the tran-

---

[1] Feet of Fines, Oxon., 29 Hen. III, m. 46, 'a die S. Johannis Baptiste In tres septimanas.'

[2] This fee of the Abbat of Bec belonged to Steventon Priory, Berks, a cell of the Abbey of Bec in Normandy. Dugdale, Vol. VI, p. 1044.

[3] Pat. 29 Hen. III, m. 6 (Appx. A. 5). Whether the island lay to the south or west of the Friary is not certain. Wood says: 'This piece of ground I suppose was part of (or at least near adjoyning to) paradise garden though wee now see it all one intire piece; for in ancient time it was divided in severall Islands, as may be seene by the arches under a ruinous stone wall to this day remaining in the same garden.' MS. F 29 a, f. 176 (Wood-Clark, II, 396). Cf. Clark's edition of Wood's 'City of Oxford,' Vol. I, p. 578, note 37. 'Paradise Garden formerly belonging to the Grey Fryers. There was a rivulet running sometimes through and made it two. The arch is in the wall to this day that parts Paradise and the Grey Friers. It came from the east part of Paradice and soe ran downe as far as the brewhouse which brewhous was formerly part of Paradise.' Elsewhere he says: 'Which isle was situated on the south side of their habitation (the rivulet called Trill Mill running between) and on the west side of the habitation of the Black Fryers; and is now belonging to Sir William Morton, Kt.' &c.; ibid, Vol. II, p. 361; cf. p. 396, n. 2, where he identifies this piece of land (i. e. the ground between the present New St., Norfolk St., and Friars St.) with the friars' *grove* as distinguished from the island.

quillity of their religion.' On the same day[1] the King ordered the Barons of the Exchequer to deduct from the fine of sixty marks,

'imposed on Henry son of Henry Simeonis because he was implicated in[2] the murder of a scholar of Oxford, twenty-five marcs, for twenty-five marcs which we owed to Henry Simeonis his father for an island in the Thames at Oxford which we have bought from him, and which said marcs he begged should be reckoned to his son in the aforesaid fine.'

The next grant is dated the 27th of November, 1246[3]. The King announces that he has handed over to the friars, for the enlargement of their premises, the whole messuage, with its appurtenances, which Laurence Wych (or Wyth), Mayor of Oxford, committed to him for that purpose, desiring them to enclose the same as they shall see fit :

'and the Sheriff of Oxfordshire was commanded to receive the messuage in place of the King for the use of the said friars.'

It is quite uncertain where this land lay, and whether Wych granted it in his public or private capacity.

For the next fifty years, excepting the undated grants of Richard Mepham and Agnes widow of Guydo, which probably belong to this period, there is no record of a gift of land to the Minorites. On the east they had already reached the permanent limit of their property[4], and the Friars of the Penitence of Jesus Christ settled about the year 1260 on the ground lying to the west. This formed the parish of St. Budoc. In 1262[5] the King allowed these friars to build an oratory here; in 1265[6] he granted them, as patron, the church of St. Budoc (which adjoined their premises, and which, owing to the removal or death of the parishioners, was too impoverished to support one chaplain), 'to make thence a chapel for themselves.' With the church they acquired[7]

'the cemetery and the houses standing in the same and belonging to the said church,'

---

[1] Liberate Roll, 29 Hen. III, m. 9 (Appx. A. 4).

[2] Or 'present at'—*interfuit*.

[3] Pat. 31 Hen. III, m. 8 (see Appx. A. 7).

[4] Ingram in his Memorials of Oxford, published 1837 (Vol. III, under St. Ebbe's), says, speaking of Pat. 29 Hen. III, m. 9: 'A great part of the wall built according to this agreement is still in existence, or at least an old wall on the same site.' Some of it, on the west side of Littlegate Street, south of Charles Street, is still to be seen. Cf. Wood, MS. 29 a, fol. 179 : 'On the east side of it (i.e. Minorites' property) . . . was the way leading from Watergate to Preachers Bridge.'

[5] Pat. 46 Hen. III, m. 11 (May 7).

[6] Pat. 49 Hen. III, m. 24 (Feb. 5).

[7] Ibid. (Feb. 8), Appx. A. 9.

with the proviso that the cemetery should always be treated as consecrated[1] ground. The value of the church was 20s. a year[2].

At the Council of Lyons in 1274 the Friars of the Penitence of Jesus Christ, or 'Friars of the Sack,' were forbidden to admit new members[3], and the Order came to an end when the old members died out. The Minorites and their friends therefore applied themselves to secure the property. As early as 1296 Boniface VIII wrote to the Bishop of Lincoln, ordering him[4] to allow the Friars Minors to take possession of the house or area of the Friars of the Sack, whenever the five remaining brethren should die or transfer themselves to other religious Orders. At the court of Clement V, the first of the Avignon popes, the claims of the Minorites were urged by John of Britanny, Earl of Richmond; and Clement issued a Bull in their favour, dated the 27th of May, 1309 (VI Kal. Jun. A° IV)[5].

'In a petition exhibited to us on your part,' runs the document, 'it is contained that owing to the narrowness of your place at Oxford, you and other friars, there flocking together to the University from divers parts of the world in great multitude, do endure manifold wants and various inconveniences. Since therefore the place of the Friars of the Penitence of Jesus Christ of the same place of Oxford adjoining your place, is shortly, as is believed, to be relinquished by the said Friars, to remain at the disposal of the Apostolic Seat, according to the tenor of the Constitution published by Pope Gregory X, our predecessor, in the Council of Lyons, it is humbly prayed us, that we deign to concede to you that place for the enlargement of your place aforesaid.'

This prayer the Pope goes on to grant 'of his special favour,' mentioning the earnest supplications of John of Britanny[6] on behalf of the friars.

The King, however, also had a claim to dispose of lands which his grandfather had granted, and which, in default of heirs or successors, legally escheated to the Crown. By Letters Patent dated the 28th of March, 1310[7], Edward II assigned to the Friars Minors the property which Henry III had previously given to the

---

[1] B. Twyne (MS. III, 13) seems to have been led astray by the word 'benedictum' into thinking there was a Benedictine church here.

[2] Placita Coronae, Oxon. 13 Edw. I, M. ½} 3, m. 55.

[3] Chronicles of Edw. I & II, Vol. I, p. 83 (R. S.).

[4] Wadding, V, p. 575, No. xxii *Ex parte dilectorum.* The date is VI Kal. Sept. An. 2.

[5] Wadding, Ann. Min. Vol. VI, p. 463.

[6] Wadding calls him 'Earl of Kichiemunda.'

[7] Pat. 3 Edw. II, m. 9 (Appx. A. 11).

PROPERTY AND BUILDINGS.

Penitentiary Friars, with the same stipulation as to the cemetery. The land is accurately described; it was contiguous to the place of the Friars Minors, in the suburb of Oxford, twenty and a half perches long from north to south, six perches wide at the south end, two and a half at the north, and four perches seven feet in the middle.

Letters Patent of the same day[1] confirmed the grant of four other parcels of ground to the Friars Minors: some of these may have been previously held by the Friars of the Sack. The 'plot of ground in Oxford,' five perches two feet from east to west, two perches and a half from north to south, conferred on the Minorites by John Wyz and Emma his wife, may have been within the walls, near the West Gate; the others were in the suburb. Henry Tyeys gave land measuring six perches by five, and lying between the site of St. Budoc's Church and the Thames (Trill Mill Stream); Richard le Lodere's land, measuring fourteen and a half perches five feet, by four perches and three feet, and stretching from the Thames to the above-mentioned place of Henry Tyeys, was included in the grant, as was a larger plot[2], measuring sixteen and a half perches from the Thames to the 'royal way,' and ten perches in breadth; which seems to have included the south part of Paradise Gardens[3].

All these places are described as adjoining the property of the Warden and Friars Minors of Oxford.

It was probably at the instance of the Crown and as a protest against the papal claims that the Minorites a few years later formally surrendered to the King the area which had belonged to the Penitentiaries, 'in its entirety as it came into their hands,' and received it back of the King's special favour in pure and perpetual alms[4].

One fragment of the Penitentiary Friars' property came into the hands of the Franciscans somewhat later. In October, 1319, an *Inquisitio ad quod Damnum*[5] was held in Oxford to decide whether Richard Cary could, without prejudice to the King or others, bestow on the Friars Minors a place in the suburb of Oxford, adjacent to

---

[1] Pat. Edw. II, m. 14 (Appx. A. 10).
[2] No donor's name occurs.
[3] This is probably the land which Wood refers to as having belonged to Thomas Fullo. The charter of Rob. Hokenorton to Osney mentions 'land which Will. Fullo held of Reginald de Sub Muro, juxta ecclesiam S. Budoci, Oxon., quae tendit a Regia Semita usque ad aquam Thamesis in profundum, et usque ad terram Radulfi Fullonis in latum, ex australi parte predicte Ecclesie.' B. Twyne, MS. III, 8–9.
[4] Pat. 12 Edw. II, m. 25 (6 March, 1319); Appx. A. 12.
[5] Inquis. a. q. D. 13 Edw. II, No. 31.

their property, and measuring five perches in length and five in breadth. The jurors declared that the grant would not be injurious to the King or others, and that Cary possessed sufficient property in the town to discharge all his civic duties. The place 'at the time when it was built' was worth 20s. a year, but now, owing to its ruinous condition, only 2s. Cary held it for a rent of 8s. a year of Johanna, wife of Walter of Wycombe, Agatha her sister, and John son of Alice, who was wife of Andrew Culvard, the heirs of Henry Owayn; they held it of the Prior of Steventon, paying 4d. a year in lieu of all services. The plot was therefore the fee of the Abbat of Bec mentioned above, and is probably the same as

'the place which the Friars of the Penitence bought of Walter Aurifaber, and they pay thence to the Prior of Steventon 2s.[1]'

A few months previously a similar inquisition [2] was held at Oxford, which resulted in an addition to the Minorite property on the east side within the wall. This was a plot of ground of the annual value of 2s., five perches by six, granted to them by John Culvard. The town, however, claimed the right,

'at all times when it shall be necessary, to have free entry and egress thence to restore, repair and defend the wall of the said town.'

In 1321 [3] Walter Morton obtained leave to grant in mortmain to the Franciscans a place with its appurtenances, measuring five perches by five, in the suburb of Oxford; and similar licence was given to John de Grey de Retherfeld [4] in 1337 to bestow on them a tenement, six perches by five, lying next their habitation on the east side within the town. This brings us to the end of the list of grants of landed property to the Oxford Minorites—a list which we may claim to be fairly complete. It is interesting to note from what classes the donors were drawn. Most of them were men of business—the leading tradesmen of the town [5]. Three of them, Laurence Wych, John Culvard, and Richard Cary, were at various times Mayors of Oxford,

---

[1] Inquis. Oxon. Capta 6 and 7 Edw. I; Brian Twyne, III, 8–9. Walter Aurifaber had a daughter named Agatha; ib. XXIV, 253.
[2] Inquis. a. q. D. 12 Edw. II, No. 47 (5 March, 18 May), Appx. A. 13; Pat. 13 Edw. II, m. 44 (8 July).
[3] Pat. 14 Edw. II, m. 10 (12 May).
[4] Pat. 11 Edw. III, pt. 2, m. 6 (19 Aug.), Appx. A. 14.
[5] Rob. le Mercer and others are commanded to help the Mayor, Peter son of Thorald, in building the city wall (Claus. 18 Hen. III, m. 23). Robert Owen and Ric. the Miller witness William of Wileford's deed, see App. The names are significant—the Mercer, the Miller, the Barber, the Tailor.

and the two latter represented the city in Parliament[1]. Richard Mepham belonged to the higher rank of ecclesiastics. Master Thomas de Valeynes seems to have been a person of some importance in Oxfordshire and the adjoining counties[2].

Buildings.

Of the buildings of the Friars Minors in Oxford we have disappointingly little information—with the exception of the boundary wall already mentioned there are no remains of their house now visible. Excavations might perhaps yield interesting results, but most of the ground is thickly built over, and the information derived from the records and other sources is rarely precise enough to enable us to identify with any certainty the sites of the various buildings.

For the first twenty years the Friary must have presented a very modest, not to say mean, appearance, and the brethren were probably contented to take the accommodation afforded by the houses, which were granted them, with little alteration. The infirmary built by Agnellus has already been noticed. After they had been nearly a year in Oxford, the friars built a small chapel[3]. In 1232, the King gave them

'thirty beams in the royal forest of Savernak for the fabric of their chapel which they are having built at Oxford,'

adding that

'if any one in the same bailiwick shall wish to give them timber, the bailiff shall permit them without hindrance to carry through the forest free of toll oaks to the number of thirty[4].'

Probably this refers to the original chapel. It had a choir where the brethren attended and celebrated divine service[5], and at, or over, the door of which stood a crucifix, or wooden cross[6]. It was here, in the choir before the altar, that Agnellus was buried in a 'leaden box,' as became the *zelator paupertatis*[7]. The chapel was pulled down when the new church was finished[8]. Under the auspices of Agnellus rose their first school, which was apparently the finest of

---

[1] Wood–Peshall, Ancient and Present State, &c., p. 355.

[2] One of this name was Commissioner of gaol delivery for Dorchester, Wycombe, Aylesbury, &c.: Pat. 54 Hen. III, m. 17 d, 12 d; and 55 Hen. III, m. 28 d.

[3] Eccleston, Mon. Franc. I, p. 9.

[4] Close Roll, 16 Hen. III, m. 9 (June 17).

[5] Eccleston, p. 20.

[6] Ibid.; and Barth. of Pisa, Lib. Conform. fol. 80.

[7] Eccleston, p. 54. Barth. of Pisa says, 'in capsa lignea,' fol. 80.

[8] Eccleston, ibid.

their early buildings[1]. Whether this was afterwards enlarged, or whether new schools were built on the same site or elsewhere, there is no longer any means of deciding.

These houses were situated within the wall, and it was not till the increase of the 'area' between 1240 and 1250 that building on a large scale was commenced between the wall and Trill Mill Stream[2]. The tendency to build was strenuously resisted by the stricter party among the friars—the party which upheld the early traditions of the Order. Eccleston relates how an Oxford friar appeared after death to the custodian and warned him that,

'if the friars were not damned for their excess in building, they would at any rate be severely punished[3].'

An obscure passage in a letter of Adam Marsh probably refers to the same tendency; even novices, he laments, are taught to neglect the things of the spirit

'for flesh and blood, for mud and walls, for wood and stone, for any kind of worldly gain[4].'

The opposition of the older generation was, however, unavailing, and a 'stately and magnificent[5]' convent began to rise. But of the new friary, too, there are but scanty notices. No English king bestowed on the house of Franciscans at Oxford that loving care which Henry III bestowed on the Minorite Church at Reading, or Edward II on the Dominican Church which rose over the tomb of his ill-fated favourite at Langley. From royal grants we learn that building was going on at the Grey Friars of Oxford in 1240, when ten oaks were given to them by the King for timber[6]. In 1245 (July 7th),

'the Sheriff of Berkshire was ordered to give to the Friars Minors of Oxford for the works of their houses sixty shillings instead of six oaks which the King gave them before[7];'

and a further grant of six oaks for timber in 1272 shows that the operations were of a protracted nature[8]. From similar sources we find that the Church, which was dedicated to St. Francis, was in

---

[1] Eccleston, p. 37, 'Scholam satis honestam.'
[2] Pat. 32 Hen. III, m. 10.
[3] Mon. Franc. I, 25.
[4] Ibid. 362: 'quasi carni et sanguini, quasi luto et lateribus, quasi lignis et lapidibus, quasi quibuscunque qualicunque compendiolo mundanis questibus totum dandum esset.'
[5] Wood, MS. F 29 a, f. 179 a.
[6] Claus. 24 Hen. III, m. 17 (Feb. 5); Liberate, 24 Hen. III, m. 19 (Feb. 7).
[7] Liberate, 29 Hen. III, m. 5.
[8] Claus. 56 Hen. III, m. 7.

process of erection in February, 1246[1], and February, 1248[2]. At the latter date the friars are again permitted to

'enclose the street which extends under the wall of Oxford from the Watergate . . . to the small postern in the wall near the Castle . . . We grant also that the north side of the chapel built and to be built in the aforesaid street may supply the interruption of the wall as far as it is to reach, the other breaches in the wall being fully repaired as before, except the small postern in the wall, through which the said friars can go and return from the new place where they now live, to the former place in which they used to live.

It would appear from this that the street was outside the wall. Mr. Parker, however, states positively that it was 'the inner road' which they were 'permitted to enclose[3]; in Wheeler's Garden, south-west of St. Ebbe's Churchyard, there used to be a line of old walling, running parallel to the city wall inside, and the space between these walls may have been the street in question[4]. It must be remembered, however, that the friars had already in 1244 acquired the road with the right to enclose it, and to throw down this section of the city wall. In 1248, therefore, we may well believe that little existed of the wall, which on the south side was never a very prominent feature. The church running due east and west would extend along and across the site of the wall, the west end being outside, the east end inside. From the south end of Paradise Place, where the wall juts out southwards for a few yards, to a point about the north end of King's Terrace, there have long been no signs of the city wall; and it is probably here that the Grey Friars' Church stood. The tradition is still preserved in the name Church Place. Of the appearance of the church we know little. The roof was tiled[5], like that of the Grey Friars' Church at Reading; it is probable the east end was flat, and there was no triforium[6]. Wood thinks that one of the eight towers which figured in the pageant at the inthronization of Warham in 1504,

---

[1] Liberate, 30 Hen. III, m. 16: 'Mandatum est Vicecomiti Oxonie quod de amerciamentis Itineris Roberti Passelewe et sociorum suorum Justiciariorum qui ultimo Itinerauerunt ad placita foreste in Comitatu suo faciat habere fratribus minoribus Oxonie iij Marcas et fratribus predicatoribus eiusdem ville iij ad fabricam ecclesie sue de dono Regis.'

[2] Pat. 32 Hen. III, m. 10.

[3] Early Hist. of Oxford, p. 298: his map of Oxford gives a street outside the wall.

[4] I am indebted to Mr. Parker for this information and suggestion.

[5] Cromwell Corresp., 2nd series, Vol. XXIII, fol. 709 b (Record Office).

[6] Cf. Walcott's 'Church and Conventual Arrangement,' on Friars' Churches, &c.

represented the tower of the Grey Friars[1]. William of Worcester has left a somewhat puzzling[2] description of the church in 1480[3].

'The length of the choir of the church of St. Francis at Oxford contains 68 steps. The length from the door (*valva*) of the choir to the west window contains 90 steps; so in the whole length it contains 150 (?) steps. The width of the nave of the said church on the east (*ab orienti parte*) contains with the aisle 28 steps. The length of the nave from the south side to the north door contains 40 steps only, and there are ten chapels in the said north nave of the church. The width of the north nave of the church contains 20 steps. The width of each chapel contains 6 steps, and so the width of the whole nave of the church with the ten chapels contains 26 steps. And each chapel contains in length 6 steps. And each glass window of the ten chapels contains three dayes (or lights) glazed.'

Reckoning William's 'steps' at half a yard each[4], and correcting his apparent mistake in addition, we find that the church measured seventy-nine yards from east to west, the choir containing thirty-four yards, and the nave forty-five. At its widest part the church measured twenty yards, ten yards of which were taken up by the north aisle. Hence the width of the nave properly so called, and of the choir, which in friars' churches is, where it exists, of the same width as the nave[5], was ten yards. The choir was aisleless, and the north aisle was probably the only one in the church: this, too, narrowed from ten yards to four towards the east end of the nave. In 1535 Friar Henry Standish, Bishop of St. Asaph, bequeathed £40 'for the building of an aisle joining to the church of the Grey friars, Oxon[6],' probably on the south side, but it is almost certain that this was never built.

The wider aisle must have extended nearly the whole length of the nave to allow space for the north door and the ten chapels, all of which were built on to the north wall. They would be in part sepulchral chantries, supported by noble families or gilds, often containing the image or shrine of some saint, while the shrine of the patron saint stood behind the high altar. They were presumably later additions, and whether the church in its original form attained

---

[1] Annals, 662.
[2] Stevens, 'Hist. of Abbeys,' &c., I, 137: 'This account appears to me very confuse and unintelligible.'
[3] Itinerarium, p. 296.
[4] Ibid. p. 83, 'Memorandum quod 24 steppys sive gressus mei faciunt 12 virgas . . . Item 50 virgae faciunt 85 gradus sive steppys mei:' and p. 281, 'quaelibet virga tres pedes,' &c.
[5] Walcott, as above.
[6] P.C.C. Regist. Hogen, qu. 26 (in Somerset House).

the proportions here described must remain doubtful. But there is no reason to suppose it was afterwards enlarged to any great extent. In the thirteenth century, benefactors, great and small, were willing and eager to help the friars to raise those splendid buildings which drew forth the fierce denunciations of later reformers; and though much of the church was doubtless built, like that at London, 'from good common alms[1],' there can be little question that the chief 'founder and benefactor' was the wealthy Richard Plantagenet, Earl of Cornwall, and King of the Romans[2]. It was in the choir of this church that his heart was buried[3]

'under a sumptuous pyramid of admirable workmanship[4].'

Here, too, five years later the remains of his third wife, Beatrice of Falkenstein, were interred, 'before the great altar[5];' and many other monuments of nobles and famous men must have given the interior of the church an imposing appearance. Among those buried here were several of the Golafres: the tomb of Sir John Golafre, who died at Quinton, Bucks, in 1379[6], was in the chancel; that of his younger brother, William, was probably in the same part of the church[7]. Sir John's illegitimate son, John Golafre, knight and lord of Langley, bequeathed his body to be buried next his father's, if he should die in England[8]; but

'at the time of his death (1396) he altered his will in that part in which he bequeathed his body to be buried in the chancel of the church of the Friars Minors at Oxford, and willed and also bequeathed his body to be buried in the Conventual Church of Westminster where our lord the King shall dispose[9].'

---

[1] Mon. Franc. I, 508, &c.

[2] Wood-Clark, II, 407. Adam Marsh was personally known to the Earl of Cornwall; in a letter to the Queen of England he mentions having been with him; Mon. Franc. I, 291: cf. ibid. 105-6, 400. A letter from Adam to Senchia, Richard's wife, is extant, ibid. p. 292. The following character of Richard is curious as being drawn probably by a Franciscan: 'Hic erga omnes mulieres cujuscunque professionis luxuriosissimus, thesaurorum collector cupidissimus et avidissimus, pauperum oppressor insolentissimus.' MS. Cott. Cleop. B xiii, f. 148: cf. Hardy, Descript. Catal. &c.

[3] He died 1270, according to Walsyngham, Ypodigma Neustriae, p. 165 (R. S.); 1272 according to Trivet, Ann. 279. The latter is probably correct: see Foedera, I, 489.

[4] J. Rouse, p. 199 (ed. Hearne). Rouse studied at Oxford, and died 1491.

[5] Chron. of Osney, 17 Oct. 1277: R. S. ed. p. 274.

[6] Wood, MS. F 29 a, fol. 179 b.

[7] Ibid.

[8] Regist. Arundel, I, fol. 155. Sir H. Nicolas reads Exon. instead of Oxon: p. 135.

[9] Ibid. fol. 155 b. The Golafre property at Fyfield now belongs to St. John's College; the President informs me that the College has no documents relating to the Golafre family.

William Lord Lovell, by a will dated 18 March, 145⅘, made provision

'to be buried at the Grayfreris of Oxenford in suche place as I have appoynted[1].'

The wills of less distinguished persons occasionally contain information as to the interior of the church. In 1430 Robert Keneyshame, Bedel of the University, willed to be buried in the Franciscan Church,

'in the midst between the two altars beneath the highest cross in the body of the church[2].'

James Hedyan, bachelor in both laws and principal of Eagle Hall, was buried in the nave[3]. Agnes, wife of Michael Norton, was in 1438 buried

'in the Conventual Church of the Friars Minors of Oxford before the image of the blessed Mary the Virgin of Pity[4].'

And in 1526 Richard Leke, 'late bruer of Oxford,' desired

'to be buried within the Graye ffreres in Oxford before the awter where the first masse is daily vsed to be saide[5].'

But more honoured than any of these was the 'fair stone sepulchre[6]' in which the body of Agnellus, the only Provincial Minister known to have been buried at Oxford, found its final resting place. For the shrine of Agnellus possessed all the fascination of miraculous association and miraculous power. When the friars, many years after his death, went in the night to remove the body from the original chapel before its demolition,

'they found the little leaden box in which it lay, together with the grave, full of the purest oil, but the body itself with the vestments uncorrupted and smelling most sweetly[7].'

Here, too, we are told, was the tomb of one greater than Agnellus; but if the statement of John Rouse, that Roger Bacon was buried among the Franciscans at Oxford, is anything more than a tradition, it was perhaps not in the church, but in the common burial place of the brethren of the convent, that the Warwick antiquary found his grave[8].

---

[1] Early Lincoln Wills (A. Gibbons, 1888), p. 186.
[2] B. Twyne, MS. XXIII, 478. He altered this part of his will in a codicil, and was buried in St. Ebbe's.
[3] Mun. Acad.: Anstey, p. 543.
[4] 'Coram ymagine beate Marie Virginis de pyte.' Oxford City Records, Old White Book, f. 90 a.
[5] P.C.C. Porch, fol. 9.
[6] Barth. of Pisa, fol. 80.
[7] Eccleston, 54.
[8] J. Rouse, Hist. p. 29: 'et modo in ordinis sui fratres Minores Oxon sepultum.'

PROPERTY AND BUILDINGS.

The cloisters, of which we find no mention till the dissolution, were no doubt situated on the south of the church, round 'Penson's Gardens.' Whether the friars were buried in the cloisters, the garth, the chapter-house, or 'the cemetery of the Friars Minors,' in which John Dongan was interred in 1464[1], or sometimes in one place, sometimes in another, is unknown. On the east of the cloisters would be the chapter-house[2]; over it, and joining the church, a dormitory[3]. On the south of the cloisters, opposite the church, stood the refectory. It is possible, but not probable, that the long narrow building stretching down towards Trill Mill Stream, which is marked in old maps of Oxford[4], was the refectory: Bridge Street marks the site. The library may have been on the west side of the cloisters, but no hint remains as to the building or its position, while the contents may be more appropriately treated elsewhere. The warden's house is equally unknown; he may perhaps merely have had rooms set apart in some one of the larger buildings[5], as was probably the case with the vice-warden[6]. From the Lanercost Chronicle we learn that in the thirteenth century the 'master of the schools' had a chamber of his own[7]; and Wiclif tells us that in his time

'Capped Friars, that beene called Maisters of Diuinitie, haue there chamber and service as Lords or Kings[8].'

Ample accommodation for guests was a marked feature in most religious houses, and there is no reason to suppose that the Oxford Franciscan Friary formed an exception to a custom which, while it excited some animosity against the apostles of poverty, tended to ensure the favour and secure the alms of the rich[9].

---

[1] Oxford Univ. Reg. A a a, fol. 213.

[2] First mention is in 1370: Anstey's Mun. Acad. 232-3.

[3] At Reading, the chapter-house and dormitory seem to have formed one building. Liberate Rolls, 23 Hen. III, m. 6, and 24 Hen. III, m. 1.

[4] Agas map of 1578, engraved by Neale 1728; Hollar's map, 1643.

[5] The warden at Reading occupied one of 'thre prety lodginges' at the Grey Friars; Cromwell Corresp., Vol. XXIII, f. 742.

[6] Cf. Inventory of the Grey Friars, Ipswich; Chapter House Bks. A $\frac{3}{11}$; 'owthe of the Vicewarden's Chamber.'

[7] P. 130.

[8] 'Two short treatises against the Begging Friars' (Oxf. 1608), p. 30; cf. Roy's Satire on Card. Wolsey, Harl. Misc., Vol. IX, p. 42, &c.

[9] See Pecock's Repressor, p. 543, on the objection that 'religiose monasteries (nameliche of the begging religiouns) han withinne her gatis and cloocis grete large wijde hi3e and stateli mansiouns for lordis and ladies ther yn to reste, abide, and dwelle;' and p. 548-50. Edward III stayed at the Grey Friars, York, in 1335 (Rymer, Foed., Vol. II, pt. ii, p. 909). In the Record Office (Excheq. Q. R. Wardrobe $\frac{24}{13}$) is a document containing details as to feasts in the Dominican Convent at Oxford in

The convent was supplied with good water by a conduit of leaden pipes, which, according to Wadding, was made in the thirteenth century by a magnate at his own expense, and extended many miles under the watersheds of the Isis and Cherwell[1]. In 1246-7 we hear that the Friars Preachers and Minors had appropriated many places on the Thames, and had made there 'ditches and walls and other things[2].' Lastly, there were three gates: one in Freren Street[3], perhaps an entrance to the church through 'Church Place;' another in St. Ebbe's Street, opposite Beef Lane[4], where St. Ebbe's Churchyard now extends; and a third—their principal entrance, which existed in Wood's time—in Littlegate Street, apparently where the latter is now joined by Charles Street[5].

This completes the list of conventual as distinct from the farm buildings, and if the account is meagre and unsatisfactory, we may try to console ourselves with William of Nottingham's retort, when a friar threatened to accuse him before the Minister General 'because the place at London was not enclosed:'

'And I will answer to the General, that I did not enter the Order to build walls[6].'

---

connexion with the burial of Piers Gaveston; the feasts were continued for four weeks. The Earl of Hereford, who spent Christmas at Grey Friars, Exeter, in 1288, found his lodgings detestable and the stench insupportable: Oliver, Monast. Exon. p. 331.

[1] 'Ex magnatibus unus rem magnam ausus est et perfecit, ut suis sumptibus a multis milliaribus Anglicanis ductis sub Isidis et Chervelli fluminum divortiis plumbeis canalibus, corrivaretur ad omnes Monasterii officinas aqua salubris in magna abundantia.' Ann. Minorum, I, 364, A.D. 1221. Wadding gives no authority for the statement.

[2] Placita Coronae, 31 Hen. III, Oxon. M ⅘ 3, f. 40: 'Jurati presentant quod fratres predicatores et fratres minores ceperunt in pluribus locis super aquam Thamesis et ibi fecerunt fossata et muros et alia.'

[3] B. Twyne, MS. XXIII, 151 (11 Hen. VII).

[4] Oxford City Records, 191.

[5] Wood, MS. F 29 a, fol. 179 a.

[6] Eccleston, p. 35.

CHAPTER III.

FRANCISCAN SCHOOLS AT OXFORD.

Learning necessary to the friars.—The first readers to the Franciscans at Oxford.—Nature of the office of lector; Grostete and Adam Marsh.—The lector and his *socius*.—Later lectors were ordinary Regent Masters.—Appointment to the lectureship.—Special regulations concerning the lectors.—System of instruction recommended by Grostete.—Lectures by friars.—Controversy with the University about theological degrees in 1253.—Controversy between the University and Dominicans, and its results.—Study of philosophy (Arts) before theology insisted on by the University.—Roger Bacon on the necessity of a preliminary training for friars.—Extortion of graces by external influence: 'wax-doctors.'—Career of a student Minorite.—On the numbers of friars sent to Oxford.—Course of study before 'opposition.'—'Opposition' and 'Responsion.'—The degree of B.D.—Exercises before inception.—The degree of D.D.: the licence.—Vesperies.—Inception.—Questions disputed on these occasions in the thirteenth century.—How far the statutable requirements as to the period of study were a reality.—Expenses at inception.—Necessary Regency.—Conditions on which dispensations were granted.—Maintenance of Franciscan students at the University.—What proportion took degrees.—Relative numbers of the various religious Orders at Oxford.

ST. FRANCIS himself was always strongly opposed to the learning of his age.

'Tantum habet homo de scientia quantum operatur,' he said, 'et religiosus tantum est bonus orator quantum operatur[1].'

But it was inevitable that the missionaries to the towns should be armed with a knowledge of theology to enable them to cope with the numerous heresies of the thirteenth century, and with a knowledge of physical science to enable them to cope with the frequent pestilences caused by the disregard of sanitary conditions[2]. In addition to this the influence of many learned men in the Order could not but be felt; and the early Franciscans in England were as zealous for learning as for good works.

---

[1] Wadding, I, 346; cf. Mon. Franc. I, xxx–xxxii.

[2] Cf. Bacon's works, *De retardatione senectutis, Antidotarius,* &c.; and Opera Inedita, 374—'regimen sanitatis.' Grostete's 'interest in physical science seems to date from his connexion with the friars.' M. Lyte, p. 30.

'They were so fervent,' Eccleston tells us, 'in hearing the divine law and in scholastic exercises, that they hesitated not to go every day to the schools of theology, however distant, barefoot in bitter cold and deep mud[1].'

Agnellus, though in Wood's words 'he never smelt of an Academy or tasted of humane learning[2],' frankly recognised the necessity. The school which he built at Oxford has already been noticed:

'but afterwards,' adds Bartholomew of Pisa[3], 'he had reason for regret, when he saw the friars bestowing their time on frivolities and neglecting needful things; for one day when he wished to see what proficiency they were making, he entered the schools whilst a disputation was going on, and hearing them wrangling and questioning, *Utrum sit Deus*, he cried: "Woe is me, woe is me! Simple brothers enter Heaven, and learned brothers dispute whether there is a God at all!" Then he sent 10*l*. sterling to the Court to buy the Decretals, that the friars might study them and give over frivolities.'

Agnellus rendered the greatest service to his Order by persuading Robert Grostete, the foremost scholar of his time, and the most influential man at Oxford, to accept the post of lecturer to the friars[4]. The exact date at which he undertook these duties is uncertain. He resigned the archdeaconries of Northampton and Leicester in 1231, but he may have been lecturer to the Franciscans some time before this; certainly he was closely connected with their house at Oxford[5]. He was resident in the University in 1234[6], and according to both Eccleston[7] and the Lanercost Chronicle[8], he gave up his lectureship only to accept the bishopric of Lincoln in 1235.

He was succeeded by Master Peter[9], who afterwards became a bishop in Scotland. The third reader was Master Roger Wesham[10], who afterwards (namely in or before 1239) was made Dean of Lincoln, and then (1245) Bishop of Coventry and Lichfield. The fourth was Master Thomas Wallensis, who,

'after he had lectured laudably at the Friars' in the same place, was appointed (in 1247) to the bishopric of St. David's in Wales[11].'

---

[1] Mon. Franc. I, 24.
[2] MS. F 29 a, f. 176.
[3] Liber Conf. fol. 79 b.
[4] Mon. Franc. I, 37.
[5] Grostete, Epistolae, p. 17 sqq., letter to Agnellus and the convent at Oxford, written between 1225 and 1231.
[6] Lyte, 'Hist. of Univ. of Oxford,' p. 29.
[7] Mon. Franc. I, 37: 'Ipso igitur ab cathedra magisteriali in cathedram pontificalem . . . translato.'
[8] P. 45: 'Vir iste primus cathedram scholarum fratrum minorum rexit Oxoniae, unde et assumptus fuit ad cathedram praelatiae.'
[9] Mon. Franc. ibid.
[10] Ibid. p. 38. The dates are from Le Neve.
[11] Ibid.

Thomas was made Archdeacon of Lincoln by Grostete in 1238, at which time he was lecturing in Paris[1]; he was then young[2] and it is probable that he was already archdeacon when he lectured to the friars at Oxford.

All these men were seculars, not friars : it was important at a time when, as Roger Bacon says[3], 'the Order of Minors was new and neglected by the world,' to secure the services of men of recognised position and ability. Of Master Peter nothing further is known. The other two were certainly close friends of Grostete[4]. Matthew Paris bears testimony to the high character and learning, the kindness and tact, of Roger Wesham[5]. Bacon ranks Thomas Wallensis among 'the wise men of old[6],' who studied foreign languages and knew the value of philology; and even Paris admits that this enemy of monks[7] was a man of lofty purpose, and accepted the bishopric of St. David's, though it was the poorest see,

'because it was in his native country, Wales, and he desired to console his wretched fellow countrymen by his presence, advice, and help[8].'

The divinity lecturer to the Franciscans or 'Master of the Schools[9],' as he was also called, had, as such, no status in the University. It is even doubtful whether he counted as a 'regent master,' unless he also lectured in the University Schools. Thus Adam Marsh protested against being required by the Masters to subscribe a new statute on the ground

'that he had three years ago retired from the office of teaching in their University[10].'

---

[1] Grostete, Ep. p. 149. In Letter xvii 'Magister Thomas Walensis' is mentioned as being in England; the date of the letter must be between 1235 and 1239 (when W. de Raleger became Bishop of Norwich); probably 1238, after Thomas had returned from Paris, before he became Archdeacon.

[2] Ibid. p. 151.

[3] Opera Ined. p. 325.

[4] Grostete, Ep. ut supra. Both received high offices in Lincoln diocese, Roger as dean resisted the bishop's claims. Paris, Chron. Majora, III, 528; IV, 391.

[5] Chron. Majora, IV, 424, 'vir moribus et scientia eleganter insignitus;' V, 644, 'vir omni laude dignissimus.' We may perhaps see a result of his contact with the Franciscans in his exhortation to the clergy of his diocese 'to preach often in the vulgar tongue, simply and without discussion, to the people, using practical not subtle arguments.' B. Twyne, MS. XXI, 280 (Episc. Coventr. '*in suis institutis MS.*').

[6] Opera Inedita, pp. 88, 428.

[7] Chron. Majora, IV, 245.

[8] Ibid. 647.

[9] Lanerc. Chron. p. 130; cf. ibid. pp. 45, 58.

[10] Mon. Franc. I, 348. The statute was to be subscribed by 'the Chancellor and all the regent masters in Holy Scripture . . . and Friar Adam called de Marisco.'

But in a letter written shortly before this, and referring to the same subjects, he mentions that he was 'lecturing on Holy Scripture' to the friars[1]. The position of the *lector* was, in fact, not unlike that of a college tutor, except that he was always a man of proved ability and long experience. To the friars he was far more than a theological lecturer; he was a trusted friend, on whose advice and sympathy and help they might reckon in all the conduct of life. Such at least was the tradition established by Grostete and carried on by Adam Marsh[2]. Both of them men versed in affairs of state, both men of acknowledged weight in the counsels of the realm[3], and fearless opponents of illegality and oppression, they not only trained the friars in theology and philosophy, but taught them to comprehend the social needs of the age.

'I return your lordship,' writes Adam to Grostete[4], 'the breviate which you wrote, "*Of the rule of a kingdom and a tyranny*," as you sent it, sealed with the seal of the Earl of Leicester;'

and Simon de Montfort had frequent consultations with the friar about his government of Gascony[5]. It was from their daily intercourse with men like these that the Oxford Franciscans became, if not the leaders, the spokesmen of the constitutional movement of the thirteenth century[6]. The corpse of Simon de Montfort was

---

[1] Mon. Franc. I, 335.

[2] For Grostete, see Lanerc. Chron. p. 45: 'The friars then going to Robert as to a pedagogue relate what has happened and beg him to say what he thought,' &c. The extraordinary activity of Adam Marsh in this and in many other spheres has been too often and too well described to detain us here: see Brewer's pref. to Mon. Franc. I, Pauli, 'Pictures of Old England,' pp. 67, 68 (extract quoted by Lyte, p. 51), and his 'Grosteste and Adam Marsh.' Cf. Bacon, Op. Ined. p. 186. Adam's description of the ideal pastor might be applied to himself. Mon. Franc. I, 445.

[3] For Adam's influence with Hen. III, see Lanerc. Chron. p. 24; Mon. Franc. I, 142 and 268 (on behalf of Earl Simon). He incurred the royal displeasure 'propter verba vitae;' ibid. 275. Cf. ibid. 335: one of the grounds on which he declines to assist the Archbishop in his visitation is 'districtum domini regis mandatum, quo interdictum fuit domino archiepiscopo ne me, velut proditorium inimicum, ad comitivam suam evocaret.' Cf. p. 387, he is summoned to Reading and London 'on matters of the highest importance, touching the sceptre and the kingdom.'

[4] Ibid. p. 110. Compare Nicholas de Lyra's commentary on Psalm xliv. quoted by J. Rouse, 'Hist. Regum Anglie,' ed. Hearne, p. 38.

[5] Mon. Franc. I, 267.

[6] Stubbs, Const. Hist. II, p. 313, n. 1: 'The sentiments not of the people but of the Universities, and incidentally of the Franciscans also, are exemplified in the long Latin poem printed in Wright's Political Songs, pp. 72-121. ... It was clearly a manifesto, amongst themselves, of the men whose preaching guided the people.'

buried by the Grey Friars of Evesham, and it is probably to the Franciscan school that the Latin poems in his honour are to be ascribed [1], as well as the form of prayer addressed to him:—

> 'Sis pro nobis intercessor
> Apud Deum, qui defensor
> In terris extiteras [2].'

The Oxford Franciscans regarded him as a saint and a martyr, though he died excommunicate, and testified to the miracles which he wrought [3].

The *lector* had also his *socius* [4], a younger friar who acted as his secretary, and whose time was almost entirely at his disposal. The position of both *lector* and *socius* will be best illustrated by two extracts from the letters of Adam Marsh.

In the first of these [5], addressed to the Provincial, he writes that he has found Friar A. de Hereford, whom the Provincial had assigned to him as his *socius*, affectionate and of good character, docile and well-read, and far more capable than 'some of those who are appointed by the counsel of the discreet to instruct in Holy Scripture.'

'I see,' he continues, 'that any friar who is associated with me to help me in my various [6] and constant toil, will have to subordinate his ecclesiastical labours and apply himself continually to supplying my defects, and directing my goings, and supporting my burdens, though this might sometimes produce in him virtue and industry and endurance. Far be from me therefore such impious tyranny, as that I should be willing to see the great gifts and spiritual progress in the said friar stunted or retarded or thwarted by any consideration of private convenience; especially as I can through the Saviour's pity, be provided, as I have heretofore been by your grace, with a competent companion without injury to the general welfare. I have also reason to think that Friar A., however great be his willingness and energy, will be unable without bodily suffering and mental disquietude to continue permanently with me, unless the stringent rules are relaxed in

---

[1] See note 6, p. 32. The poem expresses the constitutional view of monarchy with extraordinary clearness. Parts of it are translated by Mr. York Powell, 'Hist. of England,' pp. 148-9, and 152.

[2] Polit. Songs (Camden Soc.), p. 124.

[3] 'Miracula Symonis de Montfort' (printed at the end of Rishanger's Chronicle, Camden Soc. 1840), pp. 87, 95, 96. Cf. Dictum de Kenilworth, cap. 8 (Stubbs' Select Charters, pp. 420-421).

[4] Cf. Bacon, Op. Ined. 329. It was apparently in this relationship that 'Juvenis Johannes' stood to Roger Bacon.

[5] Mon. Franc. I, 314-316.

[6] Adam's position was exceptional, and his *socius* no doubt exceptionally hard-worked.

his favour (*nisi quatenus urgentia mitigat obedientiae salutaris diurnos aestus et vigilias nocturnas*).

'. . . . I ask therefore confidently, that you will, if it be not displeasing to your holy paternity, send to me without delay Friar Laurence de Sutthon, as my *socius*, if he consents, and that you will send Friar A. to London to study, as he himself greatly desires, if it be your good pleasure. And though Friar Laurence suffer some tolerable defect, he is yet peculiarly fitted to help me, though vulgar obstinacy may not think so.'

The other letter [1] is also directed to the Provincial.

'I am not a little surprised,' he writes, 'that through some excessive caution and severity, no provision has yet been made for the beloved Friar W. de Maddele, who has up to now diligently borne the burden of teaching (*eruditionis impendendae*), long since imposed on him. He is thus compelled, not only to exhaust the vital spirit by excessive studies, but also to wear out his bodily powers by writing every day with his own hand, though his strength is not the strength of stone, nor his flesh the flesh of brass. And while the other friars who have been deputed to the office of lecturing, especially those to whom he has succeeded, had great volumes and the assistance of *socii* provided for them, he alone does not seem to be cared for; though I hear that he has a pleasant faculty of lecturing, is acute in arguing, and in writing and speaking useful and acceptable to both friars and seculars. It will therefore be for you, if you please, without delay to take thought for the peace of mind and provide for the advancement (*provectui*) of those who study.'

The position of the *socius* probably altered but little after this time. That of the *lector* underwent a change. The Franciscans assimilated their system of teaching to the system in vogue in the University generally: from the time of Adam Marsh the lecturers to the Franciscans were merely ordinary Regent Masters in theology belonging to the Order. This will be evident from a comparison of the dates at which the various lecturers, whose names have been preserved, held the office: a sufficient number of these dates has now been recovered, on the indisputable evidence of contemporary records, to put the matter beyond all doubt [2].

The appointment to the lectureship was in the hands of the Provincial Chapter [3]; practically the person recommended by the leading

---

[1] Mon. Franc. I, 354.

[2] See the list of 67 *lectores* in Part II. The list is taken from the Cottonian MS. of Eccleston. In the same MS. (Cott. Nero A IX, fol. 78) is a similar list of readers at Cambridge under the heading, 'Fratrum Minorum Magistri Cantabrigie.'

[3] Mon. Franc. I, 335; cf. Harl. MS. 431, fol. 100 b, election of J. David to be lector at Hereford: Wadding, X, p. 156 (A.D. 1430); XIII, 73. At first the lecturers seem to have been appointed by the Provincial Minister (Mon. Franc. I, 37, 354), or, when a friar was sent from one province

brethren at Oxford was elected[1]. This is true of the later as well as of the earlier lectors. No Minorite could proceed to any degree unless he were first authorised to do so by papal ordinance or by the election of his Order[2].

According to the Constitutions of Benedict XII, no Minorite might lecture on the Sentences in a University (*i.e.* become B.D.),

'unless he had first lectured on the four books of the Sentences with the writings of the approved doctors in other *studia* which are in the same Order called *Generalia*,'

or in one of certain specified convents[3]. The friars of the English province were specially favoured in respect to the degree of D.D. It was decreed in the General Chapter at Rome in 1411

'that no one shall be promoted to the degree of master, unless he first go to Paris, according to the papal statutes and the general institutes, and do all that he is bound to do, *Provincia Angliae excepta*[4].'

However, the Franciscans at Oxford never obtained the right

---

[1] Mon. Franc. I, 357.

[2] Woodford in his reply to Armachamus (cap. 8) says: 'Pope Benedict ordained statutes for the order of friars Minors, of great and mature counsel, which are called among the Minorities *statuta papalia*; in these it is decreed concerning which parts of the Order ought to lecture on the Sentences at Paris, which parts at Oxford and Cambridge, how they ought to be elected in general and provincial chapters, and how consequently they ought to ascend to the doctor's degree by papal ordinance or election of the Order.' The constitutions of Benedict XII, *de studiis* (A.D. 1336), were printed in *Chronologia historico-legalis seraphici Ordinis Fratrum Minorum*, Neapoli 1650, tom. I, p. 46 (referred to in Anal. Franc. II, 165); I have not seen this book. They are omitted by Baronius et Raynaldus, Annales Eccles. Vol. XXV, p. 92 seq. to another, by the General (Ibid. 39, R. de Colebruge). In the 14th and 15th centuries, the reader had to be confirmed by the General, and might be appointed by him: MS. Canonic. Misc. 75, f. 77 b; and Wadding, X, 156. Anal. Franc. II, 240 (A.D. 1411).

They are contained in Bodl. MS. Canonic. Misc. 75, ff. 73 seq., but no mention of Oxford occurs here. The following regulations are given for Cambridge (fol. 77 b): 'Simili quoque modo, aliorum (qui) ordinabuntur ad legendum sentencias in studio Cantabrigie, duo assumantur duobus annis de provincia Anglie per ipsius provincie provinciale Capitulum eligendi, et tercius anno tercio de aliis partibus ordinis per generale capitulum tam de cismontanis quam de ultramontanis eligendus.'

[3] MS. Canonic. Misc. 75, fol. 78: 'Nullus quoque frater dicti ordinis ad legendum in prenominatis studiis (i.e. recognised Universities) sentencias assumatur, nisi prius legerit 4^{or} libros sententiarum cum scriptis approbatorum doctorum in aliis studiis qui (*sic*) in eodem ordine dicuntur generalia vel conventibus infrascriptis, vidz. . . Londoniensi, Eboricensi, . . . Novi castri, Stramforicensi (?) . . . Exoniensi,' &c. Nineteen convents in all are mentioned; only those which are, or may be, in England are here quoted. I have found no evidence to show whether this rule was or was not carried out.

[4] Anal. Franc. II, 241.

which was enjoyed by the Dominicans at Paris, of being the sole judges of the fitness of any friars of their own Order for academical degrees[1]. In the case of Adam Marsh, the term of office was one year[2]; and this was probably the general rule[3], though the readers might perhaps be re-elected in the anuual Provincial Chapter[4]. They often remained at Oxford after the expiry of their year[5], and no doubt continued to lecture, though they ceased to be *ex officio* representatives of the friars in their dealings with the University or other bodies.

Even in the earliest times it was found necessary to modify the stringency of the rule in favour of the lecturers. Visiting and good works were subordinated to their scholastic duties[6]. They were provided with more ample accommodation than the other friars, and their privacy was at certain times inviolable[7]. In the Constitutions of Benedict XII (1337) regulations for their support are given with some detail[8]. Masters, lectors, and bachelors in Universities were to be provided with the necessaries of life by the convents of the places where they lectured. But their other expenses, such as those connected with the necessary books, were to be assessed by the General or Provincial Minister and to fall on the convent from which they were sent; or, if the convent was unable to 'procure' the funds, these were to be supplied by the custody or province in which the native convent of the lecturer was situated. In addition to this, seculars and members of other religious Orders who attended the lectures, would no doubt have to pay fees[9].

We may reasonably infer that Grostete practised in the Franciscan school the system of instruction in theology which he subsequently recommended to the University. When consulted by the latter, he answered that the Regent Masters in theology ought to take the Old and New Testaments as the only sure foundations of their teaching and make them the subject of all their morning lectures, according to

[1] Lyte, p. 107.
[2] Mon. Franc. I, 232.
[3] See dates of the Oxford lectors in Part II; Harl. MS. 431, fol. 100 b, &c. The period of necessary Regency was at first one year, afterwards two.
[4] That the Chapters of the Minorites were actually held yearly in England may be seen from Pat. Roll, 1 Hen. IV, part 5, m. 7: 'ac pro capitulo suo provinciali quod in Anglia singulis annis celebratur.'
[5] e.g. Adam Marsh, T. Docking, &c.
[6] Mon. Franc. I, 40.
[7] MS. Canonic. Misc. 75, f. 11 b; Lanerc. Chron. p. 130: 'Non,' inquit (janitor), 'audeo tam mane ostiolum illius (i. e. magistri scholarum) pulsare, cum ipse studio intendat quid legere debeat.'
[8] MS. Canonic. Misc. 75, fol. 80.
[9] Mun. Acad. 428; Masters of Arts were compelled to exact their fees. Gratuitous lecturing by Franciscans is

the custom of the Doctors of Paris [1]. Roger Bacon laments the exaggerated respect which was paid to the 'Sentences' in his day, and points out that

'the learned men of old, some of whom we have seen, such as Robert bishop of Lincoln and Friar Adam de Marisco, used only the text' which was 'given to the world from the mouth of God and of the Saints [2].'

At the Friary, as in the rest of the University, much of the teaching in the theological faculty was, even in the thirteenth century, done by bachelors [3]; the admission to the degree of B.D. was accompanied by a licence to 'lecture on the book of the Sentences.' Some of the lectures would probably be for the brethren alone; others were open to the University [4]. The latter would certainly be the case when a friar delivered the lectures, which he was bound to give as 'Necessary Regent,' in his monastery. These courses seem however to have been sometimes delivered in the University Schools in School Street [5].

The academic studies of the friars were confined to the faculty of theology (in its wide mediaeval sense), and of canon law, the 'handmaid' of theology. The regulars were for the most part subject to the same statutes as the secular students in these faculties, with some important modifications.

The rules of the two Orders forbade their members to take a degree in Arts [6]. The customs of the University, on the other hand, required

always spoken of as exceptional. Thus Nic. de Burgo urges his having lectured 'pene gratis' as a reason why he should be excused the payment of his composition (Reg. H. 7, f. 117). A grace to Walter Goodfylde, S.T.B., is conceded 'condicionata ... quod legat unum librum sentenciarum publice et gratis.'

[1] Epistolae, pp. 346-7. The bibliographies in Part II will give some idea of the subjects chiefly taught by the early Franciscans: see especially John Wallensis (ethics and practical theology), Thomas Docking (biblical exegesis), Roger Bacon (physics, &c.).

[2] Op. Ined. 329. Cf. pp. 81 and 82: 'tota sapientia concluditur in sacra scriptura ... sed ejus explicatio est jus canonicum cum philosophia;' and this was the system followed by Grosteste and Adam. In the Opus Minus (p. 357), Bacon gives a curious example (after Augustine) of what he understands by 'explaining the Scriptures by natural science.' Cf. 'Les contes moralisés de Nicole Bozon, Frère Mineur,' by Miss L. T. Smith and Paul Meyer.

[3] Mon. Franc. I, 38.

[4] Cf. Wadding, IV, 14-15, on the schools of the two Orders at Paris. Tywne, MS. III, 300; Dominicans complain that the seculars 'prevent scholars from going to the schools of the friars,' &c. (1312).

[5] Cf. Lyte, p. 108; a Dominican Regent goes to the school and finds it occupied by other disputants (1312).

[6] Acta Fratrum Praedicatorum, Collectanea, II, p. 217; Archiv für Litt. u. K. Gesch. I, p. 189. Constitutions of the Dominicans in 1228: 'in libris gentilium et philosophorum non studeant,' &c. Bacon, Op. Ined. p. 426; Denifle, 'Die Universitäten,' &c. I, 701, 719-720.

that the student of theology should have graduated in Arts[1]. The issue was definitely raised in 1253[2], and we have from the pen of Adam Marsh a detailed account of the struggle[3]. In February the Chancellor and Masters of the University were formally petitioned to allow Friar Thomas of York,

'a man of high repute among the great and the many, on account of the eminence of his character, ability, learning, and experience, to ascend the chair of ordinary regent in Holy Scripture.'

The objection was then raised that he had not ruled in Arts. A committee of seven was appointed by the Masters to prepare a report, and the deliberations lasted, with a short interval, the whole of the next fortnight (Feb. 22 to March 8). On Saturday, March 8, 'the chancellor and masters and some bachelors' assembled to consider the report, which was to the effect that Friar Thomas should incept this time, but that a statute should be passed providing that for the future no one should incept in theology unless he had previously ruled in Arts in some University, and read one book of the Canon (of the Bible) or of the Sentences, and publicly preached in the University; the Chancellor and Masters reserved to themselves the right of granting dispensations, but provided against the use of undue influence of powerful patrons in procuring such 'graces' by the clause:

'but if any one shall attempt to extort a grace from the University through the influence of any magnate, he shall *ipso facto* be expelled from the society of the Masters and deprived of the privileges of the University[4].'

The report was at once accepted as the basis of a statute, to be signed by

'the Chancellor and all the regent masters in theology, and Friar Hugh of Mistretune, and the other regent masters in decrees and laws, and the two rectors (proctors) for the artists, and Friar Adam called de Marisco[5].'

Adam however refused to sign, and the meeting was prorogued till the next day, the first Sunday in Lent, only to be postponed again till Monday, when Adam, 'in the presence of the chancellor, masters, and scholars,' repeated his objections, adding others. He could not, he

---

[1] Mun. Acad. p. 25: 'Statuit Universitas Oxoniensis, et si statutum fuerit, iterato consensu corroborat,' &c.

[2] Wood gives 1251 as the date. But both the statute (Mun. Acad. 25) and the letters of Adam Marsh (Mon. Franc. I, 337—reference to controversy about the Southwark Hospital, M. Paris, An. 1252) are clear and at one on the point.

[3] Mon. Francisc. I, 338, 346 sqq.

[4] Mun. Acad. p. 25—the statute itself.

[5] The statute as it exists is not signed.

argued, agree to a statute of which he disapproved, merely to gain his immediate point. The promised 'graces' were fallacious,

'since by the opposition of any one man such a grace could be long delayed or altogether prevented; thus even the best men would be rejected, and he who was approved by divinity would be reproved by inhumanity.'

Further, it was unreasonable to require his signature, seeing that he was now almost a stranger (*quasi foras factus*), having for three years retired from the office of lecturing in their University. At length he formally washed his hands of the whole matter, withdrawing even his opposition,

'since the measure, dangerous as it was and distasteful to him, did not seem to him to be conceived in a spirit of wilful injustice,' (*non videtur secundum planum sui praeferre iniquitatem*).

He then left the assembly, while the seven commissioners withdrew to decide on the terms of the statute, which was merely a recapitulation of the original report. The Chancellor at once sent Adam the final decision, 'written with his own hand,' which the latter duly forwarded to the Provincial Minister. He left Oxford on Wednesday, the very day on which the statute was passed, while Thomas of York celebrated his 'vesperies' on Thursday and his inception on Friday, under the presidency of Friar Peter de Manners. In view of the bitterness which marked both the contemporary struggle between the University and Mendicants at Paris, and the disputes between the University and Dominicans at Oxford sixty years later, it is impossible not to be struck with the good feeling and moderation displayed both by Adam and his opponents.

The controversy at the beginning of the fourteenth century was to a large extent the sequel to the events we have just related[1]. The Dominicans in 1311 appealed first to the King, and when this proved of no avail, to the Pope, complaining that graces were frequently refused to fit candidates, and demanding the repeal of the statute of 1253. The appeal was read in the church of the Minorites,

'in the presence of a vast multitude of people there assembled on the occasion of a public sermon to the clerks,'

but the Franciscans took no active part in the matter, and the details of the struggle belong to the history of the Black Friars. The other

---

[1] The official account of the proceedings in the suit between the Friars Preachers and the University has recently been edited by Mr. Rashdall, Collect. Vol. II, Oxf. Hist. Soc.

Mendicant Orders however were no doubt involved in the odium which attached to the conduct of the Dominicans, and from this time forth the jealous feeling between the friars and the University never died out.

The issue of the controversy concerned the Franciscans no less than the Preaching Friars. In 1314 the arbitrators to whom the matter had been submitted published their award[1]. The statute of 1253 was upheld, but the right of refusing to any one, who had not ruled in Arts, the grace to incept in theology, was practically withdrawn from each individual member of Congregation and vested in the Regent Masters of the Theological Faculty.

'On such a grace being asked, every Master shall be bound to swear on the gospels . . . that he will not refuse such grace out of malice, hatred or rancour, but only for the common utility and honour of the university. And if notwithstanding this oath such grace be refused by any one, the reason of the refusal shall at once be set forth in the same Congregation of Masters in the presence of the Chancellor and proctors of the university and the Masters ruling in Theology, and within ten days or less it shall be discussed for the decision of the university whether that reason be sufficient or not. And if the reason of the aforesaid refusal be sufficient in the judgment of the Masters then ruling in Theology or of the majority of them, the refusal of the grace shall hold good; but if the reason of the refusal be insufficient in the judgment of the same persons, *eo ipso* the grace shall be granted [2].'

The Dominicans however hoped with the Pope's assistance [3] to get more favourable terms, and it was not till 1320 that they finally submitted to the University [4]. The wording of the award was certainly vague and required explanation. What, for instance, was the meaning of the expression, 'the common utility and honour of the university'? It is probably to this period that the following decree is to be referred, and it may be regarded as a gloss on the award of 1314 [5]:—

'*Item*, quod nullus de cetero, nisi prius in artibus rexerit, in disputatione

---

[1] Collectanea, Vol. II, p. 264 seq.
[2] Ibid. p. 271.
[3] John XXII issued several bulls in their favour; Anno 2, VII Kal. Nov., XVII Kal. Nov., Kal. Nov.; Anno 4, IV Id. Aug. I have not seen this last.
[4] Collect. II, 272.
[5] Mun. Acad. 391. This explanation or compromise was not suggested in any of the three bulls of John XXII, which I have seen. The Pope did not advance matters much: on this point he decreed, 'quod fratres predicatores et alii religiosi predicti ejusdem loci Oxonienses, dummodo alias ydonei fuerint, ad idem Magisterium in facultate predicta (sc. theologica), etiam si antea in artibus Magistri non fuerint, non petita, eo pretextu quod Magistri non fuissent in artibus, ab ipsis Cancellario et Magistris vel aliis, ad quos id pro tempore inibi pertinet, licentia per viam gratiae, sed per modum merae justitiae, libere assumantur.' Bull of John XXII, VIII Kal. Nov. A° 2, transcribed by Mr. Bliss from *Regesta*, Vol. 67.

solemni alicujus doctoris in theologia, publice opponere permittatur, nisi prius coram Cancellario et Procuratoribus Universitatis juramentum praestiterit corporale, quod philosophiam per octo annos, solis philosophicis principaliter intendendo, et postea theologiam per sex annos completos ad minus audierit, seu partim audierit et partim legerit, per spatium temporis supradicti: ad fidelem vero hujus statuti conservationem, noverint doctores in theologia Regentes se fore specialiter obligatos.'

The award of 1314 remained the permanent law of the University, and for the next century the friars confined themselves to insisting on the due execution of its provisions. In 1388, Richard II, hearing that, 'contrary to the decision of the aforesaid declaration you maliciously prevent the friars from taking degrees in theology,' wrote two strongly worded letters to the Chancellor, Proctors, and Regent Masters of the University, ordering them, 'under pain of our heavy displeasure,' to observe the statute of 1314[1]. In 1421, in consideration of remonstrances from the King and the Archbishop of Canterbury, the University gave a solemn undertaking to carry out the same statute, with some changes in detail[2]. So long however as the condition, that the canditate must have ruled in Arts, was inserted in the 'form of licensing to incept in theology[3],' the religious felt themselves to be at a disadvantage in comparison with the seculars, and bitterly resented their inferiority. When therefore, in 1447, the University was raising funds for the erection of the new schools, the Mendicants seized the opportunity to secure the abolition of this clause, promising in return that each friar should pay 40s. to the University at the time of receiving the licence[4]. This may however have been only a temporary arrangement: the Registers of Congregation supply little evidence as to its having been carried out[5].

The object of these statutes was partly to prevent the regulars from having an undue advantage over the seculars in the matter of theological degrees, but they must have had the effect of ensuring to the friars some preliminary training before the commencement of their

---

[1] Close Rolls, 11 Ric. II, m. 15; 12 Ric. II, m. 45.

[2] Wilkins, Concilia, III, 400.

[3] Ibid. 574-5. The same form of licensing was used for all faculties, and there was no mention of regency in Arts in the licence for the faculty of theology, strictly speaking: Ibid. 382-3. It was however contained among the conditions which the licentiate swore he had fulfilled or been dispensed from: Ibid. 391-2, 394.

[4] Ibid. 575.

[5] In 1459 John Alien, B.D. of Cambridge, supplicated for incorporation at Oxford: one of the conditions imposed was, 'quod solvat xl^s ad fabricacionem scolarum.' This condition was withdrawn the same day. Regist. Aa, f. 119.

theological studies. Roger Bacon, as usual, has a decided opinion on the necessity of such a training. Writing in 1271[1], he says:—

'During the last forty years there have arisen some in the Universities (*in studio*) who have made themselves doctors and masters of theology and philosophy, though they have never learnt anything of real value (*dignum*) and are neither willing nor able to do so on account of their '*status*.' .... They are boys inexperienced in themselves, in the world, in the learned languages, Greek and Hebrew; ... they are ignorant of all parts and sciences of mundane philosophy, when they venture on the study of theology, which demands all human wisdom. ... They are the boys of the two student Orders, like Albert and Thomas and others, who enter the Orders when they are twenty years old or less. ... Many thousands enter who cannot read the Psalter or Donatus, and immediately after making their profession, they are set to study theology. ... And so it was right that they should make no progress, especially when they did not procure instruction for themselves in philosophy from others after they entered the Order. And most of all because they have presumed in the Orders to investigate philosophy by themselves without a teacher—so that they have become masters in theology and philosophy before they were disciples—therefore infinite error reigns among them.'

The Oxford friars however could not have acquired their great scholastic reputation unless they had been better fitted than the seculars for the study of theology; and Friar William Woodford had little difficulty in pointing to many who, having entered the Order in their youth,

'wrote many works of great wisdom, which remain for the advantage of the Church[2].'

The clause of the statute of 1253 which prohibited the extortion of graces or dispensations by means of the letters of influential persons was not altogether effective. When, in 1358, the bitter feeling against the friars found a spokesman in Richard Fitzralph and again burst forth into open hostility, the clause was re-enacted in a more stringent form[3]. Any one using such letters was declared for ever incapable of holding or obtaining any degree at Oxford, and the University determined to hold up these 'wax-doctors' to obloquy.

'These,' begins a proclamation of the same year[4], 'are the names of the wax-doctors, as they are called who seek to extort graces from the University by means of letters of lords sealed with wax, or because they run from hard study as wax runs from the face of fire. Be it known that such wax-doctors are always of the Mendicant Orders, the cause whereof

---

[1] Opera Inedita, pp. lv and 399.
[2] Twyne, MS. XXII, f. 103 c (Defensorium, cap. 62).
[3] Mun. Acad. 206.
[4] Ibid. 207–8.

we have found[1]; for by apples and drink, as the people fables, they draw boys to their religion, and do not instruct them after their profession, as their age demands, but let them wander about begging, and waste the time when they could learn, in currying favour with lords and ladies. . . . These are their names: Friar Richard Lymynster incepted in theology by means of the prince's letters, and his grace contained the condition that he should incept and not lecture, but that Friar John Nutone his predecessor should continue lecturing[2]: and Friar Giuliortus de Limosano of the Order of Minors, who asserted that he was secretary of the King of Sicily, extorted from the University, or rather from the theological faculty, by letters of the King, grace to oppose.'

These instances hardly seem to justify the violent language of the proclamation, and it is uncertain to what extent the Oxford Minorites were guilty of the practice here denounced. Wiclif repeats the charge against the Mendicants generally:—

'A what cursedness is this, to a dead man, as to the world, and pride and vanitie thereof, to get him a cap of masterdom by praier of Lords[3]!'

It remains for us to give an account of the academic, or rather scholastic career of a Friar Minor at Oxford. As many of the friars entered the Order in tender years, there is no doubt that boys' schools formed part of many of the friaries[4]. There is no evidence of such a school at Oxford, but at Paris one existed where the student friars received a preliminary education[5]. It is probable that the names of friars who showed ability were sent up by the various convents to the Provincial Chapter and that a certain number were elected by the 'discreet men' there assembled to go to the University[6]. There is no evidence of any definite rule fixing the number or proportion of friars who might be sent from each convent, custody, or province, to Oxford[7]. The average number of friars living in the convent at Oxford at any time during the last quarter of the thirteenth and the

---

[1] The following passage is taken with some alterations from Richard de Bury's Philobiblon, p. 51 (edited by E. C. Thomas).

[2] I do not know to which Order these two belonged.

[3] 'Two Short Treatises,' &c., p. 30.

[4] Wadding, V, 300; statutes made at the General Chapter at Paris, 1292.

[5] Ibid. II, 382.

[6] Cf. Woodford, Defensorium, cap. 8. Friars are sent to the University by papal ordinance or election by the Order.

[7] Such as existed e. g. among the English Benedictines, one monk out of every twenty being sent to the University. Cf. the practice among the Dominicans, at Paris: 'Tres fratres tantum mittantur ad studium Parisius (sic) de provincia.' (Constitutions, c. 1235, in Archiv f. L. u K. Gesch. I, 189), and at Oxford, whither two students were sent from each province; Fletcher, The Black Friars of Oxford, p. 6.

first half of the fourteenth century was probably between seventy and eighty[1].

A friar usually completed his eight years' study of Arts, and often began his course of theology[2], at his native convent. On coming up to Oxford he at once entered on or continued his theological studies. A secular student of Divinity during his first three years attended 'cursory' lectures on the Bible and was admitted to oppose after the end of the fourth year[3]. In the friaries the course of study would in the main correspond with that adopted by the University. After six years[4] (instead of four) spent chiefly in the study of the Bible, a friar was presented by his teacher, a Regent Master of the same Order[5], to

---

[1] As the estimates of the numbers of friars and monks vary considerably, it may be worth while to give the evidence (which is entirely indirect) on which this calculation is based. In 1255, there were, according to Eccleston, 49 Franciscan houses in England and 1242 friars, giving an average of rather more than 25 to each convent (Mon. Franc. I, 10). At London, according to the *Regist. Fratrum Min. London.*, there were about 100 friars, on the average, in the fourteenth century (Ibid. p. 512). The public records give more trustworthy statistics. It was often customary for the kings on their progresses to give pittances of 4d. each to the friars of the places through which they passed. I have found no such grant to the Oxford Minorites: but the statement in the text may be compared with the following instances.

At *London* in 1243, there were *80* Minorites (Liberate, 28 Hen. III, m. 18: cf. also Q. R. Wardrobe, $\frac{4}{5}$ and $\frac{4}{5}$); August, 1314, *64* (Q. R. Wardrobe, $\frac{28}{35}$); October, 1314, *72* (Q. R. Wardrobe, $\frac{28}{35}$); 1315, *72* (Q. R. Wardrobe, $\frac{28}{35}$); 1325, *72* (Q. R. Wardrobe, $\frac{8}{5}$). At *Norwich* in 1326, *47* (Q. R. Wardrobe, $\frac{8}{5}$). At *Lynn* in 1326, *38* (Q. R. Wardrobe, $\frac{8}{5}$). At *Gloucester* in 1326, *40* (Q. R. Wardrobe, $\frac{8}{5}$). At *Cambridge* in 1326, *70* (Q. R. Wardrobe, $\frac{8}{5}$).

It is not often possible to compare the numbers in the same houses at different dates. In the northern convents, before the Black Death, there was a large decrease: thus at *New-castle* in 1299, provision was made for *68* Minorites (Q. R. Wardrobe, $\frac{8}{15}$, f. 4); about 45 years later, for *32* only (Chapter-house Books, A $\frac{1}{15}$, 149); but this may be explained by reference to the special circumstances of the North. Elsewhere we find an increase.

At *Winchester*, there were *23* Minorites in 1243 (Liberate, 27 Hen. III, m. 2); *43* in 1315 (Q. R. Wardrobe, $\frac{28}{35}$). At *Reading*, there were *13* in 1239 (Liberate, 23 Hen. III, m. 3); *26* in 1326 (Q. R. Wardrobe, $\frac{8}{5}$).

From these figures, and from the Bull of Clement V in 1309 (granting property of the Friars of the Sack to the Grey Friars), we may infer that the numbers in the Oxford convent increased rather than diminished up to A.D. 1349.

[2] Mun. Acad. 388: 'quidam in eorum primo adventu in villam Oxoniae ... ad opponendum in sacra theologia se offerunt inopinate.' Ibid. 390: 'nisi prius dictas liberales artes per octo annos integros in Universitate vel alibi rite audierit,' &c. Friars sometimes however spent the whole time at the University; see Regist. G. 6, fol. 55 a (R. Burton); H. 7, fol. 124 (J. Thornall).

[3] Mun. Acad. 389; Lyte, 223.

[4] Mun. Acad. 389. One of these years at least must be spent at Oxford; ib. 388: sometimes six or even twelve years' residence in a University was insisted on; Regist. G. 6, f. 61 b (Banester); H. 7, f. 73 (Thornall).

[5] Ibid. 204, 388: 'a doctore proprio ejusdem ordinis et Regente.'

the Chancellor and Proctors; special enquiry was then made as to his knowledge of the liberal arts, his age, morals, and stature; and if he satisfied the University officers on these points, he was admitted to 'oppose in theology[1].' Two more years elapsed before he could become a 'respondent[2].' Opposition or opponency and responsion were the two sides of a disputation: some question in theology was proposed, probably by the Master of the Schools; the opponent took one side (affirmative or negative) and *put* his case; the respondent then had to take the other side. The difficulty of the respondent's task was probably augmented by his having to answer the arguments of more than one opponent[3]. These regulations however were apparently superseded in 1358, when it was enacted that no religious who had not ruled in Arts should presume to read the Sentences until he had opposed duly and publicly a whole year in the ordinary disputations of the Masters, no other person of the same Order opposing at the same time[4]. This appears to have been the theory, and to some extent the practice, during the times about which we have any detailed information—i.e. the period covered by the early Registers. In none of the supplications and graces of the Minorites is there mention of the lapse of two years or anything approaching it between opponency and responsion; the latter exercise indeed is usually coupled with opponency, and treated as a very secondary affair[5]. A few instances will be sufficient as illustrations. In 1515 a grace was granted to Friar W. German, scholar of theology, with the stipulation that half a year should elapse between his opposition and responsion; the condition was subsequently withdrawn at German's request[6]. In 1457, Friar Gonsalvo of Portugal supplicated that he might count two terms of opponency as a year[7]; Richard Ednam in 1455 was allowed to count eight oppositions *pro completa forma oppositionis*[8]. Friar John Smith was admitted B.D. six months after he was admitted to oppose[9]. The opponent had to dispute in each of the Schools of the Masters in

---

[1] Mun. Acad. 204, 388.
[2] Ibid. 389.
[3] Cf. Univ. Reg. Vol. II, Part I, p. 22, disputations 'in Parvisis' (for B.A.).
[4] Mun. Acad. 206.
[5] The usual form of application for B.D. is: 'Supplicat frater Joannes Brown ordinis minorum et scolaris in sacra theologia quatenus studium 12 annorum in logicis philosophicis et theologicis sufficiat ut admittatur ad opponendum in novis scolis qua habita una cum responsione possit admitti ad lecturam libri sententiarum.' Reg. G. 6, f. 107.
[6] Regist. G. 6, f. 254 b: cf. ibid. f. 187, similar condition in the grace to Friar W. Walle, 1513.
[7] Reg. A a, f. 101 b.
[8] Ibid. 87 b.
[9] Reg. G. 6, f. 127 b; ibid. 160 a. John de Castro of Bologna became B.D. four days after his admission to opposition (Boase, Register, p. 93).

theology[1]; towards the end of our period, oppositions were held in the new Schools of theology[2].

After nine years spent in theological study, the friar might be admitted to read the *Sentences* of Peter Lombard publicly in the Schools[3], that is, to take the degree of B.D. On the presentation of the candidate to the Chancellor and Proctors, one at least of the Regents in theology must swear that he *knew* him to be a fit person in morals and learning, the other Regents, that they *believed* him to be such[4]. Within a year from this time[5], the new Bachelor had to begin his lectures on the *Sentences*, which he continued for a year (three terms), reading the text on most of the 'legible' days of each term, with questions or arguments pertinent to the matter, giving the accepted interpretation. He was not to raise doubtful points or attack the conclusions of another, more than once a term, except at the first and last lectures on each book of the *Sentences*[6]. In the first year also, he had to preach an examinatory sermon, which before 1303 was usually held at the Black or Grey Friars, after that date at St. Mary's[7]; another Latin sermon, '*qui non sit examinatorius*,' at St. Mary's[8]; and a third, before his inception, in the Dominican church, according to the statute of 1314[9]. In the next two years he had to continue his studies, and perhaps lecture on a book of the canon of the Bible[10]: the lecturing in this case was apparently to be done *biblice*; i. e. without commenting or discussing questions, except only on the text (*quaestiones . . literales*)[11]. Further, after the lapse of a year from the conclusion

---

[1] Reg. Aa, f. 74 b: 'oppositio in singulis scolis' (J. Sunday, 1453).

[2] Reg. G. 6, and H. 7, *passim*.

[3] Mun. Acad. 389.

[4] Ibid.: this ceremony was called 'deponing.'

[5] Ibid. 395.

[6] This seems to be the general sense of the words: 'non replicet pluries quam semel in termino, ultra introitus librorum, et cessationes eorumdem; introitus enim et cessationes librorum, ac recitatio locorum ad materiam propriam pertinens, . . . pro replicationibus minime computantur;' Ibid. 395. For these technical terms, cf. Twyne, MS. II, f. 147 b.

[7] Collectanea, II, 225, 270; Mun. Acad. 392.

[8] Mun. Acad. 395: this is the sermon which is often alluded to in the Supplications, &c. of the fifteenth century as 'sermo ad quem tenetur ex novo statuto.'

[9] Collectanea, II, 270. The registers make no mention of this sermon; it seems to have been superseded by sermons at St. Paul's, St. Frideswide's, St. Mary's, &c. See Reg. G. 6, f. 185; H. 7, f. 51 b, 110, &c.

[10] Mun. Acad. 391, 396. From the latter passage (and from statute of 1253, ibid. p. 25) it would appear that lectures on the Bible were a substitute for lectures on the Sentences: 'et aliquem librum de canone bibliae vel sententiarum Oxoniae in scholis theologiae publice legant.' This however does not seem to have been the case in reality: see *supplicat* of Friar John Sunday, Feb. 5, 145¾, in Appendix: cf. Reg. Aa, f. 54 (J. Florence), 122 (Ednam), f. 114, &c.

[11] Mun. Acad. 392, 394: 'biblice seu

of his lectures on the Sentences, he had to respond to eight Regents in theology separately (or to all if there were less than eight); all or most of these responsions were to be 'ordinary,' or at least 'concursive' (*concursivae*), and responsions at vesperies and inceptions were included in the eight[1]. Whether the rest of these responsions took place at the terminal disputations in the Theology School is not quite clear; but a later statute (1583) provides that none of these terminal disputations shall count to any one '*pro forma*[2].' The responsions were latterly held in the new schools: before these were built, in the schools of the various Masters. The Bachelor had then completed the studies necessary for the degree of S.T.P. or D.D.

These exercises seem usually to have been insisted on, more or less fully, even in the century before the Reformation. Friar John Sunday in 1454, having finished his lectures on the Sentences, supplicated for leave to incept after responding to each of the doctors and completing his course on the Bible: the grace was conceded on condition that he should respond and oppose eight times '*pro forma*,' and respond twice '*preter formam*[3].' Friar Thomas Anyden, S.T.B., supplicated (1507) that three responsions in the new schools with an examinatory sermon and '*introitus*' of the Bible should suffice that he should be admitted to incept[4]. It was rarely that three years intervened before the admission to read the Sentences and inception[5]. Thus Friar Gilbert Saunders was admitted to oppose in Nov. 1511, and incepted in July 1513[6]. Friar John Smyth was admitted B.D. in Dec. 1512, and D.D. in July 1513[7]. Another of the same name however was allowed to incept in 1507 if he had spent four years in the study of theology after taking the bachelor's degree[8].

We now come to the exercises and ceremonies connected with inception. First the grace had to be asked of Congregation; there was no fixed time for doing this[9]. Secondly came the 'deponing,' which was done by all the regent masters in the faculty present; all of them cursorie.' For the explanation of the term 'cursory lectures,' see Clark's Univ. Reg., Vol. II, Part I, p. 76.

[1] Mun. Acad. 392, 394. I do not understand '*concursivae*'; cf. note 6 on p. 81.
[2] Clark, Register of the Univ., Vol. II, Pt. II, pp. 109–110.
[3] Reg. A a, f. 79 b (printed in Appendix).
[4] Reg. G. 6, f. 47 b.
[5] Three years was theoretically the minimum; Mun. Acad. 391: the extension of the period to four years must be of later date; Clark, Reg. Vol. II, Pt. II, p. 139. An instance of the later custom is found in 1507; Reg. G. 6, fol. 22 b.
[6] Reg. G. 6, fol. 168 b, 187 b.
[7] Ibid. fol. 160, 187 b.
[8] Ibid. fol. 22 b.
[9] Registers, *passim*: cf. Clark, Register, Vol. II, Pt. I, 142 seq., for the later customs.

had to swear that they *knew* the candidate to be a fit person; he must be of good life and honest conversation and not deformed in body (*corpore vitiati*)[1]. He then received in the ordinary form the Chancellor's licence to incept, after swearing to observe the statutes of the University and to incept within a year of his admission[2].

On the day preceding the day fixed for his 'vesperies,' the licentiate sent to each Master of Theology and requested him to attend the latter ceremony[3]. Theological vesperies were in the thirteenth century held in the various schools; a Franciscan celebrated his vesperies in the school or church of the convent under the presidency of his own master[4]. At the beginning of the fourteenth century, a statute was passed enacting that every inceptor in theology should celebrate his vesperies in St. Mary's Church[5]. It does not seem that the masters in the faculty were bound to attend[6], but the prospect of an important or exciting discussion often attracted a large audience[7]. The exercises at vesperies consisted of disputations on theological questions proposed probably by the candidate[8], and announced to Congregation. All the masters present both at vesperies and at the Act had the right to bring forward their arguments in turn[9]. Thus Friar Hugh of Hertepol (c. 1280–1290) disputed 'in the vesperies before the inception of Friar John de Persole at Oxford[10].' About the same time 'Sneyt (debated) a question in the vesperies of Robert de Bromyard; Thomas of Malmesbury, preacher, responded[11].' The proceedings were terminated by a speech delivered by the presiding master in praise of the inceptor[12]. Grostete is said to have presided and given the oration at the vesperies of Adam Marsh[13].

Inception followed the next day. Even this ceremony in the thirteenth

---

[1] Mun. Acad. 379, 396.

[2] Ibid. 374, 377, 380, 450.

[3] Ibid. 432, 433. The phrase '*tenere vesperias*' (cf. ibid. 429) perhaps refers to the Master who presided, '*celebrare vesperias*,' to the incepting Bachelor. Vesperies might be held in any faculty on any day which was a *dies legibilis* among the artists; Mun. Acad. 433. Anstey (Ibid.) and Lyte (213) are mistaken in thinking that this only applied to the Faculty of Arts.

[4] Collectanea, II, 217, 222–3.

[5] Mun. Acad. 393; Collectanea, ibid.

[6] Mun. Acad. 432.

[7] Cf. Lyte, 106.

[8] This at least was the later practice;
Clark, Register of the Univ.,Vol.II,Pt.I. p.180: the statute in Mun.Acad.432 ('*quomodo Regens,*' &c.) may mean that the presiding master proposed the questions; perhaps this refers only to the Arts Faculty.

[9] See decree of 1586 in Clark, Reg. of Univ., Vol. II, Pt. I, p. 120—evidently an attempt to return to an older custom: cf. Mun. Acad. 433-4, though this probably refers only to the Act.

[10] Assisi MS., No. 158, *questio* 185: Hugh of Hertepol however probably presided in this case; see Part II.

[11] Ibid. *questio* 159.

[12] Trivet, Annals, p. 306; Lyte, 214.

[13] Bale, Script. Brit., Vol. I, p. 306: ' in vesperiis Adae.'

century took place sometimes in the churches of the friars[1]; but at the beginning of the fourteenth century, it was certainly the custom to hold the Act in St. Mary's[2]. The inceptor was admitted into the gild of Masters by one of the Masters (not the Chancellor), who was called the Father[3]. In the case of a Franciscan, the Father would usually, though not always, be a doctor of the same Order[4]. Those about to incept first read their lectures, then opened a discussion on certain questions[5]. In later times the exercises consisted of the discussion by all the inceptors, as opponents, of three questions proposed by the respondent and sanctioned by Congregation; the respondent, while statutably a D.D., was usually some M.A. or B.D. who was allowed to count this responsion *pro forma*[6]. In the more vigorous days of scholasticism, it is probable that the disputation was more of a reality—that the inceptor (who took the part of opponent) chose his own subjects[7] and was answered by a rival among the doctors[8].

Many of the questions discussed at vesperies, inceptions, and other disputations at Oxford at the end of the thirteenth century—probably in the convent of the Minorites—are preserved in a manuscript at Assisi[9]. The question on which Friar Hugh of Hertepol disputed at the vesperies of Friar John de Persole was: *An Christus in primo instanti potuit mereri perfectione.* Other questions of the same Friar Hugh were: *An deus eadem ratione formali videatur trinus et unus, An incarnacio sit possibilis.* The following are also among the questions in the same volume: *Utrum deus sit infinite potencie, Utrum virgo concepit sine semine, An intellectus sit forma corporis, An deus sit in omnibus rebus, An omnes beati equaliter participant beatitudine, An ratio ymaginis est in actuali visione dei.*

We may next enquire how far the statutable requirements as to the

---

[1] Trivet, *ut supra*.
[2] Mun. Acad. 392: 'sicut in ecclesia Virginis gloriosae honorem recipit magistralem.' Perhaps it was always unusual to hold the Act anywhere except in St. Mary's.
[3] Rashdall, Early Hist. of Oxford; Church, Quarterly Review, Vol. XXIII; Lyte, p. 213 *seq.*; Mon. Franc. I, 135.
[4] Friar John Smyth, Minorite, was created D.D. by the Abbat of Winchcombe; Reg. G. 6, fol. 31 b. Cf. Mon. Franc. I, 348.
[5] Mun. Acad. 433: 'Incepturi quidem suas legant in principio lectiones, deinde quaestiones, quas disputare voluerint, proponentes Magistris opponant.'
[6] Clark, Regist. of the Univ., Vol. II, pt. I, pp. 144, 180, 121.
[7] Mun. Acad. 433 (passage quoted in note 3 of this page).
[8] Cf. Assisi MS. No. 158, *questio* 117: 'questio domini Archidiaconi esse te in inceptione sua: respondit archidiaconus Oxon'.'
[9] No. 158 in the Municipal (formerly conventual) Library at Assisi. Some of the questions have the names of Cambridge friars attached to them (e. g. Letheringfont; and *questio* 104, frater Johannes Crussebut apud Cantebrigiam);

period of study were carried out: the only evidence obtainable is from the registers, which begin about 1450. The statutes, as we have seen, required that a religious should have studied Arts (i. e. philosophy) and Theology for fourteen years before opponency. The periods mentioned in the supplications vary from sixteen to eight years, the most usual number of years being twelve. Before inception, six more years of study were demanded, i. e. twenty in all. The period in the supplications varies from fourteen to twenty years; the usual number is eighteen. There is however reason to believe that these figures are not very exact. We have no means of checking them with regard to opponency, and the University was probably in the same position. But it frequently happened, that a friar, who had been admitted to oppose on the ground of having studied 'logic, philosophy and theology' for twelve years, supplicated two years later or less for grace to incept on the plea that he had studied the same subjects for eighteen years[1].

The expenses at inception were very heavy. The *religiosi* wore their usual habit[2], and Mendicants were exempted from the payment of 'commons' to the University[3]. Further, when several inmates of the same convent incepted on the same day, the charges (fees to the bedells and others?) were the same as for one inceptor[4]. But these details did not touch the largest expenses. According to ancient custom, every inceptor on the day of his inception feasted the Regent Masters (apparently of all faculties)[5], and Wiclif inveighs against the Mendicant Doctors for their

'great gifts and making of huge feasts of a hundred and many hundred pounds[6].'

Friar William Woodford, Wiclif's contemporary, started from London to take his D.D. with £40 in his purse[7].

Attempts were made to curtail the expenses of the friars. In his constitutions for the reformation of the Franciscan Order in 1336, Pope Benedict XII decreed[8], that

two are disputations by Minorites at Paris and *in curia*. The names of seculars and Friars Preachers also occur.

[1] See e. g. John Brown, Regist. G. 6, fol. 107, 185. Robert Sanderson, ibid. fol. 107 and 171: contrast W. German, ibid., fol. 187, 301. The generalizations in this paragraph are derived from an examination and analysis of all the entries, relating to the Franciscans, in the University Registers to the end of the year 1525.

[2] Mun. Acad. 434.

[3] Ibid. 480; cf. Regist. A a, f. 2.

[4] Ibid. 450-1.   [5] Ibid. 353, &c.

[6] Two Short Treatises, &c. (ed. 1608), p. 30.

[7] See Part II.

[8] Bodleian MS. Canonic. Misc. 75, fol. 79 b, cap. X. De expensis studencium evitandis.

'at inceptions¹ of Masters of the Order in theology, or of bachelors beginning the Sentences, they shall not spend in food and drink, except once only, more than would suffice for the moderate refection of the convent of the place where such inceptions take place. Other bachelors, lecturers or other students, both at Paris and at other *studia generalia* and *studia particularia*, shall not spend anything at their own inception or scholastic act or at the inception or act of others.'

It became usual, both among religious and seculars, to commute the expenses of the feast for a fixed money payment to the University. According to the scale fixed by statute in 1478², seculars who were able to spend at the University more than £40 and less than £100 (a year), paid twenty marks in lieu of the feast; those able to spend £100 or more, paid £20. A monk's composition was assessed at twenty marks; a friar's at ten marks or £6 13s. 4d. (equivalent to about £80 of present money). The sums actually paid by the Franciscans varied considerably. Sometimes the statutable amount was paid³. Friar John Whytwell (14$\frac{48}{50}$) paid £10⁴. Friar Richard Ednam (1463) was required to give £15, as well as a *liberata* to the Regents *ex sumptu proprio*⁵. More often (especially in the sixteenth century) a reduction of the sum was granted by the University, the concession being usually accompanied by the condition that the friar should say masses *pro bono statu Regentium*⁶. Friar Thomas Anneday was allowed to pay seven marks, 'because he is poor and has few friends⁷.' Others obtained a reduction of their composition by one half⁸; or the whole sum might be remitted under certain conditions, as in the case of Friar Nicholas de Burgo⁹. Sometimes Congregation refused to allow the full reduction asked for¹⁰.

It was further customary for inceptors to provide robes for masters and others attending their inception. Perhaps a trace of this custom may be seen in the grace to Friar Gonsalvo of Portugal, who at his inception was to

---

¹ p'nis, *principiis* (MS.).
² Mun. Acad. 353-4.
³ Regist. G. 6, f. 187 b; J. Smyth (1513).
⁴ Regist. A a, fol. 7 (printed in Boase's Reg. p. 287).
⁵ Reg. A a, f. 128; cf. ibid. 122. Ednam was probably in an exceptional position: shortly after this he became Bishop of Bangor; Le Neve, Fasti.
⁶ e. g. on Nov. 27, 1506, 'supplicat frater Johannes Smyth ordinis minorum s. t. b. quatenus secum graciose dispensetur sic quod quinque libre solvende in die admissionis sue possunt sibi sufficere pro sua composicione. Hec est concessa condicionata quod quinquies dicat missam de quinque vulneribus et ter dicat missam de trinitate pro bono statu regentium ante Pascha.'
⁷ Regist. G. 6, fol. 169 b: cf. Regist. H. 7, f. 140, S. Thornall (printed in Appendix).
⁸ e. g. W. German, W. Walle: see Part II.
⁹ Regist. H. 7, f. 117.
¹⁰ Reg. G. 6, f. 177, G. Sander.

'give a livery, i.e. *cultellos*, according to the ancient practice, to all the Regents[1].'

During the period of necessary regency, which followed inception, a secular had the right to attend all meetings of Congregation, and was bound to deliver 'ordinary' lectures publicly in the schools for the remainder of the year in which he incepted and the whole of the following year[2]. A statute of 1478 states the custom as enforced in the case of the Mendicants[3]:—

'Every one of them so incepting shall be bound to necessary regency for twenty-four months to be reckoned continuously from the day of his inception, including vacations, or he shall be regent and pay to the University according to the ancient customs; and although it happen that some other of the same Order incept within the term of the said months, he shall yet be bound to observe the foresaid form of regency, so that however only one of them come to the house of Congregation, according to the custom hitherto in use; proviso, that none of them shall omit to lecture (*expendet*) more than thirty days in a year by virtue of any grace whether general or special.'

Perhaps the exclusion of the friars, except one of each Order, from the house of Congregation and consequently from the government of the University, dates from the middle of the fourteenth century[4]. In 1454 Friar John David, S.T.P., supplicated for leave

'to resume his ordinary lecturers and exercise the acts of regent excepting the entry to the house of Congregation[5].'

Dispensations from necessary regency were often obtained. In 1452 Friar Anthony de Vallibus, D.D., asked leave to absent himself from all scholastic acts for a fortnight in order to visit his friends who were sick[6]. Friar William Walle was dispensed from fifteen days of his regency in 1518[7]; Friar John Brown from his regency during Lent in 1514[8]. Gilbert Sander and Walter Goodfeld were released from the whole of their necessary regency[9]. John Smyth obtained a similar grace as being 'warden of a convent and consequently very busy[10].' Dispensations from the sermon which was to be preached in St. Mary's within a year of inception were also very frequent[11].

These and other graces were usually granted subject to certain con-

---

[1] Mun. Acad. 755: cf. Ric. Ednam above. A monk gave robes to all the Regent Masters of Arts at his inception in 1360; Mun. Acad. 223.

[2] Mun. Acad. 419, 451, 452.

[3] Ibid. 453.

[4] Or earlier: see Mon. Franc. I, 347.

[5] Regist. A a, f. 83.

[6] Ibid. f. 62 b.

[7] Reg. H. 7, f. 6 b.

[8] Reg. G. 6, f. 207.

[9] Ibid. f. 104 b, and f. 199 b: cf. N. de Burgo, H. 7, f. 117 b.

[10] Reg. G. 6, f. 194 b: cf. T. Frances, H. 7, f. 68.

[11] Mun. Acad. 396; Reg. G. 6, f. 213 b (R. Saunderson), 214 (G. Sawnder), &c.

ditions. The recipient was often to say masses 'for the pestilence' or 'for the welfare of the Regents'[1]: or he had to lecture gratuitously on some specified book'[2] or preach a sermon[3]; or again the payment of a sum of money was imposed as a condition[4]. Thus in 1515 Friar John Flavyngur was allowed to give extraordinary lectures on a book of the Decretals,

'on condition that he would pay 6*s.* 8*d.* to the University on the day of his admission and would read two books of the Decretals[5].'

Friar Thomas Frances received permission in 1521 to incept

'on condition that he would pay 40*d.* within a month for the repair of the staff of the junior bedell of arts and would preach a sermon at St. Paul's within two years and an examinatory sermon before his degree[6].'

Franciscan students were maintained at the Universities by a system of exhibitions. These were provided sometimes by private benefactors[7], usually by the native convent of the student out of the 'common alms,' with the occasional assistance of other convents[8]. From the few traces which remain of the custom we may infer that the exhibition was generally reckoned at £5 a year, and that this sum covered the ordinary expenses of living[9]. Masters, lecturers and bachelors, as already stated, were supported by the convent in which they lectured[10]:

---

[1] Registers, *passim.*

[2] Reg. A a, f. 51 b, J. David (see Appendix); G. 6, fol. 39, Gerard Smyth; H. 7, fol. 117, N. de Burgo.

[3] Regist. G. 6, f. 39 b, W. Gudfeld (see Appendix), &c.

[4] e. g. Regist. A a, f. 119, John Alien; H. 7, fol. 119, N. de Burgo.

[5] Regist. G. 6, fol. 257 b.

[6] Regist. H. 7, fol. 51 b: cf. D. Williams (ibid.) : . . . ' predicet unum sermonem in ecclesia divi pauli London, et solvat angelum aureum ad reparationem baculi inferioris bedelli artium.' Cf. ibid. fol. 64, the same friar was to pay 12*d.* for the same purpose.

[7] See the will of William Maryner, 'citezein and salter of London,' in Somerset House (P.C.C. Fetiplace, qu. 8), A.D. 1512: 'Item, I bequeth to the exhibucion of a vertuons scoler of the said freeres Minours (of London) to be provided and ordeyned of the goode discrecion of the said wardeyn of the place, v$^\text{li}$.' Cal. of State Papers, Hen. VIII, Vol. III, p. 497 : May 24, 1521, 'to a Grey Friar for his exhibition at Oxford 8*d.*' (weekly ?).

[8] Bullarium Romanum, I, 251 (' Martiniana,' A.D. 1430), cap. X : ' . . . ita et taliter quod cuilibet studenti pro posse provideatur de suis necessariis, tam pro libris, quam pro reliquis opportunis, de communibus eleemosynis per procuratorem receptis pro quolibet conventu sive loco nativo fratris ad studium promovendi. Exhortantes strictissime in visceribus Jesu Christi ceteros fratres aliorum locorum, quod quum viderint idoneos ad studia promovendos, totis viribus eisdem impendant auxilium, consilium et favorem, . . . quaerendo pro eis eleemosynas, recommendando valentibus subvenire,' &c.

[9] See note 7: cf. Wiclif, Trialogus, IV, cap. 35 (p. 369) : ' . . . quilibet consumat annuatim in persona sua de bonis regni centum solidos et totidem in aedificationibus,' &c. Lyte, p. 93, on cost of living at Oxford: cf. Palmer, in Reliquary, Vol. XIX, p. 76; the king supported Dominicans at Langley at the rate of 3*d.* a day each, A.D. 1337.

[10] Bodl. MS. Canonic. Misc. 75, fol. 80.

but their allowance was probably not much larger than that of the ordinary student friars. Nicholas Hereford, preaching at Oxford in 1382[1], asserted that those of the Mendicants who had graduated as masters or bachelors, in addition to the ample allowance which they got from their community, begged for themselves, saying, 'I am a bachelor (or master) and require more than others, because I ought to be able to live up to my position.' (*Quia oportet me habere ad expendendum secundum statum meum.*)

It is impossible to say what proportion of the Franciscans at Oxford proceeded to a degree. In 1300 we have the names of twenty-two members of the convent: of these, ten at least were then, or because afterwards, Doctors of Divinity[2]. But the proportion of graduates to non-graduates and B.D.'s in the whole convent cannot have been nearly so large. The following statistics are derived from the University Registers[3]. From 1449 to 1463, five Franciscans obtained or supplicated for the doctor's degree; five others for that of bachelor only. From 1505 to 1538 (i. e. about thirty-three years, as some pages of the Registers are missing), twenty-five Franciscans incepted or supplicated for the degree of D.D.; twenty-six others obtained or supplicated for that of B.D. (one of them also for B.Can.L.): three more were admitted to oppose: one more supplicated for B.Can.L. The proportion of D.D.'s to B.D.'s would generally be larger than this: from 1532 to the dissolution in 1538 fourteen obtained, or supplicated for, the degree of bachelor, two only became D.D.'s: we may reasonably suppose that some of the fifteen bachelors would have proceeded to the doctor's degree had not the dissolution intervened.

The following figures will show the relative numbers of the various religious houses in Oxford[4]. The Registers from 1449 to 1463 contain the names of 10 Franciscans, 13 Dominicans, 12 Carmelites, 9 Austin Friars, 44 Benedictines, and 8 Cistercians: from 1505 to 1538, of 57 Franciscans, 40[5] Dominicans, 24 Carmelites, 23 Austins, 169 Benedictines, and 44 Cistercians.

---

[1] Twyne, MS. IV, 173.
[2] See Wood-Clark, II, 386.
[3] The Register as edited by Boase has been relied on in the main. J. Whytwell, described by Boase as a friar, was a Minorite (Reg. A a, fol. 23 b): similarly John Harvey (Acta Cur. Canc. F, f. 212 b), and J. de Castro (ibid. F, f. 263). Edward Drewe (sup. for B.A. in June, 1505) is called friar by Boase, not in Reg. G. 6, f. 1. Simon Clerkson was a Carmelite. Reg. I, 8, f. 279.
[4] Those described merely as friars or monks and whose Order I have not discovered, I have omitted in this calculation.
[5] M. Gryffith (Boase, 168) is described in one place as Dominican, in another as Franciscan: I have counted him among the Dominicans.

CHAPTER IV.

BOOKS AND LIBRARIES.

Absence of privacy.—Books of individual friars.—The two libraries, and their contents.—Grostete's bequest.—Extant manuscripts once in the Franciscan Convent.—Alleged illegal detention of books by the friars in 1330.—Richard Fitzralph's statements.—Richard of Bury on friars' libraries.—Dispersion of the books.—Leland's description of the library in his time.

IT is difficult to realise the external conditions under which the friars produced their works. At the end of the thirteenth and in the early part of the fourteenth century—the period of their greatest literary activity—privacy must have been almost unknown. Only ministers and lectors at the Universities were allowed to have a separate chamber or compartment shut off from the dormitory[1]. But there can be little doubt that, from Wiclif's time onwards[2], each Doctor of Divinity had his chamber; and every student had some place allotted to him, in which stood a *studium*, or combined desk and book-case[3]. Every student friar had books set apart for his especial use[4]; these books

---

[1] MS. Canonic. Misc. 75, fol. 11 b (Bodleian): 'Nullus frater cameram habeat clausam vel a dormitorio sequestratam, ministris exceptis et lectoribus in generalibus studiis constitutis. Nec in studiis aliorum fratrum habeantur velamina vel clausura, quominus fratres inter (? intra) existentes patere possint aspectibus aliorum.' This MS. dates from the thirteenth and fourteenth centuries, and contains '*Constitutiones fratrum Minorum*' made at various times. This extract is from the constitutions of Bonaventura as re-enacted in 1292. Cf. Mon. Franc. I, 195; Lanerc. Chron. p. 130. In the sixteenth century the Oxford Carmelites seem to have had a separate '*cubiculum*'

each; Acta Cur. Canc. EEE, f. 249 b.

[2] Wiclif, Two Short Treatises, &c., cap. 13 (p. 30). The custom seems to have been new in his time.

[3] Cf. note 1. Several grants of timber to the Dominicans '*ad studia facienda*' occur in the early records; e.g. Close Roll, 42 Hen. III, m. 2; Liberate, 45 Hen. III, m. 6; Close, 53 Hen. III, m. 6, seven oaks to the friars Preachers, Oxford, 'for the repair of their studies.' Representations of these *studia* are not uncommon in mediaeval pictures and illuminations. Savonarola's *studium* is still in the Dominican monastery of S. Marco, Florence. Cf. also M. Lyte, p. 204.

[4] Bullarium Romanum, I, 251.

were obtained by gift or bequest[1], by purchase[2] or by assignation by the Provincial[3] or Warden[4], or they had been copied out by the friar himself[5]. Alexander IV expressly declared that they were not the private property of the individual friars[6]; on the death of the friar who had had the use of them, they reverted to the convent, or were distributed to others 'by the Warden with the consent of the convent and licence of the minister[7].'

There is no reason to suppose that the friars had a chamber specially set apart as a *scriptorium*; they were comparatively free from the legal routine or 'office-work' which the administration of their vast estates imposed on the monks and their clerks. But the transcription of manuscripts was part of the regular work of the Oxford Franciscans; and it is indeed the only kind of manual labour expressly mentioned in connexion with the convent. Roger Bacon's statement[8] that he could only get a fair copy of his works made for the Pope by writers unconnected with his Order, means merely that there were no professional scribes among the Minorites of Paris.

---

[1] MS. Canonic. Misc. 75, f. 80 b: cap. x, 'de libris donatis vel legatis cuivis communitati seu persone ordinis,' &c.

[2] Cf. Burney MS. 325 *in principio*: 'Istum librum emit Johannes Ledbury, de ordine fratrum minorum, a magistro Gilberto Hundertone, de elemosina amicorum suorum.' (A.D. 1349.) In Liberate Roll, 30 Hen. III, m. 10, is a grant of ten marks to a friar, apparently a Minorite of Northampton, '*ad unam Bibliotecam emendam*.'

[3] Mon. Franc. I, 359–360. Adam Marsh writes to the Provincial, 'rogans obnixius quatenus . . . Bibliam carissimi P. de Wygornia piae recordationis eidem (sc. fratri Thomae de Dokkyng) ad usum salutarem assignare velitis. . . . Insuper non desunt qui de pretio libri memorati cumulatius, ut audio, satisfaciant.'

[4] MS. Canonic. *ut supra*; cf. Burney MS. 5, Bible belonging to Minorites of St. Edmundsbury, 'cujus usus debetur fratri Waltero de Bukenham ad vitam.'

[5] Mon. Franc. I, 349: 'Plures, aut audio, reperientur opportuni ad nunc dictum fratris obsequium (i. e. to act as Secretary to Friar Ric. of Cornwall), si scripturae quos ex studiosa praefati fratris R. (Cornubiae) vigilantia manibus suis conscripserint, singulis suae concedantur in usus utilitatis privatae, tam ad communitatis profectum ampliorem.'

[6] Bullarium Romanum, I, 110. Friars Minors promoted to bishoprics, &c. shall give up to the General or Provincial Minister 'libros et alia quae tempore suae promotionis habent,' as these must really belong to the Order. (A.D. 1255.) The books were however practically treated as private property; see e. g. a MS. in the Bodleian, Laud. Misc. 528, 'quondam Johannis Ston et Agnetis uxoris ex dono Johannis, fratris ordinis Minorum.' Cf. ibid. No. 176; Ball. Coll. MS. 133, f. 1, &c.

[7] MS. Canonic. *ut supra*, where careful and elaborate instructions are given: e. g. 'meliores seu utiliores libri semper remaneant in conventu'; 'Libri vero ad communitatem custodie pertinentes distribuantur in provinciali capitulo fratribus ejusdem custodie tantum per ministrum et diffinitores juxta disposicionem custodis et fratrum discretorum,' &c.

[8] Opera Ined. p. 13.

The vellum which Adam Marsh asked the Custodian of Cambridge to send at his earliest convenience[1], may have been intended for original compositions of the friars, but it was probably to be used for a careful fair copy of some work—perhaps a Missal or a book of the Bible. Several manuscripts, containing the works of Nicholas Gorham, are still extant, which Friar William of Nottingham copied at Oxford with 'tedious solicitude' and 'laborious diligence,' at the expense of his brother, Sir Hugh of Nottingham[2].

It was naturally in the libraries that most of the literary treasures were stored. In the fifteenth century there were two libraries in the Franciscan convent at Oxford, the library of the convent and the library of the student friars[3]. There is no evidence that either was founded by Grostete[4]. The convent probably received its first considerable collection of books from Adam Marsh, to whom his uncle, Richard Marsh, Bishop of Durham, bequeathed his library in 1226[5]. The next book we hear of at the Grey Friars is the volume of Decretals purchased by Agnellus[6]—doubtless the *Decretum* of Gratian with the additions codified by Raymund of Pennaforte and approved by Gregory IX in 1230. In 1253, Grostete,

'because of his love for Friar Adam Marsh, left in his will all his books to the convent of Friars Minors at Oxford[7].'

From a rather obscure passage in one of Adam's letters[8], this would appear to mean all Grostete's writings 'both original and translated,' not all the books which he possessed: on the other hand, a copy of St. Augustine's *De Civitate Dei* is extant which the friars received from Grostete[9]. These works of *Lincolniensis* were in the library in the middle of the fifteenth century, when Dr. Thomas Gascoigne was allowed to consult them[10]. He mentions particularly having seen a

---

[1] Mon. Franc. I, 391. The MS. of Adam Marsh's letters in the Cottonian Collection was probably written in the Franciscan Convent at Oxford.

[2] Merton Coll. MSS. 168, 169, 170, 171.

[3] Gascoigne, *Loci a libro veritatum* (ed. Rogers), pp. 103, 140. Cf. Gottlieb, *Mittelalterliche Bibliotheken.*

[4] Stevens, Wood, &c.: who however do not assert it positively.

[5] Close Roll, 10 Hen. III, m. 6 (3rd Sept.). The usual meaning of *Biblioteca* in mediaeval Latin is *Bible*, and this may possibly be the meaning here.

[6] Mon. Franc. I, 634 (from Bartholomew of Pisa).

[7] Nic. Trivet, Annales, 243.

[8] Mon. Franc. I, 185, letter to the Dean of Lincoln: 'scriptis ... tam editis quam translatis.'

[9] MS. Bodl. 198.

[10] Gascoigne, *passim*; cf. note in Balliol Coll. MS. 129, fol. 7 (the handwriting is, I think, Gascoigne's): 'et nota quod in illo armario sive libraria (sc. fratrum minorum Oxon.) sunt optimi libri et specialiter ex dono domini R. Grostete .... qui fecit plures libros ibi existentes.'

complete copy of Grostete's letters [1], his autograph gloss or exposition on the Epistles of St. Paul [2], two copies (one of them autograph) of his commentary on the Psalter [3], a treatise against luxury [4], and another *super textum* [5], both written by his own hand. Boston of Bury notices his translation of the *Testamenta XII Patriarcharum* in the same place. Friar Thomas Netter of Walden refers to a book *De Studio* by Grostete, with autograph notes by the author, which he had seen in the Minorite convent [6]; and Wadding mentions two more treatises, or rather sermons, which Grostete gave to the friars—one *De Laude Paupertatis*, the other *De Scala Paupertatis* [7]. Probably all these were in the library of the convent [8]. Another relic of Grostete preserved there was his 'episcopal sandals made of rushes [9].'

The statement that all Roger Bacon's works were in these libraries rests on the authority of John Twyne [10], but it is not probable that his writings were ever collected in one place. No doubt the works of the scholastic philosophers, and chiefly of the Franciscan schoolmen [11], formed the bulk of the library; which also contained a bibliographical compilation of considerable value, namely the *Catalogus illustrium Franciscanorum*, of which Leland often makes use [12]. St. Jerome's 'Catalogue of Illustrious Men,' was there bound up with 'many other good books [13],' his commentaries on Isaiah and Ezechiel [14], a book

---

[1] Note in Bodleian MS. quoted in preface to Grostete's *Epistolae*, p. xcvi.

[2] Gascoigne, pp. 102 and 174.

[3] Ibid. pp. 126, 177.

[4] Ibid. p. 138.

[5] Ibid. p. 126.

[6] Twyne, MS. XXI, 496: 'ex tomo 2° et lib. 5° Doctrinalis Antiquitatis Ecclesiae Th. Waldeni fratris Carmelitae de Sacramentis, cap. 77.'

[7] Annales Minorum, I, 364. The first of these sermons, if not both of them, is contained in MSS. Royal 6 E v, 7 E ii; f. 251 b; Laud. Misc. 402, f. 133; Phillipps, 3119, fol. 62. The sermon *de laude paupertatis* was preached on the feast of St. Martin to Franciscans: 'sumusque in loco paupertatis et inter professores paupertatis.' Cf. Mon. Franc. I, 69.

[8] See Gascoigne, pp. 102-3.

[9] Ibid. 140. William of Wykeham left his sandals to his college at Oxford; Register Arundel, fol. 215.

[10] '*Comment. de rebus Albionicis*,' quoted in Wood MS. F 29 a, fol. 166, and 177 b. John Twyne lived c. 1500-1581.

[11] Wood-Clarke, II, 405, books of Richard Middleton; also some writings of Robert Kilwardby, mentioned by Boston of Bury (Tanner, *Bibl.* p. xxxviii.

[12] 'Libellus praeterea est instar catalogi de eruditis Franciscanis, quem olim vidi, atque adeo legi in collegio ei sectae dicato propter Isidis Vadum.' Leland, *Script.* 268; other references to it, *ibid.* 269, 272, 289, 297, 302, 304, 315, 325, 326, 329, 406, 409, 433. It must have been compiled in the 15th century.

[13] MS. Balliol Coll. 129, fol. 7.

[14] Lambeth MS. 202, fol. 99 b: 'et preter istas omelias super Jerimiam et ezechielem, scripsit idem Jeronymus 18 libros super ysaiam prophetam et 14 libros super ezechielem, ut patet inter fratres Minores Oxonie, ubi isti libri sunt' (note by Gascoigne).

called *Speculum Laicorum*[1], and a few Hebrew and even Greek manuscripts[2].

Few only of the MSS. seem to have been preserved; very few at any rate can be identified[3]. Caius College possesses two of them, a copy of the Gospels in Greek and a Psalter in Greek[4]. The volume (already referred to) containing St. Augustine's *De Civitate Dei*, with Grostete's annotations, is now in the Bodleian[5]. A thirteenth-century MS. of some of Grostete's lesser works, with St. Augustine's *De Concordia quatuor Evangeliorum*, given to Lincoln College by Gascoigne, was perhaps obtained by him from the Franciscan library[6]. The copy of Jerome's 'Catalogue of Illustrious Men,' which Gascoigne saw in this library, appears to be extant among the MSS. in Lambeth Palace[7]. It may be reasonably conjectured that the single copy of Adam Marsh's letters[8], and some or all of the treatises bound up in Phillipps MS. 3119[9], were also kept, or at any rate written, in the Oxford con-

---

[1] Wood, Hist. et Antiq. (Latin ed.), p. 83; a note from Gascoigne: the book contained a full account of Grostete's quarrel with Innocent IV in the chapter on Excommunication. MSS. of the work are Royal 7 C. XV, and Caius Coll. 184.

[2] Wood-Clark, II, 380; cf. R. Bacon, Opera Ined. p. 88. Hebrew was taught at Oxford in the fourteenth century; Twyne, MS. XXIV, 94, 101: cf. Wadding, VI, 199, on the efforts of Friar Raymund Lully to secure the teaching of oriental languages at Oxford and elsewhere.

[3] MSS. usually contained anathemas against any one who should deface or remove them. Persons into whose possession they came would naturally seek to obliterate all traces of their former ownership; e. g. in Royal MS. 3 D. I (fol. 234 b) the words 'conventui fratrum minorum Lichefeldie' (the former owners of the book) are almost obliterated; 'a fure viz. qui codicem abstulerat,' remarks Casley: cf. Bodl. MS. Canonic. Misc. 80 (a thirteenth-century Bible), 'olim Fratrum ordinis Minorum de . . .'

[4] Nos. 348 and 403. It is not expressly stated whether the latter belonged to the Oxford Franciscans; see Smith's Catalogue, p. 166. I do not know the age of either of these MSS.; probably c. 1500.

[5] MS. Bodl. 198.

[6] Now Lincoln Coll. MS. 54: see p. 61, n. 7.

[7] Lambeth MS. 202 (sec. xiii). It cannot be certainly identified: the volume has been rebound and several leaves cut out at the end. There is nothing to indicate to what house or Order the book belonged. On fol. 81 occurs a note on the title of the '*Catalogus*' of St. Jerome, with the addition: 'Hoc Mag. Thomas Gascoigne Oxonia in Collegio de Oriell Ebor' diosic' natus; 1432.' In Ball. Coll. MS. 129, f. 7, is the note, apparently in Gascoigne's writing, 'qui liber (sc. virorum illustrium) est in armario fratrum minorum Oxonie; et continet idem liber plures alios bonos libros.' Lambeth MS. 202 contains also several treatises by St. Augustine, Isidore, &c.: see Todd's Catalogue.

[8] MS. Cott. Vitell. C. viii: cf. Mon. Franc. I, p. lxix.

[9] Among the contents are, treatises against the Mendicant Orders, Grostete's sermon in praise of poverty, Eccleston's Chronicle, *Impugnacio Fratrum Minorum per Fratres Praedicatores apud Oxon'*, and other tracts relating for the most part to the Franciscans.

vent. The following interesting notes occur in a Digby manuscript in the Bodleian[1]:—

'For the information of those wishing to know the principles of the musical art, this book, which is called *Quatuor principalia Musice*, was given by Friar John of Tewkesbury to the Community of the Friars Minors at Oxford, with the authority and assent of Friar Thomas of Kyngusbury, Master, Minister of England, namely A. D. 1388. So that it may not be alienated by the aforesaid community of friars, under pain of sacrilege.' . . . (At the end), 'This work was first finished on the 4th of August, 1351. In that year the Regent among the Minors at Oxford was Friar Symon of Tunstede, D.S.T., who excelled in music and in the seven liberal arts. Here ends the treatise called *Quatuor principalia*, which was put forth by a Friar Minor of the custody of Bristol, who did not insert his name here because some thought scorn of him' (*propter aliquorum dedignacionem*).

Sometimes, if we may believe their accusers, the Friars obtained books by less creditable means than gift, bequest, or purchase. In 1330[2] the Sheriff of Oxfordshire received a writ from the King instructing him

'to command the Warden of the Friars Minors at Oxford and friar Walter de Chatton to give back to John de Penreth, clerk, justly and without delay, two books of the value of forty shillings, which they are unjustly keeping, as he says';

failing this the said friars shall be summoned to appear before the King's justices at Westminster. The Sheriff forwarded this writ to the Mayor, but the latter declared that the friars were not subject to his jurisdiction, 'and therefore nothing was done in the matter[3].'

The friars had on all sides the reputation of being great collectors of books. Richard Fitzralph, the famous Archbishop of Armagh, was fond of exaggeration[4], and no one will accept without considerable

---

[1] Digby MS. 90; this extract is copied from the catalogue. The treatise has been printed under the name of Simon de Tunstede by E. de Coussemaker, '*Auctores de Musica*,' &c., Vol. IV, pp. 220-299 (Paris, 1876).

[2] Twyne, MS. XXIII, 488, 'ex chartophylacio civitatis Oxon. In fasciculo Brevium'; (this is not now among the City Records). The date is, 'T. meipso apud Wodestok, 28 die Martii a° regni nostri 4°,' i. e. Edward III (not II, as Twyne), who was then at Wood-stock; and the mention of P. de la Beche, sheriff, leaves no doubt on the matter (see Wood, Annals, A° 1327).

[3] Twyne, ut supra: 'In dorso brevis, ita: "Gardianus ordinis fratrum minorum et frater Walterus de Chatton confrater ejusdem Gardiani nihil habent in balliva nostra extra sanctuarium ubi possunt summoneri seu attachiari; ideo de eis nihil actum est."'

[4] e. g. his statement that in his time there were 30,000 students at Oxford.

modifications his statement, made before the Pope in 1257[1], that the friars have grown so numerous and wealthy,

'that in the faculties of Arts, Theology, Canon Law, and as many assert, Medicine and Civil Law, scarcely a useful book is to be found in the market, but all are bought up by the friars, so that in every convent is a great and noble library, and every one of them who has a recognised position in the Universities (and such are now innumerable) has also a noble library.'

Some rectors of churches, whom the Archbishop had sent to the Universities, had even been obliged to return home owing to the impossibility of getting Bibles and other theological books. Perhaps these rectors were not filled with a passionate desire to learn. In 1373 the University passed a statute against the excessive number of unauthorized booksellers in Oxford[2].

Richard of Bury mentions the great help he received from Dominicans and Franciscans in collecting his books[3], and bears testimony to the magnificence of the libraries of the Mendicants which he visited:

'there we found heaped up amid the utmost poverty the utmost riches of wisdom[4].'

But Richard of Bury notices a tendency among the 'religious' to subordinate the love of books to

'the threefold superfluous care of the belly, clothes, and houses[5],'

and the tendency became much stronger after his time. The almost[6] total absence of books in the bequests to the Oxford Franciscans in the fifteenth and sixteenth centuries is the more striking because of the frequency of such bequests to colleges. It is said that the Minorites sold many of their books to Dr. Thomas Gascoigne[7]. Certain it is that in the latter days they parted with them, just as 'forcyd by

---

[1] Sermon in Twyne, MS. XXII, 103 a–b.
[2] Mun. Acad. 233.
[3] Philobiblon (ed. E. C. Thomas), pp. 65–8.
[4] Ibid. (§ 135).   [5] Ibid. p. 47.
[6] The will of Henry Standish contains a bequest of five marks for books (1535); this is the only instance which I have found. See list of bequests in Chapter VII. On the other hand it must be remembered that a friary produced its own books.

[7] See note by Gascoigne in MS. Bodl. 198, fol. 107 (A.D. 1433): 'et nota quod omnes note et figure in margine istius libri fuerunt scripte propria manu sancte memorie Magistri Roberti Grosseteste Episcopi Lincolniensis, et librum dedit mihi sponte sub sigillo suo conventus fratrum minorum Oxonie.' Gascoigne is said to have given the books which he had from the Minorites to the libraries of Balliol, Oriel, Lincoln and Durham Colleges; this MS. was given to Durham College.

necessitie,' they parted with their jewels and plate¹. The exclusion of the Mendicant Friars from the use of the University Library by the statutes of 1412², cannot have been any real hardship to the Franciscans so long as their own library was intact. In the sixteenth century however this was no longer the case, and we accordingly find some instances of Franciscans supplicating for admission to the library of the University³. The earliest instance is in 1507; but, as the registers from 1463 to 1505 are lost, it would of course be ridiculous to attempt to draw from this fact any inference as to the date of the dispersion of the books of the Minorites. Leland visited the Friary shortly before the Dissolution, and we have from his pen the last description of the once famous library⁴:—

'At the Franciscans' house there are cobwebs in the library, and moths and bookworms; more than this—whatever others may boast—nothing, if you have regard to learned books. For I, in spite of the opposition of all the friars, carefully examined all the bookcases of the library.'

¹ Cromwell Corresp. (Rec. Office), Second Series, Vol. XXIII, fol. 709 b. Leland, who was evidently received with scant courtesy by the Franciscans, and who is consequently very bitter against them (he calls them 'braying donkeys'), remarks on the dispersion of the books: 'Nam Roberti episcopi volumina et exemplaria omnia, ingenti pretio comparata, furto ab ipsis Franciscanis, huc illuc ex praescripto commigrantibus (aut ut verius loquar) vagantibus sublata sunt'; quoted in Wood-Clark, II, 381-2.

² Mun. Acad. p. 264.

³ Register G, fol. 35 a (A. Kell); Acta Cur. Cancell. F, fol. 156 b (W. German and J. Porret).

⁴ Leland, Collect. Vol. III, p. 60. Cf. Wood-Clark, II, 381-2. Leland mentions only one library; but he probably saw all that was to be seen.

CHAPTER V.

PLACE OF OXFORD IN THE FRANCISCAN ORGANIZATION.

Learned friars as practical workers among the people.—Their sermons.—Educational organization throughout the country.—Relations of the Oxford School to the Franciscan Schools of Europe.—English Franciscans teach at foreign Universities.—Oxford as the head of a *custodia*.—Provincial chapters held at Oxford.

IF the Franciscans became leaders of scholastic thought, they were first and foremost practical workers. 'Unfitted as the works of Roger Bacon or of Raymond Lully might seem to the practical divine, it was for him, not for the philosophic disputant, whether as a missionary among the Saracens or a combatant of error and heresy at home, that these works were written[1].' In the case of Roger Bacon this is abundantly evident.

'Before all,' he writes[2], 'the utility of everything must be considered; for this utility is the end for which the thing exists.... The utility of philosophy is in its bearing on theology and the church and state and the conversion of infidels and the reprobation of those who cannot be converted[3].... The end of all sciences, and their mistress and queen,' is moral philosophy, 'for this alone teaches the good of the soul[4].'

It is difficult to resist the temptation of quoting more passages of this kind[5] (illustrating as they do the Franciscan view of life), especially as, in the dearth of records, actual instances are hard to find: one proof however may be brought that it was not all theory. Among the twenty-two Oxford Minorites, for whom in the year 1300 the Provincial, Hugh of Hertepol, claimed the episcopal licence to hear the

---

[1] Brewer, Mon. Francisc. I, p. li. See the rest of his luminous remarks there, and in his preface to R. Bacon, Opera Inedita.
[2] Opera Ined. pp. 19-20, Opus Tertium.
[3] Cf. Ibid. p. 116, on the potential value of burning-glasses in the Crusades.
[4] Ibid. 53. Cf. p. 50, ethical part of moral philosophy: 'et haec est pulchrior sapientia quam possit dici.'
[5] e.g. Opus Majus, 46; Opus Tert. pp. 3-4, 10-11, 40, 48, 84; Opus Minus, 323; Compend. Studii, 395, 397, 400 sqq., &c.

confessions of the crowds who thronged to the church of St. Francis, eight were then or afterwards doctors of divinity and theological lecturers to the Friars at Oxford, and among the others were two names of yet greater fame, Robert Cowton and John Duns Scotus[1]. It must however be added that, of the eight friars who were actually licensed by the bishop to hear confessions, none appears as having subsequently lectured or taken a degree[2].

Here however we may see how the Franciscans brought their philosophy to the test of experience in the details of everyday life; and they possessed to a remarkable degree, in spite of—perhaps because of—their learning, the power of appealing to the hearts of the people.

'It is the first step in wisdom,' said Roger Bacon, 'to have regard to the persons to whom one speaks[3],'

and his brethren followed this principle in their preaching. 'Their sermons,' says Brewer, 'are full of pithy stories and racy anecdotes; now introducing some popular tradition or legend, now enforcing a moral by some fable or allegory[4].' It has often occasioned surprise that the generation which saw the rise of poetry in England, saw also the rise of English prose—that, in a word, Wiclif was the contemporary of Chaucer. When we remember that, for a century and a half, men versed in all the learning of their time had been constantly preaching to the people in the vulgar tongue in every part of the country, we shall see less cause to wonder at the vigorous language, the clear and direct expression, of 'the father of English prose.'

For the learning of the friars was not confined to the Universities[5]. To the Franciscans Oxford was more than a place for study; it was the

---

[1] Twyne, MS. II, fol. 23, from Register of D'Alderby, bishop of Lincoln; printed in Wood, Hist. et Antiq. (Lat. ed.), p. 134, and in Wood-Clark, II, p. 386. It may seem bold to identify 'Johannes Douns' with the great schoolman, but there is no doubt he was a young friar at Oxford at the time (he lectured at Oxford c. 1304); and he is in company with many other prominent schoolmen of the time.

[2] Two of them were already D.D.'s.

[3] Opera Inedita, p. lvi. Cf. Sir Francis Bacon: 'non accipit indoctus verba scientiae, nisi prius ea dixeris quae versantur in corde ejus.'

[4] Mon. Francisc. I, li. See 'Les contes moralisés' of Friar Nicholas Bozon. Wiclif is less complimentary to Friars' sermons: they are 'japes' pleasing to the people, and 'rimes'; Select Works, III, 180. The old school of theologians, secular and monastic, and the clergy disliked them intensely.

[5] The Franciscans at Northampton receive ten oaks to build a house for their schools; Close Roll, 42 Hen. III, m. 6 (dated Oxford, June 26).

centre of a great educational organization which extended throughout the land.

'The gift of wisdom,' to quote Eccleston's words, 'so overflowed in the English province, that before the deposition of Friar William of Nottingham, there were thirty lecturers in England who solemnly disputed, and three or four who lectured without disputation. For he had assigned in the Universities students for each convent, to succeed to the lecturers on their death or removal[1].'

However, in practice this rule was not very strictly adhered to. Sometimes a friar would pursue his studies with a view to becoming reader to a particular convent[2]; but usually, when an 'extra-university' lectureship was founded or fell vacant, the convent applied to the Provincial Minister for any lecturer they chose[3]. Thus about the year 1250, the brethren at Norwich requested that Friar Eustace of Normanville should be appointed as their lecturer[4]. Eustace, after consulting Adam Marsh, declined the office with the Minister's permission, alleging in excuse his weak health and his want of the necessary training and experience; and Adam informed Robert de Thornham, custodian of the Cambridge 'Custody,' in which Norwich was situated, of the decision[5]. The appointments, like those of the Oxford lecturers, were in the hands of the Provincial Chapter, and the various convents obtained letters of recommendation from powerful patrons in support of their candidate[6]. The lecturer was appointed

---

[1] Mon. Franc. I, 38. Brewer (p. xlix) gives a misleading version of the passage. The original of the last part runs thus : 'Assignaverat enim in Universitatibus, pro singulis locis, studentes, qui decedentibus vel amotis lectoribus succederent.'

[2] e.g. Thomas of York for Oxford, Mon. Franc. I, 357.

[3] It was not necessary that he should have been at any *studium generale*. Thus the Dominicans complain that a friar who has often lectured on the sentences and Bible *extra universitatem* cannot lecture on the Bible at Oxford unless he is a B.D. *Acta Fratrum Praedicatorum*, Collectanea, II, 226. Cf. Clement IV's constitutions for the Friars Minors in 1265, Bullarium Romanum, p. 130, § 5: 'Fratres autem de ordine vestro, quos secundum institutiones ipsius ordinis conventibus vestris deputandos duxeritis in lectores, sine cujusquam alterius licentia libere in domibus praedicti ordinis legere ac docere valeant in theologica facultate (illis locis exceptis in quibus viget studium generale), ac etiam quilibet in facultate ipsa docturus solemniter incipere consuevit.'

[4] Mon. Franc. I, letter 178. It is no doubt addressed to W. of Nottingham (who died 1251), as in a letter written later than this and referring to R. de Thornham, Adam mentions 'Peter minister of Cologne,' i.e. P. of Tewkesbury, Nottingham's successor in the English Provincialate; ibid. letter 183.

[5] Ibid. letter 179.

[6] Harl. MS. 431, fol. 100 b (printed in Appx. B). Wadding, Vol. X, p. 156 (cap. viii of the '*Martiniana*,' A.D. 1430); Vol. XIII, 73.

for one year, and could be re-elected by the Provincial Chapter at the request of the convent[1]. Nor was it only to brethren of their own Order that the friars were sent. For many years a Franciscan was theological lecturer to the monks of Christchurch, Canterbury, till at length in 1314 one of his pupils was able to take his place. His teaching, wrote the monks, in grateful recollection of their 'lector,'

'in urbe redolet Cantuarie, ac plures nostre congregacionis fratres ipsius sedulos auditores ita sacre scripture aspersione intima fecundavit, quod ipsos ad lectoris officium in scolis nostris subeundum ydoneos reputamus; nos unum de fratribus et commonachis nostris predictis loco dicti fratris Roberti ad hujusmodi ministerium exequendum duximus subrogare[2].'

Thus the friars disseminated over the country, from the universities outwards, the 'New Learning' of the thirteenth century.

But the fame of the Franciscan school at Oxford was not only English, but European[3]. Friars were sent thither to study not only from Scotland[4] and Ireland[5], but from France and Aquitaine[6], Italy[7], Spain[8], Portugal[9], and Germany[10]; while many of the Franciscan schools on

[1] Harl. MS. *ut supra*. Cambridge Public Library, MS. Ee. V. 31, contains letters addressed by the convent of Christchurch, Canterbury, to the Provincial Minister and Chapter of the Friars Minors in England, requesting permission for Friar R. de Wydeheye to continue to act as master of their schools; the letter was written every year; e.g. in 1285, 1286, 1287, &c.: see ff. 21 b, 24 b, 28, 29, 34, &c.: cf. Wilkins, Concilia, II, 122.

[2] Cambridge MS. Ee. V. 31, fol. 156 b, 'Littera fratris Roberti de Fulham quondam lectoris nostri de conversacione sua.' It is doubtful whether he is the same as Robert de Wydeheye mentioned in the preceding note, and whether he had been at the University.

[3] See Archiv f. L. u. K. Gesch. d. Mittelalters, VI, 63 (A.D. 1292) and Wadding, *Sup. ad Script.* 717 (A.D. 1467); printed in Appx. B.

[4] Scotland for many years formed part of the English province. Mon. Franc. I, 32; Wadding, IV, 136.

[5] Stephen of Ireland, Malachias of Ireland, Maurice de Portu, &c.

[6] William de Prato; perhaps N. de Anilyeres, or Ayneleres, or Anivers (Mon. Franc. I, 316, 379, 380). Several English students returned to Oxford from Paris before taking their degree (e.g. Ric. of Cornwall; Mon. Franc. I, 39); and probably many came over during the dissensions at Paris in the middle of the thirteenth century. See also decree of Gen. Chapter of Milan, 1285; 'Provintia Aquitanie potest mittere unum studentem Oxonie'; Archiv f. L. u. K. Gesch. d. Mittelalters, VI, 56.

[7] See Part II, Peter Philargus of Candia (Alex. V), John de Castro of Bologna, Nic. de Burgo, Francis de S. Simone de Pisa, &c.

[8] Rymer's Foed. IV, 30. It was probably in Paris that Roger Bacon was laughed at by the Spanish scholars at his lectures; Opera Ined. 91, 467.

[9] Part II, Gundesalvus de Portugalia, Peter Lusitanus, etc.

[10] Mon. Franc. I, 313, Part II, Hermann of Cologne, Mat. Döring; Anal. Francisc. II, 242: 'Provinciae seu studia, ad quas et quae Provincia Argentinensis studentes de debito transmittere potest; videl. Oxoniae, Cantabrigiae,' &c.

the Continent, both in universities and elsewhere[1], drew their teachers from England, and, in England, mainly from Oxford. Eccleston mentions a friar who studied with him at Oxford, where his lectures, after some failures, won the admiration of Grostete; afterwards, as his fame increased, he was called by the Minister-General to Lombardy, and enjoyed a great reputation even at the Papal court[2]. Grostete, on his return from the Council of Lyons, was anxious to get Adam Marsh out of the neighbourhood of Paris as soon as possible.

'It is not safe,' he writes to the Provincial Minister, 'to let Adam stay there; for many greatly desire to keep him at Paris, especially now that Alexander of Hales and John de Rupellis are dead; and so both you and I shall be deprived of our greatest comfort[3].'

At another time[4] the General writes to the Provincial Minister of England, requesting him to send English friars to Paris to teach; it was probably on this occasion that Richard of Cornwall[5] left Oxford to win the applause of his hearers at Paris. Peckham received his early education in the schools of his Order at Oxford, and lectured at Paris and at the Court of Rome[6]. Among those whom the Oxford Convent

---

[1] Mon. Franc. I, 38: 'Usque adeo fama fratrum Angliae, et profectus in studio aliis etiam provinciis innotuit, ut minister generalis, Frater Helias, mitteret pro Fratre Philippo Walensi et Fratre Ada de Eboraco qui Lugduni legerunt.' Lyons was not a *generale studium*; Denifle, I, 223.

[2] Mon. Franc. I, 39. As the passage is of great interest, it may be quoted at some length: 'An excellent lecturer, who studied with me at Oxford, used always in the schools, when the master was lecturing or disputing, to employ himself in the compilation of original things instead of attending to the lecture. Now when he had become lecturer himself, his hearers became so inattentive, that he said he would as lief shut up his book every day and go home, as lecture; and consciencestricken he said, "By a just judgment of God, no one will listen to me, because I would never listen to any teacher." He was besides, since he consorted too much with seculars and thus paid less attention to the brethren than was usual, a living example to the others, that the words of wisdom are only learnt in silence and quiet... But after he had returned to himself and applied himself to quiet contemplation, he made such excellent progress that the Bishop of Lincoln said that "he himself could not have delivered such a lecture as he had delivered." So, as his good fame grew, he was called to the parts of Lombardy by the General Minister, and in the very court of the pope was in high repute. But at last, as he was in the extreme agony, the Mother of God, to whom he had always been devoted, appeared to him, and drove away the evil spirits, and he was held worthy, as he afterwards revealed to a friend, to enter happily to the pains of purgatory. For he told him that he was in purgatory and had great pains in his feet, because he was wont to go too often to a holy woman (*réligiosam matronam*) to console her, when he ought to have been intent on his lectures and other more necessary occupations; he begged him also to have masses celebrated for his soul.'

[3] Grostete, Epistolae, p. 334.
[4] Mon. Franc. I, 354. [5] See Part II.
[6] Peckham's Reg. p. 977, and Part II.

sent to teach in the universities of the Continent, were John Wallensis, William of Gainsborough, Roger Bacon, Duns Scotus, and William of Ockham[1]. All these names belong to the thirteenth or early fourteenth century; from that time onwards international jealousies and wars rendered the connexion of the English universities with Paris far less close, and contemporaneous with this breach was the beginning of the intellectual decline of the Order of St. Francis.

Oxford was the head of a 'custody,' which contained, according to the list given by Bartholomew of Pisa[2], seven other convents, namely, Reading, Bedford, Stamford (Linc.), Nottingham, Northampton, Leicester, and Grantham. What exactly the organization of a '*custodia*' was, it is impossible to determine; it was probably always rather indefinite, and Bartholomew of Pisa points out that in early records the word is used very loosely[3]. Perhaps it was originally intended to hold chapters of custodies[4], as well as of provinces and convents. The Custodian had in early years the right of making and enforcing byelaws in his custody; thus

'in the custody of Oxford at the head of which Friar Peter was for twelve years, the brethren did not use pillows up to the time of Friar Albert the minister[5].'

Each custody had its special characteristic, Oxford being chiefly remarkable for study[6]. Two Custodians of Oxford, Peter of Tewkesbury and John of Stamford, became Provincial Ministers[7]. At first the Wardens of the convents were appointed by the Custodian[8], but in 1240 the right of election was transferred to the convents themselves, and many friars at the same time demanded the total abolition of the Custodian's office, on the ground that it was superfluous[9]. It continued however, to exist down to the Dissolution and seems to have implied a general right of supervision; the Custodian was a kind of permanent *visitator*[10].

---

[1] For dates and authorities, see notices of these friars in Part II.

[2] Liber Conformitatum, fol. 126. This list does not always agree with Eccleston; the latter mentions e. g. a 'custody of Salisbury,' p. 27.

[3] Liber Conform. f. 99. For a curious use of the word, see Liberate Roll, 17 Hen. III, m. 10; the *custodes* of the houses of Friars Minors in Dublin were seculars and trustees of their property.

[4] Liber Conform. ibid.

[5] Mon. Franc. I, 27. In the custody of Cambridge the brethren did not use 'mantles.'

[6] Ibid.

[7] See notices in Part II.

[8] Evers, Analecta, p. 60.

[9] Ibid., and Mon. Franc. I, 48. The custodian admitted novices to profession; Archiv f. L. u. K. Gesch. VI, 89.

[10] Wright, Suppression of the Monasteries (Camden Soc.), p. 217. The word is sometimes used as equivalent to *gardianus*; e. g. Acta Cur. Cancell. H. fol. 53 b. Cf. W. of Esseby, Warden and Custodian of Oxford, Mon. Franc. I, 10, 27.

Several Provincial Chapters were held at Oxford. It was probably a Conventual, not a Provincial Chapter, before which Grostete, then 'reading the act at the Friars Minors,' preached his sermon in praise of poverty and mendicancy[1]. Here Albert of Pisa held his first chapter as Provincial Minister of England, and announced the stern principles which were to guide his government[2]. Soon after this Elias instituted a severe visitation throughout the Order, and sent Friar Wygmund or Wygred, a German, as visitor to England in 1237 or 1238[3]. He held chapters at London, Southampton, Gloucester, and Oxford[4]. At the latter place the Warden, Friar Eustace de Merc, was bitterly attacked and excluded a day and a half from the chapter, though his innocence seems to have been eventually established[5]. The inquisitorial methods adopted by the visitor raised a storm of opposition throughout the province, which found expression, on the completion of the visitation, in a Provincial Chapter held at Oxford in the summer or autumn of 1238[6]. Here a solemn appeal to Rome was formulated, and exemption claimed from all visitations, except those authorized by the General Chapter[7]. The result of this and similar appeals from the Order was the final deposition of Elias by the Pope on the 15th of May, 1239[8].

In the spring or early summer of 1248 the Minister-General, John of Parma, held a Provincial Chapter at Oxford,

'in which he confirmed the provincial constitutions concerning poverty in living and buildings (*de parsimonia et paupertate aedificiorum*). And when he

---

[1] Mon. Franc. I, 69. If we may believe Eccleston, the sermon seems hardly to have expressed Grostete's real convictions; he told W. of Nottingham in private, 'quod adhuc fuit gradus quidam superior, scilicet vivere ex proprio labore.' On this sermon, see Chapter IV, p. 58.

[2] Ibid. 55; 'in festo Purificationis,' i.e. Feb. 2nd, prob. anno 1237.

[3] Ibid. 29, 31: in the Phillipps MS. of Eccleston (fol. 75) he is called Wygerius. Jordan's Chronicle gives 1237 as the date of the visitation, 1238 as the date of the appeal; Analecta Franciscana I, pp. 18–19.

[4] Mon. Franc. I, 30. A chapter was held in London about May 18th, 1238 (Liberate Roll, 22 Hen. III, m. 11), and at Oxford soon after June 30th, 1238 (ibid. m. 15); the latter entry, dated June 30th, runs thus: 'Rex ballivis suis Oxon' salutem. Precipimus vobis quod de firma ville nostre Oxonie faciatis habere fratribus minoribus Oxon' X marcas ad sustentacionem suam et fratrum suorum qui nuper convenient ad capitulum suum apud Oxon'.' These are probably the chapters held by the visitor.

[5] Mon. Franc. I, 31.

[6] Ibid. 30.

[7] Ibid.: 'Igitur cum venissent fratres ad Romam, mox petiverunt ut fratres de cetero in suis locis visitarentur per capitulum generale,' &c. It is no doubt to these events that Grostete refers in his letters to Gregory IX and Cardinal Rinaldo Conti, Protector of the Order at Rome; Epistolae, LVIII, LIX.

[8] Wadding, Vol. III, *sub anno*.

gave the friars the option of confirming or deposing the Provincial Minister (W. of Nottingham), they unanimously asked that he might be confirmed[1].'

Eccleston states that in the same chapter the Minister-General

'recalled the brethren to unity who had begun to surpass the rest in singular opinions[2].'

For this chapter the King provided one cask of wine and the necessaries of life[3]. In 1289 three of the four Orders celebrated their Provincial Chapters at Oxford, that of the Minorites taking place on the feast of the Nativity of the Virgin (Sept. 8)[4]. No account of the proceedings remains.

The next Provincial Chapter at Oxford about which we have any information was held in 1405, at a critical period in the history of the Order in England. In 1404 'a great and very scandalous schism' arose among the Franciscans owing to the arbitrary and unconstitutional conduct of the Provincial, John Zouch[5]. The friars appealed to the Protector of the Order, the Cardinal-bishop of Sabina, who appointed Friars Nicholas Fakenham and John Mallaert commissioners, with power to depose the Provincial, if necessary. The commissioners deposed him in his absence, called a chapter at Oxford on May 3rd[6], and proceeded to elect a successor. The Vicar of the Provincial forbade the friars to attend the chapter.

'And the commissioners prayed the King to order the friars to assemble at the chapter at Oxford for the reformation of their religion; and they obtained royal briefs about this matter[7].'

John Zouche was afterwards reinstated by the Protector of the Order, but does not seem to have ever made good his authority over the English Province[8].

---

[1] Mon. Franc. I, 68. The date is fixed by the entry in Liberate Roll, 32 Hen. III, m. 7 (May 16th, 1248).

[2] Mon. Franc. I, 50; probably an offshoot of the errors of Mendicants at Paris, 1243; see Mat. Paris, Chronica Majora, Vol. IV, pp. 280-3; Martene and Durand, Thesaurus, &c., Vol. IV, p. 1686, § 8.

[3] Liberate Roll, *ut supra*: 'Mandatum est Vicecomiti Oxon' et Berkshire quod . . . cariari faciat unum dolium vini usque Domum fratrum Minorum Oxon', quibus Rex illud dedit de celario quod fuit Roberti Blundi Vinetarii, et eisdem fratribus in die Capituli sui inveniat victui necessaria de elemosina Regis' (Woodstock, May 16).

[4] Osney Chron. in Ann. Monast. IV, 318; Peckham, Register, p. 958.

[5] Eulogium Historiarum (continuatio), III, 403; Wadding, IX, 499.

[6] Eulog. Hist. III, 405. The diploma of Innoc. VII (in Wadding, IX, 499) gives the names of the commissioners.

[7] Eulog. Hist. ibid.

[8] Wadding, *ut supra*.

CHAPTER VI.

RIVALRY BETWEEN THE ORDERS: ATTACKS ON THE FRIARS.

Rivalry between Friars Preachers and Minors: proselytism.—Politics and Philosophy.—Peckham and the Oxford friars.—Evangelical Poverty.—Contrast between theory and practice.—Attack on the friars by Richard Fitzralph.—Charge of stealing children.—Wiclif's early relations to the friars.—His attack on them in his later years.—Charges of gross immorality made not by Wiclif, but by his followers.—The University and the friars: summary of events in 1382.—Unpopularity of the friars in the fifteenth century.—Foreign Minorites expelled from Oxford.—Conspiracies against Henry IV; part taken by Oxford Franciscans.—Conventual and Observant friars.

It was inevitable that a spirit of rivalry should exist between the two great Mendicant Orders; and the rivalry soon developed into antagonism. In the thirteenth century one lecturer to the Friars Minors at Oxford was removed from the convent, another was suspended from lecturing, for causing offence to the Friars Preachers and at their request[1]. An 'enormous scandal of discord,' in Matthew Paris' words[2], arose in the year 1243, each of the two Orders claiming precedence of the other. Though there is little direct evidence on the point, there is no doubt that Oxford was one of the chief scenes of conflict. The controversy was carried on by 'men of education and scholars[3],' and some details of it are preserved in the pages of Eccleston. It arose from the proselytising tendencies of the two Orders[4]. The Dominicans, according to Eccleston[5],

---

[1] Phillipps, MS. 3119, fol. 87 dorse (printed in Appx. C). This happened before 1269; the names are not given. Perhaps the explanation of the following note to the list of lectors at Oxford in Eccleston's Chronicle is to be found here: 'Notandum quod secundum alia chronica quartus magister ... hic non nominatur,' &c. Mon. Franc. I, 552.

[2] Chron. Majora IV, 279.

[3] 'Viri literati et scolares,' ibid.

[4] The proselytising fervour of the Dominicans is well illustrated in the letters of Jordan, Master of the Order, 1223-1236, *Letters du B. Jourdain de Saxe* (Paris, 1865), pp. 28, 66, &c.; p. 126: 'Apud studium Oxoniense, ubi ad praesens eram, spem bonae captionis Dominus nobis dedit' (A. D. 1230). But Jordan cherished no ill-feeling against the Franciscans: Mon. Franc. I, 22.

[5] Mon. Franc. I, 56.

'were wont to profess on the day of their entry, if they liked, as did Friar R. Bacun[1] of good memory.'

Friar Albert of Pisa, when Provincial Minister of England, obtained a bull from Gregory IX prohibiting this practice:

'the Friars Preachers were not to bind anyone so as to prevent him entering any Order he chose, nor were the friars to admit their novices to profession till the year of probation had been completed[2].'

The Dominicans on their side claimed similar privileges, and obtained a bull from Innocent IV to the effect that

'no Friar Minor should receive those bound to them (*suos obligatos*); if he did so, he should be excommunicated *de facto*; and they consented to the same privilege about those bound to us.'

Eccleston complains that the Dominicans made such good use of the bull that 'they let scarcely any one go;' and regards this equitable arrangement as a great hardship to his Order. 'But not long,' he adds, ' did this tribulation last;' Friars William of Nottingham and Peter of Tewkesbury obtained from Innocent IV a revocation of his constitution[3].

The antagonism between the two Orders did not stop here, and in many of the great questions of the day they are found on opposite sides. The Oxford Franciscans, as we have already seen, were among the staunchest supporters of Simon de Montfort; the Oxford Dominicans seem to have sided with the King. The famous Mad Parliament, which Henry III summoned to Oxford in 1258, met in the convent of the Black Friars, and Prince Edward and his retainers stayed there before the battle of Lewes[4].

The same rivalry made itself felt in the sphere of philosophy, and

---

[1] i.e. Robert, not Roger, as Leland and others have supposed; even Dean Plumptre makes this mistake; Contemp. Review, Vol. II.

[2] Mon. Franc. I, 56. A Papal letter containing the last clause and addressed to the Friars Minors is printed in Wadding, III, 400; the date is 'x Kal. April. Pontificatus anno xii,' i.e. 1238.

[3] Mon. Franc. I, 56. See letters of Innocent IV (1244) to the Friars Preachers and Friars Minors in Wadding, III, 433-5. In these the Pope refers to other letters of his forbidding either Order to receive the *obligatos* of the other; the term is now declared not to include novices during their year of probation.

[4] Fletcher, Black Friars in Oxford, pp. 6-7. John Darlington, one of the King's nominees in the committee of twenty-four appointed in 1258 to carry out reforms, was a Dominican; Pat. 50 Hen. III, m. 42; Stubbs, Const. Hist. II, 77. The confessors of the English kings were almost invariably Dominicans. Compare also the part which the Oxford Dominicans took in the Piers Gaveston struggle.

the Franciscans dealt a heavy blow at their more orthodox adversaries by impugning successfully an important doctrine of Thomas Aquinas[1]. The Angelic Doctor had held with Aristotle and against Averroes that the individualising principle was not form but matter. How then, asked his opponents, could the individual exist in the non-material world[2]? Such a doctrine was in contradiction to the mediaeval theory of heaven and the life after death; and the Church rallied to the side of the Franciscans. At Oxford, Archbishop Kilwardby, Dominican though he was, condemned this among many other errors in 1276, but the sentence seems to have had little effect at the time[3]. It was chiefly against this opinion that Peckham's measures in 1284 were directed[4]. If the Dominicans had allowed the aspersion cast on their greatest teacher to pass without serious protest when the condemnation came from one of themselves, they were anything but content to submit to the adverse judgment of one of their rivals. Peckham was attacked

---

[1] Dean Plumptre (Contemp. Rev. II, p. 376 note) identifies the 'unnamed professor at Paris,' referred to by Roger Bacon, with Thomas Aquinas, and I am inclined to agree with this suggestion. A passage in Royal MS. 7 F. VII. f. 159 (quoted in Part II, *sub* Richard of Cornwall) would at first sight seem to identify the unnamed professor with Friar Ric. of Cornwall. But there is no evidence that the latter was quoted as an authority in the schools (like Aristotle, Avicenna, and Averroes) during his lifetime (Bacon, Op. Ined. p. 30), nor could the statement that 'he never heard lectures on philosophy and was not educated at Paris or any other school where philosophy flourishes' (ibid. 31 and 327) apply to Richard (Mon. Franc. I, 39). On the other hand, all the facts mentioned about the unnamed professor coincide with what is known of Thomas Aquinas (Quétif-Echard, I, 271). It may then be assumed with some probability that we have here Bacon's judgment on his great contemporary. 'Truly,' he writes, 'I praise him more than all the crowd of students, because he is a very studious man, and has seen infinite things, and had expense; and so he has been able to collect much that is useful from the sea of authors,' but he was fatally handicapped by not going through the regular training (Opera Ined. p. 327). His followers maintain that philosophy as published in his works is complete—that nothing further can be added. 'These writings,' Bacon continues, 'have four sins : the first is infinite puerile vanity; the second is ineffable falsity; the third superfluity of volume ... ; the fourth is that parts of philosophy of magnificent utility and immense beauty and without which facts of common knowledge (*quae vulgata sunt*) cannot be understood—concerning which I write to your glory—have been omitted by the author of these works. And therefore there is no utility in those writings, but the greatest injury to wisdom.'

[2] Mullinger, Cambridge, I, 120–1.

[3] Wood, Annals, sub anno 1276, p. 306. Peckham, Reg. III, 852, &c. Kilwardby seems to have generally supported his Order against the Franciscans: see Peckham's letter to the Prior of the Friars Preachers at Oxford; he is amazed at the 'cruelty and inconsideration' of a letter of his predecessor's, in which the latter apparently made an attack on the Minorites; Register, III, 117–118.

[4] Ibid. III, 866, 898. Wood, Annals, 318 seq.; Annales Monast. IV, 297 seq.

both by the Provincial of the Black Friars in a congregation at Oxford[1] and in an anonymous pamphlet apparently by a Cambridge Dominican[2]—'a cursed page and infamous leaf,' as he describes it, 'whose beginning is headless, whose middle malignant, and whose end foolish and formless.' His action further involved the whole of the Franciscan Order in England in the storm. He was accused of 'having sown discord between the Orders[3];' and to defend himself against the charge of unduly favouring the Franciscans, he denied that he had consulted the latter on the subject and insisted on the previous condemnation of the same error by his predecessor[4]. He claimed to be actuated by no personal animus against the dead, whom he held in high honour and whom he had himself defended; his attack was directed against ignorant and arrogant men who presumed to teach what they did not know and to entice youths to the same errors. 'We cannot and dare not,' he urged, 'fail to rescue our children, as far as we can, from the traps of error;' and he forbade 'curious theologians' to defend the condemned doctrines in 'the disputes of boys' (*in certaminibus puerilibus*) at Oxford.

'We by no means,' he adds, 'reprobate the studies of philosophers, so far as they serve the mysteries of theology, but the profane novelties which, contrary to philosophic truth, have been introduced into the heights of theology in the last twenty years, to the injuries of the saints.'

The question became a matter rather of feeling than of argument; the *esprit de corps* of the rival factions was involved, and the two Orders further estranged[5].

Peckham lost few opportunities of advancing the interests of the Mendicants at the expense of the monks and secular clergy, and of his brother Franciscans against the other Orders. The discipline and morals of the nuns of Godstow had suffered owing to the proximity of their house to the university-town, and the Archbishop, in his injunctions for the better government of the same, appointed two Friars Preachers and two Friars Minors (or four of each if necessary) as permanent confessors to the Convent[6]. In 1291 he wrote to the Prior of St. Frideswide's urging him to confer the church of St. Peter le Bailey on some one devoted to the Friars Minors and

---

[1] Peckham, Reg. III, 864.
[2] Ibid. 896-901, 943.
[3] Ibid. 867.
[4] Ibid. 852, 866, 901.
[5] Peckham writes: 'Diversity of opinion among philosophers does not dissolve friendship, but among modern vain-talkers it has passed to the affection of the heart.' Reg. III, 900.
[6] Ibid. 845-852 (A.D. 1284).

nominated by them[1]. While strenuously asserting the right of the Minorites to hear confessions in spite of the opposition of the parish priests[2], he forbade the Carmelites and Austin Friars at Oxford to hear any confessions of any persons whatsoever, regular or secular, clerk or lay, male or female, and ordered the Archdeacon, if they disobeyed, to pronounce public sentence of excommunication on them[3]. Arguing that 'it was lawful to change a vow for a better one[4],' he maintained that the Franciscans might, as they had hitherto done, admit members of other religious bodies to their Order; he would, he wrote to the Chancellor of the University of Oxford, himself admit them, if he were still Provincial Minister.

'We have heard with great surprise,' he proceeds, 'that the Prior and friars of the Order of St. Augustine in Oxford are imposing the mark of excommunication on the Friars Minors of Oxford, and defaming them in many ways, for receiving one of their friars in the aforesaid canonical form. We therefore order you to go in person to the Austin friary and warn them, in our name and by our authority, to cease from these detractions. But if they assert that they have raised this tumult against the Minorites on the ground of some privilege of theirs, you shall ask them to let me have a copy of their privilege to compare with those of the Minorites which we have to maintain; and we will certainly not allow them to be molested in contravention of their privilege; nor will we endure that the Friars Minors be injuriously oppressed, for by so doing we should break the commands of the Pope[5].'

Peckham further, while condemning the erroneous opinions of the Dominicans at Oxford, denied the claim to superiority which they put forward[6]. The Franciscans claimed precedence on the ground of their humility (which of course dwindled in inverse ratio as their assertion of it grew), and of their absolute poverty. The Archbishop enunciated the formula which was condemned by the inquisitors and the Pope in the next century, and which formed, so to speak, the

---

[1] Peckham, Reg. III, 977.

[2] Ibid. 956: cf. 952, the Friars Minors and Preachers have more power than the secular priests, being *literatiores et sanctiores* than the latter. The Franciscans no doubt contrasted favourably with their neighbour, the Rector of St. Ebbe's, at this time. In 1284 the Rector of St. Ebbe's was summoned by the Archdeacon to answer to a charge of repeated adultery with the wife of a parishioner, William le Boltere; it was further alleged that to get the husband out of the way he had twice secured his imprisonment on a false charge; the second time, the unfortunate man died in gaol. Ibid. 855. Perhaps there was also a black sheep among the Oxford Franciscans about this time; an unbeliever might suspect human agency in the 'memorabile factum' related in the Lanercost Chronicle, p. 136; q. v. (A.D. 1290).

[3] Reg. I, 99–100: A.D. 1280.

[4] Ibid. III, 838–840: A.D. 1284. But see Archiv f. L. u. K. Gesch. VI. 41, 88.

[5] The passage has been somewhat condensed in translating.

[6] Reg. III, 867.

text of the controversy, '*De paupertate Christi.*' He defined the poverty of the apostles to be

'having no title to the possession of any property real or personal, private or common[1];'

the Minorites in following this example were in a state of 'perfection,' and lived a holier life than any other Order in the Church.

The claim was generally admitted, and led to the exaltation of the Minorites in the eyes of the world at the expense of the other Orders[2]. As early as 1269 a controversy on this point arose between the convents of the two Orders at Oxford. A Dominican named Solomon of Ingeham accused the Minorites of receiving money either with their own hands or through a third party[3]. The Franciscans denied the charge and demanded the punishment of Friar Solomon. The Dominicans asked them to prove the falsehood of Solomon's assertion and promised then to punish him. 'The burden of proof,' replied the Franciscans, 'lies with you who affirm, not with us who deny.' The Dominicans brought forward many instances in which they maintained that the Minorites had actually received money. These, answered the latter, were merely personal transgressions, and affected the community no more than any case of carnal sin or disobedience. The Dominicans, however, based their contention mainly on the argument that money bequeathed to the Franciscans must be received either by them in person or by intermediaries on their behalf. The Minorites answered

'that, according to the definition of lawyers, money left by will is counted among the goods of the deceased until it passes into the *dominium* and property of the legatee. But it cannot become ours by legal right or pass into our *dominium* without our consent. Thus money, howsoever it may be deposited by the executors or committed to anyone for the brethren, is always counted among the goods of the deceased as long as it remains unspent, and the executors can, by their own authority or by that of the deceased, reclaim it at pleasure. How then can it be called ours?'

---

[1] Reg. III, xcix—summary of Peckham's Liber Pauperis: 'nihil possessorie sibi intitulatum; mobile vel immobile, proprium vel commune, nil dico quod divicias saperet, vel delicias redoleret, aut secularem gloriam ministraret.' Among the questions discussed by Peckham and others at this time was, 'Utrum habere aliquid in communi minuat de perfectione.' Archiv für Litt. u. Kirch. Gesch. IV, 46, &c.

[2] Phillipps, MS. 3119, fol. 86, dorse: 'Veniunt ad nos diversi seculares et religiosi comparacionem inter statum et statum facientes, statum vestrum (i.e. Minorum) extollentes, et nostrum (Praedicatorum) in hoc deprimentes, quod nos peccuniam recipimus, vos autem non recipitis, judicantes nos in hoc minus perfectos mundi contemptores.'

[3] Phillipps, MS. 3119 fol. 86-88: printed in Appx. C.

Peace was eventually restored by the interposition of the Chancellor and leading secular masters, at whose recommendation Friar Solomon withdrew his words. It is curious that neither the document containing the account of this quarrel, nor Peckham, mention the explanation which afterwards became the accepted theory, that the ownership of the goods of the Franciscans was vested in the Pope. Yet this explanation was originally given by Innocent IV in 1245[1].

As far as the bulk of the Franciscan Order was concerned, the controversy on 'Evangelical Poverty' was purely a theoretical one[2], its ultimate importance rather accidental than real. The claim to 'this perfitnesse,' as Daw Topias contemptuously calls it, rested not on fact but on a legal construction. The friars had only the use, not the proprietorship, of their lands and houses and goods. John XXII by his bull, '*Ad conditorem canonum*,' issued on the 8th of December, 1322, and declaring that use was inseparable from proprietorship, withdrew from the Order the right of holding property in the name of the Roman See, and thus went far to destroy its theoretical claim to precedence. The whole Order, instead of the party of the *Spirituales* merely, was for a time banded against the Pope; and the dispute about a legal quibble became transformed under the hands of Ockham into an examination of the position and claims of the Papacy, and of the whole relation of Church and State.

Ockham probably studied at Oxford in his younger days, but it was no doubt later in life, and under the influence of Marsilius of Padua, that he developed the doctrines which made him 'at once the glory and the reproach of his Order[3].' In philosophy he had many followers at Oxford in the fourteenth century, and the Franciscan Convent was, like the rest of the University, divided on the questions of Nominalism and Realism[4]. The dispute concerning the poverty of Christ was not allowed to rest. It was this discussion which first brought the Archbishop of Armagh into open hostility to the friars[5]; and Wiclif men-

---

[1] Wadding, III, p. 130. Cf. Nicholas III's bull, '*Exiit qui seminat*' (1279), and Clement V's '*Exivi de Paradiso*' (1312). Peckham held that the ownership remained with the donors; Regist., Vol. III, Preface, p. c (from Peckham's declaration of the Rule in the '*Firmamentum trium ordinum*').

[2] On the whole subject see Ehrle's articles in the Archiv für Litt. u. Kirch. Gesch. on 'Die Spiritualen;' Vol. IV, p. 46 seq. contains a clear exposition of the basis of the 'theoretischer Armuthsstreit.'

[3] Lyte, Oxford, p. 118; Shirley, Introd. to Fasc. Zizan. p. xlix; R. L. Poole, Wycliffe, p. 41.

[4] e. g. among the followers of Ockham was Friar Adam Godham; among the realists, Friar John Canon, &c. Cf. Wood, Annals, I, 439.

[5] Lechler, Johann v. Wiclif, I, 218 seq.

tions the controversy as being still carried on between the two Orders in his time.

'Prechours seyn þat Crist hadde hiȝe shone as þei have; ffor ellis wolde not Baptist mene þat Crist hadde þuongis of siche schone. Menours seyn þat Crist went barfote, or ellis was shood as þei ben, for ellis Magdalene shulde not have founde to þus have washid Cristis feet¹.'

A great historian has said of the Middle Ages, that 'at no time in the world's history has theory, pretending all the while to control practice, been so utterly divorced from it².' An extract from the Patent Rolls³ will afford a striking illustration of the truth of these words as far as the learned Franciscans, the professors of evangelical poverty, are concerned. The date is February 22nd, 1378; the writ is issued in the King's name.

'Know that whereas certain horses, cups, books, money, silver vessels, and diverse other goods and chattels, which belonged to our beloved brother in Christ, John Welle of the Order of Friars Minors, doctor in theology, have been abstracted and carried away out of his dwelling in London by one Thomas Bele his servant and other evil doers, ... we have of our special favour granted to the said John all the horses, cups, books, money, vessels and other goods and chattels aforesaid, wheresoever they may be,' &c.

It was probably the glaring contrast between the lofty claims of the friars and their actual life, rather than any inferiority in their morality as compared with the secular priests, which exposed them to the bitterest denunciations and taunts of the reformers. The Mendicants were far more in sympathy with the poor than were the endowed monks, and possessed far more than the parish priests the confidence of the people⁴. Wiclif recognised this fact, while he lamented it.

Fitzralph had been deputed by Clement VI in 1349-1350 to inquire into this dispute; see his Liber de pauperie Salvatoris, edited by R. L. Poole for the Wyclif Society, 1890 (p. 273).

¹ Select English Works of J. Wyclif, I, 76. Cf. ibid. p. 20; among the 'fals lores' sown by the friars, Wiclif mentions ' of þe begginge of Crist.'

² Bryce, Holy Roman Empire, p. 121 (7th edition).

³ Pat. 1 Ric. II, pt. 4, m. 37 (printed in Appx. B). John Welle may have been Warden, though the fact would probably have been stated in the record; I have not been able to find any names of London Wardens between 1368 and 1398; Mon. Franc. I, 521, 523.

⁴ This is clearly brought out in the history of the peasant revolt of 1381, if we may trust Walsingham's account of Jack Straw's confession (Hist. Angl. II, 10): 'Postremo regem occidissemus, et cunctos possessionatos, episcopos, monachos, canonicos, rectores insuper ecclesiarum de terra delevissemus. Soli mendicantes vixissent super terram, qui suffecissent pro sacris celebrandis aut conferendis universae terrae.'

'Though it raine on the Awter of the Parish Church, the blind people is so deceived, that they will rather give to waste houses of Friars, then to Parish Churches, or to common waies, though men cattle and beasts ben perished therein[1].'

The first important attack on the friars in the fourteenth century was that led by Richard Fitzralph, Archbishop of Armagh. He had been Fellow of Balliol College before 1325 and Chancellor of the University in 1333[2]. While assailing the whole principle of mendicancy, his main charge against the friars, especially the friars at Oxford, was that of 'stealing' children, i. e. of secretly inducing them to enter the Mendicant Orders. In 1357 the Archbishop was cited to appear and defend himself before the Papal Court at Avignon; and on the 8th of November, in a solemn assembly of Pope and Cardinals, he made a great speech in defence of the parish priests against the Mendicants[3]. The Archbishop stated that, owing to the privileges of hearing confessions which the friars enjoyed, almost all youths in the Universities, and in the houses of their parents (in nearly all of which friars were to be found as '*familiares*'), had Mendicants as their confessors.

'Enticed by the wiles of the friars and by little presents[4], these boys (for the friars cannot circumvent men of mature age) enter the Orders, nor are they afterwards allowed, according to report, to get their liberty by leaving the Order, but they are kept with them against their will until they make profession; further, they are not permitted, as it is said, to speak with their father or mother, except under the supervision and fear of a friar; an instance came to my knowledge this very day; as I came out of my inn an honest man from England, who has come to this court to obtain a remedy, told me that immediately after last Easter, the friars at the University of Oxford abducted in this manner his son who was not yet thirteen years old, and when he went there, he could not speak with him except under the supervision of a friar.'

Parents were in consequence afraid to send their sons to the Universities, and preferred to keep them at home as tillers of the soil. While the numbers both of the friaries and of their inmates had enormously

---

[1] 'Two short treatises,' &c. p. 35 (cap. 17).

[2] Hist. MSS. Comm. 4th Rep. 442; Lechler, I, 217. His principal opponent was also an Oxford man, Friar Roger Conway; see notice of him in Part II.

[3] Ibid. 220 seq. (full analysis of the speech). The original is printed in Edw. Brown's Fascic. Rer. Expetend. (1695), Vol. II, under the title, *Defensorium Curatorum*. A short summary in old English will be found in Mon. Franc. II.

[4] Cf. statute of the University against 'wax-doctors' (A.D. 1358); Mun. Acad. 207–8; 'Nam pomis et potu, ut populus fabulatur, puerulos ad religionem attrahunt et instigant;' (from Richard de Bury's Philobiblon), quoted on p. 42.

increased, the number of secular students in every faculty decreased; the students at Oxford, who in his time were reckoned at 30,000, had now sunk to 6000.

Though these figures are of course preposterously exaggerated, and though the main cause of the diminution of the number of students was the Black Death, there can be no doubt of the essential truth of the accusation. In 1358 the University of Oxford passed a statute forbidding the admission of boys under eighteen to the Orders. The statute deserves to be quoted at length[1].

'It is generally reported and proved by experience, that the nobles of this realm, those of good birth, and very many of the common people, are afraid, and therefore cease, to send their sons or relatives or others dear to them in tender youth, when they would make most advance in primitive sciences, to the University to be instructed, lest any friars of the Order of Mendicants should entice or induce such children, before they have reached years of discretion, to enter the Order of the same Mendicants; and because owing to the admission of such boys to the Mendicant Orders, the tranquillity of the students of the University has been often disturbed; therefore the said University, zealous in the bowels of piety both for the number of her sons and the quiet of her students, has ordained and decreed, that if any of the Order of Mendicants shall receive to their habit in this University, or induce, or cause to be received or induced, any such youth before the completion of his eighteenth year at least, or shall send such an one away from the University or cause him to be sent away, in order that he may be received into the same Order elsewhere: then *eo ipso* no one of the cloister or community of such a friar, ... being a graduate, shall during the year immediately following, read or attend lectures in this University or elsewhere where such exercises would count as discharge of the statutable requirements in this University (*vel alibi quod in hac Vniversitate pro forma aliqua sibi cedat*); and this penalty shall be inflicted on all those of the Order of Mendicants, and the associates of all those, who shall be convicted by credible persons of having withdrawn youths in any way from the University, or from hearing philosophy.'

The friars did not deny the charge, but defended their conduct[2], and exerted themselves to the utmost to obtain a repeal of the statute. Their efforts were successful. While a suit which they had begun in the Roman Court was yet undecided, the Provincials of the four Orders laid their grievances before the King in Parliament[3]. In 1366 the obnoxious statute was formally annulled, on condition that the

---

[1] Mun. Acad. 204.
[2] Wood, Annals, I, 475 (W. Folvyle, Cambridge Minorite); Twyne, MS.XXII, f. 103 c (W. Woodford). The Oxford Dominican (?) who writes under the pseudonym of Daw Topias says in answer to this accusation, 'To tille folk to Godward, I holde it no theft.' Polit. Poems, II, 83 (R.S.).
[3] Rolls of Parliament, Vol. II, p. 290.

friars' suits at Rome and elsewhere against the University should cease¹. The latter, however, did not abandon the struggle; its influence is probably to be seen in the petition of the Commons in 1402², that no one be allowed to enter any of the four Orders under the age of twenty-one years. The King's answer was not favourable: he ordained merely that no friar should admit to his Order an infant under fourteen years without the assent of his father, mother, or guardians. The ordinance applied to the whole of England, and the petition of the Commons is a sign that the popularity of the friars had suffered under the attacks of Wiclif.

It has been clearly shown by recent criticism³ that Wiclif's enmity to the friars was confined to the last few years of his life. His earlier opponents were the monks—the *religiosi possessionati*. At one time he compares the poverty and mendicancy of St. Francis with the manual labour of St. Peter and St. Paul, in contrast with the possessions and worldly honours of the ecclesiastics of his time⁴. He seems to have been on terms of some intimacy with William Woodford, who may be regarded as the leader of the Oxford Minorites in their subsequent controversy with the reformer and his followers. Woodford relates⁵ that

'when I was lecturing concurrently with him on the Sentences⁶.... Wiclif used to write his answers to the arguments, which I advanced to him, in a notebook which I sent him with my arguments, and to send me back the notebook.'

Wiclif had indeed many points of sympathy, especially on questions of ecclesiastical polity, with the Friars Minors. He was in agreement with them and in antagonism to the monks and many of the bishops, in the opinion that the tribute to the Pope should be refused, and that the secular power was, under some circumstances, justified in depriving the Church of its possessions⁷. Eight or nine years before Wiclif

---

¹ Rolls of Parliament, Vol. II, p. 290.
² Ibid. Vol. III, p. 502, § 62.
³ Lechler, J. v. Wiclif, I, 319, 374, 585 seq.
⁴ Ibid. 588.
⁵ Twyne, MS. XXI, 502; from Woodford's *Quaestiones de sacramento altaris contra Wyclefum*, qu. 63.
⁶ 'Quando concurrebam cum eo in lectura sententiarum.' I do not know the precise meaning of the phrase: cf. Mun. Acad. 393, 'Statutum est quod duo Magistri in theologia, si velint, possunt concurrere disputando.'
⁷ See the curious account in the *Continuatio Eulogii Historiarum* of the council of bishops and lords held at Westminster under the presidency of the Black Prince in 1374, the subject of discussion being the papal tribute. Four doctors of theology were present, namely, the Provincial of the Friars Preachers, J. Owtred, monk of Durham, an opponent of the friars (see MS. Ball.

wrote his famous tract in defence of the Parliament of 1366, an Oxford friar and doctor declared in his school that the King had the right of depriving ecclesiastics of their temporalities; he was ordered by Congregation to recant this and other opinions solemnly after a University sermon, and to pay 100s. to the University [1].

When, however, Wiclif began to call in question the Church's doctrine on the Eucharist, he found himself in direct antagonism to the friars; and the quarrel, which began in a dogmatic difference in the schools[2], soon acquired a wider character. Wiclif's accusations resolve themselves really into three[3]; firstly, that the friars upheld the 'idolatrous' doctrine of the Eucharist; secondly, that they maintained the theory of the mendicancy of Christ; thirdly, that they taught the people to rely for their salvation on letters of fraternity and prayers and masses, instead of on a good life; whence a general demoralization ensued.

Coll. 149, ff. 63-5), J. Mardisle, Friar Minor, and an Austin Friar. The Archbishop said, 'The pope is lord of all; we cannot refuse him this,' 'quod omnes praelati seriatim dixerunt.' The Dominican refused to give an opinion, and suggested a hymn or mass. The monk used the old argument about the two swords. Mardisle promptly retorted with the text, 'Put up again thy sword into his place,' showing that the two swords did not mean spiritual and temporal power; 'et quod Christus temporale dominium non habebat, nec Apostolis tradidit sed relinquere docuit;' which he proved by a learned appeal to scripture, authorities, and history. The subsequent proceedings are very humorously told; Eulog. Hist. III, 337-8. Four Mendicant B.D.'s were, at John of Gaunt's wish, present at Wiclif's trial in 1377, to support him by argument in case of need. Lechler, I, 369, and note.

[1] Mun. Acad. p. 208. He is called merely 'Frater Johannes ... Doctor,' the surname and Order being omitted; but his 'heresies' are those of the Franciscans.

[2] Lechler, I, 586. Of the twelve doctors who condemned Wiclif's doctrines at Oxford in 1381 (or beginning of 1382), six were Mendicants; Tyssyngton was the only Minorite. Wood, Annals, I, 499.

[3] These are clearly stated in his treatise 'De Blasphemia, contra Fratres,' Select English Works, III, 402 seq.; Trialogus, Lib. IV, cap. 27-32. Ibid. cap. 37, another charge is added, namely, the opposition offered by the friars to the 'Poor Priests,' of which Wiclif says: 'Revera inter omnia peccata, quae unquam consideravi de fratribus, hoc mihi videtur esse sceleratissimum propter multa; emanavit enim integre ex unicordi consilio et consensu omnium horum fratrum.' The 'Poor Priests' resembled the early Friars Minors in many points, e. g. as itinerant preachers: perhaps Wiclif, when organizing the former, was led to look more closely into the ideal which the latter professed to follow; and if so, he may well have been shocked at the contrast between that ideal and the reality. One change in the life of the friars—their gradual approximation to the seclusion of the older Orders, may be illustrated by two passages from Matthew Paris and Wiclif (allowance being made for the prejudices of the writers). The friars, says the Benedictine historian, 'wandered through cities and villages,' and 'had the ocean for their cloister' (Chron. Majora, V, 529). Wiclif attacks them for living

'Popis graunten no pardoun to men bot if þei be byfore verrely contritte, bot þese freris in hor lettres speken of no contricioun [1].'

It is improbable, however, that the indulgences granted by the friars differed from the other indulgences of the Middle Ages, which in theory absolved from the temporal punishment, not from the sin and eternal punishment. Wiclif may have classed with the friars the 'pardoners' who did not belong to any of the four Orders [2]. The records relating to the Franciscan house at Oxford throw no light on the matter, which indeed belongs to the general history of the Mendicants, not to the history of a particular convent. Wiclif's charges amount practically to this: the friars were the foremost champions of the external, unspiritual form of religion, which he laboured to destroy: they were no longer leaders of thought, but obstacles to progress.

Though Wiclif's writings, especially his English writings, are full of violent invective against the friars [3], it is difficult to find in them any definite accusations of the grosser forms of immorality. One instance will sufficiently illustrate the difference between Wiclif and his followers.

'Friars also,' says the former, 'be foully envenomed with ghostly sin of Sodom, and so be more cursed than the bodily Sodomites that were suddenly dead by hard vengeance of God; for they do ghostly lechery by God's word, when they preach more their own findings for worldly muck, than Christ's Gospel for saving of men's souls [4].'

'Jack Upland' improves on this, and does not scruple to impute to the friars generally the vilest sins.

> 'Your freres ben taken alle day
> with wymmen and wifes,
> bot of your privey sodomye
> spake I not yette [5].'

At Oxford the seculars, always numerically strong and jealous of the regulars, rallied to Wiclif's standard; while the Mendicants roused

'closed in a cloister,' instead of going about among the people, 'to whom thy maie most profite ghostlie ... Charitie showld drive Friars to come out amongst the people and leaue Caymes Castels that bin so needeless and chargeous to the people.' (Two Short Treatises, &c., p. 21.)

[1] Select English Works, III, 424.

[2] Wyclif, Latin Works, *Sermones*, II, xlvii. Jusserand, *La Vie Nomade*, p. 186 seq.; Rogers' Introd. to Gascoigne's *Liber Veritatum*, p. 123.

[3] He accuses them, e.g. of 'stinking covetise,' of 'simonie and foule marchandise;' they are 'worse enemies and sleers of man's soule than is the cruel fende of hell by himself;' some of them are 'damned divels;' Two Short Treatises, Select English Works, *passim*. Latin works, *Sermones*, II. Cf. Polit. Poems (Rolls Series), I, 266:

'Ther shal no saule have rowme in helle
Of frers ther is suche throng.'

[4] Two Short Treatises, cap. 48 (printed by Vaughan, p. 254).

[5] Polit. Poems, II, 49.

the anger of the University by appealing to external authority. The friars were accused of having made use of their position as confessors to stir up the peasant revolt. On the 18th of February, 1382, the heads of the four Mendicant Convents at Oxford sent a letter to John of Gaunt, denying the charge and begging his protection[1]; all evils were attributed to them, and their lives were in danger. Their chief enemy was Nicholas Hereford. In Lent of the same year Hereford preached a University sermon at St. Mary's, in which he argued that no 'religious' should be admitted to any degree at Oxford[2]. He was appointed by the Chancellor to deliver the principal English sermon of the year at St. Frideswide's Cross on Ascension Day (May 15th), and used the opportunity to attack monks and friars and mendicancy in general[3]. On the 19th of the same month, the 'Council of the Earthquake' met at the Blackfriars in London, and condemned ten of Wiclif's conclusions as heretical and fourteen as erroneous; among the seventeen doctors of divinity who took part in the council were four Minorites, the Oxford Franciscans being represented by Hugo Karlelle and Thomas Bernewell[4]. The Archbishop sent Peter Stokes, a Carmelite, to publish the condemnation at Oxford. The Chancellor and Proctors resented this interference with their rights, and the general feeling was strong in Wiclif's favour. Stokes and his brethren went in fear of their lives; when the Carmelite 'determined' against Philip Repyngdon on the 10th of June, men were seen in the schools with arms concealed under their clothes. At length, on June 15th, the Chancellor was compelled, by the King's command, to publish the condemnation of the twenty-four conclusions;

'and he thus so roused the seculars against the religious that many of the latter feared death, the seculars crying out that they wanted to destroy

---

[1] Fascic. Zizan. 292–5: the letter is dated Oxford, 'sub sigillo priorum et gardiani conventuum et ordinum praefatorum.' The part which the Franciscans took in the peasant revolt still remains obscure. An undated letter of Richard II 'to the Minister of the Friars Minors of Dorchester' refers to an individual friar agitating among the labourers about this time; but whether before or after the rising I cannot say. The letter occurs in MS. Dd. III, 53, p. 97, in the Cambridge Public Library. 'Nous auons entenduz coment votre Confrere et obedientier du dit ordre ffrere Johan Gorry (or Grey?) fait excitacion et maintenance a les cotagiers et autres tenauntz notre cher en dieu labbe de Midelton, laborers demorantz dedeinz la Seigneurie mesme labbe, de rebeller contre le dite Abbe leur seignur es choses queles ils sont tenuz et deuient fair a lui de reson selonc la forme de lestatut fait des laborers,' &c.

[2] Fascic. Zizan. p. 305.

[3] Lyte, 264. A Latin version of the sermon is in Twyne, MS. IV, 172–4.

[4] Fascic. Zizan. 287.

the University, though really they (the religious) only defended the cause of the Church[1].'

In November the University tried to turn the tables on its adversaries; in an assembly of the clerks at St. Frideswide's, the Chancellor accused some of the orthodox party (among them a Minorite friar) of heresy[2]. But from this time the sacramental controversy tended to retire into the background, and the alliance of monks and friars, which Wiclif's attack on the faith had called into being[3], came to an end. In 1392, Henry Crompe, a Cistercian monk, who had been a prominent opponent of Wiclif, was charged with having determined on several occasions against the right of the friars to hear confessions[4]. Friar John Tyssyngton and other Minorites took part in his condemnation in a Convocation held in the house of the Carmelites at Stamford. In their anxiety to silence their adversaries, the Mendicant Orders proved false to the tradition common to all the great mediaeval Universities—the tradition of intellectual freedom; they upheld the claim of Archbishop Arundel to visit the University, and lent their support to the rigid censorship which he established[5]. But it is only fair to remember that, years before this, the authority of the Church had been invoked against the teaching of the friars themselves. In 1368 Simon Langham sent thirty errors of the friars to the University, and it was enacted that no one should presume to defend or approve these tenets in the schools or elsewhere 'on pain of the greater excommunication[6].'

The history of the fourteenth and fifteenth centuries affords many other illustrations of the hostility with which the friars, and especially the Minorites, were regarded by the University. The subject of academical degrees, and of the action taken by the University against the 'wax-doctors,' has been treated elsewhere. A statute, which probably dates from the first half of the fifteenth century, provides that both the *collatores* of University sermons shall, if possible, be seculars[7]. Wood says that in the years 1423 and 1424 there

'were nothing but heartburnings in the University occasioned by the Friers their preaching up and down against tithes.'

The chief offender, Friar William Russell, warden of the Greyfriars of

[1] Fascic. Zizan. 298, 301, 311, &c.
[2] Lyte, 273; Wilkins, *Conc.* III, 172.
[3] Polit. Poems, I, 259.
[4] Fascic. Zizan. 343-357.
[5] Twyne, MS. Vol. II, f. 229, letter of Archbishop Arundel to John XXIII, dated Aug. 20 (1410?).
[6] Wood, Annals, I, 481.
[7] Mun. Acad. 289; the statute before it is dated 1431, that after it, 1432.

London, taught that tithes might be given arbitrarily, i. e. not to the parson legally entitled to them, but 'for the pious use of the poor,' according to the will of the giver. The University of Oxford condemned this doctrine and ordained that everyone taking a degree should formally abjure it: the oath, which remained in force till 1564, runs thus:—

Insuper, tu jurabis quod nullas conclusiones per fratrem Wilhelmum Russell, ordinis Minorum, nuper positas et praedicatas, contra decimas personales, et in nostra Universitate Oxoniae, necnon in venerabili concilio episcoporum, anno Domini millesimo quadringentesimo vicesimo quinto celebrato Londoniis, solemniter damnatas, nec alicujus earum sententiam tenebis, docebis, vel defendes efficaciter publice aut occulte, nec aliquem doctorem, tentorem vel defensorem hujusmodi, ope, consilio vel favore juvabis[1].

For a similar offence another Franciscan, William Melton, D.D., was arrested at the instance of the University, and compelled to recant[2]. The Alma Mater kept a vigilant eye on her sons wherever they might be. In 1482 Friar Isaac Cusack, D.D., began to create disturbances in Ireland by preaching the old Franciscan doctrine of evangelical poverty; he was captured, sent to Oxford, and degraded and expelled the University as a vagabond and a heretic[3].

The feeling of nationality fostered by the long French wars was not without its influence on the friars in England and especially at the Universities. In 1369 the Chancellor caused a royal proclamation to be published at Carfax ordering all French students at Oxford, both religious and secular, to leave the kingdom[4]. In 1388 a royal writ was issued to the Warden of the Friars Minors in Oxford at the advice of the same convent, warning him to admit no foreign friars who might reveal to the enemy 'the secrets and counsel of our kingdom,' and to expel any such friars for whose good behaviour he would not be responsible, or who would not pray or celebrate masses for the King and the good estate of the realm[5].

Among the many problems presented by the reign of Richard II, not the least obscure is the passionate loyalty with which the Franciscans regarded his memory[6]. Yet Richard II and his councillors

[1] Mun. Acad. 376; for other references see notice of William Russell in Part II.
[2] Wood, Annals, I, 572.
[3] Ibid. 638.
[4] Twyne, MS. XXIII, 188.
[5] Close Roll, 12 Ric. II, m. 42 (Appx. B).

[6] The *Continuatio Eulogii Historiarum* gives the reasons alleged by two individual friars for their support of Richard:—(1) personal: 'teneor sibi et tota parentela mea quia ipse promovit illam,' p. 390; (2) legitimist standpoint: 'electio nulla est, vivente possessore legitimo,' p. 392.

were suspected of Lollardy, while his successor posed as the champion of orthodoxy. Henry IV, however, derived his support chiefly from the wealthy ecclesiastics, and the Lollardy of the Court of Richard II was rather political than dogmatic; the opinions prevalent at the Court were more in consonance with Wiclif's earlier teaching and with the teaching of the Franciscan Order on the need of poverty in the Church and the evils of its endowments, than with the Lollard doctrine of the Eucharist. In the early years of Henry IV the Franciscans were active in organizing conspiracies[1]; the pulpit and the confessional were used to spread disaffection against the new monarch[2]; and the failure of his campaigns was attributed to the magical arts of the Friars Minors[3]. In 1402, eight Minorites of the convent of Leicester were seized, and convicted on their own admission of having organized an armed revolt to find King Richard and restore him to the throne[4]. They were condemned to be hanged and decapitated at Tyburn, and the sentence was carried out in the sight of many thousands without any ecclesiastical protest. One of these friars was Roger Frisby, an old man and Master in Theology[5]. On the Vigil of the feast of St. John the Baptist[6]—the very day on which the rebels were to meet 'in the plain of Oxford,' his head was taken from London Bridge and brought to Oxford;

'and in the presence of the procession of the University, the herald proclaimed: "This Master Friar Minor of the convent of Leicester in hypocrisy, adulation, and false life, preached often, saying that King Richard is alive, and roused the people to seek him in Scotland;" and his head was set on a stake there[7].'

While subject to attacks from without, the Franciscan Order suffered from rival factions within. The long-standing division between

---

[1] Eulog. Hist. III, 388 seq.; Stubbs, Const. Hist. III, 36.
[2] Eulog. Hist. III, 392.
[3] Stubbs, *ut supra*.
[4] Eulog. Hist. III, 391: it is mentioned with less detail in most of the chronicles of the time, e.g. Walsingham, Otterbourne. Adam of Usk's account differs in some points; 'undecim de ordine fratrum minorum in theologia doctores,' &c., p. 82.
[5] Eulog. Hist. III, 391, where his defence before the King, or rather statement of his position, is given. Before his execution he preached on the text, 'Into thy hands, Lord, I commend my spirit.' 'Et devote recommendavit omnes qui causa mortis suae erant;' ibid. 393. His name is given by Wylie, *Henry IV*, Vol. I, p. 277. He was D.D. of Cambridge (Fascic. Zizan. 287) and perhaps had no further connexion with Oxford than that mentioned in the text.
[6] Nativitas (June 24) or Decollatio (Aug. 29)?
[7] Eulog. Hist. III, 394. The whole description of these events by the anonymous continuator of the *Eulogium* is extremely graphic and powerful; his sympathies are strongly on the side of the rebels.

the lax or Conventual, and the strict or Observant parties, at length received formal recognition in the Council of Constance (1415) when the Observants were constituted a semi-independent branch under a Vicar-General[1]. How did this arrangement affect Oxford as a *studium generale*? The Observants as a body produced few students; the reformed houses on the Continent objected to send their brethren to Paris[2]. A few foreign Observants found their way to Oxford in the fifteenth century[3]; and when later in the century Observant friaries were founded in England[4], some of their members studied in the Conventual house at the University[5]. Whether any part of the Convent was set apart for them is unknown: according to all appearance, the brethren of both branches lived together in peace and goodwill.

---

[1] Anal. Franc. II, 260.

[2] Ibid. 297; A. D. 1435: the Observants in answer to the reproach of the Conventuals ' quod non haberent magistros in theologia nec vellent studere etc., dicebant, quod studere vellent et desiderarent, sed conqueri de hoc merito deberent, quod ipsi de communitate omnes conventus, in quibus habet Ordo studium generale, vellent ipsi habere et nullum Observantibus dare, nec ipsi vellent permittere, quod ibi promoverentur ad studia, sed promotiones darent illis de sua vita. Sed et propter innumerabiles dissolutiones, quae multo adhuc amplius vigent in conventibus studiorum generalium, sicut Parisius testatur locus, qui dicitur infernus, propter inhonestates tacendas, ne aures audientium tinnire contingeret, et propter exactiones pecuniarias ampliores quam apud saeculares, multaque alia tacenda; dicebant, se cum puritate regulae non posse ibi studere.'

[3] E. g. Gonsalvo of Portugal.

[4] The first according to Wadding (XIV, 252) was Greenwich, A. D. 1480.

[5] E. g. John Billing, Ralph Creswell.

CHAPTER VII.

ILLUSTRATIONS OF THE FRIARS' MANNER OF LIFE AND MEANS OF LIVELIHOOD: BENEFACTORS.

Lost records.—Mendicancy.—Procurators and limitors.—Career of Friar Brian Sandon.—Charges of immorality against the friars.—Their worldly manner of life before the Dissolution.—Poverty of the Convent.—Sources of income.—Annual grants from the King and others.—Frequency of bequests to the friars.—List of benefactors.—Classes from which the friars were drawn.—Motives which led men to become friars.

OF the internal economy of the Franciscan house at Oxford, or indeed of any friary in England, little is known or ever can be known. The *Registrum Fratrum Minorum Londoniae* is, in Brewer's words, 'the only work of the kind extant. A painful proof, if such were needed, of the utter devastation committed when the Franciscan convents were dissolved, and their libraries dispersed[1].' We may here give some account of the records which must once have existed in every Franciscan house or province. From the earliest times an annual *compotus*[2] or balance-sheet of income and expenditure was drawn up, and if in later days this was sometimes omitted, an ex-warden was always liable to be called to render an account to his successor[3]. In each convent would also be kept a list of the brethren who died there[4]; and lists both of living benefactors and of dead, for whose souls prayers or masses were to be said[5], while many in their

[1] Mon. Franc. I, lxxi.
[2] Ibid. 8: 'Unde accidit ut Frater Angnellus, cum Fratre Salomone, gardiano Londoniae, vellet audire compotum fratrum Londoniae, quantum sc. expendissent infra unum terminum anni, cumque audisset quod tam sumptuose processisset vel satis parca fratrum exhibitio, projecit omnes talias et rotulos, et percutiens seipsum in faciem, exclamavit, "Ay me captum!" et nunquam postea voluit audire compotum.'
[3] Acta Cur. Cancell. EEE, f. 124 b (2nd Sept. 1529), printed in Appx.
[4] Wadding (VI, 108) refers to the

'tabula or index of the brethren who died there (Cologne) such as is kept commonly in the monasteries of the Order.' See the curious necrology of the Observant Friars of Aberdeen, Mon. Franciscana, II, 123-140. Lansdowne MS. 963 is said to contain notes by Bishop Kennett, 'ex obituario conventus Fratrum Minorum Guldefordiae, MS. Norwic. 671:' it is really notes from the obituary of the Friars Preachers of Guildford, now in the University Library, Cambridge; MS. Ll. II, 9.
[5] Polit. Poems and Songs, &c., Vol. II, p. 24 (R.S.). Chaucer's 'Sompnoure'

lifetime received 'letters of confraternity[1].' In the decrees of the General Chapter of Paris in 1292 it is commanded[2] that each minister should have the lives and acts of holy friars carefully collected in his province and entered in special registers, and bring them to the General Chapter; also that all notable excesses of friars, grave crimes, and credible accusations, the sentences passed and punishments inflicted on the offenders, should be noted in books kept for the purpose, preserved in the archives of the province, and faithfully handed on to each succeeding minister. The acts of Provincial Chapters were also kept[3]. Of these and similar records we have, besides the London register already alluded to, only a few letters of fraternity[4]. Of English Franciscan records originated by or relating to the convent at Oxford, not one (unless the list of lectors and the account of the controversy with the Dominicans in 1269[5] can be called records) is known to exist[6]. Any account, therefore, of the internal life of the convent must be meagre and unsatisfactory in the highest degree.

The hours and numbers of daily services seem to have differed little, if at all, from those observed in other monastic institutions[7]. We may therefore omit this subject and treat of the points which receive additional elucidation from documents relating to Oxford.

offers an explanation of the disappearance of these 'tables' (Poet. Works, Vol. I, pp. 367-8: Bohn's edition):—

'His felaw had a staf typped with horn,
A payr of tablis al of yvory,
And a poyntel y-polischt fetisly,
And wroot the names alway as he stood
Of alle folk that gaf him eny good,
Ascaunce that he wolde for hem preye.
. . . . . .
And whan that he was out atte dore, anoon
He planed out the names everychoon
That he biforn had writen in his tablis.'

Mon. Franc. II, preface, p. xxxi. Cf. Wills in Somerset House, Holder, fol. 4 (will of J. Tate); Logge, f. 121 (J. Benet); Polit. Poems and Songs, II, 29, 33; Wiclif, Two Short Treatises, &c. (Oxford, 1608), cap. 15.

[2] Wadding, V, 299-300.

[3] Some of those relating to the German provinces are given in Nicholas Glasberger's Chronicle, Anal. Franc. II.

[4] Specimens will be found in Mon. Franc. II; Surtees, Hist. of Durham, Vol. I, p. 27; Archaeologia, XI, 85; Mullinger, Cambridge, Vol. I, p. 317, mentions a letter of fraternity of a somewhat different kind.

[5] Mon. Franc. I, 552; Appendix C.

[6] The deed of W. Wileford (Appx. A. 1) is not a Franciscan record, any more than the Public Records are. I have not been able to find the seal of the Oxford Minorites. It was attached to the original letter addressed by the four Mendicant Convents to John of Gaunt, a copy of which is printed in Fascic. Zizan. pp. 292-5. This is the only mention of the seal which I can recall. There are a few special references to Oxford in the decrees of the General Chapters; see Index, under Franciscan Order.

[7] See Testament of St. Francis: 'Oure dyvyne servyce the clerkis saide as other clerkis.' Mon. Franc. I, 564. An article in the Dominican statutes of 1228 (Dist. 1, n. 4) provides that 'hours' shall be said rapidly, 'ne fratres de-

The first means of livelihood of the Mendicant Friars was naturally begging. Certain of the brethren were appointed by the Warden to 'procure' food for the convent during some fixed period[1]. There were no definite rules as to how many friars should be sent as 'procuratores' or 'limitors'[2]; the details depended on the necessities of the convent and the will of the Superior[3]. Each house had definite 'limits' assigned to it, within which its members might beg[4]. The friars went two and two, accompanied by a servant or boy[5] who carried the offerings, which were usually in kind. The friar in Chaucer's 'Sompnoure's Tale,' himself a 'maister[6]' in the schools, after preaching in the church went round the village—

' In every hous he gan to pore and prye
And beggyd mele or chese, or ellis corn[7].'

A good deal of private begging was done by the student friars to obtain the means of study[8]. Roger Bacon appealed to his brother in England, to his powerful and wealthy acquaintances, for money to carry out the commands of the Pope[9].

'But how often (he writes to the latter) I was looked upon as a dishonest beggar, how often I was repulsed, how often put off with empty hopes, what confusion I suffered within myself, I cannot express to you. Even my friends did not believe me, as I could not explain the matter to them; so I could not proceed in this way. Reduced (*angustiatus*) to the last extremities, I compelled my poor friends [10] to contribute all that they had,

votionem amittant et eorum studium minime impediatur.' Archiv. für Litt. u. Kirch. Gesch., Vol. I, p. 189.

[1] Mon. Franc. I, 10–11; Bullarium Romanum, I, 250.

[2] Wiclif, Two Short Treatises, &c., p. 31: ' and who can best rob the poore people by false begging and other deceipts shal have this Judas office.'

[3] Bullarium, ut supra. Constitutions of Martin V, cap. vi: ' Item quod omnes fratres vadant pro eleemosyna confidenter juxta discretionem Praelati praecipientis, cujus arbitrio committimus discernendum, qui congrue mittendi sunt pro eleemosyna, vel qui non.'

[4] Wadding, IX, 438; complaint of the Minorites of Cambridge in 1395 that a house of the same Order at Ware was trespassing on their *limites*, and bull forbidding the same. Cf. Polit. Songs and Poems, &c., Vol. II, pp. 21, 78.

[5] In early days they carried the offerings themselves in their ' caparones' or under their arms. Mon. Franc. I, 10–11.

[6] Poet. Works, I, 382. This poem, though banished, owing to its coarseness in some parts, from polite society, contains a more lifelike and graphic description of the English mediaeval friar than is to be found elsewhere in literature.

[7] Ibid. 367.

[8] Burney, MS. 325, quoted above, p. 56, n. 2. Cf. Twyne, MS. IV, 173, sermon of N. Hereford in 1382: ' Cum eorum limitatores satis mendicaverint pro sua communitate, statim mendicant iterum pro seipsis, et sic falsi pravi monstrant (se) esse apostatas et frangunt regulam,' &c.

[9] Opera Ined. p. 16.

[10] *Familiares homines et pauperes*, prob. students or the common people (see

and to sell many things and to pawn the rest, often at usury, and I promised them that I would send to you all the details of the expenses and would faithfully procure full payment at your hands. And yet owing to their poverty I frequently abandoned the work, frequently I gave it up in despair and forbore to proceed.'

Begging of this kind would either be unauthorized or legalized by special license. The statutes of the Order[1] enact that every convent shall have its 'procurator' or 'syndicus,' who shall transact all the legal business of the house and receive in the name of the Roman Church for the use of the friars all pecuniary alms and bequests, or all such alms and bequests as can be changed into money. The express object of these constitutions was to

'preserve the Order in its purity and prevent the brethren being immersed in secular affairs[2].'

It would appear that at Oxford in the fourteenth century the office of alms-collector was held by one of the brethren. This conclusion, however contrary to the spirit and letter of the statutes, seems warranted by a remarkable legal document of the year 1341[3]. It is the record of a suit in the Hustings Court, in which Friar John of Ochampton, Warden of the Friars Minors at Oxford, 'through Friar John de Hentham his attorney,' charged 'Richard de Whitchford minor[4],' with refusing to render an account of the sums received by him when he was 'receiver of pence of the said warden,' and with embezzling sixty shillings or more, which he obtained from various people on the Monday after the feast of St. Michael, 1340. Two of the sums are specified, namely, one mark by the hands of Richard, servant of John de Couton, and 12*s*. by the hands of Thomas of London. The Warden claimed to have suffered loss to the extent of one hundred shillings; Richard de Whitchford could not deny the receipt of the money, but on his request the court appointed two auditors, Richard Cary and John le Peyntour; to these he rendered an

---

ibid. Pref. xx): the word translated 'friends' above is *amici*. Cf. the frequent charges against the friars that they 'devour poore men's almes in wast, and feasting of Lordes and great men.' Wiclif, Two Short Treatises, &c., p. 31; Polit. Poems and Songs, &c., II, p. 28; Peacock, Repressor, 550 (R.S.).

[1] Bull of Martin IV, Kal. Feb. A° 2, recited and confirmed by Martin V, Kal. Nov. A° 10. John XXII by his Bull 'Ad Conditorem' forbade the Franciscans to use the Bull of Martin IV without special license of the Pope; Martin V allowed them to use it 'freely and lawfully.'

[2] Wadding, X, 130.

[3] Twyne, MS. XXIII, f. 266 (Oxf. City Archives): printed in Appendix B.

[4] He is not called '*frater*,' but the omission of this word before '*minor*' is not infrequent.

CH. VII.] *MEANS OF LIVELIHOOD, ETC.* 93

account, and was found to be sixty shillings in arrears; 'and,' the record continues, 'as he cannot make satisfaction he is committed to prison.'

In the fifteenth and sixteenth centuries the Oxford friars sometimes employed laymen to represent them in the courts[1]; sometimes the Warden appeared in person[2], but most of the legal business in the Chancellor's court at Oxford was undertaken by one of the brethren. From 1507 or before, to the Dissolution, this duty was entrusted to Friar Brian Sandon. His name does not occur in the University Register, and he was, though a priest[3], probably not a student; indeed, his administrative business would hardly have left him time for other occupations. Between 1507 and 1516 and between 1527 and 1534, he appears as plaintiff or defendant in some fifteen suits in the Chancellor's court[4]. Some of these afford glimpses into the life of the friars. On the 26th of March, 1512[5], Father Brian instituted an action against John Morys, his proctor, alleging that the latter

'did not according to the convention before entered into between the said friar and John Morys, bring corn to the house of the friars minors;'

and on April 5th John Morys was committed to prison 'at the instance of the provost (*preposeti*) of the friars minors for a debt[6].'

But if the friars did not grow corn, they seem to have made use of their meadows as pasture land. On the 20th of May, 1529[7], Friar Brian sued Margery, widow of John Lock, for 7s. 8d.,

'for certain cheeses which the husband of the said Margery bought from the aforesaid Brian Sanden.'

Eventually the case was submitted to the arbitration of William Clare the elder, and Edmund Irishe, bailiffs of Oxford, with the addition of a third if necessary, each party binding itself to abide by the decision of the majority under penalty of 40s., in case of disagreement, to be paid to the party willing to accept the judgment.

While these and similar actions were instituted by Brian in fufilment of the duties of his position, he was undoubtedly engaged in others of a private nature. At one time he acts as attorney for a

---

[1] e.g. Placita de Scaccario, 3 Hen. VII, m. 35; Acta Cur. Canc. ꟼ, fol. 262 b.
[2] Placita de Scacc. 4 Hen. VII, m. 34 d: cf. Acta Cur. Canc. EEE, fol. 124 b; &c.
[3] Chapter House Books, A.$\frac{3}{11}$, fol. 31 b.
[4] Acta Cur. Canc. ꟼ, ff. 5 b, 158 b, 159 b, 167, 200 b, 258 b; EEE, 72, 107, 183, 202, 238 b, 251 b, 257, 272 b, 273.
[5] ꟼ, f. 159 b.
[6] Ibid. 160.
[7] EEE, fol. 107 a–b.

priest¹. At another he is charged with wrongfully keeping a knife, the property of *dominus* Galfred Coper². In 1531³ he had a dispute with his tailor and appealed to the law, alleging

'that, whereas he had given to William Gos⁴, tailor, three yards and three quarters of woollen cloth to make him a habit, the said Gos had purloined one quarter of a yard, and that in consequence his clothes were too short (*nimis brevem et succinctam*).'

Brian having declared on oath that he had supplied the above-mentioned amount of cloth, Gos promised to give him 14d. as satisfaction. for the missing quarter of a yard. But later in the day he again appeared and charged the friar with perjury. After some more recriminations an agreement was come to out of court, and we hear no more of the habit.

That his litigious spirit should sometimes have brought Friar Brian into trouble we cannot wonder. Several times in the latter part of his career he was in danger of 'bodily injury;' in 1532⁵ he made application to have Robert Holder bound over to keep the peace, and in 1534 the judge ordered that James Penerton should not be released from Bocardo till he found sufficient sureties that he would not inflict bodily harm on Friar Brian or his friends (*familiaribus*)⁶. The same year he complained of having been libelled by one Giles Mawket, a carpenter (*fabro lignario*), in the parish of St. Ebbe's⁷. This was probably a slander on his character, which was not above suspicion. In 1535⁸ 'a woman of Radley named Anna' asserted in the Commissary's court that she was with child by Thomas Denson, Bachelor of Laws:

'qui Denson (as the record puts it, reciting the evidence of Joanna Cowper, another woman of ill-fame) egre tulit ut extraneus quisque familiaritate dicte Anne uteretur; because (it is added in the margin) he tok fryer Bryan wrastelyng wth her in a morning⁹.'

The records of the Chancellor's court contain charges of immorality against two other Friars Minors¹⁰. The first was '*dompnus*' Robert

---

¹ EEE, fol. 257, action to recover debt.
² ꟻ fol. 167.
³ EEE, fol. 183.
⁴ On the same page occurs a 'W. Gos conductor (ut asserit) stabuli cujusdam juxta collegium animarum.'
⁵ EEE, fol. 239.
⁶ Ibid. fol. 273.
⁷ Ibid. fol. 272 b.
⁸ Ibid. fol. 324 b-325.
⁹ Denson refused to clear himself by compurgation and was sentenced to three days imprisonment (commuted to a payment of 10s. to the University) for his fornication, 'to the terror of others.'
¹⁰ And a more serious one against the Carmelites; EEE, fol. 249 b.

Beste[1], who was summoned before the court together with a scholar of Broadgates Hall,

'on grave suspicion of incontinence and disturbance of the peace.' 'Then the judge commanded '*dompnus*' Beste to go to the prison house, namely le Bocardo, and remain there for half-an-hour'—

apparently while his case was considered. It does not appear what the charge against him was, or what (if any) further steps were taken[2]. His companion was warned to moderate his attentions to the same Joanna, wife of William Cooper or Cowper, of St. Ebbe's, who appeared in the trial above referred to.

Joanna seems to have taken a special interest in the Minorites. At the end of 1533[3] Friar Arthur, B.D., appealed to the court to stop her spreading evil reports against him, which she had failed to prove; she was ordered to abstain in future

'from defaming the said friar or any of his house on pain of a fine of 40*s*. to be paid to the Convent of friars minors, and banishment from the town; also that she shall not in any way lay traps (*paret .. insidias*) for the said Arthur or any of his Order or cause such traps to be laid, under the aforesaid penalties.'

But if Friar Arthur was innocent, he was peculiarly unfortunate. A few months later[4] he again appealed for protection against the libels of Nicholas Andrews and John Poker, scholars of Peckwater's Inn. At this time Dr. Baskerfeld, Warden of the Grey Friars, was acting as substitute for the Commissary, and he heard the case in the house of the Minorites. The accusation has been carefully obliterated in the Chancellor's book, evidently by the friars themselves, but the gist of it can be deciphered.

'Judex interrogavit eosdem an voluissent prefatum Arcturum accusare et denunciare: qui responderunt se nolle[5] hoc facere ...; a quibus judex petiit ... an aliquid scandalosum et d ... scirent contra dictum fratrem, et interrogavit eos quid hoc erat: et dicebant ambo hiis verbis sequentibus (tactis evangeliis); ... they saw the seyde frere Arctur in a chambre at the sygne of the Bere in all hollows parische in Oxford with a woman in a red capp .... both locked together in a chambre, and seid to the mayd of the hous, "then ba ... why ... suche ale here to be kept? It is not thy masters will and thy mistres that ony suche ale shold be kept here."'

Friar Arthur strenuously denied the accusation, and the court adjourned

---

[1] EEE, fol. 230 (A.D. 1530).
[2] Ibid. fol. 238 b; in the margin occurs the entry, 'ffryer Robert hora 1ª xviº' (sc. die Septembris).
[3] Ibid. fol. 257.
[4] Ibid. fol. 271 b (11th May, 1534).
[5] From this point the entry is crossed out.

for two hours. When it reassembled, the defendants refused to submit to Dr. Baskerfeld's jurisdiction, arguing that he was incompetent to decide a case in which one of the members of his convent was so deeply implicated. Two days later, however, they confessed before the judge that they would not swear to their original statement, and both sides promised to forgive and forget the whole matter.

Though none of these charges was actually proved, we must admit that they show that the convent was not in a healthy state on the eve of the Dissolution. There is certainly no trace of the religious fervour by which even in the latter days some of the Observant convents were honourably distinguished. We find the brethren at Oxford engaged in money transactions, lending[1] and borrowing[2], 'buying and selling[3].' Friar John Arter[4] kept a horse in the town and raised difficulties about the bill; Randulph Craycoke or Cradoc, who had charge of the horse, would not part with it till he had received 'about ten shillings for food and grass,' which sum the friar refused to pay, asserting that Randulph had worked the horse himself (*laboravit dictum equum diversis* (?) *oneribus*). The court, to which the disputants appealed, reduced the amount by 2s.; but Arter was probably unable to pay: no one appeared at the time appointed to claim the animal, 'so we sent Cradoc away with the horse until his bill should be paid.'

The Warden, Friar Edward Baskerfeld, D.D., was plaintiff in a somewhat similar case[5], in which both sides were represented by counsel. In his evidence the friar deposed that he had lent Master Richard Weston, LL.B.,

'a Roane hors of the value of 20s. in the hostel de flore de leust[6], and that he had handed over the horse to the servant of the Subdean of Excestre in the name of Richard Weston, and that he said these words, stroking (*palpando*) the belly of the horse: "how I delyver the hors sane and sound without spurre gallyng I prey you delyver hym so ageyn," and that he never saw hym to this day.'

---

[1] Acta Cur. Canc. Ꝗ, f. 158 b, 'Friar Brian and J. Loo, tactis evangeliis, swore that Brian had lent Garret Matthew 1 mark.' EEE, f. 95 b.

[2] Cf. Ꝗ, f. 210, 'Notandum quod magister Doctor Alyngdon, ord. frm. minorum promisit se soluturum W. Hows 11ˢ 4ᵈ,' &c. (Cf. ibid. fol. 194 b: 'gardianus ... obligavit se pro vicecustode domus sue quod dictus vicecustos restitueret Ric. Wynslo duas duodenas vasium electriorum 5 ly (?) platers and dyschys and 1 pece more.')

[3] EEE, f. 161: 'R. Roberts petiit ... xxvˢ sibi debitos ab eodem Roberto Puller fratre ex causa emptionis et vendicionis,' &c.

[4] Ibid. f. 74 b (1528). Prob. the same as Friar Arthur above.

[5] Ibid. fol. 270 b–271 a (1534).

[6] Fleur de Lys, near Carfax: see Wood's City of Oxford. Part of this entry is in Latin, part English, as often.

CH. VII.]   *MEANS OF LIVELIHOOD, ETC.*   97

The parties agreed to submit the dispute to the judgment of three arbitrators, and the result does not appear in the records of the court.

No doubt some of the friars had private incomes and emoluments of their own[1] (apart from the allowance or 'exhibition' which as students they still received from their native convents or from benefactors); and some may have lived outside the walls of their monastery[2]. But the convent itself was very poor; the love of many had waxed cold, and it was inevitable that in order to get a livelihood they should resort to means forbidden by their Rule.

At the beginning of the sixteenth century[3], the Warden, Dr. Goodefyld, leased one of the gardens lying within the boundaries of the convent to Richard Leke, brewer of Oxford. The terms of the agreement are unknown, but the friars thought them—or Leke's interpretation of them, very injurious to their interests, and in 1513 and 1514 demanded the repudiation of the contract. Feeling ran very high, and Leke was in personal danger; the Warden was bound over to keep the peace, and promised

'that if his friars molested Richard Leke, he would keep them in safe custody until the matter had been more fully examined.'

Again the case was referred to arbitration and the decision is unknown. It is interesting to find that Leke was fully reconciled to the friars before his death[4].

The poverty of the brethren was aggravated by the irregularity with which payments, on which they might justly reckon, were made. One of their chief sources of income was a royal grant of 50 marcs per annum during the King's pleasure, to be paid in equal portions at Easter and Michaelmas. It was first instituted by Edward I[5] in 1289,

---

[1] e. g. Friar Nic. de Burgo. See Chap. iii, on the maintenance of the students. Wadding, IV, 255; VI, 8, on 'personal annual incomes' of friars. Bequests to individual friars sometimes occur.

[2] See Part II, N. de Burgo and J. Kynton.

[3] Acta Cur. Canc. ꟻ, fol. 212 b; 197 b., 210.

[4] See his will in Appx. B. To receive annual rents from lands was declared illegal in 1302. Wadding, VI, 8. (Cf. Barth. of Pisa, *Liber Conform.* fol. 98.)

[5] Not Henry III, as often stated. This is conclusively proved by Pat. 1 Hen. VII, pt. 1, m. 4. One entry on this membrane mentions the grant of 25 marcs to the Friars Minors, Cambridge, originally made by Henry III, then follows an entry of the 27th Nov.: 'Sciatis quod nos intelligentes qualiter dominus Edwardus primus post conquestum et alii progenitores nostri ... concesserint videlicet quilibet eorum tempore suo Gardiano et Conuentui fratrum minorum Oxonie quinquaginta marcas percipiendas annuatim ad Scaccarium suum, nos,' &c. Cf. Pat. 1 Edw. II, pt. 1, m. 17, 1 Edw. IV, pt. 3, m. 25, &c.

H

and was continued by all the kings (with the exception of Edward V) to the Dissolution[1]. Sometimes the sum was paid direct from the treasury; but often (and this seems to have been the general custom as regards royal benefactions to religious houses) a sheriff or other officer was held responsible for the payment; either he was instructed to send the requisite amount to the Exchequer, or he paid the money directly; and the sums which he paid were accredited to him when he produced his accounts at the sessions of the Exchequer. As may be proved by many instances, the system did not conduce to regularity of payment. Edward II, in December 1313, ordered Richard Kellawe, Bishop of Durham[2], 'to send to our exchequer at Westminster within fifteen days of the day of St. Hilary,' ten marks in partial satisfaction of the grant[3]. But though this sum was to be the first charge on the arrears in the Durham diocese of the tax of one-half of their income[4] imposed on the clergy by Edward I (A.D. 1294), and though writs were repeatedly[5] issued to enforce payment, we find that on the 4th of June, 1315, nothing had been done, '*unde vehementer admiramur*[6].'

The fifty marks were never made a definite fixed charge on the revenues of any one county nor were they levied year by year as a single sum; each year some sheriff or bishop was made responsible for a fraction of the whole amount. The annuity was on several occasions in arrear. Thus Henry IV in the first year of his reign granted the friars 'of his abundant favour' (*de uberiori gratia nostra*) all the arrears that had accumulated during the reign of his predecessor[7]. Affairs of State made themselves felt in the Franciscan convent. In 1450 Parliament passed a general act of resumption, annulling all

---

[1] The grant is mentioned in the following records:—Exchequer Q. R. Wardrobe, 4/7 (17-18 Edward I); Patent Roll, 32 Edw. I, m. 13; Liberate Roll, 34 Edw. I, m. 1; Pat. 1 Edw. II, part 1, m. 17; Liberate Rolls, 8 Edw. II, m. 3 and 5; 9 Edw. II, m. 2; Treasury of the Receipt, 20/51 (16 Edward II); Liberate Rolls, 10, 11, and 12 Edw. III; Issue Roll of the Exchequer, 44 Edw. III, p. 78 (printed in 1835); Pat. 1 Ric. II, pt. 6, m. 21 (referring to Pat. 1 Edw. II, and 1 Edw. III); Pat. 1 Hen. IV, pt. 2, m. 21; Rolls of Parliament, Vol. IV, 195-6 (A.D. 1422, referring to the grant by Henry V); Pat. 31 Hen. VI, pt. 2, m. 32 (referring to Pat. 1 Hen. VI); Pat. 1 Edw. IV, pt. 3, m. 25; Pat. 17 Edw. IV, pt. 2, m. 28; Rolls of Parliament, Vol. V, 520, 597; Vol. VI, 90; Harl. MS. 433 (1 Ric. III); Pat. 1 Hen. VII, pt. 1, m. 4; Pat. 1 Hen. VIII, pt. 1, m. 7; Cromwell Corresp. 2nd series, Vol. XXIII, fol. 710 b.

[2] Regist. Palat. Dunelm. (ed. Hardy), Vol. II, p. 980 (11th Dec. anno 7).

[3] Ibid. p. 1065, 'in partem cujusdem annuae eleemosynae, quam de nobis percipiant annuatim.'

[4] Ibid. pp. 1027-8. Cf. Stubbs, Constit. Hist. II, 130 (3rd edition).

[5] The Durham Register contains six writs on the subject.

[6] Ibid. p. 1085.

[7] Pat. 1 Hen. IV, pt. 2, m. 21.

grants made since the King's accession, and the annuity to the friars ceased to be paid[1]. The brethren represented to Henry VI the hardships which this loss of revenue inflicted on them, and in 1453 the King ordered the arrears to be paid,

'in order that the same warden and friars may be in a happier frame of mind (*hillariorem animum habeant*) to offer up special prayers for us to the Highest[2].'

Under the circumstances we cannot be surprised if the friars sometimes took legal measures to recover the debts due to them. It was no doubt in connexion with this grant, that in 1466 Richard Clyff, 'custos' of the Oxford Grey Friars (first in person and afterwards through his attorney) sued John Broghton, late Sheriff of Kent, in the Court of Exchequer, for 100s. due to him from the preceding year, and claimed damages to the amount of ten marks[3]. In 1488, in like manner, Richard Salford, Warden of the Friars Minors at Oxford, applied to the Barons of the Exchequer to compel John Paston, Knt., late Sheriff of Norfolk and Suffolk, to pay a debt of £10 18s., and put in a claim to £10 damages; he recovered the debt, but the damages were reduced to 26s. 8d.[4] On the same day he sued Edmund Bedyngfeld, Knt., late Sheriff of the same counties of Norfolk and Suffolk, for a debt of 'seven pounds of silver' and 100s. damages; the amount of the debt and 20s. damages were awarded him[5]. The next year he again brought an action against the same Bedyngfeld and recovered the debt (£4 2s.), while the barons assessed his damages at 10s. instead of the £4 which he claimed[6]. We gather from these instances that though the annuity was usually paid and was not often much in arrear, it was not collected without considerable trouble and expense on the part of the friars. These actions involved a journey to London and the employment of an attorney[7]: they were never settled in one day, and weeks or months elapsed between the first hearing and the second.

The Grey Friars were also in receipt of annual or weekly alms

---

[1] Pat. 31 Hen. VI, pt. 2, m. 32: 'Que quidem littere nostre (Pat. of 10th Dec. A° 1) ... ratione cuiusdam actus in parliamento nostro sexto die Novembris anno regni nostri vicesimo octavo editi vacue existunt et adnullate.' Stubbs, Const. Hist. III, 143, 150 (2nd edition).

[2] Pat. *ut supra*.

[3] Placita de Scaccario, 6 Edw. IV, m. 20.

[4] Ibid. 3 Hen. VII, m. 35.

[5] Ibid. m. 35 *in dorso*.

[6] Ibid. 4 Hen. VII, m. 34 *in dorso*.

[7] In the first three of these pleas, Jacobus Bartelet was attorney for the friars; in the fourth Ric. Salford appeared all through 'in propria persona.'

from others besides the King. Durham College paid them 50s. yearly[1].

'In ye accompts of S. Ebbs made before 1542, it appears in all, y^t ye churchwardens of S. Ebbs parish paid to ye warden of ye Grey Freyers Oxon 6d. per annum[2].'

The nunnery of Godstow[3] gave every week alternately to the Friars' Preachers and Minors

'fourteen loaves of the best wheat' (*pasto*), worth in money value 8d. a week, 'for the soul of Roger Writtell; and the aforesaid friars shall have the seal of the monastery to the amount of 34s. a year.'

The nuns also gave annually to each of the four Orders of friars at Oxford 3s. 4d. in money, and 'one peck (*modium*) of oytemell and one of peas (*pisarum*) in Lent.' Among the 'perpetual alms' of Osney Abbey is mentioned a grant of 20s. to the four Orders, as the price of one ox, at Christmas, and of 4d. a week to each Orde 'according to ancient custom[4].'

A large part of their revenue was derived from bequests. To minister to the sick and the dying was one of the first duties which St. Francis practised himself and enjoined on his followers: that in this respect the English Franciscans followed his precepts may be seen in the tradition of them which remained in the memory of this country and which Shakespeare has expressed in 'Romeo and Juliet':

> 'Going to find a barefoot brother out,
> One of our order, to associate me,
> Here in this city visiting the sick,
> And finding him, the searchers of the town,
> Suspecting that we both were in a house
> Where the infectious pestilence did reign,
> Seal'd up the doors and would not let us forth.'
> (Act V, Scene II.)

But work like this receives little notice in history, and where it is mentioned it is usually upon the sordid aspect of the case—the greed for legacies—that the chroniclers insist.

In connexion with Oxford there are perhaps in the extant records only two instances of a Franciscan being found in the chamber of sickness or death. On Nov. 24, 1357, the will of Robert de Trenge[5],

---

[1] Twyne, MS. XXI, 812.
[2] Wood, MS. D 2, p. 344.
[3] Valor Ecclesiasticus, Vol. II, p. 191.
[4] Ibid. p. 223.

[5] Oxf. City Rec. Old White Book, fol. 55 b. The Warden of Merton says, 'He died in 1351, it is said of the plague.' Memorials of Merton Coll. (O. H. Soc.), p. 157.

Warden of Merton, was proved by the sworn testimony of Friar John of Nottingham of the Order of Friars Minors, and Master Walter Moryn, clerk. The will itself is dated June 14, 1351, but in the Middle Ages it was rarely that a man made his will until he felt that his hours were numbered, and although Robert de Trenge seems to have lived some time longer, he was probably now lying in expectation of death, struck down perhaps by the dreaded plague.

The other instance is of later date, namely 10th Dec., 1514[1]. A scholar, John Eustas, had died intestate at Oxford;

'at the instance of his administrators, Friar Richard of Ireland, of the Order of Minors, appeared before us (the commissary), and confessed that he had abstracted from the goods of the aforesaid dead man, without competent legal authority, two mantles and thirty-one yards of linen cloth, and in gold 13s. 4d., which goods he has still in his possession.'

A few days later Friar Richard Lorcan was ordered by the court to restore these goods under penalty of the law[2].

It is, however, in the wills of men and women of every rank and every status that we get most insight into the work of the friars as visitors of the sick. Unfortunately we possess but few wills as early as the thirteenth or first half of the fourteenth century, while for the fifteenth and sixteenth centuries, when the popularity of the friars had greatly declined, they are fairly numerous. Taking those proved in the Chancellor's court between 1436 and 1538, we find that one will in every eight, roughly speaking[3], contains a bequest to the Minorites. In the 'Old White Book' (Oxford City Records)[4], the proportion is about one to every four or five, and in the last half of the fourteenth century, one-third of the wills of Oxford citizens contain bequests to the Franciscans; and these figures are borne out by the Oxford wills scattered through the early Registers at Somerset House[5]. The legacies come from all ranks; tradesmen and

---

[1] Acta Cur. Canc. ꝗ, fol. 250 a.
[2] Ibid. 254 b.
[3] Some of the wills are not complete, e.g. those of Phil. Kemerdyn (1446), T. Cartwright (1532), and E. Standish (1533).
[4] As the Hustings Court was only concerned with freehold property in Oxford, it is rarely that the whole will is found in the Old White Book. About thirty date from 1348-9, but I do not think that any one of them is entire. Two Oxford wills of this date are among the 'Early Lincoln Wills' (p. 39), those of Ric. Cary and Alice his wife, but contain no bequests to the friars. This is perhaps the Ric. Cary who granted land to the Franciscans in 1319; his son, who died 1352, was old enough to make a will (Old White Book, f. 54).
[5] Cf. Mon. Franc. II, pp. xxvi-xxvii. 'An analysis of a considerable number of wills... from the Registers of the Norwich Consistory Court.., shows that at a time when the Grey Friars

merchants being especially well represented. Nor were the benefactors confined to Oxford and its neighbourhood: the Convent, like the University, occupied a national position. But it will be best to give as complete a list as possible of the bequests to the Grey Friars, and leave readers to draw their own conclusions.

John of St. John[1], clerk, by an undated will, probably about 1230, left half a mark to the Friars Minors of Oxford.

Martin de Sancta Cruce, Master of the Hospital of Sherburn, near Durham, left 10s. to them in 1259, with bequests to Friar Richard of Cornwall and others[2].

Boniface of Savoy, Archbishop of Canterbury, left them fifteen marks at his death in 1270[3].

Nicholas de Weston, citizen of Oxford, left them 10s. in 1271[4].

Walter de Merton, Bishop of Rochester, Chancellor of England, and founder of Merton College, bequeathed twenty-five marks to them at his death in 1277[5].

Thomas Waldere, of Wycombe, left them 2s. in 1291[6].

Amaury de Montfort[7], papal chaplain, Treasurer of York, &c. in an elaborate will dated Feb. 2nd, 130$\frac{0}{1}$, ordered that 'the goods and revenues of the aforesaid Treasury owed to him' should be divided into three parts; one-third was to be subdivided into six parts; the sixth part was to be again subdivided into three parts, one of which was to go to the Friars Preachers of Oxford, Leicester, and elsewhere; the second

were falling out of favour, every third will conveyed a gift to them.' The wills proved in the court of the Archdeacon of Oxford (now under the care of Mr. Rodman at Somerset House) begin in 1529. Between 1529 and 1538 I found twenty-nine wills, in which the town of Oxford, or some person or persons resident in Oxford, are referred to; of these, thirteen contain bequests to friars, nine of them containing bequests to the Grey Friars, either alone or (more usually) in conjunction with other Orders. In the same register, out of forty-three wills, taken at random from the years 1529-30, 1534-5, five only contained bequests to friars, three of them mentioning the Minorites.

[1] Twyne, MS. XXIII, 89. His executors according to Twyne were the Chancellor and Dean (?) of Oxford; 'sed probatum est illius testamentum ... per A. Archidiaconum Oxon;' prob. Adam of St. Edmundsbury, who held the office of Archdeacon in 1223 and 1234.

[2] *Durham Wills* (Surtees Soc.), Vol. I, p. 9.

[3] Wadding, IV, 240, quotes his will (dated 1264) from 'Historia Guicenonii,' Tom. 2, fol. 59 and 60-7, i. e. Samuel Guichenon.

[4] Twyne, MS. XXIII, 105.

[5] See abstract in Bp. Hobhouse's Life of W. of Merton, p. 45.

[6] Hist. MSS. Commission, Report V, p. 560. 'This Thomas Waldere,' says Mr. Riley, 'was probably the wealthiest man of his time in Wycombe.'

[7] Roman Transcripts at the Record Office, 'Archivio Vaticano Armar. I, Capsula 9, Num. 9.' Le Neve, Fasti, III, 159.

Ch. VII.] BENEFACTORS. 103

'fratribus Minoribus, Carmelitis, Oxonii, Leycestrie, parisius, et fratribus ordinis S. Trinitatis;'

the third, to pay any debts he might leave. As Amaury was dispossessed of the Treasurership in Aug. 1265 (after holding it only for a few months), and never recovered it, these bequests were merely a pious wish.

John de Doclington bequeathed 20s. to each of the four Orders in Oxford in 1335[1].

Nicholas Acton[2], parson of the church of Wystantowe (Salop), and owner of property in London, left the Oxford Franciscans 40s. in 1337.

William de Burchestre left them one marc in 1340[3].

John son of Walter Wrenche, of Milton, spicer, by a will dated May 4th, and proved on May 5th, 1349, gave to the Friars Preachers and Friars Minors of Oxford each ten quarters of corn[4].

Edmund Bereford[5], lord of several manors near Oxford, in his will dated Jan. 8th, 135$\frac{0}{1}$ and proved in 1354, gave, among many other pious bequests, 20s. at his death and 10s. on his anniversary to the Minorites.

'Item volo quod xij trisennalia celebrentur pro anima mea, videlicet ... in quolibet ordine fratrum j trisennale.'

Henry Malmesbury, citizen of Oxford, left them 20s. in 1361[6].

John de Bereford[7], citizen and sometime Mayor of Oxford, bequeathed 13s. 4d. to each of the Orders in 1361,

'ut habeant animam meam inter eorum missas recommendatam ... Item, cuilibet ordini fratrum predicatorum Minorum Carmelitarum et Augustinensium Oxon', die sepulture mee 2s. 6d., et in die commemorationis anime mee in mensem 2s. 6d., et die anniversarii mei 2s. 6d.'

Humphrey de Bohun, Earl of Hereford and Essex (who died 1361), devised

'to the students of each house of the four orders of Mendicants in Oxford and Cambridge £10 to pray for us[8].'

---

[1] Wood, MS. D. 2, p. 61 (Lincoln Coll. Archives).

[2] Sharpe's Cal. of Wills proved in the Court of Hustings, London, Vol. I.

[3] Wood, MS. D. 2, p. 59 (Lincoln Coll. Archives).

[4] Wood-Clark, II, 388 note. Wood, MS. D. 2, p. 540.

[5] Lambeth Registers; Islip, fol. 105–106; proved in the court of the Archbishop in Oct., in that of the Bishop of Lincoln in Nov. 1354.

[6] Twyne, MS. XXIII, 68; he belonged to the parish of St. Mary Magdalen.

[7] Ibid. 758, 'ex munimentis Coll. Merton, B 7. 13.' Twyne says he was Mayor in 29 Edw. III; but J. de St. Frideswide was then Mayor, and J. de Bereford a leading burgess. Twyne, MSS. Vol. II, fol. 8.

[8] Nichols, 'Royal and Noble Wills,' pp. 46–7.

Richard Bramptone, butcher of Oxford, in 1362, left 10s. to be divided equally among the four Orders of friars[1].

Walter de Berney[2], a wealthy citizen of London, with apparently no near relations, was a benefactor: his will, made in 1377, contains, among many similar bequests, the following:

'Item fratribus minoribus Oxon' et Cantebrig' equaliter x li.'

Richard Carsewell, butcher of Oxford, in 1389 left the house in which he lived, 'without the South Gate of Oxford toward Grantpounde,' to his executors, with instructions to sell it

'and to distribute to the poor friars minors of the money received for the said tenement, ten marks[3].'

John Ocle or *Okele*, of Oxford, 'skinner,' left in 1390, 20s. a year for three years to Friar John Schankton, of the Order of Minors, to celebrate masses for the soul of the testator and his friends, in the Franciscan church at Oxford. To the convent of Friars Minors he bequeathed 5s., to celebrate divine service for him on the day or the morrow of his death[4].

Sir John Golafre, of Langley and Fyfield, knight, by will dated Jan. 19th, 139[8], left the Minorites £10, if he were buried in their church:

'et si ita contingat quod corpus meum sepultum fuerit alibi, tunc volo quod predicti fratres minores non habeant nisi tantum x li[5].'

Richard de Gàraford, of Oxford, who was buried in the Dominican cemetery, left the Friars Minors 6s. 8d. in 1395[6].

John de Waltham, Bishop of Salisbury, left them 6s. 8d. in the same year 'to pray specially for his soul[7].'

John Maldon, Provost of Oriel, left 3s. 4d. to each of the Mendicant Orders at Oxford in 1401[8].

John Bannebury, of Oxford, left 40d. to the Grey Friars in 1401[9].

Matthew Coke, of Oxford, in the same year, bequeathed 30s. to be

---

[1] Balliol Coll. Archives, B 17. 2.

[2] Norfolk Antiq. Miscell. Vol. I, p. 400 (Early Wills from the Norfolk Registry). Sharpe's Cal. of Wills, &c., Vol. II, p. 205.

[3] Oxf. City Records, Old White Book, fol. 69 b.

[4] Ibid. fol. 71.

[5] Lambeth Registers; Arundel, Part I, fol. 155, where a memorandum is added to the effect that he was not buried at Oxford.

[6] Twyne, MSS. Vol. XXIII, 427.

[7] P. C. C. Rous, fol. 32 (at Somerset House).

[8] Register Arundel, Pt. I, fol. 198.

[9] A. Gibbons, 'Early Lincoln Wills,' p. 94 (from Burghersh's Register).

divided among the Orders of friars, 'to celebrate for my soul,' and added the hope:

'et ultra hoc spero in voluntate uxoris mee [1].'

John Thomas, priest, left by will made at Oxford 1413, 10s. to the Friars Minors there,

'to say one dirige for me with their other usual suffrages [2].'

Lady Alienora de Sancto Amando in 1426 left £8 to be divided amongst the four Orders at Oxford 'to celebrate for her soul [3].'

Robert James, Esq., lord of Borstall, left 6s. 8d. to each Order at Oxford in 1431 [4].

Agnes, wife of *Michael Norton* [5], in 1438 willed to be buried in the Minorite church at Oxford, and gave instructions that her tenement in St. Ebbe's should be sold and that

'from the money so acquired an anniversary should be held in the said church of the friars Minors of Oxford for my soul and the soul of Thomas Clamiter (?) my late husband, for the space of twenty years, the friars receiving for each such anniversary 6s. 8d.

James Hedyan, LL.B., and Principal of Eagle Hall, in 1445 bequeathed 8s. to the Franciscans, in whose church he was buried, and 20d. to Friar Giles (his Franciscan confessor?) [6].

Reginald Mertherderwa, doctor of laws and rector of the parish of St. Crida the Virgin in the diocese of Exeter, in 1447 left 6s. 8d. to each of the four Mendicant Orders at Oxford; and to the convent of Friars Minors

'to provide one breakfast or dinner among them, that they may the more devoutly pray for my soul, three shillings and four-pence [7].'

William Skelton, clerk, rector of the parish of St. Vedast, London, left the Minorites 3s. 4d. in the same year [8].

Walter Morleyse, 'de alta Sebyndon,' Co. Wilts, left them 5s. (1451) [9].

Richard Browne, alias Cordon [10], LL.D. and Archdeacon of Rochester, Canon of York, Wells, etc., provides in his will dated 1452, that if he dies in or near Oxford, every Order of friars there shall have one noble (6s. 8d.)

---

[1] Ibid. p. 96.
[2] Regist. Arundel, Pt. II, fol. 164 b: he was buried in the church of the Friars Preachers, at Oxford.
[3] Regist. Chichele, Pt. I, fol. 392 b.
[4] Ibid. fol. 425 b.
[5] Old White Book (Oxford), fol. 90.
[6] Mun. Acad. p. 543 (Acta Curiae Cancell.).
[7] Ibid. 557 : 'pro refectione unius jentaculi sive coenae inter eos habenda,' &c.
[8] Lambeth Registers; Stafford, fol. 162.
[9] P. C. C. Rous, fol. 129.
[10] Regist. Kempe, fol. 263 a–265 b; and Mun. Acad. 639–657.

'for the labour of masses and other suffrages to be said for the salvation of his soul and the souls of all the faithful dead.' Further, 'I give and bequeath to Friar David Carrewe, Minorite, Master in Theology, 6s. 8d.'

William Lord Lovell[1] made arrangements before his death 'to be buried at the Grayfreris of Oxenford;' (will dated 18 March, 145$\frac{4}{5}$, proved Sept. 1, 1455). In the arrangements a bequest would no doubt be included.

Master Philip Polton, Archdeacon of Gloucester (buried in All Souls Chapel), left 40d. to each Order of friars of Oxford by will dated 1461[2].

John Dongan in 1464 desired to be buried 'in the cemetery of the Friars Minors of the University of Oxford,' to whom he gives 40d[3].

John Russel, of Holawnton, Wilts, made his will in 1469[4].

'Also I give and bequeath to the iiij ordyrs off ffrerys w^t in þe Vniuersite, of Oxford iiij nowbles to haue myne obyte holden ther and to pray for my sowle and the sowlys of sir Robert Russell, Knyght' (and other members of the family).

William Dagvyle, gentleman, left 30s. to the five Orders of friars at Oxford in 1474[5].

William Chestur, 'marchaunte of the staple of Caleys and Citezein and Skynnere of London,' bequeathed in 1476[6],

'to euery of þe iiij ordres of ffreres in Oxenforde xxxiij$s$. iiij$d$.'

Robert Abdy, Master of Balliol College, left £4 to the four Orders of friars at Oxford in 1483[7].

Alice Dobbis, 'wif of John Dobbis of y^e town of Oxenford Alderman,' gave and bequeathed 6s. 8d. to the 'ffreris Minours' in 1488[8].

James Blacwode, of Oxford, in 1490 left to the Minorites there

'V^s et unum Gublet de Argento pouncede[9].'

Master John Martoke, elected Fellow of Merton College in 1458, left each Order of friars at Oxford 6s. 8d. (will executed 1500, proved 1503)[10].

Margaret Goldsmith in 1503 left 13s. 4d. to be divided among the four Orders[11].

---

[1] Early Lincoln Wills, p. 186.
[2] Acta Cur. Cancell. A a a, fol. 194 b.
[3] Ibid. fol. 213.
[4] Old White Book, fol. 125 b.
[5] Wood, MS. D. 2, p. 61 (Lincoln Coll. Archives).
[6] P. C. C. Wattys, fol. 174.
[7] *Testamenta Eboracensia* (Surtees Soc.), Pt. III, p. 284. The will was proved at Oxford and York.
[8] Old White Book, fol. 135.
[9] Ibid. 136.
[10] Acta Cur. Cancell. Q, fol. 48 b. Memorials of Merton Coll., 238.
[11] Ibid. f. 61.

Thomas Banke, Rector of Lincoln College, willed in 1503
'that the friars of each of the Religions in the town of Oxford should celebrate exequies for him, and that each house should receive of his goods 6s. 8d.[1]'

John Pereson (buried at St. Mary Magdalen), left the four Orders 13s. 4d. in 1507[2].

In the same year, Thomas Clarke, the executor of the will of *John Falley*, promised to pay Dr. Kynton, Minorite, 26s. 8d. in four instalments[3].

Edmund Crofton, M.A., who made bequests to Brasenose College and the convents of St. Frideswide, Osney, and Rewley, left 26s. 8d. to the four Orders (1508)[4].

William Hasard, of Magdalen College, Proctor of the University in 1495, by a will dated 19th Aug. 1509 and proved 31st Aug. of the same year, bequeathed 10s. to each house of friars,
'praying each Order to celebrate one trental for his soul with the exequies of the dead and a mass on the day of his death[5].'

'*Richard ffetiplace*, of Estshifford[6] (Berks) Squyer,' made a will in 1510 containing the entry:
'Item I bequeth to the iiij orders of freers in Oxford xxvjs. viijd., and eueryche of theym to kepe a solempne dirige and masse praying for my soule.'

'Dame *Elizabeth Elmys* of Henley upon Thamys' in 1510 left to each of the four Orders in Oxford, if she died in that neighbourhood, 10s. for a trental, &c.
'And I will that thos said places of freeres to whom my legacies shall come, Immediatly aftir shall syng in their places oon masse of Requiem w^t placebo, dirige, laudes, and commendacion[7].'

'*Sebyll Danvers*,' widow, of Waterstoke, in the diocese of Lincoln and county of Oxford, in 1511 left the four Orders 13s. 4d. to be divided equally among them[8].

Thomas Dauys, of St. Edwardstowe, Worcester diocese, in 1511 gave in his will
'to the iiij orders of freeres for iiij trentalles to be said in Oxford xls.[9]'

William Perot, of Lambourne, Salisbury diocese, in 1511 left to the 'Grey freres of Oxon xxd.[10]'

---

[1] Ibid. f. 209.
[2] Ibid. ꝗ, f. 26.
[3] Acta Cur. Cancell. ꝗ, f. 28.
[4] Ibid. f. 59.
[5] Ibid. fol. 96.
[6] P. C. C. Fetiplace, quire 1 (Shifford-on-Thames).
[7] Ibid.
[8] Ibid. qu. 2.
[9] Ibid. qu. 1–2: he bequeaths sheep to various parish churches.
[10] Ibid. qu. 7: Lambourn, Berks.

Richard Harecourt, Esquire, of Abingdon, left 26s. 8d. to the four Orders in Oxford in 1512[1].

William Besylis, Esquire, in 1515 bequeathed 'to the grey ffryers in Oxenfford vjs. viijd.'[2]

Robert Throkmorton, Knight, willed in 1518[3], that

'ther be said for my soule in as shorte a space as it may be doon after my deceas twoo trentalles in the Graye ffrieris of Worceter, ij Trentalles in the grey ffreris of Oxford, ij trentalles in the grey ffreris of Cambrygge, ij trentalles in the blake ffreris of Oxford (and same of Cambridge), and for euery of thes trentalles I will there be gyven xs. apece.'

Sir Richard Elyot, 'Knyght, one of the Kinges Justices of his commen benche,' willed in 1520, that the four Orders at Oxford and elsewhere,

'haue at my burying or moneth mynde to kepe dirige and masse for me iijs. iiijd.'[4]

John Tynmouth, Franciscan friar, Bishop of Argos, Suffragan of Sarum, and parson of Boston, left to the Grey Friars of Oxford £5: the will was made in 1523, and proved in 1524[5].

In 1526 *Richard Leke* or *Leek*[6], 'late bruer of Oxford,' bequeathed 4d. to each Grey friar of Oxford being a priest, and 2d. to each 'being noo prest;' 6s. 8d. to the friars 'to make a dyner in their owne place;' 6s. 8d. to the Warden 'to prouide for the premisses;' 20s. for altars; and an additional 10s. to be paid in three instalments, namely, 'at my burying,' 'at my monethes mynde,' and 'at my yeres mynde.'

Walter Curson, of Waterperry[7], 'gentilman,' bequeathed a legacy in these terms:

'Also I woll and gyue to the iiij orders of ffreers in Oxforde for iiij Trentalles to be doēn and had for my soule and my ffrendes soules xls. eqally to be dewyded that is to wit to euery one of them xs.' (executed 24 Nov. 1526, proved 2 May, 1527).

John Rogers (Exeter College) in 1527 also bequeathed each Order 10s.[8]

John Coles (1529), left the four Orders 13s. 4d. (his executors were M.A.'s)[9].

---

[1] P. C. C. Holder, qu. 2.
[2] Ibid. qu. 6.
[3] P. C. C. Maynwaryng, qu. 2.
[4] Ibid. qu. 24.
[5] Wood, MS. B 13, p. 14.
[6] P. C. C. Porch, qu. 9: see Appendix B.
[7] Ibid. qu. 19.
[8] Acta Cur. Canc. EEE, f. 283 a.
[9] Ibid. fol. 300 b.

John Seman, of Oxford, by will dated 1529, gave
'vnto euery one of the iiij orders of ffryours in Oxford, so that they be at my buryall and monethes mynde, x*s*.[1]'

Anthony Hall, of Swerford, a considerable landowner, desired in his will dated 1529 and proved 1530, to
'haue a trentall of masses to be said for me, the one half at our lady ffryers (i.e. Carmelites), and the other half at the gray ffryers[2].'

John Byrton, of 'Abburbury,' also a farmer or landowner, left in 1530 to the four Orders at Oxford 4*s*.[3]

Thomas Goodewyn, of Alkerton (Oxon), a large sheepfarmer, bequeathed 2*s*. 8*d*. to the 'gray ffryers of Oxford,' in 1530[4].

In 1532 *William Clare*, of Hollywell, Oxford, left 3*s*. 4*d*. to each Order of friars at Oxford[5].

Jane Foxe, of Burford, in 1535 bequeathed her lands and tenements and 'ii c (200) shepe' to her son, and 5*s*. 8*d*. 'to the iiij order of frears in Oxford[6].'

Henry Standish[7], Friar Minor, and Bishop of St. Asaph, in 1535 bequeathed
'five marcs to buy books to be placed in the library of the scholars of the friars Minors in the University of Oxford,'
ten marks to the church of the same friars, £40 for the exhibition of scholars[8] in the University of Oxford, and £40 to build an aisle in the church of the friars Minors at Oxford.

Thomas Sowche, of 'Spellusbury,' left to the 'fore orders of freers in Oxford, euery one of them iiij*d*.[9]'

Richard Elemens or *Elemeus*, of 'Welleford' (Berkshire?), in 1536 left 'vnto the Gray freers yn Oxford x*s*.[10]'

John Claymond, S.T.B., President first of Magdalen College, then of Corpus Christi College, left 20*s*. to each of the convents of friars at Oxford in 1536,
'ut celebrent in ecclesiis suis pro anima ejus[11].'

---

[1] Oxf. Wills and Adminis. Series I, Vol. I, f. 2.

[2] Oxford Wills, Series I, Vol. I, fol. 18 b. He had land in Steeple Aston, Hooknorton, &c.: among his bequests are, 'Item to our lady of pyte a shepe. Item to seynt Antony a shepe.'

[3] Ibid. f. 36 b.

[4] Ibid. fol. 58 b.

[5] Ibid. fol. 68 b. One of his sons was a canon of Osney.

[6] Ibid. fol. 103.

[7] P. C. C. Hogen, qu. 26. See notice of him in Part II.

[8] Prob. not 'religious students.'

[9] Oxford Wills, ut supra, f. 119: no date is given; the will seems to have been proved in the early part of 1536; Sowche was an owner of pasture lands.

[10] Ibid. fol. 127.

[11] Wood, MS. D. 2, p. 613.

Elizabeth Johnson, of Oxford, widow, in 1537 left

'to the four ordres of fryers four nobles to singe dirige and masse at All-hallowes churche at the buryall and moneth mynde.'

The will was proved on Jan. 12th, 153$\frac{8}{9}$,—after the suppression of the friaries[1].

Many testators authorized their executors to make due provision of trentalls and masses 'for the wealth of their souls,' without specifying where they were to be celebrated: the friars no doubt came in for a share of these. Thus Thomas Hoye, Vicar of Bampton, in 1531 gives the following instructions[2]:

'It is my will that the forsaid goodes be preysid and put to vendicion and the money therof cummyng to be ordered and distributed by myn executors for trentallys of masses off Requiem eternam and masses of the V woundes of our lord to be celebrate and said for the welthe of my soule and all Christen sowles. Amen.'

On the other hand, the parish priests or rectors of churches were legally entitled to one-fourth of the gifts, bequests, and fees given by their parishioners to the friars[3]: but it is impossible to say whether the right was generally enforced. In 1521 Leo X,

'owing to the importunate exaction of the funeral fourth by some rectors of churches,'

exempted the friars from the payment[4].

Among other sources of revenue may be enumerated the institution of annual masses for fees (of which the wills often make mention), commutations of penances for money[5], payment by the University and others for the use of their church, schools, and other buildings on various occasions[6], and collections in church[7]. At the beginning of the sixteenth century we hear of a

'gild of St. Mary in the church of the Friars Minors[8],'

which no doubt supported one or more friars to say mass in one of

---

[1] Ibid. fol. 65. The overseer of the will was Dr. J. London, Warden of New College; the witnesses Alderman Banister and W. Plummer.

[2] Oxford Wills and Adminis. Series I, Vol. I, fol. 87 b: cf. ibid. fol. 5, &c.

[3] Wadding, Vol. V, 342–3 (privilege of Boniface VIII, 1295); Mon. Franc. II, Pref. p. xvii.

[4] Wadding, Vol. XVI, p. 134.

[5] Restricted by Constitutions of 1260; Archiv. f. L. u. K. Gesch. VI, 92. Cf. Wiclif, Two Short Tracts, &c., p. 37:

'The Friars suffren men to lie in sinne, fro yere to yere, for an annual rent.'

[6] Cf. Grey Friars at Cambridge, in Willis and Clark, Architect. Hist. II, 724.

[7] Cf. Chaucer's Sompnour's Tale. Forbidden 1260; Archiv. f. L. u. K. Gesch. VI, 92.

[8] Acta Cur. Cancell. ꟼ, fol. 135 b: '... Confessus est coram nobis Ric. Barlow quod debet magistris Gilde Sancte Marie in ecclesia fratrum minorum tresdecim nobilia que mutuo a predictis magistris recepit,' &c.

the ten chapels. Of manual labour there is little evidence; the only kind mentioned is the transcription of manuscripts of which we have already spoken.

We may here say a few words on two other points. Firstly, from what classes of society were the Franciscans mainly drawn? In the thirteenth century a very large number of men of position, of high birth, were attracted to the Order; but that this was unusual may be gathered from the rejoicings which took place over converts who were '*valentes in saeculo*[1].' There is every reason to suppose that the Grey Friars, as well as the other students at the University, were mainly recruited from the sons of tradesmen, artisans, and villeins[2]. Friar Brackley, D.D. was the son of a Norwich dyer[3]; and the towns probably supplied the greater proportion of the Oxford Franciscans[4]. Secondly, what led men to take the vows of the Minorites? Excluding again the thirteenth century (when the highest motives were predominant), and confining ourselves to the later times, we must admit that, apart from those who entered the Order as boys, either from choice or at the instigation or compulsion of relatives[5]—the leading motive was a superstitious belief in the externals of religion, in the efficacy of 'the washing of cups and pots.' How strong this feeling was may be seen from the fact that Latimer was at one time in danger of yielding to it.

'I have thought,' he wrote to Sir Edward Baynton, 'that if I had been a friar in a cowl, I could not have been damned, nor afraid of death; and in my sickness I have been tempted to become a friar[6].'

[1] Mon. Franc. I. 541.
[2] Lyte 196, and note 1.
[3] Mon. Franc. II, preface.
[4] See their designations or surnames, of London, York, Nottingham, Hartlepool, &c.
[5] See e.g. John Cardmaker in Part II. The proselytising tendency has already been referred to. The number of 'apostate' friars must have been very considerable to judge from the frequent edicts against them.
[6] Cal. of State Papers, Hen. VIII, Vol. V, p, 607. Wadding, V, p. 139, Pope Martin IV was buried in a Franciscan habit, A.D. 1285. Cf. Ibid. XIV, p. 58; Polit. Poems and Songs (R. S.), II, 19, 32.

CHAPTER VIII.

THE DISSOLUTION.

Attitude of the Grey Friars towards the Reformation in its intellectual, religious, and political aspects.—The Divorce.—Visitation of Oxford in 1535.—Suppression of the friaries in 1538.—Condition of the Grey Friary.—Expulsion of the friars; their subsequent history; Simon Ludford.—Houses and site of the Grey Friars.—Dr. London tries to secure the land for the town.—The place leased to Frewers and Pye; bought by Richard Andrews and Howe; resold to Richard Gunter.—Subsequent history of the property.—Total destruction of the buildings.

THE intellectual torpor which oppressed Oxford for more than a century after the disappearance of Wiclif and his followers was due less to the repressive measures adopted by Archbishop Arundel, than to the want of vitality, of adaptability to new modes of thought, in the scholastic philosophy and method, with which the intellectual life of Oxford had for so long been identified. The University as a whole did not extend a warm welcome to the New Learning, and it was to be expected that the Mendicant Orders especially should be attached to the old state of things, with which their past greatness was connected, and to which their present position and any prestige they still possessed were due [1]. The Grey Friars consequently were inclined to oppose the revival of learning; and Tyndale no doubt classed them among 'the old barking curs, Duns' disciples and like draff called Scotists, the children of darkness,' who 'raged in every pulpit against Greek, Latin, and Hebrew [2].' Dr. Henry Standish, sometime Warden of the Grey Friars of London and Provincial Minister of England, attacked Erasmus' version of the

---

[1] The Franciscans still maintained a certain reputation as theologians: one of them was appointed each year to preach the University sermon on Ash-Wednesday; Acta Cur. Canc. ꓶ, fol. 263 a, 264 a and b; EEE, fol. 362, 363, 366 b: the custom was probably of ancient origin. Cf. also the notice of John Kynton.

[2] Lyte, Oxford, p. 435.

New Testament in a sermon at Paul's Cross and in conversation at Court, and seems to have been the recognised leader of the 'Trojan' party in England[1]. But even among the Minorites there are traces of the influence of the Renaissance. Another Provincial Minister, Richard Brynkley, was a student of Greek, and was supplied with a copy of the Gospels in Greek from the Franciscan Library at Oxford. Friar Nicholas de Burgo seems to have been one of that band of Humanists whom Wolsey attracted to Oxford, that they might propagate in his own University the learning and culture of Italy[2].

The close historical relation, notwithstanding the fundamental differences, between the intellectual movement and the religious movement, was neatly expressed in a saying current among the friars: 'Erasmus laid the egg; Luther hatched it[3].' The beginnings of the English Reformation in its religious aspect are to be sought among the educated classes, especially at Cambridge. The Minorites, while generally hostile to the new religion[4], did not take a leading part in suppressing it. And when it is remembered how very little progress the Lutheran doctrines made in England before the Dissolution, the few instances of sympathy with those doctrines recorded in the lives of Oxford Franciscans acquire a certain importance[5]. These, however, were exceptional cases. If we trace the fortunes of individual Franciscans after the Dissolution, it will be found that no generalization as to their attitude towards the Reformation can be made. A few remained loyal to the old religion[6], others embraced the new[7], and on both sides persecution was suffered for conscience'

---

[1] Calendar of State Papers, Hen. VIII, Vol. III, Nos. 929, 965. Cf. Seebohm's Oxford Reformers, 326–7.

[2] See notices of R. Brynkley and N. de Burgo.

[3] Erasmus, Opera, III, 840: 'Ego peperi ovum, Lutherus exclusit. Mirum vero dictum Minoritarum istorum magnaque et bona pulte dignum. Ego posui ovum gallinaceum, Lutherus exclusit pullum longe dissimillimum' (quoted by Mullinger, Cambridge, I, 588, n. 2).

[4] Kynton, e.g., took part in the condemnation of Luther's doctrines and books at the conference in London, April 21, 1521.

[5] See notices of John Rycks and Gregory Basset. Foxe (Acts and Monuments, IV, 642, A° 1531) says that Dr. Call, 'by the word of God, through the means of Bilney's doctrine and good life, whereof he had good experience, was somewhat reclaimed to the gospel's side.' William Call, D.D. of Cambridge, was at this time Provincial Minister of the English Franciscans. In this connexion attention may be drawn to the lectures on St. Paul's epistles delivered by Minorites; see J. Porrett and W. Walker.

[6] See notices of E. Ryley, Gregory Basset.

[7] See Thomas Kirkham (?), R. Beste, John Joseph, Guy Etton, J. Cardmaker, R. Newman.

sake¹; others again contrived to reconcile themselves with both old and new according to circumstances².

With the Reformation as a political movement, the Franciscans had more sympathy. A large section of them had, long before this, taught the supremacy of the State over the Church in all things political³; they approved in principle the confiscation of Church property for the common good⁴; and Friar Henry Standish, in defending the claim of the temporal courts to try and punish criminous clerks, together with the broad principles on which that claim rested, was only applying to present circumstances the time-honoured traditions of his Order⁵. It is true that the Friars of the Observance resisted the royal supremacy in 1534. But the supremacy claimed by Henry VIII went beyond anything asserted by his predecessors, involving, as it did in effect, the establishment of a lay jurisdiction superior to all ecclesiastical courts *in spiritualibus* as well as *in temporalibus*, constituting Henry 'a king with a pope in his belly'⁶. The Franciscans at Oxford seem, like most of the religious, to have accepted the supremacy in this extended form and to have taken the oath without demur: at least there is no evidence to the contrary⁷.

The oath administered to the monks and friars involved an acknowledgment, not only of the royal supremacy, but of the lawfulness of Henry's divorce from Katharine and marriage with Anne Boleyn, and a promise to preach the same on every occasion⁸. The attitude of the Oxford Franciscans to the divorce, so far as it can be ascertained, may be briefly stated here.

Henry attached great importance to securing a decision in favour of his divorce from the chief universities of Europe. The divorce became the all-absorbing topic at Oxford; and individual Minorites took a prominent part in the discussions. But the convent as a whole did not present a united front. Dr. Thomas Kirkham, a Franciscan, is mentioned as one of the Doctors of Divinity who opposed the

---

¹ One only, J. Cardmaker, appears to have been burnt.

² See E. Bricotte, J. Crayford, H. Glaseyere.

³ Eulog. Hist. III, 337-8. See notice of J. Mardeslay.

⁴ Cf. *Munimenta Academica*, p. 208. In this respect the Franciscans were at one with Marsiglio of Padua and Wiclif.

⁵ Cal. of State Papers, Hen. VIII, Vol. II, Nos. 1313, 1314: Brewer, Henry VIII, I, 250-3. Cf. R. L. Poole's Wycliffe, 32-3.

⁶ Gasquet, Henry VIII and the English Monasteries, I, 215.

⁷ Dixon, Church of England, I, 213; but see Gasquet, I, 248, note.

⁸ Dixon, ibid.

divorce and were ready to write against it[1]. Dr. Kynton seems to have been on the same side at first[2]; Archbishop Warham complained of his having spread calumnious reports about himself in connexion with the 'King's matter,' and demanded his punishment. But it is doubtful whether in the end Kynton had the courage of his opinions; he was one of the committee of three appointed by the theological faculty to decide the question with the assistance of thirty other members to be nominated by the smaller committee[3]. This body subsequently issued, in the name of the University, the qualified declaration in favour of the King, the tenour of which is well-known.

The most active champion of the King's cause was also a Minorite, Dr. Nicholas de Burgo, a native of Italy, who enjoyed the patronage of Cardinal Wolsey[4]. The unpopularity of the divorce, among those who were guided by their sentiments rather than by their personal interests, is shown by the treatment he received at Oxford. He was pelted with stones in the street, and the good women of the town would have 'foyled' him 'if their handys might have served their harts'[5]. In retaliation the friar caused about thirty women to be locked up in Bocardo for three days and nights[6]. As we shall see later on, his services did not go unrewarded[7]. The position of Friar Nicholas, however, was exceptional, and his action cannot be regarded as representative of the feelings of the Oxford Convent.

The causes which led to the dissolution of the monasteries do not concern us here. The friaries were not included in the Act of 1536 for the abolition of the lesser monasteries; they possessed as a rule no estates except the site on which they were built, and the gains to be derived from their disendowment were perhaps regarded as insufficient compensation for the odium which the measure would necessarily involve. The first blow had already fallen upon the Observant Friars, the fearless champions of the legality of the Queen Katharine's marriage and of the Papal supremacy. The conventuals were left alone till Henry decided on the general suppression of the religious houses throughout England. The object of the royal party was then to obtain what was called a 'voluntary' surrender of their property from the members of each religious

---

[1] Wood, Annals, anno 1530.
[2] Lyte, Oxford, 475.
[3] Wood, Annals, anno 1530.
[4] Boase, Register, 128. Cal. of State Papers, Hen. VIII, Vol. IV, Nos. 1334, 6619; Vol. V, 623; cf. V, No. 593.
[5] Wood, Annals, sub anno 1530; Lyte, Oxford, 474.
[6] Wood, ibid.
[7] See notice of N. de Burgo in Part II.

community; and among those who had the courage to offer opposition were many houses of Franciscans, 'with hom,' writes the Bishop of Dover, 'in every place I have moche besynes'[1]. But among these we cannot reckon the convent at Oxford.

In 1535 Cromwell sent his agent, Layton, and others, to Oxford to reform the University. After abolishing the study of the schoolmen[2], the visitors proceeded to deal with the religious students[3]. For the reform of the monasteries, they were armed with a set of eighty-six articles of inquiry and twenty-five injunctions[4], the real though not avowed object of which was to make monastic life unbearable and so to prepare the way for 'voluntary' surrenders[5].

'We have further,' writes Dr. Layton to Cromwell on the 12th of September[6], 'in visitynge the religiouse studenttes, emongyste all other injunctions, adjoyned that none of them for no manner of cause shall cum within any taverne, in, alhowse, or any other howse whatsoever hit be, within the towne and the suburbs of the same, upon payne onse so taken by day or by nyght, to be sent imediatly home to his cloister whereas he was professede. Withoute doubte we here say this acte to be gretly lamentede of all the duble honeste women of the towne, and specially of ther laundres that now may not onse entre within the gaittes, and muche lesse within ther chambers, wherunto they wer ryght well accustomede. I doubt not but for this thyng onely the honeste matrones will sew unto yowe for a redresse.'

It is probable, that, between this time and the summer and autumn of 1538, when the general dissolution of the friaries took place, many of the Oxford Franciscans had left their house[7]. The Friary, it will be seen, was wretchedly poor and in a ruinous condition; 'and few do geve any almys to them'[8]. The commission to visit the Oxford

---

[1] Wright, Suppression, p. 212 (Camden Soc.).

[2] 'We have sett Dunce in Bocardo,' &c. Wright, Suppression, p. 71 (quoted by Wood, Dixon, Lyte, Gasquet, &c.).

[3] Wright, ibid.

[4] Gasquet, I, 255. The articles and injunctions are printed in Wilkins, Concilia, III, 786, *seq*. They were drawn up with reference to the monks, not friars; but no distinction seems to have been made between the various classes of religious students at the Universities.

[5] Gasquet, I, 255-7.

[6] Wright, Suppression, 71.

[7] Of the nine Minorites (namely J. Tomsun, T. Tomsun, W. David, R. David, W. Browne, G. Etton, H. Glaseyere, J. Crayford, and H. Stretsham) who were admitted to opponency or to B.D. between 1534, when the troubles began, and July 1538, only one appears in the list of those desiring 'capacities' at the dissolution. Many brethren in other convents, and perhaps in this, fled to the Continent. Gasquet, II, 245-6. Cal. of State Papers, Hen. VIII, Vol. VII, Nos. 939, 1020.

[8] Cromwell Corresp. 2nd Series, Vol. XXIII, f. 711a (J. London to T. Cromwell, Aug. 14).

friaries in 1538 consisted of Dr. John London, the mayor (Mr. Banaster) and 'master aldermen' (apparently Mr. Pye and Mr. Fryer). On the 8th of July[1], Dr. London writes to Cromwell that he and his fellow-commissioners have been 'at all the places of the fryers in Oxforde,' and wishing 'to know your lordeships pleasur' on certain doubtful points, he proceeds to give an account of his work.

'At Mr. Pyei's comyng home Mr. Maier and Mr. ffryer wer at London, and forasmoch as we dowbtyd of ther spedy comyng home, and Mr. Pye and I wer creadable informyd that it wasse time to be doing among the friers[2], we went to euery place of them and tok such a vew[3] and stay among them as the tyme wolde permytt.'

After visiting the Carmelites and Austin Friars, they came to the Grey Friars.

'The Grey ffryers,' continues London[4], 'hathe prayty Ilondes behynde ther howse well woddyde, and the waters be thers also. They haue oon fayre orchard and sondry praty gardens and lodginges. It ys a great hoge howce conteynyng moche ruinose bylding. They haue impledged and solde most of ther plate and juellys forcyd by necessitie as they do saye, and that remaynyth ys in the bill. Ther ornamentes of ther church be olde and litill worthe. Ther other stuff of howsholde ys ybill worth x ƚi. They haue taken vppe the pypes of ther condytt lately and haue cast them in sowys to the nombre lxxij, wherof xij be sold for the costes in taking vppe of the pypes, as the warden saith. The residew we haue putt in safe garde. Butt we haue nott yet weyd them. And ther ys yet in the erthe remaynyng moch of the condytt nott taken vppe. In ther groves the wynde hathe blown down many great trees, wich do remayn upon the ground. Thees freers do receyve yerly owt of thexchequer of the Kinges almys l markes. Thys howse ys all coveryde wᵗ slatte and no ledde.'

Before August the 14th the doctor had sent up the plate of the Oxford friaries to Cromwell's servant in London, Mr. Thacker, and received from him 'a bill indentyd conteynyng the parcels of the sayd plate wᵗ the nombre of ownces.'[5] The following is the list of

Juelles and plate in the grey ffryers[6].

Imp'mis a crosse of sylu' and gylt . . . . . liiij vnc'.
A chales all gylt . . . . xiiij vnc'.

---

[1] Cromwell Corresp. 2nd Series, Vol. XXIII, f. 709 a (J. London to T. Cromwell, Aug. 14).

[2] The White Friars had already sold an annuity and divided the proceeds among themselves. Ibid.

[3] Or 'vow'?

[4] Ibid. f. 709 b.   [5] Ibid. f. 711 a.

[6] Chapter House Books, A$\frac{3}{11}$, f. 29 (Rec. Off.).

A nother all gylt.	xv vnc'.
A nother pcell gylt	xiij vnc'.
A nother chales pcell gylt	xiiij vnc' et di.
A pyxe of sylu' gyldyd w^t owt a cou'	xv vnc'.
A sensar of sylu' waynge	xxxij vnc'.
A payer of small cruettes gylted	ij vnc' iij qrt'.
V masers olde w^t bonds of sylu' weyng w^t the trees [1]	lxxxxij vnc'.
A black horne w^t sylu' bonde and fot weyng w^t the horne	x vnc' et di.
iij dosyn sponys	xxxiij vnc'.
A knappe [2] of the cou' of a maser	ij vnc'.

The treatment of the friars themselves was a more complicated problem. All of them seem to have been willing to become secular priests, and London urged

'that with spede we may haue ther capacyties, ffor the longer they tary the more they will wast [3].'

On the 14th of August [4] he complains that ·

'as yet we haue nott the capacities and therfor be at the chardge in fyndyng them mete and drink.'

On the 31st of August, again, he writes to Cromwell from Oxford [5]:

' I have causyd all our fower ordre of fryers to change ther cotes, and have despacchide them as well as I can till they may receyve ther capacities, for the wiche I have now agen sent uppe thys berar doctor Baskerfelde [6], to whom I do humblie besek your lordeschippe to stonde gudde lorde. He ys an honest man, and causyd all hys howse to surrender the same and to chaunge ther papistical garmentes. I wrote to your lordeschippe specially for hym to have in hys capacytie an expresse licens to dwell in Oxford, altho he wer benefycyd; and your lordeschipp then wrote that yt wasse your pleasur he and all other shulde have ther capacities according to ther desyer, and for that thys man is now an humble sutar unto your lordeschippe. He hath be a visitar of dyvers places wiche they do call custodies, and knowith many thinges as well in London as otherwise, wiche he hath promised me to declare unto your lordeschippe, if it be your pleasur he schall so do.'

The list of Oxford Grey Friars who 'wold haue ther capacytis' which was sent to Cromwell [7], contains eighteen names, thirteen of them being priests, one subdeacon, and four not in holy orders. The

---

[1] Mazer, a large drinking bowl (Skeat); 'trees' seems to mean merely wood.
[2] 'Knob.'
[3] Cromwell Corresp. *ut supra*, fol. 710 b.
[4] Ibid. fol. 711 a.
[5] Wright, Suppression, p. 217.
[6] Warden of the Grey Friars.
[7] Chapter House Books, A$\frac{3}{1\frac{1}{1}}$, fol. 31 b.

names are: Edward Baskerfelde, Warden, S.T.P.[1]; Friars Brian Sanden, Richard Roper, B.D., Rodulph Kyrswell, Robert Newman, William Brown, John Covire (or Conire or Comre), James Cantwell, Thomas Cappes, John Stafforde Schyer (?), William Bowghnell, James Smyzth, Thomas Wythman, priests; Friar John Olliff, subdeacon; and Friars Symon Ludforth, Thomas Barly, William Cok, and John Cok, *non infra sacros*.

It is not often possible to trace the subsequent career of the friars when they had been turned adrift on the world. The monks as a rule received pensions, and the entries respecting the payment of these in the Ministers' Accounts and other records, afford some clue to their fate. The Mendicants except in a few isolated cases received no pensions. Dr. London in his letter of the 8th of July[2] asked Cromwell 'what reward euery freer shall have . . . .[3] at ther departinge,' but the question no doubt refers merely to the gift of a few shillings, which was usually made to each friar on his dismissal. No instance occurs in the records of a pension having been paid to any of the Grey Friars who were at Oxford at the time of the suppression[4]. It is probable that Baskerfeld, who was an important person in the University, received a benefice with license to live in Oxford. Robert Newman seems also to have been presented to a living[5]. But the career of only one of these eighteen friars can be traced with any certainty. Simon Ludford, a native of Bedford, became an apothecary in London. On November 6, 1553, he supplicated for the degree of M.B. at Oxford after six years' study in the medical faculty. On November 27, he obtained the degree and was admitted to practise. The College of Physicians remonstrated with the University and recommended that the degree should be revoked on the ground of Ludford's ignorance. Though the University refused to withdraw its license, the ex-friar proceeded to Cambridge, but the Physicians hastened to warn the authorities there against him. They had, they wrote to the University, already examined Ludford 'on the 17th day before the Calends of March, 1553' (?), and, finding him completely ignorant of medicine, philosophy, and the liberal sciences, and distinguished only by 'blind audacity,' unanimously voted against his admission. Ludford left Cambridge, but persevered. In May 1560,

---

[1] The request that he may live in Oxford, &c., is here inserted in Latin.
[2] Cromwell Corresp. *ut supra*, f. 710 b.
[3] Several words illegible in MS.
[4] W. Vavasour is I think the only Franciscan who studied at Oxford whose pension is recorded. Cf. Gasquet, II, 453-5.
[5] See Part II.

he supplicated for the degree of M.D. at Oxford, stating that he had long practised in London by permission of the London College of Physicians. In July he incepted as M.D. of Oxford. In April 1563 he was made fellow of the College of Physicians, and he was censor of the same College in 1564, 1569, and 1572.[1]

We turn now to the Minorites who had studied at Oxford, but who were living in other convents at the time of the dissolution. Of these a considerable number obtained benefices[2], a few even rising to positions of some importance in the Church[3]. But what proportion these successful cases bore to the unsuccessful cannot be even approximately ascertained; it would naturally be higher among friars who had received a university education than among the common herd. Yet it is unlikely that a majority even of the former were presented to livings. The number of disbanded monks and friars seeking employment as priests must have been very large, and at the same time the demand for priests was growing less and less.[4] Some of the friars probably drifted into secular employments; others perhaps joined the ranks of the 'sturdy beggars' of whom so much is heard in the sixteenth century. It can hardly be doubted but that the lot of many was one of hardship and suffering.

In the eyes of Cromwell and his royal master the only question of real importance was the most advantageous disposal of the property. The buildings of the Grey Friars were of little account, and the convent was among those

'howses of freres that have no substance of lead, save only some of them haue smale gutters[5].'

The site, however, was of considerable value. Dr. London was anxious that it should be secured for the city; and his letter[6] gives a curious picture of the state of Oxford at the time of the dissolution.

'It ys rumoryd her that dyuers of the garde do intende to begge thees howsys of the Kinges hyghnes, and that with other consideracions moveth me now to be an humble petitioner vnto your lordeschippe for my neybours. We haue in Oxforde two of the Kinges grace's seruantes

---

[1] Boase, Register, p. 222; Munk, Roll of the Royal College of Physicians, 2nd ed., Vol. I, p. 64. Oxf. Univ. Arch. Reg. I, 8, fol. 138 b, 139, 139b, 190, 190b, 192b.

[2] Some dozen instances will be found in Part II; a few are rather doubtful.

[3] See J. Cardmaker, J. Crayford, Guy Etton.

[4] Private masses though declared to be meet and necessary and agreeable to God's law, in the Six Articles, were no doubt falling into disfavour.

[5] Chapter House Books $A\frac{3}{11}$, 9–10.

[6] Cromwell Corresp. 2nd series, Vol. XXIII, f. 710 a–b.

Mr. Banaster and Mr. Pye, two as burgerly and as honest men as lyveth in any town and hathe no thing to lyve vpon, nother farmes abrode nor fees saving oonly ther wages of the Kinges grace iiij*d*. a daye. Mr. Banaster ys now mayer, and Mr. Pye hath be mayer, to hys great chardge.'

The writer then urges that Mr. Banaster should have the site (' cyte ') and profits of the White Friars, Mr. Pye those of the fair of the Austin Friars.

"Mr. Pye specially hath be diligent to bring vnto the Kinges grace's hondes thees howses, and therefor I besek your gudd lordeschipp to be gudd lord vnto hym. And syns Mr. Mayer com home he ys as diligent as maye be and so is Mr. ffryer.'

London goes on to plead for his 'neybours of Oxford,'

' seying so gudd an occasion ys come wherin your lordeschipp may do vnto them the hyest benefytt that euer dydd honorable man. The greatest occasion of the povertie of thys town ys the payment of ther fee-farme. ffor thys ys customablie seen, that such as befor they haue be bayliffes hath be prety occupyers, if in ther yere corn be nott at a hie price, then they be nott able to pay ther fee-farme. And for the worschipp of ther town they must that yere kepe the better howsys, fest ther neybours and wer better apparell, wich maketh them so pore that few of them can recouer agen. If by your gudde lordeschips mediation the town myȝt haue the grey and black fryers growndes after the Kinges grace hath be answerd for the wodd and buyldinges with other thynges upon the same, and lykewyse the cytes of the Whyte and austen fryers after the decese of Mr. Banester and Mr. Pye; It wolde mervelosly helpe the town, and geve them great occasion to fall to clothynge, ffor vpon the grey and black fryers water be certen convenyent and commodiose places to sett fulling mylles vpon, and so people myȝt be sett awork. Now the baylys forcyd by necessitie taketh such tolls of such as passith by the town with catell or any maner of cariage as makith men lothe to com herbye : and Oxford ys no great thorowfare whereby moche resort schuld helpe them. Thys benefytt shuld lytill hynder the kinges maiestie and mervelosly helpe thys pouer town; and your lordeschipp schuld do a blessyd dede to helpe so many pouer men wich by ther fee-farme be notably poverischyd. And yet the Kinges grace schuld save a C markes yerly in hys cofers by reason of the grey and black fryers wich hath euery of them C (*sic*) markes by yere.'

The plan here sketched out, creditable as it is to its author, was not carried into effect. On August 10th, 1540, William Frewers and John Pye of Oxford, obtained a lease of the house and site of the Grey Friars, together with the grove containing by estimation five acres, for twenty-one years, at a rent of 20*s*. a year—half the amount of the rent which the same persons paid for the Black Friars[1]. Much of the Grey Friars' property was expressly excepted from this lease; namely, the close called 'le Churcheyarde' now held by Richard Gunter of Oxford at an annual rent of 3s. 4d., the orchard or garden called 'Paradise,' and the garden called 'Boteham,' now held by William Thomas at an annual rent of 6s. 8d. Further all large trees and shrubs were reserved to the King, together with all those buildings within the precincts of the two friaries 'which the King had commanded to be levelled or taken away.'

In 1544 the tenants seem to have opened negotiations for the purchase of the property. In the official 'particulars' sent up to the royal commissioners we read:

'These houses of ffryers ar wythin the towne of Oxford and as I haue lernyd they ar not nyghe eny of the Kinges houses neyther hys graces parkes fforestes and chase by seven myles. And what ffyne wylbe gyuen ffor the same I know not neyther can lerne. And they ar the ffermers them selues y^t desyreth to by the premysses[2].

The price which the tenants offered was probably unsatisfactory; the impecunious Pye with his wages of 4d. a day can hardly have had a chance against wealthier speculators in monastic lands. In 1544 a successful bid was made by Richard Andrewes of Hales, Esquire (Glouc.), one of the largest of these speculators[3], who as usual was acting in partnership with another, in this case John Howe. On July 14th, 1544, the King granted to these two, in consideration of £1094 3s. 2d. paid by Richard Andrewes, various monastic lands in the counties of Derby, Middlesex, Oxford, &c., including the sites of the Black and Grey Friars in Oxford[4].

'We give also and for the aforesaid consideration by these presents concede to the said Richard Andrewes and John Howe, the whole site of the house late of the friars Minors, commonly called "les Grey ffreers" within the town of Oxford now dissolved. And also our whole grove of land and wood with its appurtenances containing by estimation five acres of land, now or late in the tenure or occupation of William ffrewers and John Pye or their assigns; and our whole close of land called 'le Churcheyarde' with its appurtenances, now or late in the tenure or

---

[1] Augmentation Office Miscell. Books, Enrolment of Leases, Vol. CCXII, fol. 195 (Record Office).

[2] Particulars for Grants, Augm. Office, 35 Hen. VIII, sec. 4 (Record Office). It is among the deeds relating to Richard Andrews, but there is nothing to show that he and Howe were at that time in any sense the 'farmers' of the property.

[3] Cf. Dixon, Church of England, II, 212.

[4] Pat. Roll, 36 Hen. VIII, Part 3, m. 37; Originalia Rolls, 36 Hen. VIII, Pt. 4; V, m. 12.

occupation of James Gunter or his assigns; and our whole garden or orchard called "Paradyse," and our whole garden called Bateham or Boteham, now or late in the tenure or occupation of William Thomas or his assigns, with all and each of their appurtenances situated within the town of Oxford, lately belonging to the priory or house of the friars Minors . . . .; and all our houses, buildings, stables, granaries, curtilages, gardens (*ortos*), orchards, gardens (*gardina*), waters, ponds, vineyards, land and soil whatsoever with their appurtenances lying within the said boundary of the house of the friars Minors . . . . Which site of the late house of friars Minors and all the aforesaid houses, buildings, gardens, orchards, &c., belonging thereto, now amount (*extenduntur*) to the clear annual value of 30*s*. . . . We except however always and totally reserve out of the present concession, all the bells and the whole of the lead and glass on the said houses of the friars Minors and Preachers, except the lead and glass in the gutters and windows of the houses or mansions of the same friars: and also in like manner all the buildings and structures of the late churches, cloisters, refectories, dormitories, and chapterhouses of the said friars.'

All the property granted was to be held by Richard Andrewes and John Howe and the heirs and assigns of Richard Andrewes, in chief, 'for the service of the twentieth part of one knight's fee.' An annual rent was to be paid to the King from each parcel of property, the rent of the site of the Friars Minors being 3*s*., that of the Friars Preachers 4*s*.

The purchase was purely a matter of speculation, and the next month (August 26th, 1544), Andrewes and Howe obtained from the King, for a fine of 9*s*., license to alienate the site of the Grey Friars, with the grove, churchyard, Paradise, and Boteham, and the buildings, except those already reserved for the King, to Richard Gunter, alderman of Oxford, and Joanna his wife, and the heirs and assigns of Richard Gunter, to be held by them 'for the services due thence to us, our heirs, and successors[1].' It does not appear whether the leases of Frewers, Pye, and Thomas, were cancelled or allowed to run their course.

The subsequent history of the property is obscure, and probably would not repay an exhaustive investigation. Wood states that the land 'being shifted through severall hands doth now acknowledg also severall owners[2].'

Part of it was 'now inhabited by tanners[3].' The island or grove on the south of Trill Mill stream belonged

Originalia, 36 Hen. VIII, Pt. 4, m. xl.

[2] Wood–Clark, II, 411.
[3] Ibid. I, 310, note.

'to Sir William Moorton, Kt., Judge of the King's Bench, in right of his wife Anne, daughter and heir of John Smyth of Oxford, Gent[1].'

Writing about a century later, Peshall states that the site now forms the messuage or Tenement and large Yard of Charles Collins, Gent; the Garden, Orchard, and Tenement of Swithin Adee, M.D., late Sir James Cotter's, Bart., and the large Garden and Orchard called Paradise Garden. The Island in their possession . . . is occupied by Mr. Shirley, which serves partly for a Tan Yard and Buildings necessary thereto[2].'

In a short time little was left of the buildings—so complete was the work of destruction. 'The trees were soon cut down, all the greens trod under foot, the church thrown down, and the stones, with the images and monuments of the greatest value, scattered about[3].' The name only survived; Agas in his map (1578) puts the *Graie Friers* where the house of the Black Friars stood. 'The ruins of this college are gone to ruine,' wrote Wood, 'and almost lodged in obscurity[4]:' and the 'scanty fragments' (*rudera paucula*) which were visible to Hearne and Parkinson as they walked towards the Watergate[5] have long since vanished. Even the use to which the materials were put is unknown. Some of the stones form no doubt the foundation-work of many houses in St. Ebbe's: but while something definite is known about the materials of the Houses of the other Mendicant Orders, the records are silent respecting the greatest of the friaries[6].

[1] Wood – Clark, II, 361, 396, note.
[2] Wood–Peshall, Ancient and Present State, p. 270.
[3] Dugdale, Vol. VI, Part 3, p. 1529: Wood–Clark, II, 389.
[4] Wood–Clark, II, 411.
[5] Hearne's Pref. to Otterbourne; Parkinson was the author of *Collectanea Anglo-Minoritica.*
[6] None of the printed books, so far as I know, contain any notice of the uses to which the materials of the Franciscan convent were put. Among MS. sources, I have examined the church-wardens' accounts of Carfax (to which the Rector kindly gave me the fullest access). Wood MSS. C. 1, 'ex archivis S. Petri de Bailly;' and D. 2 (notes from parish archives). The early records of St. Ebbe's and St. Giles' are no longer to be found.

PART II.

BIOGRAPHICAL AND BIBLIOGRAPHICAL NOTICES.

CHAPTER I.

CUSTODIANS AND WARDENS.

1. W. of Esseby, Warden and Custos, c. 1225.—2. E. de Merc., Warden, 1237.—3. P. of Tewkesbury, Custos, 1236-1248.—4. J. of Stamford, Custos, 1253.—5. Martin, Warden, c. 1250.—6. Adam of Warminster, Warden, 1269.—7. J. Codyngton, Warden, 1300.—8. J. of Okehampton, Warden, 1340.—9. R. Clyff, Custos, 1465.—10. R. Salford, Warden, 1488.—11. W. Vavasour, Warden, c. 1500.—12. R. Burton, Warden (and Custos), 1508.—13. W. Goodfield, Warden, before 1513.—14. J. Harvey, Warden, 1513.—15. E. Baskerfield, Warden (and Custos), 1534.

UNLIKE the Abbots and Priors of the *religiosi possessionati*, the heads of the Mendicant Houses required no royal assent to their appointment. Their names consequently do not occur in the royal records, and to this fact is due the incompleteness of the following list of the custodians and wardens of the Grey Friars at Oxford. It is a noteworthy if not surprising fact, that not a single original work by any of these men can now be found.

William of Esseby (perhaps Ashby in Norfolk)[1], the first warden, was one of the four clerks who came to England with Agnellus in 1224; he was then a young man and a novice, having recently joined the Order in France[2], and only assumed the habit of a *professus* when he became warden at Oxford[3]. He was among the first three Minorites authorized to preach in England[4].

When the English Province was divided into custodies (c. 1226?), he was made custodian of Oxford[5]. Afterwards he was sent to found

---

[1] Jessop, Coming of the Friars, p. 36.
[2] Mon. Franc. I, p. 6.
[3] Ibid. p. 10.
[5] Ibid. p. 27.
[4] Ibid. p. 21.

the convent at Cambridge, and Eccleston draws a strange picture of him solemnly chanting the service, with one other friar and a crippled novice, in the wooden shed which served for a chapel[1]. Later William is heard of at Northampton[2]. About 1238, he was sent by Friar Wygmund, the German *visitator* of England, to visit Ireland; his mission here proved as abortive as that of the German in England; on his return he went to Cologne to join Wygmund[3]. He had ceased to be warden or custodian of Oxford before 1237[4]. He was alive when William of Nottingham became Provincial Minister, and died 'after many years' at London[5].

Eccleston gives him a high character. He was specially distinguished for his obedience.

'When Friar Gregory, the Provincial Minister of France, asked him whether he would like to go to his native land, he said, he did not know what he would like, because his will was not his own, but the Minister's; so, whatever the Minister would, he would[6].'

By his tact he did much towards winning for his Order the affection of the world, and he was instrumental in leading many fit persons of various ranks and ages 'to the way of salvation[7].'

> Cambridge Univ. Library, MS. Ii I. 24, p. 332. seq. (sec. xiv) contains a sermon by the '*Prior de Essebi de artificioso modo predicandi*,' and other sermons perhaps by the same author. Tanner and others suggest that this Essebi may be the Franciscan: but 'Prior' was a title unknown in the Franciscan Order. The author was probably a Prior of Canons Ashby.

Eustace de Merc was a member of the Oxford convent in the lifetime of Agnellus, and had license to hear confessions; he was warden at the time of the visitatorial chapter held by Friar Wygred or Wygmund in 1237-8. On this occasion many accusations were brought against him, in consequence of which he was for a day and a half excluded from the chapter; the charges are not specified and do not seem to have been proved. After fulfilling the duties of warden

---

[1] Mon. Franc. I, p. 18.
[2] Ibid.
[3] Ibid. p. 30.
[4] When Eustace de Merc was warden, and Peter custodian.
[5] Ibid. p. 6. Phillipps, MS. 3119, fol. 71, contains the following note in an old hand (cf. Bale, Scriptores, II, 41): 'Hic (W. de Esseby) aliquando temptatus a carne amputavit sibi genitalia zelo pudicicie; quo facto papam peciit et ab eo graviter correptus celebrandi divina meruit dispensacionem. Hic eciam Willemus post multos annos quievit London.'
[6] Mon. Franc. I, p. 6.   [7] Ibid.

for a long time, he became custodian of York. The date of his death is unknown.

While he always showed to others 'the sweetness of an angelic affection,' he subjected himself until the end of his life to the severest discipline; even in his earlier years, his fasts and vigils and self-inflicted stripes endangered his health, and called forth the remonstrances of his superiors [1].

Peter of Tewkesbury. It is uncertain whether 'Friar Peter, custodian of Oxford' is to be identified with Peter of Tewkesbury; but a comparison of the dates, so far as they can be ascertained, brings out nothing inconsistent with this supposition, and we shall put the facts about both of them together. Peter of Tewkesbury was warden of London about 1234; about this time he went to Rome with Agnellus and some Friars Preachers on behalf of the English prelates [2]. Agnellus confessed to him on his death-bed and constituted him his vicar [3]. When Albert of Pisa was Provincial, Friar Peter was custodian of Oxford; he held the office for twelve years (1236–48 ?) [4]. During the generalship of Haymo, 'Friar Peter, custodian of Oxford' was one of the three friars chosen for the English province to note doubtful points in the Rule [5]. In 1245 he again appears as custodian; Adam mentions having written a detailed account to him about the proceedings at or before the Council of Lyons [6]. Peter of Tewkesbury was at the general chapter of the friars at Genoa in 1244, and remained afterwards to obtain and take back two Papal bulls about the Friars Preachers and Minors, evidently the revocation of the bull providing that no Minorite should receive the *obligati* of the Preachers into his Order [7]. When John of Stamford fell ill on his return from Lyons, Peter of Tewkesbury was sent to Mantes to come back with Adam Marsh, at Grostete's request [8]. In 1250 he was minister of Cologne [9]. It was probably in the next year that he was elected fifth Provincial of England after the death of William of Nottingham [10]: he was succeded by John of Stamford about 1256 or 1257 [11]. He was

[1] Mon. Franc. I, 31, 43, 58, 61 : see Part I, Chapter I.
[2] Mon. Franc. I, 52.
[3] Ibid. 53, 54.
[4] Ibid. 28.
[5] Ibid. 48–9.
[6] Ibid. 378.
[7] Ibid. 377, 56.
[8] Grostete, Epist. 334.
[9] Mon. Franc. 63, 308, 313 : Grostete was at the Roman court at this time. Cologne was constituted a separate province in 1239. Anäl. Franc. I, 290.
[10] Ibid. 71. For date, see W. of Nottingham.
[11] Ibid. : letter LXVIII.

an intimate friend of Robert Grostete, 'from whom he often heard many secrets of wisdom.' Eccleston says of him:

'Friar Peter of Tewkesbury, minister of Germany, with God's grace defended the state of the Order against the King, legate, and many false brethren, to such an extent that the fame of the fact spread to many provinces, and his zeal of truth was invincibly proved [2].'

He was buried at Bedford [3].

John of Stamford, custodian of Oxford [4], was a man of great importance among the friars. He was at the council of Lyons in 1245 as *socius* of Adam Marsh [5]. The Pope had some thoughts of sending him with others on an embassy to the Chorasmeni, Tartars, and Saracens, who had attacked the Holy Land, but the plan was not carried out [6]. On his return, he was taken ill at Beaune, and was tended by Adam Marsh [7]. John of Stamford was one of the three friars to whom the general entrusted the confirmation of the election of William of Nottingham's successor in the office of Provincial Minister (1251) [8]. Some time after 1245 he became custodian of Oxford; he held the office in 1253 when Thomas of York incepted [9]. He joined about this time with Adam Marsh and Thomas of York in a petition to the Provincial, begging for mercy for Hugh Cote, probably a lay brother, who had stolen three horses of great value, and then repented [10]. He succeeded Peter of Tewkesbury as provincial minister about 1256 [11]. His friendship with Adam Marsh lasted to the end of the latter's life [12]: feeling that his last days were approaching, Adam begged Bonaventura, then General, to send to him John of Stamford, the English Provincial, who was at this time (1257), apparently abroad [13]. As Provincial he procured an endowment (20s. per annum) for St. Owen's Church in London, the parish in which the Minorites then had their house [14]. He is said to have died in 1264,

---

[1] Mon. Franc. 64.
[2] Ibid. 63–4.
[3] Ibid. 537, 559.
[4] Ibid. 389.
[5] This is proved by Grostete's Letters, No. cxiv. From a passage in a letter of Adam Marsh written at Lyons to the English Provincial, it would seem that Adam was at first accompanied by another 'Friar J.' and afterwards joined by J. de Stamford: 'Rogo salutari obsequio meo carissimos patres, fratres Ric. de Wauz, J. de Stanford, reliquosque fratres socios sc. et filios vestros; in quorum, si placet, sanctis recordationibus me et fratrem J. renovare velitis in Domino.' Mon. Franc. I, 378.

[6] Mon. Franc. I. 376–378.
[7] Grostete, Epist. p. 334.
[8] Mon. Franc. I, 71.
[9] Ibid. 338, 387.
[10] Ibid. 340.
[11] Ibid. 537, 559, 305.
[12] See Adam's letters to him in Mon. Franc. I, p. 387, seq.
[13] Ibid. 305, 306.
[14] Ibid. 512.

but there is no good authority for the statement[1]. He was buried at Lynn, with which place he seems to have had some previous connexion: Brewer calls him warden of Lynn[2].

Martin is mentioned in two letters from Adam Marsh to 'W., Minister of England' as warden of Oxford; but the superscription is untrustworthy and the date of the letters uncertain[3]. This Martin may have been identical with the 'Frater Martinus senex' (mentioned by Eccleston), who established the convent at Shrewsbury, and delighted in the recollection of the hardships and poverty which he had then experienced[4]. A Martin de Barton, who was also known to Eccleston, and had often seen St. Francis, came to England in the early years of the Order, and was afterwards vicar of the English Provincial and filled many other offices[5]. When custodian of York, Martin de Barton enforced the strictest poverty, only allowing so many friars to live in any place, as could be supported by mendicancy alone without incurring debts[6].

Adam of Warminster was warden in 1269; he took part in a controversy with the Dominicans at Oxford in that year, defending his Order against the charge of being 'receivers of money[7].'

John de Codyngton was warden in 1300, when he received license from the Bishop to hear confessions in the Archdeaconry of Oxford[8].

John de Okehampton was warden in 1340; all that is known of him will be found in the Appendix B.

Richard Clyff was custodian in 1465 and 1466. In the latter year he sued John Broghton, sheriff of Kent for a royal debt. He was sometime vice-warden of London and was buried in the church of the Minorites there[9].

---

[1] Dugdale Monast. VI, Pt. 3, p. 1522. Wadding says he became Archbishop of Dublin in 1284 (V, 134): this was J. of Sanford; Rymer, I, 655.

[2] Mon. Franc. I, 537; 42–43; 305, note.

[3] Letters CLXXVI and CCIII. Letter CLXXV was no doubt written to W. of Nottingham (P. of Tewkesbury being mentioned in it), but it is unsafe to ascribe the following letter to the same date. He is probably the warden referred to in Letter CC.

[4] Mon. Franc. I, 8.   [5] Ibid. 25.

[6] Ibid. 27. In Phillipps MS. fol. 74, is the note, 'Iste frater Martinus (de Barton) obiit Northamton.'

[7] Appendix C.

[8] Wood-Clark, II, 387.

[9] Exchequer of Pleas; Plea Roll, 6 Edw. IV, m. 20 (cf. chapter VII); MS. Cotton Vitell. F xii, f. 289 b.

Richard Salford was warden in 1488 and 1489; he recovered debts from Sir John Paston, sheriff of Norfolk and Suffolk, and Sir Edmund Bedyngfeld, sheriff of the same counties; the records of these suits contain the only notices of him now remaining[1].

William Vavasor was studying at Oxford and transcribing philosophical treatises in 1490 and 1491[2]. He incepted as D.D. in 1500, and was warden of the convent about the same time[3]. In Thomas Cromwell's list of learned persons not living in Oxford (A.D. 1531) is the name of 'Dr. Vavysor, Grey Friar at....'[4]. At the dissolution he was warden of the Grey Friars at York[5], and was one of the few Mendicants who received a pension; the amount was £5 a year[6].

Robert Burton was warden on April 12, 1508, when he applied to the Chancellor's Court to recover a debt.

'Eodem die dedimus terminum domino Joanni Gardener principali aule bovine ad satisfaciendum fratri Roberto Burton gardiano fratrum Minorum xxv^s viii^d sibi debitos in fine quatuor septimarum,' &c.[7]

As B.D. he supplicated for D.D. on March 8th, 150$\frac{7}{8}$ after studying for twenty years at Oxford and Cambridge, preaching two University sermons at Oxford, and six at Paul's Cross, &c.; the grace was conceded on condition that he should respond once more[8]. Afterwards he became regent of the Franciscan Schools in London. The register of the Grey Friars, London, notes among those buried in the chapel of All Saints in the Franciscan church,

frater Robertus Burton sacre theologie prof(essor quondam) Regens loci, qui obiit 8° die mensis Januarii A.D. 1522[9].

---

[1] Exchequer of Pleas, Plea Rolls, 3 Hen. VII, m. 35 (printed in App. B); 3 Hen. VII, m. 35, dorse; 4 Hen. VII, m. 17, dorse; 4 Hen. VII, m. 34, dorse.

[2] MS. Corp. Chr. Coll., Oxon, 227, fol. 46, contains *Antonii Andreae tractatus de tribus principiis naturalibus*: (In calce) scriptus per me fratrem Wyllelmum studentem Oxonie, a° incarnacionis Dom. 1419 [1491?]. Ibid. fol. 118 *Duns Scotus super Metheororum libros tres priores*: (In calce) 'Expliciunt questiones .. scripte per manum fratris Wyllelmi Vavysur eiusdem ordinis, A.D. 1491.' MS. 228 was also written by him in 1490.

[3] Wood, Fasti, p. 5.

[4] Cal. of State Papers, Hen. VIII, Vol. V, §§ 6, 18.

[5] Eighth Report of the Dep. Keeper, App. 2, under York.

[6] Misc. Books, Augment. Office, 233 (30–31 Hen. VIII), fol. 154 b.

[7] Acta Cur. Cancell. ꝗ, fol. 53 b: in the margin he is called 'custos fratrum Minorum.'

[8] Reg. G 6, fol. 55. He was still at Oxford in June 1509; Acta Cur. Cancell. ꝗ, f. 92.

[9] MS. Cott. Vitell. F, XII, fol. 277 b. Mr. Brodrick seeks to identify Robert Burton, Fellow of Merton in 1480,

CUSTODIANS AND WARDENS.

Walter Goodfield was warden shortly before 1513; as warden he leased one of the friary gardens to Ric. Leke, brewer[1]. From the University Register[2], it appears that on Nov. 27, 1506, he supplicated to be admitted to opponency and to read the sentences, after studying twelve years in logic, philosophy, and theology; on May 10, 1507, in making the same supplication, he stated that he had studied the same subjects fourteen years. He was admitted to oppose on Dec. 10, 1507. On June 3, 1508, he supplicated as B.D. for D.D.

'This grace was granted on condition that he has studied twelve years in logic, philosophy, and theology, and that he proceed before Easter, and that he preach once '*preter formam*,' after taking his degree, and read one book of the sentences publicly and gratis.'

On March 19, 15$\frac{09}{10}$, he was allowed to count a sermon to be preached on Ash Wednesday as his examinatory sermon. On May 12, 1510, he was licensed in theology. On June 27, 1510, he was dispensed '*pro suis lecturis minutis.*' On July 1, he was admitted D.D.; on Oct. 28, 1510, he was with three others appointed a judge to examine a sentence passed on Thomas Foster by the commissary[3]; and on Dec. 10, he was dispensed from his necessary regency, possibly owing to his duties as warden. He seems to have become warden of the London convent after this[4]. He died on the 6th of May, 1521, and was buried in the chapel of All Saints, in the Grey Friars Church, London[5].

John Harvey succeeded Goodfield as warden; he held the office in Feb. 151$\frac{3}{4}$[6], Feb. 151$\frac{5}{6}$[7], and probably for many years afterwards. He had ceased to be warden in 1529, when he was required by the vice-warden or sub-warden John Bacheler, in the name of the then warden, to answer certain charges made against him respecting his administration[8]. The following details are known about his scholastic career; he was admitted to oppose in theology Dec. 6, 1514, and admitted B.D. on Jan. 20, 151$\frac{4}{5}$; he was still B.D. in 1529; one of the same name took the degree of B. Can. L. on April 3, 1530, but he is not described as a friar[9].

Proctor in 1489, with the Minorite (Mem. of Merton Coll. 241); this seems to me more than doubtful.

[1] Acta Cur. Cancell. ꝫ , fol. 194: see App. B.

[2] The series of graces, &c., relating to W. Goodfield is printed in App. D.

[3] Boase, Register, p. 298.

[4] MS. Cott. Vitell. F, XII, fol. 277 : ' frater Walterus Goodfield, S.T.P. et gardianus loci.'

[5] Ibid.

[6] Acta Cur. Cancell. ꝫ , f. 212 b.

[7] Ibid. f. 261 b, 262 b.

[8] Ibid. EEE, f. 124 b. See App. B.

[9] Boase, Reg. p. 68. Reg. G 6, f.

Edward Baskerfild was probably the immediate successor of John Harvey. In Jan. 152⅞ he held some office, being then 'in London on the business of his house' and likely to stay there some months[1]; he is described as warden in 1533, as *custos fratrum minorum Universitatis Oxon'* in 1534[2], and he was warden at the time of the dissolution.

He supplicated for B.D. on April 12, 1526, after

'studying logic, philosophy, and theology for thirteen years, and preaching some sermons at Exeter and Oxford,'

was admitted to oppose on June 13, and became B.D. on Feb. 18, 152⅞[3]. He supplicated for D.D. on Dec. 9, 1531, and March 5, 153½, after sixteen years' study; and became D.D. on July 8, 1532[4]. He had previously obtained a reduction of his composition on inception first to five, and then to four marks;

'Causa est quod est pauperior quam ut possit eam summam pecunie (quinque marcas) solvere[5].'

In Oct. 1532, he was dispensed from his necessary regency. In 1533 we find him at Exeter, trying to extract from Thomas Benet a recantation of his heresies[6].

He acted as deputy of the commisary, or vice-chancellor, in 1534, 1535, 1536, and 1537[7]. In this capacity he sometimes held his court in the Franciscan convent, as, for instance, when investigating the charges of immorality against Friar Arthur[8]. His pecuniary position seems to have improved: he kept a horse in 1534[9], and in 1537, one Robert Symon was admitted to the privileges of the University as servant of Dr. Baskerfild[10].

At the dissolution he made his peace with the visitors by causing his house to surrender at once[11]. Dr. London sent him to Thomas Cromwell (Aug. 31, 1538), to obtain the 'capacities' for the Oxford

---

220. Acta Cur. Cancell. EEE, 124 b. Reg. H 7, fol. 211 b.

[1] Reg. H. 7, fol. 185.
[2] Acta Cur. Cancell. EEE, fol. 393 b, 270 b.
[3] Reg. H. 7, f. 152 b, 153; Boase, Reg. 143.
[4] Reg. H. 7, fol. 257, 262 b.
[5] Ibid. fol. 263 b, 271 b; in the latter place he is called 'pater edmundus Baskerfell frater ordinis minorum.'

[6] Foxe, V, p. 20: the Martyrologist calls him 'an unlearned doctor.'
[7] Acta Cur. Cancell. EEE, fol. 173, 270, 322, 387, &c.
[8] See Part I, Chapter VII: Acta Cur. Cancell. EEE, f. 321 a, 'Datum in edibus ffranciscanis,' &c.
[9] Part I, Chapter VII.
[10] Acta Cur. Cancell. EEE, f. 336.
[11] Wright, Suppression, p. 217.

friars, and begged Cromwell to allow him to live in Oxford 'altho he wer benefycyd.' As

'visitar of dyvers places wiche they do call custodies,'

he possessed information concerning the friars in London and elsewhere which might be useful to the King's agents, and which he was willing to impart to them. He appears to have accompanied Dr. London on his visitation after the dissolution of the friars at Oxford, and we find him on Jan. 3, 1539, receiving in conjunction with the doctor, the surrender of the Black Friars of Derby[1]. The name is spelt in a variety of ways, e. g. Baskarwild, Bascafyld, &c.; a fifteenth century MS. in the Bodleian (Laud. Lat. 114, § 3), containing *Cantica Sacra*, belonged to Edward Baskervile, D.D.

NOTE. Wood places **Herveius de Saham** among the wardens of the Grey Friars (A.D. 1285). This is a mistake based on a misunderstanding of the following passage in Peckham's Register (p. 895):

'Et ne pro defectu acquietantiae solutionem dictae pecuniae retardetis, damus magistro Herveo de Saham, auditori compoti vestri de bonis dicti defuncti, Oxoniae commoranti et regenti, et gardiano Fratrum Minorum de eadem, tenore praesentium potestatem ut soluta dicta pecunia in forma praefata, plenam vobis faciant acquietantiam de eadem' (May 6, 1285).

[1] Reliquary, Vol. XVIII, p. 21.

CHAPTER II.

LECTORS OR REGENT MASTERS OF THE FRANCISCANS.

THE following sixty-seven names are classed together under a separate heading simply because they are found in a list in an old manuscript. The list is evidently intended to include all the Regent Masters of the Friars Minors at Oxford[1] in chronological order; it seems to break off about the year 1350. Whether it is complete up to that date may be doubted; but no contemporary, or nearly contemporary, notice has been found of any Friar Minor Regent in Theology or D.D. of Oxford before 1351, whose name does not occur in this list[2].

The list is found in two MSS:—

I. British Museum; Cotton Nero A IX, fol. 77 a–b, in Eccleston's Chronicle. Names 1–5 are in the same hand as the rest of the MS.; 6–21 in a hand rather larger but not perceptibly later. On the reverse of the leaf, they are continued in a later fourteenth century hand which ends at the 58th name; then 59–66 have been added not much later (the ink has faded a good deal in this part); the last name is in a later hand, probably fifteenth century.

II. Phillipps, MS. 3119, fol. 76 (at Thirlestaine House). Names 1–21 are in the same hand as the MS., i.e. the text of Eccleston's Chronicle; another scribe has added names 22–49 inclusive; then the names are continued in another hand to Laurence Briton, where the list ends. This MS. omits Henry Cruche and Walter de Chauton, so that Laurence Briton is called the 53rd master instead of the 55th.

Lectors.

1. **Adam Marsh** or **de Marisco** was born probably at the end of the 12th century in the diocese of Bath[3]. He was educated at Oxford,

---

[1] See Part I, Chapter III. Eccleston begins the list with the words: 'Ipsi vero inceperunt ut magistri.'

[2] Except perhaps Friar W. Lemster,

but it is not certain to which Order he belonged; see notice of him, A.D. 1290.

[3] Trivet, Annals, p. 243.

where he studied under Robert Grostete[1], whose affectionate interest in him dated from his early years[2]. His brother Robert was made Archdeacon of Oxford by Grostete in 1248 and other members of the family were in the bishop's service[3]. Adam's uncle, Richard de Marisco, Bishop of Durham, from 1217 to 1226, gave him a living near Wearmouth, which he held for three years[4], and bequeathed to him his library in 1226[5]. At this time Adam was a Master, probably of Arts. Soon afterwards, at the instigation of his friend and pupil[6] Adam of Oxford, who had recently become a Minorite, he gave up 'all worldly greatness and a large income[7]' to enter the Franciscan Order at Worcester, 'through zeal for greater poverty[8].' He is said to have been appointed by the General Chapter *socius* of St. Anthony of Padua, the first theological student in the Order. The two then proceeded, according to the same authority, to study under the Abbat of St. Andrew's at Vercelli, where they made such progress in five years that the Abbat confessed that his pupils had become his teachers[9]. In 1230 St. Anthony and Adam Marsh are said to have headed the opposition to the relaxations which Elias was attempting to bring into the Order[10]; but this tradition is probably unfounded; Eccleston says nothing about it[11]. After his entry into the Order, Adam probably resided for the most part at Oxford, where Grostete was then lecturing to the Franciscans. Wood asserts that the latter presided at his inception and made the customary speech in praise

---

[1] Roger Bacon calls Grostete Adam's 'master.' Op. Ined. 187.

[2] Mon. Franc. I, 145, *ab annis juvenilibus*.

[3] Ibid. pref. lxxvii–lxxviii.

[4] Lanercost Chron. p. 58, where Adam after his death is said to have appeared to a friar and said it was well with him, 'because I have escaped the judgment, but that cursed church which I held for three years nearly gave me over to damnation.'

[5] Close Roll, 10 Henry III, m. 6.

[6] Mon. Franc. I, 15: 'fuit autem tunc socius Magistri Adae de Marisco et ad robas suas.'

[7] M. Paris, Chr. Maj. V, 619–20.

[8] Ibid. p. 16. The date of his entry must have been between 1226 (when he was *Magister* not *Frater*, Close Roll, *ut supra*), and 1230. See Grostete's Letters, pp. 17–21 written before 1231; and Wadding, II, 240. He probably entered the Order in 1227, or perhaps at the end of 1226. The entry on the Close Roll about the Bp. of Durham's library is dated Worcester, Sept. 3. Canon Creighton puts the date of Adam's entry into the Order ten years later. Dict. of Nat. Biogr.

[9] Wadding, II, 48. Evers, Analecta (Hist. of Friar Nic. Glasberger), p. 33. I have not been able to find any early authority for these statements. A letter from Adam to the Abbat of St. Andrew's is extant. Mon. Franc. I, 206. The University of Vercelli was founded in 1228, and it is probably in this year, if at all, that Adam went there. Denifle, Die Universitäten des Mittelalters, I, 290.

[10] Wadding, II, 240–1. St. Anthony died 1231.

[11] The account in Eccleston refers to the deposition of Elias in 1239. Mon. Franc. I, 45–7.

of the inceptor at the ceremony[1]; but the statement, though probable enough in itself, lacks authority and seems to have originated from a confusion between Adam and Robert Marsh[2]: it is not unlikely that Adam received his theological degree abroad. There is no direct evidence of his having lectured on theology to the friars at Oxford before 1252[3], but there can be no doubt that he began to do so not later than 1247 (when Thomas Wallensis was elected Bishop of St. David's), and he probably delivered lectures long before. He was certainly before this time one of the recognised leaders of the English Franciscans[4]. He was on a commission of three elected by the English province to report on the Rule when Haymo was general (1239-1244), and recommended that no change should be made in the statutes of St. Francis[5]. He wrote a solemn exhortation in the name of the English Minorites to Boniface of Savoy on his consecration to the Archbishopric of Canterbury in 1245[6]. William of Nottingham submitted to him the names of three friars from whom he was to select one to act as Vicar in the Provincial Minister's absence (1250?)[7] In his latter years he was one of the foremost men in the church. At the instance of the Archbishop of Canterbury and for his use, he wrote an address to the Pope on the occasion of Henry III taking the cross (1250)[8]. He addressed a long letter of advice to St. Sewalus on his appointment to the Archbishopric of York in 1255[9]. In the same year he was nominated by Alexander IV to settle a dispute between the Bishop and the Prior and Convent of Winchester[10]. He was on a Papal commission to try a cause between the King and the Bishop of St. David's, and between the same bishop and the Abbat of Gloucester[11], and on another commission appointed to examine the claims of Richard de Wiche to canonization[12]. He

---

[1] Cf. Trivet, Annals, p. 306.

[2] Mon. Franc. I, 135. Wood-Clark II, 364: Wood refers to Gascoigne, Liber Veritatum, I, 663: I have not seen the passage, which does not occur in the extracts edited by Hearne or Rogers; but Gascoigne cannot be regarded as an authority in this matter.

[3] Ibid. 232 (prob. Nov. 1252), 281, 335 (Jan. 1253), letter CXC was however probably written before this time, c. 1250, but I can find no other reference to either of the lawsuits mentioned there.

[4] Brewer in one place calls him Provincial of the Minorites (p. 613): this is a slip. Nor was he warden of the London convent; 'Frater A. Gardianus Fratrum Minorum Londini' (Mon. Franc. p. 181) was not A. de Marisco. See ibid. p. 396.

[5] Ibid. 49.

[6] Ibid. 77. Boniface was elected in 1240.

[7] Ibid. 355.

[8] Ibid. 414, seq.

[9] Ibid. 438-489.

[10] Ibid. 95, 609-612.

[11] Ibid. 342.

[12] Wadding, IV, *anno* 1256.

supported Grostete in his revolt against the scandalous nepotism of Innocent IV[1]. At Oxford his character, learning, and friendship with the great, gave him a very important position, and he acted as spokesman now of the Franciscans, now of the whole University[2]. His fame was European, and Grostete was afraid that the Parisians would secure him to supply the place of Alexander of Hales (1245)[3]. Among his correspondents and friends were many of the leading men of the age, such as Walter de Cantilupe[4], Richard de Wiche, Walter de Merton, Richard Earl of Cornwall, John of Parma, and Bonaventura. He assisted the Archbishop of Canterbury in his visitation, and accompanied Grostete to the Council of Lyons. At one time he is wanted to attend the Parliament at London[5], at another he is summoned by the Queen to Reading, to treat of 'matters touching the King and his heirs[6].' He incurred the royal displeasure by an outspoken sermon at Court (Oct. 1250)[7]; but his advice was asked and listened to by the King who afterwards called him his father[8].

'When the Jews ... had transgressed against the peace of the kingdom, so that both by the judgment of the King and the princes of the land they were judged worthy of death, he alone resisted their arguments and forbade that they should be put to death[9].'

In 1247 he was sent abroad with the Prior of the Dominicans on the King's business, and forty marks were granted to buy horses and harness for the ambassadors[10]. In 1257 he was sent with Walter de Cantilupe, Bishop of Worcester, on a similar mission, his expenses being paid out of the treasury[11]. He was no less intimate with the Earl of Leicester than with the Bishop of Lincoln. He lectures Eleanor de Montfort on her duties as a mother and wife, and on her excess in dress[12]. He speaks equally plainly to Simon de Montfort.

'Better is a patient man than a strong man,' he writes to the hot-headed earl, 'and he who can rule his own temper than he who storms a city[13].'

The friar took a keen interest in his friend's great deeds, recognised his noble qualities, and the value of his efforts 'to purge, illuminate, and sanctify the church of God,' and looked to him as the guardian

---

[1] Mon. Franc. I, 139.
[2] Ibid. I, 99, 347.
[3] Grostete, Letters, 334.
[4] Cf. ibid. p. 302.
[5] Mon. Franc. I, p. 105.
[6] Ibid. p. 152.
[7] Ibid. p. 275.
[8] Lanercost Chron. p. 24.
[9] Ibid.
[10] Liberate Roll, 31 Hen. III, m. 4 (App. B).
[11] Ibid. 42 Hen. III, m. 3.
[12] Mon. Franc. 294, 295, 298, 299.
[13] Ibid. I, 264.

of the public weal[1]. He encouraged the Earl to go forward in his thankless task of saving Gascony, and tried to win the King over to his side[2].

'If,' he writes to the Earl in 1250[3], 'you have received the answers of broken friendship and feigned affection, what else are you now suffering than what you before expected? The clear circumspection of your wisdom will remember, in how many conferences, after repeated and careful examination, we drummed into each other's ears the execrable shamelessness of seductive cunning, such as we now see; although, considering the trustworthiness of courageous fidelity, your wisdom did not think proper to decline the danger of a truly grand exploit, for the imminent suspicion merely of some stupendous dishonesty.'

With all his other occupations Adam Marsh did not neglect the poor and oppressed; he begs Grostete to assist two poor scholars relatives of the bishop; he writes to Thomas de Anesti on behalf of an able and honest schoolmaster who is in want of the very necessaries of life; a weeping widow brings her troubles to him, sure of sympathy and help[4]. His health gave way under the strain of his manifold duties and the severe discipline of his Order: he suffered from weakness of the eyes and other infirmities[5]. In 1253 he lost his lifelong friend Grostete, who bequeathed his library to the Oxford Franciscans out of love for Adam Marsh[6]. In 1256 the King and Archbishop of Canterbury tried to force him into the bishopric of Ely; his rival Hugh Balsham who had been elected by the chapter appealed to Rome and obtained a decision in his favour on Oct. 6, 1257. His candidature, probably none of his own seeking, seems to have laid the friar open to a charge of worldly ambition, which must have embittered his last days[7]. Feeling the end approaching, he wrote to Bonaventura to send the Provincial John of Stamford,

'by whom, through God's blessing, I may be directed through things transitory and my thoughts raised to things eternal[8].'

On Dec. 23, 1257, he was ordered abroad by the King[9]. He probably died on Nov. 18[10], 1258, and was buried next to Grostete

---

[1] Mon. Franc. I, 225, 264; and the long account of his trial, p.122. Cf. Part I, p.32.
[2] Ibid. 268, &c.
[3] Ibid. 266-7. A sentence at the end of the letter seems to refer to the defeat of St. Louis at Mansourah. Cf. pp. 278-9. (The translation is Brewer's.)
[4] Ibid. 137, 244, 398. See also Brewer's preface.
[5] Ibid. 305, 348, 367.
[6] Nic. Trivet, Annals, p. 243; Mon. Franc. I, p. 185.
[7] M. Paris, Chron. Majora, V, 619. Cf. Mon. Franc. I, 412.
[8] Mon. Franc. I, 305.
[9] Liberate Roll, 42 Hen. III, m. 3.
[10] W. of Worcester, *Itin.* p. 81, from Franciscan Martyrology of Salisbury.

at Lincoln[1]. Besides the treatise mentioned below, none of his works remain[2] except the letters, which, stilted and obscure in style, do not justify the title of *Doctor illustris*, with which subsequent generations honoured him[3]. His reputation as a philosopher and theologian must rest on the evidence of his contemporaries, and on the greatness of the school which he did so much to found. Matthew Paris calls him '*literatus*[4].' Grostete found him

'a true friend and faithful counsellor, respecting truth not vanity,'—'a wise man and a prudent, and fervent in zeal for the salvation of souls[5].'

His most famous pupil Roger Bacon had nothing but praise and admiration for his master, who like Grostete was 'perfect in all wisdom[6].'

Extant works:—*Epistolae*.
  MSS. Brit. Mus.: Cotton Vitell. c. viii. (sec. xiii–xiv).
    Bodl.: Digby 104, fol. 90 (sec. xiii), letter 147 only.
  Edited by Brewer, Monumenta Franciscana, I (1858).

Pastorale excerptum (perhaps merely an extract from the letters).
  MS. Vienna: Bibl. Palat. 4923, fol. 40 b–42 b (sec. xv).

2. **Ralph de Colebruge** was the second Franciscan master who lectured at Oxford. He entered the Order while regent in theology at Paris, where he won some fame; after finishing his course of lectures, he was appointed by the General of the Order to rule in theology at Oxford, probably before 1250; he was still a novice when he entered on his duties at Oxford[7].

3. **Eustace de Normaneville**, probably took the Franciscan habit at Oxford about 1250 or before[8]. His conversion was of peculiar importance to the Order,

---

[1] Lanerc. Chron. p. 58.

[2] Bale and Pits give lists of his works, but produce no authority. Leland states on the evidence of the *Catalogus de eruditis Franciscanis*, which he had seen in the Minorite convent at Oxford, that Adam wrote 'a fair number of commentaries on Holy Scripture.' One edition of Barth. of Pisa (Bononiae, 1620) mentions as his works, Elucidarium Scripturae, and Theological Lectures. This passage is not in the edition of 1510. It is not probable that the 'Ordinances for the household of Bishop Grostete,' or rather Grostete's Rules for the Countess of Lincoln, are by Adam. Mon. Franc. I, 582. Royal Hist. Soc., *Walter of Henley*, pp. xlii, 122.

[3] Not his contemporaries, as Brewer states. I do not know when the title first originated.

[4] Chron. Majora, V, 619.

[5] Epist. Nos. XX and XCIX.

[6] Op. Ined. 70, 74–5, 88, 186, 428.

[7] Mon. Franc. I, 39, and n. 1. Cf. ibid. 542, 'Rodulphus de Corbrug.' Cf. Collect. Anglo-Minoritica, 48.

[8] The good effects of Eustace's conversion were commented on by 'Peter,

'because he was noble and rich, and had laudably ruled in arts and decrees, and had been Chancellor of Oxford[1], and was about to incept in theology.'

It must have been soon after his entry that the friars at Norwich asked him to become their lecturer. Adam Marsh was deputed by the Provincial to make the proposal to him. Eustace refused the honour on the plea of ill-health and 'unprepared aptitude of mind[2].' Eccleston mentions him as the third who lectured at the Oxford Grey Friars as a master[3]. He was afterwards sent to Cambridge and was the third regent master of the Franciscans there[4].

4. **Thomas of York** (1253) is first mentioned in a letter of Adam Marsh written at Lyons, 1245; the writer sends for various books, among which is

'the chapter of the First Prophecy (Abbat Joachim?) which the beloved brother in Christ, Thomas of York had[5].'

Soon afterwards we find him consulting with Adam, Grostete, and the Vicar of the Provincial Minister, about sending English friars to Denmark[6]. He wrote to Adam about the defeat of St. Louis and

minister of England,' 1251–1256 (Mon. Franc. I, 40). But Eustace entered the Order during the ministry of W. of Nottingham. Two of the letters (Nos. 178 and 200) in which Adam Marsh mentions Eustace as a friar are addressed to 'Friar W., minister of England,' but several of these superscriptions are undoubtedly wrong and the rest consequently of little value. Letter 179, however, written at the same time as 178 and stating Eustace's refusal to lecture at Norwich, is addressed to Robert of Thornham, who was then evidently custodian of Cambridge (Mon. Franc. I, 62). In a letter to W. of Nottingham (No. 173) Adam states that this Robert was just starting for the Holy Land, and as he certainly went (Mon. Franc. I, 62), there is no reason to suppose that he delayed long. What then is the date of letter 173? That the superscription is correct is shown by the mention in the letter of Peter, minister of Cologne, i. e. P. of Tewkesbury, William's successor in England; Adam also mentions his regret at being unable to accompany Grostete to the Roman court owing to his having to assist the Archbishop of Canterbury. These details fix the date of Robert's departure (or resolution to depart) to Palestine at 1250: thus letter 179 cannot have been written later than 1250, and Eustace must have entered the Order in that year at latest. He witnesses a charter as friar in 1251; Wood, MS. D 2, p. 537.

[1] Le Neve and others place his chancellorship in 1276; Eccleston certainly says *fuerat*. Mon. Franc. I, 39, note 2, 41; Phillipps, MS. fol. 76 a.

[2] Mon. Franc. I, pp. 319, 321.

[3] Ibid. p. 39.

[4] Ibid. p. 555.

[5] Mon. Franc. I, 378. Cf. p. 395 (letter to Th. of York, 1252?), 'Mittit vobis frater Laurentius (Adam's secretary) quaternos matris prophetiae (?) pro quibus misistis,' &c.

[6] Ibid. p. 90–1. When John Erlandi became Bishop of Roskild, I do not know: he was translated to the Archbishopric of Lundia in 1254; Langebek, Script. rer. Dan. Vol. V, p. 583.

the Crusaders in 1250, and Adam sent the letter on to Grostete[1]. About the same time Adam remonstrates with him for breaking his promises, especially for omitting to send him 'the table of the Trinity' (? *tabula trinitatis*)[2]. Another letter to him from Adam Marsh refers to the anger of the King against Simon de Montfort, whose friendship Thomas seems to have enjoyed and whose party he no doubt supported. Perhaps it was before 1250 that Adam advised the Provincial Minister to instruct Thomas,

'that he should apply himself to the study of Holy Scriptures by attending the lectures of the learned and investigating their writings,'

with a view to his eventually becoming lecturer to the Grey Friars at Oxford; failing this, the writer hints that Thomas would probably be summoned abroad[3]. In the same letter he refers to his 'youthful age.' At the beginning of 1253[4] Thomas of York was presented to incept in theology at Oxford, objections were raised on the ground that he had not taken a degree in Arts. Eventually he was allowed to incept, but a statute was passed to regulate the conduct of the University on similar occasions in the future. The details of the controversy are given elsewhere[5]. The vesperies took place on Thursday, March 13th, and the inception on the following day, under the presidency of Friar Peter de Manners, apparently a Dominican; Adam Marsh, who as master of the inceptor would naturally have presided, left Oxford on March 12th. Thomas of York now became lecturer to the Oxford Franciscans[6]. He was afterwards sent to Cambridge and occurs as the sixth in the list of 'Masters of the Friars Minors' there[7]. Adam Marsh writes to him in the most affectionate terms and speaks highly of his learning, and the brightness of his intellect[8]; he describes him to Grostete as an earnest, discreet, and benevolent man, filled with a heavenly zeal for the salvation of souls[9]. According to the *Catalogus illustrium Franciscanorum* he wrote a commentary on Ecclesiastes[10].

[1] Ibid. 114–5.
[2] Ibid. 392. In the same letter is the sentence: 'Nuper mihi de curia Romana allatum est Apostolicae Sedis privilegium, pro quo laborare sui gratia voluit amantissimus frater J., domini papae nuntius.' Cf. reference to the same on p. 313 (A.D. 1250).
[3] Mon. Franc. I, 357.
[4] Ibid. 338, 346.
[5] Part I, Chapter III.
[6] Ibid. 39: but see ibid. p. 552, 'Notandum,' &c.; the last words should be 'et quintus ponitur frater T. de Eboraco.'
[7] Ibid. 555.
[8] Ibid. 357, 392–5.
[9] Ibid. 115. Cf. 393, 'Bene fecistis ... qui pro patre secundum carnem dilecti fratris J. de Beverlaco in negotio suae salutis tam consultum vigilantiae fidelis adjutorium, nec non et in caeteris praesertim ad salutem animarum pertinentibus, tam exquisita circumspectione exhibere voluistis.'
[10] Leland, Scriptores, *sub nomine*; cf. Part I, p. 58.

Frater Thomas de Eboraco super Metaphysicam Aristotelis.
MS. Florence: Laurentiana, *ex Bibl. S. Crucis,* Plut. xiv, Sin. Cod. V.

5. **Richard Rufus of Cornwall**[1] was a Master, probably of Arts, when he became a Minorite at Paris
'at the time when Friar Elias threw the whole Order into confusion' (c. 1238).

He came to England (where he made his profession) while the trial of the Minister-General was yet pending in the Roman Court[2]. He is mentioned as speaking at a chapter at Oxford soon after coming to England—probably either the visitatorial chapter or the chapter held to protest against the visitor's conduct in 1238[3]. Soon after 1250 he received a command from the General to go to Paris as lecturer, but he seems to have obtained leave to continue his studies at Oxford owing to his weak health[4]. He probably lectured on the sentences as B.D. about this time. But soon afterwards, '*ob vehementiores perturbationum occasiones*[5],' in Adam Marsh's words, he formed the 'inexorable resolution' of going to France in accordance with the General's permission: and Adam in the name of the other friars, requested the Provincial to facilitate his departure by providing him with suitable companions and the necessary manuscripts[6]. Early in 1253 again, Adam writes to the Provincial:

'I beg you to look out for some one competent to act as secretary to Friar Richard of Cornwall[7].'

---

[1] That Ric. Rufus and Ric. of Cornwall were one and the same is proved by Cotton MS. of Eccleston, f. 77, where 'rufus' is added in an old hand in the margin, and by Phillipps, MS. of Eccleston, fol. 76 a, 'Ricardus Rufus Cornubiensis.' Cf. Mon. Franc. I, 16. He is probably identical with 'Ricardus le Ruys,' whose commentary on the sentences Bale saw at Norwich, 'in claustro monachorum.' Script. II, 81.

[2] Mon. Franc. I, 16, 39.

[3] Phillipps, MS. 3119, f. 76 a. 'Iste Ricardus veniens in Angliam narravit in capitulo Oxon', quod, cum unus frater Parisius extasi staret, visum erat ei quod frater Egidius laicus sed contemplativus sedit in cathedra legens autenticas septem peticiones dominice oracionis cuius omnes auditores erant tamen fratres in ordine lectores. Intrans autem S. Franciscus primo siluit et postea sic clamavit, O quam verecundum est vobis quod talis frater laycus excedit vestra merita sursum in celo (?). Et quia inquid sciencia inflat, caritas autem edificat, plures sunt venerati fratres clerici ... in eterno regno dei.' (MS. imperf.)

[4] Mon. Franc. I, 330, 365, 366.

[5] Ibid. 360, 365. In an agreement drawn up in 1252, after a quarrel between the Northerners and the Irish in Oxford, and signed by representatives of the two parties, the name of 'Ricardus Cornubiensis' appears among the Irishmen (Wood, Annals, 246). This was no doubt a namesake of the friar, who is often confused with the friar; he is mentioned in Grostete's Epist. p. 138, Mon. Franc. I, 135, Le Neve, Fasti, II, 184, &c.

[6] Mon. Franc. I, 366.   [7] Ibid. 349.

It may then be inferred that he went to Paris in 1253, where, according to Eccleston,

'he gave cursory lectures on the sentences and was judged a great and admirable philosopher [1].'

After lecturing in Paris, he returned to Oxford, it appears, and became regent-master of the friars (c. 1255?) [2]. It was here that he developed the 'errors,' the verbal subtleties, which Roger Bacon so unsparingly denounced. Writing in 1292, Bacon says [3]:

'Et optime novi auctorem [4] pessimum et stultissimum istorum errorum [5], qui vocatus est Ricardus Cornubiensis, famosissimus apud stultam multitudinem, set apud sapientes fuit insanus et reprobatus Parisius propter errores quos invenerat et promulgaverat, quum sollempniter legebat sentencias ibidem, postquam [6] legerat [7] sentencias Oxonie, ab anno Domini 1250 [o]. Ab illo M CC L igitur tempore remansit multitudo in huius magistri erroribus usque nunc, scilicet per quatraginta annos et amplius, et maxime invalescit Oxonie sicut ibidem incepit hec demencia infinita.'

Adam Marsh, though in somewhat general terms, gives a far more flattering account of Richard [8].

Martin de Sancta Cruce, Master of the Hospital of Sherbourne, bequeathed to him in his will dated November, 1259, *unum habitum integrum*, and a copy of the Canonical Epistles [9].

Assisi MS. 176 contains a compilation ascribed by a note in a late hand to 'Master Richard Rufus of England;' the volume was in the possession of the friars at Assisi in 1373, consists of 226 leaves, and seems to contain more than one treatise: it is not rubricated.

Inc. 'Deus autem qui dives est in misericordia propter nimiam caritatem suam.'

6. John Wallensis was B.D. of Oxford before he entered the Order [10]. He must have become D.D. and regent master of the Franciscan schools at Oxford before 1260 [11]. It was probably after this that he went as lecturer to Paris, where he was honoured with the title of

---

[1] Ibid. 39. Bacon says, 'solemniter legebat;' see below.

[2] It may be considered certain that Thomas of York became lector in 1253 and that Richard succeeded him—whether immediately or not is a little doubtful; the Cotton MS. of Eccleston calls Richard *sextus* (*lector*), instead of *quintus*.

[3] Royal MS. (Brit. Mus.) 7 F, VII, fol. 81; cf. Charles, Roger Bacon, 415; the MS. is very inaccurate, Charles still more so.

[4] *Auctorem*, not in MS.

[5] MS. *errorem*.

[6] Charles reads *priusquam*.

[7] MS. *legeret*.

[8] 'Cui conversationis honestas et claritas scientiae, pietas affectionis et opinionis integritas, facultas erudiendi et disserendi subtilitas,' &c. Mon. Franc. I, 365.

[9] Durham Wills (Surtees Soc.), Vol. I, pp. 10–11.

[10] Mon. Franc. I., 542.

[11] See notice of H. de Brisingham.

Arbor Vitae[1], and where he was buried[2]. But before his death he was again in England. In October, 1282, 'Friar John Wallensis, S.T.D.,' was sent by Archbishop Peckham as ambassador to the insurgent Welsh[3]. In 1283 he was one of the five doctors at Paris who were deputed to examine the doctrines of Peter John Olivi[4]. He enjoyed a great reputation as a theologian, and the widespread and lasting popularity of his works is shown by the large number of MSS. and printed editions which have come down to us. His writings are specially illustrative of the practical side of the Franciscan teaching.

Summa de Penitentia. *Inc.* ' Quoniam provida solertia est.'
    MSS. Brit. Museum: Royal 10 A ix. f. 1–50 b (sec. xiii); 4 D iv. fol. 244 b (sec. xv)[5].
    Paris:—Bibl. Mazarine, 569, f. 86 b (sec. xiv).
    Falaise:—Bibl. Publ. 38, p. 372 (sec. xiv).
    Cf. Worcester Cathed. Libr. MS. 114 (=789) 'Jo. Wallensis ordinis Praedicatorum summa de confessione[6].'

Breviloquium de quatuor virtutibus cardinalibus, or, *de virtutibus antiquorum principum et philosophorum :* four or five parts:
    i. De justitia; ii. De prudentia; iii. De temperantia; iv. De fortitudine; v. De ordinatione virtutum (this is sometimes included in part iv). *Inc. prol.* 'Quoniam misericordia et veritas.'
    MSS. Brit. Mus.: Royal 10 A ix., f. 67 b–99 (sec. xiii); 12 E xxi, § 2, (sec. xv); Burney 360, f. 1 (sec. xv); Harleian 632, f. 25 (sec. xv).
    Oxford:—Bodl.: Bodley 58 (=2006); Laud, Miscell. 603, fol. 103 (sec. xiv).—Corp. Chr. Coll. 18[7].—Oriel Coll. 34 (sec. xiv ineuntis)[8].
    Paris:—Bibl. Nat. 3706 (sec. xiv), 6346 (xiv), 6776 f. 1–54, (xiv) imperf. at the beginning.
    Toulouse, 340. Cf. MS. St. Omer, 400 (sec. xiv). *Breviloquium de sapientia . . . sanctorum doctorum,* etc.: *inc.* 'Quoniam unica est veritas' (='quoniam misericordia et veritas?')
    Printed at Venice, 1496; Lyons, 1511 (fol. 200 *seq.*); Argentina, 1518 (fol. 151 b–164); and *sine anno et loco* (Louvain 1485?) under the title *Liber de instructione principum per quatuor partes secundum quatuor virtutes cardinales.*

Ordinarium[9], or, *Alphabetum vitae religiosae :* 3 parts:

---

[1] Barth. of Pisa, Liber Conform. fol. 81.
[2] Wadding, IV, 325.
[3] Peckham's Register, II, 421–2.
[4] Hist. Litt. de France, t. xxv, p. 178.
[5] This MS. belonged to the London Franciscans.
[6] Probably the *Summa* of John Lector of Freiburg; see p. 150.
[7] Ascribed to Thomas Wallensis.
[8] Stated to have been composed at the request of *Episcopus Maglonensis*, i.e. Magalona, Narbonne.
[9] Mentioned again by Tanner, as a different work under the title, *De ordinatione universali.*

i. *Diaetarium*; ii. *Locarium*; iii. *Itinerarium*. *Inc.prol.* 'Nunquid nosti ordinem coeli.' *Inc. pars i.* 'Quoniam omni negotio.'

MSS. Brit. Mus.: Harl. 632, f. 1 (sec. xv).
    Bodleian: Tanner 110, f. 124 (sec. xiv ineuntis); Laud, Miscell. 497 (sec. xv).
    Dublin:—Trinity Coll. 138 (=278).
    Paris:—Bibl. Nat. 3588 (sec. xiv).
    Charleville, 113 (xiv) and 272 (xiv).
Printed at Venice, 1496 (fol. 260); Lyons, 1511 (fol. 217–255); Argentina, 1518 (fol. 164).

Summa collectionum (or, *collationum*), or, *Communiloquium*, *Summa collationum ad omne genus hominum*, or, *De vitae regimine*, or, *Margarita Doctorum*, or, *Communes loci ad omnium generum argumenta*. A compendium for the use of young preachers, consisting of 7 parts:

i. De constitutione reipublice; ii. De colligatione membrorum reipublice; iii. De informacione hominum; iv. De republica ecclesiastica; v. De instructione scolasticorum; vi. De instructione religiosorum; vii. De informacione hominum ut sint parati ad mortem. *Inc. prol.* 'Cum doctor sive predicator evangelicus.' *Inc. pars i.* 'Quoniam respublica, ut dictum est, est universale quoddam corpus.' *Inc. cap. i.* 'Sed primo notandum est quod respublica est res populi.'

MSS. Brit. Mus.: Harl. 632, f. 36 (xv).
    Oxford:—Bodley 815 (=2684), f. 108 (sec. xv).—Balliol Coll. 274 (A.D. 1409).—Lincoln Coll. 67 (sec. xiv).
    Cambridge:—Peterhouse 12 or 2-3-9.—Pembroke 123. Cf. Public Library Kk II, 11 (sec. xv). 'Summa compilata a fratre Johanne Walense'—*de republica* added in the table of contents.
    Paris:—Bibl. Nat. 3488 (sec. xiv), 3935, f. 1 (sec. xv).
    Evreux 11 (sec. xiv).
    Basel, F. III. 16.
Printed at Cologne c. 1467 by U. Zell; Augsburg, 1475; Ulm, 1481; Venice, 1496 (f. 1–166); Lyons, 1511 (f. 1–139); Paris, 1516.

Floriloquium philosophorum, or, *Floriloquium sive compendiloquium de vita et dictis illustrium philosophorum*, or, *de philosophorum dictis exemplis et vitis*. 10 parts:

i. On philosophy in general; ii. On the name and profession of philosophers; iii. On the succession of illustrious philosophers and their life; iv. On the life and maxims of some less famous philosophers; v. Of divers philosophic perfections; vi. On the four principal sects of philosophers—peripatetics, stoics, academicians, and epicureans; vii. On the seven liberal arts; viii. Poets and authors of apologues; ix. On the abuses of philosophy; x. On the places where philosophic studies have been most honoured (e. g. Paris and Oxford mentioned). *Inc. prol. i.* 'Cum enim debeamus apes imitari.' *Inc. prol. operis.* 'Cum ex vita gentilium.' *Inc. opus.* 'Circa primum notandum quod diversimode describitur philosophia.'

    MSS. Brit. Mus.: Royal 6 B xi. f. 127 (sec. xiv).
        Bodl.: Laud. Misc. 603 (xiv).
        Cambridge :—Corp. Chr. Coll. 307 (xv).
        Paris :—Bibl. Mazarine 727, § 5.
        Toulouse 340, vi. (xiv).—St. Omer 622 (A.D. 1346).
        Printed at Venice, 1496 (f. 167–232); Lyons, 1511 (f. 140–194); Argentina, 1518 (f. 107–147).

Breviloquium de sapientia sanctorum. 8 chapters :

    Inc. prol. 'Cum varii sint homines omnes. . . . Licet in priori tractatulo[1].' *Inc. cap. i.* ' Sapientia enim dicitur ab eo quod est sapere.'

    MSS. Bodl.: Laud. Misc. 603, f. 99 (sec. xiv).
        Cambridge :—Corp. Chr. Coll. 307 (xv).
        Toulouse 340, vi. (xiv).
        St. Omer 622, § 3 (xiv).
        Printed at Venice, 1496 (f. 233); Lyons, 1511 (f. 195–200 b); Argentina (f. 147 b–151 b), and *sine anno et loco* (Louvain 1485 ?).

Summa justitiae, or, *Tractatus de septem vitiis ex* [*Gul. Alverno*] *Parisiensi.* 10 parts.

    i. De peccato in generali; ii. De superbia; iii. De invidia; iv. De ira; v. De avaricia; vi. De accidia; vii. De gula; viii. De luxuria; ix. De quinque sensibus corporis; x. De quibusdam peccatis, &c. *Inc. prol.* 'Summa justicie Christi fidelium est declinare a malo et facere bonum.' *Inc. opus.* 'Justicia que est via ad regnum ut supradictum est in duobus consistit.'

    MSS. Brit. Mus.: Harl. 632, f. 168.
        Cambridge : Peterhouse 89 (=1751).
    Cf. MS. Oxford :—Exeter Coll. 7, § 4 (sec. xv). *Jo. Wallensis Liber de vitiis ex Parisiensi confectus : inc.* 'Peccatum vitandum est.'

---

[1] i. e. *Breviloq. de IV virtutibus.*

Tractatus de vitiis et remediis eorum (doubtful).

Inc. 'Dicendum est de vitiis seu peccatis primo in generali.'

MS. Brit. Mus.: Royal 4 D iv. f. 226–244 (sec. xv).[1]

Cf. Anonymous *Summa de vitiis et virtutibus* in MS. Paris:—Bibl. Mazarine 924 (sec. xiv), which is compiled chiefly from the *Summa* of William Péraud.

Moniloquium vel collectiloquium. A work in 4 parts for the use of young preachers:

i. De viciis; ii. De virtutibus oppositis dictis viciis; iii. De penis; iv. De gloria beatorum.

The object is thus set forth in the prologue:

'Cum almus Christi confessor beatus Franciscus, a summo magistro Ihu Christo perfectissime edoctus et suo spiritu plenissime (?) inspiratus, in sua sacra regula monuerit fratres suos, ut in suis predicacionibus sint eorum eloquia casta et examinata ad edificacionem et utilitatem populi, annunciando eis vicia et virtutes, penam et gloriam, cum brevitate sermonis: ad occasionem dandam minoribus predicatoribus colliguntur dicta autentica sanctorum de predictis 4 annunciandis.'

Inc. prol. 'Cum almus,' &c. *Inc. opus.* 'Cum autem nostra sit intencio ut dictum est aliqua auctentica in generali colligere.' *Inc. pars i., dist. i., cap. i.* 'De primo notandum quod describitur vicium sub nomine mali.'

MSS. Brit. Mus.: Harl. 632, f. 248.

 Cambridge:—Peterhouse 87 or 2-0-4, 'De quatuor predicabilibus ad omne genus hominum.'—Pembroke Coll. 123.

 Paris:—Bibl. Nat. 6776, f. 55–352 (sec. xiv). Imperf. at the beginning; fol. 58, 'Cum autem sit intentio.'—'Explicit summa de viciis et virtutibus compilata a fratre Johanne Galensi ordinis fratrum minorum. Orate pro eo.'

 Falaise:—Bibl. Pub. 38, p. 468.

 Munich:—Bibl. Reg. 23595 (sec. xiv), 'Distinctiones predicabiles Johannis Gallensis de virtutibus.'

Legiloquium sive liber de decem preceptis, or, *De decem mandatis divinis*, or, *Summa de preceptis*.

Inc. 'Scribam eis multiplices leges. . . . Omnipotens creator omnium.'

MSS. Brit. Mus.: Harl. 632, f. 307 b (sec. xv) imperfect.

 Oxford:—Bodl. Rawlinson C. 534, f. 106 (sec. xiii): cf. Bodl. 2501, 'forte Jo. Wallensis.'—Lincoln Coll. 67, f. 143 (xiv).

 Paris:—Bibl. Mazarine 569, f. 139 b (xiv).

---

[1] The name of the author is given in a hand considerably later than the MS.

Bruges 239 (Haenel p. 756).—Falaise 38, p. 325 (xiv. ineuntis).
—Toulouse 340 (xiv).
Extracts printed by Charma, 'Notice sur un MS . . . de Falaise,' 1851.

Manipulus Florum, begun by John Wallensis, finished by Thomas Hibernicus, to whom it is usually ascribed; excerpts from the fathers, in alphabetical order.
Inc. prol. 'Abite in agro, &c. Paupercula non habet messem.'
Inc. opus. 'Abstinentia. Bonum est in cibo.'
MSS. Oxford:—Merton Coll. 129 (sec. xiv).—Lincoln Coll. 98 (xiv).
Cambridge:—Caius Coll. 402 (A.D. 1306).
Paris:—Bibl. Mazarine 1032, &c.
Troyes, 1785 (finitus A.D. 1306).—Basel, B iv. 9 (written A.D. 1324).
Printed at Piacenza 1483, Venice 1493, &c.
A similar work, ascribed in the same hand as the text to Friar John Walensis, is contained in MS. Charleville 136 (sec. xiv); inc. 'Accidia. Nota accidiosus est.'

De origine progressu et fine Mahumeti et quadruplici reprobatione prophetiae ejus, cap. xv.
Inc. 'Ad ostendendum quod Mahumetes.'
Printed at Argentina 1550. The editor, G. Fabricius says: 'hunc Galensis libellum in dissipatis Bibliothecis inventum collegi.' No MSS. of the work have been discovered, and its authenticity seems very doubtful. It is not mentioned by the earlier bibliographers, such as Philip de Bergamo and Tritheim. Except in the number of chapters, it appears to differ entirely from the *Tract. contra falsitates legis Machometi* of Peter de Pennis: Quétif-Echard I 569; MS. Chapitre de Bayeux 42.

Sermones de tempore et de sanctis.
MSS. Bodl.: 1956=NE. B. i. 14, now Bodley 50; referred to by Tanner.
Munich:—Bibl. Reg. 26941 (sec. xiv. ineuntis) contains a sermon preached at Paris by John Wallensis.
Charleville 113 § 3 (sec. xiv and xiii), *Sermones de tempore*: inc. 'Dominica prima de adventu': these are anonymous but follow some works by J. Wallensis in the MS.

Postilla super Johannem.
MSS. Vienna:—Bibl. Palat. 1533 (sec. xiv).
Florence:—Laurentiana, *ex bibl. S. Crucis*, Plut. xxvii. Dext. Cod. iii. 'Tabula super Postillam Fratris Joannis de Vallensis (*sic*) super Joannem.' The work itself is missing.

This appears to be identical with the *Postilla in Evangelium Joannis*, printed among Bonaventura's works. It is doubtful whether the commentary should be ascribed to either of these writers. (See Hist. Litt. xxv. 193-4.)

Collationes in Johannem. Ascribed also to Bonaventura, and printed among his works (edit. 1589, tom. ii): probably by the same author as the preceding *Postilla.*

Cf. MSS. Oxford:—Exeter Coll. 39 (xiv), Thomas Wallensis;—Bruges, 338, 'Joannes Anglicus super Joannem' (Haenel); or 474, 'Scripta Johannis Anglici super Johannitium' (Laude).

Commentaries on Exodus, Leviticus, Numbers, Deuteronomy, Joshua, Judges, Ruth, Ecclesiastes, Song of Solomon, Isaiah.

MSS. Oxford:—Bodl. Laud. Misc. 345 (sec. xiv), ascribed to John Wallensis.—Merton Coll. 196 (sec. xiv), and New College 30 (sec. xv), ascribed to Thomas Wallensis.—Leland mentions the same works in the library of Christ Church, Canterbury, where they were ascribed to John Wallensis (Leland *Collect.* III. 7).

The following works are sometimes assigned to John Wallensis:—

Expositio super Pater Noster.

MSS. Charleville 873 contains, according to Haenel (p. 120), Joannis Wallensis ... expositio super pater noster et dietarium super vita religiosa.' In the new catalogue this treatise is given as anonymous, the same volume, No. 272 (sec. xiv), containing the *Dietarium.*

Mondée Abbey (diocese Lisieux), Cod. 3, Joannes Galesius Ordinis Minorum super *Pater noster* (Montfaucon, p. 1333).

In fabulas Ovidii, or, *Expositiones seu moralitates in lib. i.* (?) *Metamorphoseon sive fabularum* (Leland and Tanner). This appears to be the work generally ascribed to Thomas Walleys, and, by M. Hauréau, to Peter Bercherius[1]. There is no real ground for assigning it, as Leland does, to John Wallensis.

MSS. Oxford: Bodl. Auct. F. 5. 16 (= Bodl. Sup. A. I Art. 86 or Bodl. 2581), Johannes Anglicus.
Brit. Mus.: Royal 15 C xvi, anon.
Cambridge:—Peterhouse 12 or 2-3-9 'a fratre Thoma Waleys de provincia Anglie ordinis Predicatorum.'

---

[1] *Mémoires de l'Académie des inscriptions,* t. XXX, pp. 45-55: Peter was a Benedictine who lived and wrote at Avignon from 1320 to 1340. M. Hauréau has no doubt made out his case.

Dublin :—Trin. Coll. 8, anon., but bound up with works by John Wallensis.

Reims 741 (Haenel p. 405), 'Liber fabularum a magistro Joanne Anglico compositus.'

Troyes 1627 (sec. xiv), Thomas Waleys.

Printed at Paris 1511, &c.

In mythologicon Fulgentii.

A commentary on this by John Wallensis is mentioned by Leland in the Library of the Friars Minors at Reading (*Collect.* III, 57). Many anonymous treatises on the work are extant ; e. g.

MSS. Brit. Mus.: Royal 7 C I f. 311.—Dublin :—Trin. Coll. 8 (§ 8), bound up with works of John Wallensis.

Cf. notice of John Redovallensis.

Comment. in Valerium de non ducenda uxore.

Seen by Leland in the Franciscan Library, London. The *incipit* which he gives is merely that of the work itself, and is no assistance in identifying the commentary of John Wallensis. The latter refers to the epistle in his *Breviloq. de quatuor virtutibus cardinalibus* : MS. Brit. Mus.: Royal 10 A ix, f. 83 b–84.

Cf. notice of John Redovallensis.

As to other works attributed to him with some show of reason by the older bibliographers:

De cognitione verae vitae, mentioned by Wadding, is the same as the *Ordinarium*. An anonymous treatise with this title is in Royal MS. 10 A ix. f. 109-133 (which contains some works by John Wallensis). *Inc.* 'Sapientia Dei que os muti aperuit,'

De visitatione infirmorum : Augustine's treatise on this is in the Royal MS. above mentioned (fol. 134–145).

Declaratio regulae S. Francisci (printed at Venice, 1513 in *Firmamentum Trium Ordinum*), is usually attributed to John Peckham.

Pastoralia by J. Wallensis; formerly in Harl. MS. 632, f. 261 ; (see old table of Contents); fol. 250–265 (old pagination) are missing. Boston of Bury calls this *De cura pastorali:* inc. 'Licet beatus.' Expl. 'et haec ad David.'

Collectio epistolarum decretalium Romanorum pontificum was by John Gallensis of Volterra (c. 1200): printed at Ilerda 1576, &c.: MSS. Nat. Libr. Paris 3925, A ; Toulouse 368 (sec. xiii. med.).

Indices duorum operum; an alphabetical table of contents in Harl. MS. 632, f. 133–167.

Summa confessorum ; by John Lector of Freiburg : see MSS. Troyes, 156 and 1492 (sec. xiv), &c. *Inc.* 'Quoniam dubiorum[1].'

---

[1] Another handbook for confessors is occasionally found bound up with works of John Wallensis. See MSS. St. Omer 622, § 6, *Tract. de instructione confessorum*, and Charleville 113, § 2, *Libellus de modo audiendi confessionis.*

De oculo morali; identical with the work attributed to Grostete and Peter de Limoges. *Inc.* 'Si diligenter.' It may be noticed that Boston of Bury attributes this to John Wallensis and does not mention it among Grostete's works (Tanner, Bibl. pp. xxxiii, xxxvii).

De correptione sive correctione. *Inc.*: 'Probata virtus.' *Expl.* 'Commorabitur' (Boston of Bury).

De exortatione. *Inc.* 'Qui exortatur': *Expl.* 'Moderantis' (ibid.).

De disciplina. *Inc.* 'Disciplina ad mentem instruendam' (ibid.)[1].

In quatuor libros Sententiarum. *Inc.* 'Quoniam teste B. Augustino' (Barth. of Pisa, and Ph. of Bergamo).

De arte predicandi, ascribed to John Wallensis in MS. Paris: Bibl. Mazarine 569, f. 80 b: really by Thomas Walleys.

7. **Thomas Docking**, also called Thomas Good[2], was a native of Norfolk and probably entered the Order at Norwich. In a letter written A.D. 1252–3[3], Adam Marsh asks the Provincial Minister to assign the bible of the late P. of Worcester to 'friar Thomas de Dokkyng,' who was distinguished by good morals and pleasant manners, a clear head, great learning and ready eloquence; his friends were ready to pay handsomely for the book. He was evidently a student at this time. He became D.D. and reader to the Franciscans at Oxford about 1260[4]. In 1269, when he took an active part in the controversy with the Oxford Dominicans, he is described as 'sometime reader at Oxford[5].' According to Blomefield, he was warden of Norwich and died about 1270[6]. His theological works, chiefly biblical commentaries, were long held in high repute[7]; some are still preserved.

Expositio super librum Deuteronomii.

 MSS. Brit. Mus: Royal 3 B xii (sec. xv).
  Oxford:—Balliol Coll. 28 (A.D. 1442).
  Lincoln:—Cathedral Libr. (Haenel p. 799), 'Thomas Bockering.'

Inc.: 'Simpliciores et minus expertos confessores.' It is by John Lector of Freiburg: MS. Mazarine 1322. Hist. Litt. xxv. 269.

[1] There is an error in Tanner's extracts from Bury (p. xxxiii): 'Quoniam misericordia' given as the *incipit* of *De disciplina* belongs to the preceding work, *Compendiloquium*. Cf. Bale, MS. Seld. supra 64, fol. 83; Tanner, Bibl. 435.

[2] Royal MS. 3 B. XII (sec. xv): 'Liber magistri Thome Gude, i. e. Boni, Doctoris sacre Theologie Oxonie et Ordinis Minorum, vocati Dockyng, eo quod natus fuit in villa vocata Dockyng.'

[3] Mon. Franc. I, 359–360: the letter mentions 'the irrevocable intention of Friar R. of Cornwall.'

[4] Or 1265? See notices of H. of Brisingham and W. of Heddele.

[5] App. C.

[6] Hist. of Norfolk, IV, 111; no authority is given.

[7] He is probably the 'Bokkyng' quoted by William of Ockham (Goldast, p. 957); and he is often referred to by Thomas Gascoigne.

Comment. on Isaiah.

MS. Oxford:—Ball. Coll. 29 (sec. xv).

Expositio super Epistolas S. Pauli.

MSS. Oxford:—Ball. Coll. 30 (sec. xv), containing Galatians, Ephesians[1], Hebrews.
Magd. Coll. 154, Galatians, imperf. (sec. xv).

Lectura super Apocalypsin, doubtfully ascribed to him.

MS. Oxford:—Ball. Coll. 149 f. 107. *Inc.* 'Panis ei datus. Querit propheta.'

Expositio Decalogi, Inc. 'Non habebis deos alienos in conspectu meo. Hoc est in corde.'

MS. Bodl. 2403 (=T. Bodley NE. F. 4. 9), now Bodley 453, f. 57–90[2].

Questions on St. Luke.

MS. Paris:—Bibl. Nationale, 3183, § 8 (sec. xiv).

Questio utrum Job in prosperis fuerit altior coram Deo quam in adversis.

MS. Ibid. § 11 (sec. xiv).

Comment. super Sententias, mentioned in the Catalogue of Illustrious Franciscans (Leland)[3].

8. **H. de Brisingham**[4] is probably the same as
'Frater Henricus Lector Oxoniensis Fratrum Minorum,'
who composed a *Summa de Sacramentis* in 1261[5]. He afterwards became thirteenth master of the Friars Minors at Cambridge[6]. Blomefield claims him as a Norfolk man, and says that he died about 1280[7]. He is perhaps to be identified with '*Henricus de Oxonio*

---

[1] At the end of this commentary; 'Explicit lectura H. M. et d. Dockyng super Epistolam ad Ephesios.'

[2] At the end of this MS. (sec. xv): 'Explicit expositio ffratris Thome Dockyng super preceptis decalogi secundum formam textus deutronomii quinti.' The same volume contains an anonymous treatise on the creed ('de sufficientia articulorum in Simbolo,' &c.: *Inc.* 'Est quedam mensura fidei'), which Bale (MS. Seld. sup. 64, f. 177) carelessly identifies with Docking's *Epos. decalogi*; and an anonymous treatise on the decalogue, which Tanner ascribes to Docking (*Inc.* 'Si autem vis ad vitam ingredi'): cf. MS. Laud. Misc. 524, fol. 67 b (olim Laud. F. 12).

[3] Tanner (Bibl. 230) mentions his *Correctiones in S. Scripturam,* 'MS. olim in monast. Sion;' and *Tabulam super Grammaticam Dokking,* MS. Linc. Cathed. Libr. F. 18.

[4] Brewer's reading 'A. de Brisigham' is incorrect: MSS. Cott. Nero, A IX, and Phillipps, 3119, f. 76.

[5] MS. Laud. Misc. 2, fol. 159 b.

[6] 'Frater T. Brisigham, sed incepit Oxoniae, &c.' Mon. Franc. I, 555.

[7] Hist. of Norfolk, IV, p. 114. Cf. Bale, *Script.*

Chordigerae sectae,' whose sermons were seen by Bale in the Franciscan Library at Reading [1].

The *De Sacramentis Summa* is his only extant work.

MS. Bodl. Laud. Misc. 2, f. 130 (sec. xiv. ineuntis).

9. **William of Heddele** (Durham or Northumberland?) is mentioned by Adam Marsh in a letter to the Provincial, c. 1253, as 'your desirable son Friar William de Hedele[2].' We know from another source that Heddele was reader at Oxford in 1269, when he took part in the controversy with the Friars Preachers[3]. When Prince Edward went to the Holy Land,

'he took with him,' in the words of the so-called Lanercost Chronicle[4], 'the reader and master of the Friars Minors at Oxford, Friar William de Hedley, a man beloved of God and in favour with men.'

The chronicler puts these events in the year 1266. Edward took the cross in 1268 and sailed in 1270. Friar William died on the outward voyage in the sea of Greece:

'his corpse,' continues the same authority 'being given to the waves as the custom is, followed the course of the ships for three days, until, at Edward's command, it was taken again into the vessel and afterwards committed to the earth.'

10. **Thomas de Bungay** (Suffolk) has been traditionally associated with Roger Bacon and regarded as a wizard by later generations. Very little is known of him. He perhaps entered the Order at Norwich. He lectured as D.D. in the Franciscan convent at Oxford about 1270; he seems like Roger to have attached a great importance to mathematics and may have held his views on the value of natural science and of induction. He lectured afterwards at Cambridge, being the fifteenth in the list of Franciscan masters there. He was the eighth English Provincial Minister, and was succeeded by Peckham, probably in 1275. He was buried at Northampton[5].

According to the Catalogue of Illustrious Franciscans he wrote a Commentary on the *Sentences*[6]. None of his works are printed; only one seems to be extant in MS.

De celo et mundo: 3 books. *Inc.* 'Summa cognicionis, &c. Aristoteles probat hic tres questiones in primo capitulo. Prima est

---

[1] Bale, *Script*. II, 93-4; MS. Seld. sup. 64, fol. 65 b; Wadding, *Script*. 166. This may equally well have been Henry de Apeltre, the twelfth lector.

[2] Mon. Franc. I, 360.

[3] Appendix C.

[4] Lan. Chron. p. 81.

[5] Mon. Franc. I, 537, 552, 555, 560. Blomefield, Norfolk, IV, 114. Charles, Roger Bacon, p. 24.

[6] Leland, Script. p. 302.

quod omne corpus est completum quo ad divisiones.' *Expl.*
'Hic terminantur questiones super 3 c. et m. a Magistro T. de bungeya.'

MS. Cambridge :—Caius Coll. 509, § 3 (sec. xiv. ineuntis).
Cf. MS. Bibl. Nat. Paris 16144 (sec. xiii), 'Thomas super librum de celo et mundo' (Aquinas ?).

11. **John Peckham** was born in Sussex and received his earliest education in the Priory of Lewes [1]. He took the Franciscan vows about 1250 [2]; he was then tutor to the nephew of Master H. of Anjou, perhaps in the University of Paris, but was probably for the time being residing at Oxford [3]. On entering the Order he resigned the tutorship. Adam Marsh calls him ' *Dominus Johannes de Pescham Scholaris*;' he may therefore either have had no degree at this time, or that of bachelor. He appears to have spent some time at Oxford, as in later years he expresses his gratitude for the training he received in the Franciscan convent of that University [4]. He then returned to France, studied under Bonaventura, and took the Doctor's degree at Paris, where he ruled in theology [5]. Among his pupils was St. Thomas of Cantilupe, Bishop of Hereford [6]. At Paris too he came in contact with Thomas Aquinas and probably attended his lectures. He was present when the latter submitted his doctrine about the ' Unity of form ' to the judgment of the masters in theology ;

'we alone,' the Archbishop wrote afterwards, 'stood by him, defending him to the best of our power, saving the truth [7].'

He was at Paris during the troublous times which followed William of St. Amour's attack on the Mendicants, and wrote a defence of the latter [8]. He returned to England probably about 1270 or soon after, and was admitted at Oxford to the same degree as he held at Paris [9]. He now became lecturer to the Franciscans. On May 2, 1275, he

---

[1] Peckham, *Registrum*, p. 902 : 'in ipsius vicinia coaluimus a parvo, et ab ejusdem professoribus solatia recepimus et honores.'

[2] Mon. Franc. I, 256. The date is uncertain. Adam Marsh describes him, ' quem et honestior conversatio et litteratura provectior commendabiliter illustrant.' For the spelling of the name, cf. Rymer's Foed. I, 800, ' Peschan.'

[3] This is merely a deduction from the fact that Adam Marsh wrote about his entering the Order.

[4] *Registrum*, p. 977. It is hardly necessary to add that he was not a student at Merton ; as Archbishop, he was patron of the college ; ibid. 123.

[5] Mon. Franc. I, 537, 552. Trivet, Annales, p. 299.

[6] Regist. p. 315.

[7] Ibid. 866, 898. Henry of Ghent was also present; see his *Quodlibeta*, Quodl. II, quaest. ix.

[8] Regist. III, xcvii, seq. (preface).

[9] N. Trivet, p. 299.

was with Friar Oliver de Encourt Prior of the Dominicans, appointed, by the King's writ, to decide a suit in the University which had long been under consideration in the Chancellor's court [1]. It was probably soon after this that he was elected ninth Provincial Minister and confirmed by Bonaventura [2]. He did not hold this office long, being in 1277, summoned by the Pope (Nicholas III?) to lecture on theology in the schools of the Papal Court at Rome [3]. After lecturing here for something less than two years, he was appointed Archbishop of Canterbury by Papal bull in January 1279, and consecrated by the Pope in the following March [4]. His official connexion with the Order did not cease; he was deputed by the Pope

'protector of the privileges of the Order of Minors in England,'

and frequently used his powers for the benefit of the Franciscans [5]. His relations to the Oxford Franciscans, as well as his condemnation of erroneous doctrines at the University, have already been noticed. While enforcing to the uttermost his legal rights, the Archbishop evinced a special solicitude for the poor, feeding them in time of famine, remonstrating with covetous abbats and careless landlords [6]. He himself is said to have travelled on foot, to have surpassed all in watchings and fastings and prayer, to have used none but vile garments and bedding—in fine to have lived as became one who held perfection to consist in the contempt of riches and the search for truth [7]. He died on December 8, 1292, and was buried 'among the monks' of Canterbury near Becket's tomb [8]. His heart was buried in the choir behind the High Altar at the Grey Friars of London [9]. He named as his executors the Friars Minors of Paris [10]. The Dominican Nicholas Trivet sums up his character in these words [11]:

'He was a zealous promoter of the interests of his Order, an excellent

[1] Close Roll, 3 Edw. I, m. 18, dorse.
[2] Mon. Franc. I, 537, 560. Mr. Martin says that Provincial Ministers were at this time appointed by the General: this was the case at first, but the custom was departed from as early as the time of William of Nottingham (1240). Mon. Franc. I, 59.
[3] Mon. Franc. I, 560. Trivet, 299, Lanerc. Chron. 100; Denifle, I, 301, seq.
[4] Lanercost Chron. 100, 'post biennium.' Nicholas III was elected Nov. 25, 1277; this leaves little more than a year before Peckham's nomination to the Archiepiscopate; but it is not likely that he was made lector by John XXI. Le Neve, Fasti; Milman, VI, 410.
[5] *Registrum*, pp. 210, 248.
[6] Ibid. 715, 68–9, 38–9.
[7] Lanerc. Chron. 144; Wadding, V, 53, 80: *Registrum*, I, pref. lx, xcix.
[8] Mon. Franc. I, 537.
[9] MS. Cott. Vitell. F, XII, f. 274.
[10] Rymer, I, 800. An account of his bequests to Christ Church, Canterbury, will be found in the Public Library at Cambridge, MS. E e, V, 31, f. 74 b.
[11] Annales, p. 299.

maker of songs, of pompous manner and speech, but of kind and thoroughly liberal heart.'

A careful and valuable account of his works will be found in Mr. Trice Martin's preface to Peckham's Register, Vol. III[1].

A few additions may be made to Mr. Martin's list of his extant writings.

Constitutiones Ottoboni cum expositione Peccham.

    MS. Cambridge :—Pembroke Coll. 145 (=2073). Cf. Wilkins, *Concilia*, II, 50–51.

Quaestiones ordinariae. Inc. ' Utrum theologia ex duobus.'

    MS. Paris :—Bibl. Nat. 3183 (sec. xiv); containing the questions, *Utrum theologia sit prae ceteris Scientiis necessaria Praelatis Ecclesiae,* and, *Utrum theologia ex duobus componi debuerit Testamentis.* Cf. MSS. ibid. 15805, *Quodlibeta S. Thome, J. de Pechan, Guil. de Hoxon*; and 15986, f. 238 (sec. xiii), *Responsio ad questionem Joh. de Peschant.*

Tractatus Fratris Joannis Pecham Ord. Min. contra Fratrem Rogerium (Ord. Praed.) obloquentem contra suum Ordinem (called by Tanner, *Contra Priorem Cisterciensium*). *Inc.* ' Super tribus et super quatuor sceleribus.'

    MS. Florence :—Laurentiana, *ex Bibl. S. Crucis*, Plut. XXXVI. Dext. Cod. xii. p. 25 (sec. xiv. exeuntis).

Formula confessionum. Inc. ' Sicut dicit b. Joannes.'

    MS. Florence :—Laurentiana, *ex Bibl. S. Crucis*, Plut. IV. Sinist. Cod. xi (A.D. 1433).

Scriptum super Ethicam.

    MS. Florence :—Laurentiana, *ex Bibl. S. Crucis*, Plut. XII. Sinist. Cod. xi.

12. **Henry de Apeltre** was the twelfth reader at Oxford, and seventeenth master of the Friars Minors at Cambridge. Nothing more is known about him[2].

13. **Robert Cross** or **Crouche**[3] (de Cruce) must have lectured at Oxford about 1280. In April of that year Peckham forbade an Oxford Dominican to visit a certain 'college of women' on account

---

[1] Nicholas Glasberger says that he wrote a life of St. Anthony of Padua, '*miro stilo*,' at the command of the Minister-General, Jerome of Ascoli. Anal. Franc. II, 91.

[2] Mon. Franc. I, 552, 555. See H. de Brisingham, note 5. (Appletree in Derby, or in Northampton, or Appletree-Wick in Yorkshire?)

[3] He may be the same as Robert de Sancta Cruce who went to the Minister General with a letter of recommendation from Adam Marsh (c. 1250?). Mon. Franc. I, 333.

of grave suspicion, on the accusation of Friar Robert de Cruce[1]. Leland states that he was immersed in philosophical studies to an advanced age, and when at last he betook himself to theology he showed greater skill in investigating speculative subtleties than in exploring the literal sense; the statement might be made with equal truth of most of the scholastics. He became Provincial Minister soon after 1280. The successor of John Peckham, Hugh of Bath, died within a short time of his appointment, and was succeeded by Robert Cross as eleventh minister[2]. He held the office in June 1284, when he obtained for the English Minorites exemption from the payment of a custom due to the King from all who passed to or from the Continent by the port of Dover[3]. In Sept. of the same year he held a chapter of the English Franciscans[4]; and in March 1285, he represented the English Province at the General Chapter of Milan[5]. He may have resigned the dignity at this Chapter; on Oct. 31, 1285, Peckham addresses a letter to 'W., Provincial Minister of the Friars Minors'; this must be William of Gainsborough[6]. Robert Cross was buried at Bridgwater[7]. None of his works remain. Leland mentions his commentaries on the *Physics* and the *Sentences*, on the authority of the Catalogue of Illustrious Franciscans.

14. **R. de Toftis**, called by Wood, Radulphus de Toftis.

15. **Alanus de Rodano**.

16. **Roger de Marston** or **Merscheton**[8] was D.D. of Oxford and lecturer to the Franciscans before 1290. Some questions on which he disputed, perhaps before he became doctor, are preserved in a MS. at Assisi[9]. He subsequently lectured at Cambridge as twelfth master of the friars[10]. According to Ehrle, Marston's theological and philosophical teaching bears strong resemblance in some respects to that of Peter John Olivi[11]. He became thirteenth Provincial Minister perhaps at the great Chapter of Paris in 1292,

---

[1] Peckham, Reg. 117–8.
[2] Mon. Franc. I, 537, 560.
[3] Pat. 12 Edw. I, m. 9.
[4] Peckham, Reg. 820.
[5] Pat. 13 Edw. I, m. 27.
[6] Peckham, Reg. 909.
[7] Mon. Franc. I, 537, 560.
[8] Mon. Franc. I, 552, 555, 560. Other variations are Merston (ibid. 537, and Assisi MS. 158, quest. 6) and Mirstun (Assisi MS. 158, quest. 134).
[9] Assisi MS. 158, questions 6, 134, 144. Qu. 134 runs thus: 'Disputacio Rogeri de Mirstun ordinis minorum.' (Inc.) 'Circa emanacionem eternam.' (At end): 'Ad(?) hanc questionem respondetur quod essencia est principium, quo sit omnis productio.'
[10] Mon. Franc. I, 555: 'incepit Oxoniae.'
[11] Archiv f. Litt. u. K. Gesch. d. M. III, 459; cf. 413. Are any of his writings extant except the questions at Assisi?

certainly between 1285 (when W. of Gainsborough was appointed) and 1299 (when Hugh of Hertepol was Provincial). He is said to have been warden of Norwich and to have died in 1303[1]. He was buried at Norwich[2].

17. **Alan de Wakerfeld**[3] was at Oxford in 1269, when he represented his convent on several occasions in the controversy with the Friars Preachers[4]. He was not yet lector.

18. **Nicholas de Ocham** occurs in the Assisi MS. as Hotham, Master Nicolaus de Hotham, and Frater N. de Ocham minor[5]. He lectured at Oxford towards the end of the thirteenth century. Except the *quaestiones disputatae* at Assisi, it is doubtful whether any of his works are extant[6]. Leland says:

Catalogus eruditorum Franciscanorum Nicholai Ochami meminit; cujus et depraedicat libros; *Commentarios*, videlicet, *in Sententias Petri Longobardi*, et opus, cui *De Verbo* titulus. Scripsit libellum *De latitudine oppositionum*, ingeniosi iudicium astrologi[7].

> Cf. MSS. Paris:—Bibl. Nat. 14565 f. 173 b (sec. xiv). 'Fratris Nicholai minoris replicationes;' and Cambridge:—Caius Coll. 319, 'Nicholai super 2 et 3 sententiarum, in 3 libris.'

Another Friar Nicholas Minorite, (called by Sbaralea[8], 'Specialis'), flourished about the same time as, or soon after, N. of Ocham, and wrote a chronicle on the Franciscan contest with the Pope, A.D. 1321–1328 (MS. Bibl. Nat. Paris, 5154: Extracts in Böhmer's *Fontes Rer. German.* IV, 588 seq.).

19. **Walter de Knolle** was afterwards twenty-third master at Cambridge[9].

20. **Hugh de Hertepol** or **Hartlepool** was a friar and a man of importance in Oxford in 1282, when Devorguila appointed him to be one of the two proctors to whom the government of the new college of Balliol was entrusted; the statutes of 1282 are addressed to 'Friar Hugh de Hertilpoll and Master William de Menyl[10].' It was probably

---

[1] Blomefield's Norfolk, IV, 112.
[2] Mon. Franc. I, 537.
[3] Assisi MS. 158 twice mentions *Waker*, who may be this Wakerfield. Quest. 76, and at the end of the volume 'Waker dis(putavit) R(espondit) Penn(ard).'
[4] Appendix C.
[5] In Devon's Exchequer Issue Rolls, Hen. III–Hen. VI, p. 114, there is mention of 'Master Nicholas de Ocham,' 30 Edw. I.
[6] Assisi MS. 158, questions 161–3, 165 (of considerable length), 123, 'questio in vesperiis de Hotham'; and near the end of the volume, 'questio Hotham in vesperiis cnol (?) Oxon. Respondit persel.' The last letter in the name 'Cnol' is uncertain; but it is probably Walter de Knolle, Ocham's successor at Oxford. Cf. H. de Hertepol and J. de Persora below.
[7] Tanner, Bibl. 556.
[8] Wadding, Sup. ad Script. 563.
[9] Mon. Franc. I, 552, 556.
[10] Savage, Balliofergus, p. 15.

some years later that Hugh became S.T.P. and lecturer to the Franciscan convent. His disputations seem to have been considered valuable and several of them are preserved [1]. He disputed

'in the vesperies before the inception of Friar John de Persole (i.e. Persora, his successor) at Oxford [2].'

He became fourteenth Provincial Minister, in succession to Roger Marston. The date of his appointment or election is uncertain. In April 1299 [3], we hear of him going as Provincial, with Friar W. of Gainsborough as his *socius*, to the General Chapter at Lyons; on this occasion the King gave to the two friars 10 marks. In 1300 (Aug. 7) at Dorchester (Oxon), he chose twenty-two friars of the Oxford convent and presented them to Dalderby, Bishop of Lincoln [4], with the request that he would license them to hear confessions. The bishop asked 'whether he was presenting them for all the convents in the diocese of Lincoln,' and, finding that it was only for the Oxford convent, refused to license more than four. At length a compromise was effected, and eight of the friars were licensed to hear confessions in the archdeaconry of Oxford. In 1301 [5], Hugh was again abroad, probably at the General Chapter at Genoa. In Sept. 1302, he was, with W. of Gainsborough and others, sent as ambassador to the Court of Rome to negotiate for peace with the King of France [6]. While in Italy on this mission, he attended the General Chapter at Assisi [7]; he probably did not return to England, as we are told that he was 'buried among the friars at Assisi [8].'

21. **John de Persora** or **Pershore** (c. 1390) called in the Assisi MS. John de Persole (see above, under Hertepol).

22. **John of Berwick** lectured at Oxford before the end of the thirteenth century. He was buried at Stamford. Bale identifies him with a Brenlanlius who is referred to by John Pico de Mirandola in his treatise *contra Astrologos*.

---

[1] In MS. 158 at Assisi. See Part I, Chapter III.

[2] Ibid. quest. 185.

[3] Q. R. Wadr. ⅔ (R.O.), this refutes the statement in Collect. Angl. Min. that he was unanimously elected in 1300.

[4] Wood, MS. F, 29 a, fol. 178.

[5] Q. R. Wardr. $\frac{11}{18}$, m. 1. Cf. Rymer's Foed. I, 936.

[6] Almain Roll. 30 Edw. I (R.O.). Cf. Mon. Franc. I, 514 (1302).

[7] Rodulphus, quoted by Wadding, Script. 360.

[8] Mon. Franc. I, 537. The author of 'Collis Paradisi' (?) however quotes the following epitaph: 'Hic jacet Fr. Hugo de Hergilpol Anglicus Mag. in S. T. quondam Minister Angliae, qui obiit III id. Septembris A. D. MCCC sedo. Orate pro anima ejus.' Wadding, ibid. The General Chapter met at Assisi in 1304, Archiv f. L. u. K. Gesch. VI, 67. Hugh was appointed ambassador to Rome, Sept. 9, 1302.

Joannis Anglici Ordinis Minorum Summa Astrologiae Judicialis, quae anglicana vulgo nuncupatur (doubtful).

MS. Florence:—Laurentiana, in Plut. XXIX (Montfaucon, p. 237, 299).

Printed at Venice 1489, under the name of Joannes Eschvid (*i.e.* Eshendon or Ashendon; see MS. Bodl. 3467, p. 91).

Questiones Joannis de Beroyko de Ordine Fratrum Minorum de Formis.

MS. Venice:—Bibl. S. Anton. (Tomasin, p. 9).

Leland adds: 'Collaudat eruditorum Index Franciscanorum ejus *In longobardum elucubrationes*[1].

23. **Thomas of Barneby**, wrongly called by Brewer 'Johannes de Barneby,' is identified by Wood, without much probability, with the first Senior Dean of Merton College, who was appointed by Kilwardby in 1276[2]. He is mentioned in a record dated March 20, 1326, as 'master of the Friars Minors[3].'

24. **Adam of Lincoln**, D.D. and regent master of the Franciscans at Oxford, succeeded Hugh of Hertepol as fifteenth Provincial Minister, probably in 1304[4]; he had ceased to hold the office in 1310[5]. He was one of the doctors of theology appointed in the Provincial Council of York in July 1311, to examine the charges of heresy against the Knights Templars[6]. He was buried at Lincoln. The Register of the Friars Minors of London adds: *qui fecit mirabilia*; probably some word like *opera* is to be supplied[7].

25. **William of Gainsborough**[8] must have been Provincial Minister before he lectured at Oxford[9]. He was Provincial in Oct. 1285, being the twelfth in order[10]. He was doctor of theology in

---

[1] Bale, *Script.*, I. 413; Leland, *Script.*, 326; J. Picus Mirand., *Opera Omnia* (Basel, 1572), Tom. I. *Contra Astrol.*, Book XII.

[2] Wood-Clark, II, 371. Memorials of Merton Coll. 185, n. 1.

[3] 'Fratri Barnabe Magistro fratrum Minorum;' the rest of the passage is worn away: Q. R. Wardrobe, ⅘ (R.O.). The note in MS. Merton Coll. 55, f. 261, 'memoriale fratris Thome de Barneby pro 14 solidis,' is of the fifteenth century.

[4] Mon. Franc. I, 537, 560.

[5] See notice of Richard Conyngton.

[6] Wilkins, Concilia, II, 399.

[7] Mon. Franc. I, 537.

[8] Geynysborough, Geynisboru, Geinesburgh, &c.

[9] Mon. Franc. I, 553, 'qui primus (prius ?) fuerat minister.' This was by no means unprecedented; Anal. Franc. I, 16: 'Minister Generalis ... absolvit fratrem Simonem a ministerio Theutoniae et lectorem instituit.' Cf. instances among the Dominicans, Martene, Thes. Nov. Anecd. IV, pp. 1791, 1822.

[10] Peckham, Regist. 909. Mon. Franc. I, 537, 560. Cf. Chapter House Records (R.O.), A₁₃, p. 61: 'fratri Willelmo de Geynesburg' ministro fratrum minorum in Anglia revertenti in Angliam

1294, when he was sent with Friar Hugh of Manchester, a Dominican, to the King of France, to protest against the latter's seizure of Gascony and to renounce homage in the name of the English King[1]. In 1299 he accompanied the Provincial, Hugh of Hertepol, to the General Chapter at Lyons[2]. Early in 1300 he was called by Boniface VIII to lecture on theology in the Roman Curia[3]; the King paid his expenses.

Fratri Willmo de Geynesburgh de ordine Minorum eunti ad curiam Romanam ad mandatum Pape ad legendum de Theologia in palatio ejusdem Pape, de dono Regis ad quatuor equos sibi emendos pro equitatura sua et socii sui et pro hernes' eorundem portand' versus eandem curiam, 50 marc'. Eidem de dono Regis ad expensas suas morando in eadem curia pro negotio predicto 50 marc', per manus Domini J. de Droken' liberantis eidem denar' apud London' mense Maii. Eidem de dono Regis nomine expensarum suarum eundo de Wysebech usque London' pro dictis denariis ibidem recipiendis mense predicto 26s. 8d. Summa 68 li[4].

During the two years that he remained at Rome[5], his energies were not entirely confined to his work as lecturer. Boniface was at this time endeavouring to bring the war between France and England to a close by arbitration. In Sept. 1300, Friar William of Gainsborough was appointed by Edward I to act as one of his 'proctors and special messengers' at Rome in this matter[6]; and in Sept. 1302, he was employed with Hugh of Hertepol and others in the same capacity[7]. On Oct. 24, 1302, the Pope, passing over the candidate of the Chapter, nominated William, Bishop of Worcester; the consecration took place on Nov. 25, the enthronement on June 9, 1303[8]. As a protest against the Papal interference, the King imposed a fine of 1000 marks on the new bishop[9], but granted him £100 for the expenses for his inthronization in consideration of his great need[10].

---

de Burdeg' ad expensas suas ... de dono Regis lxvi[s] viii[d] sterl';' May 13 (1287?).

[1] Trivet, Annales, 331.

[2] Queen's Remembr. Wardrobe, ¾, m. 1 (R.O.).

[3] 'Wardrobe Account 28 Edw. I,' ed. Topham, p. 164. Mon. Franc. I, 537, 553, 560, 'qui in curia Romana legit cursorie et ordinarie.' Lanerc. Chron. says he was called to the Curia to read theology ' coram cardinalibus,' p. 194.

[4] 'Wardrobe Account,' *ut supra* (May, 1300).

[5] Lanerc. Chron. 194; cf. date of his appointment to Worcester.

[6] Almain Roll, 28 Edw. I (R.O.).

[7] Ibid. 30 Edw. I.

[8] Le Neve, Fasti, III, 53. Annal. Monast. IV, 554, 555. For a full account of the inthronization, see Thomas, Survey of Worcester, App. No. 76.

[9] Pat. Roll, in Le Neve, III, 53, n. 96. Cf. Stubbs, Const. Hist. III, 308–9.

[10] Thomas, Survey, App. No 77; cf. Ann. Monast. IV, 556.

William still continued to be employed in affairs of state[1]. In March 1307, at Carlisle, he demanded and obtained from the Papal nuncio the excommunication of the murderers of John Comyn[2]. On March 22, he was appointed to accompany Prince Edward on his journey to France to claim the hand of Isabella[3]. Later in the same year he was sent on an embassy to Rome in connexion with the same affair[4]. On his return journey[5] he died at Beauvais (Sept. 17); as nearly all his attendants died at the same time, it was believed that the calamity was due to poison[6]. The bishop was buried among the Friars Minors at Beauvais[7].

26. John Basset.

One of this name is said to have written *Chronica* in English; he was probably much later than this friar. Tanner, *Bibl.* 79.

27. **Thomas Rondel** or **Rundel**[8] was lecturer at Oxford in the last years of the thirteenth century, having previously read the sentences at Paris[9]. In 1309 he was one of the commissioners or inquisitors appointed to hear the accusations against the Knights Templars; he is then described as master of theology, and probably resided in the convent at London[10], where he was buried[11].

28. **Adam of Howden** or **Hoveden** or **Houdene**[12] was D.D. and probably regent master of the Franciscans at Oxford in 1300. He was one of the twenty-two friars presented by Hugh of Hertepol on July 26 of this year, to receive the bishop's license to hear confessions at Oxford, and was one of the eight actually licensed[13]. He afterwards read at Cambridge as the twenty-ninth master of the Friars Minors[14]. An 'Adam de Houdene' was chamberlain to W. of Gainsborough, Bishop of Worcester (1302–7), but he was not a friar.[15]

A sermon of his preached on the feast of Epiphany is in MS. Oxford, New Coll. 92, f. 82 b[16].

---

[1] Cf. Rymer's Foed. I, p. 979.
[2] Lanerc. Chron. 206.
[3] Rymer's Foed. I, 1012; Lanerc. Chron. 210.
[4] Rot. Rom. 1 Edw. II, m. 10 (Le Neve); Thomas, Survey, App. No. 78.
[5] Thomas, ibid.
[6] Lanerc. Chron. 210.
[7] Mon. Franc. I, 537, 553.
[8] Assisi MS. 158, quest. 119: 'Disputavit Gilbertus (Stratton?); Respondit Rundel minor.'
[9] Phillipps MS. 3119, fol. 76, 'qui legerat sentencias Parisius.'
[10] Wilkins, Concil. II, 336, 337, &c.; cf. 370, 'presentibus magistris minorum et predicatorum, gardiano minorum,'&c.
[11] Mon. Franc. I, 553.
[12] Phillipps MS., *ut supra*.
[13] Wood MS. F, 29 a, f. 178.
[14] Mon. Franc. I, 556.
[15] Pat. 14 Edw. II, m. 9.
[16] 'In festo Epiphanie; Minorum; Houdene.' The MS. dates from the latter part of the 14th cent., but we may without much hesitation identify 'Hou-

29. **Philip of Briddilton** or **Bridlington** was contemporary with Adam of Hoveden, and like him was licensed as D.D. by the Bishop of Lincoln to hear confessions in 1300[1]. He responded in the schools to Master Richard de Heddrington or Herington on the question '*an omnes beati equaliter participant beatitudine*[2],' a problem which agitated western Christendom in the early fourteenth century.

30. **Peter de Baldeswell**[3] was at Oxford in 1300, when he was presented by the Provincial to the Bishop of Lincoln, but not licensed to hear confessions[4]. He was not then D.D.

31. **John de Horley**, co. Oxon or Surrey (the same applies to him as to P. of Baldeswell).

32. **Martin of Alnwick** was a member of the Oxford convent in 1300; he was among the twenty-two friars for whom Hugh of Hertepol sought to obtain license to hear confessions, and was one of those rejected. He was not a D.D. at this time[5]. He took his degree and lectured at Oxford between 1300 and 1311. In the latter year he was summoned to Avignon to take part in the controversy between the Conventual and Spiritual Franciscans, as one of the four advisers of the General Minister. The matter was tried by a commission of cardinals and theologians; Martin and his fellows pleaded the cause of the Conventuals, or Community of the Order. The case was adjourned to the Council of Vienne and decided by the bull *Exivi de Paradiso* (which was published in the last session of the Council, May 6, 1313) in favour of the better section of the Conventuals[6]. Martin of Alnwick was evidently one of the leading Franciscans of the time. According to Bale he died 1336 and was buried at Newcastle[7].

> A universal chronicle, '*Flores temporum seu chronicon universale ab urbe condita ad annum* 1349,' is sometimes attributed to him; Leland, e. g. says: 'Catalogus quoque Franciscanorum scriptorum Chronicorum Alaunovicani meminit' (Tanner, Bibl. 515). See also MS. Arundel 371 (sec. xv). This is the chronicle of Hermann Gigas based

dene' with Adam of Hoveden, as the other preachers mentioned belong to the end of the 13th century, e.g. Henry de Sutton, friar minor, Symon de Gandavo, Chancellor (Oxford), &c.

[1] Wood MS. F, 29 a, f. 178.
[2] Assisi MS. 158, quest. 179. Ric. de Hederington succeeded to the prebend of Ailesbury in 1290. Le Neve, II, 95.

[3] Brewer's reading Haldeswel is wrong. The Phillipps MS. also reads Baldeswelle.
[4] Wood MS., *ut supra*.
[5] Wood MS., *ut supra*.
[6] Archiv f. Litt. u. Kirch. Gesch. II, 361; III, 39; IV, 28 seq.
[7] Script. cent. V, 26.

on the well-known chronicle of Martinus Polonus (printed 1750). In the preface Hermann says that he has followed, 'inter modernos, Martinum Romane sedis penitenciarium (?) de ordine fratrum predicatorum' (Ar. MS. 371, f. 2).

Several philosophical treatises by *Martinus Anglicus* are extant in MS. Vienna :—Bibl. Palat. 4698 (sec. xiv).

33. **Robert of Beverley.**

34. **Richard de Coniton** or **Conyngton** (co. Cambridge or Huntingdon) was at Oxford in 1300 and was one of the friars to whom the Bishop of Lincoln refused the right to hear confessions[1]. He became D.D. and lecturer to the Franciscans between 1300 and 1310. He was afterwards thirty-first master of the Minorites at Cambridge[2]. He was sixteenth Provincial of England, and held the office in 1310[3]. About this time the Order was disturbed by the violent antagonism of the two parties within it—the 'Community,' the lax or moderate party which comprised the majority and included the official heads of the Order, and the strict or 'Spiritual' party. A papal investigation into the causes of dispute and into the observance of Rule by the Order was instituted, and the leaders of each party summoned to the Curia. Richard Conyngton as Provincial was the official representative of the English Franciscans at Avignon and Vienne (1301–1313)[4]. He was buried at Cambridge[5].

He is said by Leland and Bale to have written a treatise *De Christi Dominio* against Ockham in defence of the papal authority[6].

Wadding states that he had seen Richard's *Commentary on the Sentences* in the Vatican[7]. Bale mentions his exposition on the seven penitential psalms, *ex monasterio Nordovicensi*[8].

Tractatus Magistri Richardi Conyglon Ministri Angliae de paupertate contra opiniones Fratris Petri Joannis (*Olivi*). Inc. 'Beatus qui intelligit super egenum et pauperem. Ps. Praecedit actus meritorius.'

MS. Florence :—Laurentiana, *ex Bibl. S. Crucis*, Plut. XXXVI, Dext. Cod. xii (sec. xiv *exeuntis*).

35. **Thomas of Pontefract** was at Oxford in 1300; when the bishop of Lincoln refused to grant him license to hear confessions.

[1] See above.
[2] Mon. Franc. I, 556.
[3] Ibid. 538, 560. Reports of Hist. MSS. Commission, IV, 393 a, letter of Gonsalvo, Minister General to 'Friar R. minister of England,' 1310.
[4] Archiv f. Litt. u. K. Gesch. II, 356; III, 39; Wadding, VI, 171.
[5] Mon. Franc. I, 538, 553. Bale gives 1330 as the date of his death.
[6] Leland, Script. 331 ; Bale, I, 404.
[7] Wadding, VII, 168.
[8] MS. Bodl., Seld. supra 64, fol. 160.

He became D.D. and lecturer in theology some years after this. In July 1311 he was one of the inquisitors appointed to extort confession of heresy from twenty-four Templars in the Province of York [1].

36. **Peter de Sutton**; 'jacet Stanfordiae,' i.e. Stamford, co. Lincoln [2].

37. **Ralph of Lockysley**[3] or **Lockeleye**[4] was regent master at Oxford about 1310. He was buried at Worcester [5]. According to Bale (I, 366) he wrote *De paupertate evangelica*, &c.

38. **William of Schyrbourne** (1312) was at Oxford in 1300; he was one of the friars presented by the Provincial for license to hear confessions, and rejected by the bishop of Lincoln [6]. He was master of the Friars Minors in 1312, and in this capacity gave some support to the Dominicans in their controversy with the University [7].

Leland says: 'Ejus extant *Quodlibeta Theologica*, lib. i.' (?) [8].

39. **William of Nottingham** is confounded with the fourth Provincial Minister by Wadding, Bale, Pits, and the Register of Friars Minors of London [9]. In a work attributed to him, but really composed by his namesake, occurs the following note, in a hand of the fifteenth century [10]—

'This Notyngham was secular canon and precentor of the Church of York' (and in another hand), 'afterwards he became a friar of the order of St. Francis.'

In the absence of any confirmatory evidence, no weight can be attached to this statement. No William of Nottingham occurs in Le Neve's *Fasti*. At the beginning of the fifteenth century a John of Nottingham held two prebends and was treasurer of York: and he may be the person referred to in the first part of the note; it is worthy of remark

---

[1] Wood MS., *ut supra*; Wilkins' Concilia, II, 399; Lea, Hist. of the Inquisition, III, 301.

[2] Mon. Franc. I, 553. Cf. Digby MS. 154, f. 37 (sec. xiii, xiv); Letters of Friars P. de S. and others, to Roger de Merlawe, c. 1290–1300 (v. ibid. f. 38).

[3] MS. Cott. Nero, A, IX.

[4] MS. Phillipps, 3119; Brewer's 'Rockysley' is a mistake.

[5] Mon. Franc. I, 553.

[6] Wood MS. F, 29 a, &c.

[7] Twyne, MS. III, 327 (Acta fratrum Praedicatorum). 'Item Fratri Henrico Croy conventus fratrum Praedicatorum antedicti, Baculario Sacrae Theologiae pro Inceptione in Theologia se disponenti, responsiones ad hoc secundum statuta Universitatis praedictae necessario requisitae per magistrum Willelmum de Schireburn magistrum Fratrum Minorum et alios etiam magistros prius concessae, de ordinatione ipsorum Cancellarii et Procuratorum ac quorundam aliorum magistrorum, sunt penitus denegatae.' (Oxf. Hist. Soc. Collectanea, II, 241.)

[8] Tanner, Bibl. 668. Harl. MS. 5398 (§ 3) contains a Sermon attributed to John Schyrborn.

[9] Mon. Franc. I, 70, 538.

[10] Ball. Coll. MS. 33.

that the MS. originally came from York. William of Nottingham must have been reader to the Franciscans soon after 1312. While regent in theology at Oxford he was largely occupied in transcribing MSS., especially the works of Nicholas de Gorham, the expenses being defrayed by his brother *Dominus* Hugh of Nottingham[1]. He succeeded Richard Conyngton as seventeenth Provincial Minister[2]. In 1322 he was at the General Chapter of Perugia, and, with the other ministers, signed the famous letter in which the Franciscans declared that the doctrine *De paupertate Christi* was not heretical but sane and catholic; this was the beginning of the revolt of the whole Order (as distinguished from the Spirituals) against John XXII[3]. According to Bale he died Oct. 5, 1336[4]. He was buried at Leicester[5].

Bale ascribes to him *Determinatio pro lege Christianorum*, lib. i. *Inc*. 'Numquid deus posset revelare aliquam legem.'

'Ex Redingensi Minoritarum cenobio.' (MS. Seld. sup. 64, f. 215.)

40. **John de Wylton** lectured at Oxford in 1314: in February of that year he appears, as representative of the Minorites, in a list of twelve regent masters in theology (i. e. the theological faculty for the time being), who condemned as heretical eight articles, chiefly concerning the nature of the Trinity, in the convent of the Austin Friars[6]. Wood[7], Bale[8], and Tanner[9], call him an Austin Friar. Bale states that he studied and lectured as master at Paris, and says that John Baconthorpe, in his commentaries on Books I and II of the Sentences, speaks of him with high praise[10]. His works seem to have perished[11].

41. **John de Crombe** (Cott. MS.) or **Crombre** (Phil. MS.) was perhaps a native of Combs in Suffolk: he was buried at Oxford[12].

Compendium theologicae veritatis per fratrem Johannem de Combis,
  lib. vii. *Inc*. 'Veritatis theologie cum superni.'

MS. Cambridge :—Caius Coll. 193.

---

[1] Merton Coll. MSS. 166, 168, 169, 170, 158.
[2] Mon. Franc. I, 538, 560.
[3] Wadding, VI, 396–7: he confuses William Provincial of England with William of Ockham; VII, *sub anno* 1323.
[4] MS. Seld. sup. 64, fol. 215.
[5] Mon. Franc. I, 538.
[6] Mun. Acad. p. 100.
[7] Annals, *sub anno* 1270; elsewhere Wood calls him John Middleton, Minorite, ibid. p. 386.
[8] Script. Brit. I, 365.
[9] Bibl. p. 778.
[10] I have not found this reference; Baconthorpe's commentaries on Sentences I and II fill a folio volume of 378 leaves (Milan, 1510).
[11] According to the Old Catalogue, MS. Bodl. 783 contains a treatise by a John Wylton (the monk of Westminster?); the entry is erroneous; the MS. (now Laud. Misc. 677) contains nothing about John Wylton.
[12] Mon. Franc. I, 553.

Anonymous in MSS. Charleville 19 (written A.D. 1337), and Metz 448 (sec. xv): generally ascribed to Albertus Magnus and printed at the end of tom. xiii. of his works, Lyons 1651.

42. **William of Alnwick** is possibly identical with the friar called Roger of Alnwick in the list of Oxford Franciscans presented to the bishop of Lincoln in 1300[1]. After lecturing at Oxford (c. 1315–1320?), he was sent to the University of Naples, as Doctor of Theology[2]. He was present at the General Chapter of Perugia in 1322, and joined with the other leading men in the Order in declaring that the doctrine of Evangelical Poverty was not heretical[3]. In 1330 he was made bishop of Giuvenazzo near Bari[4]. He is said to have died at Avignon in 1332[5]. Bartholomew of Pisa mentions him among the famous Franciscan theologians of the English nation[6]; William Woodford places him among

'inceptores ordinis Minorum qui egregie scripserunt super sententias[7].'

Questiones Almoich super primum Sententiarum.

Questiones Almoich in 1 et 2 Sententiarum[8].

    MSS. Padua :—Bibl. S. Anton. (Tomasin, p. 61 b, 62 b.)

    Cf. MS. Ball. Coll. 208 (sec. xiv), an abridgment of the commentary of Duns Scotus on the 2nd book of the Sentences by 'Master William of Alnwick, Friar Minor.'

43. **William Herberd** or **Herbert**, if we may credit the Lanercost Chronicle, which is usually trustworthy at this period, was at Paris in 1290[9]. From his place in the list of masters, it might be inferred that he lectured at Oxford about 1315–1320. But if the following works ascribed to him are genuine, he must have flourished not much later than 1250–60. They are preserved in a fourteenth-century MS. formerly in the library of Henry Farmer of Tusmor, Oxon, now in the Phillipps Library at Thirlestaine House[10].

---

[1] Wood MS., *ut supra*. Another William of Alnwick was bishop of Norwich and Lincoln in the fifteenth century.

[2] Mon. Franc. I, 553: 'postea apud Montem Bononiae Neapoli legit; demum Episcopus.'

[3] Wadding, VI, 396; Anal. Franc. II, 129: 'Hugo de Novo Castro et Gulielmus de Almuchia, sacrae theologiae doctores.'

[4] Wadding, VII, 112, 169, 'ex Regest. Rob. Regis Siciliae.'

[5] Bale and Pits.

[6] Lib. Conform. f. 81 b, 'Almoith.'

[7] MS. Harl. 31, f. 96 b.

[8] Tanner, Bibl. 354, says his commentaries on the Sentences 'extant impr. . . . Lip.' (?)

[9] P. 135, a curious story about the Jews at Paris; 'frater W. Herbert, qui vidit,' &c.

[10] Bernard's Catalogues, Tom. II, no. 9159: Phillipps Catal. No. 8336; the same volume contains some works of Friar Nicholas Bozon ('Boioun'). I have not had an opportunity of examining these works of Herbert's, which are probably of some value.

Sermo Fratris Willielmi Herebert in Ecclesia B. Mariae Virginis Oxon; in haec verba: 'Dixit mater Ihu ad eum, Vinum non habent.'

Sermo ejusdem Fratris in Ecclesia B. Mariae Oxon. in translatione S. Edmundi Archiepiscopi in haec verba: 'Homo quidam erat dives et induebatur purpura,' etc.

(St. Edmund was translated in 1247; the words however must mean *in festo translationis*, i.e. June 9th.)

Ejusdem Fratris Epistolae summo Pontifici, Episcopo Coventrensi et Lichfeldensi (Roger of Wesham?), Symoni de Montfort, etc.[1]

Historica quaedam de Papis Romanis (*anon.*).

Tractatus de Veneno et Antidotis (*anon.*).

Hymns in old English[2], quibus haec notula adjicitur: 'Istos Hympnos et Antiphonas transtulit in Anglicum non semper de verbo in verbum, sed frequenter sensum aut non multum declinando, et in manu sua scripsit frater Willielmus Herebert; qui usum horum autem habuerit, oret pro anima dicti Patris.'

William Herbert was buried at Hereford, which was probably his native convent[3].

44. **Thomas of St. Dunstan** (Kent?).

45. **John of Reading** (de Radingia) was buried at Avignon. He had probably gone to the papal curia in connexion with the revolt of Michael de Cesena and William of Ockham[4].

> Cf. MS. Florence:—Laurentiana, *ex Bibl. S. Crucis*, Plut. XXXV, Dext. Cod. xi, *Primus Fratris Joannis de Padingia* (=*Radingia?*), S.T.D. ord. Min. (*super sententias?*).

46. **John of Thornton**; the name is uncertain; it may be Jornton; the Phillipps MS. reads Zortone.

47. **Richard of Drayton**, was buried at Shrewsbury[5].

48. **Robert of Leicester** seems to have been a protégé of Richard Swinfeld, bishop of Hereford, to whom he dedicated his first extant work in 1294[6]. He was S.T.P. and in residence at Oxford in 1325, and probably lecturer to the friars about the same time. In this year he was associated with Nicholas de Tyngewick, M.D. and S.T.B. as '*Magister Extraneus*' of Balliol College[7]. The two were called upon to decide whether the statutes of the College allowed the members to attend lectures in any faculty except that of Arts, and ordained 'in the presence of the whole community' that this was not permissible.

---

[1] Not mentioned in the Phillipps Catalogue.
[2] *Inc.*: 'Ha troe yat art so vayr y kud;' Phill. Catal.
[3] Mon. Franc. I, 553.
[4] Ibid. 554.
[5] Ibid.
[6] MS. Digby, 212, f. 2.
[7] Hist. MSS. Commission, Report IV, 443 (deed in Ball. Coll. Archives).

Among those present in the Hall of Balliol when the decision was proclaimed was Richard Fitzralph, afterwards Archbishop of Armagh, the great opponent of the Mendicant Orders [1]. Bale and Pits say that Robert died at Lichfield in 1348; 'but,' adds Wood, 'I suppose 'twas sooner.'

De compoto Hebreorum aptato ad Kalendarium, four parts with prologue; composed A.D. 1294. *Inc. prol.* 'Operis injuncti novitatem, pater meritis insignissime, magister et domine R. Dei gratia Herfordensis antistes ecclesie.'

Compotus Hebreorum purus. Inc. 'Prima earum est a creacione mundi.'

Commentariolus supra tabulas in tractatu primo supra recensito descriptas (or, *De ratione temporum*), written in 1295. *Inc.* 'Ad planiorem et pleniorem prescripti tractatus intelligenciam.'

These three works are contained in MS. Bodl. Digby 212 (sec. xiv).

Distinctiones.

MS. Cambridge:—Pembroke Coll. 220, § 1; 'Enchiridion poenitentiale ... ex distinctionibus ... Rob. de Leycester (aliorumque).'

De paupertate Christi.

Attributed to him by Leland [2].

49. **Walter de Foxisley**, or **Ffoxle** in Phillipps MS. (Norfolk or Wilts?).

50. **Henry Cruche.** A sermon by 'H. de Cruce, Minor,' is in Merton Coll. MS. No. 248, f. 170. This name is omitted in the list given in the Phillipps MS.

51. **John de Ratforde** (cf. 63rd master).

See MS. Bodl. Digby 216, f. 40, containing three theological questions to which the name 'Ratforde' is prefixed; the MS. dates from the fourteenth century: the questions are: '*an quilibet adultus teneatur laudare Deum; utrum ex sui meriti vel demeriti circumstantiis juste debeat augeri vel minui pena; utrum ad omnem actum creature rationalis concurrat necessario Dei efficientia specialis.*'

52. **John de Preston** [3].

---

[1] Hist. MSS. Commission, Report IV, 443 (deed in Ball. Coll. Archives).

[2] Leland's authority was probably the Catalogue of Franciscan writers in which R. of Leicester was mentioned: 'colligo hunc (Robertum) fuisse Guil. Hereberti synchronium, instructus serie Catalogi *De Scriptoribus Franciscanis*, editi;' *Scriptores*, p. 304.

[3] A monk of this name is mentioned in MS. 24 of Corp. Chr. Coll. Cambridge, A.D. 1348.

53. **Walter de Chauton**[1] is no doubt identical with **Walter de Chatton**, who with the warden was summoned to appear in the Mayor's Court, to answer a charge, brought against the convent, of wrongfully keeping two books, in 1330[2]; he evidently held some official position at this time, presumably that of regent master. He is said to have been warden of Norwich, probably his native convent, and to have taught theology there[3]. He was one of the D.D.'s whom Benedict XII consulted in drawing up his Statutes for the Franciscan Order in 1336[4]. This fact lends some support to Bale's statement that he became papal penitentiary and died at Avignon in 1343[5]. Bartholomew of Pisa mentions him among the famous writers of the Order; William of Woodford among those who entered the Order in their youth, and 'wrote many works of great wisdom[6].'

Cathon sur les Sentences [W. Chatton[7] or R. Cowton?].
    MSS. Paris:—Bibl. Nat. 15886, 15887 (sec. xiv), two copies.

Questio fratris Galtheri magistri . . . de schaton, que est secunda in ordine primi sui in prologo. Inc. 'Utrum Deus possit creare.' *Expl.* 'Et ideo non est simile.'
    MS. Cambridge:—Public Library, Ff. III, 26, f. 122, 123, 130 b.
    Cf. MS. Harl. 3243, fol. 55, *Adam Wodham de divisione, etc. contra Chatton.*

54. **John de Ridevaus, Rideval**, or **Redovallensis**, sometimes called John de Musca, according to Bale[8], flourished about 1330. Of the works attributed to him, the Commentary on Fulgentius seems to be the same as that attributed to John Wallensis; similarly perhaps with the commentary on the letter of Valerius to Rufinus; the moral exposition of the Metamorphoses seems to differ from that ascribed to Thomas Walleys and Peter Bercherius.

---

[1] Chtantton (*sic*) in MS. Nero A, IX; omitted in Phillipps MS. The name is given in a variety of forms: Certhanton or Certanton (Wood), Southampton (Brewer), Catton, Gathon, Chattodunus (Leland), Ceton, Cepton, Tepton (Barth. of Pisa, Pits, &c.), Schaton (N. Glasberger, Analecta Francisc. II, 166), Canton ('Chronologia historico-legalis seraphici Ordinis Fratrum Minorum,' Neapoli, 1650; quoted ibid. note 5), Chvaton (Baronius-Raynaldus).

[2] Twyne, MS. XXIII, 488, from the Oxford City Records; cf. Part I, ch. iv.

[3] Blomefield, Hist. of Norfolk, IV, p. 112. There is a Catton near Norwich.

[4] Baronius-Raynaldus, Ann. Ecclesiast. Vol. XXV, p. 92; Anal. Franc. II, p. 166.

[5] Script. Brit. I, 420.

[6] Liber Conformitatum, f. 81 b; Defensorium, cap. 62 (Twyne, MS. XXII, 103 c).

[7] Woodford refers to 'Chatone's' commentaries on the Sentences; MS. Harl. 31, ff. 61, 96.

[8] Script. I, p. 409.

Lectura super Apocalypsi.
> MS. Venice:—St. Mark, Class. I, Cod. 139, fol. 110–119 (sec. xiv), 'Extracta de lectura fratris Joannis Rydelbast super Apocalypsi, ordinis Minorum.'

'*Commentarius super Fulgencium continens picturas virtutum et viciorum sub ymaginibus deorum et dearum quos colebat vana superstitio paganorum editus a fratre J. de Ridevall de ordine fratrum minorum.*' Inc. 'Intencio venerabilis viri Fulgencii.'
> MSS. Cambridge:—Pub. Libr. Ii II, 20, f. 121–162 (sec. xv); and Mm I, 18, § 6 (xv).
> Worcester Cathed. Libr. 154 (=Bernard 829).
> Venice:—St. Mark, Class. I, Cod. 139, f. 121–136 (xiv).

'*Ovidii Metamorphoseos fabule* ccxviii *moraliter exposite.*' Inc. 'In hujus expositionis initio.'
> MSS. Cambridge:—Pub. Libr. Ii II, 20, f. 162–199 (anon. but in the same writing as the *Comment. super Fulgencium* which it follows).
> Worc. Cath. Libr. 89 (=764), 'Jo. Risdevallus.'

In Valerium ad Rufinum de uxore non ducenda. Inc. 'Loqui perhibeor.'
> Cf. MSS. Cambridge:—Pub. Libr. Mm I, 18, § 5; and London:—Lambeth Palace 330 (xv).

Commentaries on St. Augustine's De Civitate Dei. Inc. 'Magnus dominus et laudabilis nimis in civitate Dei.'
> MSS. Oxford:—C.C.C. 186 and 187 (sec. xv *ineuntis*); on books 1, 2, 3, 6, and 7, by 'Jo. Rydevallis' or 'Rydewall,' Friar Minor[1].

55. **Lawrence Briton** is perhaps the same as Laurentius Wallensis mentioned by Tanner, who wrote a dialogue on free will[2]. A sermon by him is preserved in Merton College, MS. 248, f. 170. He flourished about 1340. A Dominican of the same name was S.T.P. of Paris in the thirteenth century[3]. Among the MSS. mentioned in the old catalogue (1381) at Assisi[4], is a '*Summa mag. fratris Laurentii Vualensis Anglici ordinis Minorum;*' this is perhaps a mistake for Johannes Wallensis.

56. **John de Rudinton** or **Rodyngton** belonged to the custody

---

[1] Cf. MS. Seld. sup. 64, f. 75.
[2] Tanner, Bibl. p. 473: 'MS. olim in bibl. Sion.' The work is however printed and ascribed to Laurence Valla (see Panzer, Ann. Typ.).
[3] Archiv f. Litt. u. Kirch. Gesch. II, 171.
[4] Fratini, *Storia ... del Convento di S. Francesco in Assisi* (Prato, 1882), p. 205.

of Oxford, and the convent of Stamford[1]. He was D.D. of Oxford[2], nineteenth Provincial Minister of England[3], and is described in the Register of the Grey Friars of London as 'vir sanctissimus[4].' He was buried at Bedford[5]; Bale and his followers mention 1348, the date of the first great pestilence, as the year of his death.

Joannes Rodinchon in lib. i. Sententiarum.
    Included by Joannes Picardus in his *Thesaurus Theologorum* (A.D. 1503)[6].

Johannis de Rodynton determinationes theologicae.
    MS. Munich :—Bibl. Regiae, Cod. Lat. 22023 (sec. xiv).

Quaestiones super quartum librum Sententiarum (by the same author ?).
    MS. ibid. fol. 18.

Questiones super quodlibeta rodincon.
    MS. Bruges, 503 (sec. xv).

57. **John de Howden** (c. 1340).

[John Hoveden of London, S.T.P. and author of many works, was not a friar; he died A.D. 1275: Tanner, *Bibl.* 415.]

58. **T. Stanschaw**, called by Brewer, G. Stanforth[7], by others, Thomas Stanchaw, Straveshaw, &c., was a Minorite of Bristol[8]. Bale says:

'obiit Avenione A.D. 1346. Ex quodam Minoritarum registro[9].'

Some sermons in MS. Merton Coll. 248 (sec. xiv *exeuntis*) are ascribed to 'Stanschawe.'

A number of works are attributed to him by Bale, 'ex Bibliotheca Nordovicensi,' and 'ex officina Roberti Stoughton[10].'

59. **Edmund Grafton**.

60. **Stephen Sorel**.

61. **Adam Wodham** or **Godham** was one of the most famous of the later Franciscan schoolmen[11]. He is said to have lived chiefly at

---

[1] Mon. Franc. I, 560; Tanner, Bibl. 638.

[2] Mon. Franc. I, 554, 560, 538. Cf. John Major, Gesta Scotorum, I, cap. 5.

[3] Mon. Franc. I, 538, 554.

[4] Ibid. 538.

[5] Ibid.

[6] Willott, Athenae, pp. 237–8. According to Sbaralea, the *Thesaurus* was approved in 1503, parts were printed at Milan in 1506, and the entire work was preserved in the Franciscan Library at Assisi; Wadding, Sup. ad Script. p. 451.

[7] The 'G' is certainly wrong; the initial 'T' is inserted in a later hand in Cott. MS. The name is doubtful; MS. reads Stansch or Stanfth.

[8] Tanner, Bibl. 691.

[9] MS. Seld. supra 64, fol. 175; Script. I, 427–8.

[10] MS. and Script. *ut supra*.

[11] Barth. of Pisa, Liber Conformitatum, f. 81 b; Wadding, VI, 344. John Major, who edited a version of his Sentences in 1512, calls him : ' Vir modestus, sed non inferioris doctrinae aut ingenii quam Ockam,' Gesta Scot. Lib. IV, cap. 21.

Norwich, London, and Oxford [12], and was probably reader in theology at several convents in succession. He was a follower of William of Ockham in philosophy and probably attended his lectures. He may be the Adam to whom Ockham's *Summa logices* was addressed [1]. The date of his lecturing as regent master at Oxford is unknown; it must have been about 1340 or soon after. He was perhaps the 'Frater Adam magister in sacra theologia de Anglia,' who went to Basel in 1339 to consult Friar James de Porta on some miracles alleged to have been wrought there [2]. He died, if we may believe Bale, at Babwell in 1358 [3].

Comment. in IV libros Sententiarum, abbreviated by Henry of Oyta. *Inc. prol.* 'Ista est lex Adam.'

MSS. Paris:—Bibl. Nat. 15892 and 15893 (sec. xiv) [4].

Bruges, 162, 'Magistri Adae lecturae super IV. Sententiarum' (?).

Toulouse, 246, the abbreviated version of the lectures of Adam Godham or 'Adam de Vodronio' by Henry de Hoyta, written in the Franciscan convent at Paris, A.D. 1399.

Rouen, 581 (sec. xiv-xv).

Printed at Paris, 1512. Perhaps some of the MSS. cited above contain the original work of Adam Wodham. See Wadding, *Sup. ad Script.* 2-3.

Quaestiones variae philosophicae et theologicae, by Godham and others [5].

MS. Brit. Mus.: Harl. 3243 (sec. xiv).

Comment. super Cantica Canticorum.

MS. formerly in the Franciscan Library in London (Leland, *Collect.* III, 49).

Postilla super Ecclesiasticum, Lib. I.

'Ex registro Decani Nordovicensis' (Bale MS. Bodl. Seld. sup. 64).

Determinationes, or, *Determinationes XI*. *Inc.* 'Utrum officina.'

Mentioned in *Catalogus illustrium Franciscanorum*, and by Bale (MS. *ut supra*) 'ex bibliotheca Nordovicensi [6].'

---

[12] Tanner, Bibl. 329; Wadding, VIII, 139; J. Major's preface to Wodham's Sentences, ed. 1512.

[1] Wadding, Sup. ad Script. 327.

[2] Analecta Franciscana, II, 177.

[3] Bale, Script. I, 447.

[4] In the Bibliothèque de l'Arsenal, MS. 514 (*olim* 551) has the note: 'Verisimile est authorem hujus libri esse magistrum Adamum de Rodromo' (i.e. Wodham). The MS. really contains only Peter Lombard's Sentences without any commentary.

[5] Cf. notice of Walter Chatton.

[6] Bale adds that he wrote *Sententias et conclusiones*, Lib. I, 'Absolutio criminis sive peccati' (on the power of the Mendicants to hear confessions, especially against Wetheringsete), *ex officina Ricardi Kele*; *Sententias Oxoniensis consilii*, Lib. I, 'Sententie septem ponuntur' (?). MS. Bodl. Seld. sup. 64, fol. 9. For Wetheringsete or Wetherset, see Tanner, Bibl. 759.

62. **Robert de Redclive.**

63. **Thomas Radford** (cf. 51st master).

64. **John Went** or **Gwent** was a native of the Bristol custody[1]. He probably incepted in theology and lectured to the Friars at Oxford about 1340 or soon after. His character for holiness was such that he was believed to have wrought miracles in his lifetime[2]. He succeeded John de Rodyngton as Provincial Minister, being the twentieth in Order, probably between 1340 and 1350[3]. Bale adds:

'he died at Hereford A.D. 1348, as I have found in a register of the Minorites[4].'

It is however not improbable that he found only the first statement in the register and added the date. Both the catalogues of the Provincial Ministers state that he was buried at Hereford[5].

65. **Thomas Oterborne** can hardly have written the chronicle generally ascribed to him. The chronicle itself bears no marks of having been written by a Franciscan; even the notices of the Order given in Walsingham and the Eulogium Historiarum are sometimes omitted, and usually shortened, in the so-called Otterbourne. But apart from this, the evidence of dates is fairly conclusive: the chronicle, as edited by Hearne, leaves off abruptly in the year 1420, and Hearne puts Otterbourne's death at 1421. Pits and Wood suppose from MSS. which end in 1411 that the writer died in that year. Hearne says

there are not wanting MSS. which bring the history hardly beyond Edward III.'

But even assuming the existence of such MSS. it is practically impossible that they can have been the work of the Franciscan doctor. Thomas Oterborne must have lectured at Oxford before 1350. It is true that the last nine names of lectors given in the list are in a more recent hand than the earlier ones; but the names of Went and Oterborne are in the same writing, and there can be no reasonable doubt that they were contemporaries. The dates of Oterborne's two immediate successors at Oxford are unknown[6], and the list of lectors here comes to an end. We cannot therefore know whether there were any more lectors before Simon Tunstede. Assuming that he was the

---

[1] Mon. Franc. I, 560.
[2] Ibid. 538.
[3] W. of Nottingham, 17th Minister in 1322; Thomas Kingesbury, 26th Minister in 1380; the dates between these are uncertain.
[4] Script. Brit. I, 432.
[5] Mon. Franc. I, 538, 560.
[6] Unless the conjecture about J. Valeys is correct.

sixty-eighth lector, we may naturally conclude that the sixty-fifth read several years before him, i.e. several years before 1351 when Simon was 'regent among the Minorites at Oxford[1].' It is therefore most probable that Thomas was reader not later than 1345. The historian was perhaps the Thomas Otterburn who became rector of Chingford in 1393 and was ordained priest in 1394[2].

66. **John Valeys**[3] was perhaps the Friar John Wells who took a prominent part in the disputed election to the Chancellorship in 1349, as a supporter of John Wyllyot, fellow of Merton, whose conduct seems to have been of a peculiarly riotous and lawless character[4]. He may possibly be the John Welle, S.T.P. and Friar Minor[5], who was robbed by his servant in London in 1377; some curious details about this affair will be found in Appendix B.

67. **Richard Malevile** of the London Custody (c. 1350?); this name is added in a still later hand.

[1] Digby, MS. 90, f. 6 b (14th century), in Bodleian.
[2] Tanner, Bibl. 567. The chronicle is in Brit. Mus. MS. Cotton, Vitell. F, IX.
[3] The name is unfortunately not clearly written in the Cott. MS: it may be *Vilers*: cf. Memorials of Merton Coll. p. 199.
[4] Wood, Annals, A.D. 1349.
[5] Pat. 1 Ric. II, pt. 4, m. 37.

CHAPTER III.

FRANCISCANS WHO STUDIED IN THE CONVENT AT OXFORD, OR HAD SOME OTHER CONNEXION WITH THE TOWN OR THE UNIVERSITY.

Agnellus or Angnellus of Pisa was custodian of Paris before becoming first Provincial of England[1]. He is said to have been made Provincial by St. Francis in 1219[2]; the order as given by Francis a S. Clara[3] is as follows:

'Ego frater Franciscus de Assisio Minister Generalis praecipio tibi fratri Agnello de Pisa per obedientiam, ut vadas ad Angliam, et ibi facias officium Ministeratus. Vale. Frater Franciscus de Assisio.'

It may be doubted whether this letter is authentic, nor is the date beyond dispute. It may be considered as certain that Agnellus did not come to England till September 1224[4]. He was then a deacon, and about thirty years of age[5]. He landed with eight others at Dover, went to Canterbury, and thence to London, establishing houses and receiving novices. Such was his humility that he long refused the order of priesthood, and only at length consented, when the Provincial Chapter had procured a command from the General Chapter, that the order should be conferred on him[6]. He was a zealous guardian of the primitive poverty of the Rule of St. Francis, and would only allow houses to be built or areas to be enlarged where it was absolutely necessary[7]. He urged the demolition of a conventual building called *Valvert* at Paris, and forbade the enlargement of the house at Gloucester: he had the infirmary at Oxford built so low that a man could

---

[1] Mon. Franc. I, p. 5.
[2] Wadding, I, 303; Anal. Franc. II, pp. 14-15.
[3] Christ. Davenport, Opera omnia (Duaci 1665), Tom. I, Hist. Minor, p. 2: he adds, 'Originale meo adhuc tempore in Episcopio Audomarensi servabatur.'
[4] Mon. Franc. I, p. 5. Cf. Lanerc. Chron. p. 30; Annals of Worc. p. 416 (Ann. Monast. IV).
[5] Mon. Franc., ibid.
[6] Ibid. 53-4.   [7] Ibid. 34, 35, 36-7.

scarcely stand upright in it. He built a school at Oxford of more generous proportions, and encouraged the love of learning in the Order[1]. The choice of Grostete as the first master of the Minorites was due to Agnellus[2]. He was, according to Matthew Paris, on familiar terms with the King, and was one of his counsellors[3]. In December, 1233, he offered his services as peace-maker between Henry III and the rebellious Earl Marshall, though his efforts to induce the latter to submit were unavailing[4]. It would seem to have been after this that he went to Rome on some business of the English prelates[5], and he may also at the same time have attended a General Chapter in Italy[6]. On his return, he was seized with dysentery at Oxford; it was believed that his health had never recovered from the severities to which he was exposed while labouring for peace in the winter of 1233[7]. He recommended that the General Minister, Elias, should be requested to appoint Albert of Pisa, or Haymo, or Radulf of Rheims, as his successor. He constituted Peter of Tewkesbury his Vicar, and made his last confession to him. He died at Oxford in great pain, crying continually, ' *Veni, dulcissime Jesu.*' The exact date of his death is uncertain; it was probably early in 1235[8]. He was, says Eccleston,

'a man specially endowed with natural prudence and foresight, and conspicuous for every virtue[9].'

He was buried in a wooden or leaden coffin in the choir of the chapel before the altar. When this chapel was superseded by the larger church, the friars came by night to remove the body; they found the coffin and the grave

'full of the purest oil, the corpse with its garments incorrupt and smelling most sweetly.'

His bones were laid with due pomp in 'a fair stone sepulchre' in the new church, and the miracles which were wrought at his tomb were a source of honour and profit to the Convent at Oxford[10].

---

[1] Mon. Franc. I, 37; cf. Barth. of Pisa, fol. 79 b.
[2] Mon. Franc. ibid.
[3] Chron. Majora, III, 257: 'familiaris erat domino regi et consiliarius ipsius.'
[4] Ibid. Cf. p. 251; Mon. Franc. I, 52; Ann. Monast. I, 92.
[5] Mon. Franc. ibid.
[6] He was present at the translation of the body of St. Francis in 1230; ibid. 5.
[7] Mon. Franc. I, 52-4, account of his death, &c.
[8] This is supported by MS. Cott. Nero A. IX, f. 70 b: 'A° domini MCC 35 frater Agnellus ... obiit,' and Cott. Cleop. B. XIII, f. 146 b.
[9] Mon. Franc. I, 52.
[10] Ibid. 54; Barth. of Pisa, fol. 79, 80; 126, 'miraculis pluribus decoratus.'

Richard de Ingewrthe or **Indewurde** (Norfolk) is named second in the list of friars who came over with Agnellus in 1224. He was a priest and advanced in years; according to Eccleston he was the first Minorite who preached to the people '*citra montes.*' With three other friars he established the first house of Franciscans in London (at Cornhill); he then proceeded to Oxford with Richard of Devon, hired a house of Robert le Mercer in St. Ebbe's, and thus founded the original convent in the University town. The two companions then went on to Northampton, where they again hired a house and founded a friary. Richard of Ingewrthe afterwards became custodian of Cambridge, which was specially noted for its poverty under his rule. In 1230, when Agnellus attended the General Chapter at Assisi, he was associated in the Vicariate of the English Province with Henry de Ceruise or Treviso, a lay-brother from Lombardy. Soon after this he was sent by the General, John Parens, as Provincial Minister to Ireland. At length he was released from the office in General Chapter by Albert of Pisa (c. 1239), set out as a missionary to Palestine, and died there[1].

Richard of Devon, a young acolyte, was the third of those who came over with Agnellus. He accompanied R. of Ingewrthe from Canterbury to London, Oxford, and Northampton;

'and (in Eccleston's words) left us many examples of longsuffering and obedience. For after he had traversed many provinces in obedience to commands, he was for fifteen years worn out by frequent quartan fevers and remained continually at Romehale[2].'

Adam of Oxford was a master before he entered the Order[3]. The account of his conversion given by Eccleston[4] is as follows:

Master Adam of Oxford, of worldwide fame[5], had made a vow that he would do anything he was asked to do 'for the love of the blessed Mary;' and he told this to a certain recluse, who was a friend of his. She revealed his secret to her friends, that is, to a monk of Reading, another of the Cistercian Order, and a Friar Preacher; telling them that they could gain such a man in such a way; not wishing that Adam should become a Friar Minor. But the Blessed Virgin did not permit anyone in

---

[1] Mon. Franc. I, 5–7, 7, 9, 10, 27. I have found no authority for the form 'Kingesthorp' which Leland, and his followers Bale and Pits, substitute for Ingewrthe, except a late marginal note in Phillipps MS. 3119, f. 71.

[2] Mon. Franc. I, 6, 7, 9, 10. Bale's statement that R. of Devon and W. Eton 'seipsos castrabant' is probably without any foundation, so far as the former is concerned; see William of Esseby.

[3] Mon. Franc. I, 15. In the Phillipps MS. of Eccleston he is called 'Ada de Exonia' (fol. 72 b).

[4] Ibid. 15–16.

[5] '*Toto famosus orbe,*' probably when Eccleston wrote, i.e. after Adam's death.

his presence to make the needful request; but deferred it to another time. One night he dreamed that he had to cross a bridge, where some men were throwing their nets into the stream, endeavouring to catch him: but he escaped this with great difficulty and reached a very peaceful spot. Now when by the divine will he had escaped all others, he went casually to see the Friars Minors, and during the conversation Friar William de Colvile, the elder, a man of great sanctity, said to him: 'Dear master, enter our Order for the love of the Mother of God and help our simplicity.' And Adam immediately consented to do so, as if he had heard the words from the lips of the Mother of God.

He assumed the habit on January 25[1], probably A.D. 1227. He was at this time assistant, or secretary[2], to the great Adam Marsh, whom he soon afterwards induced to join the Franciscans. Shortly after this, Adam of Oxford went to Gregory IX, and was at his own desire sent to preach to the Saracens[3]. From a letter of Grostete's, addressed to Agnellus and the Convent of Friars Minors at Oxford, relating to this subject, and written in or before 1231[4], we learn that Adam had formed the resolution of going to preach to the infidels before he entered the Order, and that he was induced to take this latter step partly because it was likely to add to his influence as a missionary. Grostete urges the Friars not to grieve for his loss:
'for the light of his knowledge is so bright that it ought to be concentrated most there where it may dissipate the thickest darkness of infidelity.' 'Have no fear,' the writer continues, 'that he will be cut off from the "Sacred Page;" he has humility, and no "*haeretica pravitas*" will slip in.'

He died at Barlete, and miracles are said to have been wrought by his relics or his memory[5].

William of York, 'a solemn bachelor,' was probably an Oxford man, as he entered the Order on the same day as Adam of Oxford[6].

Adam Rufus[7] studied under Grostete in the early part of the thirteenth century, presumably at Oxford. A letter from 'Robert Grostete called Master,' written perhaps before he held any preferments, i.e. before 1210, addressed to 'Master Adam Rufus,' is extant; it is a treatise on the nature of angels, and Grostete asks Adam to inquire diligently the opinions of the wise men, with whom he converses, on the subject. In another letter written about 1237,

---

[1] 'In die conversionis Sancti Pauli;' Mon. Franc. I, 15.
[2] 'Fuit autem tunc socius Magistri Adae de Marisco et ad robas suas;' ibid. [3] Ibid. 16.
[4] Letter II (pp 17-21): Grostete was then Archdeacon of Leicester, an office which he resigned in 1231.
[5] Mon. Franc. I, 16.
[6] Ibid. 15.
[7] See Grosseteste, Epistolae, Nos. I, XXXVIII, and p. 449.

Grostete mentions having heard of Friar Ernulphus, papal penitentiary, from 'Friar Adam Rufus of good memory,' formerly his beloved pupil and friend. It may be inferred from his connexion with Grostete and Ernulphus or Arnulfus, Vicar of the Order of Minorites[1], that the Order which he entered was that of the Franciscans.

Henry de Reresby, who entered the Order abroad, was vicar of the custodian of Oxford about 1235 or before. He was made first provincial of Scotland by Elias, but died before he could enter on his duties[2]. According to Leland's notes from Eccleston he died at Leicester; according to another account, at Acre in Norfolk[3]. After his death he appeared to the custodian of Oxford, and said that,

'if the friars were not damned for excess in buildings, they would at any rate be severely punished,' and added, 'if the friars said the divine service well, they would be the sheep of the Apostles[4].'

Walter, a canon of Dunstable, and **John,** a novice of the same priory, escaped from their house through a broken window and joined the Franciscans at Oxford in 1233. Walter afterwards returned with three Minorites to the Chapter of Dunstable, seeking absolution. After submitting to corporal punishment, he was absolved; he was further ordered to restore the books and clothes (*quaternos et pannos*) which he had taken with him, and to deliberate for a year—i.e. during his noviciate—whether the discipline of the Order which he had entered was more severe than that of the Order he had left; if it were so, he was to remain a Minorite; if not, he was to return to Dunstable. John was found by the Prior of Dunstable at London and similarly absolved: he afterwards went to Rome[5].

John of Reading, who became Abbat of Osney in 1229[6], joined the Minorites in 1235, probably at Northampton[7]. He is probably the Abbat to whom Bartholomew of Pisa refers as having assisted with his own hands at the building of the Franciscan Church at Oxford[8]. He was certainly at Oxford about 1250, when Adam Marsh wrote

---

[1] Mon. Franc. I, 45, 47. [2] Ib. 25, 32.
[3] Ibid. 549, cf. p. 32: 'Fratrem Albertum in loco Leycestriae ... recepit.' Leland's notes are from the Phillipps MS. of Eccleston, which differs in some respects from the Cotton and York MSS. But Phillipps MS. fol. 74 adds in a marginal note in an old hand, ' obiit autem in Acria, plenus dierum.'
[4] Ibid. 25.
[5] Annals of Dunstable, anno 1233 (Ann. Monast. III, 133-4).
[6] Annals of Osney, p. 70 (Ann. Monast. Vol. IV)
[7] Ibid. 82; cf. Mon. Franc. I, 16. M. Paris under the year 1241 writes, 'the Abbat of Osney smitten with pusillanimity of mind, left the Order of the great doctor Augustine and migrated to the Order of Minors, wishing to try the novelty;' IV, 163.
[8] Liber Conform. fol. 79 b.

FRANCISCANS IN THE OXFORD CONVENT.

to the Provincial that he was in ill-health and requested that Friar Adam de Bechesoueres, the physician of the Order, might be sent to Oxford to attend him[1]. Another 'Frater Johannes Anglicus de Redingis' was Visitor of Germany in 1229, and Minister of Saxony 1230–1232 [2].

Albert of Pisa did not, as stated by Bartholomew of Pisa and others, accompany Agnellus to England. He was (according to Eccleston) Minister of Hungary, Germany (1223–1227), Bologna, the March of Ancona, the March of Treviso, Tuscany, perhaps of Spain in 1227[3]. He was one of the three recommended by Agnellus as fit persons to succeed him as Provincial of England, but he was not appointed by Elias till almost a year after the death of the first Minister[4] (c. 1236). He reached England on December 13, and celebrated a Provincial Chapter at Oxford on February 2 [5]. On another occasion Eccleston tells us—

'Friar Albert was present at the sermon of a young friar at Oxford; and when the preacher boldly condemned loftiness of buildings and abundance of food, he rebuked him for vainglory[6].'

Soon after his arrival, Albert appointed lecturers at London and Canterbury[7], though he does not appear to have been a learned man himself. His connexion with Oxford was slight, and his acts as Provincial can hardly claim a place here. After remaining two years and a half in England, he went to Rome to take part in the proceedings against Elias[8]. On the deposition of the latter (May 15, 1239), Albert was elected Minister General. He died in the same or the following year[9] and was buried at Rome[10].

---

[1] Mon. Franc. I, 320 (letter 178); for the date see p. 139, n. 8.

[2] *Chronica Fratris Jordani* in Anal. Franc. I, 17, 18.

[3] Mon. Franc. I, 54; Wadding, Annales III, 22. The period of his ministry in Germany is given by Jordan, Anal. Franciscana I, 11, 16; the authority for his ministry in Spain is Chronica Anonyma, ibid. 284.

[4] Mon. Franc. I, 53, 54.

[5] Ibid. 55.   [6] Ibid. 60.

[7] Ibid. 38.   [8] Ibid. 58, 47.

[9] The list of General Ministers in the Reg. Fratrum Minorum Londoniae states: 'Frater Albertus Pisanus fuit iv^{us} generalis, et ministravit tribus annis; qui prius fuit minister in provincia Angliae.' Mon. Franc. I, 553. Eccleston mentions no space of time, but states that Haymo was made Minister of England in the same Chapter in which Albert was elected General, that he 'ministered one year in England, and was afterwards elected General' (ibid. 57, 59). There is no reason to suppose that Haymo resigned the Provincialate before he became General. The early dates in the Registrum are untrustworthy. Further, a note to the Phillipps MS. of Eccleston (fol. 76, *dorse*) says, in a list of General Ministers: 'quintus fuit frater Albertus de Pysis bonus et sanctus homo qui non vixit in ministerio nisi sex mensibus et migravit ad dominum.' The handwriting of the note is about contemporary with that of the text.

[10] Mon. Franc. I, 48, 58.

Ralph of Maidstone, bishop of Hereford 1234–1239, resigned his see in December, 1239, and was admitted into the Franciscan Order by Haymo[1]. He took this step in accordance with a vow, made perhaps before he became bishop[2]. It is uncertain at which convent he took the habit. Bartholomew of Pisa states that he helped with his own hands to build the church at Oxford[3]. It is not improbable that he was there for some time. He was a Master of Paris, noted for his learning, and was among the 'famous Englishmen' who left Paris owing to the disputes in 1229 and settled at Oxford on the invitation of Henry III[4]. According to a later addition in one of the MSS. of Eccleston's Chronicle, he lived five years after assuming the habit, staying for the most part in the convent of Gloucester[5]. The Dunstable Annals state that he was, for a time at any rate, rendered incapable by a fall from a rock, but whether this took place before or after he became a friar is not quite clear[6]. He died at Gloucester (c. 1245) and

'was buried in the choir of the brethren, in the presbytery, on the north side under an arch[7].'

A most interesting relic of the friar-bishop is now in the British Museum. Royal MS. 3 C. xi, a copy of the New Testament with gloss (sec. xiii), belonged to the Friars Minors of Canterbury,

'*ex dono Fratris Radulphi de Maydenestane, quondam Episcopi Herefordensis.*'

> He wrote a *Commentary on the Sentences* when he was Archdeacon of Chester (c. A.D. 1220). This is mentioned in a treatise on the Sacraments, '*secundum Mag. R. de Maidinstan archidiaconum Cestrensem super Sententias.*'
>
> MS. London: Gray's Inn, 14, f. 28-32 (sec. xiii).

William of Nottingham was marked out by nature for a Mendicant Friar.

'He told me,' writes Eccleston, 'that when he was living in his father's

---

[1] Mon. Franc. I, 58. Eccleston gives a somewhat confused account of the vision relating to the event; the vision seems to have appeared to Haymo. See Annals of Tewkesbury (R. S.), *sub anno* 1239; and Mon. Franc. I, 542 (A.D. 1239).

[2] M. Paris, Chron. Majora, IV, 163; Hist. Angl. II, 374: 'Magister Radulphus de Madenestane, vir quidem moralis et eliganter literatus, sed ordini Praedicatorum (!) fidei interpositione obligatus.' Barth. of Pisa, Lib. Conform. f. 82, 101 b; an account of the vision in consequence of which he became a Minorite.

[3] Liber Conform. f. 79 b.

[4] M. Paris, Chron. Majora, III, 168; cf. ibid. III, 305. Lyte, Oxford, p. 31.

[5] Mon. Franc. I, 59, note 1. This passage does not occur in the Phillipps MS. of Eccleston.

[6] Ann. Monast. III, pp. 148, 156.

[7] Mon. Franc. I, 59, n. 1.

house and some poor boys came begging alms, he gave them of his bread, and received the crust from them, because it seemed to him, that hard bread, which was asked for the love of God, was sweeter than the delicate bread which he ate and his companions; and so, to make their bread sweet like this, the little boys went and begged in their turn (*ab invicem*) for the love of God[1].'

William's brother, Augustine, was also a Minorite; he was first in the household of Innocent IV, accompanied the Patriarch of Antioch, the pope's nephew, to Syria, and at length became bishop of Laodicea[2]. William himself successfully championed the interests of his Order against the Dominicans at the Roman Curia[3]. At one period he lived for some time in the Franciscan convent at Rome, where, though (to quote his own words)

'the brethren had no pittance except chestnuts, he grew so fat that he often blushed[4].'

He acted as vicar for Friar Haymo in England (1239), and in 1240 was himself

'elected and confirmed Provincial Minister by those to whom the appointment had been entrusted[5].'

He had never held any subordinate office, such as that of custodian or warden[6]. He was a diligent student of the Scriptures, and seems to have attended Grostete's lectures at Oxford[7]. As minister, he was energetic in furthering the study of theology, and in developing the educational organization of the Franciscans in England[8]. During his ministry, the friary at Oxford was greatly enlarged[9]. Evidence of his popularity was given in the Chapter held at Oxford by the General Minister, John of Parma (c. 1248), when the friars unanimously refused to sanction his deposition[10]. He was 'absolved' from the ministry in the General Chapter of Metz, and sent on behalf of the Order to the Pope[11]. It was probably in this Chapter, that, with the assistance of John Kethene and Gregory de Bosellis, he carried a decree 'almost against the whole Chapter,'

'ut privilegium indultum a Domino Papa de recipienda pecunia per procuratores penitus destrueretur; et expositio Regulae secundum dominum

---

[1] Mon. Franc. I, 72; Phillipps MS. f. 80 b reads *pueri* for *plurimi* in line 3.
[2] Mon. Franc. I, 62.
[3] See Part I, chapter vi.
[4] 'Ut plurimum erubesceret,' Mon. Franc. I, 72.
[5] Ibid. 59.
[6] Ibid.
[7] Ibid. 69.
[8] Ibid. 38, 69, Part I, chapter v.
[9] Part I, chapter ii.
[10] Mon. Franc. I, 68.
[11] Mon. Franc. I, 70.

Innocentium, quantum ad ea in quibus laxior esset quam Gregoriana, suspenderetur[1].'

The cause of his deposition is unknown, but the event excited the displeasure of the English friars, who called a Provincial Chapter and unanimously re-elected him[2]. A letter from Adam Marsh, congratulating him on this second election and urging him not to decline the office is extant[3]. But William of Nottingham was already dead. When he reached Genoa on his mission to the Pope, his *socius*, Friar Richard, was struck down by the plague;

'while others fled, he remained to comfort his companion, and like him he was struck down and died[4].'

The date of the Chapter of Metz, and consequently of William's death, is not quite certain; it was probably in the spring or early summer of 1251[5]. A few extracts from the chronicle of Eccleston (who knew him personally) will illustrate the character of the man.

He sat very long in meditation after matins, and was unwilling to attend to confessions and consultations at night, as his predecessors had done.... Above all things, he was careful to avoid the vice of suspicion. Familiarities of great persons and of women he most studiously avoided, and, with wonderful magnanimity, thought nothing of incurring the anger of the powerful for the sake of justice. He used to say that great persons entrap those familiar with them by their advice, and women with their mendacity and malice turn the heads even of the devout by their flatteries. He studied with all diligence to restore the good name of those who were defamed, provided that he thought them penitent, and to comfort the hearts of the desolate, especially of those who held offices in the Order[6].

He represented the tendency to a less strict interpretation of the Rule in regard to money than had hitherto obtained in England, holding that—

'the friars might in a hundred cases lawfully contract debts, and might with their own hands dispense the money of others in alms. He said further that it was right after a visitation to amuse oneself a little in order to distract the mind from what one had heard[7].'

---

[1] Mon. Franc. I, 32. Eccleston says this took place in the Chapter of Genoa, i.e. either 1244, or 1254. But the letter of Innocent IV here referred to was published on Nov. 14, 1245; while W. of Nottingham and Elias, who was also mentioned (*ibid.*), were dead before 1254: see Ehrle, Archiv für Litt. u. Kirch. Gesch. Vol. VI, p. 31, n. 6. The declaration of the rule by Gregory IX (*Quo elongati*) is given in Wadding II,
244: that by Innocent IV, *ibid*. III, 129.

[2] Ibid. 70, 303.
[3] Ibid. 373.
[4] Ibid. 70.
[5] English Historical Review for Oct. 1891.
[6] Mon. Franc. I, 70.
[7] Ibid. 71. Cf. declaration of the Rule by Innocent IV, on debts; Wadding, III, 129–130.

The following story may be regarded as an instance of his cynicism or knowledge of human nature:—

'He used to narrate that St. Stephen, the founder of the Order of Grammont, placed a chest in a secret and safe place, and forbade anyone to go near it during his life. The brethren were very inquisitive, and after his death could not refrain from breaking it open, and they found only a piece of parchment with the words; Brother Stephen salutes his brethren and prays them to guard themselves from the laity. For just as you held the chest in honour, as long as you did not know what was in it, so they will hold you in honour [1].'

That the well-known *Commentary on the Gospels*, called also *Unum ex quatuor*, or *De concordia evangelistarum*, by Friar William of Nottingham, was by this William, and not by his namesake, the seventeenth provincial of the English Minorites [2], is proved by Eccleston's words (Mon. Franc. I, p. 70)—

'.... Verba Sancti Evangelii devotissime recolebat; unde et super unum ex quatuor Clementinis (Phillipps MS. f. 80 reads *Clementis*) canones perutiles compilavit, et expositionem quam idem Clemens fecit complete scribi in ordine procuravit.'

The commentary was founded on the work of Clement of Langthon [3], and the number of MSS. of it still in existence attest its popularity in the Middle Ages.

    The work comprised 12 parts. *Inc.* 'Da mihi intellectum.'

    MSS. Brit. Museum: Royal 4 E ii. (A.D. 1381); readers are asked to pray 'pro anima Fratris Willielmi de Notingham, qui studio laborioso predictam Expositionem ex variis compilavit.'

    Oxford:—Bodl.: Laud. Misc. 165 (sec. xiv ineuntis), Balliol Coll. 33 (sec. xiv exeuntis). Merton Coll. 156 and 157 (sec. xiv). Magdalen Coll. 160 (sec. xv). St. John's Coll. 2 (sec. xv).

    Cf. Merton Coll. 68, fol. 121 (sec. xv), 'Questiones quas movet Notyngham in scripto suo super evangelia extracte secundum ordinem alphabeticum per Mag. Joh. Wykham.' *Inc.* 'Abel. Queritur super:' Lincoln Coll. 78 (sec. xv), a similar work: *Inc.* 'Abraham. Queritur super illo dicto.'

Comment. in Longobardum, perhaps by the other W. of Nottingham.

    Mentioned in the Catalogue of Illustrious Franciscans (Leland, *Script.*).

A. of Hereford (c. 1248) was assigned by the Provincial to Adam Marsh as his secretary. Adam thought him too able a man to be kept

---

[1] Mon. Franc. I, 59.

[2] To whom it is attributed by the Reg. Frat. Minorum Lond. Mon. Franc. I, 538.

[3] Tanner, Bibl. 183. MSS. Oxford, St. John's Coll. 2, prologue; Mag. Coll. 160 *in calce* (see Coxe's Catalogues); and Brit. Mus. Royal MS. 4 E, ii.

in this subordinate position; his learning and eloquence marked him out for a teacher and preacher; many of those appointed by the Provincial Chapter to lecture on theology were far inferior to him. In addition to this his health would not stand the constant strain to which the secretary of the indefatigable doctor was necessarily subjected. Adam therefore requested the Provincial to send him to London to pursue his studies, as A. of Hereford himself desired [1].

Laurence de Sutthon was the friar whom Adam Marsh suggested to the Provincial as A. of Hereford's successor. A 'Friar Laurence' was with Adam in 1249, and the latter wrote to Thomas of York, probably after 1250:

'Friar Laurence sends you the books of the mother of philosophy (?) for which you sent [2].'

Hugo de Lyndun seems to have been a weak brother at Oxford —weak in mind and body—whom Adam Marsh took under his especial care (c. 1253) [3].

John of Beverley was a friar at Oxford when Martin was warden, and was known to Adam Marsh. Friar Thomas of York laboured for the salvation of the father of this J. of Beverley [4].

Gregory de Bosellis was the first lecturer to the friars at Leicester [5] (c. 1240 ?). He was at the General Chapter of Genoa (1244) or Metz when he supported W. of Nottingham, Minister of England [6]; and he was Vicar of the Province at the time of the same Minister's death [7]. He was with the Earl and Countess of Leicester in Gascony [8], and went to the papal court with the Archbishop of Canterbury in 1250 [9], when the rules of the Order against riding on horseback were relaxed in his favour [10]. He had studied at some University, probably at Oxford, and was capable of filling Adam Marsh's place as lecturer to the friars there, though it does not appear whether he ever actually did so [11].

Thomas of Maydenstan, an invalid novice at Oxford, c. 1253;

---

[1] Mon. Franc. I, 314-5.
[2] Ibid. 315, 374, 395.
[3] Ibid. 360, 364: 'Cui me spiritualiter inter mortales teneri fateor.'
[4] Ibid. 317, 393.
[5] Ibid. 38.
[6] Ibid. 32.
[7] Ibid. 70.
[8] Ibid. 307, 368, 380.
[9] Ibid.
[10] Ibid. 369. Cf. Bodl. Tanner MS. 223, f. 161, a license from Innocent IV to the Friars accompanying the Archbishop, 'equitare et subtelares et capas portare,' Aug. 2, 1249.
[11] Mon. Franc. I, 380.

Adam Marsh hearing a rumour that he was to be sent away from Oxford begged the Minister to let him remain,

'as it is believed that his removal would do injury to the souls of several persons of whose conversion no slight hope is entertained.'

The brethren at Oxford joined in the request[1].

Thomas Bachun of the Convent of Nottingham was recommended by Adam Marsh as a suitable person to act as private secretary or amanuensis to Friar Richard of Cornwall, when the latter was about to proceed to Paris, 1252. It is however uncertain whether he was appointed or whether he studied at Oxford[2].

Adam de Bechesoueres or **Hekeshovre**[3] occurs several times in Adam Marsh's letters as the chief physician among the early English friars. Thus at one time Adam writes to John of Stamford, custodian of Oxford, requesting him to allow a poor sick scholar named Ralph of Multon, a friend of the writer's, to consult Friar A. de Bechesoueres, who has already done him good. The famous Walter de Merton went to him once with a letter of introduction from Adam Marsh. He was wanted again at Oxford to attend Friar John of Reading, formerly Abbat of Osney. Adam Marsh recommended Grostete to consult him about his health. At another time we hear of him going to the General Minister in France, with a 'supplicatory letter' from Adam Marsh;

'he promised,' adds the latter in a letter to the English Provincial, 'to return to England soon and humbly submit in all things to the regular discipline.'

N. of Anivers, Anilyeres or **Aynelers,** a youth of ability, fair learning and great promise, was ordered by the Minister General to go to France, probably about the year 1248. Adam Marsh, anxious that the best should be done both for the young friar and the Order, after consultation with Peter of Tewkesbury, custodian of Oxford, obtained leave from the Provincials of England and France for him to stay for a year or two in England, the consent of the General being also secured:

'it is thought,' adds Adam in his letter to the Minister of France, 'that he will at present find the requisite helps to the successful study of letters more easily obtainable in England than anywhere else.'

N. de Anivers was therefore allowed to spend a year in theological

---

[1] Mon. Franc. I, 357–8.
[2] Ibid. 349.
[3] Ibid. 137, 320, 333, 388, 405.

study at Oxford, Cambridge or London. Adam Marsh maintained his interest in his welfare, and, after the year was over, requested the Minister of France to allow him to continue his studies in England up to the ensuing Pentecost: it is probable that he was a pupil of Adam's at Oxford[1].

William of Pokelington (Yorkshire) entered the Order about 1250 and made his profession at Oxford in 1251[2]. He was then a master. Shortly before this he had been ill and perhaps took the vows on his recovery[3]. He was an intimate friend of Adam Marsh and at one period acted as his secretary[4]. Adam employed him several times as messenger to Grostete[5], who had a high opinion of him and liked to have him as a companion[6].

Walter de Madele, Maddele or **Maddeley** studied in the Franciscan Convent at Oxford (c. 1235 seq.). While here, he ventured to disregard the custom which forbade the friars to wear shoes.

'It happened,' says Eccleston[7], 'that he found two shoes, and when he went to Matins, he put them on. He stood therefore at Matins, feeling unusually self-satisfied. But afterwards when he was in bed, he dreamt that he had to go through a dangerous pass between Oxford and Gloucester called "*boysalix*" (?), which was infested by robbers; and when he was descending into a deep valley, they rushed at him from both sides, shouting, "Kill him!" In great terror he said that he was a Friar Minor. "You lie," they cried, "for you do not go barefoot;" and when he put out his foot confidently, he found that he was wearing those same shoes: and starting in confusion from sleep, he threw the shoes into the middle of the courtyard.'

Walter was '*socius*' or secretary to Agnellus and was at Oxford at the time of the latter's death (1235)[8]. Later he was in Germany with Peter of Tewkesbury, minister of Cologne, and returned to England in 1249 with Friar Paulinus, perhaps a German, in obedience to Peter[9]. He enjoyed a considerable reputation as a theologian and was lecturer at a Franciscan Convent. Adam Marsh once sent for him to come and see him at Oxford.

'I conferred with him as you desired,' he writes to the Provincial[10], 'about investigating the meaning of Holy Scripture in the original books of

---

[1] Mon. Franc. I, Letters clxxv, ccxiv, ccxv. He may have been a Frenchman by birth.
[2] Ibid. 118.
[3] Ibid. 229.
[4] Ibid. 133.
[5] Ibid. 133, 137.
[6] Ibid. 103, 118.
[7] Ibid. I, 28.
[8] Ibid. 53.
[9] Ibid. 308.
[10] Ibid. 353 5.

the saints, and he professed himself very ready to do this or anything else which you thought fit to enjoin on him.'

This was not the only subject discussed at the interview. The English Minister suspected Walter of a desire to go abroad and of having obtained from the General the promise of a lectureship in some foreign convent or University. The Provincial had indeed just received an order from the General to send some English friars to teach at Paris, and perhaps Madele's name was mentioned. Madele however denied the imputation, and Adam recommended the Provincial to keep him in England, sending other friars to Paris, and to remedy his grievances. Though he had long taught theology with success, no competent provision had been made for him; he had not only to exhaust his mind by studies but also to wear out his body by writing daily with his own hand, as he lacked the 'great volumes and the assistance of companions,' which had been provided for his predecessors in the office. Eccleston refers to him as dead when he wrote his chronicle[1]. None of Madele's writings[2] have been preserved.

G. of St. Edmund: Adam Marsh wrote to the Provincial (W. of Nottingham) on behalf of Martin the warden and the other friars at Oxford, requesting him to order without delay

'that Friar G. de Sancto Eadmundo be restored to the convent of friars at Oxford[3].'

Thomas of Eccleston, the earliest historian of the Franciscan Order in England, was probably a native of Lancashire[4]. All that is known of him is contained in his Chronicle. He was an inmate of the London Convent when William of Nottingham was minister (1240–1250), and speaks from his own experience of the poverty and hard fare of the brethren there[5]. He was a student at Oxford in the lifetime of Grostete, whether before or after the latter became bishop is not clear[6]. He knew the earliest converts to the Order in England, and enjoyed the intimacy of William of Nottingham[7]. His history is dedicated to Friar Simon of Esseby—perhaps Ashby in Norfolk or Lincolnshire[8]. In the preface he states that he had been

---

[1] Mon. Franc. 28.
[2] Ibid. 355, 'in scriptis et eloquiis tam fratribus quam saecularibus utilis et acceptus.'
[3] Ibid. 364.
[4] Lewis, Topog. Dict. Cf. Mon. Franc. I, lxvi. The name Eccleston occurs in the title of the York MS., Mon. Franc. I, p. 1.
[5] Mon. Franc. I, p. 9; cf. 17.
[6] Ibid. 39.
[7] Ibid. 10, 13, 71, &c.
[8] Ibid. p. 1, p. lxvi, Jessopp, 'The Coming of the Friars.'

collecting and arranging materials for twenty-five years, and explains his object in writing.

'Every upright man ought to judge his life by the examples of better men, because examples strike home more directly than the words of reason.' Other Orders have lives of their holy brethren; this Chronicle is intended similarly to edify the Franciscans by giving them some account of those who have sacrificed their all to enter the Order and observe the Rule of St. Francis[1]. From this point of view, chronology was of little importance, and there is scarcely a date in the whole book. It is impossible to give the exact date at which the Chronicle was finished; the deaths of William of Nottingham and of Innocent IV are mentioned[2]; and the work was probably not completed before 1260. It is certainly the narrative of a contemporary, often of an eye-witness, and, apart from the manifest sincerity of the author, the accuracy of the details can in some instances be tested by independent and trustworthy authority. To take one example; Eccleston's account of the reception of the friars at Cambridge (pp. 17, 18) may be compared with the following entry in Close Roll 22 Hen. III, m. 12, (June 15 1238):

Rex ballivis suis de Cantebr' salutem. Sciatis quod concessimus fratribus Minoribus de Cantebr' domum illam cum pertinenciis in Cantebr' que fuit Magistri Benjamin Judei et quam prius vobis concesseramus ad Gayolam nostram (*or* vestram) inde faciendam, ad clausum domorum predictorum fratrum dilatandum, salvis domino feodi serviciis et redditibus ei inde debitis. Et idem vobis precipimus quod eisdem fratribus de domo predicta plenam saisinam habere faciatis.

The following MSS. of the Chronicle '*De adventu Fratrum Minorum in Angliam*' are extant, all dating from the early fourteenth century.

- (1) A mutilated MS. in the Chapter Library at York; Brewer's text for the earlier portion of the Chronicle is founded on this.
- (2) Brit. Mus.: Cotton Nero A ix was used by Brewer as the guide for the later part: this MS. begins with *Collatio IX* (i. e. *Collatio VIII* in the York MS.).
- (3) A fragment of the earlier portion of the Chronicle is contained in a MS. at Lamport House; this has been printed by Howlett in Mon. Franc. II; it supplies most of the chapters wanting in the Cottonian MS., of which it probably formed a part.
- (4) No. 3119 of the MSS. of Sir T. Phillipps (Thirlestaine House, Cheltenham), contains the whole Chronicle, though without many of the incidents which occur in the York and Cotton MSS. Neither Brewer nor Howlett knew of its existence. A short

---

[1] Mon. Franc. I, p. 1. [2] Ibid. 66, 70.

account of it will be found in 'The English Historical Review,' Oct. 1890, p. 754.

In the same volume of MSS. is the treatise *De impugnatione*, etc., printed in the Appendix C: Bale and Pits ascribe this to Eccleston, but without sufficient authority.

Roger Bacon is said on the authority of John Rous[1] to have been born at or near Ilchester in Dorsetshire. He came of a wealthy perhaps noble family; he speaks of one brother as rich, of another as a scholar. He was probably nephew of Robert Bacon the Dominican. Roger's family espoused the royal cause in the Barons' war and suffered great losses[2]. The year 1214 is usually given as the date of his birth. The date is an inference from the following passage written in 1267:

'I have laboured much at sciences and languages, and it is now forty years since I first learnt the alphabet; and I was always studious; and except for two of those forty years I have always been *in studio*[3].'

The last phrase probably means 'at a University' or some place of study. Boys of ten or twelve years frequently began their education at Oxford, and it is likely that Bacon went there at an early age[4]. Roger of Wendover relates that Friar Robert Bacon preached before the King at Oxford in 1233, and fearlessly rebuked him for listening to evil counsellors, especially Peter des Roches. Matthew Paris gives the story with the following addition:

'a clerk of the court of a pleasant wit, namely, Roger Bacun, ventured to make this joke: "My lord King, what is most harmful to men crossing a strait, or what makes them most afraid?" The King replied, "Those men know who occupy their business in great waters." "I will tell you," said the clerk, "*Petrae et Rupes*[5]."'

It cannot be regarded as certain that this Roger Bacon was the

---

[1] Hist. Regum Angl. pp. 29, 82. In John Argentein's *Loci communes*, written about 1476 (MS. Ashmole, 1437, p. 155) is the note: 'Hic Rogerus fuit filius Fugardi, et creditur quod erat Rogerus Baconus natus apud Witnam juxta Oxoniam.'

[2] Ibid. 82, 'de generosa prosapia.' Op. Ined. pp. 13, 16: 'Misi igitur fratri meo diviti in terra mea, qui ex parte regis consistens, cum matre mea et fratribus et tota familia exulavit, et pluries hostibus deprehensus se redemit pecunia; et ideo destructus et depauperatus, non potuit me juvare, nec etiam usque ad hunc diem habui responsum ab eo.' Cf. ibid. p. 10.

[3] Op. Ined. p. 65.

[4] The report that he was educated at Brasenose Hall is merely a tradition founded on a foolish legend. Historical fictions die hard. In 1889, Mr. W. L. Courtney writes in the *Fortnightly Review*, Vol. XLVI, p. 255, R. Bacon 'seems to have been educated at Brasenose College in Oxford, although Merton College has also laid claim to the honour of his youthful learning.' Merton College was not founded till Roger was advanced in years; Brasenose College was founded more than two centuries after his death.

[5] Chron. Majora, IV, 244-5.

famous friar. The name was not uncommon; e.g. a Roger Bacon, a Thomas Bacon, and a Peter Bacon occur in Pat. Roll 3 Edw I. On the other hand Roger was certainly in Oxford in or before this year. He states that St. Edmund, Archbishop of Canterbury, lectured at Oxford in his time, i.e. Edmund Riche who became Archbishop in 1233[1]. At this period too, Roger attended Grostete's lectures and made the acquaintance of Adam Marsh, for both of whom he always retained the greatest admiration. He found in them that sympathy with and understanding of his experimental method, which were denied him in later life[2]. It was doubtless his connexion with these men that led Roger to enter the Franciscan Order. When or where this took place is unknown: perhaps at Oxford before the death of Grostete. He had clearly reached years of discretion when he took the step. This may be inferred from his denunciation of those who entered the Orders as boys and begun the study of theology before they had been grounded in philosophy[3]. It is also implied in such passages as these:

'When I was in another state, I wrote nothing on philosophy.' 'Men used to wonder before I became a friar that I lived owing to such excessive labour[4].'

He began his studies on positive science before 1250[5], and had by 1267 spent more than 2,000 *librae*[6].

'on secret books and various experiments and languages and instruments and tables.'

It is not necessary to assume that this sum was expended before he joined the Franciscan Order; he could, and undoubtedly did, obtain money by begging to carry on his experiments[7]. Roger left Oxford for Paris some time before 1245; he states that he had seen Alexander of Hales with his own eyes[8], and he heard William of Auvergne

---

[1] Comp. Stud. Theol. Royal MS. 7, f. vii, f. 154 (quoted in Charles, p. 412; Brewer, p. lv). The origin of the tradition that Roger wrote a life of St. Edmund seems to be a passage in M. Paris, Chron. Maj. V, 369, where the historian says that he was supplied with details for the life of St. Edmund by *Robert* Bacon. The confusion between the two Bacons is continually recurring. Even in Luard's edition of Grostete's Letters there is an unfortunate misprint; on p. 65 Roger Bacon should be Robert.

[2] Op. Ined. pp. 70, 75, 82, 88, 91, 186–7, 329, 428, 472, 474.

[3] Ibid. 327, 425.

[4] Ibid. 13, 65.

[5] Ibid. 59; he writes in 1267, 'Nam per viginti annos quibus specialiter laboravi in studio sapientiae, neglecto sensu vulgi,' &c.

[6] Ibid.: this seems almost incredible; the Parisian *libra* at this time appears, from Paucton and Le Blanc, to have been a sum of 20 *solidi*, not (as Plumptre asserts) 'a silver coin about the size of the more modern franc.'

[7] See Part I, chapter vii.

[8] Op. Ined. 325. A. of Hales died 1245.

dispute on the *Intellectus Agens* before the whole University: William died in 1248[1]. Roger was in France in 1250 when he saw the chief of the Pastoureaux, and remarked that

'he carried in his hand something as though it were sacred, as a man carries relics[2].'

He is said by Rous to have been made D.D. of Paris and to have been incorporated as D.D. at Oxford[3]. When he returned to Oxford is unknown; probably soon after 1250. He must have lectured at this time; he won some fame, as he says himself[4], but without doubt made many enemies. About the year 1257 or 1258—when Adam Marsh could no longer protect his great pupil—Roger was exiled from England and kept under strict supervision in Paris for ten years[5]. In 1263 he wrote an astronomical treatise called *Computus Naturalium*[6]. Soon after this, a clerk named Raymund of Laon mentioned Bacon's name to the Cardinal Bishop of Sabina and roused the latter's interest in his discoveries[7]. Bacon sent a letter in reply to the Cardinal's communication: this has not been preserved. In 1265 the Cardinal became Pope Clement IV. On 22nd of June 1266, Clement wrote requesting Roger to send him a fair copy of the work which Raymond had mentioned, setting forth the remedies he proposed, '*circa illa, quae nuper occasione tanti discriminis intimasti;*' the friar was to do this, in spite of any constitution of his Order to the contrary, secretly and without delay[8]. The Pope's supposition that the work was already written was erroneous;

'for,' writes Roger[9], 'whilst I was in a different state of life, I had written nothing on science; nor in my present condition had I ever been required to do so by my superiors; nay, a strict prohibition has been passed to the contrary, under penalty of forfeiture of the book, and many

---

[1] Charles, p. 10; Op. Ined. p. 74.
[2] Opus Majus, p. 190 (edition of 1750).
[3] Hist. Reg. Angl. p. 82.
[4] Op. Ined. p. 7, 'famam studii quam retroactis temporibus obtinui.' His name does not occur in the list of masters of the Friars Minors at Oxford; a note appended to that list says, that 'according to other chronicles the fourth master is not mentioned here nor have I elsewhere found his name.' Mon. Franc. I, 552; Phillipps MS. 3119, fol. 76. May not this have been Roger Bacon? That his name should be suppressed is not to be wondered at. (The Reg. of Friars Minors at London adds after the name of John of Parma, General Minister, 1247-1256: 'Hic etiam scripsit fratri Rogero Bakon tractatum qui incipit, "Innominato magistro."' This treatise usually ascribed to Bonaventura is really addressed to a secular.)
[5] Op. Ined. p. 7; Charles, 24-25.
[6] See below.
[7] Op. Ined. p. xiv, seq.
[8] Ibid. p. 1.
[9] Ibid. p. 13.

days' fasting on bread and water, if any book written by us (i.e. the Franciscans) should be communicated to strangers[1].'

However, although the book was not yet written, and notwithstanding endless difficulties, want of money, want of mathematical and other instruments and tables, the restrictions of the Rule, jealousy of his superiors and brethren who, he says,

'kept me on bread and water, suffering no one to have access to me, fearful lest my writings should be divulged to any other than the Pope and themselves[2]'—

the Opus Majus, the Opus Minus, and the Opus Tertium, were sent to the Pope within fifteen or eighteen months after the arrival of the papal mandate[3]. 'Such a feat' says Brewer, 'is unparalleled in the annals of literature.' The Pope probably used his influence in behalf of Roger, as the latter seems to have returned to England about this time and to have been freed from annoyance[4]. The works sent to Clement he regarded merely as handbooks; at the same time that he was writing them, he was engaged on a larger work which was to embrace the whole range of sciences as then understood[5]. He was working at this in 1271[6]. His attacks on all classes, including his own Order, became even more violent than hitherto. In 1277 and 1278 synods were held at Paris and Oxford to condemn erroneous doctrines. The repressive movement extended to the Franciscans; in 1278, Jerome of Ascoli, the Minister General, held a Chapter at Paris, and among other friars Roger Bacon was condemned '*propter quasdam novitates*[7].' He is believed to have remained in prison for fourteen years. Jerome of Ascoli, who became Pope Nicholas IV in 1288, died in 1292. Raymond Gaufredi, a man of liberal views, was elected General in 1289, and released many friars who had been imprisoned for their opinions by his predecessors. In 1292 he held a General Chapter at Paris, and it is probable that among the friars here set free was Roger Bacon[8].

---

[1] This statute was included in the *Constitutiones Generales*, passed in the General Chapter of Narbonne, 1260; the fast imposed was of three days' duration; Archiv f. L. u. K. Gesch. d. Mittelalters, Vol. VI, p. 110.

[2] Op. Ined. p. xciv, from Wood's *Antiquitates* (said to be taken from the *Opus Minus*).

[3] Op. Ined. p. xlvi. Bacon's difficulties are fully described in Brewer's preface.

[4] Charles, p. 35.

[5] See below; and Brewer, Op. Ined. xlviii, seq.

[6] Op. Ined. p. lv.

[7] Charles, 36-7; Wadding, II, 449. No record or contemporary account of the trial remains.

[8] This tradition receives some support from a note appended to the *Verbum abbreviatum* of Raymund Gaufredi, Sloane MS. 276 (sec. xiv), printed in *Sanioris Medicinae . . . de arte chymiae*,

It is certain that the last work of Roger's of which we have any notice was written in 1292[1]. The date usually assigned for his death (1294) is a pure conjecture[2]. John Rous says that he was buried among the Friars Minors at Oxford[3].

Such then is the chronological outline of his life, as far as it can be ascertained. A list of his works will be more useful than a short account of his character or philosophy.

Roger Bacon's Works were neglected and regarded with a pious horror in the Middle Ages[4]. The result is that many of those which have survived at all have reached us in a fragmentary state. 'It is easier,' said Leland, 'to collect the leaves of the Sibyl than the titles of the works written by Roger Bacon.' The difficulty has to a considerable extent been removed by Mr. Brewer's valuable preface to the *Opera Inedita*, and by the labours of M. Charles. The following account of Roger Bacon's works is based chiefly on these two writers. Some additions have been made and some rearrangement attempted.

Miscellaneous works, lectures, &c., probably early:—

Computus naturalium, an astronomical treatise, is the earliest work of Bacon's to which a date can be assigned; it was written A.D. 1263-4. *Inc.* 'Omnia tempus habent.'

MSS. British Museum: Royal 7 F viii. fol. 99-191 (sec. xiii).
Oxford: University College, 48.
Douai 691, § 2.
Summary printed by Charles, *Roger Bacon*, pp. 355-8.

&c., Frankfurt, 1603, p. 285: 'Et ipse Rogerus propter istud opus ex praecepto dicti Reymundi a fratribus ejusdem ordinis erat captus et imprisonatus. Sed Reymundus exsolvit Rogerum a carcere quia docuit eum istud opus.' Cf. ibid. p. 265, and Sloane MS. 692, f. 46.

[1] Namely, *Compendium studii theologiae*.

[2] In Royal MS. 13 C i, fol. 152, is the following note in a hand of the 15th or 16th century: 'Anno Christi 1292 in festo Sancti Barnabe (June 11) obiit Rogerus Bacon professor theologie et quasi eruditus ut magister in octo scienciis liberalibus ubi alii clerici non posuerunt preter vii sciencie' ('scie' in MS.).

[3] Hist. Reg. Angl. p. 29.

[4] John Twyne says that the friars at Oxford fastened all his works with long nails to the shelves of their library and let them rot there. Jebb reasonably calls the accuracy of this statement in question, Op. Majus, p. xi (ed. 1750). Bacon's influence however on his age was slight: 'not a doctor of the 13th or 14th century,' says Charles, p. 42, 'quotes Bacon; not one combats or approves his opinions.' In an anonymous treatise, *De recuperatione sanctae Terrae*, addressed to Edward III, c. 1370, the author recommends the study of mathematics, 'propter plures earum utilitates, praecipue tactas in libello super utilitatibus hujusmodi confecto per fratrem Rogerum Bacon de ordine Minorum;' printed in Bongars, Orientalis Hist. Tom. Secund. (1611), p. 339. W. Woodford refers to his 'curious book,' *De retardatione senectutis*, Brown, Fasc. Rerum, Vol. I, p. 197. Some of his contemporaries, such as Bungay, Peckham, William de Mara, seem to have been more generally influenced by him

De termino Paschali, an earlier work, to which Bacon refers in the *Computus naturalium*; (Charles, p. 78).

Questions on Aristotle's physics.

MS. Amiens 406, f. 1-25; cf. MS. Bodl. Digby 150, fol. 42 (sec. xiii), 'Summa Baconis.'

Quaestiones super librum physicorum a magistro dicto Bacon.

MS. Amiens 406, fol. 26-73.

De vegetabilibus (gloss on this work then attributed to Aristotle).

MS. Amiens 406 (intercalated in the preceding work).

In Aristotelis Metaphysica.

MS. Amiens 406, fol. 74.

Tractatus ad declaranda quaedam obscure dicta in libro Secreti Secretorum Aristotelis. Inc. 'Propter multa in hoc libro contenta qui liber dicitur Secretum Secretorum Aristotelis sive liber de regimine principum.'

MS. Bodl.: Tanner 116, fol. 1 (sec. xiii exeuntis); the same MS. fol. 16, contains Aristotle's supposititious *Secretum Secretorum* 'cum glossa interlineari et notis Rogeri Bacon.'

Questiones naturales mathematice astronomice, &c. 'Expliciunt reprobationes Rogeri Baconis.'

MS. Paris:—Bibl. Nat. 16089, f. 93 (sec. xiii-xiv).

Bacon in Meteora. Inc. 'Cum ad noticiam impressionum habendam.'

MS. Bodleian: Digby 190, fol. 38 (sec. xiv ineuntis).

Processus fratris Rogeri Bacon . . . de invencione cogitacionis (astrological fragment). *Inc.* 'Notandum quod in omni judicio quatuor sunt inquirenda, scil. natura planetae.'

MS. Bodl.: Digby 72, fol. 49 b, 50 (sec. xiv-xv).

De somno et vigilia.

MSS. Bodl.: Digby 190, f. 77: *Inc.* 'De somno et vigilia pertractantes, Perypateticorum sentenciam potissime sequemur.'

Cambridge:—Publ. Library Ii, vi. 5, fol. 85 b-88 (sec. xiii). *Inc.* 'Sompnus ergo et vigilia describuntur multis modis.'

Logic :—

Summulae Dialectices, an elementary treatise on logic, characterised by Charles, who expresses a doubt as to its authenticity, as very dry, unimportant, and intended for lecturing purposes. *Inc.* 'Introductio est brevis et apta demonstratio.' 'Expliciunt sumule magistri Roberti (*sic*) Baccun.'

MS. Bodl.: Digby 205, f. 48 (sec. xiv).

Syncategoremata. Inc. 'Partium orationis quaedam sunt declinabiles.'

MS. Bodl.: Digby 204, fol. 88 (sec. xiv).

Summa de sophismatibus et distinctionibus. Inc. 'Potest queri de difficultatibus accidentibus.'

MS. Bodl.: Digby 67, fol. 117 (sec. xiii); fragment.

Tractatus de signis logicalibus. Inc. 'Signum est in predicamento relationis.'

MS. Bodl.: Digby 55, fol. 228 (sec. xiii).

Opus Majus, written A.D. 1266–1267; 7 parts. *Inc.* 'Sapientiae perfecta consideratio consistit in duobus.'

MSS. of the whole work: Oxford:—Bodl. Digby 235 (sec. xv and xiv).

    Dublin:—Trinity Coll. 81 (=221); a transcript of this is in Trinity Coll. Cambridge.

    Paris:—Bibl. Mazarine 3488 (sec. xviii).

    Rome:—Vatican 4086 (Montfaucon's Catal. p. 114), 'Rogerii Baconi causae universales in septem partes distinctae'; probably the *Opus Majus*.

Parts I–VI edited by Jebb, 1733: reprinted at Venice 1750.

The parts often occur separately.

I. *On the four causes of human ignorance:* authority, custom, popular opinion, and the pride of supposed knowledge.

    MS. Brit. Museum: Cott. Jul. F vii. fol. 186.

II. *On the causes of perfect wisdom in Holy Scripture*, or, *On the dignity of philosophy*.

III. *On the usefulness of grammar*.

    This part, Charles points out (p. 62), is not perfect in Jebb's edition: see *Opus Tertium*, cap. XXVI, XXVII.

IV. *On the usefulness of mathematics*.

    MSS. London:—British Museum: Cotton, Tib. C. V. (sec. xiv); Julius D. V. 'De utilitate scientiarum'; Julius F vii. fol. 178 (sec. xv), 'Declaratio effectus verae mathematicae.' And fol. 180, 'De moribus hominum secundum complexiones et constellationes.'

    Royal 7 F vii, p. 1 (sec. xiii), 'Pars quarta compendii studii theologiae'; pp. 82–125, 'Descriptiones locorum'; pp. 133–140, 'De utilitate astronomiae,' or 'Tractatus de corporibus coelestibus.'

    Sloane 2629, f. 17, 'De utilitate astronomiae.'

    Also Lambeth Palace Library 200 (sec. xv), 'De arte mathematica.'

    Oxford:—Bodl. E Musaeo 155, p. 185 (sec. xv ineuntis), 'Pars quarta in qua ostendit potestatem mathematicae in scientiis et rebus et occupationibus hujus mundi.' Univ. Coll. 49 (sec. xvii).

Paris:—Bibl. Nat. 7455 A (sec. xv), 'De utilitatibus scientiae mathematicae verae.'

Cf. Bodl.: Digby 218, f. 98 (sec. xiii-xiv).

Printed, except the last two chapters, by Combach, Frankfurt 1614, under the title: 'Specula Mathematica in quibus de specierum multiplicatione... agitur,' &c.

V. *Perspective and Optics.*

MSS. London:—Brit. Mus.: Royal 7 F vii. p. 125 (sec. xiii), 'De visu et speculis'; 7 F viii. f. 47 (sec. xiii), 'Perspectiva quedam singularis,' 'Perspectiva R. Bacon, liber secundus.'

Sloane 2156, f. 1 (A.D. 1428), and 2542 (sec. xv): Addit. 8786, f. 84, 'Incipit tractatus de modis videndi.'

Oxford:—Bodl. Digby 77 (sec. xiv) and 91 (sec. xvi).

Paris:—Bibl. Nat. 2598, f. 57 (sec. xv).

Venice: —St. Mark, Classis XI, Cod. 10 (sec. xiv).

Rome:—Vatican (Cod. Lat.) 828, f. 49 (A.D. 1349).

Printed by Combach, Frankfurt 1614, under the title, 'Rogerii Baconis Angli... Perspectiva.'

VI. *Experimental Science.*

MSS. Brit. Mus.: Sloane 2629 (sec. xvi), extracts.

Oxford:—Bodl.: Digby 235, p. 389; Canon. Misc, 334, fol. 53, 'Alius tractatus ejusdem Fratris Rogeri extractus de sexta parte compendii studii theologiae.' Univ. Coll. 49.

VII. *Moral Philosophy. Inc.* 'Manifestavi in precedentibus quod cognitio linguarum.'

MSS. Brit. Mus.: Royal 8 F ii. f. 167-179 (sec. xv), three parts out of six.

Bodl.: Digby 235, p. 421 [1].

Omitted in Jebb's edition: extracts printed by Charles, pp. 339-348. Printed at Dublin 1860 (?) [2].

Opus Minus, written in 1266-7, was mainly an abstract of the *Opus Majus* with some additions on the state of scholasticism, on alchemy practical and speculative, and on astronomy. Charles gives the following description of it. It consisted of 6 parts:

i. Introduction or dedicatory letter; ii. Practical alchemy; iii. Explanation of the *Opus Majus*; the order of the sciences inverted, i. e. they were arranged according to their dignity, moral philosophy first; iv. Treatise on the seven sins of Theology; v. Speculative alchemy, or, *De rerum generationibus* (see below); vi. *De Coelestibus.*

Of this work only the fragment edited by Brewer (*Opera Ined.*

---

[1] Cf. MS. Sloane 2629, f. 54 b; *inc.* 'Moralis philosophia est finis omnium Scientiarum aliarum'; only a few lines.

[2] Charles, Roger Bacon, p. 62, n. 7: I have not seen this edition and can get no information about it.

311–390) from MS. Bodl. Digby 218, has been discovered. This includes a few pages of Part ii., all of iii., most of iv., and part of v. Wood quotes a passage from the *Opus Minus* which does not occur in this fragment (*Opera Ined.* xciv. n. 1). From this it has been assumed that he had access to a MS. of the *Opus Minus* now lost; but the passage is quoted by Leland, and probably copied from him by Wood. It may perhaps occur in some other work of Bacon's; thus the passage quoted in *Op. Ined.* pp. xcvii–xcviii, from which Brewer argues that 'Wood must have seen some other copy of the *Opus Minus* not now discoverable,' occurs in Brewer's edition of the *Opus Tert.* pp. 272–3.

Part of the blank on p. 375 is to be filled up from the *Opus Majus, Pars VI, Exemplum II*, where the passage '*Est autem—curabit et*' occurs, word for word. How much of the *Opus Majus* was here inserted is doubtful; probably to the end of *Exemplum II*. Thus MS. Bodl. Canonic. Miscell. 334, f. 53, begins with the words, '*Corpora vero Adae et Evae,*' *Opus Minus*, p. 373, and leaves off with the words, '*et alibi multis modis,*' which occur at the end of *Opus Majus, Pars VI, Exemp. II*.

The last part of the *Opus Minus* is wholly wanting in Brewer's edition. The subject of this part may be gathered from Bacon's words in *Opus Tert.*, cap. xxvi (p. 96):

'Nunc igitur tangam aliquas radices circa haec quas diligentius exposui in Secundo Opere, ubi de coelestibus egi': and (p. 99) 'Sed in Opere Minore ubi de coelestibus tractavi, exposui magis ista.'

In Digby MS. 76, fol. 36 seq. (sec. xiii) is a treatise on this subject, forming part of the *Physics* in the great *Compendium Philosophiae* (see below). It is not improbable, that, before being incorporated in this larger work, it formed part of the *Opus Minus* sent to the Pope; on fol. 42 are the words:

'et est nunc temporis scilicet anno domini 1266.'

Opus Tertium, written in 1267 (see *Opera Ined.* p. 277), 75 chapters.
  MSS. London:—Brit. Mus: Cotton Tiberius C. V. (sec. xiv); also Lambeth Palace Library, 200 (chapters 1–45).
    Oxford:—Bodl. E Musaeo 155 (sec. xv ineuntis); and Univ. Coll. 49 (A.D. 1617).
    Cambridge:—Trinity College, MS. Gale (transcript of the Cotton MS.).
    Douai, 691 (sec. xvii), wanting chapters 38–52: this MS. has been described by Victor Cousin, *Journal des Savants* for 1848 (5 articles).
  Printed in Bacon's *Opera Inedita* (Rolls Series), pp. 3–310.

Charles has been misled by a passage in the work called '*Communia Naturalium*' into thinking that this latter formed part of the *Opus Tertium*; Charles, *R. Bacon*, pp. 65, 83-4; his description of *Opus Tertium* is consequently erroneous. The passage is from the Mazarine MS. of the *Communia Naturalium* (i.e. No. 3576), fol. 85:

'Quod est improbatum in secunda parte primi operis, deinde in hoc tertio opere explanavi hoc et solvi objectiones.'

These words refer to Bacon's doctrine that the *intellectus agens* is not part of the soul, but God and angels. This is insisted on in the *Opus Tertium*, cap. xxiii, and it is not likely that Bacon would do more than refer to it again casually in the course of the same work. The relation of the *Opus Tertium* to the *Commun. Nat.* is probably as follows: the latter was written or begun first. Bacon repeatedly mentions that he was, while writing his three *Opera* for the Pope, engaged on a larger work, *Scriptum Principale*, which he did not send to Clement[1]. Much of this larger work naturally found its way, probably in a summarised form, into the *Opus Tertium* as we know it, the treatise actually sent to the Pope.

Tractatus de multiplicatione specierum, or, *De generatione specierum et multiplicatione et corruptione earum*, is inserted by Jebb in the *Opus Majus*, pp. 358-445, between Part v and Part vi. The subject is however discussed in Part iv, which is often quoted or referred to in Part v. In the *De multiplicatione*, &c. (p. 368), are the words:

Ut tactum est in communibus naturalium.

Again (p. 358):

Recolendum est igitur quod in tertia parte hujus operis tactum est, quod essentia, substantia, natura, potestas, potentia, virtus, vis, significant eandem rem, sed differunt sola comparatione.

There is nothing about this in the third part of the *Opus Majus*; but it is found in the *Communia Naturalium*. The treatise *De multiplicatione specierum* was therefore part of a work of which the *Communia Naturalium* formed the third part. This large work was according to Jebb, the *Opus Minus*; according to Charles, the *Opus Tertium*[2]; according to Brewer, the encyclopaedic *Compendium*

---

[1] Op. Ined. 60. 'Patet igitur quod scriptum principale non potui mittere.'

[2] Charles is somewhat inconsistent; in spite of Bacon's words, 'tertia parte hujus operis,' he refers the two treatises to separate works — the *Communia Naturalium* to the *Opus Tertium*, the *De multiplicatione* (rightly) to the fourth part of the *Compendium Philosophiae* (pp. 61, 89).

Philosophiae. Brewer is no doubt right; the *De multiplicatione* was intended as a sub-section of the great treatise on Physics.

How then did the treatise come to be regarded as part of the *Opus Majus*, and to be inserted in the MSS. of that work? There can be little doubt that it was, in its original form, the treatise on rays sent to the Pope with the *Opus Majus*, but as a separate work (*Opera Ined.* pp. 227, 230). The references to the *Communia Naturalium* are not inconsistent with this hypothesis: (1) the treatise on rays does not seem to have been written specially for the Pope, and consequently references to works which he could not know were not unnatural; (2) Bacon had already begun the encyclopaedic work, but found it impossible to get it finished or send it to the Pope (*Opera Inedita,* pp. 60, 315).

Inc. 'Primum igitur capitulum circa influentiam agentis habet tres veritates.'

> MSS. London :—Brit. Mus.: Royal 7 F viii. f. 13 ; *inc.* 'Postquam habitum,' &c. Addit. 8786, fol. 20 b : *inc.* 'Postquam habitum est de principiis rerum naturalium ': Sloane 2156, f. 40 (A.D. 1428) ; *inc.* 'Postquam,' &c.
> Oxford :—Bodl. Digby 235, p. 305 (inserted in the *Opus Majus*).
> Dublin :—Trinity Coll. 81 (in the *Opus Majus*).
> Paris :—Bibl. Nat. 2598 (sec. xv): *inc.* 'Postquam,' &c.
> Bruges, 490 (sec. xiii), called *Philosophia Baconis.*

Printed in Jebb.

De speculis (on burning mirrors). *Inc.* 'Ex concavis speculis ad solem positis ignis accenditur.

> MS. Oxford :—Bodl. Ashmole, 440 (sec. xvi); cf. Digby 71.

Printed at Frankfurt 1614, in Combach's *Specula Mathematica,* p. 168.

Speculi Abnukefi compositio secundum Rogerium Bacon. Inc. 'Quia universorum quos de speculis ad datam distanciam.'

> MS. Bodl.: Canonic. Misc. 408, fol. 48.
> Cf. Brit. Mus. Cott. Vesp. A ii. f. 140.

Compendium Philosophiae, an encyclopaedic work, which if completed would have formed a kind of revised and enlarged edition of the *Opus Majus, Opus Minus,* and *Opus Tertium.* In the *Communia Naturalium,* cap. i. (MS. Bodl. Digby 70) Bacon gives a sketch of his plan. The work was to consist of four volumes, and to treat of six branches of knowledge, viz., vol. i. Grammar and Logic; vol. ii. Mathematics; vol. iii. Physics; vol. iv. Metaphysics and Morals. This *Compendium* seems to have been known also as *Liber sex scientiarum.* The latter title is found in the collection printed at Frankfurt in 1603[1] in MSS. Bodl. Canonic. Misc. No. 334, fol. 49 b; *ibid.*, No. 480, fol. 33; and E. Musaeo 155, p. 689. In each of these MSS. the same passage is quoted, as follows:

Dicta fratris Rogerii Bacon in libro sex scienciarum in 3° gradu sapiencie, ubi loquitur de bono corporis et de bono fortune et de bono et honestate morum. (*Inc.*) In debito regimine corporis et prolongatione vite ad ultimos terminos naturales . . . miranda potestas astronomie alkimie et perspective et scienciarum experimentalium. Sciendum igitur est pro bono corporis quod homo fuit immortalis naturaliter. . . . . . (*Expl.*) ut fiant sublimes operaciones et utilissime in hoc mundo, etc.

Charles identifies the *Liber sex scientiarum* with the *Opus Minus*; but this passage does not occur in the extant portion of the *Opus Minus* which deals with the same subject and expresses the same ideas (*Opera Ined.*, p. 370 seq.). It seems probable therefore that this passage is an extract from the section on Alchemy in vol. iii. of the *Compendium Philosophiae*.

Vol. I. *Grammar and Logic.* A portion of this has been edited by Brewer, *Opera Ined.*, pp. 393–519, under the title *Compendium Studii Philosophiae*. It was written in 1271, and contains an introduction on the value of knowledge and the impediments to it, and the beginning of a treatise on grammar.

MS. Cott. Tiberius C. V. (sec. xiv).

Two other treatises on grammar by Roger Bacon are extant, and probably formed part of the *Comp. Phil.*[2]:

(1) *Inc.* 'Primus hic liber voluminis grammatici circa linguas alias a Latino. . . . Manifestata laude et declarata utilitate cognitionis grammatice' (chiefly on Greek grammar).

MSS. Brit. Museum: Cotton Jul. F viii. f. 175 (sec. xv), a fragment.
Oxford:—Corpus Christi Coll. 148 (sec. xv); Univ. Coll. 47 (sec. xvii).
Douai, 691 § 1 (sec. xvii), copied from Univ. Coll. MS. 47.

(2) *Inc.* 'Oratio grammatica autem fit mediante verbo.' 'Explicit summa de grammatica magistri Rogeri Bacon.'

MS. Cambridge:—Peterhouse, 1, 9, 5, James 3 (sec. xiv).

Vol. II. *Mathematics*; 6 books:

i. *Communia mathematicae*; ii–vi. Special branches of mathematics.

---

[1] *Sanioris medicinae*, p. 7, where a passage on alchemy is quoted.

[2] Digby MS. 55 contains a treatise on grammar falsely attributed to Bacon; *inc.* 'Scientia est ordinatio depicta in anima.' See Opera Ined. p. lxv.

Liber i. *Inc.* 'Hic incipit volumen verae mathematicae habens sex libros. Primus est de communibus mathematicae, et habet tres partes principales.'

> MSS. British Museum: Sloane 2156, f. 74–97 (sec. xv), ending in the second part of the first book.
> Bodl.: Digby 76, fol. 48 (sec. xiii), containing the remainder of the first book (?). *Inc.* 'Mathematica utitur tantum parte.'

Libri ii–vi. An extant fragment of a commentary on Euclid by Bacon may have belonged to this part; in *De Coelestibus* (*Comp. Phil.* vol. iii.) he often refers to his commentary on the Elements of Euclid (Charles, p. 85).

> MS. Digby 76, f. 77–8 (sec. xiii).

A treatise, *De laudibus mathematicae*, expressing the same ideas as Part iv. of the *Opus Majus*, may have been intended as an introduction to this volume.

> MS. Royal 7 F vii. fol. 141–152: cf. Digby 218, f. 98.

Vol. III. *Physics.* First came general physics (1 book), then particular sciences (3 books).

Liber i. *Communia Naturalium*, divided into 4 parts.

> MSS. Brit. Mus.: Royal 7 F vii. f. 84 (sec. xiii), *Liber Naturalium*. 'Hoc est volumen naturalis philosophiae in quo traditur scientia rerum naturalium, secundum potestatem octo scientiarum naturalium quae enumerantur in secundo capitulo; et habet hoc volumen quatuor libros principales, Primum scilicet *De communibus ad omnia naturalia*; secundum *De Coelestibus*; tertium *De Elementis, mixtis, inanimatis*; quartum *De vegetabilibus et generabilibus.*' (This MS. ends at the third part of the first book).
> Bodl.: Digby 70 (sec. xiv). *Communia Naturalium. Inc.* 'Postquam tradidi grammaticam' [Desinit ad init. cap. vii].
> Cf. Digby 190, f. 29 (sec. xiv ineuntis). *De principiis naturae*; beginning illegible.
> Paris:—Bibl. Mazarine 3576; olim 1271, f. 1–90 (sec. xiv). 'Incipit liber primus Communium naturalium Fratris Rogeri Bacon, habens quatuor partes principales, quarum prima habet distinctiones quatuor. Prima distinctio est de communibus ad omnia naturalia et habet capitula quatuor. Capitulum primum de ordine scientiae naturalis ad alias. (*Inc.*) Postquam tradidi grammaticam secundum linguas diversas.'

Extracts printed by Charles, pp. 369–391.

Libri ii, iii, iv. The special natural sciences, according to the Royal MS. just quoted, were treated in three books. They were seven[1] in number, as Bacon enumerates them in the second chapter of the first part of the *Communia Naturalium*.

'Praeter scientiam communem naturalibus, sunt septem speciales, videlicet perspectiva, astronomia judiciaria et operativa, scientia ponderum de gravibus et levibus, alkimia, agricultura, medicina, scientia experimentalis.'

Liber ii. (1) *Optics* or *Perspective* (a version of the *De multiplicatione specierum*). *Inc.* 'Ostensum quippe in principio hujus Compendii Philosophiae.'

MSS. Brit. Mus: Royal 7 F vii. p. 221 (sec. xiii), fragment, called 'Quinta pars Compendii theologiae'; and Addit. 8786, fol. 2 (fragment).

[Cf. Bodl. Digby 183, fol. 49 (sec. xiv) ?]

See the references under *Tract. de multiplicatione specierum.*

(2) *Astronomy*, or, *De coelo et mundo.*

MSS. Oxford:—Bodl. Digby 76, f. 1 (sec. xiii), *Compendium Philosophiae.* *Inc.* ' Prima igitur veritas circa corpora mundi est quod non est unum corpus continuum et unius nature.' *Ibid.* fol. 36, *De corporibus coelestibus, sc. de zodiaco, sole, etc. Inc.* ' Habito de corporibus mundi prout mundum absolute constituunt' (cf. *Opus Minus*). Cf. Ashmole 393 I, f. 44 (sec. xv), ' Veritates de magnitudine... planetarum. Tractatus extractus de libris celi et mundi,' etc. Also, Univ. Coll. 49, De corporibus coelestibus.

Paris:—Mazarine 3576, *De coelestibus* (five chapters). *Inc.* ' Prima igitur veritas.'

(3) *Gravity, Scientia ponderum de gravibus et levibus.*

Cf. *Tractatus trium verborum.*

Liber iii. (4) *Alchemy*, or, *De elementis*[2].

Liber iv. *De vegetabilibus et generabilibus*[3].

(5) *Agriculture.*

See note in Brewer, *Opera Ined.* p. li.

(6) *Medicine.*

(7) *Experimental Science.*

Vol. IV. *Metaphysics and Morals.*

Inc. 'Quoniam intencio principalis est innuere nobis vicia studii theologici que contracta sunt ex curiositate philosophie.'

---

[1] Royal MS. 7 F vii (see above) speaks of eight sciences, i. e. including what Bacon calls ' scientia de communibus naturalibus.'

[2] See the works under the heading, *Alchemy*: cf. 'Excerpta ex libro sex scientiarum' in *Sanioris medicinae*, &c. (Frankfurt, 1603), p. 7 : 'Quarta vero scientia non modicam habet utilitatem ... et est Alchymia speculativa.'

[3] The *Breve Breviarium* includes a treatise *De vegetabilibus et sensibilibus*, and another *De medicinis et curis corporum*; edition of 1603, pp. 228 and 156; MS. Bodl. E Musaeo 155, pp. 549 and 553.

MSS. Bodl.: Digby 190, fol. 86 b (sec. xiii-xiv). 'Methaphisica fratris Rogeri ordinis Fratrum Minorum, de viciis contractis in studio theologie' (25 lines).

Paris:—Bibl. Nat. 7440 (sec. xiv), fol. 38-40, fol. 25-32. 'Incipit metaphysica Rogeri Baconis de ordine praedicatorum' (fragment).

It is, however, probable that these MS. fragments ought to be referred to Bacon's last work, the *Compendium Studii Theologiae*, rather than to the *Compendium Philosophiae*.

Compendium studii theologiae, Bacon's last work, bears the date 1292 ('usque ad hunc annum Domini 1292'). Extracts from it are printed by Charles, pp. 410-416. This work consisted of six parts or more.

Part i. *On the causes of error.*

Part ii. *Logic and grammar in reference to theology.*

These two parts are extant (though not complete) in MS. British Museum, Royal F vii. pp. 153-161 : there is a long gap between pp. 154 and 155.

According to this MS. the work consisted of two parts:

'Incipit compendium studii theologiae et per consequens philosophiae ut potest et debet servire theologicae facultati, et habet duas partes principales ; prima liberali communicatione sapientiae investigat omnes causas errorum, et modos errandi in hoc studio.... Secunda pars descendit ad veritates stabiliendas et ad errores cum diligentia exterminandos.'

Part v. is preserved in Royal MS. 7 F. viii. f. 2 (sec. xiii) (almost complete); it is a treatise on *optics*.

Incipit: ' Acto prologo istius quintae partis hujus voluminis quam voco compendium studii theologiae, in quo quidem comprehendo in summa intentionem totius operis, extra partem ejus signans omnia impedimenta totius studii et remedia, nunc accedo ad tractatum exponens ea quae necessaria sunt theologiae de perspectiva et de visu.'

Part vi. is mentioned in Part v.: it is to be a treatise, '*De multiplicatione Specierum.*'

In Part iv. also the words '*in partibus sequentibus*' occur.

Alchemy was treated in the *Opus Minus* and in the *Compendium Philosophiae*. Bacon divides it into (1) Speculative alchemy, 'the science of the generation of things from elements'; (2) Practical alchemy, 'which teaches us how to make noble metals and colours,' &c., and the art of prolonging life (*Opus Tertium*, cap. xii). Wood mentions a treatise of Bacon's *De rerum generationibus*, of which he had seen two copies varying much. These may have been the versions in the *Opus Minus*[1] and the *Compendium Philosophiae*[2]. A number of works on alchemy and medicine ascribed to Bacon have been preserved, some of them are undoubtedly genuine, others apocryphal.

Epistolae fratris Rogerii Baconis de secretis operibus artis et naturae et de nullitate magiae [or, *De mirabili potestate artis et naturae*].

The work consists of a letter or collection of letters in ten or eleven chapters, the last five of which Charles considers doubtful, addressed perhaps to William of Auvergne (who died in 1248), or to John of London, whom Charles identifies with John of Basingstoke (d. 1252).

Inc. cap. 1. 'Vestrae petitioni respondeo diligenter. Nam licet.'

MS. Brit. Mus: Sloane 2156, p. 117.

Printed at Paris 1542; at Oxford 1594; Hamburg 1613; in Zetzner's *Theatrum Chemicum*, 1659; and by Brewer in *Rog. Bacon Opera Inedita*, App. I.

The three following treatises were printed at Frankfurt in 1603, under the title, *Sanioris medicinae magistri D. Rogeri Baconis angli de arte chymiae scripta*, &c., and elsewhere.

Summary of Avicenna's *De anima*. *Inc.* 'In illius nomine qui major est.'

MS. Bodl: Ashmole 1467 (sec. xvi). [Cf. Charles, *R. Bacon*, p. 59; *Opera Ined.* p. 39.]

Breve Breviarium, or, *De naturis metallorum in ratione alkimica et artificiali transformatione*, or, *Coelestis alchymia*, or, *De naturis metallorum et ipsorum transmutatione*.

Divided into two parts, speculative and practical alchemy; the work contains no doubt some of the ideas incorporated in the *Opus Minus* and the *Comp. Philosophiae*. The date is uncertain.

Inc. 'Breve breviarium breviter abbreviatum.'

MSS. Brit. Mus: Sloane 276, f. 4 (sec. xv–xvi).

Bodl.: Digby 119, fol. 64 (sec. xiv); and Bodl. E Musaeo 155, p. 513.

Paris:—Bibl. Nat. new Latin collection, No. 1153. (Abbey of St. Germain).

Tractatus trium verborum, or, *Epistolae tres ad Johannem Parisiensem*; namely:

i. 'De separatione ignis ab oleo,' or, 'De modo projectionis';
ii. 'De modo miscendi'; iii. 'De ponderibus.' *Inc.* 'Cum ego Rogerus rogatus a pluribus.'

---

[1] Printed in Opera Ined. p. 359 seq.

[2] The special treatise on alchemy in this work does not seem to be extant. Cap. vii of the *Communia Naturalium* begins, '*De generacione*. Habito ergo de principiis naturalibus generacionis.'

MSS. British Museum: Cotton Julius D.V.; Harleian 3528, f. 174;
Sloane 1754, 'Mendacium primum, secundum, et tertium.'
Oxford:—Bodl: Digby 119, f. 82 (sec. xiv ineuntis); Ashmole
1448, pp. 1-25 (sec. xv); Corpus Christi Coll. 125, f. 84^b;
University Coll. 49.

Fragment on alchemy, without title.

MS. Paris:—Bibl. Nat. 2598, f. 138 (sec. xv), 'Explicit de subjecto
transmutationis secundum Rogerum Bachonis.' It perhaps
occurs in one of his larger works.

*Libellus Rogerii Baconi . . . de retardandis senectutis accidentibus et
de sensibus conservandis* (11 chapters). This work is assigned
by Charles to the year 1276. *Inc. prol.* 'Domine mundi ex
nobilissima stirpe originem assumpsistis.' *Inc. cap.* 1. (De
causis senectutis). 'Senescente mundo senescunt homines.'

MSS. Brit. Museum: Sloane 2320, fol. 56.
Bodl.: E. Musaeo 155, pp. 591-637 (sec. xiv-xv); Canonic. Misc.
334, fol. 1 (sec. xv); and 480, fol. 1 (sec. xv).
Printed at Oxford in 1596 (and in English, London 1683).

Antidotarius, a second part of this work. *Inc.* 'Post completum
universalis sciencie medicacionis tractatum.'

MSS. Bodl.: Canonic. Miscell. 334 (fol. 21^b to 25), and 480 (fol. 16);
E Musaeo 155, p. 645. Cf. MS. Canon. Misc. 480, fol. 38^b-47, below.

Liber Bacon de sermone rei admirabilis, sive de retardatione senectutis.
Inc. 'Intendo componere sermonem rei admirabilis domino
meo fratri E, cujus vitam deus prolonget.'

MSS. Bodl.: E Musaeo 155, pp. 655-666; Digby 183, fol. 45 (sec. xiv
exeuntis); Canonic. Miscell. 334, fol. 25-31.

De universali regimine senum et seniorum. Inc. 'Summa regiminis
senum universalis est hoc ut dicit Avicenna.'

MSS. Brit. Mus.: Sloane 2629, fol. 57.
Bodl.: Canon. Miscell. 334, fol. 18^b-21^b; 480 (*explicit* fol. 16);
and E Musaeo 155, p. 638.

De graduacione medicinarum compositarum. Inc. 'Omnis forma inherens.'

MSS. Bodl. Canon. Misc. 334, fol. 32; 480, fol. 23^b (the author's name
is obliterated in the MS.).

Tractatus de erroribus medicorum[1]. *Inc.* 'Vulgus medicorum.'

MSS. Oxford: Bodl. Canon. Misc. 334, fol. 42; 480, fol. 30 (author's
name obliterated); E Musaeo 155, pp. 669-689. Corpus Ch.
Coll. 127 (sec xv).

---

[1] Sloane MS. 3744, p. 71 (sec. xv) contains *Errores secundum Bacon. Inc.* 'Scito enim quod omne corpus aut est elementum aut ex elementis compositum.' According to Charles (p. 71) this is the *De Erroribus medicorum*.

Canones practici de medicinis compositis componendis, 'Cap. i. Extractum de libro septimo Serapionis qui est antidotarium suum et est theoricum capitulum.' (13 chapters.) *Inc.* 'Necesse est illi qui vult componere medicinas.' 'Explicit tractatus de compositione medicinarum per fratrem rugerium bacon editus.'

MS. Bodl. Canon. Misc. 480, fol. 38^b–47.

De leone viridi (on the manufacture of mercury); only the summary by Raymund Gaufredi is extant. *Inc.* 'Verbum abbreviatum.'

MSS. Brit. Mus. :—Sloane 692, f. 46 (sec. xv). Oxford :—Corpus Chr. Coll. 277. Printed at Frankfurt, 1603 (*Sanioris medicinae,* p. 264), &c.

A number of works on alchemy are attributed to Roger Bacon erroneously or without any probability.

De consideratione quintae essentiae; 3 books.

The author was a Franciscan who entered the Order at Toulouse[1]. *Inc. opus.* 'Dixit Salomon sapientie cap. vii. Deus dedit mihi.'

MSS. Bodl.: Canonic. Misc. 334, fol. 59^b. 'Primus liber de consideracione quinte essencie omnium rerum transmutabilium. In nomine domini nostri Jhesu Christi. Incipit liber de famulatu philosophie ewangelio domini Jhesu Christi et pauperibus euangelicis viris Amen.' Fol. 94^b, 'Explicit liber quinte essencie secundum fratrem Rogerium Bacun de ordine minorum.'

Bodl. E Musaeo 155, pp. 431–507. 'Explicit liber tertius de consideracione 5te essencie secundum magistrum Rogerum Bacon, correctus et scriptus per Johannem Cokkes manibus suis propriis Oxon[2].'

Brit. Museum: Sloane 2320, f. 73 (sec. xv–xvi).

Paris :—Bibl. Nat. 7151 (xv).

Venice :—St. Mark, vol. IV. Cl. XIV., Cod. 39.

De expulsione veneni. Inc. 'Ista subscripta sequerentur post capitulum de hiis que expellunt venenum.'

MS. Bodl. E Musaeo 155, p. 507 (not expressly ascribed to Bacon in the MS.: see Brewer, *Op. Ined.* p. xl.).

Speculum alchemiae. Inc. 'Multifariam multisque modis.'

MSS. Brit. Museum: Addit. 8786, f. 62; 15,549; Sloane 3506 (English translation).

Bodl.: Ashmole 1416, f. 101 (sec. xv).

Printed in Zetzner's *Theatrum Chemicum,* vol. ii., A.D. 1659; in Manget's *Theasurus,* vol. i., &c., &c.

---

[1] Charles, R. Bacon, p. 76. It is often, perhaps rightly, attributed to John de Rupescissa.

[2] Brewer reads, 'Explicit liber tertius De Consideratione quartae Sententiae S. Magistri per Rogerum Bacon,' &c. His whole account of this MS. is not very trustworthy; Op. Ined. p. xxxix.

Speculum alchemiae. *Inc.* 'Speculum alchemiae quod in corde meo figuravi.'
: MS. Brit. Mus.: Harl. 3528, fol. 185.

Speculum secretorum, or, *Liber secretorum.* *Inc.* 'In nomine Domini . . . ad instructionem multorum circa hanc artem.'
: MSS. Brit. Mus.: Sloane 513, f. 178^b (sec. xv).
: Oxford:—Bodl.: Digby 28, f. 61 (sec. xiv); Digby 119, f. 90^b; Ashmole 1467, f. 208^b, and 1485, p. 117 (sec. xvi). Also Corpus Christi Coll. 125, f. 86.
: Printed at Frankfurt, 1603 (p. 387).

Secretum secretorum naturae de laude lapidis Philosophorum. *Inc.* 'Secretum secretorum naturae audiant secreti quae loquor.'
: Printed at Frankfurt, 1603 (pp. 285–291).

Rogerina major et minor, two medical treatises; neither by Bacon: one is by a Roger Baron.
: MSS. Bodl. 2626; Cf. MS. St. Omer 624 (sec. xiii); Charles, *R. Bacon,* p. 75, *note.*
: Cambridge, Publ. Libr. Ii, I. 16 (sec. xiv) and Ee, II. 20.
: Brit. Mus.: Sloane 342, f. 146 (sec. xiii).

De Magnete. *Inc.* 'Amicorum intime, quamdam magnetis lapidis.'
: MS. Bodl. E Musaeo 155, pp. 414–426 (anon.): Charles (p. 18) ascribes it to Peter de Maricourt.

Calendar, wrongly attributed to Bacon; made by a Minorite at Toledo 1297, and extracted from the *Tabulae Toletanae.*
: MS. Cott. Vesp. A. II. f. 2; Cf. *Opus Majus* p. 140 (ed. Venet, 1750).

Semita recta alchemiae (or, *Liber duodecim aquarum*).
: MS. Brit. Mus.: Sloane 513, f. 181^b–188^b (sec. xv): 'Explicit semita recta alkemie secundum Magistrum Rogerum Bakun.'
: Cf. MS. Sloane 276, f. 21, an anonymous work on the same subject, differing somewhat from the above.
: Bodl.: Ashmole 1485, pp. 173–188 (sec. xvi), 'Liber aquarum.'

Thesaurus spirituum, four treatises on the influence of planets, &c. *Inc.* 'Hec est doctrina omnium experimentorum.'
: MS. Brit. Museum: Sloane 3853, f. 3–40 (sec. xv). 'Hec est tabula libri sequentis.... a quodam viro venerabili ordinis Minorum fratre summa composita et ordinata, et a diligencia M. Rogero Bakon ordinis Minorum nuper recognita, qui quidem liber pro omnibus hujus mundi experimentis sufficit,' &c.
: 'Explicit liber qui secundum Robertum Turconem et Rogerum Bakon fratrem Minorum Thesaurus spirituum nuncupatur.'
: Cf. MS. Sloane 3850, f. 129^b, *De nigromantia,* extracted from the above.

De fistula.
> MS. Sloane 238, f. 214ᵇ–216ᵇ (sec. xv). 'Secundum Rogerum Bacon ut habetur in libro qui dicitur Thesaurus pauperum[1].'

Necromanciae. Inc. 'Debes mundare manus et pedes ante visionem characterum.'
> MS. Sloane 3884, f. 44ᵇ (sec. xv–xvi) : 'Haec sunt quae Rogerus Bacon de pura necromancia dixit.'

Other worthless recipes, fragments, &c., attributed to Bacon will be found in MSS :—
> Bodl. 3, 349, 'Index simplicium'; Ashmole 1423, iv. pp. 1–7 'Opus,' 'Opus Commune,' 'De conclusionibus'; Sloane 692, f. 102, 'Finalis conclusio'; Harl. 2269, art. 1; Cott. Jul. D. V. 'De colore faciendo'; Digby 196, f. 163ᵇ, 'Septem virtutes naturae'; Ashmole 1485 (sec. xv), various.

De intellectu et intelligentia, and *De nutrimento,* which Charles considers genuine, are printed among the works of Albertus Magnus.
> MSS. Bodl.: Digby 67, f. 107 (sec. xiv), anon: and Digby 55, f. 193, anon: Alb. Magnus, *Opera,* V. p. 239 and 175 (Lugd. 1657).

Tractatus de veritate theologiae in septem partes distributus, perhaps by Robert Bacon. *Inc.* 'Flecto genua mea ad patrem domini nostri Jesu Christi.'
> MS. Bodley 745 (=2764) (sec. xiv) pp. 113–188: 'Incipit tractatus fratris B.' Part i. de trinitate dei; ii. de creatura dei; iii. de corruptela peccati; iv. de incarnacione verbi; v. de gratia spiritus sancti; vi. de medicina sacramentali; vii. de statu finalis judicii.

Tractatus super Psalterium, probably by Robert Bacon.
> MS. *ibid.* pp. 193–497. 'Incipit tractatus fratris R. Bacun, super psalterium. Beatus vir qui.'

Excerptiones Rogeri Bacon ex auctoribus musicae artis; or correctly, *Excerptiones Hogeri abbatis,* &c.
> MS. Cambridge:—Corp. Chr. Coll. 260 (*olim* 189).
> Cf. MS. Milan:—Ambrosiana, *Rogerii de Baccono de generatione et corruptione, de Musica, de prospectiva* (Montfaucon, p. 523). Cf. Opera Inedita, 295 *seq.*

De sacrae scripturae profundis misteriis authore Rogero Bacon.
> MS. London:—Gray's Inn, 17 (sec. xv); the title is in a later hand. It is probably a version of the Expositiones Vocabulorum de singulis libris Bibliae Rogeri compotistae monachi S. Eadmundi;

---

[1] Cf. MSS. Sloane 284 (sec. xiv), 477 (A. D. 1309), and 2411; Digby 150 (sec. xiii), f. 106, '*Extracciones a Thezauro pauperum,* libro scil. preceptorum medicinalium.'

MSS. Oxford:—Bodl. Laud. Misc. 176 (sec. xiv); Magd. Coll. 112 (sec. xv).

John, Roger Bacon's favourite pupil, was certainly not John of London[1], or John Peckham[2]. On the other hand it is impossible to identify him with any known scholastic doctor. It is not certain whether he was a friar or whether he was ever at Oxford. About 1260 Roger Bacon found him probably at Paris, as a poor boy of fifteen eager to learn, but forced to beg his bread and to serve those who gave him the necessaries of life[3].

'I caused him,' says Roger[4], 'to be taken care of and instructed for the love of God.'

The boy repaid his master's care. Wishing to send a fit interpreter of his works to the Pope, Bacon writes[5],

'I chose a youth whom for five or six years I have had instructed in languages and mathematics and optics, in which is all the difficulty of what I send; and I instructed him gratis with my own mouth after I received your command, feeling that I could not at present have another messenger after my own heart.'

There was no one at Paris who knew so much of the roots of philosophy as did *juvenis Johannes*; he was 'a virgin, not knowing mortal sin,' and 'an excellent keeper of secrets[6].' John was sent to Clement with the *Opus Majus* and other treatises[7] in 1267, the other works, *Opus Minus* and *Opus Tertium*, being sent later and probably by other messengers. From this time we have no authentic information about him, and do not know whether he fulfilled Bacon's expectations:

'he has that which will enable him to surpass all the Latins, if he lives to old age and builds on the foundations which he has[8].'

Robert de Ware, in Hertfordshire[9], entered the Order at Oxford between 1265 and 1268. In the prologue of his only extant work,

---

[1] John of London was a master, and contemporary of Roger's; Op. Ined. p. 34. 'Juvenis Johannes' was aged 20 or 21 in 1267, and had no experience in teaching, ibid. 61.

[2] The dates are conclusive; Peckham entered the Order as a young man, not as a boy, in the lifetime of Adam Marsh; Mon. Franc. I, 256. 'Juvenis Johannes' was about 12 years old when Adam died.

[3] Op. Ined. 63.

[4] Ibid. 61.

[5] Ibid.

[6] Ibid. 62.

[7] Namely, a treatise on rays, Op. Ined. p. 230, and an elaborate one on mathematics and judicial astrology, ibid. 270; John took also a concave lens, ibid. p 111.

[8] Ibid. 62.

[9] MS. Gray's Inn Libr. 7, f. 62, 'a quadam villa proxima que dicitur Herteford.'

addressed to his younger brother John, he gives the following account of his conversion [1] :—

> I was the eldest son of my father; at a tender age, tenderly beloved, I was designed for a life of study. At length I came to Oxford, and then I entered the Order of Friars Minors. At this my father was exceedingly grieved, and did all in his power to force me to leave the Order, sending my mother and brother and relatives and other friends to me, with intreaties and promises; and, I am told, with the help of some powerful persons, he made every exertion to secure my liberation in the court of Ottobon, who was then acting as legate in England [2]. At length finding himself thwarted because I would not give my consent, he became so embittered against me that he absolutely refused to see me or speak with me, nor could any of my friends pacify him. One day even, when I had come to his gates with my companion-friar, and wished to enter, he refused me admittance by his servants, drew his sword, and swore with a mighty oath that he would kill me if I presumed to enter.

At length the father was stricken down by a mortal disease, and, warned in a vision, he relented towards his son. The latter was summoned hastily from London, and reconciled to his father, who before his death gave proof of his devotion to the Order of St. Francis.

Twenty-five discourses on the Virgin Mary, by friar Robert de Ware. Inc. prol. " Aue rosarium scripturarum per areolas."

> MS. London:—Gray's Inn, 7, f. 62-138: (sec. xiii). No title; the name of the author is given in a hand of the fourteenth century.

Walter de Landen, William Cornish, William de Wykham, Dyonisius, and **Robert de Cap(e)ll,** were Franciscans at Oxford, and took part in the controversy with the Dominicans in 1269. All that is known about them will be found in Appendix C.

Nicholas de Gulac was at Oxford in 1269. Suffering from stone and despairing of life, he at length prayed the Lord

'to cure him by the merits of his martyr Earl Simon de Montfort.'

On the next morning as he rose from his bed '*ut commingeret,*' the stone fell at his feet, and he had no pain before or afterwards, being completely cured on Easter Tuesday, 1269; to this miracle witness was borne by the whole convent of Minorites at Oxford [3].

Laurence of Cornwall, to whose miraculous recovery from fever, after prayer to Simon de Montfort, the same Friar N. de Gulac bore witness, was probably at Oxford about the same time [4].

---

[1] MS. Gray's Inn Libr. 7, f. 62.
[2] Ottobon came to England in November, 1265, and left in July, 1268.
[3] *Miracula Symonis de Montfort,* p. 96 (Camden Soc. 1840).
[4] Ibid. p. 95.

Stephanus Hibernicus, called also **Stephen of Exeter** and **Stephen of Oxford**, was born in 1246, and became a Minorite at 'Mutifernana' in 1263. These facts are contained in the *Annales Montis Fernandi* (*sive Minoritarum Multifernanae*) *ab a°* 45 *usque ad an.* 1274, the authorship of which is usually ascribed to Stephen[1]. It is very doubtful whether he was at Oxford.

The *Annales* are extant in 'MS. Bibl. Arch. Armachani,' according to Hardy; formerly MS. Clarendon 19, f. 32-44 (Bernard).

William of Ware, or **William Warre**, **Guaro**, **Varro**, &c., born at Ware in Hertfordshire, entered the Order in his youth, according to William Woodford[2]. It is not improbable that he studied at Oxford, but there is no authority for the statement[3]. He was S. T. P. of Paris, where most of his life was spent[4]. He is said to have been a pupil of Alexander of Hales[5] (d. 1245), and master of Duns Scotus[6], who went to Paris in 1304. He was called *doctor fundatus* by later writers[7].

His *Commentaries on the Sentences* were seen by Leland in the Franciscan Library, London[8], and are now extant in the following MSS.:

Oxford:—Merton Coll. 103, 104 (sec. xiv). *Inc.* 'Utrum finis per se et proprius theologie.'

Toulouse, 242, § 1 (sec. xiv), anon. *Inc. ut supra*.

Troyes, 661, § 1 (xiv). 'Questiones super I et III lib. Sentent.' ascribed to Duns Scotus. *Inc. ut supra*.

Troyes, 661 § 2 (xiv). 'Questiones Wareti super tertium librum Sententiarum.' *Inc.* 'Queritur utrum incarnacio sit possibilis Quod non. Incarnacio est quedam.'

Vienna :—Bibl. Palat. 1424, and 1438 (xiv).

Florence :—Laurentiana, *ex Bibl. S. Crucis*, Plut. xxxiii, Dext. Cod. i (sec. xiii).

Padua, Bibl. S. Antonii, *in Pluteis* xxiv and xxii. (Tomasin, pp. 62ª, 60ᵇ.)

---

[1] Hardy, Descript. Catal. Vol. III, p. 207, No. 352. Wadding, Script. 218, Sup. ad Script. p. 667.

[2] Twyne MS. XXII, 103 c. (Defensorium, cap. 62). Perhaps he is the 'Frater G. de Ver' who was at the London convent, c. 1250, Mon. Franc. I, 328.

[3] Bale (I, 323) and Pits.

[4] Pits calls him S.T.P. of Oxford; his name does not occur in the list of Franciscan masters. Wadding (VI, 48) says that Duns Scotus was made S.T.P. at Oxford when Ware was called to Paris. This is incorrect; Duns was never doctor of Oxford; see notice of him.

[5] Dugdale, Monast. Vol. VI, Part III, p. 1529 (from Fr. a S. Clara).

[6] Barth. of Pisa, Liber Conform. f. 81, 'Johannes Guarro Anglicus magister Scoti.' Duns Scotus mentions him twice in his works, Wadding, VI, 45. Cf. Bibl. S. Antonii, at Padua, MS. *in Pluteo* XXII, *in calce*: 'Varro professionis Minoritae Doctorum Jubar et praeceptor Divi Scoti famosus'; quoted by Tomasin, p. 60 b.

[7] Willot, Athenae, p. 166.

[8] Collectanea, III, 51.

Richard Middleton is said by Bale, Wood, and others, to have studied at Oxford, but they produce no evidence for the statement [1]. He was B.D. at Paris in 1283 [2], when with other doctors and bachelors he was appointed to examine the doctrines of Peter Johannis Olivi. He appears to have incepted as D.D. soon afterwards [3], and is reckoned among the masters of Duns Scotus. Like many other famous doctors of his Order, he is said by Wadding to have written on the Immaculate Conception [4]. According to Willot he was known at Paris as *Doctor solidus et copiosus, fundatissimus et authoratus* [5]: at the Council of Basel he was referred to as *Doctor profundus* [6].

Commentum super iv. Sententiarum. Inc. prologus, 'Abscondita produxit.'

MSS. Oxford:—Bodl. 2765 (now Bodley 744)—Balliol Coll. 198 (sec. xiv)—Merton Coll. 98, f. 118 (sec. xiv).
Cambridge:—Caius Coll. 303—Pembroke Coll. 111, 113.
Canterbury:—Cathedral Lib. 4.
Munich:—Bibl. Regia, 3549 (sec. xv) and 8078 (sec. xiii–xiv).
Printed at Venice 1489, at Venice *sine anno*, and Venice 1507–9, &c.

Quaestiones quodlibetales (two parts). *Inc. Pars I.* 'Queritur utrum Deus sit summe simplex.'

MSS. Oxford:—Merton Coll. 139, fol. 2 (sec. xiv).
Troyes, 142 (xiv); *Pars II incipit ut supra.*
Florence:—Laurentiana, *ex Bibl. S. Crucis*, Plut. xvii, Sin. Cod. vi (sec. xiv *ineuntis*).

Quodlibeta tria. (The first contains 22 questions; the second 31; the third 27.) *Inc.* 'In nostra disputacione de quolibet.'

MSS. Oxford:—Merton Coll. 139, f. 162 (sec. xiv).
Paris:—Bibl. Nat. 14305 (sec. xiii) *Questiones de quolibet*; this may contain either the *Quodl. tria* or the *Questiones Quodlib.*, or both.

---

[1] A 'Richard Middleton' was fellow of Merton *sub* Edw. III; of course he is not to be confounded with the Minorite doctor.

[2] Wadding, IV, 54, 121. Archiv f. L. u. K. Gesch. III, 417. This date is sufficient to show that he cannot have finished the *Summa* of Alexander of Hales at the command of Pope Alexander IV, as Davenport (Francis a S. Clara) alleges, Opera, Tom. I, Hist. Minor, p. 12. The *Summa* was finished by Friar William of Middleton, D.D. of Paris (and probably fifth master of the Franciscans at Cambridge), who died 1261, Wadding, IV, 57; Lanerc. Chron. 70; Mon. Franc. I, 555.

[3] Archiv, &c., II, 296 (from Angelus de Clarino, Hist. Tribulat.).

[4] Wadding, VI, 13; and Willot, Athenae.

[5] Athenae, 314–315; the two last epithets are applied to him in the edition of his Quodlibets printed at Venice in 1509.

[6] Wadding, Sup. ad. Script. 633; this is the earliest instance which I have found of the special application of any such title to Richard Middleton.

Toulouse, 738 (sec. xiii).
Florence :—Laurent. *ut supra*.
Printed at Venice 1509, Paris 1519, and Brescia 1591.
De gradibus formarum.
MS. Munich 8723, fol. 175 (sec. xiv and xv).
Quaestiones disputatae, by R. Middleton and others.
MS. Assisi (see Fratini, p. 203).
Sermo fratris Ricardi de dilatatione sermonum (?). *Inc.* 'Quoniam emulatores estis.'
MS. Oxford :—Merton Coll. 249, f. 175 (sec. xiii).

William de la Mare, de Mara, or **Lamarensis**, may have studied at Oxford[1] before he went to Paris, where he was a disciple of Bonaventura. In 1284 he published a criticism of Thomas Aquinas, called *Correctorium operum fratris Thomae*[2], which afterwards won for him the title of standard-bearer of the Anti-Thomists[3]. This treatise, which may perhaps be still extant in an Italian library, is generally known only through the reply to it, attributed sometimes to Aegidius Romanus, but with more probability to Richard Clapwell[4]. 'The serious part of the work of William de Lamarre,' says M. Charles, 'seems directly inspired by Bacon[5].' He had no doubt come under Roger's influence either at Oxford or Paris. William de Mara appears also to have written in favour of a strict observance of the Rule of St. Francis. In a dispute on the interpretation of the Rule in 1310, Friar Ubertino de Casali, one of the leaders of the 'Spiritual' party, quoted, in support of his views,

'the opinion of St. Francis expressed in his Rule, and of Pope Nicholas in his Declaration, of Friar Bonaventura in his Apologia, of Friars Alexander and Rigaldus . . . and of Friar John de Peckham in his book on Evangelical

---

[1] It is always assumed that he was an Englishman; the available evidence on the point is slight. MS. Borghes. 322, f. 174 a (sec. xiv) has the note: 'Hic loquitur (Petrus J. Olivi) stulte contra fratrem G. de Mara et communem opinionem.' MS. Borghes. 358, f. 227 b (sec. xiv): 'Magister Guillelmus de Anglia habet duas sententias in instrumentis duobus datas contra doctrinam P(etri) J(oannis) . . .' &c. The second William here is probably W. de Mara (Archiv f. L. u. K. Gesch. III, 472–3). B. of Pisa and Tritheim say nothing about his nationality. The name was not uncommon in England; see e.g.

Pat. Roll, 10 Edw. I, m. 7 dorse; Le Neve, Fasti, vol. iii; cf. forest of Mara, or Delamere in Cheshire.

[2] Charles, Roger Bacon, p. 240. Cf. B. of Pisa, Liber Conform. fol. 81 : 'scripsit . . . contra fratrem Thomam de Aquino correctorium componendo.'

[3] Wadding, Sup. ad Script. 323.

[4] This reply was printed at Cologne, 1624 (Charles, ibid.), and at Cordova in 1701. See Merton Coll. MS. 267; MS. in Bibl. S. Anton. Venet. in pluteo xviii; Boston of Bury, in Tanner, Bibl. p. xxxviii.

[5] Charles, Roger Bacon, pp. 240–1.

Perfection, and of Friar William de Mara, who were all solemn masters of our Order¹.'

From this it is clear that William died before 1310.

Some of his writings are extant in MS.

Summa Fratris Gul. de Mara contra D. Thomam.

    MS. Venice:—Bibl. S. Anton. *in Pluteo* xix (Tomasin).

Correctorium Fratris Gul. de Mera . . . secundum dicta D. Thomae de Aquino contra correctorium Fratris Joannis (?) *de Crapuel Ordinis Praedicatorum*—perhaps the printed *Defensorium seu Correctorium.*

    MS. *ibid. in Pluteo* xviii.

Quaestiones de natura virtutis, by 'Gulielmus de le Maire, ordinis Minorum.'

    MS. Brit. Museum:—Burney 358 (sec. xiv)—mutilated at the beginning.

Sermo Fratris Guillermi de la Mare regentis in Theologia. (On St. Peter.) *Inc.* 'Precurrens ascendit in arborem sycomorum. . . . Fratres orate ut sermo Dei currat et clarificetur.'

    MS. Troyes, 1788 (sec. xiv).

Expositio libri Physicorum Aristotelis; and *Comment. in libros* 1, 2, et 3, *Sententiarum*².

    MSS. Sta Croce, Florence 380, 381, 382, 383; mentioned in Wadding, *Sup. ad Script.* These MSS. are now in the Laurentiana, *ex Bibl. S. Crucis,* Plut. xxxiv. Sin. Codd. iv, v, vi, vii, but they do not seem to contain the *Physics.*

Quaestiones tres philosophicae per Gulielmum (*de Mara?*) *de Anglia, fratrem ordinis Minorum. Inc.* 'Est dubitacio utrum lineam componam ex punctis.'

    MS. Bodl. Canon. Misc. 226, f. 76 (sec. xv). There seems no reason for attributing these to W. de Mara rather than to William of Ockham, or any English Minorite named William³.

John of Oxford, Friar Minor, was ordained priest by Peckham in 1284⁴.

Richard de Slekeburne (co. Durham), confessor of Devorguila, played an important part in the foundation of Balliol College: this

---

¹ Anal. Franc. II, 115.

² 'Scripsit super sententias ad opus domini fratris Bonaventure multa superaddendo et multa quodlibeta faciendo.' B. of Pisa, Liber Conform. f. 81: cf. Tanner, Bibl. 223.

³ Other works attributed to him by Sbaralea (Wadding, Sup. ad Script.), viz. *Paraphrasis Musaei* and *Sylvarum libri quatuor,* are by W. de Mara, Bishop of Constance in the fifteenth century.

⁴ Peckham's Reg. p. 1040.

CH. III.] *FRANCISCANS IN THE OXFORD CONVENT.* 217

has already been referred to[1]. There is no direct proof that Friar Richard was himself at Oxford. Several documents relating to him are preserved in the Balliol College Archives, and described in the Reports of the Hist. MSS. Commission[2].

(1) A letter of Devorguila to him, in which she speaks of 'the alms of the poor scholars of our House of Balliol now studying at Oxford,' and urges Friar Richard by all means in his power to promote the perpetuation of the said house, A.D. 1284.

(2) A grant by the executors of Sir John Balliol of sums to the scholars, with the consent of Devorguila and at the advice of Friar R. de Slekeburne (three deeds, 1285-1286).

(3) A confirmation by Friar Richard of another grant by Sir J. Balliol's executors of debts due to Sir John: the confirmatory deed is dated Coventry, 1287.

William of Exeter was summoned in 1289 from Oxford by Deodatus, Warden of the Friars Minors of Exeter[3], to assist him in choosing a new site for the convent[4].

William of Leominster is placed among the Franciscans by Pits, but it is not certain that he belonged to this Order[5]. He was a friar and master of Oxford in 1290; in this year his name appears as one of the masters who gave their consent on behalf of the University to the compromise, effected by the intervention of the King and his council, concerning the right of the bishop of Lincoln to confirm the Chancellor-elect[6]. Bale states that he had seen this friar's *Collationes Sententiarum* and *Quaestiones Theologiae*, at London, '*in quadam officina*'[7].

John Bekinkham appears to have been an Oxford Minorite; he was one of the friars to whom the royal alms of 25 marks was paid by the exchequer in 1289 or 1290[8].

---

[1] Part I, chapter i.
[2] Report IV, pp. 442-4.
[3] Oliver, Monasticon Diocesis Exon. p. 331. He is not to be confused with his namesake, the opponent of Ockham: he may possibly be the author of the *Tractatus de octo Beatitudinibus* in MS. Laud. Misc. 368, fol. 106 (sec. xiv).
[4] Cf. Inquisitio ad quod damnum 20 Edw. I (Nov. 1291), in Mon. Franc. II, 289.
[5] His name does not occur in the list of *lectores*, as it probably would have done had he been a Franciscan; this inference however cannot be drawn with any certainty.
[6] Rolls of Parliament, I, 16 a. Lyte, p. 127. The name of ' Frater Willelmus de Leominstre' stands first in the list of the five *magistri* who represented the University.
[7] Script. II, 98. Cf. MS. Seld. sup. 64, fol. 48, 'ex officina Joannis Cocke.'
[8] Excheq. Q. R. Wardrobe, $\frac{4}{1}$, 17-18

John de Clara was executor of Hugh de Cantilupe, Archdeacon of Gloucester, in 1285; he was at this time at Oxford[1]. In 1289 or 1290 he appears, in conjunction with John Bekinkham, as receiving the royal grant of 25 marks in the name of the Oxford Convent[2]. In 1299 he was entrusted with 10 marks out of the royal exchequer for the expenses of Hugh of Hertepol and William of Gainsborough, who were going to the General Chapter at Lyons[3]. In 1301 he was sent with instructions to find the Provincial Minister with all speed, and received of the royal bounty 24s. 3d. for his expenses[4].

John Russell was private chaplain to Edmund, Earl of Cornwall, in 1293. In a letter to Raymund, General Minister of the Friars Minors, dated Aug. 29, 1293[5], the Earl thanks the Minister

'pro vestris muneribus preciosis, cultellis vestris videlicet nobilibus de corallo atque insigni vase tiriaco, que in octavis virginis gloriose per manus dilecti et domestici nostri fratris Johannis Rossel .... recepimus .... Dat' in manerio nostro de B. (Beckley?)[6] prope Oxon',' &c.

Russell wrote about the same time to *dominus* R. de M. (Roger de Merlawe):

'Veni ad capitulum fratrum nostrorum Oxon', proponens vos personaliter visitasse; sed jam istud iter impedivit debilitas corporalis[7].'

This John Russell was contemporary, and probably identical, with the twenty-second master of the Franciscans at Cambridge[8].

Postilla in Cantica Canticorum.   *Inc.* 'Cogitanti mihi Canticum.'

    MS. London:—Lambeth Palace, 180, f. 1 (sec. xv).

Lectura super Apocalypsim.   *Inc.* 'Statuit septem piramides. . . . Accedens ad expositionem.'

    MS. Oxford:—Merton Coll. 172, fol. 106 (sec. xiv), manu Will. de Nottingham.

De potestate imperatoris et pape.

    Formerly in the King's Library, according to Bale (MS. Seld. supra 64, fol. 163b, 193): it is not mentioned in Casley's Catalogue.

Edw. I (R.O.): 'per manus fratrum Johannis de Bekinkham et Johannis de Clara xvi^{li}. xiii^s iiii^d.'

[1] Peckham, Regist. p. 895.
[2] Excheq. Q. R. Wardrobe, $\frac{4}{5}$ (R.O.).
[3] Excheq. Q. R. Wardrobe, $\frac{8}{9}$, m. 1.
[4] Ibid. $\frac{11}{12}$ (m. 1): 'ffratri Johanni de Clare de ordine Minorum pro expensis suis et conductione equitature pro se et socio suo eundo cum magna festinacione ad diversa loca pro fratre Hugone de Hertpoul ministro ordinis sui querendo ad consensum expedicioni negociorum predictorum prestandum per manus proprias apud Berkhamstede eodem die (March 29) xxiiij^s iij^d.' The business mentioned was connected with a bequest to the Mendicant Orders by Edmund, Earl of Cornwall.

[5] MS. Digby 154, fol. 38.
[6] Kennet's Parochial Antiquities, I, 362.
[7] MS. Digby 154, fol. 37 b.
[8] Mon. Franc. I, 556.

Henry de Sutton was warden of the Grey Friars, London, in 1302 [1], and 1307, when the King (Edward I) gave him 40 marks 'pro pitancia fratrum Minorum in capitulo suo generali celebrando apud Tolosam in festo Pentecost proximo [2].

He procured a legacy of 2 marks annually from Henry Waleys, Mayor of London, for his convent [3]. The evidence of his connexion with Oxford is very slight. His name occurs as the author of a sermon in a collection of sermons which were probably delivered at Oxford at the end of the thirteenth century [4].

William Mincy, William de Newport, Roger de Barton (Cheshire), **Robert de Gaddestyn** or **Gaddesby, John de Westburg, Robert de Mogynton** (Derby), Franciscans at Oxford in 1300, were on the 26th of July in that year presented at Dorchester by Hugh of Hertepol the Provincial, and licensed by Dalderby, Bishop of Lincoln, to hear confessions, grant absolution, and enjoin penances, in the Archdeaconry of Oxford. They were not at this time, and probably never became, doctors of divinity [5].

John de Stapleton, A.D. 1300, was similarly presented by the Provincial, but rejected by the Bishop. The Register of the Friars Minors at London says:

'Friar John de Stapilton, heir to great wealth and lordship, spurning wife and heritage, became a Friar Minor.'

It is doubtful whether this refers to the same person [6].

Adam de Corf, Peter de Todworth, Walter Bosevile, and **Roger de Alnewyck**, were in like manner presented by the Provincial and rejected by the Bishop, A.D. 1300. They were not at this time D.D's. Nothing further is known of them, unless Roger de Alnewyck is to be identified with William of Alnwick, 42nd reader at Oxford [7].

John Duns Scotus [8] was a Franciscan at Oxford in 1300. In

---

[1] Mon. Franc. I, 514.

[2] Exchequer, Q. R. Wardrobe, Accts. $\frac{12}{17}$, 35 Edw. I. (R.O.)

[3] Mon. Franc. I, 512-3. See ibid. 518: 'Octavam fenestram vitrari fecit frater Henricus de Sutton, gardianus.'

[4] MS. New Coll., Oxford, 92; among other preachers mentioned is Simon of Gaunt, Chancellor of the University in 1291.

[5] Wood MS. F 29 a, f. 178 (i.e. Wood-Clark, II, 386).

[6] Ibid., and Mon. Franc. I, 552.

[7] Wood MS. ibid.

[8] There is no evidence as to the place of his birth (the note which Leland triumphantly quotes—Merton Coll. MS. 59—was written in 1455, and contains the baseless statement that he was fellow of Merton College); and the only

the list of friars presented to the Bishop of Lincoln he appears as 'Johannes Douns'[1]; the Bishop refused to grant him license to hear confessions. Soon afterwards Duns lectured on the four books of the *Sentences* as B.D. at Oxford[2]. At the end of 1304 he was called to Paris to incept as D.D. The letter of the General Minister recommending this choice is given by Wadding[3], who however has misunderstood it. For this reason, and because it illustrates some points in the educational system of the Minorites, the letter may be quoted in full[4].

In Christo sibi carissimis Patribus, Guillelmo Guardiano Parisiis, vel ejus Vicario et Magistris, Frater Gondisalvus gaudens in Domino.

Ad expeditionem dilecti in Christo Patris Aegidii de Legnaco, de quo per litteras vestras certificatus existo, cum de alio (ut moris est) eodem calculo praesentando providere oporteat, et cum, secundum statuta Ordinis, et secundum statuta vestri Conventus, Baccalaureus hujusmodi praesentandus ad praesens debeat esse de aliqua provincia aliarum a Provincia Franciae, dilectum in Christo Patrem Joannem Scotum, de cujus vita laudabili, scientia excellenti, ingenioque subtilissimo, aliisque insignibus conditionibus suis, partim experientia longa, partim fama, quae ubique divulgata est, informatus sum ad plenum, dilectioni vestrae assigno, post dictum patrem Aegidium, principaliter et ordinarie praesentandum. Injungo nihilominus vobis ad meritum salutaris obedientiae, quatenus praesentationem hujusmodi cum solemnitate solita sine multo dispendio facere debeatis; si tamen constiterit vobis, quod dominus Cancellarius velit duos simul licentiare de nostris, volo et placet mihi, quod frater Albertus Methensis, si ad Conventum redire poterit, cum praefato fratre Joanne debeat expediri. In quo casu mando et ordino, quod dictus frater Albertus antiquitatis merito prius incipere debeat, dicto fratre Joanne sub eo postmodum incepturo. Valete in Domino et orate pro me. Datum in loco Esculi provinciae Marchiae Anconitanae, XIV Kal. Dec. anno MCCCIV.

Duns probably taught at Paris till 1307. Wadding, indeed, asserts

evidence of his nationality is the name 'Scotus,' and a note in the catalogue of the library at Assisi, written 1381: 'Opus super quatuor libros sententiarum mag. fratris Johannis Scoti de Ordine Minorum qui et doctor subtilis nuncupatur, de provincia Hiberniae.'

[1] Wood-Clark, II, 386. He must have attained the age of thirty by this time; Archiv f. L. u. K. Gesch. VI, pp. 128-9.

[2] Wadding (VI, p. 48) cites some passages bearing on the date. Duns' great work on the *Sentences* is called *Scriptum Oxoniense*, but I do not know how far the name can be traced back; Merton Coll. MSS. 60, 61, 62, date from the middle of the 15th century. Barth. of Pisa however says: 'Hic primo in Anglia Oxonie Sentencias legit. Deinde in studio Parisiensi.'

[3] He says, e. g. on the authority of the letter, that Duns was at Paris in 1304; the letter implies exactly the opposite; he was in 'some province other than the province of France.'

[4] Wadding, VI, 51, from Petrus Rodulphus, 'qui eas ex ipso exscripsit autographo.'

that he was sent to Cologne by the General Minister in 1305 [1]; but this is almost impossible, and the description which Wadding gives of the scene is derived from later and unhistorical tradition. The statement, however, that he was appointed Regent by the friars in the General Chapter at Toulouse in 1307 sounds more plausible [2]; he may have been made the first Regent at Paris, or he may have been sent at this time as lector or Regent of the Franciscan schools at Cologne. At any rate there seems no reason to distrust the notice of his death which Wadding quotes from the list of friars who died at Cologne [3].

'D. P. frater Joannes Scotus, sacrae Theologiae Professor, Doctor Subtilis nominatus, quondam lector Coloniae, qui obiit anno MCCCVIII, VI Idus Novembris.'

This entry, though certainly not contemporary, was probably derived from some authentic record. Duns' title of *Doctor Subtilis*, though it does not seem to have been given him in his lifetime, is of considerable antiquity. It is mentioned by Bartholomew of Pisa at the end of the fourteenth century [4], and by the MS. Catalogue at Assisi, written in 1381 [5].

A collected edition of his works was printed at Lyons in 1639. Many of the works included in these twelve folio volumes are considered doubtful by the editors [6].

Some few treatises not included in this edition are assigned to him.

Johannis Scoti super Apocalypsin notulae. Inc. liber: 'Liber iste principaliter dividitur in tres partes.' (Doubtful.)

MS. Bodl. :—Laud. Misc. 434, f. 1 (sec. xiv).

[*Ejusdem ?*] *super S. Matthaei Evangelium notae. Inc.* 'Liber generacionis,' &c.: 'Sicut fluvius de loco voluptatis egrediens.' (Doubtful.)

MS. *ibid.* f. 75.

---

[1] Wadding, VI, 107.
[2] Ibid. 51. The passage is usually understood to refer to his regency at Paris. No record of the Chapter remains.
[3] Ibid. 116. The statement that he died at the age of 34 or 43 is a pure guess. The tradition of his having been buried alive when in a trance is found in St. Bernardin of Siena; Wadding, VI, 114.
[4] Liber Conform. f. 81.
[5] Archiv f. L. u. K. Gesch. I, 368, n. 1. Ehrle adds that the epithet occurs in some MSS. which he puts in the first half of the fourteenth century; ibid.
[6] See the critical notice prefixed to each work in the Lyons edition; and *Hist. Litt.* Vol. XXV, pp. 426–446.

'*Utrum pluralitas formalitatum possit stare cum simplicitate divine essencie.*'

MS. Bodl.: Digby 54, f. 123 (sec. xv).

De perfectione statuum[1]. *Inc.* 'Quod status prelatorum sc. pastorum ecclesie.'

    MSS. Oxford:—Merton Coll. 65, f. 119 (A. D. 1456).
        Cambridge:—Public Library Dd. III. 47 (sec. xv); Corpus Christi Coll. 107, fol. 77–93a (sec. xv).
        Florence:—Laurentiana, *ex Bibl. S. Crucis,* Plut. xxxvi, Dext. Cod. xii, p. 101 (sec. xiv *exeuntis*).

Opusculum Doctoris Subtilis super aliquos canones Arzachel. (Doubtful.)
    MS. Cambridge:—Public Library 1017, f. 14–15 (sec. xv). Cf. Tanner, *Bibl.* p. 689, *sub* ' Stantonus.'

Tractatus Johannis Duns Scoti de lapide philosophorum. (Apocryphal.)
    MS. Paris:—Bibl. Nat. 14008, f. 156.

Robert Cowton, or **de Couton** (co. York), according to W. Woodford, entered the Order when young[2]. He was at Oxford in 1300, when the Provincial asked the Bishop of Lincoln to license him, among others, to hear confessions, but Robert was among the rejected[3]. At this time he was not a doctor. According to Bale and Pits he studied philosophy at Oxford and theology at Paris: there can be little doubt that he obtained the degree of D.D. in the latter University. His title of 'the pleasant doctor[4]' is not vouched for by any early authority.

If we may draw any inference from the number of MSS. preserved, few works by any Franciscan were more in demand in England[5] in the fourteenth and fifteenth centuries than the *Commentaries* of Robert Cowton *on the Sentences.* The following MSS. contain them, or parts of them.

    London:—Brit. Mus. Royal 11 B. i. 11 B. iv.—Gray's Inn, 20.

---

[1] Rejected by Wadding without good reason: *Hist. Litt.* xxv, 447.

[2] Twyne MS. XXII, 103 c.

[3] Wood MS. F 29 a, 178: 'Rob. de Couton' is the eighteenth in the list of twenty-two names.

[4] '*Doctor amoenus* vulgo vocatus est.' Pits, p. 443 (anno 1340).

[5] I have not found any mention of Robert Cowton in any foreign library, unless 'Cathon' in Bibl. Nat. Paris MSS. 15886–7, be for Cowton. Valentinelli proposes to identify Cowton with 'Frater ven. doctor Robertus Anglicus ordinis Minorum,' the author of a *Dialogus de formalitatibus inter Ochanistam et Dumsistam* (sic): *inc.* 'quod verbis vituperii satis abundas'; MS. Venice; St. Mark, Vol. I. Class. V, Cod. 24 (sec. xv). The author was probably later than Cowton; perhaps Robert Eliphat.

Oxford:—Univ. Coll. 76, f. 455—Balliol 192, 199, 200, 201—Merton 91, 92, 93—New College 290—Exeter 43—Lincoln 36.
Cambridge:—Caius Coll. 281, 324—Peterhouse 73, 75—Pembroke 107.

Malachias of Ireland is said by Wadding to have been a Franciscan and B.D. of Oxford, c. 1310. According to the same writer, he preached before Edward II, and was not afraid to rebuke the King to his face[1].

Libellus septem peccatorum mortalium, or, *Tractatus de Veneno* (often wrongly ascribed to Grostete.)

MS. Brit. Mus.: Cott. Vitell. C. xiv, § 6.
Printed at Paris 1518.

Walter Brinkley or **Brinkel** (co. Cambridge), called by Willot 'the Good Doctor,' 'the ancient Doctor and Sophist[2],' is said by Bale to have been a doctor of Oxford and to have flourished A.D. 1310. Bale and Pits give a list of his works, but nothing of a trustworthy nature appears to be known about him[3].

John of Winchelsea, S.T.P. and Canon of Salisbury, a fellow of Merton in the reigns of Henry III (?) and Edward I, entered the Minorite Order in his old age at Salisbury, and died during the year of his noviciate, A.D. 1326[4].

John Canon is said to have flourished c. 1320, and to have attended the lectures of Duns Scotus at Oxford and Paris[5]. Wood, referring to the *regestrum Oriell*, says that his

'philosophicall treatises were soe much esteemed among the students of this University that they were read to them by their tutors and by logick lecturers in each society[6].'

---

[1] Ann. Min. VI, 176: Wadding refers vaguely to 'Irish MSS.' Cf. Bale, Script. II, 242-3. Dict. of Nat. Biography.

[2] Willot, Athenae, 83. Bale, Vol. II, p. 52: 'Sophisticus doctor et scriptor antiquus.' William Woodford refers on several occasions to 'Doctor antiquus' on the *Sentences*; Harl. MS. 31, f. 79, &c.

[3] Bale gives these notes in MS. Seld. sup. 64, fol. 16 b: *Brynkcley ... scripsit distinctiones theologicas*, lib. I; 'Ad sciendam primam originem et finalem'; *ex Ramesiensi monasterio. Brenkyll Minorita scripsit lecturam sententiarum*, lib. IV; 'Utrum per aliquam disciplinam vel scientiam'; *ex Coll. Regine Oxon. Brinquilis Minorita anglus scripsit super sententias*, lib. IV; 'Sit aliqua conclusio theologica'; *Ex bibl. Carmel. Parisiensium.*

[4] Mon. Franc. I, 543; Brodrick, Mem. of Merton Coll., 197-8; Bale, Script. I, 391.

[5] Tanner, Bibl. 150. All Souls MS. 87 (A.D. 1473), 'Joannis Scoti discipulus.' The note in Peterhouse MS. 2-4-2, 'studiit Oxon et Paris,' is in a late sixteenth-century hand.

[6] Wood-Clark, II, 402.

Comment. in libros octo Physicorum Aristotelis. Inc. prol. 'Venite ad me omnes qui laboratis.' *Inc. opus.* 'Utrum substancia finita.'

Of the MSS. of the work, which are very numerous, the oldest appears to be Lambeth MS. 100, f. 103, which Todd refers to the thirteenth century.

Printed at Padua 1475[1], St. Albans 1481, Venice 1481, 1487, 1492, &c.

John Stanle, friar, was appointed to receive at the Exchequer the royal grant of 25 marks payable at Easter 1323 to the Friars Minors at Oxford[2].

'**Philippus a Castellione Aretino**' (Castello near Arezzo) in the Tuscan province, is described by Wadding as, '*in theologia magister insignis apud Oxonienses.*' He flourished 1316, and wrote treatises on the poverty of Christ[3].

William of Ockham, 'Auctor nominalium,' 'Doctor singularis,' 'Doctor invincibilis[4],' was born probably towards the end of the thirteenth century. Whether he was a pupil of Duns Scotus is doubtful. He studied at Oxford in the early years of the fourteenth century, and became B.D. there[5]. After this he was called to Paris, where he incepted as D.D. Here he became acquainted with Marsiglio of Padua, over whom, according to Pope Clement VI, he exercised a powerful influence[6]. It is probable that he was present at the famous Chapter of Perugia (1322), though he was not (as is usually asserted) Provincial of England[7]. From the first he took a prominent part in the struggle against the Pope[8]. He was

---

[1] At the end of the work in this edition: 'Expliciunt questiones super octo libris phisicorum Aristotilis doctoris profundissimi fratris Johannis canonici ordinis fratrum minorum Anno 1475 ... Padue impresse.' At the end of the volume: '... compilatum a domino iohanne marbres magistro in artibus tholose et canonico,' &c. The *explicit* of Book I and Book II attributes these *quaestiones* to 'Doctor canonicus magister Petrus Casuelis ordinis minorum.'

[2] Record Off. Treasury of Receipt, 25/16.

[3] Wadding, Ann. Min. VI, 246.

[4] Wood says that Ockham received the last title from the Pope. Annals, I, 439.

[5] Lambeth MS. 221 (sec. xiv), fol. 308 b; among 'modern Oxonians,' singled out for special praise, is 'Occam inceptor in theology.' Barth. of Pisa, Liber Conform. f. 81 b, calls him 'Bacalarius formatus Oxonie.' Cf. MS. Bibl. Mazarine, Paris, 894 (sec. xiv), 'Questiones super primum librum Sententiarum de ordinacione fratris Guillelmi de Okham de ordine fratrum Minorum, Oxonie.'

[6] Riezler, *Die literarischen Widersacher der Päpste*, &c. pp. 35, 141.

[7] Wadding, VI, 396; Riezler, p. 71, &c. The English Provincial was William of Nottingham.

[8] Wadding cites a letter of John XXII dated Kal. Dec. A° VIII (1323), ordering the Bishops of Ferrara and Bologna to inquire into a report that

imprisoned at Avignon about the end of 1327, and a process was instituted against him in the Curia

'because of many erroneous and heretical opinions which he had written[1].'

He remained in custody for seventeen weeks, and refused to modify his opinions. It is said that a 'rich and noble lady,' in admiring recognition of his staunch defence of 'Evangelical Poverty,' gave him 70 florins[2]. On May 25, 1328, he fled from Avignon with Cesena, the General Minister, and Bonagratia, joined the Emperor in Italy, and was excommunicated[3]. In Feb., 1330, he accompanied Louis to Bavaria, and lived henceforth for the most part in the Franciscan Convent at Munich[4]. His literary activity was enormous, as may be seen from the list of his works. He took a direct part in the affairs of state, being present at the Councils of Rense and Frankfurt in 1338[5]. From this time his writings, hitherto largely theological, became more distinctly political[6]. In spite of excommunication, he continued to support the Emperor's cause till Louis' death in 1347, and even later[7]. But now few only of the rebel friars were left: Cesena died in 1342, Bonagratia in 1347; and in 1349 Ockham sent back the seal of the Order to the orthodox General Minister, and professed his desire to be reconciled to the Church[8]. Clement VI authorized the General Minister to absolve Ockham and his associates on their confessing in set form their errors and heresies, and promising to obey the Pope and his successors. Whether Ockham subscribed the papal formula, nothing remains to show. The date of his death is uncertain; it may however be concluded that he died at Munich not before 1349[9].

PHILOSOPHICAL AND THEOLOGICAL WORKS.

Commentarii in Porphyrii librum: in Aristotelis Praedicamentorum

Ockham had upheld the doctrine of Evangelical Poverty in a public sermon; if so, he was to be sent to Avignon within a month. Ann. Min. VII, 7, 23.

[1] Anal. Franc. II, 142. Among the writings must have been the treatise *De paupertate Christi*, which Leland and Wadding mention, but which has not been identified. Cf. also Wadding, VII, 81-2, who states a work written at Avignon in 1328 was afterwards inserted in the *Dialogus*.

[2] Riezler, 71.
[3] Ibid. 68-71; Anal. Franc. II, 143.
[4] Riezler, 76-7.
[5] Ibid. 95 seq.
[6] Ibid. 82.
[7] In his treatise on the election of Charles, the creature of the Pope.
[8] Wadding, VIII, 12-13, where the letter of the Pope to the General Minister, with the form of absolution, is given.
[9] Riezler; Wadding, VIII, pp. 10-11.

librum (or *De decem generibus*): *in Aristotelis de Interpretatione libros duo: in libros Elenchorum.*

MSS. Oxford:—Bodl. Canonic. Misc. 558, fol. 1, 24, 63ᵇ, 93 (sec. xiv).
Paris:—Bibl. Nat. 14721.
Bruges 499, *olim* 59 (sec. xiii ?).
The first three of these works (and perhaps the last) were printed at Bologna in 1496, under the title *Expositio aurea super totam artem Veterem.*

In his Catalogue of the Bruges MSS., Haenel reads *ethicorum* instead of *elenchorum.* Ockham seems to have written no distinct work on morals, though another is attributed to him by a careless blunder. Caius College MS. 200, § 3, contains, according to Smith's catalogue, *Correcciones Occami* (*Occani* in the old catalogue of 1697) *in Oculum moralem.* The MS. really reads:

' Correcciones octaui capituli de Ira. (*Inc.*) nisi tibi iratus fuissem. Refert eciam Valerius. (*Expl.*) et ei reuelauit archana. Cum igitur sobrietas.'

In other words, it is merely a fragment of chapter viii. of the well-known *Oculus moralis* attributed to Grostete or Peter de Limoges. See e.g. MS. Bodl. Laud. Misc. 677, fol. 180 b, 2nd column.

Summa logices (*ad Adamum*): 3 parts. *Inc.* 'Dudum me frater et amice. . . . Omnes logicae tractatores.'

MSS. London:—Brit. Mus., Arundel 367 (sec. xiv).
Cambridge:—Caius Coll. 464¹: 'Logica Gul. de Occham in sex tractatus divisa,' viz. (1) de terminis, (2) de propositionibus, (3) de Sillogismo simplici, (4) de S. demonstrativo, (5) de S. topico, (6) de S. elenchorum, (written at Magdeburg, A. D. 1341): also Peterhouse 217.
Paris:—Bibl. Nat. 6430, 6431, 6432 (sec. xiv); Bibl. Mazarine 3521 (sec. xiv).
Laon 431 (sec. xiv).
Basel F ii. 25 (written at Oxford, A. D. 1342).
Florence:—Laurentiana, *ex Bibl. S. Crucis*, Plut. xii. Sin. Cod. ii (sec. xiv), six books.
Printed at Paris 1488, Venice 1522, Oxford 1675, &c.

Quaestiones in octo libros physicorum. *Inc.* 'Valde reprehensibilis.'
MS. Oxford:—Merton Coll. 293 (sec. xiv). Cf. Vienna:—Bibl. Palat. 5460 (sec. xv).
Printed at Rome 1637².

---

[1] On the last fly-leaf is a rude portrait of the author.

[2] According to Tanner, one of Ockham's works on the Physics was printed at Strasburg in 1491.

In the Bibl. Nat. at Paris, MS. 17841 (sec. xv) contains *Quest. Okam super lib. Physic. et quotlibeta.* The first leaf seems to have been misplaced; *inc.*, '(U)trum deus sit super omnia diligendus: quod non.' The second leaf begins: 'Circa materiam de conceptu questio (?) utrum conceptus sit aliquid fictum': the questions on the physics end on fol. 26. They appear to differ from the above[1].

Questiones Ockam super phisicam et tractatus ejusdem de futuris contingentibus.

MS. Bruges 469 (sec. xiv).

Summulae in libros physicorum (called by Leland, *De introitu scientiarum*): 4 parts. *Inc. prol.* 'Studiosissime saepiusque rogatus.' *Inc. Pars. I.* 'Solent ante preambula indagare sapientes ante scientie ingressum de ipsis scientiis. . . . Primo de ejus unitate.'

MS. Rodez, 56, p. 107 (sec. xv), 'Philosophia naturalis.'

Printed at Venice 1506, and elsewhere.

Quaestiones (or *Commentarii*) *in quatuor libros Sententiarum. Inc.* 'Circa prologum primi libri Sententiarum quero primo utrum sit possibile intellectui viatoris.'

MSS. Oxford:—Balliol Coll. 299, f. 7 (sec. xiv); Merton College 100 (sec. xiv).

Paris:—Bibl. Nat. 15561, f. 246 (sec. xv).

Basel A vi. 12.

Printed at Lyons 1495, &c.

Ockham's commentary on the first book of the *Sentences* was probably composed when he was B.D. of Oxford; it is longer than his commentaries on the other three books together, and is often found séparate.

MSS. Oxford:—Merton Coll. 106 (sec. xiv).

Cambridge:—Caius Coll. 325.

Paris:—Bibl. Mazarine 894 (sec. xiv), 'de ordinacione fratris Guillelmi de Okham de ordine fratrum Minorum Oxonie.'

Troyes 718 (sec. xiv).

Printed separately (at Strasburg) in 1483.

It is possible that the commentaries on the last three books exist in a fuller form in the following MSS. than in the printed editions:—

MSS. Paris:—Bibl. Nat. 16398 (sec. xv), books 3 and 4; Cf. ibid.

---

[1]. Another work on the Physics ascribed to Ockham was preserved at Assisi, and perhaps is there still: *inc. prol.* 'Philosophos plurimos': *inc. opus.* 'Iste liber dividitur in duas partes.' (Wadding, *Sup. ad Script.* 328.)

16708, f. 253ᵇ (sec. xiv), 'Circa tertium Sententiarum secundum Okkam.'

Munich :—Bibl. Reg. 8943 (sec. xv), books 2, 3, and 4.

Quodlibeta septem. Inc. quodl. i. qu. i. 'Utrum possit probari per rationem naturalem quod tantum unus sit deus: quod sic.'

 MSS. Paris :—Bibl. Nat. 16398, f. 173 (sec. xv), and 17841, fol. 28 (sec. xv) : the latter ends abruptly near the beginning of the fourth quodlibet.

 Venice :—Bibl. S. Anton. (Tomasin, p. 11 b).

Printed at Paris 1487, Argentina 1491.

At the end of the edition of 1491 : 'Expliciunt quotlibeta septem venerabilis inceptoris magistri Wilhelmi de Ockam anglici, veritatum speculatoris acerrimi, fratris ordinis minorum, post ejus lecturam Oxoniensem (super sententias) edita.'

De motu, loco, tempore, relatione, praedestinatione et praescientia Dei, et quodlibetum.

 MS. Basel F ii. 24.

 Cf. MS. Paris:—Bibl. Nat. 14715, f. 82ᵇ (sec. xiv); 14909, f. 102ᵇ; 14579, f. 345; 14580, f. 110ᵇ. *Incipiunt* : ' Quia circa materiam de predestinatione et prescientia sunt opiniones diverse.'

De successivis. Inc. 'Videndum est de locis.'

 MS. Paris :—Bibl. Nat. 16130, f. 121 (sec. xiv). Cf. MS. Bruges, 500.

Propositio an sit concedenda ; essentia divina est quaternitas.

 MS. Basel A vii. 13.

De sacramento altaris, and *De corpore Christi* : 2 treatises[1]. *Inc. i.* 'Circa conversionem panis.' *Inc. ii.* 'Stupenda super munera largitatis.'

 MSS. Oxford :—Balliol Coll. 299, f. 196 (sec. xiv); Merton College 137 (sec. xiv).

  Rouen, 561 (sec. xv).

 Printed at Argentina 1491, at the end of the *Quodlibeta* ; at Paris (1490?), and Venice 1516.

Centiloquium theologicum. Inc. prol. 'Anima nobis innata eo potius naturaliter appetit cognoscere suum finem, quo pre ceteris appetentibus omnibus corruptibilibus creatis ratione ditata ad ymaginem et similitudinem dei celsius eminentiusque figuratur.'

 Printed at Lyons 1495, at the end of the *Sentences*.

---

[1] The first, consisting of three *quaestiones*, is called : 'Tractatus quam gloriosus de sacramento altaris, et in primis de puncti, linee, superficiei, corporis, quantitatis, qualitatis et substantie distinctione,' &c. The second contains forty-one chapters : 'Incipit accessus ad tractatum de corpore Christi.' *Explicit* : ' hec tamen simpliciter falsa est, corpus Christi est quantitas in sacramento altaris.'

Quaestiones Ocham in terminabiles Alberti de Saxonia.
  MS. Padua :—Bibl. S. Joannis in Viridario (Tomasin, p. 37).
Sermones Occham, by William or Nicholas of Ockham?
  MS. Worcester :—Cathedral Library 74 quarto (=Bernard, Tom. II. 918).
Notes or disputations on theology and philosophy, to which the name 'Okam' is appended.
  MS. Paris :—Bibl. Nat. 15888, f. 163, 174, 181.
Gul. Qcham quedam scripta.
  MS. Venice :—Bibl. SS. Joannis et Pauli (Tomasin, p. 25^b).

POLITICAL WORKS.

The dates are taken for the most part from Riezler.

Opus nonaginta dierum (written between 1330 and 1333). *Inc. prol.* 'Doctoris gentium et Magistri Beati Pauli.'
  MS. Paris :—Bibl. Nat. 3387, fol. 1-163 b (sec. xv).
  Printed at Louvain 1481, Lyons 1495, and in Goldast's *Monarchia,* II. 993-1236.
  This treatise corresponds to *Dialogus,* Part III, Tract vi. *de gestis fratris Michaelis de Cesena* (see below).

Epistola ad Fratres Minores in Capitulo apud Assisium congregatos, A.D. 1334. *Inc.* 'Religiosis viris fratribus minoribus universis A. p. Millesimo cccxxxiiii. in festo Petri apud Assisium congregatis frater Guilhelmus de Ocham fidem defensare.'
  MS. Paris :—Bibl. Nat. 3387, fol. 262 b-265 a (sec. xv).

This has not been printed and is not mentioned by Riezler; it is distinct from the letter of Cesena to the Friars Minors about to assemble in Chapter at Perpignan or Avignon, dated April 25, 1331 (printed Lyons 1495), and the letter of Cesena to all the Friars Minors, dated Jan. 24, 1331 (printed ibid.; Goldast, II. 1238, and Riezler, 248, give 1333 as the date of this last letter).

Dialogus[1] *inter magistrum et discipulum de Imperatorum et Pontificum Potestate ;* 3 parts:

  i. *De fautoribus haereticorum libri septem* (written A.D. 1342 or 1343). *Inc.* 'In omnibus rebus curiosus existis.'

  ii. *De dogmatibus Johannis XXII, tractatus duo* (A.D. 1333 or 1334). *Inc.* 'Verba oris ejus iniquitas et dolus.'

---

[1] Ockham did not write the *Disputatio inter militem et clericum.* See Riezler, 144-8.

iii. *De gestis circa fidem altercantium* (A.D. 1342-3). (1) De potestate papae et cleri; 4 books. (2) De potestate et juribus Romani imperii; 3 books. *Inc.* 'Discip. Salomonis utcumque sequendo vestigia.'

 MSS. London:—Brit. Mus. Royal 7 F xii, §§ 1 and 2 (sec. xv), Parts I and II; Harleian, 33 (sec. xv), Parts I and II; Addit. 33243 (sec. xv), Parts I and II; also Lambeth Palace Library 168 (sec. xv), Parts II and III.
 Oxford:—St. John's College, 69 (sec. xv), Part I.
 Paris:—Bibl. Nat. 3657 (sec. xiv) Part I, fol. 1-208; Part II, fol. 289-321; Part III, Tractatus ii, fol. 210-287, breaking off with the words *nec antedicte sedis scil. Romane antistitem* in Lib. 3, cap. 16 of Tract. ii; also 14313 (A.D. 1389), Parts I and II; 14619, fol. 121-166 (sec. xv), Part III, Tractatus ii, breaking off in Lib. 3, cap. 16 of Tract. ii, as above; 15881 (sec. xiv), Parts I, II; and Part III, Tractatus ii, breaking off in Lib. 3, cap. 16, as above.— Bibl. de l'Arsenal 517, fol. 17-303, Parts I, II, and III, ending with the words '*Magister Hoc multis racionibus improbatur. Primo* . . .', in Chapter 17 of the 3rd book of Tractatus ii of Part III [1],—Bibl. Mazarine 3522 (sec. xiv), fol. 149-198, Part III, Tract. ii, ending in Cap. 16 of Lib. 3; fol. 200-246, Part III, Tract. i; fol. 246-297, Part III, Tract. ii, ending with Cap. 23 of Lib. 3, *passibilis et mortalis.*
 Rome:—Vatican, Bibl. Regin. Sueciae, 90; cf. 79, 'de potestate papae.' (Montfaucon.)
 Dijon 340 (sec. xv), Parts I, II, and III, ending with the words '*pro nunc tibi sufficiant*,' as in the printed editions.
 Auxerre 252, f. 88 (sec. xiv), containing Part III, Tract. ii (3 books).
 Avignon 185, containing Part I.
 Toulouse 221 (sec. xiv), Parts I, II, and Part III, Tractatus ii, which is called Tractatus iii in the MS.
 Basel A vi. 5, Parts I, II, and III.
 Florence:—Laurentiana, *ex Bibl. S. Crucis*, Plut. xxxvi. Dext. Cod. xi (sec. xiv), Parts I and II.
 Venice:—St. Mark, Vol. I, Cl. viii. Cod. 7 (sec. xv), Part I, book 6.
 Printed at Lyons 1495; reprinted in Goldast's *Monarchia* II, 398-957.

Part III, according to the scheme drawn up in the Prologue [2], was to consist of nine treatises:

 i. De potestate papae et cleri; ii. De potestate et juribus Romani

---

[1] I do not know whether this MS. contains Tractatus i of Part III; probably, like most of the MSS., it omits it.
[2] Goldast, Monarchia, II, 771.

Imperii; iii. De gestis Johannis XXII; iv. De gestis Domini Ludovici de Bavaria; v. De gestis Benedicti XII; vi. De gestis fratris Michaelis de Cesena; vii. De gestis et doctrina fratris Geraldi Odonis; viii. De gestis fratris Guilhelmi de Ockham; ix. De gestis aliorum Christianorum, regum, &c.

The edition of 1495, of which Goldast's is a reprint, ends at the 23rd chapter of the 3rd book of Treatise II, with the words:

'passibilis et mortalis. Et haec de tertia parte Dialogorum pro nunc tibi sufficiant.'

The last sentence Goldast surmises to be an addition of the editor, Ascensius; but it occurs at the end of the Dijon MS., and both Goldast and Riezler are probably mistaken in thinking that Ascensius had the whole work before him and arbitrarily omitted Treatises III–IX[1]. These were probably never written. The Lambeth MS. (the only MS. in England which contains Part III) and one version in the Mazarine MS. end with the words 'passibilis et mortalis,' like the printed editions, with the colophon (in Lambeth MS.): 'Dyalogorum venerabilis Guillermi Okam finis.' The five other MSS. in Paris, which contain Part III, leave out the last seven chapters of the printed edition, and the Auxerre and Toulouse MSS. likewise do not go beyond the third book of Treatise II. It is possible that the Vatican and Basel MSS. may supply the remaining treatises; but this is unlikely. About the year 1400, Peter d'Ailly, who must have had exceptionally good opportunities for getting information[2], wrote a summary of the *Dialogus*[3]. In this he omits Treatise I of Part III, and concludes with the 16th chapter of the third book of Treatise II (like the Parisian MSS.), adding:

' et non plus de hoc notabili opere potui reperire '[4].

---

[1] Goldast, Monarchia, II, 957; Riezler, 263. Goldast speaks of six treatises only as missing, being apparenty under the impression that he has printed three. The subdivisions are very confusing, and lead to many mistakes.

[2] He was B.D. of Paris in 1373; D.D. in 1380; Chancellor in 1389; Bishop of Cambrai in 1396; Cardinal in 1411; he died in 1425. Oudin, Scriptores, III, p. 2293.

[3] MS. Paris, Bibl. Nat. 14579, fol. 88—fol. 101 b: ' Explicit abbreviatio Dyalogi Okan quam fecit magister Petrus de Alliaco Episcopus Cameracensis et postea cardinalis.'

[4] Ibid. f. 101 b. His nomenclature differs from that used here and (generally though not consistently) in the printed editions: thus he calls ' Pars I ' *Tractatus primus*; ' Pars II,' *Tractatus secundus*; ' Pars III, Tract ii ' (the only portion of Part III known to him), *Tractatus tertius*. Thus fol. 98 b: ' Tractatus tertius est de viribus Romani imperii et habet 5 libros.' Books 1, 2, and 3, correspond to those printed in Goldast (Pars III, Tract. ii, Libri 1,

Several of Ockham's other works correspond in substance to the projected treatises of Part III; these will be noted in due course.

Defensorium (de paupertate Christi) contra Johannem XXII (written between 1335 and 1349). *Inc.* 'Universis Christi fidelibus. . . . Primus error est quod Dominus noster.'
Printed at Venice 1513, and by Edw. Brown, Fascic. Rerum expetend. II, 439-464.

De imperatorum et pontificum potestate; 27 chapters or paragraphs. *Inc. prol.* 'Universis Christi fidelibus presentem tractatulum inspecturis, frater Willelmus de Okkham.' *Inc. cap.* i. 'Si reges et principes ecclesiarum.'
MS. Brit. Museum: Royal 10 A, xv (sec. xiv).

Tractatus adversus errores Johannis XXII, or *Compendium errorum papae* (written between 1335 and 1338). *Inc.* 'Secundum Bokkyg (?) super sacram scripturam.'
MSS. London:—Lambeth 168, fol. 289-314 (sec. xv).
Paris:—Bibl. Mazarine 3522, fol. 298-310 (sec. xiv).
Printed at Louvain 1481, Lyons 1495, and in Goldast II, 957-976.
Cf. *Dialogus*, Part III, Tract. iii.

Opusculum adversus errores Johannis XXII. Inc. 'Non invenit locum penitencie Johannes XXII. . . . Ut pateat evidenter, quod retractatio quam Johannes XXII fecisse refertur, ipsum ab hereticorum numero non excludit.'
MS. Paris:—Bibl. Nat. 3387, fol. 175-213^b (sec. xv).

Tractatus ostendens quod Benedictus Papa XII nonnullas Johannis XXII haereses amplexus est et defendit; 7 books (written c. 1338). *Inc. prol.* 'Ambulavit et ambulat insensanter non re sed nomine Benedictus XII in viis patris sui Johannis vidz. XXII.' *Inc. lib. i*, 'Dogmatum perversorum que Johannes XXII pertinaciter tenuit.'
MS. Paris:—Bibl. Nat. 3387, fol. 214^b-262^a (sec. xv).
Cf. *Dialogus*, Pars III, Tract. v.

Tractatus oquā (sic) *de potestate imperiali. Inc.* 'Inferius describuntur allegaciones per plures magistros in sacra pagina approbate per quas ostenditur evidenter quod processus factus et sentencia lata in frankfort per dominum lodowicum quartum dei gracia

---

2, 3): Book 4 discussed whether the emperor should defend the rights of the Roman Empire by arms 'etiam contra papam cardinales et clerum'; Book 5 treated 'de rebellibus, proditoribus, ... Romani imperii.' These two books were not known to Peter d'Ailly, and are not now to be found.

Romanorum imperatorem.' The decree of Louis referred to is dated Aug. 6, 1338[1].

MS. Rome:—Bibl. Apostol. Vaticana, Codd. Palat. Latin. No. 679. Pars I, fol. 117 (sec. xv).

Cf. Boehmer, Fontes rerum Germanicarum, Vol. IV, p. 592, 'ex libro Nicolai Minoritae de controversia paupertatis Christi 1324-1338.' *Inc.* 'Subsequenter ponuntur articuli et describunter de juribus imperii.'

Octo questiones super potestate ac dignitate papali, or *De potestate pontificum et imperatorum* (written between 1339 and 1342). *Inc.* 'Sanctum canibus nullatenus.' *Inc. quest.* 1. 'Primo igitur queritur utrum potestas spiritualis et laicalis suprema.'

MSS. Paris:—Bibl. Nat. 14603, fol. 147-216 (sec. xiv): 'Explicit tractatus venerabilis, theologi Guillelmi Okam de potestate pape.' —Bibl. Mazarine, 3522, f. 104-148 (sec. xiv).

Cf. MS. Rome, Vatican, Bibl. Reg. Sueciae, 79, *De potestate Papae*; and 375, *De potestate utriusque jurisdictionis*.

De jurisdictione Imperatoris in causis matrimonialibus, A.D. 1342. *Inc.* 'Divina providentia disponente.'

Printed at Heidelberg 1598; and in Goldast I, 21. It is of doubtful authenticity; see Riezler, 254.

De electione Caroli IV (written 1347-9). *Inc.* 'Quia sepe viri ignari.'

See Riezler, p. 271, 303, who refers to Höfler, Aus Avignon, 13.

The following treatises by Ockham are mentioned by Leland, Wadding, and others, but have not been identified.

I. *Philosophical.*

De pluralitate formae, contra Sutton (Leland, Tanner).

De invisibilibus (Leland).

Tractatus incip.: 'Dominus potest facere omne quod fieri vult non includit contradictionem':—

seen by Leland in the Franciscan Library, London (Collect. III, 49): Tanner identifies it with *Defensorium Logices*. Perhaps it is the same as *Dialectica Nova*: *inc.* 'Contradictio in Deo non est.' (Bale, Pits).

Comment. in Metaphysicam.

Tanner refers to MSS. Peterhouse 217 (where however no mention of it occurs), and Caius Coll. K. 5 (?), perhaps a mistake for H. 5 = 464, which contains Ockham's logic.

---

[1] Analecta Franciscana II, 169 sqq.

Leland adds:

Vidi etiam tres libros Ochami, quorum primus *De privatione, de materia prima, de forma* quae est principium, et *De forma artificiali*; secundus vero *De causis materiali, formali, efficiente, finali*; tertius *De mutatione subita* tractat.

[Cf. *Quaestiones in lib. Physic?*]

De perfectione specierum (Wadding). *Inc.* 'Quia Magister.'

II. *Political.*

De paupertate Christi et Apostolorum (Tritheim, Wadding).
> This is probably incorporated in the Dialogus (see Wadding, Ann. Min. VIII, 81–2). Cf. MS. Florence:—Laurentiana, *ex Bibl. S. Crucis*, Plut. xxxi. Sin. Cod. iii (sec. xiv).

De actibus hierarchicis, lib. i (Wadding).
> Wadding, *Sup.*: 'citat Joan. Picus Mirandulanus in sua Apologia quaest. 1.'

Errorum quos affinxit papae Johanni, lib. i (Wadding). *Inc.* 'Locuti adversum me lingua.'
> (Probably identical with one of the extant treatises.)

Defensorium (against the pope); mentioned by Leland, Bale, &c. *Inc.* 'Omni quippe regno desiderabilis.'
> This is the *Defensor pacis* of Marsilius of Padua.

NOTE.—In his catalogue of Vatican MSS., Montfaucon mentions, among *Praecipui codices MSS. Bibliothecae Vaticanae*, '947, ad 956 Guill. Occhami opera.' See Montfaucon, *Bibl. Bibliothecarum MSS.* p. 100.

Henry de Costesey or **Cossey** (Norfolk) is reckoned among the Oxford Franciscans by Bale and others, but without evidence. He was forty-sixth Master of the Minorites at Cambridge (c. 1336)[1], and is said to have died at Babwell[2].

Commentarius super Apocalypsim. *Inc.* 'Apocalypsis Jhesu Christi quam.... Dividitur enim iste liber sicut alii libri in prohemium et tractatum.'
> MSS. Bodl.: 2004=NE. B. 3. 18, now Bodley 57. Laud. Misc. 85, fol. 67 b (sec. xiv).
> Cambridge:—Pembroke Coll. 175.

Comment. super Psalterium. *Inc.* 'Aperiam in psalterio.'
> MS. formerly in the Franciscan library, London[3]: quoted in MS. Bodl. Laud. Misc. 213, f. 192 (sec. xv).

---

[1] Mon. Franc. I, 556. Tanner (Bibl. 202) confounds him with another H. de Costesey in the fifteenth century.

[2] Bale, I, 409.

[3] Leland, Collect. III, 49.

John de Hentham was a Minorite in the Oxford Convent in 1340, when he acted as attorney for the warden [1].

Hugh de Willoughby or **Wylluby**, S.T.P., was the Chancellor of the University in 1334. He held the prebend of Barnby, in the diocese of York, in 1338. It is not known when he became a Franciscan; but it was no doubt in his declining years [2].

Peter de Gaieta was elected in the General Chapter at Assisi, c. 1340, to take the degree of B.D. and lecture on the *Sentences* at Oxford. When the appointment of a friar to read the *Sentences* at Paris was discussed in the General Chapter at Marseilles in 1343, Peter obtained many votes. In the same year the degree of Master in the University of Naples was conferred on him by the command of Pope Clement VI. He had previously lectured on the *Sentences* there, and been Minister of the Provinces of Apulia and Terra Laboris [3].

John Lathbury (Bucks), said to have been a native of the Reading friary [4], was D.D. of Oxford and flourished about the middle of the fourteenth century [5]. The evidence for the date is found in his own most famous work [6]; the passage may be quoted as an authentic specimen of a subject of conversation between two Oxford Franciscans:

'Item anno domini 1343 in capitulo provinciali Londoniis celebrato, et in Oxonia plurimis vicibus prius et post in studio secum commoranti, frater Hermanus de Colonia fratri Johanni de Latthebury retulit viva voce, quod in patria sua est quedam villa que vulgariter dicatur Enger, de qua Anglia vocaliter derivatur, et prope illam villam ad distanciam unius miliarii est quedam quercus, arbor ingens et antiqua, ad quam ipse cum esset puerulus ex more patrie cum reliquis concurrebat. Nam omni nocte nativitatis Christi, quasi nocte media, quercus illa glandes grandes et perfectas subita apparicione ex se profert et producit copiose. Unde et incole illius patrie annuatim illa nocte ad illum locum turmatim ex consuetudine concurrunt, et ibi cum luminibus et lanternis vigilantes, horam solitam expectant et

---

[1] Twyne MS. XXIII, 266; cp. Part I, Chapter VII.

[2] Wood, Hist. et Antiq. II, 398; Le Neve, Fasti III, 465, 170; Mon. Franc. I, 542.

[3] Wadding, VII, 291.

[4] According to Bale he left several of his works to the convent at Reading; I have not found the authority for this statement. See Tanner, Bibl. 469. Adam de Lathbury was Abbat of Reading monastery in 1233. Dugdale, Vol. VI, Part III, p. 1509.

[5] The assertion that he flourished in 1406 rests on a misunderstanding of the *explicit* in MS. Merton Coll. 189: 'explicit secundum alphabetum et sic totum opus est completum A. D. 1406.' This of course only refers to the writing of the MS.

[6] *Liber moralium in Threnos*, cap. 106; Merton Coll. MS. 189, fol. 172 dorse.

explorant, bibentes, edentes, ludentes et noctem insompnem ducentes, habentes secum lapides, baculos et saculos pro fructu arboris excuciendo et asportando.'

There appear to have been two contemporary Minorites of the same name and family. Bale, after mentioning the commentaries of John Ridevaus on the letter of Valerius to Rufinus and the mythologies of Fulgentius, adds[1]:

'Hos libros cum multis aliis Joannes Lathbury senior contulit juniori Joanni Lathbury A.D. 1348. Ex cenobio Minorum Radinge.'

The elder died at Reading at an advanced age in 1362, the younger at Northampton in 1375[2]. It is not clear which of the two was the author.

The best known work of John Lathbury is his *Commentary on Lamentations*, or *Liber moralium in Threnos Hieremiae*, or *Lectura super librum Threnorum*. *Inc.* 'Juxta mores modernorum.'

   MSS. Oxford:—Merton Coll. 189—Exeter Coll. 27, &c.
   Printed at Oxford in 1482, being one of the first books issued by the Oxford press.

Distinctionum liber theologicarum, or *Alphabetum morale*. *Inc.*
   'Abstinendum est a carnalibus delitiis.'
   MSS. Brit. Mus.: Royal 11 A xiii (sec. xv).
       Oxford:—Exeter Coll. 26 (sec. xv), with the note 'Johannes Latbury, doctor de ordine fratrum minorum, qui fecit lecturam super librum Trenorum, compilavit istum tractatum. Cambridge:—Peterhouse 96.

De luxuria clericorum.
   Extracts from this treatise of Lathbury's are in MS. Bodl. James 19 (Cf. Bernard's Catal. I, 260 b), from MSS. in Exeter College: the treatise itself seems to be extracted from the *Distinctiones*.

De timore et amore Domini, &c., *secundum Johannem Lathbury, Thomam de Alquino . . . aliosque.*
   MS. Oxford:—Magd. Coll. 93 (A.D. 1438); perhaps merely excerpts from some other work.

Super Acta Apostolorum. *Inc.* 'Superedificati estis supra fundamentum apostolorum.'
   Mentioned by Bale (MS. Seld. sup. 64, fol. 89) 'ex musaeo Rob. Talbot.'

Hermann of Cologne was a contemporary and friend of John Lathbury at Oxford, c. 1343[3]. It is impossible to identify him with

---

[1] MS. Selden, supra 64, fol. 75.
[2] MS. Selden, supra 64, fol. 89, 'ex quodam Minoritarum registro.'
[3] See notice of Lathbury.

any of the other Hermanns who belonged to the Minorite Order at this time: e.g. Hermann of Saxony, the lawyer (fl. 1337), or Hermann Gygas, the historian [1].

Robert (or John?) Lamborne,
'the son of a baron, and the last heir of that barony, entered the Order in London [2].'

He became confessor to Queen Isabella in 1327[3], and he still occupied this office, 'though he was so attenuated that he was almost or quite blind,' in 1343, when Clement VI granted him certain privileges [4]. It is however very doubtful whether he was ever at Oxford. The name occurs in the Old Catalogue of Fellows of Merton College, under the reign of Edward III. If the two are identical, Lamborne ought to be placed in the Catalogue under Edward II, as he was clearly a friar in 1327; but there is no good reason for assuming their identity: Robert Lamborn of Merton may be a mistake for Reginald Lamborn [5]. Friar John (?) Lamborne, confessor to Queen Isabella, was buried in the choir of the Grey Friars Church, London [6].

Reginald Lambourne was B.D. of Merton College (c. 1350–1360), where he was a pupil of the famous mathematicians, William Rede and John Ashendon [7]. He then entered the Benedictine Order, was at Eynsham Abbey in 136¾ and 1367, and incepted D.D. as a monk [8]. He afterwards took the Franciscan habit at Oxford, and died at Northampton [9].

Epistola a Reginaldo Lambourne, monacho simplici Eynshamensi, ad quendam Johannem London, de significatione eclipsium lunae 'hoc anno instante, 1363.'

[1] Wadding, Script. 116; Sup. ad Script. 341.

[2] Mon. Franc. I, 541.

[3] Record Office, Roman Transcripts, Regesta, Vol. V, f. 80–81, 1 Clement VI; 'per sexdecim annorum spatium continue institit.'

[4] Record Office, Roman Transcripts, ibid. He has permission to continue to reside in the London convent, to have a decent chamber, one friar as *socius*, one clerk, two servants, and to dispose of his books and other property.

[5] Mem. of Merton, p. 208.

[6] 'Item versus finem chori ex parte Boriali a stallis sub fune lampadis jacet sub longo lapide ffrater Johannes Lamborn confessor Regine Isabelle et filius Baronis et ultimus heres illius baronis.' MS. Cott. Vitell. F XII, fol. 276.

[7] Mon. Franc. I, 543; Mem. of Merton, 208.

[8] Mon. Franc. ibid.; MS. Digby 176, fol. 50, 40.

[9] Mon. Franc. ibid. He may be the same as Langberg or Langborow, fellow of Merton in 1357, and S.T.P., who is said to have become a Minorite. Simon Lamborn, fellow of Merton in 1347, Proctor in 1361, and S.T.P., is also said to have entered the Order, but Wood reasonably supposes this incident to have been borrowed from the life of Reginald Lambourne. Memorials of Merton, 208–9.

Epistola a Reginaldo Lambourne monacho Eynshamensi [ad. Gul. Rede ut videtur] a° 1367, *de conjunctionibus Saturni Jovis et Martis cum prognosticatione malorum inde in annis* 1368–1374 *probabiliter occurrentium.*

MS. Bodl.:—Digby 176, fol. 50, and 40 (sec. xiv).

Robert Eliphat flourished in the middle of the fourteenth century; he is placed among the Masters of the English Province by Bartholomew of Pisa[1]. Pits states that he was famous at Oxford and Paris[2]. There can be little doubt that he is identical with **Robert Alifax** or **Halifax**, the fifty-sixth Master of the Franciscans at Cambridge[3].

Robertus Haliphax de sententiarum libris I et II.

MS. Assisi 161 (sec. xiv).

Primus Eliphat super sententias.

MSS. Paris:—Bibl. Nat. 14514 (sec. xiv).

Vienna:—Bibl. Palat. 1511, f. 110–120 (sec. xiv).

Quaestiones Rob. Eliphat.

MSS. Paris:—Bibl. Nat. 14576 (xiv), 15561, f. 243 (xv), 15880 (xiv), 15888, f. 181, (xiv)[4].

Gilbert Peckham, fellow of Merton in 1324 and 1339, may be identical with the fifty-ninth Master of the Minorites at Cambridge[5].

William Tithemersch (co. Northampton), 'of the custody of Oxford,' was sixty-first Master of the Minorites at Cambridge, and twenty-first Provincial, about 1350; he was succeeded by Roger Conway, and was buried at Bedford[6].

William Scharshille (co. Stafford),

'formerly a justiciary under Edward III, gave away all his temporal goods and entered the Order, with great honour, at Oxford[7].'

The date is not specified. A William de Shareshull, who is no doubt the same person, was ordered to attend a parliament in Scotland for the confirmation of a treaty between Edward III and Edward Balliol, in 1333; he is mentioned as a justice of assize in 1337, and he was appointed one of the examiners of some ecclesiastical petitions to Parliament in 1351[8]. In 1356 'Dominus Willhelmus de Schars-

---

[1] Liber Conform. f. 81 b.

[2] Pits, p. 443. Bale is less definite, 'Anglorum gymnasia... petiit.' I, 416. Cf. Wadding, VII, 170 (A.D. 1334).

[3] Mon. Franc. I, 557. Tanner mentions him as Robert Eliphat, and 'Aliphat Anglus, Gregorii Ariminensis auditor'; Bibl. pp. 259, 36.

[4] Cf. also p. 222, note 5, above.

[5] Mon. Franc. I, 557; Mem. of Merton Coll., 195, 346.

[6] Mon. Franc. I, 557, 560, 538.

[7] Mon. Franc. I, 541.

[8] Rymer's Foed. Vol. II, Part. II, pp. 870, 991; Vol. III, Part. I, p. 230.

hull' appears among the witnesses to an indenture between the University of Oxford and Richard d'Amory[1].

Richard Lymynster and **Giuliortus de Limosano** are mentioned in a University decree as 'wax-doctors' of the Mendicant Orders at Oxford in 1358. It is uncertain to which Order the former belonged. The latter was a Minorite from Sicily, who tried to obtain the degree of B.D. by means of letters from the king of England[2].

Jerome of St. Mark is said to have been a Minorite and Bachelor of Oxford, and author of a treatise on logic. His date—or even the century in which he lived—is unknown[3].

John of Nottingham was a member of the Oxford Convent in the middle of the fourteenth century: he was one of the witnesses to the will of Robert de Trenge, Warden of Merton, and perhaps his confessor; the will was executed 1351, and proved 1357[4].

Roger Conway, of the convent of Worcester and D.D. of Oxford, in 1355 obtained papal license to live in the Franciscan Convent of London

'for the spiritual recreation of himself and of the nobles of England,'

who were said to flock in great numbers to this friary; Roger was to be subject to the rules of the house like any other friar[5]. In 1357 he came forward as the champion of the Mendicant Orders against the Archbishop of Armagh, and wrote and preached in London 'on the poverty of Christ' and the right of the friars to hear confessions[6]. According to one account

'he strenuously defended his Order in the Curia against Armachanus[7].'

In 1359 Innocent VI issued a bull confirming the decree *Vas electionis* of John XXII,

'at the instance of Roger Coneway of the Order of Friars Minors, who asserts that he needs these letters on behalf of the said Order[8].'

He was twenty-second Provincial Minister of England[9], and

---

[1] Mun. Acad. pp. 173-180.
[2] Ibid. 208. See pp. 43-3 above.
[3] Tanner, Bibl. 509.
[4] Oxf. City Records, Old White Book, fol. 55 b.
[5] Wadding, VIII, 106, 457; the papal letter is dated, IV Idus Feb. A° III; Mon. Franc. I, 561.
[6] Wadding, VIII, 127; Wood, Annals, sub anno 1360.
[7] Mon. Franc. I, 538.
[8] Copy in Lambeth MS. 1208, f. 99 b-100: 'Copia bulle quam frater Rogerus Coneway optinuit in Romana curia anno Christi 1359; III Non. April, A° VII.' The date in Todd's Catalogue is wrong. For the papal decree referred to, see *Corpus Juris Canon., Extravag. Communium Liber* V, Tit. III, cap. 2.
[9] Mon. Franc. I, 538, 561.

perhaps held the office at the time of the controversy with Richard Fitzralph[1]. Bale and Pits state that he died in 1360; it is not improbable that he lived several years longer. He was buried in the choir of the Grey Friars Church, London[2].

A book formerly belonging to Roger Conway is preserved among the MSS. of Gray's Inn; Codex 1, formerly 17 (=1584 in Bernard)—

'*Joannes Cassianus de Institutis Egyptiorum Coenobiorum.* Cui haec notula apponitur: "Iste est liber Fratris Rogeri de Coneway[3]".'

Defensio Religionis Mendicantium, against Armachanus, or *De confessionibus per regulares audiendis contra informationes Armachani*; known also by the opening words of the treatise (preface): 'Confessio et pulchritudo.'

> MSS. Oxford:—Bodl. sup. A I, art. 95; also Corpus Christi Coll. 182, fol. 37 (sec. xv).
> Cambridge:—Public Library Ii. iv. 5. fol. 15 (sec. xv); also Corpus Christi Coll. 333 (sec. xv).
> Paris:—Bibl. Nationale 3221, fol. 206-46 (see. xv); and 3222, fol. 117, under the title: 'Quedam informacio contra intentionem domini Ricardi Archiepiscopi Armachani super decretali *Vas electionis,* edita a ffratre Rogero Conewey magistro in Theologia de ordine fratrum minorum.'
> Vienna:—Bibl. Palat. 4127, f. 221 (sec. xv).
> Printed at Lyons 1496; Paris 1511 (among the works of Armachanus); and in Goldast, *Monarchia* II, p. 1410, (under the name 'Chonoe').

Intellectus fratrum de constitutione Vas electionis quo ad Negativam ibidem definitam. Inc. 'Verumptamen quia iste dominus Reverendus dicit quod intellectus fratrum est erroneus.'

> MS. Paris:—Bibl. Nat. 3222, fol. 133^b-158^b: it is anonymous in this MS., but is attributed to Roger Conway by Bale, MS. Seld. sup. 64, fol. 157^b, and Tanner, Bibl. 197. The same MS. contains the *Replicationes* of Armachanus against this work, ff. 159 sqq.

Quaestiones tres de Christi paupertate et dominio temporali. Inc. 'Questio est hic de mendicitate; or 'Utrum Christus hominum perfectissimus.'

> MS. Vienna:—Bibl. Palat. 4127, f. 249-269 (sec. xv).

---

[1] His *Defensio Mendicantium* was written at the command of some superior; see cap. III (Goldast, Monarchia, Tom. II): 'Ad quem (Armachanum) dignatus est me rogare quidam venerabilis pater ac magister, qui me potuit obligare mandato, quod eiusdem Domini dictis et calumniis pro viribus obviarem.'

[2] MS. Cott. Vitell. F XII, f. 274 b.

[3] This volume, and MS. 12 in the same library (containing the 'Moralities' of Nicholas Bozon), were given by Conway when Minister to the Franciscans of Chester.

Wadding (*Script.* p. 212) gives the second *incipit* and says: 'Habeo MSS.' These may be now in some Italian library; perhaps in the Franciscan Convent at Rome, or MS. Vatican 3740, 'Tractatus diversorum super quaestione de paupertate Christi et Apostolorum' (Montfaucon, p. 110).

Simon Tunstede, de Tunstude, or **Donstede,** is said by Bale to have entered the Order at Norwich, where, according to Blomefield, he afterwards became Warden of the Franciscan Convent[1]. He was Regent Master of the Friars Minors at Oxford in 1351[2], and according to contemporary evidence was 'skilled in music and in the seven liberal arts[3].' He wrote on the Meteorics of Aristotle[4], and made some alterations in the horologe called *Albion*, invented in 1326 by Richard of Wallingford, Abbat of St. Albans, and in the book which the Abbat wrote about his invention[5]. He became twenty-third Provincial Minister in succession to Roger Conway about 1360[6]. He was buried among the Poor Clares of Brusyard in Suffolk[7]; Bale and Pits mention 1369 as the year of his death.

A work on music, *Quatuor principalia musicae,* or *De musica continua et discreta, cum Diagrammatibus,* has been erroneously ascribed to Tunstede[8]; it was composed by a Minorite during Tunstede's regency at Oxford, and perhaps under his supervision.

MSS. London :—Brit. Mus. Addit. 8866 (sec. xiv).
Oxford:—Bodleian; Digby 90 (sec. xiv); Bodley 515 (=2185) (sec. xv).
Printed in E. de Coussemaker's *Auctores de Musica,* &c. Paris 1876.

Robert de Wysete, Wyshed, or **de Wycett,** D.D. of Oxford, succeeded Tunstede as twenty-fourth Provincial (c. 1370?)[9]. He was buried in the choir of the Grey Friars' Church in London[10].

MS. Worcester Cathed. Library, fol. No. 35 : ' Wyneshed de motu de locali et aliis Physicis' (?); but the name here is probably an error for *Swynshed*; see MS. Cambridge, Caius Coll. 499.

---

[1] Hist. of Norf. IV, p. 131.
[2] Digby MS. 90, *in calce.*
[3] Ibid.
[4] Leland, Script. ; the work does not appear to be extant. Wadding suggests that the commentary printed among the works of Duns Scotus (Vol. II) may be by Tunstede.
[5] Laud. Misc. MS. 657 (sec. xv) ; cf. Pub. Libr. Cambr. MS. Mm III, 11. For representations of Wallingford and the clock, see MSS. Cott. Claud. E IV, f. 201 ; Nero D VII, &c.
[6] Mon. Franc. I, 538, 561.
[7] Ibid.
[8] See Part I, chapter iv: the treatise is printed under the name of Simon Tunstede in E. de Coussemaker's *Auctores de Musica med. Aevi,* Nova Series, Vol. IV, pp. 220-298. Paris, 1876. The treatise, according to the editor, is very important, and forms in some sort the transition between the thirteenth and fourteenth centuries.
[9] Mon. Franc. I, 538, 561.
[10] MS. Cott. Vitell. F XII, f. 274 b.

John Mardeslay or **Mardisle**[1], probably a Yorkshireman, incepted as D.D. at Oxford before 1355. Early in this year he disputed with the Dominican, William Jordan, in the Chapter-house and Chancellor's schools at York, *de conceptione B. Mariae Virginis*, upholding the Immaculate Conception[2]. His manner of disputation gave offence, and the Chapter of York issued letters testifying to his good conduct (April 10, 1355)[3]:

'in putting forward his opinion he behaved amicably, modestly and courteously, without introducing any abuse or improprieties whatsoever.'

He was certainly an able debater. In 1374 he was summoned with three other Doctors of Divinity to a council at Westminster, over which the Black Prince and the Archbishop of Canterbury presided[4]. The subject of discussion was the right of England to refuse the papal tribute. The Archbishop and bishops said: 'The pope is lord of all, we cannot refuse him this tribute.' A monk of Durham brought forward the old argument about the two swords. Mardeslay at once replied with the text 'Put up again thy sword into his place,'

'showing that the two swords did not mean temporal and spiritual power, and that Christ had not temporal diminion; which he proved by the scriptures and gospels, by quotations from the doctors, by the example of the religious who leave worldly goods, and by the decretals; and he related how Boniface VIII claimed to be lord of all kingdoms, and how he was repulsed in France and England.'

At the end of the day's sitting, the Archbishop said, 'There were good counsels in England without the friars.' The prince answered, 'We have had to call them because of your fatuity; your counsel would have lost us our kingdom.' The next day the papal party yielded. Between this date and 1380 Mardeslay was twenty-fifth Provincial Minister[5]. The date of his death is uncertain; he was buried at York[6].

Thomas of Portugal studied at Oxford and Paris, c. 1360, and lectured at Lisbon and Salamanca. He was elected in the General Chapter to lecture on the *Sentences* at Cambridge, and was promoted to the degree of D.D. in the University of Toulouse by Pope Gregory XI in 1371[7].

---

[1] The forms Mardiston (Brewer) and Marcheley (Leland, Bale, Pits) are wrong; they are derived from MS. Cott. Nero A IX, f. 103, where the name, though indistinct, is certainly Mardisley.

[2] Tanner, Bibl. 509; Wadding, Script. 146; Bale, Pits.

[3] Tanner, ibid; *in Registro capituli S. Petri Ebor.*

[4] Eulog. Hist. III, 337–8.

[5] Mon. Franc. I, 538, 561: cf. notice of Th. Kyngesbury.

[6] Mon. Franc. ibid.

[7] Wadding, VIII, pp. 239, 249.

Ch. III.] *FRANCISCANS IN THE OXFORD CONVENT.* 243

Philip Zoriton (?), according to Wadding 'professor in the Universities of Oxford and Cambridge,' received the insignia of the *magisterium* at the hands of Friar Francis de Cardaillac S.T.P. in 1364[1]. Zoriton appears to be a mistake for **Torinton** or **Torrington**. Philip Torrington S.T.P. was made Archbishop of Cashel in 1373[2]. He was sent by Richard II as ambassador to Urban VI, and, on his return in 1379, urged the English king to invade France in support of the Pope, against the Antipope Clement VII. Philip died in 1380[3].

Dalmacus de Raxach and **Franciscus de Graynoylles** of the kingdom of Aragon, friars Minors residing at Oxford for the purposes of study, obtained royal letters of protection on Feb. 22nd, 1378[4].

Francis de S. Simone de Pisis, called 'of Empoli,' is mentioned by Bartholomew of Pisa as having studied at Oxford[5], where he perhaps became D.D. He flourished in the fourteenth century; according to Wadding, 1376.

Determinatio Magistri Francisci de Empoli de materia montis (?)
   MS. Florence:—Laurentiana, *ex Bibl. S. Crucis,* Plut. xxxi, Dext. Cod. xi (sec. XIV *or* XV).

John Hilton, D.D. of Oxford, 'determined' in the schools against Ughtred Bolton monk of Durham, in defence of his Order. Bale and Pits state that he died at Norwich, 1376[6].

Determinationes de paupertate fratrum, et de statu Minorum, lib. ii.
   Inc. 'Articulus pertractandus sit.'
   Mentioned by Bale, 'Ex bibliotheca Nordovicensi'[7].

Quaestiones.
   One or both of these works may be the *Opera Joannis Hilton* in *Bibl. Eccles. Cathed. Sarisbur.* MS. 94 (Bernard).

Hubert of Halvesnahen (?) Bachelor of Paris, Oxford and Cambridge, and '*destinatus Lector Oxoniae,*' received the degree of

---

[1] Wadding, Vol. VIII, p. 178.
[2] Rymer's Foed. Vol. III, pt. II, p. 995. In a papal letter of 1376 he is described as 'conservator privilegiorum Fratribus Ordinis Minorum in Hibernia a Sede Apostolica concessorum specialiter deputatus,' Wadding, VIII, p. 592. Cotton, Fasti Eccles. Hibern. I, 89.
[3] Wadding, VIII, 298 (see notice of H. of Halvesnahen). Chronicon Angliae 1328–1388 (R. S.), p. 222.
[4] Rymer's Foed. IV, 30.
[5] B. of Pisa, Liber Conf. fol. 81 b: 'suis determinationibus Oxonie factis.' Wadding, VIII, 333.
[6] Bale, Pits; Willott, *Athenae,* 229.
[7] MS. Seld. sup. 64, fol. 80.

Master in 1376 by papal commission at the hands of Friar Philip (Torrington), Archbishop of Cashel, who was then staying at Avignon[1].

William de Prato, of the Order of Minorites, a native of Paris, was in 1363 raised to the degree of Master in the University of Paris by the Pope. In the papal letter[2] to the 'Chancellor of the Church of Paris,' it is stated that he had

'studied many years at Oxford and lectured in the theological faculty, and obtained the license of teaching in the said faculty and the honour of Master; he desired to lecture in the same faculty at Paris, and to give to his country what he had acquired elsewhere by studious labours.'

The Pope bids the chancellor admit him freely on the papal authority

'ad legendum determinandum disputandum et ceteros actus Magistrales exercendum,'

just as though he were D.D. of Paris. The letter is dated XV Kal. Dec. A° II. In 1370 he was sent to the Tartars by the pope, as bishop of Pekin and head of the Franciscan mission in Asia[3]. The papal letter[4] constituted him ruler of the Friars Minors in the lands

'Saracenorum, Alanorum, Gazarorum, Gothorum, Schytarum, Ruthenorum, Jacobitarum, Nubianorum, Nestorianorum, Georgianorum, Armenorum, Indorum, Mochitarum.'

De eruditione Principum, by William de Prato, *ordinis Praedicatorum* (?)[5].

MS. Vatican, Bibl. Reginae Sueciae, cod. 1960 (Montfaucon).

John Somer, of the Convent of Bridgwater[6], was at Oxford in 1380[7]. It does not appear whether he was a doctor either at this time or afterwards. He enjoyed a great reputation as an astronomer, and is said to have made use of the astronomical researches of Roger Bacon[8]. Chaucer refers to him in his treatise on the Astrolabe[9].

---

[1] Wadding, Vol. VIII, p. 332. The original document from which these facts are derived is not given in the *Regestrum* at the end of the volume: the date would be, Greg. XI, A° 6.

[2] Wadding, VIII, 166, 500.

[3] Ibid. 221, seq.

[4] Dated, VII Kal. April, A° VIII (Urban V).

[5] Quétif and Echard (II, 136 b), mention a Dominican writer, William Piati or Prati, who flourished 1540, but do not assign this treatise to him.

[6] MS. Cott. Domit. A II, f. 1.

[7] MS. Cott. Faust, A II, f. 1.

[8] Bale, Script. I, 513; he is said to have written *Calendarii castigationes* (*inc.*: 'Corruptio calendarii horribilis est'), which I have not found. MS. formerly in Caius College (perhaps now No. 141?). Cf. R. Bacon, Op. Ined. p. 272.

[9] Edit. Skeat, p. 3.

Somer is often coupled with the contemporary astronomer Nicholas of Lynn[1], and it is possible that the following passage in Mercator's *Atlas*, which is supposed by Hakluyt and others to refer to Nicholas, relates to John Somer[2].

'That which you see described in this table of those foure Iles is taken from the journal of James Knox of Bolduc or the Busse[3], who reporteth[4] that a certaine English Friar, minorite of Oxford, a Mathematician, hath seene and composed the lands lying about the Pole, and measured them with an astrolabe, and described them by a Geometrical instrument.'

To this account John Dee[5] adds the date 1360, and calls the friar a 'Franciscan of Lynn'; Hakluyt (among other details) gives the name as 'Nicholas de Lynna a Franciscan Friar.' Nicholas of Lynn was a Carmelite[6]. On the other hand, supposing that the story has a good foundation, it is more likely that the adventurous Friar was a native of some seaport on the East coast than of a Western town like Bridgwater.

Tertium opusculum Kalendarii (A.D. 1387–1462), composed
'ad instantiam nobilissime Domine, Domine Johanne Principisse Wallie, ... ac matris ... Ricardi secundi ..., ad meridiem tamen Universitatis Oxonie, ex precepto reverendi Patris, fratris Thome Kyngesburi, Ministri Anglie, ... a fratre Johanne Somur (*or* Semour) ordinis minorum, A. D. 1380.'

    MSS. Brit. Mus.: Royal 2 B viii. (sec. xiv). Cotton Faustina A II, f. 1-12; and Cotton Vesp. E VII. f. 4-22.
    Bodl.: Digby 5, f. 73 (sec. xiv).

Cronica quaedam brevis fratris Johannis Somour ordinis sancti Francisci de conventu ville Briggewater.

    MS. British Museum; Cott. Domit. A II, f. 1-6ᵇ.
    The framework of the annals may be by John Somer: the entries are short and scattered—some being later than the middle of the 15th century—and in different hands. Several refer to Bridgwater, e.g. *ad annos* 1241, 1411. *Ad. an.* 1433 is the entry: 'E(clipsis) solis universalis 17 die Junii in festo S. Botulphi secundum fratrem som."

---

[1] E.g. by Chaucer (*ut supra*).

[2] Mercator's Atlas, translated by Hexham, Vol. I, p. 44; Hakluyt, I, 134.

[3] Elsewhere called 'Jacobus Cnoyen Buscoducensis,' or 'of Hartzeuan Buske' (i.e. Bois-le-Duc, Mr. R. L. Poole informs me): I can find nothing about him.

[4] The Latin edition of Mercator, A.D. 1606, adds '(quod tamen ab alio prius accepit)'.

[5] Quoted, without a reference, in Hakluyt, I, 135.

[6] MS. Arundel 207, *ad calcem*: 'ego frater Nicholaus de Linea, ord. beate Dei genetricis Marie de Monte Carmeli.'

His astronomical and astrological writings are frequently quoted:

Bodl. Laud. Misc. 674 (sec. xv), fol. 24; *Regulae ad sciendum nati vitam secundum Jo. Somer, Ord. Minorum*; fol. 24^b: 'Hoc receptum inveni scriptum de propria manu J. Somour de ordine Minorum.' See also fol. 42^b, ... and fol. 99^b of the same MS.

Bodl. Digby 88 (sec. xv), 'An extracte of freer John Somerys Kalender, of ille days in the yere,' fol. 62^b.

Cf. Digby 119, fol. 25^b.

Hugh Karlelle (Carlisle) and **Thomas Bernewell**, Oxford Minorites, were among the Doctors of Theology who condemned Wiclif's twenty-four conclusions at the council held at Blackfriars, London, on May 21st, 1382 [1].

William Woodford or **Widford** was one of the most determined opponents of the Wicliffites. Wadding's desire [2] to claim this 'extirpator of heretics' as a fellow-countryman has led him to identify William Woodford with the comparatively unknown Friar William of Waterford. There is no ground for this identification, and dates make it almost impossible [3]. In his earlier days at Oxford, probably when he was B.D., Woodford was on friendly or even intimate terms with Wiclif. When the two were lecturing on the Sentences, they carried on a courteous interchange of arguments and opinions on Transubstantiation [4].

Woodford's earliest extant work, of which the date is known, was composed in 1381; it consists of theological lectures under the title, '72 *questiones de Sacramento Altaris*,' in answer to Wiclif's 'Confession,' and was written in great haste; these lectures were delivered, perhaps at the Grey Friars London, within five weeks of the publication of the 'Confession [5].' He does not seem to have been D.D. at this time. On the subject of his inception, a curious piece of information has been preserved in a MS. of the 15th century;

'when he was going from London to Oxford to incept in theology he fell among robbers, who took from him £40 [6].'

In 1389 he was regent master in theology among the Minorites at Oxford, and as such lectured in the schools of the Minorites against the adherents of Wiclif [7]. In 1390 when he also lectured at Oxford on the

---

[1] Fascic. Zizan. p. 287.
[2] Ann. Min. IX, 129, &c.
[3] Waterford wrote a treatise in 1433; Wadding, IX, 129; Woodford lectured at Oxford before 1381.
[4] Twyne MS. XXI, 502. See above,
p. 81.
[5] Fascic. Zizan. 517, 523.
[6] MS. Exeter Coll. 7, f. 4.
[7] MS. Digby, 170; at the end of the third *determinatio*.

same subject, he was vicar of the Provincial Minister[1]. Among his pupils was Thomas Netter of Walden, afterwards Provincial of the Carmelites and reputed author of the *Fasciculi Zizaniorum*[2]. Woodford appears now to have resided mainly at the Grey Friars, London: in 1396 he obtained from Boniface IX a papal sanction of the special privileges and graces which he enjoyed in this convent; the chief of them was the right to a private chamber or house[3]. According to Bale and Pits he died, and was buried at Colchester in 1397[4]. His name however appears among those buried in the choir of the Grey Friars Church, London.

'Et ad ejus (sc. Willelmi Goddard) dexteram sub lapide cruce exarato Jacet bone memorie et hereticorum extirpator Acerimus frater Willelmus Wydford doctor Egregius et minister[5].'

The date of his death is uncertain; but one of his works seems to have been written in the reign of Henry IV[6].

Woodford's writings, dealing as they did for the most part with the question of the hour, were very popular and often copied.

Commentaries on *Ezechiel, Ecclesiastes, S. Luke* (cap. 6-9), *S. Paul's Epistle to the Romans.*

> British Museum MS. Royal 4 A xiii (sec. xiv)[7].

De sacramento Eucharistiae, or, 72 *quaestiones*.   *Inc.* 'Ratione solemnitatis jam instantis.'

> MSS. Brit. Museum: Royal 7 B iii. § 2, (sec. xiv): Harl. 31, fol. 1-94 (sec. xv), and 42 fol. 1 (sec. xv).
>
> Oxford:—Exeter Coll. 7, fol. 4 (sec. xv); St. John's Coll. 144 (sec. xv).

Determinationes quatuor; lectures at Oxford 1389-1390. *Inc.* 'Utrum motiva.'

> MSS. Brit. Mus.:—Harl. 31 (sec. xv. ineuntis): 1st lecture fol. 124-132; 2nd 132-163b; 3rd 163b-170; 4th 170-181: Harl. 42, f. 1-124.
>
> Oxford:—Bodleian 2766, f. 69; 2224, p. 33 (=Bodley 393); 3340; Digby 170, f. 1-33 (sec. xiv. exeuntis): this last MS.

---

[1] MS. Digby, fol. 33.
[2] Fascic. Zizan. 525, n. 2.
[3] MS. New Coll. 156, fly-leaf; printed in App. B.
[4] See Tanner, Bibl. 785.
[5] MS. Cott. Vitell. F, XII, f. 274 b.
[6] Namely, *De causis condemnationis articulorum* 18, &c.: see below.

[7] This MS. (f. 112) contains also *Philosophia naturalis* (*inc.* 'Queris, venerande dux Normannorum'), erroneously ascribed to Woodford, really composed by William de Conchis: cf. MS. Bodl. Digby 107; Tanner, Bibl. p. 194.

begins in the second determination with the words: 'et nullum predictorum est impedimentum legitimi matrimonii.'

De causis condempnacionis articulorum 18 *dampnatorum Johannis Wyclif*, 1396. Probably written later; Henry is mentioned as King of England (*Fasc. rer.* p. 264).

    MSS. British Museum:—Royal, 8 F xi. (sec. xv); Harl. 31, f. 95: Harl. 42, f. 125.

        Oxford:—Bodl. 2766, § 1. [and Bodl. 3629, p.216 ?]—Merton Coll. 198 § 3 (sec. xv) and 318, f. 84 (xv)—C. C. C. 183, f. 23 (xv).

    Printed, Brown, *Fascic. rerum expetendarum*, I, 190–265.

De sacerdotio novi testamenti. Inc. 'Utrum sacerdotium Novi.'

    MSS. British Museum:—Royal 7 B. III. § 1.

    Oxford:—Merton Coll. 198 fol. 14 (xv ineuntis).

Defensorium mendicitatis contra Armachanum, or, *Defensorium contra Armachanum, in Octavo libello de mendicitate Christi.* Inc. 'Postquam dominus Armachanus.'

    MSS. Oxford:—Magdalen Coll. 75 (sec. xv).

        Cambridge:—Publ. Library, Ff. I. 21, f. 1–257.

De erroribus Armachani, or, *Excerptiones xlii. errorum Armachani.* Inc. 'Quoad errores domini Armachani contentos.'

    MSS. Cambridge:—Publ. Libr. Ff. I. 21, f. 258–265.

    Oxford:—New Coll. 290 fol. 258.

Responsiones contra Wiclevum et Lollardos, or, *ad lxv. quaestiones Wiclevi contra fratres.* Inc. 'Primo quaeritur quot sunt ordines.'

    MS. Oxford:—Bodl. 2766, p. 41. (= T. Bodl. super O. I. Art. 9).

De veneratione imaginum.

    MS. Brit. Mus.:—Harl. 31, f. 182–205; anon. and imperfect at the beginning, but probably by Woodford; 8 chapters. *Inc. cap.* 2. 'Aliter tamen senciunt doctissimi Christiani, oppositum ostendentes per naturam, per artem, per historiam, per scripturam.'

Epistola Episcopo Hereford. de decimis et oblacionibus contra Gualterum Britte:

    referred to by Woodford in *De causis condempnacionis* etc., but no longer extant; *Fasc. Per. Expetend.* I. 220, 222.

Super quinque capitula Evangelii S. Matthaei:

    mentioned by John Wheathamstede among the books which he had transcribed, but not now to be found: (Tanner, from MS. Cott. Otho, B. IV; this MS. was burnt in the Cotton library fire).

Questions on God and angels, 'fratris Willelmi ex Wodeford junioris.'

    MS. Oxford:—Ball. Coll. 63, f. 100 (sec. xiv).

Other works attributed to him :

De oblationibus fiendis in locis sanctorum, and *De peregrinationibus ad loca sancta*, mentioned by Tanner (*Bibl.* 785), appear to be the same as *Determinatio, An sancti sint orandi, vel oracio fienda sit sanctis*, an anonymous treatise in Harl. MS. 31, § 7.

Summa de Virtutibus is identical with the *Summa* by William de Wodeford, Abbat, in Caius Coll. Cambridge, MS. 454.

Tractatus de Religione, addressed to Cardinal Julian Caesarinus in 1433, was the work of William of Waterford (Tanner *Bibl.* p. 364, Wadding ix, 129).

Peter Philargi or **Philargus de Candia** (afterwards Pope Alex. V) is said to have been of very humble origin, and to have begged his bread of necessity [1]. Early in life he joined the Franciscans, who soon recognised his ability. He was sent to England in his youth and studied first at Norwich, and then at Oxford, where he became Bachelor of Theology [2] (c. 1370?). He lectured on the *Sentences* at Paris in 1378 [3], and obtained the degree of D.D. in that University [4]. In 1402 he became Archbishop of Milan, in 1405 Cardinal, and in 1409 he was elected Pope at the Council of Pisa, being then more than seventy years old and famous for learning and piety [5]. His brief pontificate was chiefly remarkable for the favours and privileges which he lavished on the Mendicant Friars. He died on May 3rd, 1410, it was believed of poison administered by order of his successor John XXIII [6]. He is described by an English chronicler as 'jocundus vir et eloquens in Latina lingua et Graeca, solemnis et nominatissimus Doctor in Theologia [7].'

Lectures on the Sentences.
    MSS. Basel A II. 22. 'Conclusiones textuales super Magist. Sentent.'
        Paris :—Bibl. Nat. Fonds de Cluni 54, =1467 of the Latin Addit. MSS. (sec. xiv) fol. 8. 'Expl. collectiva pro primo principio fratris Petri de Candia, quam compilavit Parisius, aº Mº CCCº LXXVIIIº XXIIIIᵃ die mensis Septembris, et XXVIII die ejusdem mensis in scolis legit, etc.'
        Venice:—St. Mark, Vol. I, Cl. III, Cod. 110 (A.D. 1382), *Questiones in lib.* 1 *Sentent.*, being lectures at Paris in 1379.—

---

[1] Wood, Hist. et Antiq. Milman, Lat. Christ. VIII, 121.

[2] Eulog. Hist. III, 415 (R.S.). Gascoigne, *Lib. Veritatum*, 161 : Cotton MS. Cleop. E II, fol. 262 b, a letter of Henry IV to Alexander V : the king reminds him, 'qualiter a juventute vestra fuistis in regno Anglie, ac eciam in preclaro Universitatis Oxonie studio conversatis, quodque multos honores et bona quamplurima suscepistis ibidem.'

[3] Bibl. Nationale (Paris), Fonds de Cluni, Cod. 54, fol. 8.

[4] Gascoigne, ibid.

[5] Milman, *ut supra*.

[6] Eulog. Hist. III, 415. Gascoigne, 154.

[7] Eulog. Hist. III, 414, 415.

Ibid. Cod. 111 (A.D. 1394), *Questiones in lib. 2 et 3 Sentent.*
'Explicit lectura super sententias ven. mag. fratris Petri de Candia ordinis Minorum A.D. 1390 compilata tempore quo Parisiis legebat sententias, quas de verbo ad verbum ut jacet suis scolaribus in scolis antedicti ordinis prolegebat.

Officium Visitationis B. V. Mariae, compiled by Peter when Bishop of Novara.

MS. Florence:—Laurentiana, *ex Bibl. S. Crucis*, Plut. xxv. Sin. Cod. ix.

Prosae vel Sequentiae quinque, by Peter then Archbishop of Milan.
MS. Ibid.

Praefationes Ambrosianae.

MS. Rome:—Archiv. Basilicae S. Petri (Montfaucon, p. 158).

Conclusiones Petri de Candida Cardinalis Mediolanensis, S. T. P., pro moderno schismate auferendo (urging that a general Council should be called).

MS. Brit. Mus.:—Harl. 431, fol. 30[b]. Cf. *ibid.* fol. 33[b], 34[b], 35; and Cambridge:—Emmanuel Coll. I. § 29, *Conclusiones P. de Candia positae in Concilio.*

De obligationibus Epistola.

Oxford:—Bodl. Canonic. 278, fol. 65.
Florence:—Bibl. Leopoldina (Laurentiana), Cod. Gaddian. 188 (sec. xv).

Thomas Kyngesbery, Kynbury, de Kyngusbury, D.D. of Oxford, was twenty-sixth Provincial Minister from 1379 or 1380 to 1390 or 1392[1]. At the beginning of his ministry, which coincided with the beginning of the great Schism, he obtained from the Minorites, both in Provincial Chapter and in the separate convents, an oath of obedience to Urban VI[2]. He appears to have been on terms of some intimacy with the royal family[3], and about 1390 or 1392[4] Richard II urged Boniface IX to appoint him by provision to the next vacant bishopric: the king describes him as

'virum, prout experiencia certa et ejusdem fama preclaris diffusa virtutibus nobis constat, sciencie, vite, ac morum honestate perspicuum, et per omnia graciosum, nedum in sciencia speculativa, sed in verbi dei predicacione multipliciter preexpertum.'

This recommendation appears to have had no result: perhaps Kyngesbery died about this time. He was buried at Nottingham[5].

---

[1] Mon. Franc. I, 538, 561; Cott. MS. Vesp. E VII, f. 7; Digby MS. 90, f. 6 b; Bodl. MS. 692, f. 33.
[2] Bodl. MS. *ut supra.*
[3] Ibid. Cf. notice of John Somer.
[4] Bodl. MS. *ut supra.* As to the date, see English Hist. Review, Oct. 1891.
[5] Mon. Franc. I, 538.

Though none of his writings remain, it may perhaps be inferred, from the fact that he is twice mentioned in connexion with scientific works by Minorites, that he was a patron of science in the Order[1].

John Tewkesbury, Minorite, gave a treatise called ' *Quatuor principalia musicae* '
'to the Community of the Friars Minors at Oxford, with the authority and consent of Friar Thomas de Kyngusbury, Master, Minister of England, A.D. 1388[2].'

John Tyssyngton subscribed the decree of the Chancellor Berton, condemning Wiclif's twelve 'conclusions' on the sacraments, in 1381[3]; he is the only Franciscan among the ten doctors whose names appear, and was regent master of the Friars Minors at this time[4]. Soon afterwards Tyssyngton made an elaborate reply to Wiclif's *Confessio* on Transubstantiation in the Franciscan Schools at Oxford, and issued the lecture as a treatise[5]; though this composition bears marks of undue haste, it was considered to be of great value and was ordered to be kept in the University Archives[6]. In 1392 Tyssyngton was at the Council of Stamford where the heresies of Henry Crompe, consisting chiefly of conclusions against the friars, were condemned[7]. He succeeded Thomas Kyngesbery as twenty-seventh Provincial[8]. Bale and Pits give 1395 as the year of his death: he was buried at London[9].

The only work of his extant is the *Confessio contra confessionem Johannis Wiclif*, above referred to.

John Schankton, of the Order of Minors, appears to have been confessor of John Okele, skinner of Oxford. The latter, in his will dated October 20th, 1390, left Schankton 20*s* a year for three years, 'to celebrate masses for my soul and the souls of all those to whom I am in any manner bound, and the souls of all the faithful dead, in the conventual church of the Minorites at Oxford:'

---

[1] See notices of John Somer and John Tewkesbury.

[2] Digby MS. 90, f. 6 b. A writer of the same name is mentioned by Bale and Pits, *sub anno* 1350. One was Fellow of Merton, c. 1340: see Tanner, Bibl. 706.

[3] Fascic. Zizan. 113 (R.S.).

[4] Eulog. Hist. Contin. III, 351 (R.S.).

[5] Fascic. Zizan. 133-180. That the work was originally a lecture is proved by MS. in Corp. Chr. Coll. Cambr. No. 331, p. 583 (sec. xv), 'Explicit confessio magistri et fratris Johannis Tassyngton (*sic*) de ordine Minorum et S.T. doctoris, quam edidit, et in scholis fratrum minorum Oxoniis determinando promulgavit ... A.D. 1381.'

[6] Fascic. Zizan. p. 133, note 2, &c., and Eulog. Hist. *ut supra*. Mr. Shirley says, ' Tyssyngton has evidently never seen most of the books he quotes; and the references are often false.' He attempts to give the general sense of the passages he refers to, apparently from memory.

[7] Fascic. Zizan. 357.

[8] Mon. Franc. I, 538, 561.

[9] Ibid. 538.

if Schankton died in the course of those three years, he was, before his death, to appoint another friar to fulfil the wishes of the testator[1].

John Romseye, D.D., succeeded W. Woodford as regent master of the Friars Minors in 1389[2]. He was buried in the Chapel of All Saints in the Grey Friars' Church, London[3].

John Wastenays, Inceptor in theology at Oxford, and possibly one of the 'wax-doctors,' is mentioned in the following letter given under the privy seal, *temp.* Richard II[4]:

'Tres cher et bien ame. Nous vous prions, que, en ce que notre cher en dieu frere Johan Wastenays de lordre dez Menours, Commenceour en theologie, ad affaire deuers vous touchant son commencement en la Vniuersitee doxon, lui veullez faire la grace et le fauour que bonement purrey, sauuant lez estatutz et lez priuileges de la vniuersitee auantdicte. Donne souz, etc. (i.e. souz notre priue seal).'

Jacob Fey of Florence studied at Oxford in 1393, when he transcribed a manuscript formerly kept in the library of Santa Croce, Florence, now in the Laurentian library[5]. The colophon runs:—

'Explicit compilatio quædam diversorum argumentorum recollectorum a diversis doctoribus in Vniversitate Oxoniæ ordinata satis pulchre per Reverendum Fratrem ... [6] S.T. Mag. ejusdem Vniversitatis de Ordine Carmelitarum, scripta per me Fratrem J. Fey de Florentia Ordinis Minorum in Conventu Oxoniæ anno Domini MCCCXCIII die sequenti festum 40 Martyrum ad laudem Domini nostri Jesu Christi. Amen.'

Fey was inquisitor in his native land in 1402[7].

Nicholas Fakenham (Norfolk) enjoyed the favour and patronage of Richard II. He was doctor of Oxford and twenty-eighth Provincial Minister of the Order in 1395. On the 5th of November in that year, on the occasion apparently of his inception, he 'determined' at Oxford on the papal schism by command of the king. This lecture has been preserved[8]; the introduction may be given here, somewhat abbreviated.

---

[1] Oxf. City Rec. Old White Bk. fol. 71 a.

[2] MS. Digby 170: 'Explicit 3ᵃ determinatio sive lectio magistri et fratris W. Woodford contra Wyclevystas Oxon. A.D. 1389 in scolis Minorum, et die vesperiarum fratris Johannis Romseye proximi magistri regentis.' MS. Bodl. 393, fol. 58 b reads, 'anno domini MºCCCºLXXXXIXº.'

[3] MS. Cott. Vitell. F XII, f. 277 b.

[4] MS. Dd. III, 53, p. 101, in the Public Library at Cambridge; Richard occurs as king in the two succeeding entries and in several on the preceding page. That this is Richard II is clear, (1) from the writing; (2) from the mention on p. 97, of the Statute of Labourers.

[5] Laurentiana, *ex Bibl. S. Crucis*, Plut. XVII, Sin. Cod. X.

[6] Name erased in MS.

[7] Bandini's *Catal. Cod. Lat. Mediceæ Laurentianæ*, tome IV, pref. p. xlii.

[8] Harl. MSS. No. 3768, fol. 188. Transcript in Twyne MSS. XXII, 223.

'Our mother, the Roman Church, is full of troubles and calamities. Yet her daughter, the University of Paris, alone has tried to comfort her: Paris has borne the burden and heat of the day, and may well upbraid us. We too must work for the union of the Church and the reformation of peace. I therefore, promoted to the degree of Master though unworthily, through zeal for the religion of Christ and for the Church of God, and by reason of the command of our lord the King, propose to move some matters pertaining to the proposition, in the form of a question, not as a formal *determinator*, but rather as a friendly speaker (*familiaris concionator*), now on one side, now on the other, now as an impartial person. In these writings I wish to say nothing against the Catholic Church or good morals or Pope Boniface; if I do so inadvertently I submit to the Chancellor and others in authority.—Touching the reformation of the desolate Church, I ask whether there is any reasonable way of restoring it to its original unity.'

Then he treats learnedly about the schismatical churches and shows that the Church can be reformed only by the punishment of those who have disturbed its peace—namely, the Cardinals.

He ceased to be Minister some years before his death. In 1405 he was with Friar J. Mallaert appointed papal commissary to examine into the charges made by the English Minorites against John Zouche, then Provincial Minister. The commissaries deposed Zouche; and on the latter's reappointment by papal authority, refused to obey him [1]. According to Bale he died 1407 [2]; he was buried at Colchester [3].

At the end of the '*determinatio*' in Harl. MS., 3768 (fol. 196) is the note:

'et incipiunt alie conclusiones ejusdem de eodem scismate cum epistola directa domino Karolo Regi Francorum pro reformacione scismatis prenominati.'

Some 'conclusions' then follow.

(**Richard**) **Tryvytlam** or **Trevytham** seems to have flourished about 1400; Hearne suggests that he was the same as Robert Finingham, a Franciscan who lived about 1460 [4], but this is a quite unwarranted assumption. Tryvytlam is only known from his rhymed Latin poem, '*De laude Universitatis Oxoniae*,' a defence of the friars and attack on the monks. From the poem it is clear that he was an Oxford friar, and one line points to his having been a Franciscan:

'Minorum ordinem proclamat impium,' etc. [5].

---

[1] Wadding, IX, 499; Eulog. Hist. Contin. III, p. 403, seq.
[2] MS. Seld. sup. 64, fol. 134 b, 'ex quodam Minoritarum registro.'
[3] Mon. Franc. I, 538.
[4] Hearne's edition of Tryvytlam's poem in App. Vitae Ric. II (Oxon. 1729), p. 344, note 2.
[5] Ibid. p. 358 (speaking of 'Owtrede' of Durham).

Among the assailants of the mendicants he mentions by name Ughtred of Durham, who flourished in the reign of Richard II. His poem has been edited by Hearne (Oxon. 1729), from a fifteenth century MS. then in the possession of Roger Gale, Esq.

> MS. Paris:—Bibl. Nationale, MS. 1201 (sec. xv) contains: *Ricardi Trevithelani Supplicationes ad beatam Mariam Virginem.*

William Auger or **Anger**, according to Leland[1], studied in the Franciscan convent at Oxford, and was afterwards made Warden of the Grey Friars at Bridgwater, where he died and was buried, A.D. 1404[2].

John Edes, Edaeus, or **of Hereford,** is said to have been a Minorite of Oxford, and to have written commentaries on many of Aristotle's works, as well as on the Sentences and Apocalypse[3]. He afterwards retired to Hereford, where he was elected warden, and where he died in 1406[4].

> *Quedam constituta* (?)[5] *Johannis Ede de ordine minorum. Inc.* 'Triplex fuit beneficium abrahe, viz. preeleccio, conversacio, propagacio ... Questio utrum personarum accepcio sit peccatum.'
>
> MS. Oxford:—Bodley 815 (=2684 in Bernard) f. 1-8, a fragment (sec. xv). The MS. (fol. 1) contains the note: 'Habetur liber complete inter fratres minores Hefordie' (*sic*)[6].

William Butler or **Botellere** was regent master of the Minorites at Oxford in 1401, when he lectured against the translation of the Bible into English[7]. He occurs as the thirtieth Provincial Minister and successor to John Zouche[8]. He was probably the person elected by the Chapter at Oxford on the 3rd of May, 1406, on the deposition of Zouche[9]. Though the latter was afterwards restored, he does not

---

[1] Script. 401.

[2] Bale, Script. II, 57. A 'Hugo Angerius' flourished in 1338, but he was probably not a friar nor an Englishman; MS. Bibl. Nat. Paris, No. 5155, § 6.

[3] 'Dr. J. Ede Herfordensis Minorita scripsit inter cetera opus egregium, sc. lecturam in apocalypsim lib. 1. Ex scriptis Th. Gascoigne.' Bale in MS. Seld. sup. 64, fol. 36 b.

[4] Leland and Bale, who refer to the *Catalogus eruditorum Franciscanorum.*

[5] 'Opuscula quaedam Theologica,' in Bernard's Catalogue.

[6] In MSS. Paris, Bibl. Mazarine, 287 and 288 (sec. XIV) is a *Tabula originalium ... compilata a fratre Johanne Lectore Herfordensi ordinis fratrum Minorum.* This work, though ascribed by Possevin and Tanner to J. of Hereford, is by John Lector of Erfurt. Wadding, Script. 139, Sup. ad Script. 415.

[7] Merton Coll. MSS. No. 67, f. 202 seq.: at the end, 'Explicit determinacio fratris et magistri Will. Buttiler ordinis minorum regentis Oxonie, A.D. 1401.'

[8] Mon. Franc. I, 538, 561.

[9] Eulog. Hist. Contin. III, 405. The year is fixed by the words, 'Nuntius missus inveniens generalem mortuum.' Henry of Ast died in 1405. Wadding, IX, 267.

Ch. III.] *FRANCISCANS IN THE OXFORD CONVENT.* 255

seem to have been generally recognised in England, and was in 1408 made Bishop of Llandaff[1]. Butler's tenure of office seems to have been reckoned from 1408. A new ordinance was made at this time that no Provincial of the Minorites should remain in office more than six years[2]. William Butler resigned in 1413 or 1414, but was reinstated by Pope John XXIII[3]. Whether he actually entered on his duties again does not appear. The date of his death is unknown. Bale and Pits state that he was buried at Reading[4]. The Catalogue of Illustrious Franciscans, as quoted by Leland, calls him 'Flos universitatis temporibus suis.'

Besides the treatise against the English translation of the Bible (Merton Coll. MS. 67) he is said to have written *De indulgentiis papalibus. Inc.* 'Articulus pro finali cessatione lecture sentenciarum'[5].

Vincent Boys, D.D. of Oxford, was elected thirty-first Provincial on the voluntary retirement of W. Butler in 1413. Butler was reinstated by the Pope and the election of Boys quashed; but no stigma was to attach to the latter[6]. Tanner mentions a David Boys, Carmelite, c. 1450[7].

Peter Russel was D.D. of Oxford[8], and taught also in Spain. On November 25th, 1399, Martin, king of Aragon, gave him power

'legendi docendi et dogmatizandi ubique locorum sui regni *Artem generalem* ceterosque libros Raymundi Lulli.'[9]

He was the thirty-second Provincial of England, and retired from the office in 1420, having presumably held it for six years[10].

He wrote or lectured in defence of Mendicancy. MS. Bodleian, Digby, 90, f. 200, contains a reply to him:

'Determinacio magistri Johannis Whytheed de Hibernia in materia de mendicitate contra fratres; in quo respondet pro Radulpho Archiepiscopo Armachano contra fratrem Petrum Russel.'

Robert Wellys or **Wallys**, D.D. of Oxford, was elected thirty-third Minister on Russel's retirement in 1420. Martin V empowered the

---

[1] Le Neve. Wadding, IX, 320, 499.
[2] Wadding, IX, 493-4. Cf. Eulog. Hist. Cont. III, 409.
[3] Wadding, IX, 356, 529: the papal letter is dated XVI Kal. Jun. A° IV (May 17, 1414).
[4] The list of Provincials in the Reg. Fratrum Minorum, London, has 'Frater Willielmus Butler, doctor Oxoniae, jacet...'
[5] Bale, in MS. Seld. sup. 64, fol. 215, from MSS. in the Franciscan Friary at Reading.
[6] Mon. Franc. I, 539, 561; Wadding, IX. 356, 529; Wadding calls him 'Bors.'
[7] Bibl. p. 118.
[8] Mon. Franc. I, 538.
[9] Wadding, Sup. ad Script. 608.
[10] Wadding, X, 53; Mon. Franc. I, 538, 561.

Minister of the Roman province to confirm the election, but Wellys died in France before he had assumed the duties of his new office[1].

Thomas Chayne, Minorite D.D., was one of the five friars appointed by Congregation in 1421 to decide what should be done with the pledges placed in the chests 'before the first pestilence[2].' He was buried in the chapel of All Saints in the Church of the Grey Friars, London[3].

Hugo David was D.D. and regent master of the Oxford Franciscans about 1420[4]. On the deposition of Roger Dewe or Days, Provincial Minister, in 1430, Hugo David and John (?) Wynchelse were appointed vicars of the province[5].

Determinacio Fratris et Magistri Hugonis Davidis, ordinis Fratrum Minorum, in Universitate Oxoniensi Regentis, utrum penitens, peccata sua confessus Fratri Licentiato, teneatur eadem rursus confiteri proprio Sacerdoti.

MS. Paris:—Bibl. Nationale, 3221, § 5 (sec. xv).

Robert Colman is said to have been a Minorite of Norwich[6]. He was S.T.P. and Chancellor of the University in 1419[7]. In 1428 he attended as Minorite D.D. the diocesan synod at Norwich, where inquisition was made into the heresies of William Whyte[8]. He is said to have induced Walter Clopton, Knight, chief justice of England, to enter the Order in his old age[9]. Leland says :

'Illud non est silentio praetereundum, catalogum illustrium Franciscanorum accurate Colemannum laudare, ac peritissimum carminis pronunciare'[10].

Matthias Döring studied at Oxford in his youth[11], and perhaps entered the Franciscan Order there. He was certainly a Minorite in

---

[1] Mon. Franc. *ut supra.* Wadding, X, 53.

[2] Mun. Acad. 274-5 (R.S.).

[3] MS. Cott. Vitell. F XII, fol. 277 '. . . jacet in plano frater Thomas Cheyny, doctor theologie.'

[4] MS. Bibl. Nat. Paris, 3221, § 5.

[5] Wadding, X, 169 : perhaps *Thomas* Wynchelse, who in 1427, 'famosissimus doctor illius ordinis reputabatur;' the only John Wynchelse, Minorite, mentioned elsewhere, died a novice about 1326. See notice of him.

[6] Bale, I, 563. Blomfield, Norfolk, IV, 115.

[7] Le Neve, *Fasti,* Vol. III. Wood, Hist. et Antiq. Oxon, II, 404.

[8] Fascic. Zizan. p. 417.

[9] Bale, Pits, &c. Clopton was chief justice under Richard II ; see e. g. Close Roll, 13 Ric. II, part 2, m. 4, *in dorso.*

[10] Leland, Script. 433.

[11] His epitaph contains the lines :

'Anglia gaudet eum doctum fecisse magistrum,

. . . .

Inbibit Oxonie musis nova pocula morum.'

See B. Gebhardt, *Matthias Döring der Minorit,* Sybel's Hist. Ztschr. for 1888, pp. 251, 293-4. Most of the statements here are derived from Gebhardt's article, a general reference to which will suffice. Cf. Wadding, Annales, XI, 49, 180 ; XII, 276, &c.

1422, when he matriculated at Erfurt as 'lector Minorum'[1]. He seems to have been lecturing in the Franciscan Convent at Erfurt some time before this event; his lectures on the first book of the Sentences were finished on April 21st, 1422. He may have been at Oxford about 1415 and perhaps took the degree of B.D. there. In 1423, at any rate, he appears as B.D., and became Provincial Minister of Saxony in 1427[2]. He was one of the representatives of the University of Erfurt at the Council of Basel in 1432, where he played a leading part[3]. In 1433 he was sent by the Council as ambassador to Eric, king of Denmark. Soon after this he returned to Erfurt. In 1438 he wrote a pamphlet entitled '*Confutatio primatus papae*,' with the object of enlisting the support of the secular princes on the side of the Council against the pope. He seems himself to have been a trusted friend of his Margraf, Frederic of Thüringen.

In his relations to his Order he appears as a consistent champion of the Conventuals against the stricter Observants. In 1443 he was elected General Minister of the former, and held the office till 1449. In 1455 his name occurs among the Conventual Provincial Ministers; after a struggle with the Archbishop of Magdeburg on behalf of the Conventuals he resigned the Provincialate in 1461, and retired to Kyritz, leaving the Archbishop in possession of the field. Döring however seems to have been left in peace till his death, July 24th, 1469. His chief works besides the treatise already mentioned were a *defence of Nicholas de Lyra* against Paul Burgos, written between 1434 and 1440 (printed several times; e.g. at Basel, 1507); *a defence of the miraculous blood of Wilsnach*; and his *Chronicle*; the latter was compiled from notes taken at different times from the end of the thirties onwards; and embraces the period from 1420 to 1464. It has been twice edited, by Mencken and by Riedel; both editions are said to be inaccurate.

William Russell, 'of the Convent of Stamford in the diocese of Lincoln,' argued that a religious might lie with a woman without mortal sin; this thesis was discussed and condemned in the Convocation of Canterbury at St. Paul's on October 12th, 1424, and

---

[1] Ibid. p. 251. Weissenborn, *Acten der Erfurter Univ.* part I, p. 122.

[2] Anal. Franc. II, 287.

[3] He brought forward a 'propositio circa Hussitarum articulum; de Donatione Constantini, num justo titulo clerici possideant bona Ecclesiarum temporalia quae Sylvestri a Constantino sint collata, in concilio Basiliensi 1432 ad disputandum proposita.' Gebhardt, 257. Several of his discourses at the Council are preserved in Balliol Coll. MSS. 164, 165.

Russell submitted to the decision of the clergy[1]. On May 15th, 1425, he again appeared before Convocation to answer the charge of having publicly held and preached on Jan. 28th, 1425, that tithes need not be paid to the parish priest, but might be applied by the tithe-payer '*in pios usus pauperum*'[2]. At this time Russell was warden of Friars Minors of London[3]. At first he tried to defend his doctrine, then submitted. The Archbishop enjoined on him, as a penance, that he should next Sunday after service solemnly renounce his error in set form[4] at Paul's Cross. At the time appointed Russell did not appear and was in consequence excommunicated. The proceedings against him dragged on for some time. On July 11th, a letter of the University of Oxford in condemnation of his doctrines was exhibited, and later a similar letter from Cambridge; and on the 13th it was decreed

'that he should be judged and condemned as a heretic and schismatic.'

Meanwhile, Russell, now no longer warden, fled to Rome 'to defende the forsaide erronye doctrine'[5]. On August 12th, 1425, he was imprisoned by order of the Pope, first in the Pope's, then in the 'Soldan's' prison. The following January he escaped from prison and fled to England, where he was received for one night by the Friars Minors of London. He seems to have remained at large for more than a year. He surrendered or was captured in March, 1427, and on the 21st of that month, in accordance with the papal decision, he read in English a complete recantation of his doctrine on tithes at Paul's Cross[6], and was then handed over to the Bishop of London to be imprisoned during the Pope's pleasure. He was at liberty again in 1429 when he incepted as D.D. at Oxford, and paid £10 to the University instead of giving a feast to the Regents[7]. The University showed its hatred of his teaching by adding to the oaths which had to be

---

[1] Twyne MS. XXIV, p. 129 (from Reg. Chichele, part II, fol. 35).

[2] 'Into pitous use of pore men.' Wilkins, Conc. III, 456. The whole process against Russell will be found in Wilkins, Conc. III, 438–462.

[3] Ibid. 434. Cf. Mon. Franc. I, 520: 'ad has expensas (i.e. for the tiling of a roof in the London convent) dedit gardianus Russell iii libras.'

[4] Given in English, Wilkins, Conc. III, 438.

[5] Ibid. 456. Russell says himself, 'Y ... went to the court of Rome supposyng ther to have be socured.' Ibid. 457.

[6] Ibid. 457–8.

[7] If it be the same, but he is here described as an Austin Friar. See the receipt for the £10, executed in the names of the proctors, and dated Feb. 1, 14$\frac{28}{29}$, in Oxf. Univ. Archives, F 4, f. 15. 'Noverint universi per presentes nos ... recepisse ... de Fratre Willelmo Russell ordinis Augustinencium decem libras sterlingorum virtute cujusdam gracie sibi concesse de commutacione convivii debiti in die incepcionis sue.'

taken by every inceptor in every faculty[1], a disavowal of Russell's teaching on tithes[2]. The oath has already been quoted at length in Chapter VI.

Super Porphyrii Universalia compendium, by William Russell, Friar Minor.

Comment. in Aristotelis Praedicamenta, anonymous, but probably by the same author.

MS. Oxford :—Corpus Christi Coll. 126, fol. 1, and fol. 4.

William de Melton in 1427 went about the country preaching against tithes,

'and teaching seditious doctrines among the common people in many places by uncircumcised words.'

He had probably taken a degree at Oxford, as the University was appealed to to stop his preaching. The University wrote to the Duke of Gloucester and the King's Council, and secured his arrest. Melton was brought back to Oxford, and is said to have recanted over and over again on his knees[3]. He is probably the same as William Melton of the Friars Minors, S.T.P.[4], who was preaching at York in 1426, on the subject of the mystery plays.

'He commended the play to the people, affirming that it was good in itself and very laudable; but for several reasons he induced the people to have the play on one day and the Corpus Christi procession on the second, so that the people might be able to come to the churches on the festival'[5].

Roger Donwe or **Days**, D.D. of Oxford, became thirty-fifth Provincial Minister in succession to John David between 1426 and 1430; in the latter year he was 'for just causes deposed by the Minister General.' He was buried at Ware[6].

Richard Leke or **Leech**, D.D. of Oxford, was thirty-sixth Provincial Minister between 1430 and 1438. He was buried at Lichfield[7].

---

[1] Mun. Acad. 376.
[2] Ibid. 270, note 1. Wood, Annals, pp. 569-570.
[3] Wood, Annals, *sub anno* 1427. Correspondence of Bekynton (R. S.), Vol. II, pp. 248-250.
[4] 'Sacre pagine professor.' Drake, *Eboracum,* App. 29, translates this, 'professor of holy pageantry.' This curious mistake is repeated by the editor of Mon. Franc. Vol. II, preface, p. xxviii.
[5] York Mystery Plays, by Lucy Toulmin Smith, p. xxxiv (the extract is from the York City Records, Book A, fol. 269).
[6] Mon. Franc. I, 539, 561. Wadding, X, 169, 'Friar Roger Dewe.' Wilkins (Conc. III, 458) prints a letter from Archbishop Chichele to 'fratri Johanni David S.T.P. et ordinis fratrum Minorum in Anglia ministro generali,' dated March 2, 1425, 'et nostrae translationis anno XII'—i. e. 1426, new style.
[7] Mon. Franc. ibid. Wadding, XI, 49.

Thomas Radner or **Radnor**, of the custody of Bristol and the Convent of Hereford, D.D. of Oxford, was Provincial in 1438, being the thirty-seventh in order. He was buried at Reading [1].

John Feckyngtone, 'of the Order of Minors in Oxford,' was one of the two Rectors of Balliol College in 1433, his colleague being Richard Roderham, S.T.P. The Rectors, having, at the instance of the College, inquired into the working of the statutes, recommended a change in the clause of the first statute which provided that the Master of the College, if he received a benefice of the clear annual value of £10, was thereby incapacitated from holding his office.

'In witness whereof, because our seals are known to few, we have procured that the seal of the Chancellor of the University of Oxford should be appended to these presents. Given at Merton College, April 19, 1433'[2].

The matter was submitted to the Bishop of London, who cancelled the objectionable clause [3].

John Whytwell, Minorite, on February 7th, 144$\frac{3}{8}$, was allowed to count twenty oppositions *pro completa oppositione*[4]. On January 25th, 144$\frac{9}{50}$, it was decided in solemn congregation, that one-half of the £10 paid by this friar at his inception as D.D. should be placed in the Rothbury Chest to be used for the partial redemption of the University jewels, and that the other half should be given to the proctors in payment of certain sums owed to them by the University [5].

John Argentine supplicated for B.D. on October 20th, 1449, on the ground that he had studied philosophy for nine years, theology for seven, and had opposed and responded formally four times. The grace was conceded [6]. In 1470 a John Argentine challenged and disputed against all the Regents of Cambridge; he does not appear to have been a friar [7]: he was probably the John Argentine, M.D. and D.D., who was physician to the princes Edward and Arthur, and held several prebends and livings in the dioceses of Ely, Lichfield,

---

[1] Mon. Franc. ibid. Wadding, XI, 49, *in Registro Ordinis* (says the latter) is a list of the 'Rectors of the Provinces,' A. D. 1438: in England 'Magister Thomas Roidnor.'

[2] Original in Ball. Coll. Archives (described in Hist. MSS. Com. Report, IV, p. 443).

[3] Statutes of the Oxford Colleges, Vol. I, Balliol, p. xx.

[4] Register, A a, fol. 23 b.

[5] Ibid. f. 7. (Boase, p. 287.)

[6] Reg. A a, fol. 36.

[7] MS. Cott. Julius F VII, f. 165: 'Actus magistri Jo. Argentyn publice tentus in Univ. Cantebrigie,' &c. in verse. Above, some notes are written: 'natus de Kyrkeby,' 'de collegio Regis in (Cantebrigia?).'

Wells, and London, between 1487 and 1508 ¹. One of the same name, with the degree of B.D. was Provost of King's College, Cambridge, from 1501 to 1507 ².

Antony de Valle or **Vallibus** was admitted B.D., February 6th, 1448/9 ³. He incepted as D.D. before March 22nd, 145½, when he was permitted

'to absent himself from every scholastic act for a fortnight, that he might be able to visit his friends who were sick' ⁴.

John David, on March 4th, 1450/1, was allowed to curtail his period of opponency and take the B.D. degree, on condition that he would lecture on the first book of Isaiah in the public schools ⁵. He became D.D. before June 5th, 1454, when he received permission

'to resume his ordinary lectures after the feast of St. Thomas next ensuing (July 3rd), and to resume the acts of a Regent, except entry into the house of Congregation' ⁶.

Another of the same name was lecturer to the Franciscans of Hereford before 1416, D.D. of Cambridge, and thirty-fourth Provincial Minister in 1426 ⁷.

David Carrewe, S.T.P., in 1452 received 6s. 8d. under the will of Richard Browne, alias Cordon, LL.D., Archdeacon of Rochester, &c., and benefactor of the friars of Oxford and elsewhere ⁸. This Carrewe is probably identical with the Friar **David Carron**, S.T.P., who, in 1448, was with Friar Nicholas Walshe, S.T.B., appointed commissioner to elect a Provincial of the Minorites in Ireland on the deposition of William O'Really: their choice fell on Gilbert Walshe, a relative of Nicholas, but O'Really was afterwards reinstated by the Pope ⁹.

John Foxholes (co. York) on April 14th, 1451, was allowed to count opponency from Michaelmas term to Easter as his complete opposition, on condition that he should preach one Latin sermon in addition to those which he was bound to deliver by the University statutes ¹⁰; this was equivalent to a supplication for B.D.

---

¹ Tanner, Bibl. 48; Le Neve, *Fasti*, I, 597, 587, 620.
² Le Neve, III, 683.
³ Reg. A a, fol. 2.
⁴ Ibid. fol. 62 b.
⁵ Reg. A a, fol. 51 b.
⁶ Ibid. fol. 83.
⁷ Harl. MS. 431, fol. 100 b; Mon. Franc. I, 539, 551; Wilkins, Concil.
III, 459.
⁸ Mun. Acad. p. 649. In the will of R. Mertherderwa (A.D. 1447) mention is made of a friar David Carn Dominican, S.T.P. of Oxford; Ibid. p. 558.
⁹ Wadding, Ann. Min. XII, 10-11, who adds, 'I have these from certain Vatican records.'
¹⁰ Reg. A a, fol. 53.

We venture to identify John Foxholes with **John Foxalls** or **Foxal**, Minorite, who lectured at Bologna and some other University[1]. In 1475 he was appointed Archbishop of Armagh by the Pope, but died in England within a year or two, probably without having visited his diocese[2].

He was the author of several works[3]—

Expositio Universalium Scoti. *Inc.* 'Creberrime instantiusque rogatus.'

Printed at Venice, 1508 and 1512, under the name *Joannes Anglicus*.

Opusculum super libros Posteriorum.

MS. Paris:—Bibl. Nationale, 6667 (A.D. 1501).

Printed at Venice, 1509 (?).

Opusculum de primis et secundis intentionibus, juxta mentem Scoti, Mayronis, Aureoli, Boneti, et Antonii Andreae. *Inc.* 'Quoniam materia de primis.'

MS. Florence, *olim* Bibl. S. Crucis (*nunc* Bibl. Laurent. ?).

Expositio super metaphysicam Antonii Andreae.

MS. *olim penes Waddingum*[4].

John Sunday, on May 17th, 1453, was allowed to count 'opposition in each of the schools' for about seven months, together with eighteen additional oppositions, as equivalent to the statutable opposition of one year[5]. On June 10th, he was admitted B.D.[6] On February 5th, 145$\frac{3}{4}$, after finishing his lectures on the Sentences, he supplicated for D.D., and grace to incept was conceded under certain conditions[7].

Richard Treners, S.T.B., obtained a grace on December 2nd, 1454, to substitute one additional Latin sermon after taking his degree (of D.D.) for two responsions before the degree[8].

William Goddard the elder, 'Doctor Oxoniae Disertissimus,' succeeded Thomas Radnor, according to the Register of the Grey Friars of London, as thirty-eighth Provincial Minister[9]. Radnor was

---

[1] 'Dum Bononiae legebam,' quoted by Sbaralea; Wadding, Sup. ad Script. 420.

[2] Cotton, Fasti Eccles. Hibern. III, 17.

[3] Sbaralea has collected from his extant works references to works not as yet discovered; Wadding, Sup. ad Script., 420.

[4] Wadding, Script. 20; Sup. ad Script. 68, 420.

[5] Reg. A a, fol. 74 b.

[6] Ibid. fol. 75.

[7] Ibid. fol. 79 b, printed in Appendix.

[8] Ibid. fol. 86 b.

[9] Mon. Franc. I, 539. English Hist. Review, Oct. 1891.

minister in 1438, and it is probable that Goddard was not his immediate successor. At any rate, the latter was a leading man among the friars, and probably provincial minister between 1450 and 1460. Bishop Reginald Pecock wrote a letter addressed *Doctori ordinis fratrum minorum Godard*, in which

'he calls the modern preachers pulpit-bawlers (*clamatores in pulpitis*)'[1].

A little later, the friar had his revenge. On November 27th, 1457, Pecock, being convicted of heretical opinions, abjured at Paul's Cross.

'And doctor William Gooddard the elder, that was provinciall of the Greyfreeres, apechyd hym of hys erysys'[2].

He was living in London many years after this event. In the will, dated March 6th, 147½, of John Crosby, 'citezein and grocer and alderman of London,' is the clause:

'Item, I bequeth to maister Godard thelder doctoure of dyvynyte to pray for my soule C^s'[3].

Similar bequests follow to the prior of the Austin Friars of London and to the provincial of the same Order. From this entry it would appear that Goddard was not provincial of the Minorites in 1472. From the distinguished position which he evidently occupied in 1457, and from the passage in the Grey Friars' Chronicle quoted above, it might be assumed that he had already held the office and retired. But William Goddard is mentioned as provincial in a record dated Dorchester, October 4th, 1485[4]. Was this Goddard *senior* or *junior*? For there were two Franciscans of this name in the fifteenth century. There is nothing to show that the younger Goddard was ever provincial minister; he was warden of the London convent, but was not buried in the choir, where all the ministers mentioned in the Register were buried[5]. Further, the Register of the Grey Friars states that the younger Goddard died on September 26th, 1485, i.e. before the record was drawn up. The Register is, however, in the matter of dates absolutely untrustworthy. Without further evidence it seems impossible

---

[1] Gascoigne, *Loci e libro veritatum*, p. 100. Tanner (Bibl. p. 584) gives a reference to this letter: 'MS. in Bibl. Gualteri Copi.' It is probably still among the MSS. at Bramshill House, Hants. The date of the letter is not given.

[2] Chronicle of the Grey Friars of London (Camden Soc.), p. 20.

[3] P.C.C. Wattys, fol. 180 a.

[4] Francis a S. Clara, Hist. Minor, pp. 37–8.

[5] MS. Cott. Vitell. F XII, f. 282 b. 'In capella Apostolorum ... in medio sub lapide jacet ffrater Willelmus Goodard sacre theologie doctor gardianus loci et precipuus benefactor ejusdem qui obiit 26º die mensis Septembris, A.D. 1485.' On fol. 310 he is called 'frater Willelmus Goddard junior.'

to decide with certainty which of the two was provincial in 1485; and, if it was the elder, whether he held office twice. William Goddard the elder was buried in the choir of the Franciscan Church in London.

'Ad cujus (Johannis Hastyng', comitis Pembrochie) dexteram in plano sub lapide jacet venerabilis pater et frater Willelmus Goddard doctor egregius et ordinis fratrum minorum in anglia Minister benemeritus. Qui obiit 30º die Mensis Octobris aº domini 1437'[1].

Aqua vite secundum doctrinam magistri Godard per Johannem Grene medicum scriptum; a short receipt in English.

MS. Brit. Mus.:—Sloane 4, p. 77 (c. A. D. 1468).

Richard Ednam supplicated on January 27th, 145⅘, that eight oppositions should stand for the complete opposition required by the statutes[2]; the grace was conceded without conditions, and Ednam was admitted B.D., November 28th, 1455[3]. On April 2nd, 1462, he supplicated for D.D., promising to pay £10 on the day of his inception; the grace to incept was granted on condition

'that he should incept within a year and give the Regents the usual livery'[4].

He did not take advantage of this grace, and on May 24th, 1463, he again supplicated for D.D.; the grace was conceded on condition

'that he should incept before the feast of St. Thomas (July 3rd), pay £15 on the day of his inception, and give a separate livery to the Regents at his own expense'[5].

He was at this time clearly not in the position of a simple mendicant. In March, 146⅘ he was made Bishop of Bangor[6]. The next year[7] he was allowed to appropriate a benefice 'owing to the smallness of the income of the episcopal table.' He died in 1496[8].

Gundesalvus (Gonsalvo) of Portugal was admitted to oppose in theology in April, 1456[9]. In February, 145⁶⁄₇, he supplicated that he might reckon the two terms, during which he had been opponent, as a year, and proceed to the bachelor's degree[10]. On May 29th, 1459, having performed the exercises required for the doctor's

---

[1] MS. Cott. Vitell. F XII, fol. 274 b. The date is obviously wrong. In the margin 1497 is written in a later hand, but crossed out.
[2] Reg. A a, fol. 87 b.
[3] Boase, Reg. p. 24.
[4] Reg. A a, fol. 122; see App.
[5] Reg. A a fol. 128; see App.
[6] Le Neve, *Fasti*, I, 103.
[7] 'XIX Kal. Feb. anno 1466.' Wadding, Vol. XIII, p. 356.
[8] Le Neve, *ut supra*.
[9] Reg. A a, fol. 14 b.
[10] Ibid. fol. 101 b.

degree, he supplicated for grace to incept in theology, 'notwithstanding that he had not ruled in Arts.' The grace was conceded on condition that he should incept in the first week of the next term, and

'give a livery, i.e. *cultellos*, according to the ancient custom, to all the Regents'[1].

Among the Observant friars of Portugal who died in 1504 to 1505 was

'venerandus pater frater Gundisalvus, qui bis Vicarius Provincialis fuit'[2].

> *Gundessalvi Libri de Divisione Philosophiae*, Bodl. MS. 2596 (Bernard) are probably not by this friar: cf. Cambridge MSS. No. 1025 (in Bernard): and Bibl. Nat. Paris, 16613 'Gumdissalvi Liber de anima' (sec. xiii).

John Alien, B.D. of Cambridge, was on December 1st, 1459, incorporated as B.D. at Oxford under the following conditions: (1) he was to respond twice in the first year of his incorporation, and (2) to preach once to the University in the same period; (3) he was to pay 40s. to the building of the schools, and (4) oppose twice before his incorporation. The last two conditions were on the same day withdrawn at Alien's request[3]. He may be the same as Friar John Alen, S.T.P., sometime warden of the convent at London, where he was buried, in the Chapel of All Saints[4].

Richard Rodnore and —— **Roby**, 'friars of the Order of St. Francis,' at Oxford, had a quarrel in 1461, in consequence of which Roby procured from the Archbishop of Canterbury an inhibition to prevent Rodnore being admitted to the degree of D.D. At the inception on June 27th, 1461, the Commissary refused to recognise the inhibition, Rodnore took his degree, and three persons who had been employed in presenting the Archbishop's command were imprisoned by the Congregation of Regents as 'disturbers of peace and violators of privileges,' and suspended from their office in the University[5].

Laurentius Gulielmi[6] **de Savona**, a man of noble birth, and friar of the Province of Genoa, was for five years a pupil of Friar Francis

---

[1] Reg. A a, fol. 117; printed in Mun. Acad. 755.
[2] Anal. Franc. II, 536.
[3] Reg. A a, fol. 119.
[4] MS. Cott. Vitell. F XII, fol. 277. 'Sub secunda parte tercie fenestre jacet Johannes Alen pater Magistri quondam de capella Johannes (sic) ducis Bedfordie et in eodem loco jacent frater Johannes Alen S.T.P. quondam gardianus loci filius Johannis Alen,' &c.
[5] Mun. Acad. 683.
[6] Wadding adds 'de Traversagnis;' Script. 160; Ann. Vol. XIV, p. 232.

of Savona (who in 1471 became Pope Sixtus IV), at Padua and Bologna[1]. After this Laurentius lectured at Paris and Oxford[2]. In 1478 he was at Cambridge, writing on rhetoric[3]. In April, 1485, he dates a letter to William Waynflete, in praise of his foundation of Magdalen College, 'in almo Conventu S. Francisci Londonii,' where also he seems to have written his *Triumphus Amoris Domini nostri Jesu Christi*[4]. He subsequently returned to Savona, where he died in 1495 at the age of eighty-one[5].

His treatise *Nova Rhetorica* or *Margarita eloquentiæ*, &c., was printed at St. Albans in 1480[6].

Arenga fratris Gwilhelmi Sauonensis de epistolis faciendis. Inc. 'Conquestus mecum es.'

MS. Munich:—Bibl. Regia, 5238 (sec. xv).

Fratris Laurentii Gulelmi de Traversagnis de Saona, ord. Min., S. Pag. Prof., in libros septem dialogorum, sive directorium vitae humanae, seu directorium mentis in Deum. Inc. prol. 'Quum plures nationes:' written at Savona, 1492[7].

MS. Venice:—St. Mark, Vol. IV, Cl. x. Cod. 246.

Isaac Cusack, or **Cusag**, in 1473, obtained letters from the University testifying to his learning and good conduct, and certifying that he had incepted as D.D., and

'laudably fulfilled his regency and all that pertains to the solemnity of such a degree.'

Armed with this testimonial, he went over to Ireland with a Dominican named Dionisius Tully; and the two friars

'preached publickly that Christ preached from door to door, that Pope John was a Heretic, and such like, telling the People withal, that they in their proceedings had been encouraged by the University of Oxford.'

In 1482 the University, hearing of their doings, had them arrested with

---

[1] Wadding, ibid. and Sup. ad Script. 484.

[2] Ibid. His connexion with Oxford may be inferred from his *Epistola nuncupatoria* to Waynflete, in which he speaks of the site, building, library, &c., of Magdalen College, Lambeth MS. 450; Wharton, *Anglia Sacra*, I, 326.

[3] See *explicit* of his *Rhetorica* (ed. 1480): 'compilatum autem fuit hoc opus in Alma universitate Cantabrigie, A.D. 1478, die et 6 Julii.'

[4] Lambeth MS. *ut supra*.

[5] Wadding, Script. 161.

[6] Macray, Annals of the Bodleian, 2nd edition, p. 376, says 1489.

[7] See also Wadding, *Script*, 160, 161. 'Habentur ejus monumenta Saonae apud Minores MSS. ... Magnam librorum copiam eo in conventu coacervavit.'

the co-operation of the Archbishop of Dublin, and sent back to Oxford. Being convicted of heresy, they were (according to Wood) 'after recantation degraded and rejected the University as vagabonds.' There seems to be no authority for Wood's surmise, that they were afterwards reconciled to the University 'by their complaints to great persons'[1].

William Dysse in 1477 represented the Friars Minors of Oxford in the Court of Chancery. He may have been warden, more probably permanent or temporary 'syndicus' of the house[2].

Menelaus (Menma) McCormic or **McCarmacan** is said to have studied at Oxford. He was promoted to the see of Raphoe in 1484, died on May 9, 1515 or 1516, and was buried in the Minorite Convent of Donegal[3].

— **Wy3ht**. The proctors in their accounts for the year ending April 17, 1482,
'reddunt compotum de compositionibus 4 Doctorum Theologie, viz. Morgan, Browne, et Richeford, fratrum ordinis predicatorum, et Wy3ht ordinis minorum, 26^{li} 13^s 4^d.'[4]

Mauritius de Portu, or **O'Fihely**, a native of County Cork, studied first at Oxford, then became regent of the Franciscan Schools at Milan in 1488, and regent doctor in theology at Padua in 1491, where he was honoured with the title of '*Flos Mundi.*' He was minister of Ireland in 1506 and took a prominent part in deposing the General, Ægidius Delphinus, in the first *capitulum generalissimum* at Rome in that year. In 1506 also, he was made Archbishop of Tuam by Julius II. He was present at the Lateran Council in 1512, and died the next year; he was buried among the Grey Friars of Galway[5].

[1] Wood, Annals, Vol. I. p. 638. Oxf. Univ. Archives, F 4, f. 123 b, 145 a (Letter 313).
[2] Pat. 17 Edw. IV, Part II, m. 28. His business related to the royal grant of 50 marks a year. 'Nos autem, pro eo quod littere predicte casualiter sunt amisse, sicut ffrater Willelmus Dysse coram nobis in Cancellaria nostra personaliter constitutus sacramentale prestitit corporale, et quod idem frater Willelmus litteras illas si eas imposterum reperiri contigerit nobis in eandem Cancellariam nostram restituet ibidem cancelland' tenorem irrotulamenti litterarum predictarum ad requisicionem prefati Willelmi duximus exemplificand' per presentes. In cujus, &c. T. R. apud Westmonasterium XIIIJ die Novembris.'
[3] Cotton, Fasti Eccles. Hibern. III, 349.
[4] Wood MS. D 2, p. 340.
[5] Wood, *Athenae*, I, 16-18; Wadding, Ann. Vol. XV, pp. 312, 422. He is said also to have superintended for some years the press which Ottaviano Scotto opened at Venice in 1480; Cotton, Fasti Eccles. Hibern. IV, p. 11.

For his writings, most of which have been printed, see Tanner, *Bibl.* p. 605, Wood, *Athenae* I, 16–18. They relate for the most part to works of Duns Scotus, 'whom (Wood remarks) he had in so great veneration that he was in a manner besotted with his subtilties.' The *Distinctiones ordine alphabetico* by 'Frater Mauricius Anglus' cannot be by Mauritius de Portu; they exist e. g. in a fourteenth-century MS. in the British Museum (Royal 10 B. xvi), and in a thirteenth-century MS. at Paris[1].

Petrus Pauli de Nycopia, friar, who transcribed a work of Duns Scotus at Oxford, c. 1491, was probably a Minorite[2].

John Percevall, D.D. of Oxford, was Provincial Minister about 1500[3]. There appears to have been a contemporary writer of the same name, a Carthusian, who studied at Oxford and Cambridge. Among those buried in the choir of the Grey Friars, London, 'in plano sub lapide jacet venerabilis pater et frater Johannes Persevall doctor egregius et ordinis minorum in anglia minister qui obiit 16 die Mensis Decembris, Aº Domini 1505º '[4].

Thomas Roger, warden of the Grey Friars of Gloucester, is mentioned in the following record of the Chancellor's Court; it is to be regretted that no explanation of the circumstances is forthcoming. 'Ultimo Februarii 1499 (=Feb. 29th, 1500) W. Botehill de Gloucestre, scitatus coram nobis ad instanciam fratris Thome Roger gardiani fratrum minorum Gloucestrie, prestitit juramentum corporale quod ipse in persona sua propria comparebit Gloucestrie responsurus obiciendis sibi pro parte dicti Gardiani et hoc citra ffestum Pasche proximum '[5].

John Kynton is once only described as a Minorite in the records. 'Eodem die (October 24th, 1507) Thomas Clarke executor testamenti Joannis Falley promisit se soluturum domino doctori Kynton ordinis Minorum xxviˢ viiiᵈ [6].'

He was *senior theologus* in 1503, and acted as commissary or Vice-Chancellor in 1503, 1504, 1507, 1510, 1512, 1513; 'Dr. Kyngton, *senior theologus*,' was commissary in 1532[7]. Kynton preached the University sermon on Easter Sunday in 1515[8]. He

---

[1] MS. Bibl. Mazarine, 1019; the author is here called 'Frater Mauricius Belvacensis ordinis fratrum Minorum.'

[2] MS. C.C.C. Oxford, 227, f. 1 : 'Expliciunt questiones doctoris subtilis super secundo et tertio de anima Oxonie scripte per fratrem Petrum Pauli de Nycopia. Lord Jhesu mercy.' Cf. notice of William Vavasour.

[3] According to Wood he became D.D. about 1500, *Fasti*, 6.

[4] Wood, *Athenae Oxon.* I, 5–6. Cooper, *Athenae Cantab.* I, pp. 6, 521. MS. Cott. Vitell. F XII, fol. 275. Mon. Franc. I, 539.

[5] Acta Cur. Cancell. Ⅎ, f. 30.

[6] Acta Cur. Cancell. Ⅎ, f. 28.

[7] Ibid. f. 27, 49 b, 54, 78 : Ⅎ, f. 106 b; EEE f. 159. Boase, Register, p. 161; cf. 296.

[8] Acta Cur. Cancell. Ⅎ, f. 263.

was Divinity reader to Magdalen College, and afterwards third Margaret Professor of Divinity: the latter post he resigned on October 5th, 1530[1]. He was one of the theologians deputed by the University to confer with Wolsey on the condemnation of Luther's books in 1521; he was further one of the committee appointed by the king's command to examine more thoroughly the Lutheran doctrines at Oxford in the same year[2]. He also took a prominent official, though not very decisive, part in the proceedings at Oxford in connexion with the king's divorce[3]. He was buried in Durham College Chapel;
'for,' writes Wood, 'on a little gravestone there, yet remaining, is written this: "Obiit Johannes Kynton, Frater Minor, sacræ Theologiæ professor, 20 Januar. 1535"[4].'

John Smyth, B.D., on June 30th, 1506, obtained grace to incept with the condition
'that he shall say the mass *Salus populi* thrice for the good estate of the regents.'
In January, 150$\frac{6}{7}$, he supplicated for the same grace, which was granted,
'conditionata quod habet studium 4^{or} annorum in sacra theologia post gradum bacallariatus.'
He was licensed on January 22nd, and incepted on January 26th, under Richard Kidderminster, Abbat of Winchcombe, paying £5 for his composition. In July 1507, he was dispensed from the duty of 'deponing' for that term, and in June 1508 he was allowed to postpone a sermon till the next term[5].

John Hadley was B.D. in June, 1506[6].

Christopher Studeley supplicated for B.D. on November 18th, 1506, after studying for ten years. He was buried at the Grey Friars, London, 'between the choir and the altars.'
'Et ad capud ejus (i. e. J. Seller, D.D. warden of London) sub lapide jacet frater Xpoforus Studley electus [gardianus?] qui obiit 10 die mensis Marcii A.D. 157° (*sic*) '[7].

---

[1] Wood, *Athenae*, 94.
[2] Wood, ibid. Lyte, 456.
[3] Lyte, 475.
[4] Wood, ibid. Several other references to him are found in the records of the Chancellor's Court: his servant, William Cooper, was convicted of an assault on a scholar in 1509, Acta Cur. Cancell. ℋ, f. 94 b; in 1513 he took Richard Leke into his service. See App.

B; see also EEE, fol. 265 a.
[5] Reg. G 6, fol. 22 b, 27 b, 29 b, 30, 31 b, 43, 58 b.
[6] Reg. G 6, fol. 18. R. Hadley was one of the Observants *qui fugam petierunt* in 1534; Cal. of State Papers, Hen. VIII, Vol. VII, No. 1607.
[7] Reg. G 6, f. 26 b. MS. Cott. Vitell. F, XII, fol. 288.

Ambrose Kell, Friar Minor, and scholar of theology, in March, 150⁶/₇, obtained from Congregation the right of free entry into the University library on taking an oath not to injure the books [1].

Gerard Smyth, on May 4th, 1507, obtained grace to oppose and proceed to the B.D. degree, after fifteen years' study, on condition 'quod legat tres primas questiones Scoti' [2].

He was admitted B.D. on February 6th, 150⁷/₈ [3]. He was still B.D. in 1510, when he was appointed to preach the University sermon on Ash Wednesday [4].

Brian Sandon, Sandey, or **Sanden** was *Syndicus*, legal advocate and bursar of the Franciscan Convent at Oxford from 1507 or before till the dissolution. A sketch of his career has already been given [5].

Peter Lusetanus, or **de Campo Portugaliensis,** supplicated for B.D. on June 15th, 1506, after studying for eight years. He was admitted to oppose on May 10th, 1507, and appears as B.D. in the following March. He supplicated for D.D. in June 1509 [6].

John Banester supplicated for B.D. on October 24th, 1508, after studying for sixteen years '*in universitate et extra.*'
'Hec est concessa conditionata, una quod habet studium 6 annorum in universitate; alia quod predicet semel preter formam in ecclesia b. Virginis' [7].

Thomas Rose, scholar of theology, was admitted to oppose on March 150⁸/₉ [8].

Thomas Anyden as B.D. supplicated for D.D. on November 20th, 1507: the grace was conceded on condition that he would proceed before next Easter. On the same day, at his request, the condition was graciously cancelled. He was still B.D. in December, 1512. He is probably identical with '**Thomas Anneday,** frater ordinis minorum et Inceptor in s. theologia,' who supplicated on April 12th, 1513,

'quatinus graciose secum dispensetur sic quod solvat tantum septem marcas de compositione sua, causa est quia est pauper et habet paucos amicos.'

---

[1] Reg. G 6, f. 35 a.
[2] Ibid. fol. 39.
[3] Ibid. fol. 51 b.
[4] Acta Cur. Canc. Ŧ, fol. 264 b; the entry is crossed out.
[5] See Part I, chapter VII, where references will be found.
[6] Reg. G 6, fol. 18 b, 39 b, 55. Boase, p. 46.
[7] Reg. G 6, fol. 61 b.
[8] Reg. G 6, fol. 72 (two entries about him). Another Thomas Rose, born c. 1488, is mentioned by Foxe (Acts and Monuments, VIII, 581–590); he was a priest but not a friar (ibid. 585).

CH. III.]   *FRANCISCANS IN THE OXFORD CONVENT.*   271

'Friar Thomas Anyday' incepted July 4th, with three other Minorites, and paid the above sum[1].

Roduricus admitted to oppose in theology, June 12th, 1509; he is perhaps the same as Roderic Witton, Franciscan, mentioned by Pits and Tanner[2].

Walter Goldsmyth was appointed to preach on Ash Wednesday, $15\frac{09}{10}$[3].

John Tinmouth, or **Maynelyn**, Franciscan of Lynn, was educated at Oxford and Cambridge. He was warden of the Grey Friars of Colchester in 1493. In 1511 he resigned the rectory of Ludgershall, Bucks. In 1510 he had been made suffragan bishop of Lincoln with the title bishop of Argos; he held this office till his death. He was vicar of Boston in Lincolnshire in 1518. In the same year he became a brother, and in 1579 Alderman, of the Gild of Corpus Christi in Boston. He died in 1524, desiring in his will to be buried at Boston,

'to the end that his loving parishioners, when they should happen to see his grave and tomb, might be sooner moved to pray for his soul.'

He left £5 to each of the Franciscan houses at Lynn, Oxford, and Cambridge. He is said to have written a life of St. Botolph[4].

Alexander Barclay, D.D. of Oxford, the translator and part-author of the *Ship of Fools*, entered the Franciscan Order after 1514. He died in 1552[5].

Henry Standish, of Standish in Lancashire, was D.D. of Oxford, and appears to have studied also at Cambridge[6]. He was one of the court preachers at the beginning of Henry VIII's reign, and frequently received payments for his services: the earliest grant to him in the State Papers was a sum of 20s. for preaching in 1511[7]. In 1514 the King gave £10 to Dr. Standisshe and the Friars Minors for charges at the general chapter to be holden at Bridgwater[8]. The next year

---

[1] Reg. G 6, fol. 47 b, 161, 169, 187 b.

[2] Boase, Reg. p. 66. Tanner, Bibl. 638.

[3] Acta Cur. Cancell. T, fol. 266 b; perhaps a mistake for Walter Goodfield?

[4] Cooper, Athen. Cantab. I, 31. Notes and Queries, 1st Series, Vol. XII, p. 430. MS. Wood, B. 13, p. 14. Thompson's Boston (ed. 1856). Stubbs,

Regist. Sacrum Anglic. p. 143. Dugdale, *Monasticon*, Vol. VI, p. 1511.

[5] Wood, *Athenae*, 205. Dict. of National Biography.

[6] Wood, *Athen. Oxon.* I, 92-4. Cooper, Athen. Cantab. I, 55.

[7] Cal. of State Papers, Hen. VIII, Vol. II, pp. 1450, 1467, 1470, 1474, 1477; Vol. III, p. 1555.

[8] Ibid. Vol. II, p. 1465.

the friar was in debt to the extent of 100 marcs[1]. Standish was probably at this time warden of the Grey Friars of London[2]. The time during which he was Provincial Minister cannot be determined[3]. In 1515 he attended a council of divines and temporal lords summoned by the King to consider a sermon preached by Richard Kidderminster, Abbat of Winchcombe, on benefit of clergy. The Abbat maintained that a recent act which deprived 'murderers, robbers of churches, and housebreakers' of their clergy if they were not in holy orders, was contrary to the law of God and the liberties of the Church. The Franciscan doctor defended the act, arguing that

'it was not against the liberty of the Church, because it was for the weal of the whole realm.'

Soon afterwards he was summoned to answer for his opinion before Convocation. He appealed to the King, and Henry quickly brought the bishops to submission by an assertion of the royal supremacy and a threat of *praemunire*[4]. Standish thus won the goodwill of the court; he possessed the confidence of the people. The feeling against foreign traders was now very bitter in London, and in 1517 one John Lincoln, acting as spokesman of the citizens, urged the warden of the Franciscans

'to take part with the commonalty against the strangers'

in a sermon he was to deliver on Easter Monday[5]. Standish refused, wisely, as the event showed; for an inflammatory sermon the next day resulted in a serious riot. In 1518 Standish obtained the bishopric of St. Asaph by royal influence, in spite of the opposition of Wolsey[6]. In 1524 he was sent as royal ambassador to Denmark[7]. In 1528 he was one of the 'counsellors appointed for the hearing of poor men's causes in the King's Court of Requests'[8].

His administration of his diocese was not altogether blameless. His Vicar-General, Sir Robert ap Rice, was indicted for extortions on the King's tenants in 1533, and relatives of Sir Robert had, three years

---

[1] Cal. of State Papers, Hen. VIII, Vol. II, No. 1370.
[2] He was certainly warden in 1515. Cal. of State Papers, Hen. VIII, Vol. II, No. 1313.
[3] Mon. Franc. I, 539.
[4] Cal. of State Papers, Hen. VIII, Vol. II, Nos. 1313, 1314; Brewer, Hen. VIII, I, 250-253.
[5] Brewer, I, 245-250.
[6] Le Neve, *Fasti*, I, 73. Cal. of State Papers, II, Nos. 4074, 4083, 4089.
[7] Strype, Ecclesiastical Memorials, I, i. 90. Rymer, XIV, 12.
[8] Eighth Report of the Deputy Keeper, App. 2, No. 5, p. 167.

previously, been indicted for maintaining thieves and had not yet been punished[1].

But Standish is best known as a champion, probably the foremost champion, of the 'Old Learning' in England. He was, there can be little doubt, the Franciscan theologian who in 1516 tried to organize a combined critical attack on the writings of Erasmus[2]. It was some years later—in 1520—that he preached at Paul's Cross against Erasmus' edition of the New Testament, and inveighed against his writings in conversation at court[3]. He consequently became the object of the famous scholar's satire and invective, and his memory has suffered accordingly.

In 1528, when the royal divorce suit was proceeding, he became Katharine's chief counsellor, being apparently chosen by the queen herself[4]. During the long trial, however, he showed little of the boldness which characterised Fisher's conduct, and Katharine seems not unreasonably to have entertained some suspicion of his sincerity[5]. He was present at the coronation of Anne Boleyn, June 1533[6]. That he was willing to admit the royal supremacy[7] is not surprising. He proposed to add to the King's Articles (which required the surrender, by Convocation, of the legislative powers of the clergy), the words:

'Provided that the King allow those constitutions which are not contrary to the law of God or of the realm to be put in execution as before[8].'

He died on July 9th, 1535[9]. His will is dated July 3rd, 1535[10]. He desired to be buried 'inter fratres Minores' (London?).

'Item pro sepultura mea quadraginta libras. Item pro Tumba erigenda xiij^{li}. vj^s viij^d in ecclesia fratrum minorum ubi contigerit corpus meum quiescere. Item pro exhibicione scolarium in Universitate Oxonie quadraginta libras. Item pro edificatione Insule ecclesie fratrum Minorum Oxonie quadraginta libras.'

His bequest of £5 to buy books for the Oxford Franciscans, and his appointment of two executors to distribute his own library should make us hesitate to accept unreservedly the charge of 'gross ignorance' which Erasmus brings against him[11]. Among other legacies may be

---

[1] Cal. of State Papers, Hen. VIII, Vol. VI, Nos. 62, 1379.
[2] Seebohm, Oxford Reformers, 326-7.
[3] Cal. of State Papers, Hen. VIII, Vol. III, 929, 965.
[4] Brewer, II, 304, 306.
[5] Ibid. 339, 346.
[6] Cal. of State Papers, Vol. VI, No. 661.
[7] See ibid. Vol. V, App. 9.
[8] Dixon, Church of England, I, 106.
[9] Le Neve, *Fasti*, I, 73.
[10] P.C.C. Hogen, qu. 26.
[11] Cal. of State Papers, Hen. VIII, Vol. III, No. 929. Cf. Seebohm, Oxford Reformers, 383-4.

noticed £40 to the Church of St. Asaph '*pro pavimento chori*,' 20 marcs to the Carmelites of Denbigh 'to build their cloister,' £10 to the Minorites of London for thirty trentals, £40 to the parish church of 'Standisshe,' and a messuage in 'Wrixham' to Nicholas Rygbye. The will was not allowed to pass uncontested; 'for the law is plain, that when a religious man is made a bishop, he cannot make a will'[1]. Cromwell seems to have exacted heavy fines from the executors and legatees[2].

Robert Sanderson supplicated for B.D. on Jan. 22, 151$\frac{0}{1}$, after studying twelve years. On May 30, 1511, he petitioned

'quatenus gratiose secum dispensetur ut respondeat sine aliqua oppositione propter defectum schole. Hec est concessa et conditionata quod replicet in scholis post responsionem.'

In April 1513, as B.D., he obtained grace to proceed to D.D., stating that he had studied for eighteen years. In June his composition was reduced by four nobles (= 26s. 8d.), on condition

'that he will tell no one except those whom it concerns.'

He incepted on July 4, 1513, paying £5 8s. 8d[3]. At the time of the dissolution he was warden of the Grey Friars at Richmond in Yorkshire[4].

John Brakell obtained grace to oppose and proceed to the B.D. degree on Jan. 27, 151$\frac{0}{1}$, after studying for fourteen years[5].

John Brown, having studied for twelve years, supplicated for B.D. on Jan. 22, 151$\frac{0}{1}$; he obtained the Chancellor's license Nov. 19, 1512. In June 1513, he supplicated as B.D. for D.D., after eighteen years' study. The grace was conceded

'sic quod semel predicet in ecclesia B. M. V. infra annum, et non utatur aliqua gratia generali vel speciali pro sua necessaria regentia infra annum.'

The second condition was afterwards deleted. Brown incepted on Feb. 20, 151$\frac{3}{4}$, his composition being reduced by five marcs[6]. On July 6, 1513, he appeared in the Chancellor's Court as witness of the indenture between Dr. Goodfield, ex-warden, and Richard Leke[7].

John Smyth was admitted to oppose in June 1511, after studying

---

[1] Cal. of State Papers, Hen. VIII, Vol. IX, 34.
[2] Ibid. 34, 35, 607, 771; X, 522.
[3] Reg. G 6, fol. 107, 122 b, 171, 182 b, 168 b, 187 b (and 213 b).
[4] Eighth Report of the Deputy Keeper, App. II.
[5] Reg. G 6, fol. 107 b.
[6] Reg. G 6, fol. 107, 168 b, 185, 200, 205 b, 206, 207, 215.
[7] Acta Cur. Canc. Ħ, fol. 194. See Part I, chapter VII.

for fourteen years, and to the degree of B.D. in Dec. 1512. Six months later he was licensed in theology, and allowed to incept as having studied for eighteen years, with one responsion in the new schools and two sermons *in diebus Parasceues* at the Friars Minors. At his inception he paid £6 13s. 4d. He was dispensed from his necessary regency

'quia est gardianus alicujus loci et sunt ei magna negotia'[1].

Harmon, friar, who was admitted to oppose on Jan. 26, 151¼, is perhaps identical with 'Friar Simondez Harm,' lector of the Grey Friars of Leicester in 1538[2].

Gilbert Sawnders, after sixteen years' study, was admitted to oppose in Nov. 1511, provided

'he said the mass *de Spiritu Sancto* five times for the good estate of the regents, and preached *in propria persona* at St. Mary's before Easter.'

In 1512 he was appointed to preach the sermon on Ash Wednesday[3]. On April 13, 1513, he supplicated for D.D. In May he asked that 40s. might be deducted from his composition; he was allowed to deduct 20s.; this was afterwards increased to four nobles,

'et nemini revelabit nisi quarum interest.'

He incepted on July 4, and paid £4 6s. 8d. In the following November he was dispensed from his necessary regency, and in Feb., 1514, from a sermon[4]. He died on July 16, 1533, and was buried in the Chapel of All Saints at the Grey Friars, London[5].

John Sanderson, B.D., supplicated for D.D. on Dec. 14, 1512, having studied for sixteen years,

'cum oppositione et responsione (?) in novis scolis et responsione in capitulo (?) generali cum introitu biblie'[6].

William German, or **Germyn**, or **Germen**, in Nov. 1511 obtained leave from the Chancellor to enter the University library[7]. He supplicated for B.D. on July 3, 1513, after studying 'logic, philosophy,

---

[1] Reg. G 6, fol. 127 a, b, 160, 168 b, 185 a–b, 187 b, 194 b.
[2] Boase, Reg. p. 79; 8th Report of the Deputy Keeper, App. 2, p. 27.
[3] Acta Cur. Canc. ꟻ, fol. 264.
[4] Reg. G 6, fol. 133 b, 171 b, 177, 168 b, 187 b, 199 b, 214.
[5] MS. Cott. Vitell. F. XII, fol. 277.
[6] Reg. G 6, fol. 160.
[7] Acta Cur. Canc. ꟻ, fol. 156 b.

and theology' for twelve years¹. He was still only *scolaris sacre theologie* in June, 1515, when he asked

'quatenus illa particula olim posita in sua gratia, viz. quod sit medietas anni inter oppositionem et responsionem possit deleri. Hec est concessa, sic quod dicat unam missam de spiritu sancto pro bono statu regentium, et aliam de trinitate, et aliam de recordare².'

In Nov. 1516, he obtained grace to incept, and asked for a reduction of his composition by one-half, which was probably granted³. He did not, however, become D.D. till June, 1518⁴. He was one of the executors of Henry Standish, Bishop of St. Asaph (*d.* 1535), who left

'omnes libros meos distribuendos secundum discrecionem magistri Johannis Cudnor S.T.D., nunc gardiani fratrum Minorum Londoniensium et magistri Willelmi German eiusdem facultatis, et cuilibet ipsorum quinque marcas pro labore⁵.'

Alyngdon, Doctor, friar Minor, in Jan. $15\frac{13}{14}$

'promised to pay William Hows 11*s.* 4*d.* before the fourth Sunday in Lent under penalty of the law⁶.'

Richard Lorcan, an Irish Franciscan, 'subtracted' some goods and money of John Eustas, a scholar, who died intestate, in 1514, and was ordered by the Chancellor's Court to restore them⁷.

John de Castro of Bologna was admitted to oppose on Dec. 6, 1514, and to read the *Sentences* four days later⁸. He made the following entry with his own hand in the Register of the Chancellor's Court (*sub anno* 1514):

'In die cinerum ego frater Joannes ordinis minorum italus de Castro Bononiensi praedicabo sermonem dante domino⁹.'

Radulph Gudman on May 23, 1515, obtained grace to oppose, &c., after studying for twelve years

'in hac universitate et Cantibrigie et in partibus transmarinis¹⁰.'

---

¹ Reg. G. 6, fol. 187.
² Ibid. fol. 254 b. ³ Ibid. fol. 301.
⁴ Reg. H. 7, f. 1. See also ibid. f. 22.
⁵ P.C.C. Hogen, qu. 26.
⁶ Acta Cur. Canc. ⁊, f. 210; another Alyngton is mentioned in Boase's Register, p. 99; for W. Hows, see Boase, Reg. p. 80.

⁷ Acta Cur. Cancell. ⁊, f. 250, 254 b. See Part I, chapter vii. A secular named Richard Lorgan is mentioned in Boase's Register, p. 128.
⁸ Reg. G. 6, fol. 220.
⁹ Acta Cur. Cancell. ⁊, fol. 263. Wadding (*Script.* 148) mentions another Minorite of the same name.
¹⁰ Reg. G. 6, fol. 253 b.

William Walle, having studied for twelve years, obtained grace to oppose, with the stipulation that six months should intervene between his opposition and responsion (July 3, 1513). He incepted in June or July, 1518, and half his composition was remitted. In Dec. 1518, he was dispensed from his regency for a fortnight [1].

John Flavyngur or **Flanyngur**, scholar of Canon Law, supplicated on June 20, 1515,

'quatenus studium octodecim annorum in eodem jure et in jure civili cum multis lecturis publicis in cathedra doctoris et multis aliis locis sufficiat ut admittatur ad lecturam extraordinariam alicujus libri decretalium. Hec est concessa sic quod solvat vj^s viij^d Universitati in die admissionis sue et legat duos libros decretalium [2].'

It is curious that a scholar should, before attaining the degree of B.Can.L., lecture as a Doctor: most of the instruction in civil and canon law was given by Bachelors [3].

Thomas Peyrson, elected Fellow of Merton College in 1520, is said to have entered the Order of Observant Friars while still a B.A. [4] Perhaps he is confused with

'Johannes Perse (*or* Person) electus et cursor theologie hujus loci (London), qui obiit 18 die Mensis februarii 1527,'

who was buried at the Grey Friars, London, *inter chorum et altaria* [5]. Thomas Peyrson was an Observant Friar at Lynn in 1534, probably as a prisoner: he was still there at the dissolution [6].

John Porrett or **Parott** obtained leave, on Nov. 19, 1511, to enter the University library [7]. He supplicated for B.D. on April 26, 1520, having studied for sixteen years. He was not admitted till May, 1526, after fourteen years' study (?) [8]. Early in the next year he applied to have his composition reduced to £4: this was granted on condition that he would proceed at the next act, say five masses for the regents, and interpret the epistles of Paul to the Galatians

---

[1] Reg. G. 6, fol. 187, 301; H. 7, fol. 1, 6 b.
[2] Reg. G. 6, fol. 257 b.
[3] Lyte, p. 222.
[4] Brodrick, Memorials of Merton College, p. 251.
[5] MS. Cott. Vitell. F XII, fol. 288 b, 313.
[6] Cal. of State Papers, Vol. VII, No. 1607. Eighth Report of the Deputy Keeper, App. II, p. 30. One of this name was Rector of Gedleston, Herts., from 1551–1558; Newcourt, Repert. I, 827. Another was vicar of Clacton-parva and died before Jan. 1523 (ibid. II, 155).
[7] Acta Cur. Cancell. H, fol. 156 b.
[8] Reg. H. 7, fol. 156 b.

before Easter. He does not appear to have fulfilled these conditions: on May 23, the same grace was conceded,

'because he is very poor and scarcely has what is necessary to take a degree,'

with the condition that he should read the first epistle of the Corinthians publicly in his house, *schedulis fixis hostio ecclesie b. Marie Virginis*[1], after graduating. He incepted on July 8. On Oct. 10, 1527, he was dispensed from his necessary regency as being Warden of the Grey Friars of Boston: he was, however, to continue to deliver his ordinary lectures till All Saints' Day[2].

David Williams, B.D., was allowed to incept, after fourteen years' study, on condition of preaching at St. Mary's and St. Paul's, continuing his studies at the University for two years, and paying a 'golden angel' to repair the staff of the inferior bedell of arts (Jan. 24, $152\frac{0}{1}$)[3]. In April his examinatory sermon was at his request postponed till after his degree:

'Causa est quia dicit se plura beneficia a parentibus consequuturum si fuerit inceptor quam non[4].'

On May 13, he supplicated

'quatenus graciose secum dispensetur ut posset iterum circuire non obstante aliquo statuto in oppositum. Hec est concessa et conditionata; conditio est quod non circuerat [circueat?] ante festum Penthecostes' (i.e. May 19)[5].

The meaning of this is not clear; perhaps he had already 'gone round' once and failed to incept at the ensuing Congregation[6]. Having secured a reduction of his composition to £4, he incepted on July 9[7]. In Oct. he obtained a dispensation from all scholastic acts till the first Sunday in Advent, 'because he has to preach on that day[8]'. In Feb. of the next year, he was dispensed from his necessary regency[9].

---

[1] To ensure publicity.
[2] Reg. H. 7, fol. 40, 153, 161 b, 171 b, 177 b, 178 b.
[3] Ibid. fol. 51 b. David Williams B. Can. L. must be a different person, Boase, p. 104.
[4] Ibid. fol. 61. For similar dispensation to him, see ibid. fol. 64 (May 5).
[5] Ibid. fol. 63; on *circuitus*, see Clark, Reg. of the Univ. Vol. II, Part I, p. 42.
[6] He was, however, not licensed till June 3, 1521; Reg. H. 7, fol. 58 b.
[7] Ibid. fol. 64, 69.
[8] Ibid. 72.
[9] Ibid. fol. 78; cf. 75, 70 b.

William Curtes was admitted to oppose on April 20, 1520. Soon afterwards he obtained permission

'to respond in the new schools without having any opposition there previously.'

In Feb. 152½, as B.D. he supplicated for D.D., having studied arts and theology for eighteen years.

'Hec gratia est concessa sic quod solvat xl d^{os} ad reparationem baculi inferioris bedelli sue facultatis et quod predicet sermonem ante gradum susceptum et quod procedat ante pascha [1].'

Richard Clynton supplicated for B.D., after eight years' study, April 26, 1521. Among the conditions imposed was one

'that he should celebrate three masses for the plague and another for peace [2].'

Thomas Frances, B.D., had grace to incept (after sixteen years' study) on condition of paying 40d. to mend the staff of the sub-bedell of arts, preaching at St. Paul's within two years, and preaching an examinatory sermon before his degree (Jan. 24, 152$\frac{0}{1}$). He incepted on July 9, 1521, having three days before obtained a dispensation from his necessary regency,

'because he is warden in some convent of his Order and cannot continue in the University.'

The conditions on which this was granted were:

'(1) that he should say the Psalter of David before Michaelmas; (2) that he should celebrate seven masses for the good estate of the Regents; (3) that he should pay his debts to the University before going away [3].'

John Thornall, on Nov. 19, 1521, having studied for sixteen years, was allowed to proceed to B.D., on condition

'quod studuit hic vel in alia universitate per xii annos.'

He was admitted B.D. in June, 1523, and obtained grace to incept in May, 1524, after 'studying fifteen years in this University.' His composition was reduced to five marcs on condition

'quod solvat illas quinque marcas in primis suis inceptionibus,'

and that he should incept before Easter [4]. He failed to do so, and on July 11, 1525, was permitted to pay £5, instead of his full compo-

---

[1] Reg. H. 7, fol. 38, 40 b, 78.
[2] Ibid. fol. 61.
[3] Ibid. fol. 38, 51 b, 68, 69.
[4] Ibid. fol. 73, 104 b, 124, 127, 130.

sition, with the stipulation that he should distribute 10*s.* for the use of poor secular scholars[1]. He incepted on July 17. In Oct. he was dispensed for all scholastic acts for twenty 'legible' days,

'because he has promised to preach at two places which are forty miles distant from each other[2].'

At the Dissolution he was living at the Grey Friars, London[3].

Nicholas de Burgo an Italian Minorite, native of Florence, B.D. of Paris, was incorporated B.D. of Oxford in Feb. 152⅔[4]. A year later (Jan. 25) he supplicated for the Doctor's degree, stating that he had studied seventeen years, seven of them having been spent in Oxford[5]. On the same day he prayed that his composition to the University on his inception might be remitted[6].

'Causa est quia est alienigena et anglice nescit, preterea multos hic labores suscepit, legendo publice in hac academia hoc septennio, et pene gratis, et lecturus est quoque perpetuo, et hic remoraturus, modo dignati fuerint magistri Regentes tantum gratiarum sibi impartire. Hec gratia est concessa sic quod legat unum librum sacre theologie publice et gratis post gradum ad designationem Domini Cancellarii.'

A few days later he was dispensed from nearly all his necessary regency, promising to preach 'on some day when there shall be a general procession[7].' In March, being 'unable to procure all that was necessary to him,' he was allowed to postpone his inception till after Easter, paying a fine of 20*s.* to the University. The fine was afterwards remitted and a sermon substituted, as Nicholas alleged extreme poverty (June 20)[8]. He incepted shortly after this. His dispensation from necessary regency seems to have lapsed, for in Oct. he obtained leave to absent himself for ten 'legible' days,

'because he had been bidden to preach a sermon within twenty days,'

and had not time to fulfil the duties of regent[9]. He preached at St. Peter's-in-the-East on Ash Wednesday, 1528[10]. He was patronized by Wolsey, but whether he came to England at the Cardinal's invitation is doubtful. In Nov. 1528, 'Fryer Nicholas of Oxford' received £5 as a reward from Wolsey[11]. In 1529 the King desired that the

---

[1] Reg. H. 7, fol. 140; App. D.
[2] Ibid. 142 b, 143.
[3] Eighth Report of Deputy Keeper, App. II, p. 28.
[4] Reg. H. 7, fol. 82 b, 98 b.
[5] Ibid. fol. 116 b.
[6] Ibid. fol. 117.
[7] Ibid. fol. 117 b.
[8] Ibid. fol. 119, 125 b.
[9] Ibid. fol. 129 b; in this entry he is described as Doctor.
[10] Acta Cur. Cancell. EEE, fol. 362.
[11] Cal. of State Papers, Hen. VIII, Vol. V, p. 304.

friar should have a benefice[1]; payments to him from the Privy Purse and other sources are frequently found[2]. The Italian friar had made himself useful by advocating the King's divorce[3]. He was perhaps the

'Franciscan, who was one of the chief writers in favour of the King,'

and who consorted with Dr. Barnes, the Austin Friar and friend of Luther[4]. His advocacy of the divorce rendered him very unpopular[5], and perhaps after the fall and death of his old protector, Wolsey, he felt his position less secure. In Dec. 1531, he came to London, having 'disposed of his stuff at Oxford,' to ask leave to return to Italy for his health. It was thought impolitic to let him go, 'he being so secret in the King's great matter as he has been,' and means were found to keep him in England[6].

Wolsey had already appointed him public reader in theology at Cardinal College, in succession to Thomas Brynknell, at a yearly salary of 53s. 4d., besides commons[7]; and in 1532, Henry VIII. re-appointed him to the chair of divinity[8]. He was also divinity

[1] Cal. of State Papers, Hen. VIII, Vol. IV, No. 5875.

[2] In a list of monthly wages for July, 1529, there is a payment of £6 13s. 4d. to 'Friar Nicholas, one of the King's spiritual learned counsel;' in Feb., 1530, he received £3 15s. by the King's command: ibid. Vol. V, p. 304. See ibid. Vol. IV, No. 6187 (25), a grant of denization to 'Nicholas Delborgo, Minorite, S.T.P.,' Jan. 21, 1530.

[3] In conjunction with Stokesley and Edw. Fox he wrote (A.D. 1530) a book on the King's marriage, which Cranmer translated into English with alterations and additions: Cal. of State Papers, VIII, 1054; cf. Vol. VII, 289. He is probably the 'Friar Nicolas, a learned man and the King's faithful favorer,' who was employed in negotiating with the University of Bologna for a decision favourable to the divorce (1530): Cal. of State Papers, Vol. IV, No. 6619. But there was another Friar Nicholas at this time who was employed by the Pope, Wolsey, Henry VIII, and other princes. This was a German Dominican, Nicholas de Scombergt or Schomberg, usually called Friar Nicholas or Fra Niccolo. He came to England in 1517, the same year that N. de Burgo began to teach in Oxford. He was in England in 1526, and hoped to be made cardinal. In Oct. 1532 he was on his way to Capua (from England?): a few months previously, Dr. Nicholas of Oxford (i. e. probably N. de Burgo) was trying to leave England. These facts are taken from the Calendars of State Papers, Hen. VIII, Vols. II-V.

[4] Cal. of State Papers, V, 593 (Dec. 21, 1531).

[5] See Part I, chapter viii.

[6] Cal. of State Papers, V, 623.

[7] Ibid. Vol. IV, 6788, ii, iv, vii.

[8] Ibid. V, 1181. When, after Wolsey's fall, Cardinal College was in danger of suppression, Dr. Nicholas extracted an admission from the King as to the fate of the rich vestments and ornaments which had been sent to London to have the Cardinal's arms removed; 'he had begged of the King "whitze copies for the high days of Our Lady." The King said, "Alack! they are all disposed, and not one of them is left."' Tresham to Wolsey, May 12, 1530; Cal. of State Papers, Vol. IV, No. 6377.

lecturer in Magdalen College. In Jan. 1533, he writes to Thomas Cromwell,

'I have performed the duties of reader bestowed on me by the King, and for greater advantage I have added public lectures. I have received no remuneration, for those who distribute the King's gifts do so arbitrarily. I have often asked in vain. Mr. Baxter retains the profits of my benefice, and has not paid me the money due Michaelmas last[1].'

This appeal was not fruitless: in June, 1533, Dr. Nicholas de Burgo received £6 13s. 4d. from Cromwell[2]. In 1534 he was still at Oxford, and acted as substitute for the Commissary in the Chancellor's Court[3]. Next year he obtained permission to return to Italy. In Oct. he wrote to Henry VIII, expressing a hope that he would be allowed to retain his fellowship at Oxford (*locus collegii*), and his benefice[4]. In the same year he resigned the divinity lectureship at Magdalen College[5]. In July 1537 he again wrote to the King from Italy, renewing his previous request; he was at present prevented by trouble and illness from coming to England, but hoped to come next month[6].

Thomas Kirkham was admitted B.D. in 1523, after twelve years' study[7]. In 1526 he supplicated 'that four years' study after the degree of Bachelor' might entitle him to incept. He became D.D. in July, 1527, his composition being reduced to £4, 'because he is very poor,' and in November he was dispensed from the greater part of his necessary regency as warden of the Grey Friars at Doncaster[8]. He continued to hold this office till the Dissolution[9]. He was, in Wood's words, 'a very zealous man against the divorce of King Henry VIII from Queen Katharine[10].'

He seems to have obtained Church preferment immediately after the Dissolution. In Feb., 1539, Thomas Kirkham was admitted to the rectory of St. Mary's, Colchester[11], and in 1548, to that of St.

---

[1] Cal. of State Papers, Vol. VI, No. 75. The benefice was worth 25*l*. a year; ibid. IX, 645.

[2] Ibid. Vol. VI, No. 717.

[3] Acta Cur. Cancell. EEE, f. 274.

[4] Cal. of State Papers, IX, 645.

[5] Ibid. 1120.

[6] Ibid. XII, ii, 282.

[7] Reg. H. 7, f. 110, June 8; Boase calls him Robert Kyrkeham in this place (pp. 131, and 118).

[8] Reg. H. 7, f. 104 b, 156 b, 160 b, 180 b; App. D.

[9] Eighth Report of the Deputy Keeper, App. II, p. 19. See will of Thomas Strey, lawyer of Doncaster (Nov. 14, 1530), in *Testamenta Eboracensia* (Surtees Society), Vol. V, pp. 294–7: 'Item I bequeth to Master Doctor of Grey Freres xxvj^s viij^d to bie hym a cotte... Theis beyng witnes of this my said will, Sir Thomas Kirkham, doctor of dyvynyte and warden of the Freres Minours in Doncaster' (and three others).

[10] Wood, *Fasti*, 75.

[11] According to Newcourt (Repert. II, 174) this living was vacant by his death before Jan. 22, 1551. There may have

Martin's, Outwich: he resigned the latter living in 1553 or 1554[1]. From these dates it is clear that he had joined the Protestant party.

Richard Brinkley (co. Cambridge), D.D. of Cambridge, and 'Minister General of the Order of Minors throughout all England,' was incorporated D.D. of Oxford on June 26, 1524[2]. There is a discrepancy about the dates, which seems to admit of no satisfactory explanation. A Minorite called Peter Brikley was S.T.B. of Cambridge in 1524. 'Brinkley frater minor' was admitted D.D. of Cambridge in 1527, when he paid £5 6s. 8d. 'pro non convivando[3].' He was buried at Cambridge[4].

An illuminated copy of the Gospels in Greek, now MS. Caius College 403, was lent to him out of the Franciscan Library at Oxford, as the following inscription on p. 1 testifies,

'Iste liber est de con(ventu) fratrum minorum Oxonie omissus et accommodatus fratri Ricardo Brynkeley Magistro.'

Another MS. in the Caius College Library (No. 348), containing the Psalter in Greek, has this note (p. 113):

'here xeeld be nō qweyr' off ye nūbyr off 8, ffor her' ys all q ffr. Ric. Brynkcley[5].'

Edmund Bricott, **Brycoote**, or **Brygott**, born about 1495[6], supplicated for B.D. in Jan. or Feb. 152$\frac{5}{8}$, having studied ten years 'here and at Paris.' He was admitted to oppose on June 13, and became B.D. on June 28. In Jan. 152$\frac{7}{8}$, he obtained grace to incept after fourteen years of study. He was licensed in Feb. 15$\frac{29}{30}$. In June he obtained a reduction of his composition to £5 on the score of poverty, and a dispensation (in advance) from his necessary regency, because he was warden of some house of Minorites. He incepted in July, 1530[7]. He was warden of Lynn at the Dissolution[8]. Like so many others, he seems to have gone with the times; he held the living of Thorley, Herts., from 1545 to 1562; was collated to the

---

been two of the same name. Sir Thomas Kyrkeham, priest, was among those arrested for conspiring at the Grey Friars London to refuse a subsidy to the King in 1531. Foxe, V, 57.

[1] Newcourt, I, 419.
[2] Reg. H. 7, f. 126.
[3] Wood, *Fasti*, 68: he refers to Cambridge tables at the end of Mat. Parker's Antiq. Brit. Eccles. first edition; these are not in the edition of 1572. Cooper, *Athen. Cantab.* I, 34, 527.
[4] Mon. Franc. I 539.
[5] Smith, Catalogue of Caius Coll. MSS. p. 197, 166.
[6] Foxe, VI, 215.
[7] Reg. H. 7, fol. 150, 153, 184 b, 210 b, 234, 235, 237.
[8] Eighth Report of the Deputy Keeper, App. II.

rectory of Wiley, Essex, in 1547, to that of Hadham, Herts, in 1548; and became Prebendary of St. Paul's in 1554. He probably died in 1562[1].

Thomas Knottis was admitted B.D. in May, 1527. He may be the same as the Thomas Knott who supplicated for B.A. in 1522; if so, he became a Franciscan after that date[2].

Anthony Papudo, of Portugal, was admitted to oppose in June, 1526, and B.D. in May, 1527[3].

William Walker supplicated for B.D., June 3, 1527, after studying fourteen years. The grace was conceded on condition

'that he will read the Epistles of St. Paul to the Ephesians and the Galatians in his house' (*in edibus suis*, i. e. the Franciscan Convent)[4].

Robert Knowlys supplicated for B.D. in Jan. 152$\frac{4}{5}$[5]. In Oct., 1529, as B.D., he obtained grace to incept, after eighteen years' study,

sic quod procedat in proximo actu, et legat 2^m et 3um Scoti super sententias in Domo sua, et faciat sermonem latinum in templo Dive Virginis intra annum post gradum susceptum, et alium etiam intra annum anglice intra universitatem[6].

His composition was reduced to £5, owing to his poverty (June 22, 1530). He was dispensed from his necessary regency,

'because he was lecturing in some house of the Order of Friars Minors' (June 28, 1530).

He incepted D.D. in July, 1530[7].

John Arture kept a horse in Oxford in 1528[8]. In May, 1533, he supplicated for B.D., after fourteen years of study; he was to preach, before Christmas, a sermon at St. Mary's,

'another from the pulpit (*e suggestu*) of St. Paul's London, and another *e pulpito* at Westminster[9].'

In Dec. of the same year he sued Joanna Coper for libel: the

---

[1] Wood, *Fasti*, 83; Newcourt, *Repertorium*; Foxe, VI, 215 (his evidence at the trial of Gardiner). Burnet, Reformation, II, i. 582, a curious account of Bonner's visitation of Hadham in 1554. Strype, Life of Grindal, p. 88.
[2] Reg. H. 7, fol. 169 b; Boase, 124.
[3] Ibid. fol. 153, 169 b.
[4] Ibid. fol. 174. Cf. Newcourt, Repert. II, 114; Will. Walker, Vicar of Burnham, Essex, 1557-1582.
[5] Boase, p. 145.
[6] Reg. H. 7, fol. 218 b; adm. to incept Feb. 1, 15$\frac{29}{30}$, ibid. 210 b.
[7] Ibid. fol. 234, 235 b, 237.
[8] Acta Cur. Cancell. EEE, fol. 74 b, Part I, chapter vii.
[9] Reg. H. 7, fol. 288.

scandal about him, and his doings 'at the sign of Bear' (May, 1534) have already been noticed. Soon afterwards he was again in trouble, and had to give bail for his appearance whenever he should be required to answer certain charges, which are not specified in the register [1]. About this time (1534-5) he was appointed warden of the Grey Friars of Canterbury, according to his own account, by the King, 'against the heart of the provincial [2].' There was continual war between himself and the brethren of the house. Each side accused the other of hostility to the King. Arthur wrote that he kept the observance somewhat strict because the friars rebelled against the King and held so stiffly to the Bishop of Rome [3]. On the other hand a brother whom Arthur had imprisoned brought an accusation of disloyalty against him. This seems to have been founded on a sermon which Arthur was said to have preached in the Church of Herne on Passion Sunday, 1535 [4], in which he 'blamed these new books and new preachers for misleading the people' and discouraging fasts, prayers, and pilgrimages, especially to the shrine of St. Thomas.

'And he said, if so be that St. Thomas were a devil in hell, if the Church had canonized him, we ought to worship him, for you ought to believe us prelates though we preach false.'

Further he did not pray for the King as head of the Church, nor for the Queen. As the result of this charge, Arthur was thrown into prison by Cromwell's orders, and an Observant, 'his mortal enemy,' was made his keeper, while another friar was appointed warden. Fearing to be starved, Arthur escaped to France, and wrote letters from Dieppe to a servant of Cromwell, and to Browne, the Provincial Prior of the Austin Friars, praying for his own recall and urging the punishment of his enemies [5]. He appears to have returned, if the dates in the Calendars are correct, and to have been again arrested on Aug. 21, 1537 at Cromwell's command by 'Cardemaker [6].'

John Baccheler was vice-warden or sub-warden of Grey Friars in 1529 and in 1534. At the latter date he became one of the sureties for Friar Robert Puller. In June, 1533, he supplicated for B.D., after studying twelve years: the grace was conceded on condition of his preaching at St. Mary's and Paul's Cross, but it does not appear whether the friar took advantage of it [7].

---

[1] Acta Cur. Cancell. EEE, fol. 257, 271 b, 380 b, Part I, chapter vii.
[2] Cal. of State Papers, VIII, 789.
[3] Ibid.
[4] Ibid. 480.
[5] Ibid. 789.
[6] Ibid. XII, ii, 557.
[7] Acta Cur. Cancell. EEE, fol. 124 b, 161 : the date 1534 is uncertain, Reg. H. 7, fol. 290.

Gregory Based, or **Basset**, B.D., was at one time suspected of heretical leanings and subjected to persecution.

'For in Bristol (writes Foxe, referring to John Hooker as his authority) he lay in prison long, and was almost famished, for having a book of Martin Luther, called his Questions, which he a long time privily had studied, and for the teaching youth a certain catechism[1].'

He afterwards abjured, and, to prove his orthodoxy, took a prominent part in the examination and condemnation of Thomas Benet, who was burned at Exeter in 1533[2]. On December 20, 1534 (?), he came forward as one of the sureties of Friar Robert Puller, for a debt of 25s., in the Chancellor's Court at Oxford[3]. He was still alive in Mary's reign, and is mentioned by Foxe as 'a rank papist,' in connexion with the trial of Prest's wife, a half-witted woman, who was burned as a heretic at Exeter in 1558[4]. In 1561 a warrant was out for the arrest of 'Friar Gregory, alias Gregory Basset, a common mass-sayer,' who was lying hid, it was thought, in Herefordshire[5].

Robert Beste was summoned before the Chancellor's Court on September 30, 1530, to answer a charge of 'incontinence and disturbance of the peace:' he does not appear to have been convicted. He continued to reside at Oxford during the next few years. In 1539 he became vicar of St. Martin's in the Fields; he supported the reformation, and was expelled from his vicarage on Mary's accession. He was afterwards reinstated, and resigned the living before January, 1572[6].

Nicholas Sall, admitted B.D. March, 153½[7].

John Rycks, according to Wood, spent some time among the Grey Friars at Oxford[8]. In 1509, John Rickes, M.A. (who may have been the same person), was elected fellow of Corpus Christi College, Cambridge[9]. In a list of Franciscans written in Cromwell's hand, and dated September 13, 1532, 'Father Rykys' appears as warden of the Observant Convent at Newark (Notts.)[10].

---

[1] Foxe, Acts and Monuments, V, 20.
[2] Ibid. p. 20 seq.
[3] Acta Cur. Cancell. EEE, f. 161 a. There is no year marked on this leaf; on fol. 159, the years are 1534, 1536; on fol. 164, 1528; on fol. 170, 1533.
[4] Acts and Monuments, VIII, 501; he is probably the 'old friar' mentioned ibid. p. 500.
[5] Strype, Annals, I, i. 415.
[6] Acta Cur. Cancell. EEE, f. 230, 257, 270 b, 380 b. Newcourt, *Repertorium*, I, 692.
[7] Boase, Reg. 168.
[8] *Athenae Oxon.* I, 101.
[9] *Athen. Cantab.* I, 61. It seems very doubtful whether these notices refer to the same person.
[10] Cal. of State Papers, Hen. VIII, Vol. V, No. 1312.

Ch. III.] FRANCISCANS IN THE OXFORD CONVENT. 287

'At length in his last days (being then esteemed a placid old man), when he saw the pope and his religion begin to decline in England, he became a zealous protestant [1].'

He died at London A.D. 1536 [2]. His works are as follows:—

The image of divine love. Inc. 'Consideryng in my mind how.'

Printed at London 1525 [3].

Against the blasphemies of the papists [4].

Otto Brunsfelsius. A very true Pronosticacion with a Kalendar gathered out of the moost auncyent Bokes of ryght Holy Astronomers for the yere of our Lorde MCCCCCXXXVI, and for all yeres hereafter perpetuall. Translated out of Latyn into Englyshe by John Ryckes Preest [5].

Printed at London 1536 : dedicated to Thomas Cromwell.

John Nottingham, or **Nottynge**, supplicated for B.D. in October, 1532, after studying for twenty years. He was admitted to oppose in November of that year; but in an entry two years later he is not described as B.D [6].

Edward Ryley was allowed to proceed B.D. in June, 1533, after sixteen years' study, on condition of preaching at St. Mary's and St. Paul's [7]. He was warden of the Franciscan Friars of Aylesbury in 1534, and as such took the oath of Succession [8]. He seems to have remained loyal to the old religion; he held several livings in Mary's reign, namely, Wakering Parva, and Peldon in Essex (A. D. 1555), St. Mary at Axe (1556), which was united to the parish of St. Andrew Undershaft in 1561 ; he resigned the living St. James Garlickhithe, London, in 1560, and that of Stisted, Essex, in 1561 [9].

John Williams was admitted to oppose in 1533, after studying fourteen years. On May 4, 1534, in the dispute about a horse, already referred to, between Dr. Baskerfeld and Richard Weston, he was called as a witness on behalf of the former. In January, 153$\frac{6}{7}$,

---

[1] Wood, *Athenae Oxon.* 101.
[2] Ibid.
[3] Tanner, Bibl. p. 648; Bale (MS. Seld. sup. 64, f. 76 b) gives the Latin *incipit* for this work, 'ex museo Nicolai Grimoaldi.'
[4] Wood, and Tanner, *ut supra.*
[5] Ames, Typographical Antiquities, pp. 486–7.
[6] Reg. H. 7, f. 273 b, 264 b, 310 b.
[7] Ibid. f. 289 b.
[8] Cal. of State Papers, Vol. VII, 665, 'Edward Tyley, S.T.B.' Burnet, Reform. I, ii. 205, 'Edward Tryley, S.T.B.'
[9] Newcourt, *Repertorium.* Strype, Life of Grindal, p. 79.

Baskerfeld bound himself on pain of imprisonment to produce John Williams when required, to answer charges brought against him; the nature of the charges does not appear[1].

William Browne was admitted B.D. in January, 153$\frac{4}{5}$. He was at Oxford when the friary was dissolved[2].

John Tomsun, 'Ordinis Franciscani,' was admitted to oppose on October 17, 1534[3]. The name appears among the twenty-seven names appended to the deed of surrender of the Grey Friars, London, November 12, 1538[4].

Robert Puller was at Oxford about 1534; Richard Roberts, scholar of Broadgates Hall, brought an action against him for the recovery of

'xxv solidos sibi debitos ab eodem Roberto Puller fratre ex causa emptionis et vendicionis.'

John Bacheler and other friars engaged to pay the debt[5].

John Notly, or **Snotly**, Minorite, was appointed to preach the University sermon at St. Peter's (in the East?) on Ash Wednesday, 153$\frac{5}{6}$[6].

David Whythede was at Oxford in January, 153$\frac{5}{6}$, when the warden bound himself to produce him in the Chancellor's Court whenever required[7].

John Joseph, a Minorite of Canterbury, supplicated for B.D. in June, 1533, after studying for twelve years. He was licensed D.D. in 1541, and incepted in 1542, as *vir litteris ac moribus ornatissimus*. He was dispensed from his necessary regency

'quia astringitur ad residentiam nec hic diutius manere poterit.'

It is evident that he held some benefice at this time. In 154$\frac{2}{3}$, he was dispensed from a sermon owing to ill-health[8].

---

[1] Reg. H. 7, fol. 287, 284 b. Acta Cur. Cancell. EEE, fol. 271, 380 b. Part I, chapter viii.

[2] Ibid. 303 b. Part I, chapter viii.

[3] Ibid. f. 303 b.

[4] Reports of the Deputy Keeper, Rep. 8, App. II, p. 28.

[5] Acta Cur. Cancell. EEE, fol. 161, 230.

[6] Ibid. fol. 366 b.

[7] Ibid. fol. 380 b. The year is not certain. I have found no evidence to connect him with David Whitehead, protestant preacher, who was recommended by Cranmer for the Archbishopric of Armagh, fled on Mary's accession, and became English pastor at Frankfurt; Strype, Life of Cranmer, 393, 399, 450.

[8] Reg. H. 7, f. 290; I. 8, f. 84 b, 85, 88 : Boase, p. 175.

FRANCISCANS IN THE OXFORD CONVENT.

He was one of Cranmer's chaplains, and a zealous member of the reforming party, and was appointed preacher at Canterbury by Cranmer[1]. In 1546 he became Rector of St. Mary-le-Bow[2]. In 1547 he was made one of the commissioners for the visitation of the dioceses of Peterborough, Lincoln, Oxford, Coventry, and Lichfield[3]. In 1549 he preached at Paul's Cross against the observance of Lent[4], and, on another occasion, as substitute for the Archbishop, against the rebellions in that year, concerning

'the subdewynge of them that dyd rysse in alle iij places, and how mysery they ware browte unto, and there he rehersyd as hys master dyd before that the occasyone came by popysse presttes[5].'

In 1550 he was presented to a prebend in the Church of Canterbury[6]. On Mary's accession he was deprived of his preferments, being married. He fled to the Continent[7].

Hugh Payne, Observant Friar of Newark, who opposed the King's divorce and upheld the papal supremacy in 1533–4, may have studied at Oxford before he entered the Order; a Hugh Payne supplicated for B.A. in 1523[8].

Richard Risby, warden of the Friars Observant at Canterbury, was executed on May 5th, 1534, for being implicated in the conspiracy of the Nun of Kent. It is doubtful whether he was identical with Richard Rysby, B.A., Fellow of New College in 1506[9].

William David supplicated for B.D. in November, 1534, after studying arts and theology for thirteen years[10]. The grace was conceded, and in February, 1535, he obtained permission to defer his 'Opposition' until after he had taken the degree[11]. He may be the Dr. David, Grey Friar, who assisted at the condemnation of Thomas Benet for heresy at Exeter in 1533[12].

Richard David, 'Ordinis Franciscani,' admitted to oppose, October 17, 1534[13].

---

[1] Chronicle of the Grey Friars of London (Camden Soc.), p. 62; Strype, Cranmer, 229; Wood, *Fasti*, 114.
[2] Newcourt, Repert. I, 439.
[3] Strype, Cranmer, 209.
[4] Ibid. 295.
[5] Chron. of the Grey Friars, p. 62.
[6] Wood, *Fasti*, 114; Rymer, *Foedera*, XV, 237.
[7] Wood, ibid.; Strype, Cranmer, 450, 468–9.
[8] Boase, Register, p. 131; Cal. of State Papers, Vol. VI, Nos. 836, 887, 1370; VII, 923, 939, 1020, 1607, 1652; Gasquet, I, 166, 181–2. Cf. ibid. II, 420?.
[9] Boase, Register, p. 71; Gasquet, I, chapter iv; Froude, II, 178.
[10] Reg. H. 7, f. 310 b.
[11] Ibid. f. 315.
[12] Foxe, Acts and Mon. V, 20.
[13] Reg. H. 7, f. 303 b.

Thomas Tomsun supplicated for B.D. in November, 1534, after studying philosophy and theology for fifteen years *hic et Cantabriæ*, and was admitted on January 29, 153⅘ ¹. With Gregory Basset, he became surety for his fellow friar Robert Puller in December, 1534 (?) ².

One of this name was rector of Lambourne, Essex, in 1546 (and died before April 16, 1557), and rector of Beamont, Essex, in 1555 (died before 1559) ³.

John Billing was admitted B.D. in 1537, after seven years' study ⁴. His name occurs in a list of Observant Friars of the year 1534, as having fled to Scotland ⁵.

Guy Etton, or **Eton**, was admitted to oppose in January, 153⅘, and was admitted B.D. in the same month. In October, 1535, he was allowed to substitute for a sermon at St. Mary's,

'concionem ruri vel in suo monasterio ad placitum ⁶.'

In 1553 (in Edward VI's reign) he was granted license to preach. In Mary's reign he took refuge at Strasburg with John Jewell. In 1559 he obtained the archdeaconry and a prebend of Gloucester, which he held till 1571 or later. In 1576 he was instituted Vicar of St. Leonard's, Shoreditch, and died before June 14, 1577 ⁷.

Anthony Brookby (Brockbey, Brorbe), sometime student in Magdalen College, a man learned in Greek and Hebrew, entered the Franciscan Order apparently after leaving the University. Bourchier calls him licentiate in theology at Oxford; Francis a S. Clara, Doctor of Theology. He attacked the King's anti-papal and anti-monastic measures, was thrown into prison, tortured, and at length (July 19, 1537) strangled with his own cord ⁸.

John Forest, who entered the Franciscan Order at Greenwich, about the age of seventeen, is said by Wood to have been instructed afterwards in theology among the Friars Minors of Oxford, and to have

---

¹ Reg. H. 7, 308 b, 303 b.
² Acta Cur. Cancell. EEE, f. 161.
³ Newcourt, Repert. II.
⁴ Reg. I. 8, fol. 21 b, 23.
⁵ Cal. of State Papers, Hen. VIII, Vol. VII, No. 1607; perhaps in connexion with the conspiracy of the Nun of Kent, or with the refusal of the Observants to take the Oath of Succession.
⁶ Reg. H. 7, f. 303 b; I. 8, f. 9.

⁷ Strype, Memorials, II, ii. 277; Life of Parker, II, 52; Wood, *Fasti*, 98–9; Le Neve, *Fasti*, I, 446, 447; Newcourt, Repert., I, 687. Wood says he was Archdeacon of Gloucester in Edward's reign.
⁸ Wood, *Fasti*, 106–7. Gillow, Bibliograph. Dict. of the Engl. Catholics I, 313; Bourchier (ed. Paris, 1586), p. 11.

CH. III.] FRANCISCANS IN THE OXFORD CONVENT. 291

supplicated for B.D. There seems to be no evidence in support of this statement. Forest was burnt in 1538, aged sixty-four, for denying the royal supremacy [1].

John Taylor alias **Cardmaker**, of Exeter, entered the Franciscan Order when under age [2]. In Dec. 1532, after studying sixteen years at Oxford and Cambridge, he obtained grace to proceed to B.D. [3] He was warden of the Grey Friars at Exeter in 1534 [4]. At the time of the Dissolution he preached against the Pope [5]. In 1543 he became vicar of St. Bride's in Fleet Street [6], then prebendary, and in 1547 Chancellor of Wells [7]. In the reign of Edward VI. he married a widow (by whom he had a daughter) [8], and was appointed reader in St. Paul's, where he lectured three times a week [9];

'his lectures were so offensive to the Roman Catholic party, that they abused him to his face, and with their knives would cut and haggle his gown [10].'

On the accession of Mary he tried to escape to the continent, disguised as a merchant; he was caught, committed to the Fleet, and afterwards removed to the Compter in Bread Street [11]. Convened before Gardiner and others, he appears to have shown some signs of wavering at first.

'You shall right well perceive,' he wrote to a friend, 'that I am not gone back, as some men do report me, but am as ready to give my life as any of my brethren that are gone before me; although by a policy I have a little prolonged it, ... That day that I recant any point of doctrine, I shall suffer twenty kinds of death [12].'

He was convicted of heresy, deprived of his preferments, and burnt with others at Smithfield on May 30, 1555 [13].

John Crayford or **Crawfurthe** supplicated for B.D. in April,

---

[1] Wood, *Athenae*, I, 107; Gasquet, I, 192–201.
[2] Foxe, Acts and Monuments, VII, p. 79.
[3] Reg. H. 7, f. 276 b.
[4] Oliver, Monast. Exon. 331.
[5] Wood, *Fasti*, 92.
[6] He resigned the living in 1551; Newcourt, Repert. I.
[7] Le Neve, *Fasti*, I, 177.
[8] Cooper, Athen. Cantab. I, 126–7.
[9] Ibid., and Wood, *Fasti*.
[10] Wood, *Fasti*: his manner was not conciliatory: 'he sayd opynly in his lector in Powlles that if God ware a man he was a vj or vij foote of lengthe with the bredth, and if it be soo, how canne it be that he shuld be in a pesse of brede in a rownde cake on the awter: what an ironyos oppynyone is this unto the leye pepulle.' Grey Friars Chron. p. 63.
[11] Strype, Eccl. Mem. III, i. p. 322; Foxe, VI, 627.
[12] Foxe, VII, 84.
[13] Strype, Eccles. Mem. III, i. 166, 347.

1537, after studying fourteen years at Oxford and Cambridge[1]. He was the last warden of the Grey Friars at Newcastle-on-Tyne, and surrendered his house to the King on Jan. 9, 1538/9[2]. In 1543 he was presented by Henry VIII to a canonry in Durham Cathedral. He became vicar of Midford in Northumberland in 1546, and resigned the living in or before 1561. He died in 1562, bequeathing legacies to several of the canons, grammar-scholars, and others connected with the church of Durham. To the library he left St. Augustine's works in ten volumes, St. Basil in Greek and Latin, and Rabbi Moses in print; and to Sir Stephen Holiday, all St. Cyprian's works. He willed his body to be buried in St. Michael's, Wytton-Gylbert, if he died there; otherwise in Durham Cathedral[3].

Hugh Glaseyere supplicated in 1535 that fourteen years' study might suffice for his admission to oppose and read the *Sentences*. He was admitted to oppose on July 13, and B.D. on July 14, 1538[4], i.e. on the day of the dissolution of the Oxford friary. His name, however, does not appear in the list of Minorites at Oxford 'who would have their capacities.' He conformed to the various changes in religion. In November, 1538, he was instituted to the rectory of Hanworth, Middlesex, on the presentation of the King; he resigned it in 1554. In 1546 he was appointed to the rectory of Harlington, which he held till his death[5]. In 1541 he was appointed by Cranmer to the difficult post of commissary-general of the Archbishop at Calais[6]. In 1542 he was made canon of Christchurch, Canterbury[7]. In Edward's reign he was reckoned 'an eager man for reformation,' and preached at Paul's Cross (1547) that the observation of Lent was only

'a politic ordinance of man, and might therefore be broken of men at their leisure'[8].

In 1553 he was presented by Queen Mary to the rectory of Deal[9].

---

[1] Reg. I. 8, fol. 22. Another of the same name was D.D. of Cambridge (1536), and Master of University College, Oxford (1546). Boase, p. 120; Wood, *Fasti*, 123; Cooper, Athen. Cantab. Reg. H. 7, fol. 227 b, I. 8, f. 16 b, 112. The ten vols. of St. Augustine (ed. 1529) given by him are still in the library of the Dean and Chapter.

[2] Eighth Report of the Deputy Keeper, App. II.

[3] Cooper, Athen. Cantab. 70, 532; Le Neve, *Fasti*, III, 308; Hutchinson's Durham, II, 170; Durham Wills, Vol. I, 194 (Surtees Soc. 1835), 'Crawfurthe.'

[4] Reg. I. 8, fol. 6 b, 35 b.

[5] Newcourt, *Repertorium*, I, 629, 632.

[6] Strype, Memorials, II, i. 40; *Life of Cranmer*, 126, 133.

[7] Le Neve, *Fasti*, I, 54.

[8] Wood, *Fasti*, 108; Strype, Mem. II, i. 40; Tanner, Bibl. 327.

[9] Rymer, Foed. XV, 350.

In March, 1558, Cardinal Pole appointed certain commissioners for the suppression of heresy in his diocese, among them being Hugh Glazier, S.T.B.[1] Hugh did not survive the persecution in Kent which followed. On the 27th July, 1558, 'Magister Glasier, sacellanus cardinalis,' was buried at Lambeth [2].

Henry Stretsham supplicated for B.D. in May, 1538, having studied twelve years at Oxford and Cambridge; he was to preach at St. Mary's and in some other church *intra Universitatis precinctum* [3].

Richard Roper, B.D., was one of the Franciscans at Oxford who desired 'to have their capacities' at the dissolution [4].

Radulph Kyrswell, or **Creswell**, was an Observant Friar at Reading in 1534, having probably been sent there as a prisoner for refusing to acknowledge the royal supremacy. At the time of the dissolution he was at Oxford, and as priest supplicated for a 'capacity' [5].

Robert Newman was one of the priests among the Oxford Franciscans at the dissolution who asked for 'capacities.' He became vicar of Hampton in 1541, joined the reforming party, and was deprived of the living on the accession of Mary [6].

John Comre (?), James Cantwell, Thomas Cappes, William Bowghnell, James Smyth, Thomas Wythman, were among the priests in the Franciscan Convent who asked for 'capacities' at the dissolution [7].

John Staffordeschyer, priest, was at Oxford when the friary was suppressed [8]. John Stafford, who was warden of the Grey Friars at Coventry in 1519 and 1538, when he surrendered his house to the King on the 5th October, seems to have been a different person [9].

---

[1] Strype, Mem. III, ii. 120, who gives 1558 as the date. Burnet puts this commission in 1557; Reformation, Vol. III, Part i, p. 502.

[2] Tanner, Bibl. 327: Hugh's successor at Harlington was instituted on Jan. 17, 155$\frac{8}{9}$; Newcourt, *ut supra*.

[3] Reg. I. 8, fol. 37. Henry Strensham was rector of St. George's, Botolph Lane, London, from 1541-4; Newcourt, *Repertorium*.

[4] Chapter House Books, A $\frac{8}{11}$, p. 62.

[5] Chapter House Books, A $\frac{8}{11}$, pp. 2, 62; Cal. of State Papers, Vol. VII, No. 1607. Cf. Gasquet, I, 191-2.

[6] Chapter House Books, A $\frac{8}{11}$, p. 62; Newcourt, Repert. I, 624,

[7] Chapter House Books, A $\frac{8}{11}$. One Thomas Cappes was priest of St. Mary Magdalen, Old Fish Street, London, in 1540, and got into trouble for his Protestant tendencies; Strype, Eccles. Memorials, I, p. 566; he is not mentioned in Newcourt's Repert. I, 453.

[8] Ibid.

Foxe, Acts and Monuments, IV.

John Olliff, sub-deacon, after asking for a 'capacity' on the dissolution of the Oxford friary, joined the Grey Friars of Doncaster and was among the ten brethren who signed the surrender of that house on November 20th, 1538 [1].

Thomas Barly, **William Cok**, and **John Cok**, who were not in holy orders, desired 'capacities' at the suppression of the Oxford Convent [2]. A John Cooke subscribed the surrender of the Grey Friars of Cambridge [3].

Simon Ludford was a Minorite at Oxford at the dissolution. An account of his subsequent career has been given in Part I, Chapter VIII [4].

557; 8th Report of the Deputy Keeper, App. II, p. 17.

[1] Chapter House Books, A $\frac{3}{11}$, p. 62; 8th Report of the Deputy Keeper, App. II, p. 17.

[2] Ibid. *ut supra*.

[3] Eighth Report of the Deputy Keeper, App. II, p. 14; the deed is not dated.

[4] Boase, p. xi; 222; Reg. I. 8. fol. 138 b, 139, 139 b, 190, 190 b, 192 b.

APPENDIX A.

DOCUMENTS RELATING TO THE ACQUISITION OF LANDED PROPERTY BY THE GREY FRIARS.

1. William son of Richard Wileford (c. 1228).—2. Robert son of Robert Oen (1236).—3. Royal license to the Friars to enclose their lands (1244).—4. Purchase by the King of an island in the Thames (1245).—5. Grant of the same island to the Friars (1245).—6. Thomas de Valeynes, grant of two messuages (1245).—7 Laurence Wyche, grant of a messuage (1246).—8. Royal license to enclose (1248).—9. Royal grant to the Friars of the Sack (1265).—10. Grants from various persons (1310).—11. Grant by the King of the property of the Friars of the Sack to the Minorites (1310).—12. Regrant of the same (1319).—13. John Culvard, Inquisitio ad quod damnum (1319).—14. Grant by John de Grey de Rotherfield (1337).

1

Grant of a house by William de Wileford.

The following document is by far the earliest private deed relating to the English Franciscans now extant[1], and very few grants in the Public Records are of greater antiquity. The original is to be found in the Oxford City Archives (No. 17). It is not dated, but it was executed during the mayoralty of John Pady, who held the office from 1227 to 1229[2]. The document is in excellent preservation, and the seal of W. de Wileford is still attached.

Notum sit uniuersis Christi fidelibus, quod ego Willelmus filius Ricardi de Wileford concessi dimisi et liberaui Johanni Pady, tunc maiori Oxonie, et Andree Halegod et Laurencio Halegod et Philippo Molendinario et ceteris probis hominibus Oxonie, illam domum meam in parochia Sancte Abbe in Oxonia que aliquando fuit Ricardi de Wileford patris mei cum omnibus pertinentibus eiusdem domus, ad hospitandum fratres minores in perpetuum. Et si ita contigerit quod fratres minores a uilla Oxonie discesserint, et ibi amplius manere noluerint, ad hospitandum ibi aliquos probos uiros in elemosina, saluo

---

[1] Except, I think, one mentioned in the Reports of the Historical Manuscripts Commission, but I have mislaid my reference to this.

[2] Wood-Peshall, City of Oxford, p. 355.

quod dicti probi homines Oxonie et eorum heredes faciant Capitalibus dominis illius feodi annuale seruicium quod ad predictam terram pertinet, et reddendo michi et heredibus meis annuatim unam libram cymini ad festum Sancti Michaelis pro omni seruitio. Et ego dictus Willelmus et heredes mei warantizabimus predictum mesuagium cum pertinenciis predictis probis hominibus hereditarie sicut prediuisum est contra omnes homines et feminas, pro hac autem mea concessione dimisione liberatione et warantizatione predicti probi homines Oxonie ex elemosyna collecta dederunt michi quadraginta tres marcas sterlingorum. Et ut hac predicta rata permaneant huic scripto sigillum meum apposui.

Hiis testibus, Pentecost et Henrico filio Tome tunc prepositis, Roberto Oein, Henrico filio Henrici, Petro filio turoldi, Ricardo Mol(endinario), Ricardo Taillur, Milone draparer, Benedicto Mercer, Radulpho Palmer, Willelmo clerico, et aliis.

2

Grant of a house by Robert Oen, A.D. 1236.

Close Roll, 20 Hen. III, m. 9.

Rex Maiori et probis hominibus suis Oxon' salutem. Quia per litteras vestras nobis directas accepimus quod sponte suscepistis in vos onus muragii ville Oxon' quod ad platiam quam Robertus filius Roberti Oen tenuit iuxta domos fratrum minorum Oxon', et quam idem Robertus eisdem fratribus dedit in augmentum mansionis sue: Vobis mandamus quod eisdem fratribus de predicta platia plenam seisinam habere faciatis; Ita quod predictus Robertus, qui prius fuit liber hospes prioris et fratrum sancti Johannis Jerusalem in Anglia in predicta platia, eandem libertatem habeat in corpore domus sue in qua nunc manet alibi in eadem villa in parochia sancti Michaelis ad portam Borealem. Teste ut supra (i.e. Rege apud Gloucestriam iii⁰ die Julii).

3

License to enclose their possessions and throw down part of the old wall, A.D. 1244.

Pat. 29 Hen. III, m. 9 (printed in Mon. Franc. I. 616).

Pro fratribus Minoribus Oxon'. Rex concessit fratribus minoribus Oxon' ad maiorem quietem et securitatem habitacionis sue, quod possint claudere uicum qui extenditur sub muro Oxon' a porta que

APPENDIX A.

dicitur Watergat' in parochia Sancte Ebbe usque ad paruum posticum eiusdem muri uersus castrum; Ita quod murus karnollatus similis reliquo muro eiusdem municipij fiat circa prefatam habitationem incipiens ab occidentali latere dicte porte de Watergat', et se extendens uersus austrum vsque ad ripam tamisie et inde protendens super eandem Ripam uersus occidentem vsque ad feodum Abbatis de Becco in parochia Sancti Bodhoci, iterum reflectatur uersus Aquilonem usquequo coniungatur cum ueteri muro prefati Burgi iuxta latus orientale prenominati posticij (*sic*) parui. Rex etiam concessit eisdem ad continuandum locum nouum cum ueteri, quod possint prosternere de muro antiquo quantum extenditur habitatio ipsorum infra eundem. Saluo tamen semper nobis et heredibus nostris, Regibus Anglie, libero transitu per medium loci noui, in quolibet aduentu nostro ibidem. In cuius, etc. Teste Rege apud S. Albanum, xxii die Dec.

Et mandatum est vicecomiti Oxon', Maiori et Balliuis Oxon', quod id fieri permittant. Teste ut supra.

4

Island in the Thames, A.D. 1245 (see below).

Liberate Roll, 29 Hen. III, m. 9.

Rex Baronibus de Scaccario salutem. Allocate Henrico filio Henrici Simeonis in fine lx marcarum quem fecit nobiscum eo quod inponebatur ei quod interfuit interfectioni cuiusdam scolaris Oxon' xxv Marcas quas debuimus Henrico Simeonis patri suo pro quadam Insula in aqua Tamisis apud Oxoniam quam ab eo emimus, et quas ipse petebat eidem filio suo in fine predicto allocari. Teste ut supra (i.e. King at Windsor, April 22nd).

5

Grant of the island to the Friars Minors, A.D. 1245.

Pat. 29 Hen. III, m. 6 (printed in Mon. Franc. I. 615.)

Pro fratribus Minoribus.

Rex omnibus salutem. Sciatis quod ad ampliacionem aree in qua de nouo hospitari ceperunt ffratres Minores Oxon', assignauimus Insulam nostram in fluuio Thamis' quam emimus ab Henrico filio Henrici Simeonis, concedentes eis et volentes, quod ipsi pontem fieri faciant ultra brachium illud Thamis' quod currit inter insulam predictam et domos suas, et quod Eandem Insulam ad securitatem domorum suarum et tranquillitatem Religionis sue muro uel alio modo, sicut sibi uiderint expedire, faciant includi. In huius Rei testimonium etc. Teste ut supra (i.e. Rege apud Westmonasterium xxii die Aprilis).

Et mandatum est vicecomiti Oxon' quod Insulam illam eis habere faciat. Teste Rege apud Wind(esor) xxiiij die Aprilis.

6

Grant of two messuages by Thomas de Valeynes, 1245.

Feet of Fines, Oxon; 29 Hen. III, m. 40.

Hec est finalis concordia facta in curia domini Regis apud Westmonasterium a die Purificacionis beate Marie (Feb. 2nd) in Tres septimanas, anno regni Regis Henrici filii Regis Johannis vicesimo Nono, coram Henrico de Bathonia, Rogero de Thurkelby, Roberto de Notingham, Jollano de Nevill, Gilberto de Preston et Johanne de Cobeham, Justiciariis, et aliis domini Regis fidelibus tunc ibi presentibus. Inter Thomam de Valeynes querentem et Symonem filii Benedicti et Leticiam uxorem eius Inpedientes, de duobus Mesuagiis cum pertinentiis in suburbio Oxon' unde placitum Warantie carte summonitum[1] fuit Inter eos in eadem curia, scilicet quod predicti Symon et Leticia recognoverunt predicta mesuagia cum pertinentiis esse ius ipsius Thome, ut illa que Idem Thomas habet de dono predictorum Symonis et Leticie; Habenda et Tenenda eidem Thome et heredibus suis de capitalibus dominis feodi illius imperpetuum, faciendo inde omnia seruicia que ad predicta mesuagia pertinent. Et predicti Symon et Leticia et heredes ipsius Leticie Warantizabunt, adquietabunt, et defendent eidem Thome et heredibus suis predicta mesuagia cum pertinentiis per predicta seruicia contra omnes homines imperpetuum. Et pro hac recognitione, Warantia, adquietancia, defensione, fine et concordia, Idem Thomas ad peticionem predictorum Symonis et Leticie attornauit et assignauit predicta mesuagia cum pertinentiis in augmentum aree in qua hospitantur fratres minores Oxon' commorantes, in puram et perpetuam elemosinam, liberam et quietam ab omni seculari seruicio et exactione in perpetuum. Et preterea idem Thomas dedit et concessit predicte Leticie unum mesuagium cum pertinentiis extra portam Aquilonarem Oxon' in angulo de Horsmongharestrete iuxta terram Reginaldi Gamages, simul cum fabrica quam Hugo Marescall tenet, que scilicet Mesuagium et fabricam Benedictus le Mercer pater predicti Symonis aliquando tenuit; Habenda

[1] MS. Sum̄.

et Tenenda eisdem Symoni et Leticie et heredibus ipsius Leticie de capitalibus dominis feodi illius imperpetuum, faciendo inde omnia seruicia que ad predicta tenementa pertinent: Ita tamen quod non licebit predicto Symoni predicta tenementa dare, vendere, assignare, vel legare, vel aliquo alio modo alienare, quominus illa tenementa remaneant predicte Leticie et heredibus suis in perpetuum.

7

Grant of a messuage by Laurence Wych, A.D. 1246.

Pat. 31 Hen. III, m. 8.

Pro fratribus Minoribus Oxon'. Rex omnibus etc. Salutem. Sciatis quod (ad) amplificationem aree ffratrum Minorum Oxon' assignauimus eis totum mesuagium illud cum pertinenciis quod laurencius Wych maior noster Oxon' nobis reddidit et commisit ad amplificationem aree predictorum ffratrum, concedentes eis et uolentes, quod, ad securitatem domorum suarum et tranquillitatem religionis sue, muro uel alio modo, sicut sibi uiderint expedire, illud faciant includi. In cuius etc. Teste Rege apud Clarendon xxvij die Nouembris.

Et Mandatum est vicecomiti Oxon' quod mesuagium illud loco Regis recipiat ad opus eorundem ffratrum.

8

License to enclose their new possessions; the city wall to be repaired, A.D. 1248.

Pat. 32 Hen. III, m. 10 (printed in Mon. Franc. I. 617).

Pro fratribus minoribus Oxon'.

Rex omnibus etc. salutem. Noueritis nos intuitu pietatis concessisse ut vicus qui extenditur sub muro Oxon' a porta que dicitur Watergat' in parochia Ste. Ebbe vsque ad paruum posticum eiusdem muri uersus Castrum claudatur propter maiorem securitatem et quietem fratrum minorum iuxta dictum vicum habitancium, quamdiu domino loci placuerit. Saluo tamen nobis et heredibus nostris, Regibus Anglie, libero transitu per medium Noui loci in quolibet aduentu nostro ibidem. Concedimus etiam ut latus aquilonare capelle in prefato vico constructe et construende suplere (*sic*) possit prenominati muri interruptionem, quantum se extendere debet, ceteris eiusdem muri rupturis in integrum reparatis ut prius, excepto paruo posticu in dicto muro, per quod possint dicti fratres ire et redire de nouo loco in quo modo hospitantur ad priorem locum in quo prius hospitabantur. In cuius, etc. Teste Rege apud Westmonasterium, x die febr'.

This concession is repeated and confirmed in Patent Roll 18 Edw. III. m. 19 (A.D. 1344).

9

Royal grant to the Friars of the Penitence of Jesus Christ or Friars of the Sack, 1265.

Pat. 49 Hen. III, m. 24.

As the Minorites subsequently obtained the 'area' of the Friars of the Sack, records relating to this property will naturally find a place here. On May 7th, 1262, the king gave them permission,

quod in area sibi collata[1], quam habent in parochia ecclesie Sancti Boduci Oxonie, in qua ius patronatus habemus, oratorium construere possint ad diuina ibidem celebranda (Pat. Roll 46 Hen. III, m. 11).

On February 5th, 1265, he made them a further grant (Pat. 49 Hen. III, m. 24), and on February 8th, 1265, this second grant was again made in greater detail (ibidem). It is this last which is here quoted.

Pro fratribus de penitencia Ihū Xpī Oxon'. Rex episcopo Lincolniensi salutem. Cum ecclesia sancti Budoci in suburbio Oxon' nostri patronatus per amocionem et decessum parochianorum eiusdem ecclesie iam in tantum depauperata sit et adnullata, quod fructus et obuenciones eiusdem ad sustentacionem vnius capellani ministrantis in eadem non sufficiunt, vt veraciter accepimus; ac fratres de penitencia Ihu Xpī quendam situm habeant ibidem contiguum ecclesie predicte, in quo domos suas construxerunt, deo famulari proponentes ibidem: nos, intuitu caritatis et pro salute anime nostre et animarum antecessorum et heredum nostrorum, dictis fratribus ecclesiam predictam cum cimiterio eiusdem et domibus existentibus in eodem et ad ecclesiam eandem pertinentibus, quantum ad nos pertinet, concessimus pro nobis et heredibus nostris habendam sibi et successoribus suis, videlicet ad faciendam inde sibi capellam in qua diuina celebrare possint inperpetuum, ita quod cimiterium predictum tanquam cimiterium benedictum in statu suo remaneat. In cuius, etc. Teste Rege apud Westmonasterium, octauo die februarii. Et habent dicti fratres litteram aliam (?) sub hac forma, 'Rex omnibus etc.'[2]

[1] For the grant of this area by the Abbat and Convent of Osney, at the instance of Ela Longespee, Countess of Warwick, see Wood-Clark II, p. 474.

[2] This is a reference to the letter dated May 7, 1262, already mentioned; Pat. 46 Hen. III, m. 11. The word 'aliam' is not quite clear; it may be alteram.

APPENDIX A. 301

10

Grants from various persons, A.D. 1310.

Pat. 3 Edward II, m. 14.

Rex omnibus ad quos etc. salutem. Sciatis quod de gratia nostra speciali concessimus et licenciam dedimus pro nobis et heredibus nostris quantum in nobis est, dilectis nobis in Christo Gardiano et fratribus de ordine Minorum Oxon', quod ipsi de Johanne Wyz et Emma uxore eius quandam placeam terre in Oxonia continentem in se ab oriente versus occidentem quinque perticatas et duos pedes terre et ab aquilone versus austrum duas perticatas terre et dimidiam: et de Henrico Tyeys quandam placeam terre iacentem inter placeam in qua ecclesia Sancti Budoci edificata fuit et aqua (*sic*) Thamisis, que quidem placea continet in se sex perticatas terre in longitudine et quinque perticatas terre in latitudine; et quandam aliam placeam terre extendentem se ab aqua Thamisis vsque ad predictam placeam terre que fuit Ricardi le Lodere, et continentem in se in longitudine quatuordecim perticatas et dimidiam et quinque pedes terre et in latitudine quatuor perticatas et tres pedes terre: et quandam aliam placeam terre continentem in se in longitudine ab aqua Thamisis vsque ad viam regalem sexdecim perticatas terre et dimidiam et in latitudine decem perticatas terre, placee dictorum Gardiani et fratrum ibidem contiguas; adquirere possint habendas sibi et successoribus suis ad elargacionem placee sue predicte imperpetuum, statuto de terris et tenementis ad manum mortuam non ponendis edito non obstante. In cuius, etc. Teste Rege apud Westmonasterium xxviij die Marcij; per ipsum Regem.

11

Grant of the property of the Friars of the Penitence of Jesus Christ to the Friars Minors, A.D. 1310.

Pat. 3 Edward II, m. 9.

Rex omnibus ad quos etc. salutem. Licet de communi consilio regni nostri statutum sit, quod non liceat viris Religiosis seu aliis ingredi feodum alicuius ita quod ad manum mortuam deueniat sine licencia nostra et capitalis domini de quo illa (*sic*) immediate tenetur; Volentes tamen dilectis nobis in Christo Gardiano et fratribus de ordine Minorum Oxon' gratiam facere specialem, concessimus et licenciam dedimus pro nobis et heredibus nostris, quantum in nobis est, eisdem Gardiano et fratribus, quod ipsi quandam placeam terre in suburbio Oxon' placee dictorum Gardiani et fratrum in eadem villa contiguam, continentem viginti perticatas terre et dimidiam in longitudine, et sex perticatas terre in latitudine ad capud australe, et ad capud boriale duas perticatas et quatuor pedes terre, et medio inter capud australe et capud boriale quatuor perticatas et septem pedes terre, in qua placea aliquo tempore fuit quedam ecclesia parochialis sancti Budoci cum quodam cimiterio pertinente ad eandem ecclesiam, quam quidem placeam cum dicto cimiterio dominus H. quondam Rex Anglie auus noster per cartam suam dedit et concessit fratribus de ordine de penitencia Iħu X̄p̄i Oxon' pro quadam capella ibidem construenda in qua diuina celebrare possent: Ita quod cimiterium predictum tanquam cimiterium benedictum in suo statu remaneret, sic(ut) per quandam inquisicionem per dilectum et fidelem nostrum Walterum de Gloucestria Escaetorem nostrum citra Trentam de mandato nostro inde factam et in Cancellaria nostra retornatam est compertum de predictis fratribus de penitencia Iħu X̄p̄i, perquirere possint et tenere sibi et successoribus suis ad elargacionem placee sue predicte imperpetuum, Ita tamen quod Cimiterium predictum tanquam benedictum in suo statu remaneat imperpetuum. Nolentes quod predicti Gardianus et fratres aut successores sui ratione premissorum per nos vel heredes nostros, Justiciarios, Escaetores, Vicecomites aut alios balliuos seu Ministros nostros quoscunque occasionentur, molestentur in aliquo, seu grauentur. In cuius, etc. Teste Rege apud Westmonasterium xxviij die Marcii per ipsum Regem.

12

Regrant of the property of the Friars of the Penitence of Jesus Christ to the Friars Minors, A.D. 1319.

Pat. 12 Edward II, part 2, m. 25.

This document was probably intended as a protest against the claim implied in the papal grant of the same property, as already explained (Chapter II), or perhaps merely as an additional confirmation of the friars' title.

Pro fratribus de ordine minorum Oxon'. Rex omnibus ad quos etc. salutem. Sciatis quod cum fratres de ordine Minorum Oxon' totam illam aream que quondam fuit fratrum de penitencia Iħu X̄p̄i Oxon' in suburbio Oxon' aree dictorum fratrum de ordine Minorum ibidem contiguam de eisdem fratribus de penitencia Iħu X̄p̄i adquisivissent, et iidem fratres de ordine Minorum aream illam adeo integre sicut ad manus suas devenit, nobis dederint et in manus nostras reddiderint habendam nobis et heredibus nostris imperpetuum: Nos, ob affectionem quam ad dictum ordinem fratrum Minorum gerimus et habemus, volentes eis graciam facere specialem, dedimus eis et concessimus pro nobis et heredibus nostris, quantum in nobis est, aream predictam nobis sic redditam cum pertinenciis, habendam sibi et successoribus suis fratribus eiusdem ordinis apud Oxoniam commorantibus, ad elargacionem aree sue predicte, in liberam puram et perpetuam elemosinam, salvo iure cuiuslibet. In cuius, etc. Teste Rege apud Eboracum vi^{to} die Marcii, per ipsum Regem.

13

Inquiry held at Oxford, A.D. 1319, into the advisability of allowing John Culvard to grant land to the Friars Minors.[1]

Inquisitio ad quod damnum 12 Edw. II, No. 47.

Edwardus dei gracia Rex Anglorum dominus hibernie et dux Aquitanie, Magistro Ricardo de Clare Escaetori suo vltra Trentam, salutem. Mandamus vobis, quod per sacramentum proborum et legalium hominum de Balliua vestra, per quos rei veritas melius sciri poterit, diligenter inquiratis, si sit ad dampnum vel preiudicium nostrum aut aliorum, si concedamus Johanni Culuard de Oxonia, quod ipse quandam placeam terre cum pertinenciis in Oxonia, manso dilectorum nobis in Xpo Gardiani et fratrum de ordine minorum in eadem villa ex parte orientali contiguam, continentem in se in longitudine sex perticatas terre et in latitudine quinque perticatas terre, dare possit et assignare eisdem Gardiano et fratribus habendam et tenendam sibi et successoribus suis ad elargacionem mansi sui predicti imperpetuum, necne. Et si sit ad dampnum vel preiudicium nostrum aut aliorum, tunc ad quod dampnum et quod preiudicium nostrum, et ad quod dampnum et ad quod preiudicium aliorum, et quorum, et qualiter, et quo modo; de quo vel de quibus placea illa teneatur, et per quod seruicium, et qualiter et quo modo; et quantum valeat per annum in omnibus exitibus iuxta verum

---

[1] The following petition to the King (Parliamentary Petitions, 4299, in the Record Office), probably refers to this grant, or possibly to the grant of Richard Cary (p. 20); the petition is undated. 'A notre seigneur le Roi si luy plest prient les poures freres Menours de Oxenford qil lour voille graunter la mortificacioun de vne place en Oxenford qe ne vaut qe deux souz per an auxicome retourne est en la chauncellrie et qe est a nuly preiudice.' *Endorsed*; 'Soit veu(?) lenqueste et le Roi en dirra sa volonte.'

valorem eiusdem; et qui et quot sunt (*sic*) medii inter nos et prefatum Johannem de placea predicta; et que terre et que tenementa eidem Johanni remaneant vltra donacionem et assignacionem predictas, et vbi et de quo vel de quibus teneantur, et per quod seruicium, et qualiter et quod modo, et quantum valeant per annum in omnibus exitibus; et si terre et tenementa eidem Johanni remanencia vltra donacionem et assignacionem predictas sufficiant ad consuetudines et seruicia tam de predicta placea sic data quam de aliis terris et tenementis sibi retentis debita facienda, et ad omnia alia onera que sustinuit et sustinere consueuit, vt in sectis, visibus franci plegii, auxiliis, tallagiis, vigiliis, finibus, redempcionibus, amerciamentis, contribucionibus, et aliis quibuscumque oneribus emergentibus sustinenda. Et quod idem Johannes in assisis iuratis et aliis recognicionibus quibuscumque poni possit, prout ante donacionem et assignacionem predictas poni consueuit. Ita quod patria per donacionem et assignacionem predictas in ipsius Johannis defectum magis solito non oneretur seu grauetur. Et inquisicionem inde distincte et aperte factam nobis, sub sigillo vestro et sigillo eorum per quos facta fuerit, sine dilacione mittatis et hoc breue. Teste me ipso apud Eboracum, v die Marcii, anno regni nostri duodecimo.

Inquisicio capta coram Escaetore domini Regis citra Trentam apud Oxoniam xviii⁰ die Maii anno regni Regis Edwardi filii Regis Edwardi duodecimo, secundum formam breuis huic inquisicioni consuti, per sacramentum Johannis de Coleshull, Willelmi Pennard, Rogeri Mymekan, Gilberti de Grensted, Thome Somer, Willelmi de Whatele, Roberti de Watlington, Johannis de Gunwardeby, Johnnis de Ew, Henrici de Edrope, Ricardi de Hethrop, et Willelmi de Eueston. Qui dicunt per sacramentum suum, quod non est ad dampnum nec preiudicium domini Regis nec aliorum, si dominus Rex concedat Johanni Culuard de Oxonia quod ipse quandam placeam terre cum pertinenciis in Oxonia, manso Gardiani et ffratrum de ordine minorum in eadem villa ex parte orientali contiguam, continentem in se in longitudine sex perticatas terre et in latitudine quinque perticatas terre, dare possit et assignare eisdem Gardiano et ffratribus, habendam et tenendam sibi et successoribus suis ad elargacionem mansi sui predicti imperpetuum: Ita tamen quod communitas ville Oxon' in omnibus temporibus quando necesse fuerit liberum habeat introitum et egressum ibidem ad murum ville predicte reficiendum reparandum et defendendum. Et dicunt quod predicta placea tenetur de Willelmo de Adreston' in capite per seruicium vnius denarii per annum pro omni seruicio; et quod predicta placea valet per annum ij^s in omnibus exitibus iuxta verum valorem eiusdem; et quod non sunt plures medii inter dominum Regem et prefatum Johannem de placea predicta nisi predictus Willelmus de Adreston'. Et dicunt quod eidem Johanni vltra donacionem et assignacionem predictas remanent sexaginta solidi terre tenement' et redditus in eadem villa que de domino Rege tenentur in capite pro seruicio ij sol' per annum pro omni seruicio. Et dicunt quod terre et tenementa eidem Johanni remanencia ultra donacionem et assignacionem predictas sufficiunt ad consuetudines et seruicia tam de predicta placea sic data quam de aliis terris et tenementis sibi retentis debita facienda, et ad omnia alia onera que sustinuit et sustinere consueuit. Et quod idem Johannes in assisis iuratis et aliis recognicionibus quibuscumque poni possit, prout ante donacionem et assignacionem predictas poni consueuit. Ita quod patria per donacionem et assignacionem predictas in ipsius Johannis defectum magis solito non oneretur seu grauetur. In cuius rei testimonium predicti Jurati huic Inquisicioni sigilla sua apposuerunt. Dat' predictis die, anno, et loco.

The license to alienate this land was granted to John Culvard on the 8th of July of the same year, and is entered in the Patent Roll for 13 Edw. II, m. 44. The same year similar inquisition was held to consider the petition of Richard Cary to grant land to the Friars Minors at Oxford; Inquis. ad quod damnum 13 Edw. II, no. 31.

14

Grant of a parcel of ground by John de Grey de Rotherfield,

A. D. 1337.

Pat. Roll II, Edw. III, pt. II, m. 6.

A certain interest attaches to this deed as recording the last gift of land to the Oxford Minorites, of which evidence remains—probably the last gift ever made.

Pro Gardiano et fratribus ordinis Minorum Oxon' de acquirendo ad elargacionem mansi.

Rex omnibus ad quos, etc. salutem. Licet de communi consilio regni nostri statutum sit, quod non liceat viris religiosis seu aliis ingredi feodum alicuius ita quod ad manum mortuam deueniat sine licencia nostra et capitalis domini de quo res illa immediate tenetur; Volentes tamen dilectis nobis in Christo Gardiano et fratribus ordinis minorum in villa Oxon' graciam facere specialem; concessimus et licenciam dedimus pro nobis et heredibus nostris, quantum in nobis est, dilecto et fideli nostro Johanni de Grey de Retherfeld, quod ipse quandam placeam terre cum pertinenciis in villa predicta manso predictorum Gardiani et fratrum ibidem ex parte orientali contiguam, continentem in se in longitudine sex perticatas terre et in latitudine quinque perticatas terre, dare possit et assignare eisdem Gardiano et fratribus, habendam et tenendam sibi et successoribus suis ad elargacionem mansi sui predicti imperpetuum: et eisdem Gardiano et fratribus, quod ipsi placeam predictam cum pertinenciis a prefato Johanne recipere possint et tenere sibi et successoribus suis predictis ad elargacionem mansi sui predicti imperpetuum, sicut predictum est tenore presencium, similiter licenciam dedimus specialem. Nolentes quod predictus Johannes vel heredes sui, seu predicti Gardianus et fratres aut successores sui, racione statuti predicti per nos vel heredes nostros inde occasionentur in aliquo seu grauentur Saluis tamen capitalibus dominis feodi illius seruiciis inde debitis et consuetis. In cuius, etc. Teste Rege apud Westmonasterium, xix die Augusti.

APPENDIX B.

MISCELLANEOUS DOCUMENTS.

1. Food for the Friars Minors, etc. (A.D. 1244).—2. Adam Marsh as royal *nuncius* (A. D. 1247).—3. For the same (A. D. 1257).—4. The Church of the Minorites used as a Sanctuary (A. D. 1284–5).—5. Royal grant of 50 marcs (A.D. 1289).—6. Decree of the General Chapter at Paris (A.D. 1292).—7. Royal grant of 50 marcs; tally on the sheriff of Oxford for half the amount (A.D. 1323); evidence of payment.—8. 'Receptor denariorum gardiani Fratrum Minorum Oxon' (A. D. 1341).—9. Goods and chattels of Friar John Welle, S.T.P. (A.D. 1378).—10. Expulsion of foreign Friars Minors from Oxford (A.D. 1388).—11. Friar William Woodford; confirmation of his privileges by Pope Boniface IX (A.D. 1366.)—12. Appointment of a lecturer to the Convent at Hereford (c. A.D. 1400).—13. Decree of the General Chapter at Florence (A.D. 1467).—14. Recovery of debt from a Sheriff (A.D. 1488).—15. Documents relating to the lease of a garden at the Grey Friars to Richard Leke (A.D. 1513–1514).—16. Extracts from the will of Richard Leke (A.D. 1526).—17. An ex-warden called to account (A.D. 1529).

1

Food for Friars Minors, &c., A.D. 1244.

Liberate Roll, 29 Hen. III, m. 14.

Mandatum est Balliuis Regis Oxon' quod de firma ville sue habere faciant fratri Rogero Elemosinario Regis die Mercurij in crastino sancte Lucie Virginis decem Marcas ad pascendum mille pauperes et fratres predicatores et minores Oxon' pro anima domine Imperatricis sororis Regis in aniuersario ipsius Imperatricis sicut ei iniunxit Rex. Et computetur etc. Teste ut supra (King at Woodstock, Dec. 12th).

2

Adam Marsh as royal *nuncius*, A.D. 1247.

Liberate Roll, 31 Hen. III, m. 4.

Rex Thesaurario et Camerario salutem. Liberate de Thesauro nostro Herberto de Denmade quadraginta marcas ad Equos et Harnesium emendum ad opus[1] . . . Mathei Prioris Prouincie ordinis

---

[1] The edge of the parchment is worn away here.

fratrum predicatorum et fratris Ade de Marisco, quos mittimus In Nuncium ad partes transmarinas, et ad expensas eorundem. Teste Rege apud Clarendon' xviii die Julii.

3

For the same A.D. 1257.

Liberate, 42 Hen. III, m. 3.

Rex Vicecomiti Kancie salutem. Precipimus tibi quod venerabili Patri W. Wygornensi Episcopo et fratri Ade de Marisco, quos mittimus in nuncium nostrum ad partes transmarinas, facias habere festinum passagium in portu nostro Douor' et illud aquietes et computetur[1] tibi ad scaccarium. Teste me ipso apud Westmonasterium, xiij die Decembris, anno regni nostri xlij°.

Rex Thesaurario et Camerario, etc. Liberate[2] Johanni Marscallo nostro xj^{li} ij^d pro iiij equis emptis ad opus nostrum et liberatis per preceptum nostrum iiij^{or} fratribus ordinis predicatorum et minorum euntibus in nuncium ad partes transmarinas, et lxix^s vij^d obolum pro expensis eorundem equorum et garcionum custodientium eos per xxxv dies. Liberate etiam eidem Johanni lxvj^s ix^d pro hernesiis emptis ad opus fratrum predictorum ... Teste ut supra (Rege apud Westm' xxi die Dec.).

4

The Church of the Minorites used as a Sanctuary, A.D. 1284-5.

Assize Roll 710, m. 55 [3].

Adam de Kydmersford posuit se in Ecclesiam fratrum minorum Oxon' et cognouit se esse latronem de pluribus latrociniis et abiurauit regnum coram Coronatore. Nulla habuit catalla.

5

Royal grant of 50 marcs, 1289.

Exchequer, Queen's Remembrancer, Wardrobe Acc^{ts} $\frac{4}{5}$, Anno 17-18, Edw. I.

This is the earliest mention which I have found of the annual grant of 50 marks to the Oxford Minorites. After reciting the similar grant to the Friars Preachers, the record goes on (11th October):—

---

[1] Comp^r.
[2] This entry occurs a few lines before the foregoing on the same membrane; it probably refers to the same embassy.
[3] Formerly 'Placita de juratis et assisis et corone 13 Edw. I, Oxon, $\frac{M}{\frac{5}{2}}$ } 3, m. 55.'

Et ffratribus Minoribus Oxon', percipientibus similiter annuatim a Rege in subsidium sustentacionis L marcas, scilicet eodem modo ad duos terminos pro Elemosina Regis predicti; de termino Sancti Michaelis anno presenti per manus ffratrum Johannis de Bekinkham et Johannis de Clara, xvi^{li} xiij^s iiij^d.

Later in the same document occurs this entry:—

Pro Scaccario. ffratribus Minoribus Oxon' percipientibus[1] annuatim L marcas de Elemosina Regis ad sustentacionem suam ad duos anni terminos, vid. ad festum Sancti Michaelis et ad Pasch', pro eadem Elemosina de termino Sancti Michaelis anno xvj^{mo} finiente et de termino pasche anno xvij^o xxxiij^{li} vj^s viij^d.

6

Decree of the General Chapter at Paris, A.D. 1292.

The following extract is reprinted from Ehrle's 'Die ältesten Redactionen der Generalconstitutionen des Franziskaner-Ordens,' in the 'Archiv für Literatur- und Kirchengeschichte des Mittelalters,' vol. VI. p. 63. The Franciscan School at Oxford evidently had at this time a greater reputation and greater popularity than those at Cambridge and London. But why the burden should be especially heavy during the long vacation is not quite clear. Can the Mendicant Friars have been to any large extent dependent on the alms of the secular scholars?

Memoriale ministro Anglie. Ut tempore vacacionis maioris onus conventus Oxonie aliqualiter relevetur, ordinat generale capitulum, quod studentes ibidem de provinciis inter ipsam Oxoniensem et Londonensem et Canteb[*rigiensem*] conventus pro tertia parte, connumeratis aliis studentibus extraneis, qui in prefatis Londonensi et Cantebrugiensi conventibus fuerint, ad ministri provincialis arbitrium dividantur.

7

Royal grant of 50 marcs; tally on the Sheriff of Oxford for half the amount, A.D. 1323; evidence of payment.

R.O. Exchequer, Treas. of Receipt $\frac{3}{35}$.

Gardiano et conventui ordinis fratrum Minorum Oxon' —— xvj^{li} xiij^s iiij^d.

Liberatum eisdem xxv die Maij. In vna tallia facta .... Coll' x^a et

---

[1] p̄c.

vj^{ta}[1] in comitatu Oxon' et Liberata fratri Johanni de Stanle videlicet pro hoc termino Pasche de illis quinquaginta marcis per annum quas Rex eis concessit ad scaccarium percipiendas de elemosina Regis ad voluntatem suam per breue de Liberate datum apud Westmonasterium primo die Aprilis anno xvj°. persolutum et est inter breuia de hoc termino.

8

'Receptor Denariorum,' A.D. 1341.

Brian Twyne MS. xxiii. 266.

This document—the prosecution of the collector of alms by the Warden of the Oxford Friars Minors for embezzlement —seems to be the only one of the kind extant. As Twyne points out, we should naturally have expected the suit to be tried by the Chancellor, not by the Mayor and Bailiffs of Oxford[2]. The original is no longer to be found in the City Archives, and is probably irretrievably lost. Twyne's reference is: 'Ibid. (i.e. Oxford City Archives) Husteng' Oxon' tent. ibid' die D (*lunæ* crossed out) proxim' post festum Epiphaniæ Domini, a° Ed. 3^i 14°.' (Jan. 134$\frac{0}{1}$.)

Ricardus de Whitchford minor summonitus fuit ad respondendum fratri Johanni Ochampton Guardiano ordinis fratrum Minorum Oxon' de placito computi, et unde idem Gardianus per fratrem Johannem de Hentham attornatum suum queritur quod praedictus Ricardus iniuste non reddit computum de tempore quo fuit receptor denariorum ipsius Gardiani, etc.: et ideo iniuste, quia idem Gardianus dicit quod praedictus Ricardus die Lunae proximo post festum Santi Michaelis anno regni regis praedicti 14° (i.e. A.D. 1340) recepit apud Oxoniam de denariis dicti Gardiani per manus diversorum ad summam 60 solidorum et amplius, viz. per manus Ricardi famuli Johannis de Couton j marc, per manus Thomae de Lundon xij^s, etc., ad computum inde reddendum cum inde requisitus fuerit, etc.: unde idem Gardianus saepius postea venisset ad praedictum Ricardum et ipsum rogasset ut computum ei inde reddidisset, etc.; idem Ricardus computum inde reddere recusavit et adhuc recusat, etc.: unde dicit quod deterioratus est et

---

[1] *Sic.*

[2] Cf. Twyne MS. xxiii, 252, for an appearance of the Warden before the Mayor's Court in 1287. 'Rot. Cur. die Lunae Oxon. proxim. post festum assumptionis B. Mariae a° regni R. Edw. I. 15°. Memorandum quod Johannes de Westover et Isolda uxor ejus venerunt ad curiam istam et obtulerunt se clam(antes) versus Gardianum fratrum minorum Oxon. qui venit, et petunt partes licentiam concordandi, et habent.'

APPENDIX B. 311

damnum habet ad valorem c^s et inde producit sectam, etc.: et praedictus Ricardus venit et non potest dedicere receptionem praedictam et petit Auditores, etc.: et sic per curiam dantur ei Auditores, viz. Ricardus Cary et Johannes le Peyntour, etc.: et idem Ricardus postea computavit coram praefatis Auditoribus de summis praedictis, et invenitur in arreragiis de 60^s, unde non potest satisfacere, ideo committitur custodiae quousque, &c.

9

Goods and chattels of Friar John Welle, S.T.P., A.D. 1378.

Patent Roll, 1 Ric. II, Part 4, m. 37.

It is doubtful whether the following extract is entitled to a place in this work. There is no evidence that Friar John Welle had any connection with Oxford[1]; but we venture to print the document here as illustrating in some degree the actual manner of life of a Franciscan Doctor of Divinity of the later 14th century.

Pro fratre Johanne Welle. Rex omnibus ad quos etc. salutem. Sciatis quod, cum quedam equi, salices (*sic*), libri, moneta, vasa argentea, ac diuersa alia bona et catalla, que fuerunt dilecti nobis in Xpo fratris Johannis Welle de ordine fratrum Minorum in theologia doctoris, extra hospicium suum London' per quendam Thomam Bele servientem suum et quosdam alios malefactores nuper elongata et asportata fuerint, quorum quidem bonorum et rerum aliqua, vna cum persona dicti Thome, per suspicionem occasione eiusdem mesprisionis apud villam. nostram Cantebrigg' arestata existunt, sicut per prefatum fratrem Johannem coram nobis plenius est testificatum; Nos, de gracia nostra speciali, concessimus eidem Johanni omnia, equos, calices, libros, monetam, vasa et alia bona et catalla predicta, vbicumque fuerint, seu eciam denarios de eisdem bonis et catallis, in casu quo idem Johannes eosdem denarios in manibus dictorum malefactorum seu aliorum, quibus iidem malefactores partem eorundem bonorum et catallorum vendiderint peruenientes, inuenire poterit, ac eciam bona et catalla per eosdem malefactores de denariis per ipsos de dictis bonis et catallis, que fuerunt dicti Johannis, receptis empta, habenda de dono nostro,

---

[1] He is probably to be identified with 'Johannes Vallensis Anglus, qui diu Londinii Theologiam docuit,' who was promoted to the *Magisterium* in 1368 by order of Pope Urban V, 'laureante fratre Bernardo de Guasconibus, ministro Tusciae, et Fratre Simone Bruni in Universitate Tolosana;' Wadding, vol. viii. p. 209. Wadding (viii. p. 533) gives a letter addressed to John Welle, Minorite, S T.P. and papal chaplain, A.D. 1372.

si ea ad nos tanquam forisfacta seu confiscata occasione eiusdem mesprisionis de iure debeant pertinere. In cuius, etc. Teste Rege apud Westmonasterium, xxii die ffebruarii. per breue de priuato sigillo.

10

Expulsion of foreign Friars Minors, A. D. 1388.

Close Roll, 12 Ric. II, m. 42.

De certis fratribus expellendis. Rex dilectis sibi in Christo Gardiano ordinis fratrum Minorum de Oxonia ac fratribus Anglicis, de consilio Conuentus eiusdem ordinis ibidem, qui nunc sunt vel qui pro tempore fuerint, salutem. Quibusdam certis de causis nos et consilium nostrum intime monentibus, vobis inhibemus firmiter iniungentes, ne aliquos fratres alienigenas ordinis vestri predicti, nisi tantum eos pro quibus respondere volueritis quod ipsi secreta et consilium regni nostri aduersariis nostris in scriptis seu alio modo minime reuelabunt, in dictam domum vestram vobiscum moraturos ex nunc recipiatis, et si aliquos huiusmodi fratres alienigenas in dicta domo vestra ad presens comorantes, pro quibus in forma predicta respondere nolueritis, habeatis seu qui ordinacionibus dictorum ordinis et Conuentus humiliter parere ac missas, si sacerdotes fuerint, deuote celebrare, seu aliud diuinum seruicium sibi iniunctum facere, aut pro nobis et statu dicti regni nostri specialiter orare noluerint, prout alii fratres indigene dicti ordinis faciunt et tenentur: tunc eos omnes cuiuscumque gradus fuerint ab eadem domo vestra et Vniuersitate dicte ville Oxon' de tempore in tempus penitus expelli faciatis, Et hoc sub incumbenti periculo nullatenus omittatis. Teste Rege apud Oxoniam tercio die Augusti.

11

William Woodford: confirmation of his privileges by Boniface IX, A.D. 1396.

MS. New College 156.

This document is bound up at the beginning of vol. 156 of the New College MSS. The first half of the last two lines has been torn away. Compare the letter of Innocent VI to Roger de Conway in Wadding *Annales*, vol. viii. p. 457.

Bonifacius episcopus servus servorum dei Dilecto filio Wilhelmo Wodford ordinis fratrum Minorum professori, in Theologia Magistro,

Salutem et apostolicam benedictionem. Religionis zelus, litterarum sciencia, vite ac morum honestas, aliaque laudabilia probitatis et virtutum merita, super quibus apud nos fidedigno commendaris testimonio, nos inducunt ut te favoribus apostolicis et graciis prosequamur. Exhibita siquidem nobis nuper pro parte tua peticio continebat, quod quidam locus in Conventu domus fratrum Minorum londonien' quem obtines, et nonnulla aliqua privilegia et gracie per superiores tuos tibi fuerunt concessa. Quare pro parte tua nobis fuit humiliter supplicatum, ut tibi, quod locum quoadvixeris cum omnibus Cameris et pertinenciis suis retinere valeas, concedere ac huiusmodi privilegia confirmare de benignitate apostolica dignaremur. Nos igitur tuis in hac parte supplicacionibus inclinati, tibi, ut predictum locum cum omnibus Cameris et pertinenciis suis quoadvixeris retinere et possidere, et quod ab eo absque rationabili causa nullatenus amoveri valeas, auctoritate apostolica concedimus ac huiusmodi privilegia et gracias, si alias rite tibi concessa fuerint, confirmamus per presentes, Constitucionibus apostolicis ac statutis et consuetudinibus dicti ordinis contrariis non obstantibus quibuscunque. Nulli ergo omnino hominum liceat hanc paginam nostre concessionis et confirmacionis infringere vel ei ausu temerario contraire. Si quis autem hoc attemptare presumpserit indignacionem om . . . . et Pauli Apostolorum ejus se noverit incursurum. Dat' Rome apud sanctum petrum . . . . . Pontificatus nostri Anno septimo.

12.

Appointment of a lecturer to the Convent at Hereford, c. **1400**.

Harl. MS. 431, fol. 100 b.

This letter illustrates the educational organisation—the 'University Extension System'—of the Franciscans. Friar John David, the lecturer mentioned, was D.D. of Cambridge[1] and does not appear to have studied at Oxford; but original documents relating to the subject are so scarce that no apology will be necessary for inserting the letter here.

The writer, John Prophet, was Dean of Hereford from **1393** to **1407**[2]. John David was Provincial Minister in **1425**[3].

---

[1] Mon. Franc. I, 539.
[2] It is clear that J. Prophet was Dean of Hereford when this letter was written; in another letter, referring to the same appointment, he writes: 'Cum predecessores mei decani et Capitulum herefordenses fundatores in parte domus confratrum vestrorum hereford' dinoscantur existere.' Harl. MS. 431, f. 100 b.
[3] Wilkins, Concilia III, 459.

Scribit J. Prophete Prouinciali et Capitulo generali (*sic*) ad admittendum quemdam fratrem J. Dauid in Lectorem et Regentem Domus Hereford'.

Venerabiles ac religiosi viri in Christo carissimi. Post votiue salutis ac salutacionis affectum: cum omnes de conuentu fratrum vestrorum hereford' in votis iam habeant ac desideriis intensis affectent, vt instruor, fratrem Johannem Dauid, cum prepollens virtutibus ac litterarum sciencia preditus et acceptus, vt dicitur, existat eisdem, suum ibidem habere lectorem eciam et regentem anno proximo iam futuro, vt ex sua inibi per tanti temporis interuallum exhibenda presencia feliciori valeat gubernari regimine. Vestram reuerenciam presentibus censui deprecandum ex corde, quatinus, desiderijs atque votis huius predicti Conuentus graciosius annuentes de predicto fratre Johanne, sub quo prefatus Conuentus maximam in religione ac scolastica disciplina dinoscitur obtinere proficiendi fiduciam, in hoc venerabili prouinciali vestro Capitulo eidem Conuentui eciam harum precium mearum intuitu dignemini, si placeat, prouidere; claro si libeat considerantes intuitu, quod Conuentus ille predictus, qui in perfeccione religionis et fame consueuerat hactenus haberi prefulgidus nisi celerius prouideatur eidem, ad lamentabilem, vt informor, in breui videbitur deuenire ruinam: Quod siquidem per ipsius confratris Johannis presenciam, vt speratur a multis Conuentui predicto beneuolis et amicis, apcius quam per alium poterit euitari. Ad scribendum communi vestro cetui venerando pro expedicione felici votiui desiderij supradicti Conuentus, pro tanto quod in fratrem de Conuentu predicto receptus existo, ac de cognacione mea non pauci Conuentui predicto beneuoli pro bono inibi exercendo regimine ad idem videre desiderant, et parentes mei et alij de genere meo multi in Conuentuali ibidem tumulantur ecclesia, multo procliuior sum effectus. Itaque super isto, vt vtilis effectus inde exequi videatur, cogitare dignetur vestra reuerencia prelibata. Omnia conseruare etc.

13

Decree of the General Chapter at Florence, A.D. 1467.

In the *Definitio studiorum* quoted by Sbaralea (Wadding, Sup. ad Script. p. 717) from the Acts of this Chapter, occurs the following clause.

Ad provinciam Anglie possunt mittere omnes provincie Ordinis, scil. ad Studium Oxoniarum, Cantabrigie, et ad alia studia ejusdem provincie.

APPENDIX B.

14

Recovery of debt from a Sheriff, A. D. 1488.

Exchequer of Pleas; Plea Roll, 3 Hen. VII, m. 35.

Pro Ricardo Salford querente versus Johannem Paston Militem nuper vicecomitem Comitatuum Norff' et Suff' defendentem in placito debiti per billam.

Ricardus Salford Gardianus ffratrum Minorum Oxon' venit coram Baronibus huius Scaccarii vicesimo die Maii hoc termino per Jacobum Bartelot attornatum suum et queritur per billam versus Johannem Paston Militem nuper vicecomitem Comitatuum Norff' et Suff' presentem hic in Curia eodem die, super compoto suo de officio suo predicto hic ad hoc Scaccarium reddendo, per Edmundum Dorman' attornatum suum, de eo quod predictus nuper vicecomes ei debet et iniuste detinet decem libras decem et octo solidos argenti; Et pro eo iniuste, quod, cum dictus Rex nunc pro diuersis debitis in quibus indebitatus fuerat prefato querenti, inter alia assignasset eidem querenti decem libras decem et octo solidos predictos per quandam talliam curie hic ostensam eandem summam continentem leuatam ad Receptam Scaccarii dicti domini Regis apud Westmonasterium, terciodecimo die Maii anno regni dicti domini Regis tercio, pro ffratribus Minoribus Oxon', prefato querente tunc Gardiano ffratrum Minorum predictorum existente, de et super prefato iam defendente per nomen Johannis Paston nuper vicecomitis dictorum Comitatuum Norff' et Suff' percipiendam de ipso de exitibus balliue sue et de pluribus debitis suis; Et licet predictus querens decimo septimo die Maii dicto anno tercio apud villam Westmonasterium in Comitatu Midd' per quendam Jacobum Bartelot adtunc seruientem suum monstrauerit et ad deliberandum optulerit talliam predictam cuidam Edmundo Dorman' adtunc attornato predicti nuper vicecomitis iam defendentis super compoto ipsius nuper vicecomitis hic ad hoc Scaccarium faciendo pro solucione decem librarum decem et octo solidorum predictorum habenda secundum effectum tallie predicte, ac tunc et ibidem ipse querens requisiuit prefatum nuper vicecomitem iam defendentem ad ei soluendum x^{li} $xviij^s$ predictos iam in demanda; Quo quidem decimo septimo die Maii ipse iam defendens ibidem satis habuit in manibus suis de dictis exitibus balliue sue predicte prouenientibus et de pluribus debitis predictis, vnde ipse tunc soluisse potuit prefato querenti x^{li} $xviij^s$ predictos secundum effectum tallie predicte; Ipse tamen nuper vicecomes iam defendens x^{li} $xviij^s$ illos siue aliquam inde parcellam prefato querenti nondum soluit, set hoc facere contradixit et adhuc contradicit; et vnde predictus querens deterioratur et dampnum habet ad valenciam decem librarum. Et hoc offert etc.

Et predictus nuper vicecomes, per predictum attornatum suum presens etc., petit auditum bille predicte, et ei legitur etc.: qua audita dicit quod ipse ad presens non est auisatus ad respondendum prefato Ricardo Salford in premissis. Et petit diem inde loquendi vsque Octavis sancte Trinitatis citra quem etc.: quod per curiam concessum est ei. Et idem dies datus est prefato Ricardo Salford hic etc.— Ad quem diem (xxv die Junii, *in margin*) predictus Ricardus Salford venit hic per predictum attornatum suum et petit quod predictus nuper vicecomes ei respondeat in premissis. Et super hoc idem nuper vicecomes ad respondendum prefato Ricard Salford in premissis hic solempniter exactis etc., non venit set fecit defaltam etc. Et super hoc idem Ricardus Salford petit iudicium suum in premissis et debitum suum predictum vna cum dampnis suis predictis sibi in hac parte adiudicari etc. Super quo, visis premissis per Barones predictos habitaque inde deliberacione pleniori inter eosdem, consideratum est per eosdem Barones quod predictus Ricardus recuperet versus prefatum nuper vicecomitem debitum suum predictum decem librarum decem et octo solidorum predictorum, et dampna sua, tam occasione iniuste detencionis debiti predicti, quam pro misis custagiis et expensis suis circa sectam suam predictam in hac parte appositis (?), taxata per eosdem Barones ad viginti sex solidos et octo denarios, que quidem summe in toto se attingunt ad summam duodecim librarum quatuor solidorum et octo denariorum; et quod predictus nuper vicecomes sit in misericordia domini Regis, etc.

15

Documents relating to the lease of a garden at the Grey Friars to Richard Leke, A. D. 1513–1514.

Acta Curiae Cancellarii, Oxford Univ. Archives, ꝗ, fol. 194, 197, 210, 212.

Eodem die (June 10, 1510) dominus doctor Kynton accepit sibi in seruientem Ricardum Leke pandaxatorem promittens sibi 6^s 8^d annuatim aut unam robam, quem juratum ad privilegia admisimus (fol. 194).

Eodem die gardianus fratrum minorum Oxon' promisit, quod ab isto die de cetero, donec maior communicacio in causa, que euidencius in quadam indentura inde confecta liquet, inter prefatum gardianum

APPENDIX B.

et Ricardum Leke habeatur, non impediet, aut impediri procurabit per se aut per alium, quominus predictus Ricardus Leke uti valeat jure et libertate sibi concessis secundum effectum dictarum indenturarum prefato Ricardo concessarum (*ibid.*).

Eodem die gardianus predictus promisit in verbis sacerdocii quod litem istam et causam motam non trahet ad extra que pendet inter prefatum gardianum et Ricardum Leke predictum (*ibid.*).

6º die Julii comparuit coram nobis doctor Goodefyld ordinis minorum et olim gardianus eiusdem loci, qui fide media confessus est Ricardum Leke recepisse in firmam ab eodem, tempore prioratus sui, et conuentu eiusdem loci, quemdam ortum infra cepta sua secundum tenorem cuiusdam indenture inde confecte, quam indenturam affirmat eadem fide fuisse legittime factam. Hoc idem testificante fratre vocato Brown bacallario sacre theologie eiusdem loci (*ibid.*).

(Aug. 12). Gardianus fratrum Minorum promisit fide data quod seruabit pacem domini regis pro se et suis, quantum in illo est, aduersus Ricardum Leke, et si contingat fratres suos perturbare predictum Ricardum, quod retinebit eos in salua custodia quousque res maturius possit examinari, si possit deuenire in noticiam eorum (fol. 197^{h}).

(Jan. 23, 151$\frac{3}{4}$). Comparuit coram nobis gardianus fratrum minorum et constituit suum procuratorem Magistrum Carew cum clausulis necessariis, etc. (fol. 210).

Eodem die Mr. Carew nomine procuratoris pro ecclesia fratrum minorum petiit restitucionem in integrum aduersus quemdam contractum indentatum inter predictos fratres et Richardum Leke cuius datum est, etc., et causa est quia predicta Ecclesia ut asseruit est grauiter lesa et in futuro erit, ad quod probandum accepit terminum viz. istum diem ad octo dies (*ibid.*).

(Feb. 19). Comparuit coram nobis eodem die Ricardus Leke, et conquestus est de fratre Johanne Haruey, gardiano fratrum minorum, de et super quodam contractu indentato inter eos pro quodam gardino et expensis factis circa idem infra precinctum fratrum predictorum: et post multa communicata amicabilia inter partes predictas, tandem compromiserunt se expectare laudum, arbitramentum, et determinacionem Johannis Cokkes, legum doctoris, et Willelmi Balborow, utriusque juris bachularii, in alto et in basso, in omnibus causis, negociis, et querelis, motis vel mouendis, inter predictos fratrem et Ricardum, concernentibus se et conuentum suum, pro predicto gardino, edificio murorum, et occasione eorundem, a principio mundi usque in presentem diem; ita quod feratur sentencia siue laudum per predictos arbitros citra festum annunciationis B. Virginis . . . . (fol. 212^b).

16

Extracts from the will of Richard Leke, A.D. 1526.

Prerog. Court of Canterbury, Register Porch, quire 9.

In the name of God amen. In the yere of our Lorde god a Thousand fyve hundred twenty and six; The first day of May, I Richard Leke, late Bruer of Oxford, beying of hole and perfite mynde and sike of body, make my testament and last wille in this maner and fourme folowing, ffirst I bequethe my soule to almighty god to our blissed lady saint marye and to all the holy company of hevyn, my body to be buried w^t in the graye ffreres in Oxford before the awter where the first masse is daily vsed to be saide . . . Item I will that my body be first brought to the Church of saint Ebbe, and there dirige and masse to be songe for me. Item I bequeth to two hundred prestes two hundred grotes to say dirige and masse at saint Ebbys and at the gray freres with other parishe Churches the day of my burying . . . Item I bequeth to euery gray frere being prest w^{t}in the gray freres in Oxford iiij^d, and to euery gray frere there being noo prest ij^d, to dirige and masse for my soule the day next after my burying. Item I bequeth to the said gray freres vj^s viij^d to make a dyner in their owne place, and also other vj^s viij^d to the wardeyn of the same gray freres to prouide for the premisses. Item I bequeth to the said wardeyn of the gray freres xx^s to prouide the awters to be prepared and ornated w^t apparell for prestes to say masse w^{t}in the said freres. Item I bequeth to euery oon of the foure orders of freres in Oxford x^s to be paid after the maner and fourme folowing, that is to say, at my burying iij^s iiij^d, at my monethes mynde iij^s iiij^d, and att my yeres mynde iij^s iiij^d. And also to bringe me to Churche I woll the foresaid iiij orders, and there to synge dirige and masse for my sonle and to receyue their money after the manner aboue expressed . . .

The will was proved on the 26th of July, 1526.

17

An ex-warden called to account, A.D. 1529.

Acta Curiae Cancellarii, EEE, fol. 124 b.

(*Secundo die Sept.*) Comparuit coram nobis (sc. Commissario) Johannes Bacheler ordinis minorum Oxon' vicegardianus eiusdem ordinis, qui petiit, nomine gardiani eiusdem domus, a patre Johanne Harwey S.T.B., eiusdem ordinis et loci dudum gardiano, quosdam fideiussores produci ad reddendum compotum super omnibus et singulis que eidem obicientur ex parte gardiani moderni; qui pater Johannes in fideiussores produxit Willelmum Symcokes et Willelmum Plummer Oxon', qui pro predicto Johanne Harwey fideiubebant in summa x librarum sterlingorum, dicto gardiano et ordinis prefati conuentui soluendorum, si dictus Johannes Harwey citra festum Pasche proximum legittime compotum non reddidit secundum formam petitionis prefati gardiani, cum ab eo requisitus et licite monitus.

APPENDIX C.

CONTROVERSY BETWEEN THE FRIARS PREACHERS AND FRIARS MINORS AT OXFORD, A.D. 1269.

This curious treatise, here printed for the first time, is preserved in Vol. 3119 (ff. 86–88) of the Phillipps MSS. at Thirlestaine House. The MS., a folio with two columns on each page, is written in a clear upright hand of the late 13th or early 14th century. The work, which appears to have been unknown to Wood, is attributed by Bale and Pits to Eccleston, probably merely because it is bound up with a copy of Eccleston's Chronicle: the MS. itself gives no clue as to the author, and the style bears no close resemblance to that of Eccleston. It is clearly the work of an Oxford Minorite who was an eyewitness of, and probably a participator in, the events which he records. The treatise is interesting as affording a glimpse from the inside into the life of the Oxford friars, and as showing the shifts and quibbles to which the Franciscans were compelled to have recourse in order to establish their claim to be professors of 'perfect poverty.'

Impugnacio fratrum Minorum per fratres Predicatores apud Oxoniam.

A.D. MCCLXIX circa quadragesimam venerunt fratres predicatores de conventu Oxon', viz. Salomon de Ingeham et Robertus de novo Mercato[1] pro quibusdam negociis expediendis ad domum fratrum Minorum Oxon'. Cumque tractarent de negociis suis cum tribus fratribus minoribus, viz. Waltero de Landen, Willelmo Cornubienci, Alano de Wakerfelde, nacta quacumque occasione, dixit frater Salomon: 'Vos fratres Minores peccuniam recipitis per interpositas personas sicut nos in personis propriis.' Respondens frater Alanus dixit: 'Noli, frater, ita dicere, quia nobis est verbum hoc verbum scandali et religioni nostre cedit in derogacionem et nobis omnibus in manifestam offensionem; cum non recipiamus nec recipere possimus, et certi sumus de nostra veritate quod non recipimus.' Ffrater Salomon cum impetu sponte[2] (?) manum suam ad crucem in pariete depictam juravit

---

[1] Afterwards Prior of Friars Preachers. London, Q.R. Wardrobe ⅘ (21 Edw. I).

[2] spc̄. some word like 'elevans' or 'erigens' is wanted to complete the sense.

dicens: 'In crucifixo juro quod vos recipitis;' et adjecit: 'Ego non sum magnus clericus nec homo magne litterature, et tamen constanter hoc affirmo, et in presencia pape, si necesse fuerit, affirmabo.' Et cum esset pluries increpatus ut taceret, sepius idem replicans affirmabat. Hec in presencia duorum predicatorum et trium Minorum quos supra memoravimus facta sunt, ideo certam probacionem habent.

Post hec fratres Minores, hiis non obstantibus, caritatis obsequia predictis predicatoribus exhibuerunt, et accepto caritatis indicio, versus domum suam conduxerunt. Cumque starent in porta fratrum Minorum, frater Alanus ait, qui solus ibi tunc aderat cum predicatoribus: 'Ffrater Salomon, rogo in lege fraterne caritatis, ut verbum istud offensionis et scandali de cetero de ore tuo non procedat, quia plane tibi facio constare, quod non recipimus peccuniam per nos nec per alios; nec de professione nostra recipere possumus.' Respondit frater Salomon: 'Ex verbis tuis sic arguo: vos de non recipiendo peccuniam votum fecistis; hec est major; assumo—et recepistis; ac concludo; ergo vos estis in statu dampnacionis.' Ad hec frater Alanus respondit: 'Majorem concedimus, minorem negamus, quia simpliciter falsa est; et ideo non est mirum si conclusio sit falsa.' Hiis dictis recesserunt fratres. Ad hec non modicum fratres turbati, tum propter imposicionem tum propter imponendi modum. Habita ergo deliberacione diligenti, de consilio discretorum, missi sunt duo de minoribus ad predicatores, rogantes humiliter errata corrigi et delinquentem regulariter emendari. Post modicum temporis spacium, missi sunt duo de predicatoribus ad minores pro pace reformanda, viz. frater Vincencius le Sauvage et frater Robertus de novo Mercato; qui fratribus minoribus in unum convocatis hoc inicium proposuerunt. 'Ffratres nostri petunt, quod vos doceatis fratrem Salomonem errasse et falsum vobis imposuisse, et extunc fratres nostri manum correctionis apponent et delinquentem juxta peccata regulariter emendabunt.'

Ex parte minorum fuit responsum sic: 'Vos affirmatis nos peccuniam recipere, et ideo partem affirmativam tenetis; nos negamus, et negativam tenemus. Unde, si ad probacionem accedendum sit, vestrum est probare, non nostrum; quia affirmative, non negative, incumbit probacio.' Quo dicto tacuerunt predicatores. Hec de substancia nuncii.

Extra ordinarie proposita fuerunt ista verba, dicente fratre Roberto de novo Mercato: 'Videtur sic posse persuaderi quod vos recipitis peccuniam per interpositas personas ad minus. Pono quod aliquis moriatur et in testamento suo unam summam peccunie vobis leget.

Quero cujus sit illa peccunia. Defuncti non est, quia nichil proprietatis in ea aut in re alia defunctus habet aut habere potest; vivencium enim et non moriencium est jus et proprietatem in rebus habere, et in eis dominium vendicare. Executorum non est, constat. Ergo aut omnino nullius erit, aut vestra erit.'

Ad hec frater Minor dupliciter respondit; primo per instanciam sic: 'Ponatur quod illa peccunia legaretur alicui fabrice alicujus ecclesie; quero, cujus esset illa peccunia. Non executorum, constat; et secundum te non est defuncti. Sed qua racione non est defuncti? Si defunctus unde defunctus nichil proprietatis in rebus habet, nec fabrice illius ecclesie erit, ut videtur; cum non sit major racio a parte fabrice non viventis, quam a parte defuncti non viventis, ut videtur. Non est ergo necessarium dicere quod legatum semper transit in dominium legatarii. Et ideo peccunia quamvis nobis legetur, non est necesse dicere quod sit nostra. Ad quod accedit quod nunquam in dominium consensimus, et nobis invitis et contradicentibus nullo modo in dominium nostrum transire potest: vero ipsam tanquam nostram petere possimus aut debemus nullo jure. Ex quo patet quod racio vestra non valet.'

Secundo fuit sic responsum, quod, secundum diffinicionem jurisperitorum, peccunia legata in bonis annumeratur defuncti, quousque transierit in dominium et proprietatem legatarii. 'In jus autem nostrum aut dominium nullo modo potest transire, nobis invitis et non consentientibus. Unde, qualitercumque peccunia ab executoribus deponatur seu apud quemcumque pro fratribus reponatur, quam diu manet inexpensa, semper in bonis defuncti annumeratur, et possunt eam executores, auctoritate propria vel defuncti, repetere quando volunt. Quomodo[1] ergo dicetur nostra? nullo modo.'

Ad hec predicatores, ut suam contra minores sentenciam roborarent, plures casus personales proposuerunt, in quibus asserebant fratres minores non posse excusari quin peccuniam per se vel per alios recepissent. Ad hec frater minor respondit, dicens quod hoc in nullo modo derogat communitati; quia communitas religionis a principio tales transgressores punit et parata est semper punire, ubicumque fuerint inventi. Item transgressio talium nullo modo probare potest, quod fratres stent cum transgressione sue professionis, sicut vero[2] lapsus carnis aut contumax inobediencia, si contingeret, quod absit, alicujus persone singularis.

Circa hanc ergo materiam verbis cessantibus, dictum est a parte

---

[1] Quō.
[2] (or *nec*?)

Minorum: 'Mirum est, cum tot sint status religiosorum et tot status secularium tam in clero quam in populo, sicut cernimus, quare diligencius et curiosius (in) statum nostrum quam aliorum exploratur, et omnibus aliis tacentibus vos soli verba de statu nostro tintinatis[1] (?) et de professione discutitis.' Respondit frater Vincencius le Sauvage, 'Hec est,' inquit, 'racio. Veniunt ad nos diversi seculares et religiosi, comparacionem inter statum et statum facientes, statum vestrum extollentes, et nostrum in hoc deprimentes, quod nos peccuniam recipimus, vos autem non recipitis, judicantes nos in hoc minus perfectos mundi contemptores. Nos modo in declaracionem veritatis et status nostri exaltacionem, dicimus vos hoc facere per interpositas personas quod nos facimus in propriis personis.' Et cum inculcando quereretur a fratre Vincencio, quare in ista materia haberent contra minores faciem sic obstinatam, respondit: 'Quia nunquam duos fratres minores in hoc articulo inveni consencientes.' Cui cum esset responsum ex parte minorum; 'En octo sumus congregati omnes unanimes et uno corde et ore idem sencientes et asserentes;' respondit, 'Certe verum est, sed si seorsum vos haberem in privata collacione, non ita esset; eciam vos duos,' demonstratis fratribus Willelmo de Wykham et Dyonisio, 'habita seorsum collacione, invenirem discordes et de vobis diversa elicerem.' Ista turbato animo et impetu sponte[2] (?) proferens, non minus fratri suo proprio quam eciam ipsis fratribus minoribus offensionis materiam dedit. Quod cum averteret, ad pedes fratrum se projecit in terram, culpam confitendo. Cui frater suus proprius, verba contumeliosa equanimiter non ferens, sic ait: 'Cum mihi capud fregeris, penam[3] dabis.' Quo dicto domum redierunt fratres.

Hic transeo unum diem in quo miserunt fratres minores ad predicatores iterum postulantes sibi satisfieri, et errata regulariter corrigi; quibus erat pacifice et mansuete responsum a parte predicatorum et de emenda humiliter facienda promissum. Set in solucione promissi inventi sunt minus habentes, unde tantum[4] facta fuit negocii dilacio.

Cum vero pendente tempore predicatores juxta promissa nichil facerent, minores injuriam personalem non multum ponderantes, sed injuriam communitatis sue conniventibus oculis dissimulare non poterant, et ideo de consilio discretorum miserunt ad predicatores iterum, duo postulantes. Primum est, quod principalis transgressio

---

[1] t^utínat.'
[2] MS. tenā.
[3] spt̄.
[4] (tamen ?)

facta per fratrem Salomonem emendaretur; secundum est, quod fratres pacifici et mansueti ex parte eorum ad tractandum de negocio pacis et amoris mitterentur. Quo petito, habita deliberacione, missi sunt quatuor predicatores ad minores, quorum principalis fuit frater Willelmus de Stargil. Qui, convocatis minoribus, hoc nuncium ex parte fratrum suorum proposuerunt: 'Ffrater Vincencius, qui insolenter apud vos se habuit in nuncio faciendo, fuit in nostro capitulo a proprio socio fratre Roberto de novo mercato accusatus, a suo superiore correptus, et secundum exigenciam sue religionis punitus.' Quo dicto, siluit: et cum expectarent minores de principali responsum, sc. de facto fratris Salomonis, nihil est auditum. Et cum peterent responsum sibi dari de principali, responsum istud secundarium non multum ponderantes, respondit frater Willelmus de Stargil predicator pro se et suis sociis, se non esse ad hoc missos. Hec de substancia nuncii.

Extra ordinarie autem proposita ista verba fuerunt, dicente fratre Thoma de Docking: 'Mirum est, quod vos non cessatis nos impugnare in articulo de recepcione peccunie, et hac racione, vos dicitis quod nos recipimus per interpositam personam; nos e contra (?) negamus et dicimus quod non. Mota est ergo lis et controversia inter nos et vos, et ideo oportuit per judicem determinari, quia per nos non potuit. Demigravimus ad judicem non quemcumque sed summum pontificem, et ad illum qui regulam nostram dictavit et mentem beati francisci, eodem papa sibi ipsi testante, novit. Ipse pro nobis sentenciavit. Quid ultra queritis? quid impugnatis?' Et adjecit idem frater Thomas de Docking, dicens: 'Occurrit racio idem dictans, talis peccunia a quocumque data seu quocumque titulo pro fratribus apud quemcumque deposita nunquam est nostra; ergo nunquam recepimus eam nec per nos nec per interpositam personam.'

Ad hoc respondit frater W. de Stargil, predicator, dicens: 'Sic possem arguere de capa quam porto que nunquam fuit mea, nec erit nec est; et tamen ego recepi eam.' Ad hoc obvium fuit instanciam non valere; Sic, 'quamvis tu non habeas personalem proprietatem in capa tua, ordo tamen tuus totus et communitas ordinis tui in ea proprietatem habet; sed nec persona nec communitas ordinis nostri aliquam proprietatem habet nec habere potest in peccunia a quocumque oblata, data, seu deposita. Preterea in assercione vestra hoc inconveniens incurritis. Nos habemus regulam qua utimur secundum declaracionem domini pape qui eam juxta mentem beati francisci declaravit. In sua declaracione dicit, quod nos ipsam declaracionem cum regula observando peccuniam non recipimus per interpositam personam. Vos ergo, si insistitis contrarium asserendo, notam mendacii, ut videtur, domino pape inponitis.' Respondit frater predicator: 'Absit a nobis hec presumpcio, sed plane videtur quod dominus papa non declaravit regulam juxta mentem beati francisci et ipsius regule.' Ad hec frater Thomas de Docking sic opposuit: 'Papa in sua declaracione dicit quod intencionem beati francisci plenius novit, et ad hoc persuadendum idem papa in sua declaracione tres raciones posuit: prima, quia longam familiaritatem cum eo traxit, in qua solent homines secreta cordium suorum mutuo communicare; secunda, quia in condendo predictam regulam sibi astitit cum esset in minori officio constitutus; tercia, quia in optinendo ipsius regule confirmacionem eciam sibi non defuit. Si ergo papa dicit et racionibus convincit, se nosse intencionem beati francisci, ex quo eciam sequitur declaracionem factam juxta intencionem ejusdem sancti, quid dicetis?'

Ad hoc quidam predicator dixit: 'Nullo modo videtur quod papa novit intencionem beati francisci, quod probo sic. Voluntas testamentaria fuit beati francisci, quod fratres nullo modo quererent litteras expositorias a sede apostolica, sed hoc non obstante quesierunt et papa annuente optinuerunt. Non solum ergo fratres sed et papa contra intencionem ejus fecerunt; ex quo videtur quod intencionem ejus non noverunt; quia si ipsam novissent contra ipsam non fecissent.'

Ad hoc frater Minor: 'Esto quod racio sit bona, cum illacio sit satis mirabilis. Ex hac racione probatur papam vel mentitum esse vel falsum dixisse; ipse enim dixit, plenius novimus intencionem ipsius sancti. Preterea, ut ad unum sit dicere de testamento suo quod non novimus, non respondemus, sed regulam quam observare promisimus parati sumus defendere. Accedit ad hoc, quod nec fratres nec dominus papa fecerunt contra intencionem beati francisci, quam in condendo regulam habuit, sed contra intencionem petende declaracionis. Nec in hoc pape potuit in aliquo prejudicari in facienda declaracione, maxime cum apud eum resideat plena potestas et auctoritas tocius ecclesie gubernande. Quo etiam in sua declaracione dicente et probante, ut patet inspicienti, hoc non potest nec debet in aliquo fratribus prejudicari.'

Inter hec et alia que proponebantur, ait frater W. de Stargil: 'Scimus quidem quia regulam et regule declaracionem ab eo qui potuit declarare, habetis et utramque observatis; hoc et nobiscum confitemur. Sed quomodo vos peccuniam non recipiatis, non videmus.' Ad hoc ffrater Thomas Docking sic respondit: 'Frater karissime, audeo plane dicere, quod si habitum secularem haberes quem ante habitum tue religionis portabas, facillime veritatem mee professionis tibi persuaderem; et ad spacium vii psalmorum quam nos videmus luce ipse clarius videres.'

Hiis ergo transactis transivimus ad principale, petentes iterum quod ipsi responderent nobis de principali, ipsum accessorium de quo factum est nuncium non ponderantes. Respondit frater W. sicut prius, dicens se non posse nec debere hoc facere, cum non esset ad hoc missus; tamen peticionem nostram libenter fratribus suis nunciaret. Quo facto domum redierunt fratres.

Hic transeo alium diem, in quo missi sunt de minoribus duo ad predicatores, quibus facte fuerunt multe promissiones de correctione facienda, sed in solvendo promissum inventi sunt iterum minus habentes, ut videtur: unde tantum fuit dilacio negocii. Interim pendente tempore et fratribus predicatoribus nichil respondentibus, supervenit prior provincialis predicatorum[1] Oxoniam. Ffratres Minores pro pace mutua reconsilianda[2] et servanda miserunt[3] ad eum, cum humilitate postulantes, excessum corrigi et sibi regulariter satisfieri. Prior vero provincialis, habita deliberacione et facta diligenti inquisicione per fratres suos, sic respondit: 'Ego claudam os fratris de cetero ne presumat talia dicere contra vos, et ego ipse dicam sicut vos ipsi, cum de illo articulo agitur, dicitis; et ut alii fratres sic dicant, pro viribus inducam. Fratrem vero Salomonem, quem vos esse transgressum (dicitis), aliter punire non possum, quia plane sicut dixit ita et sentit, nec induci potest ad contrarium, quia sua consciencia est quod vos estis receptores peccuniarum ad minus per interpositas personas; unde ego contra leges consciencie non possum. Misissem autem ipsum pro culpa dicenda sua ad vos, sed timui ne ipse plus vos provocasset et fierent novissima pejora prioribus.' Hic nota quod frater non dixit ex surrepcione, sed ex plena deliberacione. Hec de substancia nuncii.

Extra ordinarie autem allocutus priorem predicatorum quidam de minoribus cum mansuetudine predicatoris[4] et obsecrans, ut ipse partes suas de pace lesa reparanda et reparata jam fovenda vigilanter juxta discrecionem a deo sibi datam interponeret. Adjecit autem dictus frater minor cum mansuetudine dicens: 'Mirum est quod ita

---

[1] Robert Kilwardby.
[2] *Sic.*
[3] This word is added in the margin in a later hand. [4] p'toris.

extranee de re nobis manifesta quidam de vestris senciunt, maxime cum peccunia a quocumque legata seu donata nunquam ad dominium nostrum transeat. Et propterea nullo modo dici possumus receptores non per nos nec per interpositas personas.' Respondit prior provincialis cum mansuetudine dicens: 'Unum est quod videre non possumus. Cum peccunia in usus vestros quocumque titulo deputata multociens sit apud multos deposita, et cum post deposicionem transeat a dominio conferentis nec cedat in dominium depositarii— hoc, inquam, est quod videre non possumus, quin peccunia illa in vestrum cedat dominium.'

Ad hoc respondit frater minor, quod peccunia, quocumque titulo ad usus fratrum deputata, nunquam in eorum dominium transeat juxta declaracionem domini pape, sed possunt fratres in suis necessitatibus recursum habere ad recipientem, qui auctoritate domini principalis potest fratribus, si vult et non aliter, subvenire; quia jure debiti nullo modo fratribus tenetur, nec nomine deposti aliquid[1] exigere possunt ab eodem. Auctoritas ergo et dominium peccunie quocumque titulo tradite permanet penes ipsum tradentem, intantum quod nunquam transit nec transire potest in fratrum dominium ullo jure: unde dicit[2] dominus papa quod principalis potest eam repetere si vult, quamdiu manet inexpensa.

Ad hoc prior: 'Quid si peccunia penes ipsum recipientem est centum annis aut plus remanserit?' Ad hoc frater Minor: 'Non plus juris habent fratres nostri in peccunia in fine C annorum aut cujuscumque alterius spacii quam in fine prime diei. Et hoc parati sumus probare, et pro loco et tempore mundo manifestare.'

Ad hoc attonitus prior cum admiracione dixit: 'Vere si hoc constaret, mundo non sic habundaretis sicut habundatis.' Respondit frater Minor: 'Quomodocumque habundancia se habeat, veritatem professionis narro.' Tunc exclamans quidam predicator, cujus nomen ad presens ex causa retineo, factum eorum ut videtur non approbans, ait: 'Eya, domine deus, verba que de vobis facimus ex malis que de nobis dicitis occasionem[3] sumunt.'

Interim dum hec agebantur, fratres minores inter se contulerunt, et habito consilio miserunt ad priorem provincialem gratias agentes de sua oblacione, rogantes quod frater Salomon, ex quo consciemiam suam non deponit nec culpam suam recognoscere proponit, pro mutua pace concilianda et servanda, de loco, ex quo pacem perturbavit, amoveretur. Respondit prior se super hoc velle deliberare.

---

[1] MS. ad.   [2] *Dicit* inserted in a later hand.   [3] MS. occōsionē.

Habita vero deliberacione, sollempnes nuncios de ordine suo mittens, sic respondit: 'Frater Salomon pro conventu Oxon' fratribus suis est multum necessarius et utilis sicut bonus et ministerialis, in tantum eciam ut difficile esset mihi invenire alium eis ita utilem et necessarium, et ideo grave esset ipsum amovere. Item pro peccato privato, publica pena non debet adjungi. Hoc autem fieret si frater Salomon de loco suo ad alium locum amoveretur. Unde peticio de dicto fratre amovenda non videtur consona racioni. Nec debetis turbari, quia peticionem vestram in hac parte non fulcio, quia, ut videtur, id quod vobis primo optuli debet sufficere, viz. quod os ejus per obedienciam claudatur, et ne de cetero a(liqua) sinistra contra puritatem regule vestre dicere presumat.'

Ffacta ista responsione nuncii ex parte prioris tres faciebant peticiones. Prima fuit, quod pro dicto unius stulti communitas fratrum minorum non turbaretur; secunda fuit, quod caritas mutua ut olim omnimodis signis ostenderetur. Tercia fuit quod regula nostra cum exposicione vel exposicionibus eis ad tempus ostenderetur, ab illis tantummodo et non ab aliis quam nos nominare decrevimus inspicienda. Hec de substancia nuncii.

Extra ordinarie autem facta sunt verba ista, dicente fratre Minore: 'Si stultus de sua stulticia corrigendus est, mirum est quod fratrem Salomonem non corrigitis, qui in sua stulticia manet; quem eciam vos ipsi stultum nominatis, cum petitis quod propter dictum unius stulti communitas fratrum minorum non turbetur. Item si peccatum est corrigendum, maxime vobis qui estis professores veritatis, mirum est quod fratrem Salomonem non corrigitis, quem peccasse probatis, cum pro eo allegatis quod pro peccato privato publica pena non sit injungenda.'

Post hec fratres Minores, habita diligenti deliberacione, perpendentes quod fratres predicatores a principio in toto processu aut id negocium distulerunt aut dissimulaverunt aut a principali diverterunt, ut videtur, miserunt ad eos fratres diffinitive sic respondentes; 'Pendente principali, videtur fratribus quod peticionibus vestris accessoriis non sit respondendum; unde ad huc petunt fratres quod frater Salomon, qui pacem mutuam turbavit, ammoveatur; ad quod movere[1] potest pax et tranquillitas mutua utriusque ordinis, que est magis ponderanda quam utilitas ministerialis unius persone. Ad hoc autem quod vos dicitis, quod penitencia publica peccato privato non sit imponenda, sic responderunt fratres; quod quamvis ammoveatur, peccatum suum non

---

[1] or *monere*.

publicatur. Est enim pene omnium sentencia una, tam secularium quam religiosorum, quod fratres vestri[1] conventuales ad prelacias et ceteras dignitates, et studentes ad doctorum officia exercenda, cum gloria et non cum ignominia, frequenter emittuntur et de loco ad locum transferuntur. Unde ad huc petunt vel quod ammoveatur vel quod culpam suam confiteatur. Et ad hoc movere debet, quod fratres Minores in consimili casu personas multum dissimiles, viz. lectores, in tantum humiliaverunt, quod pro levi occasione unum valde graciosum ad pacem vestram conservandam de conventu suo ammoverunt, et alium suspenderunt per annum a predicacione et confessione; et usque hodie manet a lectione suspensus. Ad hoc autem quod vos dicitis, quod nobis debet sufficere, quod os ejus obstruatur, ne mala de nobis loquatur, respondent fratres, quod non debet sufficere, quia ad hoc tenetur de communi lege caritatis eciam si nunquam aliquem offendisset.' Cum vero fratres non solum bis aut ter, sed eciam sepcies, pro correctione transgressionis postulanda missi fuerunt, nec est eis in aliquo satisfactum, dicunt quod nolunt ulterius vexari, sed si predicatores noluerint hac vice satisfacere, sedebunt in domo paciencie sue, expectantes tempora meliora. Hec de substancia nuncii.

Extra ordinarie autem fuit responsum a parte predicatorum ad racionem de ammocione facienda sic: 'Ffratris minorum delictum contra predicatores fuit publicum, et ideo non fuit mirum si publice ammoveretur; sed istius fratris predicatoris peccatum fuit privatum, et ideo non est simile.' Ad hoc frater Minor: 'Esto quod illius fratris ammocio, cum esset persona valde gravis, in cujus comparacione, secundum judicium humane estimacionis, frater Salomon est persona multum humilis, movere non debeat; saltem moveat vos quod alius lector fuit ammotus a loco suo pro pace vestra servanda, qui eciam cum se in presencia quorundam predicatorum excusaverat, nichil contra eum habuerunt nec habere potuerunt.'

Post hec, pendente dissencionis tempore et predicatoribus nihil super petita respondentibus, urgente quadam necessitate, prior provincialis predicatorum repente de Oxonia recessit; qui nacta temporis opportunitate rediit, ne (?) incepta feliciter consummaret. Quadam vero die, clam fratribus Minoribus, credentes fratres predicatores negocium[2] melius agere per seculares magistros, necnon et dissencionem et ejus occasionem celerius quam per semet ipsos extirpare, rogatus est dominus Cancellarius cum magistris quatuor de sollempnioribus tocius universitatis, ex parte predicatorum in causa dissencionis fortiter

---

[1] *Vestri* inserted in a later hand.   [2] *Suum* inserted in another hand.

instructi, subito et occulte venerunt, et fratres Minores convocari rogaverunt, antequam de responsione facienda aliquid deliberarent aut deliberare potuerunt[1]. Convocatis igitur minoribus, ex parte predicatorum, processum dissensionis supra memoratum quamquam incomplete recitaverunt, hoc nuncium adicientes: 'Petunt fratres predicatores et nos cum ipsis petimus, consilium in id ipsum dantes, quod vos descendatis in formam pacis et unitatis. Ipsi enim parati sunt, vobis, juxta racionis exigenciam et discrecionem arbitrancium, regulariter per omnia satisfacere[2].' Inculcando vero adjecerunt: 'Nos invenimus predicatores ad omnia secundum racionis exigenciam paratissimos, iniantes quantum possunt forme pacis et unitatis et fraterne caritatis; utinam in vobis contrarium non inveniamus.' Hec de substancia nuncii et consilii.

Ffacta autem ista peticione, deliberans penes se sicut potuit, quidam frater Minor sic ait: 'Magistri mei et amici karissimi, duo verba tantum ad presens vobis propono, unum pro devota gratiarum accione, aliud pro humili peticione. Primo enim regracior vobis pro labore vestro, quod vos pro nobis pauperibus dignati estis tantum laborare, non minores gratiarum acciones exsolvens, quam zelum dei habentes pro forma pacis et unitatis insudatis. Secundo peto quod, sicut hodie principaliter pro predicatoribus laborastis, secundario pro nobis, ita cras placeat vobis laborare principaliter pro nobis, secundario pro predicatoribus, ut, vobis in unum ubicumque placuerit convenientibus, super petita cum deliberacione respondeam, et totum processum plenius manifestem.' Magistri vero instabant ut statim eis responderetur, si fieri posset bono modo. Minores vero ad eorum instanciam ab eis paululum divertentes, habita deliberacione, responderunt communiter ad omnia que magistri ex parte predicatorum recitaverunt, in qua nimirum responsione non declinabant in aliquo a responsionibus supra memoratis; adicientes quod, sicut predicatores, ita et semet ipsos, ad formam pacis et unitatis paratos invenirent. Hec de responsionis substancia.

Extra ordinarie autem facta fuerunt verba disputacionis magne inter seculares magistros, fratribus minoribus nichil opponentibus aut respondentibus; ubi fratres perpenderunt quod fuerunt contra eos graviter informati. Ipsi vero habili cautela redimentes tempus pertraxerunt in longum. Unde, pendente tempore, accidit quod bedellus universitatis missus fuit eciam bis ex parte universitatis, dominum Cancellarium

---

[1] The whole sentence is utterly ungrammatical, but quite intelligible.

[2] *Satisfacere* inserted in another hand.

pro quadam incepcione advocare; quo vocato una cum magistris aliis recessit. Magistrorum nomina, qui cum ipso ex parte predicatorum venerant, erant hec: Magister Johannes de Wyntun', Magister Hugo de Corbrug', Magister Hugo de Hevesham, Magister Willelmus [1] Pomay. Nomen vero Cancellarii, Magister N. de Ewelm'.

Interim pendente tempore, minores quesierunt consilium, quid facto opus esset discucientes. Ffacta vero discussione in hoc consenserunt, quod amicos eorum, de quibus specialiter confiderant, convocarent, et eos secundum veritatem de toto processu informarent. Convocatis autem quinque de majoribus tocius universitatis, frater unus capitulum regule sue de recepcione peccunie, et ejusdem declaracionem secundum dominum papam factam, recitavit. Quesivit frater si magistri intelligerent. Respondit Magister, persona multum sollempnis, in utroque jure peritus, Johannes le Gras nomine: 'Intelligo quidem ego.' Et incepit volvere capitulum et revolvere, et super hoc sermonem continuare. Qui ita proprie vitam fratrum communem et vivendi modum quem tenebant, et secura consciencia tenere poterant, instinctu nescio quo descripsit, quasi ipse inter fratres vitam fratrum per longa tempora duxisset. Admiratus quidam frater quod ita proprie loquebatur, quesivit an super hoc ab aliquo fratre fuisset informatus. Magister respondit et cum juramento asseruit, se nunquam verbum super hoc a fratre Minore prius audisse, adiciens hec verba: 'Ponamus quod papa nunquam declarasset capitulum id, eciam secundum jura communia possetis regulam vestram sancte et sincere observare. Nec dico vobis aliud quam jura civilia et canonica communiter dicunt. Unde mirabile est, quod vobis imponitur recepcio peccunie ad utilitatem vestram quocumque titulo deputate, ex quo in dominium vestrum non transit nec transire potest ullo jure, sed semper remanet dominium et auctoritas peccunie penes principalem dominum, et eam repetere potest quando volt quamdiu manet inexpensa.' Et inculcando adjecit dicens: 'Fratres, non oportet ut in hoc casu timeatis. Ego enim sum paratus pro ista veritate defensanda curiam adire romanam, si necesse esset, et aliquis se opponeret impudenter.' Magister Adam de Norfolk' hoc idem sentit et idem dixit. Alii vero facta super hoc longa disputacione idem senserunt.

Post hec ffrater unus totum processum a principio supra memoratum eis enarravit. Quo audito obstipuerunt. Magistrorum vero nomina qui ex parte minorum venerant hec fuerunt; Magister Johannes de Maydeston, Archidiaconus Bedeford', Magister Thomas de Bek',

[1] *de la* inserted in another hand.

Magister Johannes le Gras, Magister Stephanus de Wytun', Magister Adam de Norfolk'.

Post hec de istorum magistrorum consilio, rogaverunt minores magistros, qui ex parte predicatorum venerant, ut iterum plenius veritatem audituri convenirent. Qui cum venissent, et in uno loco cum magistris, qui ex parte minorum venerant, congregati essent, unus minorum sic exorsus est, dicens: 'Magistri boni, sicut scitis, ex infirmitate condicionis humane orta fuit quedam dissensio, persuadente generis humani inimico, inter predicatores et nos; et[1] injuria incepit a predicatoribus; petimus nos bis regulariter satisfieri. Oblata fuit quedam satisfactio, sed non sufficiens nec plena, ut videbatur; et cum Minores amplius habere non poterant, paciencer meliora tempora expectabant. Negocium autem id publicare eciam amicis suis nolebant duplici racione; primo quia timebant animos infirmorum scandalizare, secundo quia injuria a predicatoribus incepit et absque correccione a suis superioribus dissimulata fuit, cum esset correccio pluries petita; et ideo non poterant minores, ut videtur, hiis et aliis causis, negocium istud publicare, nisi aliqua[2] verba dicerent que in predicatorum derogacionem sonarent, unde minus in conspectu secularium commendabiles redderentur. Igitur contra infirmorum scandala et contra predicatorum derogacionem sanctam cautelam adhibentes prudenter tacuerunt et humiliter dissimulaverunt. Modo autem quia predicatores primo amicis suis divulgaverunt, urgente quadam necessitate, eciam minores suis amicis publicare voluerunt.'

Quo dicto, incepit idem frater omnes in communi informare sicut prius specialiter Minorum amicos informabat. Quo facto ceperunt Magistri, qui prius ex parte predicatorum venerant, aliqualiter magis pie quam prius sentire. Facta igitur longa disputacione, de discretorum consilio facta deliberacione, ait frater Minor: 'Magistri karissimi, nos parati sumus per omnia in hac causa stare arbitrio vestro et provisive discretioni in forma pacis et unitatis, scientes quod nunquam sitivimus nec adhuc sitimus penam fratris, sed tantum correccionem et emendam. Nec multum ponderamus fratris emissionem de suo loco, sed omnis satisfaccio, quantacumque exilis, que precludit viam et occasionem resumendi de cetero consimilia verba contra nos, potest et debet nobis sufficere. Tamen, si placet, duas peticiones vobis facio; primo, ut sic provideatis de forma pacis ut non detur[3] predicatoribus

---

[1] One letter, prob. c̄ (=cum) is illegible here, owing either to intentional erasure or a flaw in the parchment.

[2] MS. aᵃ (alia?).

[3] *detur* inserted in another hand.

aut fratri, qui deliquit, occasio iterum delinquendi. Nec hoc dico sine causa, quia si decreveritis ipsum non errasse nec deliquisse, in futuro tempore, nacta aliquali occasione, posset dicere, "sic et sic pro isto tempore dixi, toti universitati constabat, nec[1] judicabat me in aliquo deliquisse; quare eciam modo similiter non dicerem?" Hec future dissensionis occasio piis cautelis est precludenda. Secundo peto quod vos, ex quo vobis constat secundum jura, prout quidam vestrum[2] dicunt, quod frater ille est in errore consciencie, Priorem suum provincialem adeatis et persuadeatis ei, quod ipse informet fratrem suum ad conscienciam contrariam, ut videlicet errorem deponat, et pie, sicut debet, de Minoribus senciat.' Quod quidam se securos (?) sponderunt. Hec de substancia negocii.

Extra ordinarie autem allocutus est Gardianum in secreto unus de magistris sollempnibus, Johannes le Gras nomine, sic dicens: 'Ffrater karissime, fratres vestri non deberent[3] in aliquo turbari si fratres predicatores de eis mala dixerint, quia pro constanti habeatis, quod quo pejora de vobis dixerint, deterius eciam eis in hominum estimacione eveniet, nec vobis cedet aut cedere potest in nocumentum, si tantum[4] claustra labiorum custodieritis et bona de ipsis semper predicaveritis.'

Cui Gardianus hec verba dixit: 'Unum est de quo doleo et verecundor nimis, et inde est quod fratres multum verecundantur; videlicet, quod istius dissensionis noticia jam inter seculares est publicata, et que per nos discuti poterat, per ipsos est discussa.'

Ad hoc Magister: 'Nolite in hoc contristari aut verecundiam pati, sed magis gaudere et diem letum ducite, et hac racione; Modo manifesta est nobis omnibus veritas, que prius fuit occulta; unde nos, qui sumus majores tocius universitatis, jam veraciter super facto isto informati, alios informabimus. Sed et ego omni quo possum conatu omnes informare studebo, et ipsos precipue predicatores conabor informare.'

Superveniens autem Magister alius, Hugo de Evesham nomine, hoc exaggerando inculcavit, dicens: 'Crede mihi, ffrater Gardiane, quod nos quinque magistri, qui prius ex parte predicatorum venimus ad vos, eramus omnes heri in presencia predicatorum constituti, ubi eciam prior ipse provincialis non defuit; nec memini me unquam in vita mea forciorem disputacionem audivisse, opponentibus nobis pro facto vestro secundum diffinicionem utriusque juris et exigenciam racionis,

---

[1] nº (nullo) or uº (vero) in MS. : or nᶜ (nec)?
[2] vrᵐ.
[3] *non deberent* inserted in another hand.
[4] MS. *cum* ?

predicatoribus communiter respondentibus; facta vero longa disputacione, ita predicatores omnes racionibus vexavimus et convicimus, quod sedentes omnes in pace et obstupescentes tacuerunt, in tantum quod prior ipse provincialis, inter alios plus motus et spiritu sancto plenius, ut arbitror, informatus, dixit : " Eya, dilectissimi Magistri, quid plura ? quid ulterius inculcatis ? Ecce ego paratus sum discalciatis pedibus Minores, si vultis, adire et eis per omnia satisfacere."' Adjecit autem Magister Hugo Corbrug' occasionaliter hec verba in predicatorum presencia dicens, 'Karissimi, audeo plane dicere, quod ille qui dicit eos recipere peccuniam per se vel per interpositam personam, qui declaracionem domini pape super regulam fratrum Minorum observaverit (sic), audeo inquam plane dicere, quod nec jura novit nec terminos juris.' Alias autem in predicatorum eorundem absencia dixerunt Magistri Johannes le Gras et Adam de Norfolch'; 'Eciam si papa nunquam regulam declarasset, possent eam fratres absque prevaricacione observare, maxime cum peccunia ad eorum utilitatem quocumque titulo deputata nunquam in dominium eorundem transeat[1] ipsis invitis.' Et cum supplicaret Gardianus Magistro Stephano de Witon' quod propter deum fratres predicatores secretius juxta scita legum informaret, zelo accensus magister A. de Norf' dixit : 'Mirum est quid ipsi habent intromittere se de professione vestra, et de regula vestra verba tintinare, cum nec sunt superiores vestri, nec in aliquo spectat ad eos vos corrigere, si, quod absit, contingeret vos in aliquo contra professionem vestram aliquid attemptare. Quod autem petitis de informacione facienda juxta scita legum, non est necesse sic petere; sed petas ut juxta veritatem vestram informentur, omni eciam jure consopito.' Et adjecit Magister Stephanus dicens: 'Non solum paratus sum predicatores pro vobis informare, sed eciam personaliter pro causa vestra curiam adire romanam.'

Interim pendente tempore, iverunt Magistri quinque primo nominati, quorum principalis fuit Cancellarius, ad predicatores, et efficaciter pro parte minorum persuadentibus, tandem fratrem Salomonem, qui offensam fecerat, de assensu et voluntate sui prioris provincialis necnon fratrum suorum, ad fratres minores duxerunt, cum quo venerunt quinque[2] fratres predicatores subscripti; Adam de Lakeor, cum socio Willelmo de Hodum'[3], eorum cursore de sentenciis, Radulphus de Swelm', quondam prior localis Oxon', Iohannes de Mesley, tunc eorum visitator. Fuerunt eciam cum predictis quinque

---

[1] *transeat* inserted in another hand.
[2] Only four mentioned.
[3] Afterwards lector at Paris, and Provincial Prior of England.

APPENDIX C.

Magistris, sex fratres minores subscripti; Adam de Werministre, tunc Gardianus, Thomas de Doking, quondam lector Oxon', Willelmus de Heddel,' tunc lector Oxon', Dyonisius, Robertus de Cap(e)ll', Alanus de Wakefend'. In quorum omnium conspectu pro bono pacis frater Salomon hec verba nomine culpe in scriptis recitavit, et recitata eciam in scriptis Gardiano tradidit; verba autem sunt hec: 'Per illa verba que protuli, non intellexi quod vos receperitis vel recipitis per vos vel per alios peccuniam contra regulam vestram et ejus interpretacionem, nec intendebam communitati vel ordini derogare. Et si ex modo dicendi fuistis provocati, doleo, et peto quod remittatis.' Hic finis negocii et reformacio pacis, per omnia benedictus deus in secula amen.

Memorandum autem quod cum extra ordinarie facta essent verba inter magistros seculares de veritate processus memorati, dixerunt inter se[1], aliquid in processu propositum est falsum et calumpniabile, et maxime quod pro fundamento erat positum. Ffrater N. predicator, nunquam se fecisse illam racionem, ubi est conclusio de statu dampnacionis, manifeste dicit, sed dicit fratrem Alanum minorem fecisse premissas. Ipse vero subintulit; 'Si ita est sicut vos dicitis, sequitur conclusio de statu dampnacionis.' Aliud autem calumpniabile non receperunt. Quod cum minoribus constaret, vocatus fuit frater Alanus minor, in conspectu Cancellarii et Magistri Johannis de Wynton' requisitus super hoc, dixit: 'Verum est, solus ego frater Minor eram in porta cum eis, et ideo probacionem non habeo; sed tantum confido de veritate fratris Roberti de Novo Mercato et ipsius eciam Salomonis, quod si ipsi requisiti dicant in veritate deliberate consciencie, quod frater Salomon ipsam racionem non fecit, ego libenter subiciam me pene, tanquam sufficienter essem de falsi imposicione convictus.' Post hec ait unus ffrater Minor: 'De ista racione magna vis non est, quia de racione cujus (?) non disputamus, sed de hoc quod ipse nobis imposuit, quod negare non potuit, scilicet peccunie recepcionem, emendam quesivimus et emendam, benedictus deus, recepimus.' Terminata fuit ista dissensio Anno domini MCCLXIX Non' Junii.

[1] *se* added in margin.

APPENDIX D.

SUPPLICATIONS AND GRACES FROM THE REGISTERS OF CONGREGATION.

John David.

($145\frac{0}{1}$). 4° die Marcij supplicat etc. ffrater Johannes Dauid ffrater ordinis sancti ffrancisci, quatinus eius oppositio, incepta in termino sancti Michaelis vltimo et continuata vsque ad festum Pasche proximum, sufficiat sibi pro completa forma sue oppositionis.

Hec gratia est concessa sub condicione quod legat primum librum ysaie in scolis publicis. (Regist. Aa. fol. 51 b.)

(June 5, $145\frac{4}{5}$). Supplicat frater Johannes Dauid ordinis minorum et doctor sacre pagine quatinus secum graciose dispensetur vt valeat post festum sancti Thome proximo sequens resumere lecciones ordinarias et regentis actus exercere, ingressu in domum congregacionis dumtaxat excepto.

Hec gratia est simpliciter concessa, et ab altero procuratore etc. (Ibid. fol. 83.)

John Sunday; inception.

(Feb. 5, $145\frac{3}{4}$). Supplicat etc. frater Johannes Sunday de claustro minorum qui compleuit lecturam sentenciarum quatinus cum singulis responderit doctoribus completaque lectura Biblie, incipere valeat in theologica facultate.

Hec gratia est concessa et condicionata 2^{ci} condicione; prima condicio est quod octo vicibus respondeat pro forma et octies opponat; 2^a condicio est quod bis respondeat preter formam et sub hiis condicionibus etc. (Regist. Aa. fol. 79 b.)

Richard Ednam; inception.

(April 2nd, 1462). Supplicat frater Ricardus Ednam, bacallarius sacre theologie, quatinus 8 argumenta, 8 responsiones, introitus biblie, lectura libri sentenciarum, sermo examinatorius, sermo ad quem tenetur ex nouo statuto, sufficiant sibi ad effectum quod possit admitti ad incipiendum in sacra theologia, ita quod die inceptionis sue soluat

APPENDIX D.

Vniuersitati x li. Hec gratia est concessa condicionata; condicio est quod incipiat infra annum; alia condicio quod det Regentibus liberatam consuetam. (Reg. Aa. f. 122.)

(May 24th, 1463.) Supplicat frater Ricardus Ednam de ordine Minorum quatinus tres responsiones, introitus biblie, introitus libri sententiarum, sermo examinatorius, sermo ad quem tenetur ex nouo statuto, sufficiant sibi ad effectum quod possit admitti ad incipiendum in sacra theologia. Hec gracia est concessa cum multis condicionibus; prima est quod incipiat ante festum S. Thome, 2^a quod soluat xv li. in die inceptionis sue, 3 quod det liberatam regentibus distinctam ex sumptu proprio. (Ibid. f. 128 a.)

Supplications and Graces of Walter Goodfield,
Warden of the Franciscans.

(Nov. 27, 1506). Eodem die supplicat frater Walterus Goodfelde ordinis minorum et scolaris sacre theologie, quatenus studium xii annorum in logicis philosophicis et theologicis sibi sufficiat ut admittatur ad opponendum in sacra theologia, qua oppositione habita vna cum responsione in nouis scolis possit admitti etc. Hec est concessa contra quod legat tres primas questiones canonici publice et gratis ante pascha; 2^a quod dicat vnam missam *de quinque vulneribus*, cum ista colecta *Deus summa spes*, pro anima primi fundatoris vniuersitatis, et aliam missam *de trinitate* pro bono statu magistrorum regentium. (Regist. G. 6. f. 27 b.)

(May 10, 1507). Supplicat frater Walterus Gudfeld ordinis minorum quatenus studium 14 annorum in logicis philosophicis theologicis sufficiat ad opponendum in nouis scolis qua oppositione habita vna cum responsione in eisdem possit admitti ad lecturam libri sententiarum. Hec est concessa conditionata quod predicet vnum sermonem preter formam infra annum. (Ibid. fol. 39 b.)

(June 16, 1507). Supplicat frater Walterus Goodfyld ordinis minorum et sacre theologie scolaris quatenus vnus sermo per eum post gradum susceptum dicendus ei sufficiat pro gradu baculariatus in sacra theologia. Hec est concessa simpliciter. (Ibid. fol. 41 b.)

(He was admitted to oppose on Dec. 10, 1507.)

(June 3, 1508). Supplicat frater Walterus Goodfylde, ordinis minorum et sacre theologie baccalarius, quatenus 4^{or} responsiones in nouis scolis cum introitu biblie, vna cum sermone examinatorio, sufficiant ei ut admittatur ad Incipiendum in eadem facultate. Hec est concessa conditionata quod habuit studium 12 annorum in Logicis philosophicis theologicis et quod procedat ante pascha et quod semel predicet semel (*sic*) preter formam infra annum post gradum et quod legat vnum librum sententiarum publice et gratis. (Ibid. fol. 58.)

(Jan. 24, 150$\frac{8}{9}$). Supplicat frater Walterus Goodfyld ordinis minorum et bachallarius sacre theologie quatenus studium quod habuit post gradum bachallariatus cum quattuor responsionibus cum sermone examinatorio et introitu biblie sufficiat ad incipiendum in eadem. (Ibid. fol. 67 b.)

(March 19, 15$\frac{09}{10}$). Supplicat frater Walterus Gudfylde (B.S.T.) quatenus sermo per eum dicendus in die cinerum possit stare pro sermone suo examinatorio. Hec gratia est concessa simpliciter. (Ibid. fol. 82 b.)

(On May 12, 1510, he was licensed in theology, fol. 86.)

(June 27, 1510). Supplicat frater Walterus Gudfyld, ordinis minorum et in sacra theologia licentiatus quatenus si contingat eum realiter incipere in sacra theologia secum gratiose dispensetur pro suis lecturis minutis. Hec est concessa sic quod compleat toto isto tempore et postea secundum dispositionem commissarii tunc presentis. (Ibid. f. 92.)

(He was admitted DD on July 1, 1510.)

(Dec. 10, 1510). Supplicat frater Walterus Gudfylde doctor sacre theologie quatenus secum gratiose possit dispensari pro sua necessaria regencia secundum dispositionem commissarii. Hec est concessa et ille disposuit post proximum actum. (Ibid. fol. 104 b.)

John Thornall, July 11, 1525.

Eodem die supplicat frater Johannes Thornall ordinis minorum et licenciatus in sacra theologia, quatenus cum eo graciose dispensetur ut composicio sua diminuatur ad quinque Libras; causa est quia est admodum pauper et uix habet pecunias necessarias pro gradu suscipiendo.

Hec gracia est concessa, et condicionata, quod causa non sit ficta, et celebret unam missam contra pestem, aliam pro bono statu regentium, et compleat necessariam regentiam, et distribuat decim solidos illarum peccuniarum jam diminutarum in vsum pauperum scolarium secularium. (Reg. H. 7, fol. 140.)

Thomas Kirkham, Nov. 14, 1527.

Eodem die supplicat Mr. Thomas Kyrkam doctor in sacra theologia in ultimo Actu Creatus et necessarius Regens quatenus cum oe graciose dispensetur pro sua necessaria Regentia: causa est quia est gardianus cuiusdam loci ordinis minorum in villa Dancastrie, unde non potest commode hic adesse et interesse actibus scolasticis ad quos teneretur Racione sue necessarie Regentie. Hec gratia est concessa et condicionata ut faciat quinque missas de 5 vulneribus celebrari pro bono statu Regentium et continuet lectiones suas usque ad proximum actum. (Reg. H. 7, fol. 180 b.)

INDEX.

A.

A., warden at London, 136, *n.* 4.
A., of Hereford, secretary to Adam Marsh, 33; biographical notice of, 185.
Abburbury, 109.
Abdy, Robert, Master of Balliol, bequest, 106.
Aberdeen, Observant friars at, 89, *n.* 4.
Abingdon, monks of, 2, 12, *n.* 2; mentioned, 108.
Acre (Palestine), 8.
Acre (Norfolk?), 180.
Acton, Nic., bequest, 103.
Adam of Bechesoueres, physician, 181; notice of, 187.
Adam of Bury St. Edmund's, Archdeacon of Oxford, 102, *n.* 1.
Adam of Corf, friar Minor, 219.
Adam Godham : see Adam Wodham.
Adam of Hekeshovre : see Adam of Bechesoueres,
Adam of Hoveden or Howden, lector, mentioned, 163; notice of, 162.
Adam of Kydmersford, robber, 308.
Adam de Lakeor, Dominican, 334.
Adam of Lathbury, abbat of Reading, 235, *n.* 4.
Adam of Lincoln, lector and provincial, notice of, 160.
Adam Marsh or de Marisco, upholds Franciscan poverty, 4, and *n.* 8, 11, 22; books bequeathed to him, 57; royal ambassador, 7, 307-8; influence at Oxford, 8; relations to Walter de Merton, 9, and Richard Earl of Cornwall, 25, *n.* 2; friendship with Simon de Montfort, 32, Grostete, 32, 48, 57, Walter of Madele, 189, Roger Bacon, 192, 193; lecturer to the friars at Oxford, 31-32, 36, 37, 186, 188; letters illustrating the position of lector and socius, 33-4, 56, *n.* 3; his socius, 185, 186, 188; controversy on theological degrees in 1253, 38-9;

his activity and reputation, 32, *n.* 2, 3; 67; at the Council of Lyons, 127, 128; obtains a papal privilege, 141, *n.* 2; his letters, 57, *n.* 1, 59; mentioned, 57, 65, 128, 129, 139, *n.* 8, 140, 141, 142-3, 151, 153, 154, 156, *n.* 3, 179, 181, 184, 186, 187, 189, 211; biographical notice, 134-139.
Adam of Norfolk, secular master, 331, 332, 334.
Adam of Oxford, missionary, 7; pupil of Adam Marsh, 135; biographical notice, 178.
Adam Rufus : see Rufus.
Adam of Warminster, warden at Oxford, notice of, 129; controversy with Dominicans, 333-5.
Adam Wodham, lector, nominalist, 77, *n.* 4, 170, 226; notice of, 172.
Adam of York, lectured at Lyons, 66, *n.* 10.
Adee, Swithin, 124.
Adreston (Adderstone?), see William of.
Ægidius de Legnaco, 220.
Ægidius Delphinus, general minister, 267.
Ægidius Romanus, 215.
Agas, Map of Oxford, 124.
Agatha (daughter of Walter Goldsmith?), 20.
Agnellus of Pisa, first provincial, comes to England, 1-2, 125; character of the province under him, 3; royal ambassador, 7; opposes extension of areas, 13; builds infirmary and school at Oxford, 3, 21, 30; secures Grostete as lecturer, 30; holds provincial chapter at Oxford, 69; buried there, 21, 26; mentioned, 57, 89, *n.* 2, 126, 127, 178, 179, 181, 188; biographical notice, 176.
Agnes, widow of Guido, grant of land to the Franciscans at Oxford, 14, 15, *n.* 2, 17.
Ailly, Peter d' : see Peter.

342 INDEX.

Alan of Rodan, lector, 157.
Alan of Wakerfeld, lector, 158, 320, 321, 335.
Albert the Great, Dominican, mentioned by Roger Bacon, 42; works ascribed to, 167, 210.
Albert of Metz, 220.
Albert of Pisa, provincial, his sayings, 4, 6; knew St. Francis, 6, *n*. 7; his connexion with the Oxford friary, 3, *n*. 7, 68; policy as minister, 7, 13, 72; opinion of the English province, 11, *n*. 3; mentioned, 2, *n*. 1, 127, 177, 178, 180, *n*. 3; notice of, 181.
Alexander IV, pope, 136, 214, *n*. 2.
Alexander V, pope, mentioned, 66, *n*. 7; biogr. notice of, 249.
Alexander of Hales, 67, 137, 192, 213, 214, *n*. 215.
Alien, John, mentioned, 41, *n*. 5, 53, *n*. 4; biogr. notice, 265.
Alienora de S. Amando, bequest by, 105.
Alifax, Rob.: *see* Eliphat.
Alkerton, 109.
Alnwick: *see* Martin, Roger, William, of.
Alyngdon, doctor, mentioned, 96, *n*. 2; 276.
Amaury de Montfort, *see* Montfort.
Ambassadors, Franciscans employed as, 7, 128, 137, 138, 144, 159, 161, 162, 177, 243, 272, 307-8.
Amory Richard d', 239.
Amour, William de St.: *see* William.
Ancona, march of, 181.
Andrewes, Richard, of Hales, buys site of Grey and Black Friars, Oxford, 122, 123.
Andrews, Nic., of Peckwater's Inn, 95.
Anesti, Thomas of: *see* Thomas.
Anger: *see* Auger,
Anivers (Anilyeres, Aynelers), Nic. de: *see* Nicholas.
Anjou, master H. of, 154.
Anna of Radley, 94.
Anneday, Thomas, mentioned, 47, 51; biogr. notice, 270.
Anthony of Padua, St., 135, 156, *n*. 1.
Anthony Papudo, biogr. notice, 284.
Anthony de Vallibus, 52; biogr. notice, 261.
Antioch, Patriarch of, 183.
Antonius Andreas, 130, *n*. 2, 262.
Anyden, Thomas: *see* Anneday.
Apeltre, Henry of: *see* Henry.
Apulia, Franciscan province, 235.
Aquinas, St. Thomas : *see* Thomas.
Aquitaine, Friars from, at Oxford, 66.
Aragon, Minorites from, at Oxford, 243; Peter Russel teaches in, 255.

Arctur, John: *see* Arthur.
Arezzo: *see* Philip of Castello.
Argentina: *see* Strasburg.
Argentine John, biogr. notice, 260; cf. 191, *n*. 1.
Argos, bishop of: *see* Tinmouth.
Aristotle, 73.
—— Commentaries on 254.
—— —— De coelo et mundo, 153.
—— —— Ethics, 156.
—— —— Logic, 225-6, 259, 262.
—— —— Metaphysics, 142, 196, 233.
—— —— Meteorics, 130, *n*, 2, 196, 241.
—— —— Physics, 157, 196, 216, 224, 226, 227.
—— —— [Secretum Secretorum], 196.
—— —— [Vegetabilia], 196.
Armagh, Archbishops of: *see* Richard Fitzralph; Foxholes, J.: *see also* 288, *n*. 7.
Arnulphus, vicar of the Order, 180.
Arter: *see* Arthur, John.
Arthur or Arter, John, Friar Minor, charges against him, 95-6, 132; kept a horse, 96; biogr. notice, 284.
Arthur, prince, 260.
Arundel, Thomas, Archbp., 85, 112.
Ascensius, editor of Ockham's *Dialogus*, 231.
Ascoli: *see* Jerome of.
Ashby, 125, 189; prior of Canons Ashby, 126.
Ashendon, John, mathematician, 160, 237.
Asia, Franciscan mission, 244.
Assisi; MS. at, 143; burial at, 159: general chapters at, 159, 177, 178, 229, 235.
Auger, William, biogr. notice, 254.
Augustine, St., work in the Franciscan Library, Oxford, 57; mentioned, 150, 292.
Augustine, brother of William of Nottingham, 183.
Aureolus, 262.
Aurifaber, Walter: *see* Goldsmith.
Austin Canons, join Minorite Order, 180.
Austin Friars, 7, *n*. 2, 75, 80, 263, 281, 285.
Auvergne, William of: *see* William.
Averroes, 73.
Avignon, 163, 164, 167, 168, 170, 172, 239: *see* Clement V; Ockham imprisoned at, 225; General Chapter at, 229.
Aylesbury, 163, n. 2; Grey Friars of, 287.
Aylmer, John and Christiana, property granted to Minorites, 16.
Ayneleys: *see* Nicholas of Anivers.

B.

Babwell, Grey Friars at, 56, *n.* 4, 173; *see* Bury St. Edmund's.
Bacheler, John, Friar Minor, vice-warden at Oxford, 131, 288, 318; biogr. notice, 285.
Bachun, Thomas, biogr. notice, 187.
Bacon, Sir Francis, quoted, 64, *n.* 3.
Bacon, Peter, mentioned, 192.
Bacon, Robert, Dominican, signs charter of Henry III for the University, 9; professed on day of entry, 68; uncle of Roger Bacon, 191; preaches to the King, *ib.*; life of St. Edmund by, 192, *n.* 1; works by, 196 (?), 210.
Bacon, Roger, buried at Oxford, 26; quoted, 31; on the study of theology, 37, 42; nature and object of his writings, 37, *n.* 1, 63, 64; writings in the Franciscan Library at Oxford, 58; lectures to Spanish students, 66, *n.* 8, at Paris, 68; sends works to the pope, 56; begs for alms, 91; pupil and friend of Grostete and Adam Marsh, 135, *n.* 1, 139; his pupil John, 33, *n.* 4, 211; his opinion of Thomas Aquinas, 73, and Richard of Cornwall, 143; influence on Bungay, 153, W. de Mara, 215, and J. Somer, 244; biographical notice, 191-5; works, 195-210.
Bacon, Roger, mentioned, 192.
Bacon, Thomas, mentioned, 192.
Baconthorpe, John, Carmelite, 166.
Balborow, William, 317.
Baldeswell : *see* Peter de.
Balliol College : *see* Oxford.
Balliol, Edward, 238.
Balliol, Sir John de, 9, 217.
Balsham, Hugh, Bishop of Ely, 138.,
Bampton, Vicar of, 110; Hugh of, *see* Hugh of Bath.
Banaster or Banister, Alderman and Mayor of Oxford, visits the friaries, 110, *n.* 1, 117, 121.
Banester, John, mentioned, 44, *n.* 4; biogr. notice, 270.
Bangor : *see* Ednam, Ric. Bp. of.
Banke, Thomas, Rector of Lincoln Coll., bequest, 107.
Bannebury, John, bequest, 104.
Barbeur, William le, and Alice his wife, 16, 20, *n.* 5.
Barclay, Alexander, 271.
Bari, 167.
Barlete, 179.
Barlow, Richard, debt, 110, *n.* 8.
Barly, Thomas, Friar Minor, 119, 294.
Barnby, prebend, 235.
Barneby, Thomas of : *see* Thomas.

Barnes, Dr., Austin Friar, 281.
Baron, Roger, work by, 209.
Bartelot, Jac., attorney, 99, *n.* 7, 315.
Bartholomew of Pisa, quoted, 2, 6, *n.* 4, 30, 72, 167, 170, 180, 181, 182, 238, 243.
Barton : *see* Martin de, Roger de.
Based : *see* Basset.
Basel, mentioned, 173 ; Council of, 214, 257.
Basil, St., works of, 292.
Basingstoke : *see* John of.
Baskerfield, Edward, Warden at Oxford, 95, 288; his horse, 96, 287; surrenders his house, 118, 119; biogr. notice, 132.
Basset, Gregory, Minorite, mentioned, 113, *n.* 5, 6; 290; biogr. notice, 286.
Basset, John, lector, 162.
Bath, 2, 134; *see* Henry of, Hugh of.
Baxter, Mrs., 282.
Baynton, Sir Edw., 111.
Beamont, 290.
Beatrice of Falkenstein, wife of Ric. Earl of Cornwall, buried at Oxford, 25.
Beaune, 128.
Beauvais, W. of Gainsborough buried at, 162 : *see* 268, *n.* 1.
Bec, fee of the Abbat of, in Oxford, 16, 20, 297.
Beche, Phil. de la, Sheriff, 60, *n.* 2.
Bechesoueres : *see* Adam of.
Becket, Thomas, Archbishop, 155, 285.
Beckley, 218.
Bedford, Minorite convent in the Oxford custody, 68; burials at, 128, 172, 238.
— Simon Ludford, Friar of, 119.
— Duke of, 265, *n.* 4.
— Archdeacon of, 331.
Bedyngfeld, Edmund, Sheriff, 99, 130.
Bek' : *see* Thomas de.
Bekinkham : *see* John.
Bele, Thomas, servant of Friar J. Welle, 78, 311.
Benedict XII, pope, constitutions for Friars Minors, 35, 36, 50-1, 170.
— Attacked by Ockham, 231, 232.
Benedict le Mercer of Oxford, 16, 296, 298; Symon, son of : *see* Simon.
Benedictines ; students at the Universities, 43, *n.* 7.
— Franciscan lecturers to, 66.
— Monks enter Minorite Order, 2, 237.
Benet, John, will mentioned, 90, *n.* 1.
Benet, Thomas, martyr, 132, 286, 289.
Benjamin, Jew of Cambridge, 190.
Bercherius, Peter, 149, 170.
Bereford, Edmund, bequest, 103

344 INDEX.

Bereford, John of, Mayor of Oxford, bequest, 103.
Bergamo, Philip of: see Philip.
Berkhamstede, 218, *n.* 4.
Berkshire, Sheriff of, 22.
Bernard of Gascony, Minister of Tuscany, 311.
Bernardin of Siena, St., 221, *n.* 3.
Bernewell, Thomas, at Council of the Earthquake, 84, 246.
Berney, Walter de, bequest, 104.
Berton, William, Chancellor, 251.
Berwick: see John of.
Beste, Robert, charge of incontinence, 94-5; joins reformation, 113, *n.* 7; biogr. notice, 286.
Besylis, William, bequest, 108.
Beverley: see John of.
— Robert of.
Bible, the study of the, 36-7, 38, 44, 46, 47, 61, 65, *n.* 3, 141, 183, 185, 188, 197, 261, 275, 277, 279, 336-8.
— MSS. of, in possession of the Friars; 56, notes 2, 3, 4, 57, 58 and *n.* 14, 59 and *n.* 3, 113, 143, 182, 283.
— An Oxford Franciscan lectures against the translation of, into English, 254.
— Works on, 139, *n.* 2, 210.
— Commentaries on books of Old Testament, 32, *n.* 4, 141, 147, 149, 151, 152, 164, 173, 210, 218, 234, 235, *n.* 6, 236, 247.
— New Testament, edited by Erasmus, 273.
— — Commentaries on Gospels, 148, 149, 152, 185, 217, *n.* 3, 221, 247, 248.
— — Acts, 236.
— — Epistles of St. Paul, 58, 113, *n.* 5, 152, 247, 277, 278, 284.
— — Revelation, 152, 171, 218, 221, 234, 254.
Billing, John, Observant, 88, *n.* 5, 290.
Bilney, Thomas, martyr, 113, *n.* 5.
Black Death, 3, *n.* 7, 44, *n.* 1, 80, 172.
Black Friars: see Dominican Order.
Blacwood, James, bequest, 106.
Blund, Rob., vintner, 70, *n.* 3.
Bockering: see Thomas Docking.
Bohun, Humphrey de, E. of Hereford and Essex, bequest, 103.
Bokkyg: see Thomas Docking.
Boleyn, Anne, 114, 273, 285.
Bologna, Albert of Pisa, Minister of, 181; Bishop of, 224, *n.* 8.
— John Foxalls lectures at, 262.
— see 266, 281.
Bologna: see John de Castro.
Boltere, William le, of St. Ebbe's, 75, *n.* 2.
Bonagratia, friar, 225.

Bonaventura, general minister, mentioned, 11, *n.* 1, 128, 137, 139, 154, 155, 215, 216, *n.* 2.
— Works ascribed to, 149, 193, *n.* 4;
— his constitutions, 55, *n.* 1.
Bonetus, 262.
Boniface VIII, pope, grants land to Minorites at Oxford, 18; calls W. of Gainsborough as lecturer to Rome, 161: see also 242.
— IX, pope, 247, 250, 253, 312-3.
Boniface of Savoy, Abp. of Canterbury, bequest, 102; mentioned, 32, *n.* 3, 136, 137, 138, 139, *n.* 8, 186.
Bonner, Bp., visits Hadham, 284, *n.* 1.
Bordeaux, 160, *n.* 10.
Borstall, 105.
Bosellis: see Gregory de.
Boscvile: see Walter de.
Boston, parson of: see J. Tinmouth.
— Gild at, 271.
— Grey Friars at. 278.
Boston of Bury, 58, 150, 151.
Botehill, W., 268.
Botolph, St., life of, 271.
Bowghnell, William, Friar Minor, 119, 293.
Boys (Bors), Vincent, biogr. notice, 255.
'boysaliz,' 188.
Bozon, Nicholas, 37, *n.* 2, 64, *n.* 4, 167, *n.* 10, 240, *n.*
Brackley, Friar John, of Norwich, 111.
Brakell, John, Minorite, 274.
Bramptone, Ric., bequest, 104.
Brenlanlius: see John of Berwick.
Brewer, Mr., quoted, 63, 64, 89, 129, 194, 208, *n.* 2.
Brian Sandon: see Sandon.
Bricott, Edmund, biogr. notice, 283.
Bridgwater, Grey Friars at, 157, 244, 245, 254; chapter at, 271.
Bridlington or Briddilton: see Philip of.
Brikley, Peter, Cambridge Franciscan, 283.
Brill, 5.
Brinkley, Ric., provincial, studies Greek, 113; biogr. notice, 283.
Brinkley or Brinkel, Walter, biogr. notice, 223.
Brisingham, A., H., T., of: see Henry of.
Bristol, Minorites of, 60, 172, 174, 260, 286.
Britanny, John of, E. of Richmond, benefactor of the friars, 18.
Briton, Laurence: see Laurence.
Britte, Walter, 248.
Broadgates Hall : see Oxford.
Broghton, John, Sheriff, 99, 129.
Bromyard: see Rob. of.
Brookby (Brorbe), Anthony, Minorite, catholic martyr, 290.

INDEX.   345

Brown, John, sup. for B.D. 45, *n.* 5, 50, *n.* 1, 52; biogr. notice, 274.
Browne, Oxford Dominican, 267.
Browne, provincial of Austin Friars, 285.
Browne, Ric. (alias Cordon), bequest, 105, 261.
Browne, William, Minorite, 116, *n.* 7, 119, 288, 317.
Bruni: *see* Simon.
Brunsfelsius, Otto, 287.
Brusyard (Suffolk), Poor Clares of, 241.
Brygott: *see* Bricott.
Brynkley: *see* Brinkley.
Brynknell, Thomas, 281.
Bucks, 271.
Bukenham: *see* Walter de.
Bungay: *see* Thomas of.
Burchestre, William de, bequest, 103.
Burford, 109.
— *see* Henry of.
Burgo: *see* Nicholas de.
Burnham (Essex), 284, *n.* 4.
Burton, Robert, warden at Oxford, 44, *n.* 2; biogr. notice of, 130.
Bury: *see* Boston of.
— *see* Richard of.
— St. Edmund's: *see* Adam of: *see* Babwell; monk of, 210.
Butler, William, regent master and provincial, biogr. notice, 254-5.
Byrton, John, bequest, 109.

C.

Calais, staple of, 106; commissary general, 292.
Call, William, provincial minister, leans to reformation, 113, *n.* 5.
Cambrai, 231.
Cambridge, mentioned, 311.
— reformation begins at, 113.
— University, 258, 260.
— Caius College, 59, 226.
— Corpus Christi College, 286.
— King's College, 260, 261.
— Austin friar at, 7, *n.* 2.
— Carthusian at, 268.
— Dominicans at, 74, 103, 108.
— Franciscans at; custody, 57, 65, 68, *n.* 5, 139, *n.* 8, 178.
— — friary; foundation, 126; burial at, 283; grant of a house, 190; gifts and bequests, 97, *n.* 5, 104, 108, 271; numbers, 44, *n.* 1; *limites*, 91, *n.* 4; dissolution, 294.
— — schools, 34, *n.* 2, 35, *n.* 2, 66, *n.* 10, 110, *n.* 6, 309, 314; Oxford Franciscans study or lecture in, 130, 140, 141, 153, 156, 157, 158, 162, 164, 214, 218, 234, 238, 242, 243 (2), 261, 265, 266, 271, 276, 283, 290, 291, 293.
— — *see also* 49, *n.* 9, 80, *n.* 2, 113, *n.* 5, 119, 313.
— Jew of: *see* Benjamin.
— Mendicant Orders at, 103.
Cambridgeshire, 164, 223, 283.
de Campo Portugaliensis: *see* Peter Lusetanus.
Candia: *see* Alexander V.
Canon, John, realist, •77, *n.* 4; biogr. notice, 223.
Canterbury: Archbishops: *see* Arundel, Thomas; Becket; Boniface of Savoy; Cranmer, Thomas; Edmund Rich; Kilwardby, Robert; Langham, Simon; John Peckham; Warham, William; *also* 41, 81, *n.* 7, 84, 155, 242, 258, 265.
— convocation of, 257.
— preachers at, 289.
— Christchurch, monastery: Franciscan lectures at, 66.
— — Peckham's burial and bequest, 155, and *n.* 10.
— — shrine of St. Thomas Becket, 285.
— — canon, 292.
— Franciscans at, 2, 176, 178, 285, 288, 289; their school, 181.
— — MS. belonging to, 182.
Cantilupe: *see* Hugh, Thomas, Walter, of.
Cantwell, James, at Oxford at Dissolution, 119, 293.
Capell: *see* Robert de.
Cappes, Thomas, at Oxford at Dissolution, 119, 293.
Capua, 281, *n.* 3.
Cardaillac: *see* Francis de.
Cardmaker, John, entered Minorite order young, 111, *n.* 5; becomes reformer, 113, *n.* 7, 120, *n.* 3; arrests Friar Arthur, 285; burned, 114, *n.* 1; biogr. notice, 291.
Carew, Mr., 317.
Carlisle, 162: *see* Hugo Karlelle.
Carmelites, 75, 80, 84, 85, 103, 245, 255, 274.
Carn, David, Dominican, 261, *n.* 8.
Carrewe, David, Minorite bequest to, 106; biogr. notice of, 261.
Carron, David: *see* Carrewe.
Carsewell, Richard, bequest, 104.
Carthusian monk, 268.
Cartwright, Thomas, 101, *n.* 3.
Cary, Richard, Mayor of Oxford, grants land to the Franciscans, 19-20, 303, *n.* 1, 305; represents Oxford in Parliament, 21; auditor, 92, 311; will, 101, *n.* 4.
— — Alice his wife, 101, *n.* 4.

INDEX.

Castello : *see* Philip of.
Castro : *see* John de.
Casuelis : *see* Queswell.
Catalogus illustrium Franciscanorum, 58, 139, *n.* 2, 141, 152, 153, 157, 158, 160, 163, 169, *n.* 3, 173, 185, 254, 255, 256.
Catton (Norwich), 170, *n.* 3 : *see* Walter de Chatton.
Ceruise : *see* Henry de.
Cesena : *see* Michael de.
Charles IV, Emperor, 225, *n.* 7, 233.
Charles VI, King of France, 253.
Charles, M., life of Roger Bacon, 195, 215.
Chatton : *see* Walter de.
Chaucer, 64, 89, *n.* 5, 91, 244.
Chayne, Thomas, biogr. notice, 256.
Cheshire, 215, *n.* 1, 219.
Chester, archdeacon of, 182 ; Franciscans at, 240.
Chestur, William, bequest, 106.
Chichele, Henry, Abp., 258, 259.
China, Franciscan mission in, 244.
Chingford, 175.
Chorasmeni, 128.
Cistercians, 85, 156, 178.
Clacton Parva, 277, *n.* 6.
Clamiter, Thomas, 105.
Clapwell, Richard, Dominican, 215, 216.
Clara : *see* John de.
Clare : *see* Richard of.
Clare, William, bailiff of Oxford, 93 ; bequest, 109.
Clarendon, documents dated at, 299, 308.
Clarke, Thomas, 107, 268.
Claymond, John, president of Magdalen and C.C.C., bequest, 109.
Clement IV, pope, constitutions for Minorites, 65, *n.* 3 ; relations to Roger Bacon, 91, 193-4, 200, 201, 211.
Clement V, pope, grants property to the Oxford Franciscans, 18, 44, *n.* 1, 302 ; bull, 77, *n.* 1.
Clement VI, pope, 224, 225, 235, 237.
Clement VII, antipope, 243.
Clement of Langthon, 185.
Clerkson, Simon, Carm., 54, *n.* 3.
Clopton, Walter, chief justice, Minorite, 256.
Clyff, Richard, custodian at Oxford, 99 ; notice of, 129.
Clynton, Richard, Minorite, 279.
Cobeham : *see* John of.
Cocke, John, bookseller, 217, *n.*
Codyngton : *see* John de.
Cok, John, Minorite, 119, 294.
— William, Minorite, 119, 294.

Coke, Matthew, bequest, 104.
Cokkes, John, scribe at Oxford, 208.
— — LL.D., 317.
Colchester, Grey Friars, 247, 253, 271.
— rector of St. Mary's, 282.
Colebruge : *see* Ralph de.
Coles, John, bequest, 108.
Coleshull : *see* John of.
Collins, Charles, 124.
Colman, Robert, Minorite, Chancellor of Oxford, 256.
Cologne, 126 ; Franciscans at, 89, *n.* 4 ; *studium* at, 221.
— minister of : *see* Peter of Tewkesbury.
— *see* Hermann of.
Colvile : *see* William de.
Combis : *see* John de Crombe.
Combs (Suffolk), 166.
Comre, John : *see* Covire.
Comyn, John, murder of, 162.
Confessions : Franciscan friars as confessors, 63-4, 74-5, 79, 105, 110, 126, 127, 129, 159, 162, 163, 177, 219, 220, 239, 251.
— works on, 144, 173 *n.* 6, 239-240, 256.
Coniton : *see* Richard de Conyngton.
Constance, canon of, 216, *n.* 3.
Constantine, donation of, 257, *n.* 3.
Conti : *see* Rinaldo.
Conway, Roger : *see* Roger.
Conyngton : *see* Richard de.
Cooper, Joanna, wife of William, 94, 95, 284.
Cooper, William, 269, *n.* 4.
Coper, Galfred, 94.
Corbrug : *see* Hugh de ; Ralph de Colebruge.
Cordon : *see* Browne, Ric.
Corf : *see* Adam of.
Cork, county, 267.
Cornish, William, Minorite, 212.
Cornwall, Archdeacon of, 9.
— Earls of : *see* Edmund ; Richard.
— *see* Laurence of ; Richard of, secular ; Richard Rufus of, Franciscan.
Cossey, or Costesey : *see* Henry of.
Costard, John, and Margery his wife, 16.
Cote, Hugh, 128.
Cotter, Sir James, 124.
Countess (Comitissa), Jewess at Oxford, 9.
Couton : *see* John de.
Coventry, 217, 289 ; Grey Friars, dissolution, 293 : *see* Roger of Wesham.
Covire, John, Minorite, 119, 293.
Cowton : *see* Robert.
Cradoc, or Craycocke, Ralph, 96.

Cranmer, 281, *n.* 3, 288, *n.* 7, 289, 292.
Crayford, or Crawfurthe, John, Minorite, 120, *n.* 3; biogr. notice, 191.
Creswell, Ralph, Observant, 88, *n.* 5, 119, 293.
Crofton, Edmund, bequest, 107.
Crombe: *see* John de.
Crompe, Henry, Cistercian, 85, 251.
Cromwell, Thomas, reforms university, 116; disposes of friars and their property, 120; letters to, 117, 118, 119, 282; mentioned, 130, 132, 274, 285, 286, 287.
Crosby, John, citizen of London, 263.
Cross, Crouche (de Cruce): *see* Robert.
Croy, Henry, Dominican, 165, *n.* 7.
Cruche (de Cruce): *see* Henry.
Crusades, 7, 8, 63, 136, 138, *n.* 3, 140, 153, 195, *n.* 4: *see also* Missionaries.
Crussebut, J., Cambridge Minorite, 49, *n.* 9.
Cudnor, John, warden of Grey Friars, London, 276.
Culvard, Andrew, and Alice his wife, 20.
— John, Mayor of Oxford, grants land to Minorites, 20, 303-5; represents Oxford in parliament, 21.
Curson, Walter, bequest, 108.
Curtes, William, Minorite, 279.
Cusack, Isaac, preaches in Ireland, 86; biogr. notice, 266.
Cyprian, St., works of, 292.

D.

Dagvyle, William, bequest, 106.
Dalderby, John, bishop of Lincoln, 63-4, 129, 159, 162, 163, 164, 165, 167, 219, 220, 222.
Dalmacus de Raxach, Minorite from Aragon, 243.
Danvers, Sebyll, bequest, 107.
Darlington, John, Dominican, 72, *n.* 4.
David, Hugo, regent master, biogr. notice, 256.
— John, lecturer to Minorites at Hereford, 34, *n.* 3, 261, 313-14; provincial minister, 259.
— John, D.D., Oxford, 52, 53, *n.* 2, 336; biogr. notice, 261.
— Richard, Minorite, 116, *n.* 7, 289.
— William, Minorite, 116, *n.* 7, biogr. notice, 289.
Davys, Thomas, bequest, 107.
Daynchurch: *see* Oliver de Encourt.
Days, Roger: *see* Dewe.
Deal, 292.
Dee, John, 245.
Delamere, forest, 215, *n.* 1.
Delphinus, Ægidius, general minister, 267.

Denbigh, Carmelites of, 274.
Denmade: *see* Herbert.
Denmark, English friars wanted for, 140; king of, 257; Standish sent to, 272.
Denson, Thomas, 94.
Deodatus, warden at Exeter, 217.
Derby, surrender of the Black friars, 133.
Derbyshire, 122, 156, *n.* 2, 219.
Devon: *see* Richard of.
Devorguila, wife of John Balliol, 9, 158, 216-7.
Dewe, Roger, provincial, 256; notice of, 259.
Dieppe, 285.
Divorce of Henry VIII: *see* Henry VIII.
Dobbis, Alice, bequest, 106.
Docking: *see* Thomas.
Doclington, John of, bequest, 103.
Dominican Order, constitutions of, 1228, 37, *n.* 6, 90, *n.* 7.
— Master of: *see* Jordan.
— in England, 7, 8, 55, *n.* 3, 61, 72, 73, *seq.*, 80, 81, *n.* 7, 127, 137, 156, 178, 183, 307, 308, 326, 334, *n.* 3.
— — *see* Cambridge, Derby, Guildford, Langley Regis, Leicester, London, Oxford.
Doncaster, Grey Friars at, 282, 294, 339.
Donegal, Minorites of, 267.
Dongan, John, buried in Grey Friars' cemetery, 27; bequest, 106.
Donstede: *see* Simon Tunstede.
Donwe, Roger: *see* Dewe.
Dorchester (Oxon.), 63, 159, &c.: *see* Hugh of Hertepol.
Dorchester (Dorset), Friars Minors at, 84; mentioned, 263.
Dorchester: *see* Warin of.
Döring, Matthias, Minorite, 66, *n.* 10; biogr. notice, 256.
Dorman, Edmund, 315.
Dorsetshire, 191.
Dover, 2, 157, 176, 308; bishop of, 116.
Draper: *see* Milo.
Drayton: *see* Richard of.
Drewe, Edward, 55, *n.* 3.
Droken', J. de, 161.
Dublin, Friars Minors of, 68, *n.* 3.
— Archbishops of, 129, *n.* 1, 267.
Duns: *see* John Duns Scotus.
Dunstable, canons of, become Franciscans, 180.
Dunstan: *see* Thomas of St.
Durham, bishops of, *see* Ric. Marsh, Ric. Kellawe, Ric. of Bury.
— tax on clergy in the diocese, 98.
— Church of, 292; library, *ibid.*
— County, 153, 216.

348   INDEX.

Durham College : *see* Oxford.
Dyonisius, Minorite, 212, 323, 335.
— Tully, Dominican, 266.
Dysse, William, Minorite, 267.

E.

Eccleston : *see* Thomas of.
Edes, John, biogr. notice, 254.
Edmund, Earl of Cornwall, 218.
Edmund, St. (Rich), Abp. of Canterbury, 168, 192.
Edmund : *see* G. of St.
Ednam, Ric., Minorite, bishop of Bangor, 45, 46, *n.* 10, 51, 52, *n.* 1, 336–7 ; biogr. notice, 264.
Edrope : *see* Henry of.
Edward I, employs Minorites as ambassadors, 7, 161 ; his Crusade, 8, 153 ; stays at the Black Friars, Oxford, 72 ; grant to the Oxford Minorites, 97, 308–9 ; grant to friars in General Chapter, 219.
Edward II, assigns to the Minorites the property of the Friars of the Sack in Oxford, 18–19, 301–3 ; supports Dominicans at Langley Regis, 22, 53, *n.* 9 ; grant to the Oxford Minorites, 98, 309 ; marriage with Isabella, 162 ; mentioned, 223.
Edward III, stays at the Grey Friars, York, 27, *n.* 9 ; mentioned, 60, *n.* 2, 238, 239, 300.
Edward IV, 98.
Edward V, 98.
Edward VI, 291, 292.
Edward, the Black Prince, 81, *n.* 7, 242.
Edward, prince, 260.
Elemeus, Ric., bequest, 109.
Elias, general minister, 67, *n.* 1, 69, 135, 142, 177, 180, 181, 184, *n.* 1.
Eliphat, Robert, 222, *n.* 5 ; biogr. notice, 238.
Elmys, Elizabeth, bequest, 107.
Ely, bishopric of, 138, 260.
Elyot, Sir Ric., judge, bequest, 108.
Empoli : *see* Francis de S. Simone.
Encourt : *see* Oliver de.
Enger (near Cologne), curious custom at, 235.
Erasmus, 112, 113 ; relations to Henry Standish, 273.
Erfurt, University, Franciscans at, 257 ; 254, *n.* 6.
Eric, King, of Denmark, 257.
Erlandi, John, bp. of Roskild, 140, *n.* 6.
Ernulphus : *see* Arnulphus.
Eschvid, John : *see* Ashendon.
Esseby : *see* Simon of.
— *see* William of.
Essex, Archdeacon of, 49, *n.* 8 ; Earl of : *see* Bohun.

Essex, 284, 287, 290.
Eton, William : *see* Will. of Esseby.
Etton, Guy, Minorite, and reformer, 113, *n.* 7, 116, *n.* 7, 120, *n.* 3 ; biographical notice, 290.
Eueston : *see* William of Euston.
Eustace de Merc, warden at Oxford, compelled to eat fish, 6 ; excluded from chapter, 69 ; biogr. notice, 126.
Eustace de Normanville, lector, declines to lecture at Norwich, 65 ; biogr. notice, 139.
Eustas, John, scholar, dies intestate, 101, 276.
Evangelical Poverty, dispute concerning, 75–8, 86, 129, 163, 164, 166, 167, 225, 266, 320–335 ; *cf.* 92.
— works on, 164, 165, 169, 215–6, 222, 224, 232, 234, 239, 240, 243, 248, 255, 266 ; *cf.* 320–335.
Evesham, Simon de Montfort, buried at, 33 (*see Corrigenda*).
— *see* Hugh of.
Ew, *see* John of.
Ewelme, *see* N. de.
Exeter, diocese of, 105 ; dean of, 7 ; subdean, 96.
Exeter : Grey Friars' house at, 27, *n.* 9, 217, 291 ; *studium* at, 35, *n.* 3.
— friars preach at, 132.
— persecution at, 132, 286, 289.
— Adam of : *see* Adam of Oxford.
— Stephen of : *see* Stephen of Ireland.
— *see* William of.
Eynsham, abbey, 237.

F.

Fabricius, G., quoted, 148.
Fakenham : *see* Nicholas of.
Falkenstein : *see* Beatrice of.
Falley, John, 107, 268.
Farmer, Henry, of Tusmor, 167.
Faversham : *see* Haymo of.
Feckyngtone, John, Minorite, Rector of Balliol Coll., 10 ; biogr. notice, 260.
Ferrara, bp. of, 224, *n.* 8.
Fetiplace, Ric. bequest, 107.
Fey, Jacob, biogr. notice, 252.
Fisher, John, 273.
Fitzralph : *see* Richard.
Flavyngur, John, Minorite, lectures on decretals, 53 ; biogr. notice, 277.
Flemengvill : *see* Robert de.
Florence, general chapter at, 314.
— friars Preachers at, 55, *n.* 3.
— *see* Fey (Jacob), Nicholas de Burgo.
Florence, John, Minorite, 46, *n.* 10.
Foliot, Alice, 15, *n.* 2.
Folvyle, W., 80, *n.* 2.

INDEX.

Foreign friars at Oxford: *see* Oxford.
Forest, John, Catholic martyr, 290.
Foster, Thomas, 131.
Fox, Edward, 281, *n.* 3.
Foxal, Foxalls: *see* Foxholes.
Foxe, Jane, bequest, 109.
Foxholes, John, Minorite, biogr. notice, 261-2.
Foxle: *see* Walter de.
France; kings of, and country, 138, *n.* 3, 140, 159, 161, 243, 253, 285.
French students expelled from Oxford, 86.
French Minorites at Oxford, 66, 187, 244; expelled, 86.
— *see* Paris.
— Provincial of the Minorites in, 126, 187.
— Rob. Wellys, dies in, 256.
Frances, Thomas, inception, 52, *n.* 10, 53; biogr. notice, 279.
Francis, St., of Assisi, 1, *n.* 1, 129, 176; appears in visions, 2, 142, *n.* 3; church at Oxford dedicated to, 22, 24; his condemnation of learning, 29; mentioned, 6, *n.* 7, 81, 100, 129, 177, *n.* 6.
— his Rule, observance and relaxations, 7, 11, 14, 22, 29, 33, 36, 55, 69, 91, 97, 127, 135, 136, 147, 176, 181, 183, 186, 187, 188, 190, 193, 194, 215, 325, 327, 328, 331: *see* Gregory IX, Benedict XII.
Francis de Cardaillac, 243.
Francis de Graynoylles, Minorite from Aragon, 243.
— de Mayronibus, 262.
Francis de S. Simone (of Pisa or Empoli), 66, *n.* 7; biogr. notice, 243.
Francis of Savona (Sixtus IV), 265-6.
Franciscan Order, General Chapters, 11, 35, 66, *notes* 6 and 10, 90, 127, 135, 157, 159, 161, 166, 167, 176, 177, 178, 183, 186, 194, 218, 219, 221, 224, 229, 235, 242, 267, 275 (?), 309, 314.
— Decrees relating to Oxford, 35, 66, *notes* 6, 10, 309, 314.
— *see* Evangelical Poverty.
— England; character of the Order in, 4, *n.* 1, 11, *n.* 3, 13, 14, 27, *n.* 9, 29-30, 61, 69, 78-9, 82-3, 100, 101, *n.* 5, 111, 113, 115-6, 129, 320, *seq.*
— — Provincial Chapters; held annually in England, 36, *n.* 4, 66, *n.* 1.
— — at Oxford, 4, 5, 69, 70, 126, 142, 181, 183, 184, 218, 254.
— — elsewhere, 69, and *n.* 4, 157, 176, 184, 235, 250, 271, 314.
— — records of the, lost, 89, 90.
— Provincial Ministers of England, appointment or deposition of, 1, *n.* 1, 70, 127, 128, 177, 181, 183-4, 253, 254, 255, 256, 259.
Franciscan Order in England, custodies, 68, 125, 133.
—*Studia*: *see* Cambridge, Oxford.
— — 34 and *n.* 3, 35 and *n.* 3, 44, 51, 64, *n.* 5, 65, 186, 188, 189, 249, 270, 275 (276), 277, 284, 309, 311, 313-4, 314.
— Lecturers, appointment or election of, 30, 34, and *n.* 3, 35, *n.* 2, 36, 43, 65, 66, 139, 140, 141, 142, 177, 181, 183, 186, 189, 220, 235, 242, 313-4; *cf.* 329.
— Monastic school at Canterbury presided over by a Franciscan, 66.
— Monks and Canons enter the Franciscan Order, 2, 3, 180, 237.
— — Other friars become Minorites, 75.
— Limit to age of admission to Order, 80-1.
— Dress of the Friars, 4.
— Letters of Fraternity, 82, 90.
— Suppression of the friaries, 116; pension to a Franciscan, 130.
— Political teaching, 32-3, 81-2, 84, 85, 86, 87, 114, 137, 141, 191, 242, 272.
— — works on politics, 144, 145, 218, 229-234, 244.
— Individual friars: privileges granted to, 141, *n.* 2, 237, *n.* 5, 239, 247, 312.
— — alms and exhibitions, 53-4, 91-2, 97.
— — bequests, 102, 104, 105, 106, 107, 108, 143, 251, 261, 263, 268, 282, *n.* 9, 318.
— — private property, 78, 96, *n.* 1, 108, 109, 271, 273, 311.
— Spiritual and Observant Friars, 77, 88, 89, *n.* 4, 96, 114, 115, 163, 164, 166, 215, 257, 265, 269, *n.* 6, 277, 285, 286, 289, 290, 293.
— Rivalry between Mendicant Orders, 71, *seq.*, 127, 183: *see* Dominican Order in England.
— Convents: *see* Aberdeen, Aylesbury, Babwell, Bedford, Boston, Bridgwater, Bristol, Brusyard (Poor Clares), Cambridge, Canterbury, Chester, Colchester, Coventry, Doncaster, Donegal, Dorchester, Dublin, Evesham (*see Corrigenda*), Exeter, Galway, Gloucester, Grantham, Greenwich, Hereford, Ipswich, Leicester, Lichfield, Lincoln, London, Lynn, Newark, Newcastle, Northampton, Norwich, Nottingham, Oxford, Reading, Richmond, Salisbury, Shrewsbury, Southampton, Stamford, Ware, Winchester, Worcester, York.

Franciscan Order : *see* Ambassadors.
— — *Catalogus illustrium Francisca-norum.*
— — Confessions.
— — Heresies.
— — Missionaries.
Frankfurt, council of, 225, 232; mentioned, 288, *n.* 7.
Frederic II : *see* Isabella, wife of.
Frederic of Thüringen, 257.
Freiburg : *see* John Lector of.
Frewers : *see* Fryer.
Friars : *see* Austin Friars ; Carmelites ; Dominicans ; Franciscans ; Sack, friars of the ; Trinitarians ; and Mendicant Orders.
Frideswide, St. : *see* Oxford.
— *see* John of.
Frisby, Roger, Minorite, executed, 87.
Fryer, William, alderman, visits Oxford friaries, 117, 121 ; obtains lease of Grey Friars, 121, 122.
Fugardi, Rogerus filius, 191, *n.* 1.
Fulgentius, commentaries on, 170.
Fulham : *see* Robert de.
Fullo, Radulph, Thomas, William, 15, *n.* 2, 19, *n.* 3.
Fyfield, 25, *n.* 9, 104.

G.

G. de Sancto Edmundo, biogr. notice of, 189.
Gaddesby or Gaddestyn : *see* Robert de.
Gaieta : *see* Peter of.
Gainsborough : *see* William of.
Gallensis, Gualensis : *see* John Wallensis.
Gallensis, John, of Volterra, 150.
Galway, Franciscans of, 267.
Gamages, Reginald, land in Oxford, 298.
Garaford : *see* Richard de.
Gardener, John, principal of Beef Hall, 130.
Gardiner, Stephen, trial of, 284, *n.* 1; mentioned, 291.
Gascoigne, Thomas, Chancellor of Oxford, on the Franciscan library, 57–9, 61, *n.* 7; quoted Thomas Docking, 151, *n.* 7.
Gascony, Simon de Montfort in, 138, 186.
— seized by French King, 161.
Gaufredi : *see* Raymund.
Gaunt, John of, Earl of Lancaster, 81, *n.* 7, 84.
Gaveston, Piers, 22, 27, *n.* 9.
Gedleston (Gilstone ?), 277, *n.* 6.
Genoa, general chapters at, 127, 159, 184, *n.* 1, 186.
— Franciscan province, 265.
— plague at, 184.

Gerald Odonis, Spiritual Minorite, 231.
German, William, Minorite, 45, 50, *n.* 1 and 8 ; admitted to Univ. library, 62, *n.* 3 ; biogr. notice, 275.
Germany, provincial ministers of, 128, 160, *n.* 9, 181, 188 : *see* Wygmund.
— Minorites from, at Oxford, 66, 237, 256.
Ghent : *see* Henry of ; Simon of.
Gigas : *see* Hermann Gygas.
Gilbert of Grensted, of Oxford, 304.
Gilbert Peckham, Minorite, fellow of Merton, biogr. notice, 238.
Gilbert of Preston, 298.
Gilbert (Stratton), 162, *n.* 6.
Giles, friar, 105.
— (Egidius), Minorite, 142, *n.* 3.
Giuliortus de Limosano, wax-doctor, 43 ; biogr. notice, 239.
Giuvenazzo, bp. of, 167.
Glaseyere, Hugh, Minorite, 116, *n.* 7 ; biogr. notice, 292.
Gloucester, Abbat of, 136 ; Archdeacons of, 106, 218, 290 ; Minorites at, 44, *n.* 1, 69, 176, 182, 268.
— mentioned, 188, 296.
— duke of, 259.
— *see* Walter of.
Goddard, William, provincial, 247 ; biogr. notice, 262–4.
— Warden, London, 263.
Godham : *see* Adam Wodham.
Godstow, nunnery ; reformed by Peckham, 74 ; alms to Oxford friars, 100.
Golafre, Sir John, buried at Grey Friars, Oxford, 25.
— John, lord of Langley, benefactor, 25, 104.
— William, buried at Grey Friars, Oxford, 25.
Goldsmith, Margaret, bequest, 106.
Goldsmith, Walter, Minorite, 271.
Goldsmith, citizen of Oxford, 15, 20.
Gonsalvo, minister general, 164, *n.* 3, 220.
Gonsalvo of Portugal, Observant Minorite, 45, 66, *n.* 9, 88, *n.* 3 ; inception of, 51–2 ; biogr. notice, 264.
Good (Gude), Thomas : *see* Thomas Docking.
Goodewyn, Thomas, bequest, 109.
Goodfield (Goodfylde, Gudfeld), Walter, Warden at Oxford ; 36, *n.* 9, 52, 53, *n.* 3 ; leases land, 97, 317 ; mentioned, 271, *n.* 3, 274 ; biogr. notice, 131.
— graces to, 337–8.
Gorham, Nicholas, works of, 57, 166.
Gorry (or Grey), John, Minorite of Dorchester, agitates among labourers, 84, *n.* 1.
Gos, William, tailor, 94.

INDEX. 351

Grafton, Edmund, lector, 172.
Grammont, Order of, 185.
Grantham, Minorite Convent in the Oxford custody, 68.
Gras: *see* John le.
Gratian, *decretum* of, 57.
Graynoylles: *see* Francis de.
Greek, study of, 42, 59, 112, 113, 249, 283, 290.
Greenwich, Observant friary, 88, 290.
Gregory IX, pope, 8, 57, 69, 72, 179, 184; explanation of the Rule of St. Francis, 325, 327, 331, 334.
Gregory X, pope, 18.
Gregory XI, pope, 242.
Gregory, provincial minister of France, 126.
Gregory de Bosellis, Minorite, 183; biogr. notice, 186.
Gregory of Rimini, 238, *n*. 3.
Grene, John, 264.
Grensted: *see* Gilbert.
Grey de Retherfeld, John, gives land to Minorites, 20, 305–6.
Grey Friars: *see* Franciscan Order.
Grostete, Robert, bishop of Lincoln; his sayings, 6; influence at Oxford, 8; lectures to the Franciscans, 30, 32, 67, 69, 177, 180, 183, 189, 192; bequeaths books to the Franciscans, 57–9, 138; friendship with Adam Marsh, 48, 67, 127, 135, seq.; influence on Roger Bacon, 37, 139, 192; sermon in praise of poverty, 69; quarrel with Innocent IV, 59, *n*. 1; works ascribed to, 151, 223, 226: *see also* 4, 61, *n*. 7, 62, *n*. 1, 128, 140, 141, 179, 187, 188, 189.
Gryffith, Maurice, Dominican, 54, *n*. 6.
Guaro: *see* William of Ware.
Gudman, Ralph, Minorite, 276.
Guido: *see* Agnes.
Guildford, Dominicans at, 89, *n*. 4.
Gulac: *see* Nicholas de.
Gunter, James, has lease of part of the Grey Friars, 123.
— Richard and Joanna, have part of the Grey Friars' property, 122, 123.
Gunwardeby: *see* John of.
Gwent : *see* Went, John.

H.

H. M., 152, *n*. 1.
Hadham, 284.
Hadley, John, Minorite, 269.
— R., Observant, 269, *n*. 6.
Haldeswel : *see* Peter of Baldeswell.
Halegod, Andrew, citizen of Oxford, 295.
— Laurence, citizen of Oxford, 295.

Hales: *see* Alexander of.
— *see* Andrewes, Ric.
Halifax, Rob.: *see* Eliphat.
Hall, Anthony, bequest, 109.
Halvesnahen: *see* Hubert of.
Hampton, 293.
Hanworth, 292.
Hanyden: *see* Anneday.
Harecourt, Ric., bequest, 108.
Harlington, 292.
Harm', Simondez, 275.
Harmon, 275.
Harvey, John, warden at Oxford, 54, *n*. 3, 132, 317, 319; biogr. notice, 131.
Hasard, William, proctor, bequest, 107.
Hastings, John, E. of Pembroke, 264.
Hauréau, M., 149.
Haymo of Faversham, 7, *n*. 7; provincial of England, 14, 177, 181, *n*. 10, 182, 183; prefers manual labour to mendicancy, 14; general minister, 11, 127, 136.
Hearne, Thomas, 124, 174.
Hebrew, taught at Oxford, 59, and *n*. 2 ; at reformation, 112, 290.
Heddele, Hedele, Hedley: *see* William of Heddele.
Heddrington, *or* Herington, Ric., 163.
Hedyan, James, buried in Franciscan Church at Oxford, 26; bequest, 105.
Hekeshovre: *see* Adam of Bechesoueres.
Henley, 107.
Henry III, King of England, grants to friars at Oxford, 5, 13, 14, 16, 17, 18, 21, 22, 69, 70, 296–300, 307–8; Cambridge, 97, *n*. 5; Reading, 22; calls Mad Parliament at Oxford, 72; takes cross, 136; relations to Adam Marsh, 137–8; mentioned, 177, 191, 302; his queen, 137.
Henry IV, 70, 81, 87, 98, 247, 248, 249, *n*. 2.
Henry V, 98, *n*. 1.
Henry VI, 98–99; his council, 259.
Henry VII, 98, *n*. 1.
Henry VIII, grant to Oxford Minorites, 98, *n*. 1; royal supremacy, 114, 272, 273, 287, 289, 291, 293; divorce, 114–15, 269, 273, 280–1, 282; suppression of monasteries, 115, 290; treatment of the friars' property in Oxford, 120, 122; court preachers of, 271; appoints N. de Burgo reader at Cardinal College, 281, 282: *see also* 285, 292.
Henry of Apeltre, lector, 153, *n*. 1; biogr. notice, 156.
Henry of Ast, minister general, 254, *n*. 9.
Henry of Bath, 298.

352 INDEX.

Henry of Brisingham, lector, 143, *n*. 11, 151, *n*. 4; biogr. notice, 152.
Henry of Burford, Minorite, 11.
Henry of Ceruise, vicar of the provincial, 178.
Henry of Costesey (Cossey), biogr. notice, 234.
Henry Cruche, lector, 134, 169.
Henry de Edrope (Heythrop?), of Oxford, 304.
Henry of Ghent, 154, *n*. 7.
Henry, son of Henry, citizen of Oxford, 296.
Henry Lector, of Oxford, 152, 156.
Henry of Oyta, 173.
Henry of Reresby, 22; biogr. notice of, 180.
Henry Simeonis, his island in the Thames, 16, 17, 297.
Henry Standish: *see* Standish.
Henry Stretsham: *see* Stretsham.
Henry of Sutton, 162, *n*. 16; biogr. notice, 219.
Henry, son of Thomas, bailiff of Oxford, 296.
Hentham: *see* John of.
Herberd, Herbert, Herebert, William, lector, 169, *n*. 2; biogr. notice, 167-8.
Herbert of Denmade, 307.
Hereford, Grey Friars at, 254, 260; school, 34, *n*. 3, 261, 313-4; burials at, 168, 174, 254.
— bishop of: *see* Ralph Maidstone, Thomas of Cantilupe, Swinfeld (Ric.), 248.
— dean of, 313.
— Earl of, stays at Grey Friars, Exeter, 27, *n*. 9: *see* Bohun.
— *see* A. of.
— J. of: *see* Edes, John.
— Nicholas, sermon against the friars, 54, 84, 91, *n*. 8.
Herefordshire, 286.
Heresies, eastern, 8, 63, 179: *see* Knights Templars.
— Franciscan, 70, 82, 85-6, 166, 167, 257-9, 266-7: *see* William of Ockham.
— at Oxford, 70, 73, 82, 85, 86, 166.
— elsewhere, 251, 256, 263.
— *see* Reformation.
Hermann of Cologne, Minorite student at Oxford, 69, *n*. 10, 235; biogr. notice, 236.
— Gygas (*or* Gigas), 163, 237.
— of Saxony, 237.
Herne, church of, 285.
Hertepol: *see* Hugh of.
Hertford, 211, 213.
Hertfordshire, 277, *n*. 6, 283, 284.

Hertilpoll: *see* Hugh of Hertepol.
Herveius de Saham, Chancellor, 133.
Hevesham: *see* Hugh of Evesham.
Heythrop: *see* Richard of.
Hibernicus, &c.: *see* Ireland.
Hilton, John, biogr. notice, 243.
Hoger, abbat, 210.
Hokenorton (Hooknorton), 15, *n*. 2, 19, *n*. 2, 109, *n*. 2.
Holawnton (Wilts.), 106.
Holder, Robert, 94.
Holiday, Sir Stephen, 292.
Horley: *see* John of.
Hotham: *see* Nicholas of Ocham.
Hoveden *or* Howden: *see* Adam of, John of.
Howe, John, buys sites of Friaries at Oxford, 122, 123.
Hows, Will., 96, *n*. 2, 276.
Hoye, Thomas, vicar of Bampton, will of, 110.
Hoyta: *see* Henry of Oyta.
Hozon (Hotham?): *see* William of Hodum.
Hubert of Halvesnahen, biogr. notice, 243.
Hugh Balsham, 138.
— of Bampton, or Bath (Bathampton?), provincial, 157.
— of Cantilupe, 218.
— of Corbrug, secular master, 331, 334.
— of Evesham, 331, 333.
— of Hertepol, lector and provincial: proctor of Balliol Coll., 10; disputes at Oxford, 48, 49; presents twenty-two friars to the bishop for license to hear confessions at Oxford, 63, 129, 162, 163, 164, 165, 167, 219, 220, 222; employed as ambassador, 7, *n*. 10, 161; mentioned, 158, 160, 218; biographical notice of, 158-9.
— Karlelle, at the council of the earthquake, 84, 246.
— of Lyndun, biogr. notice, 186.
— of Manchester, Dominican, 161.
— of Mistretune, Dominican, 38.
— of Newcastle, 167, *n*. 3.
— of Nottingham, 57, 166.
— Willoughby (Wylluby), chancellor and Minorite, notice of, 235.
Humphrey de Bohun: *see* Bohun.
Hundertone, Master Gilbert, 56, *n*. 2.
Hungary, Minorite province, 181.
Hussites, 257, *n*. 3.

I.

Ilchester, R. Bacon born at, 191.
Ingeham: *see* Solomon of.
Ingewrthe: *see* Richard of.
Innocent IV, pope, 59, *n*. 1, 72, 77, 136, 137, 183, 184, 190.

INDEX.

Innocent VI, pope, 239, 312.
Inquisition, 160, 162, 165, 252.
Ipswich, Grey Friars at, 27, *n.* 6.
Ireland; Friars from, study at Oxford, 66; visitation of, 126; provincial ministers of, 178, 261, 267: *see* 142, *n.* 5, 243, *n.* 2, 266.
— *see* Carrewe (David); Cusack (Isaac); Hubert of Halvesnahen; John Duns Scotus (?); Lorcan, Ric.; Malachy of Ireland; Maurice de Portu; Menelaus McCormic; Stephen of Ireland; Thomas of Ireland; Whythead, John.
Irishe, Edmund, bailiff of Oxford, 93.
Isabella, wife of Frederick II, 6, 307.
— wife of Edward II, 162, 237.
Italy, 281, 282; friars from, at Oxford, 66: *see* Agnellus; Albert of Pisa; Francis of S. Simone; Fey (Jacob); John de Castro; Laurentius Gul. de Savona; Nicholas de Burgo; Peter of Gaieta; Philip of Castello.

J.

J., friar Minor, at Council of Lyons, 128, *n.* 5.
'Jack Upland,' Lollard writer, 83.
James de Porta, Minorite, 173.
James, Rob., bequest, 105.
Jerome (St.), works of, in Franciscan library, Oxford, 58.
Jerome of Ascoli (Nicholas IV), general minister, 156, *n.* 1; holds chapter at Paris, 194.
Jerome of St. Mark, notice of, 239.
Jewell, John, 290.
Jews, protected by Adam Marsh, 137: *see also* 9, 167, *n.* 9, 169, 190.
Joanna, princess of Wales, 245.
Joanna, wife of Walter of Wycombe, 20.
John XXI, pope, 155, *n.* 4.
John XXII, pope, bulls in favour of the Dominicans at Oxford, 40; controversy with the Franciscans, 77, 92, *n.* 1, 158, 166, 224–5, 229 *seq.*, 239, 266.
John XXIII, pope, 249, 255.
John, friar, Dr. of Oxford, advocates disendowment, 82.
John, Minorite, gives away a book, 56, *n.* 6.
John, Roger Bacon's pupil, 33, *n.* 4; biogr. notice, 211.
John of Basingstoke, 206.
— of Bekinkham, Minorite, 217, 218, 309.
— of Berwick, lector, biogr. notice of, 159.

John of Beverley, Minorite, 141, *n.* 9; biogr. notice, 186.
— Canon: *see* Canon.
— de Castro (Bologna), Minorite, 45, *n.* 9, 54, *n.* 3, 66, *n.* 7; biogr. notice, 276.
— de Clara, 309; biogr. notice, 218.
— of Cobeham, 298.
— of Codyngton, warden, biographical notice, 129.
— of Coleshull, citizen of Oxford, 304.
— of Couton, benefactor of the friars 92, 310.
— de Crombe, lector, biogr. notice, 166.
— Duns Scotus, presented for license to hear confessions, 64; lectures abroad, 68; mentioned, 112, 116, *n.* 2, 130, *n.* 2, 167, 213, 223, 224, 241, *n.* 4, 262, 268, 270, 284; biographical notice of, 219–222.
— of Dunstable, joins Oxford Franciscans; notice of, 180.
— of Ew, of Oxford, 304.
— Feckyngtone: *see* Feckyngtone (John).
— Gallensis of Volterra, 150.
— of Gaunt: *see* Gaunt.
— le Gras, secular master, expounds Franciscan Rule, 331—334.
— of Gunwardeby, of Oxford, 304.
— of Heutham, 'syndicus,' 92, 235, 310.
— of Hereford: *see* Edes, John.
— of Horley, lector, 163.
— of Hoveden or Howden, lector, 172.
— (of Kent), papal nuncio, 141, *n.* 2.
— of Kethene, Minorite, 183.
— of Lathbury, Minorite, 236; biogr. notice, 235 (*cf.* 56, *n.* 2).
— Lector of Erfurt, 254, *n.* 6.
— Lector of Freiburg, 144, *n.* 150.
— of London, 206, 211.
— London, 237.
— London, warden of New College: *see* London.
— of Maidstone, archdeacon of Bedford, 331.
— Mardisle: *see* Mardisle.
— Marshall, 308.
— of Meslay, visitor of the Oxford Dominicans, 334.
— Nottingham, Minorite, 287.
— of Nottingham, Minorite, witnesses a will, 101, 239.
— — treasurer of York, 165.
— of Okehampton, warden, 92, 310; biogr. notice, 129.
— of Oxford, Minorite, 216.
— Parens, minister general, 178.
— of Parma, minister general, praises the English province, 11, *n.* 3; holds chapter at Oxford, 69, 70, 183; friend

of Adam Marsh, 137: *see also*, 187, 193, *n.* 4.
John Peckham (Pecham, &c.), royal commissioner, 9; at Oxford, Paris, and Rome, 67; condemns errors at Oxford, 73; relations to Thomas Aquinas and Dominicans, 73, *seq.*; favours Franciscans, 74, sends John Wallensis as ambassador, 144; works by, 150, 215; influenced by Roger Bacon, 195, *n.* 4; mentioned, 153, 156, 157, 211; biographical notice, 154.
— of Persole, Pershore, lector, 48, 49, 158, *n.* 6; biogr. notice, 159.
— le Peyntour, auditor, 94, 311.
— Picard, 172.
— of Preston, lector, 169.
— of Ratforde, lector, 169.
— of Reading, abbat of Osney, joins Franciscans, 3; mentioned, 187; biographical notice, 180.
— of Reading, lector, 168.
— of Reading, minister of Saxony, 181.
— de Ridevaus, lector, 150, 236; biogr. notice of, 170-1.
— of Rodyngton or Rudinton, lector and provincial, 174; notice of, 171.
— de Rupellis, Minorite, 67.
— de Rupescissa, Minorite, 208, *n.* 1.
— of St. Frideswide, mayor, 103, *n.* 7.
— of St. John, bequest, 102.
— of Sanford, Abp. Dublin, 129, *n.* 1.
— of Stamford, custodian of Oxford, 187; Provincial, 68, 138; at Lyons, 127; biographical notice, 128.
— de Stanle, Minorite, 224, 310.
— of Stapleton, biogr. notice, 219.
— of Tewkesbury, Minorite, gift to library, 60, 251.
— of Thornton, lector, 168.
— Tynmouth : *see* Tinmouth, John.
— Tyssyngton : *see* Tyssyngton.
— Wallensis, lector, 37, *n.* 1, 170; at Paris, 68; biogr. notice, 143; works, 144-151.
— Wallensis, Minorite, 311, *n.* 1.
— of Waltham, bishop of Salisbury, bequest, 104.
— of Ware, 212 ; *cf.* 213, *n.* 6.
— of Westburg, Minorite, 219.
— of Westover, and Isolda, his wife, 310, *n.* 2.
— of Winchelsea, Minorite, notice of, 223 ; *cf.* 256.
— of Wylton, lector, biogr. notice, 166.
— — monk, 166, *n.* 11.
— de Wyntun, secular master, 331, 335.
— of Zortone : *see* John of Thornton.
Johnson, Elizabeth, bequest, 110.

Jollan of Nevill, 298.
Jordan of Saxony, Master of Friars Preachers, 71, *n.* 4.
Jordan, William, Dominican, 242.
Jornton : *see* John of Thornton.
Joseph, John, Minorite, 113, *n.* 7 ; biographical notice, 288.
Julian Caesarinus, cardinal, 249.
Julius II, pope, 267.

K.

Karlelle : *see* Hugo.
Katharine of Aragon, 114, 115, 273, 282: *see* Henry VIII.
Kell, Ambrose, Minorite, admitted to University library, 62, *n.* 3 ; 270.
Kellawe, Ric. bp. of Durham, 98.
Kemerdyn, Phil., 101, *n.* 3.
Keneyshame, Robert, bedell, his will, 26.
Kent, 168; sheriff of, 99, 129, 308.
— nun of, 289, 290, *n.* 5.
— persecution in, 293.
Kethene : *see* John of.
Kidderminster, Ric., abbat of Winchcombe, 49, *n.* 4, 269, 272.
Kilwardby, Rob., Abp. of Canterbury, 73, 160; provincial of the Dominicans, 326, 327, 328, 329, 333, 334; upholds private judgment, 326.
Kingesthorpe, Ric.: *see* Ric. of Ingewrthe.
Kingsbury : *see* Thomas of Kyngesbery.
Kirkby, 260, *n.* 7.
Kirkham, Thomas, Minorite, 113, *n.* 7; opponent of King's divorce, 114; grace to, 338 ; biogr. notice, 282.
Knights Hospitallers, house in Oxford, 13.
Knights Templars, 160, 162, 165.
Knolle : *see* Walter de.
Knottis, Thomas, biogr. notice, 284.
Knowlys, Rob., Minorite, 284.
Knox, James, of Bois-le-Duc, 245.
Kydmersford: *see* Adam.
Kydmynster, Ric.: *see* Kidderminster.
Kynton, John, 97, *n.* 2, 107, 112, *n.* 1, 316; opposes reformation, 113 ; attitude to divorce, 115; biographical notice, 268.
Kyritz, 257.
Kyrswell : *see* Creswell, Ralph.

L.

Lakeor: *see* Adam de.
Lamarensis : *see* William de Mara.
Lambeth Palace, MS. from Franciscan library, Oxford, 59.
— burial at, 293.
Lambourn (Berks) 107, (Essex) 290.

INDEX. 355

Lambourn, Reginald, fellow of Merton Coll., Minorite, biogr. notice, 237.
— Robert (*or* John), Minorite, biogr. notice of, 237.
— Simon, of Merton Coll., 237, *n.* 9.
Lancashire, 189, 271.
Lancaster : *see* Gaunt, John of.
Landen : *see* Walter de.
'Lanercost Chronicle,' written by an Oxford Minorite, 1, *n.* 1, 27, 30, 167.
Langberg, of Merton Coll., 137, *n.* 9.
Langham, Simon, Abp. of Canterbury, 85.
Langley (Regis), Dominicans at, 22, 53, *n.* 9.
— *see* Golafre, John.
Laodicea, bp. of, 188.
Laon : *see* Raymund of.
Lathbury : *see* John of.
Latimer, Hugh, bp. of Worcester, 111.
Laurence Briton (Wallensis), lector, 134, 171.
— of Cornwall, Minorite, 212.
— of Sutthon, *socius* of Adam Marsh, 34, 140, *n.* 5 ; biogr. notice, 186.
Laurentius Gulielmi de Traversagnis de Saona, biographical notice of, 265.
Layton, sent to reform the University, 116.
Lector : *see* John.
Ledbury, John, buys a book, 56, *n.* 2 (*cf.* John Lathbury).
Legnaco : *see* Ægidius de.
Leicester, four Orders at, 103.
— Dominicans at, 102.
— Minorite convent, in the Oxford custody, 68 ; lectures at, 186, 275 ; rebel friars at, 87 ; burials at, 166, 180.
— Earl of : *see* Montfort, Simon de.
— Grostete, archdeacon of, 179, *n.* 4.
— *see* Robert of.
Leke (Leech), Ric., provincial, 259.
Leke, Ric., brewer, buried at Grey Friars, Oxford, 26 ; lease of land to, 97, 131, 274, 316–8 ; bequests, 108, 318 ; servant of John Kynton, 269, *n.* 4, 316.
Leland, John, visits Franciscan library, 62 ; on R. Bacon's works, 195 ; mentioned, 149, 150, 199.
Lemster : *see* William of Leominster.
Leo X, pope, 110.
Letheringfont, Minorite, Cambridge, 49, *n.* 9.
Letitia, wife of Simon, son of Benedict, 15, 298–9.
Lewes, battle, 72 ; priory, 154.
Lichfield, Minorites of, 59, *n.* 3 ; burials at, 169, 259.
— bp. of : *see* Roger Wesham.

Lichfield, diocese, 260, 289.
Limoges : *see* Peter of.
Limosano : *see* Giuliortus de.
Lincoln, burials at, 139, 160.
— bishops of : *see* Grostete, Richard of Gravesend, Sutton (Oliver), Dalderby.
— William of Alnwick, Suffragan of, 271.
— archdeacon of, 9 ; diocese of, 257, 289.
— *see* Adam of.
— John, citizen of London, 272.
Lincolnshire, 189, 271.
Lisbon, University, 242.
Llandaff, bp. of, 255.
Lock, Margery, 93.
Lockylsey : *see* Ralph of.
Lodore : *see* Richard le.
Lollards, 83, 87, 248 : *see* Wiclif.
Lombard, Peter : *see Sentences.*
Lombardy, an Oxford Minorite teaches in, 67.
London : Austin Friars, 263.
— Black Friars, council of the Earthquake at, 84, 246 ; prior of, 320, *n.* 1.
— Grey Friars : foundation, 2, 176, 178.
— — house and convent, 28, 89, *n.* 2, 128, 132, 180, 189, 239, 258, 263, 266, 274, 280, 311 ; numbers, 44, *n.* 1.
— — political meeting at, 282, *n.* 11.
— — privileges to inmates, 237, 239, 247, 312–3.
— — property of a London Minorite, 78, 311.
— — church, 25.
— — — burials in, 126, 129, 130, 131, 155, 162, 240, 241, 247, 251, 252, 256, 263, 264, 265, 268, 269, 273, 275, 277.
— — Chapters at, 69, and *n*, 4, 235.
— — custody, 175.
— — schools, 35, *n.* 3, 130, 172, 181, 186, 188, 246, 277, 306, 311.
— — — exhibition for a London Minorite, 53, *n.* 7.
— — library, 144, *n.* 5, 150, 173, 233, 234.
— — dissolution, 288.
— — Wardens, 78, *n.* 3, 83, 89, *n.* 2, 112, 127, 131, 136, *n.* 4, 212, 258, 263, 265, 269, 272, 276.
— — Vice-warden, 129.
— bishops of, 10, 258, 260 281, *n.* 3, 284, *n.* 1 ; diocese, 261.
— St. Paul's, convocation at, 257 ; prebendary of, 284 ; Cardmaker reader in, 291.
— — Cross, sermons, 46, *n.* 9, 53, 113,

356 INDEX.

130, 258, 262, 263, 278, 279, 284, 285, 287, 289, 292.
London, Parishes; St. Andrew Undershaft, 287; St. Bride's, Fleet Street, 291; St. George's, Botolph Lane, 293, n. 3; St. Leonard's Shoreditch, 290; St. Martin's in the Fields, 286; St. Martin's Outwich, 283; St. Mary at Axe, 287; St. Mary at Bowe, 289; St. Mary Magdalen, Old Fish Street, 293, n. 7; St. Owen's, 128; St. Vedast's, 105.
— Bridge, head of a Franciscan rebel on, 87.
— Smithfield, burnings at, 291.
— Compter (prison), 291.
— Fleet (prison), 291.
— College of Physicians, 119–120.
— Parliament at, A. Marsh called to, 137; 32, n. 3.
— foreign traders in, 272.
— mentioned, 99, 103, 104, 106, 281.
— see John of; Thomas of.
London, Dr. John, Warden of New College, 110, n. 1, 166, n. 8; Visits the Oxford friaries, 117–121, 132; and other friaries, 133.
Longespee, Ela, countess of Warwick, 300, n. 1.
Loo, J., 96, n. 1.
Lorcan, Richard, Irish Minorite at Oxford, 101, 276.
Louis IX (St.), King of France, 138, n. 3, 140.
Louis of Bavaria, emperor, 225, 231, 232.
Lovell, William Lord, buried in Grey Friars Church, Oxford, 26, 106.
Ludford, Simon, Minorite, becomes apothecary and physician, 119, 294.
Ludgershall, 271.
Lull, Lully, Raymund, 59, n. 2, 255.
Lundia, abp. of, 140, n. 6.
Lusetanus: see Peter.
Luther, Martin, 113, 269, 281, 286.
Lymynster: see Richard.
Lynn, Grey Friars, numbers, 44, n. 1, 283; burial at, 129; mentioned, 271.
— — Observant at, 277.
Lyons, council of, 15, 18, 67, 127, 128, 137, 140.
— general chapter at, 159, 161, 218.
— Franciscan school at, 66, n. 10.
Lyra: see Nicholas de.

M.

McCarmacan, or McCormic: see Menelaus.
Madele: see Walter of.
Magalona (Montpellier), bp. of, 144, n. 8.

Magdeburg, abp. of, 257
Mahomet, works on, 148.
Maidstone: see John of; Ralph of; Thomas of Maydenstan.
Major, John, 172, n. 11.
Malachias of Ireland, Minorite, student at Oxford, 66, n. 5; 223.
Maldon, John, provost of Oriel, bequest, 104.
Malevile, Richard, lector, 175.
Mallaert, John, Minorite, 70, 253.
Malmesbury, Henry, bequest, 103.
— see Thomas of.
Manchester: see Hugh of.
Manners: see Peter of.
Mansourah, battle of, 138, n. 3, 140.
Mantes, 127.
Mara, forest of, 215, n. 1.
— see William de Mara.
Marbres, John, 224, n. 1.
Mardisle (Mardeslay), John, provincial, argues against papal tribute, 81, n. 7, biogr. notice, 242.
Maricourt (Maharncuria): see Peter de.
Marseilles, general chapter, 235.
Marsh (de Marisco): see Adam; Richard; Robert.
Marshall, Earl, 7, 177.
Marshall, Hugh, his tenement in Oxford, 16, 298.
— John, 308.
Marsilius of Padua, 77, 114, n. 4, 224, 234.
Marston: see Roger.
Martin IV, pope, 92, n. 1, 111, n. 6.
— V, pope, constitutions for Friars Minors, 53, n. 8, 65, n. 6, 92, n. 1, 255.
— king of Aragon, 255.
— Warden at Oxford, mentioned, 186, 189; biogr. notice, 129.
— the old, Minorite, 129.
— of Alnwick, lector, biogr. notice, 163.
— de Barton, Minorite, 129.
— de Sta. Cruce, bequests, 102, 143.
Martinus Polonus, 164.
Martoke, John, fellow of Merton, bequest, 106.
Mary, the Virgin, works on, &c., 49, 67, n. 2, 212, 214, 242, 250, 254; cf. 178-9.
Mary, queen, 286, 287, 288, 289, 290, 291, 292, 293.
Maryner, William, citizen of London, 53, n. 7.
(Matthew), provincial of Dominicans, signs Charter for University, 8; ambassador, 137, 307.
Matthew, Garret, 96, n. 1.
Matthew Döring: see Döring.

INDEX. 357

Maurice de Portu, Minorite at Oxford, 66, *n.* 5; biogr. notice, 267.
Mawket, Giles, carpenter in Oxford, 94.
Maynelyn: *see* Tinmouth, John.
Mayronis: *see* Francis de Mayronibus.
Mediavilla: *see* Richard Middleton.
Melitona, Middleton, Milton: *see* William of Middleton.
Melton: *see* William de.
Mendicant Orders, 78, 79, 80–85.
— bequest to, 218, *n.* 4.
— pensions at the Dissolution, 119, 130.
— provincials of, 80.
— *see* Oxford, Mendicant Orders at; Richard Fitzralph, Wiclif.
Menelaus MacCormic, or MacCarmacan, biogr. notice, 267.
Menyl: *see* William de.
Mepham, Ric., archdeacon of Oxford, grants land to the Minorites, 15, 17, 21.
Merc: *see* Eustace of.
Mercator's Atlas, 245.
Mercer: *see* Benedict le.
Mercer: *see* Robert le.
Merlawe: *see* Roger de.
Merschton: *see* Roger Marston.
Mertherderwa, Reginald, bequest, 105, 261, *n.* 8.
Merton: *see* Walter de.
Merton College: *see* Oxford.
Meslay: *see* John of.
Metz, general chapter, 183, 186: *see* Albert of.
Michael de Cesena, general minister, 168, 225, 229, 231.
Middlesex, 122, 292.
Middleton, John: *see* John de Wylton; Richard; William of Middleton.
Midelton, abbey of, 84, *n.* 1.
Midford, 292.
Milan, general chapter, 66, *n.* 6, 157; Franciscan schools, 267.
— abp. of, 249.
Miller: *see* Philip, and Richard.
Milo, draper of Oxford, 296.
Milton (near Oxford), 103.
Mincy, William, Minorite at Oxford, 219.
Minorites: *see* Franciscan Order.
Mirandola, J. Pico de, 159, 234.
Missionaries, friars as, 7, 128, 139, *n.* 8, 140, 178, 179, 183, 244.
Mistretune: *see* Hugh of.
Mogynton: *see* Robert de.
Monks, 78, 114, 119; attacks on, 81, 253: *see* Benedictines, Cistercians, Oxford.
Montfort, Amaury de, bequests, 102, 103.

Montfort, Eleanor de, 137, 186.
— Simon de, Earl of Leicester, friend of Adam Marsh and Grostete, 32, 137; honoured by the Franciscans, 32-3, 72, 141, 212; letter to, 168; Gregory of Bosellis with, 186.
Morgan, Oxford Dominican, 267.
Morleyse, Walter, bequest, 105.
Morton, Walter, grants land to Minorites, 20.
Morton, Sir William, 16, *n.* 3, 124; Anne his wife, 124.
Moryn, Walter, 101.
Morys, John, 93.
Moses, Rabbi, works, 292.
Muliner: *see* Miller.
Multifernana (Meath diocese), 213.
Multon, Ralph de, scholar, 187.
Munich, 225.
Musca: *see* John de Ridevaus.
Mymekan, Roger, of Oxford, 304.

N.

N. de Ewelme, Chancellor, takes part in controversy between Dominicans and Franciscans, 77, 329, 330, 331, 334, 335.
Naples, University, William of Alnwick teaches at, 167; Peter of Gaieta, D.D. of, 235.
Narbonne, 144, *n.* 8; general chapter at, 194, *n.* 1.
Netter, Thomas, of Walden, Carmelite, 58; pupil of W. Woodford, 247.
Nevill: *see* Jollan of.
Newark, Observant Friars of, 286, 289.
Newcastle, Grey Friars, numbers, 44, *n.* 1; school, 35, *n.* 3; burial at, 163; dissolution, 292: *see* Hugh of.
Newman, Rob., Minorite, reformer, 113, *n.* 7, 119; has a living, 119; biogr. notice, 293.
Newmarket: *see* Robert of.
Newport: *see* William of.
Nicholas III, pope, 77, *n.* 1, 155, 215.
— IV, pope: *see* Jerome of Ascoli.
— of Anivers, 66, *n.* 6; biogr. notice, 187.
— de Burgo, lectures at Oxford, 36, *n.* 9, 53, *n.* 2, 66, *n.* 7; his composition remitted, 51: *see* 97, *n.* 1; humanist, 113; supports royal divorce, 115; biogr. notice, 280.
— of Fakenham, commissioner to depose provincial, 70; biogr. notice, 252.
— de Gulac, biogr. notice, 212.
— Hereford: *see* Hereford.

Nicholas, of Lynn, Carmelite, 245.
— de Lyra, Minorite, 32, *n.* 4, 257.
— of Ocham, lector, mentioned, 229; biogr. notice, 158.
— de Schomberg, *or* Scombergt, German Dominican, 281, *n.* 3.
— Specialis, Minorite historian, 158, 233.
— de Tyngewick, 10, 168.
— of Weston, citizen of Oxford, bequest, 102.
Norfolk, 99, 125, 130, 151, 169, 178, 180, 189, 234, 252, 315 : *see* Adam of.
Normanville: *see* Eustace of.
North Pole, voyage of an Oxford Franciscan to, 245.
Northampton, Grey Friars, foundation, 126, 178; in the Oxford custody, 68; school, 64, *n.* 5; a friar of, 56, *n.* 2: *see also* 180; burials at, 129, *n.* 6, 153, 236, 237.
— archdeacon of, 4.
Northamptonshire, 156, *n.* 2, 238.
Northumberland, 153, 292.
Norton, Agnes, buried in the Franciscan Church, Oxford, 26; bequest, 105.
Norwich, Grey Friars at, numbers, 44, *n.* 1; school, 64, *n.* 5, 65, 139, *n.* 8, 140, 172, 249: *see also* 111, 151, 153, 158, 170, 241, 243, 256.
— library, MSS. in, 172, 173.
— bp. of, 31, *n.* 1, 167, *n.* 1.
— synod, 256.
Notly, John, Minorite, 288.
Nottingham, Grey friars at, in the Oxford custody, 68, 187, 250: *see* Augustine of; Hugh of; John of; Robert of; William of (2).
— county, 286.
Nottynge : *see* John Nottingham.
Noyf, Roger, 12, *n.* 2.
Nutone, John, friar, lectures at Oxford, 43.
Nycopia : *see* Peter Pauli de.

O.

Observant Friars : *see* under Franciscan Order.
Ocham : *see* Nicholas of; William of Ockham.
Ochampton : *see* John of.
Ockham : *see* William of.
Ocle or Okele, John, bequest, 104, 251.
Oen or Owen, Robert, citizen of Oxford, 296.
Oen or Owen, Robert, son of Robert, 13, 20, *n.* 5, 296.

O'Fihely : *see* Maurice de Portu.
Oliver de Encourt, Dominican, 9, 155.
Olivi : *see* Peter John Olivi.
Olliff, John, Minorite, 119, 294.
O'Really, William, provincial of Ireland, 261.
Oterborne, Thomas, lector, biogr. notice of, 174.
Ottaviano Scotto, printer at Venice, 267, *n.* 5.
Otto Brunsfelsius, 287.
Ottobon, legate, 156, 212.
OXFORD: ENDOWED ORDERS.
 Monks, expenses at inception, 51, 52; inception of a monk, 237.
— numbers of students (Benedictine and Cistercian), 54.
 Dissolution, 116, *n.* 4, 119: *see* Benedictines, and Monks.
 Bec, fee of the abbat of: *see* Bec.
 Osney Abbey (Austin Canons), 15, *n.* 2, 19, *n.* 2, 100, 107, 109, *n.* 5, 300, *n.* 1: *see* John of Reading.
 Rewley Abbey (Cistercians), 107.
 St. Frideswide's (Austin Canons), 15, *n.* 2, 46, *n.* 9, 74, 84, 85, 107: *see* John of St. Frideswide.
 MENDICANT ORDERS.
 alms and bequests, 54, 100, 103–110, 318.
 feasts and expenses at inception, 50, 51, 246.
 necessary regency, 52.
 numbers of students, 54.
 excluded from congregation, 52, 261, 336.
 — library, 62.
 attacks on and unpopularity of, 40, 79, 84, 90, *n.* 6.
 support Abp. Arundel, 85.
 wax-doctors, 43, 239, 252.
 visitation and suppression, 116, 117, 124.
 Austin Friars, 75, 103, 121, 160; 258, *n.* 7: *see* Oxford, Mendicant Orders.
 Carmelites, 55, *n.* 1, 75, 84, 94, *n.* 10, 103, 109, 111, 121, 252: *see* Oxford, Mendicant Orders.
 Dominicans, receive the Minorites, 2; controversies with them, 59, *n.* 9, 71–8, 129, 151, 153, 155, 156, 158, 212, 320–335; *cf.* 80, *n.* 2.
 — provincial prior signs charter for the University, 8.
 — controversy with the University, 39–41, 65, *n.* 3, 165.
 — academical exercises at the Black Friars, 46, 49.

INDEX. 359

OXFORD :—MENDICANT ORDERS.
Dominicans, schools and scholars, 37, notes 4, 5, 6; 43, *n.* 7, 267.
— numbers, 54.
— prior of the, 9, 73, *n.* 3.
— Mad Parliament at, 72; Edward (I) stays at, *ibid.*
— feasts at the burial of Piers Gaveston, 27, *n.* 9.
— accused of stirring up rebellion, 84.
— burial at, 104.
— alms, 6, 23, *n.* 1, 55, *n.* 3, 100, 307, 308.
— bequests to, 102, 103, 104, 105, 106, 107, 108, 109, 110; 261, *n.* 8.
— (Preachers' Bridge, 17, *n.* 4.)
— Dissolution, 118; lease of the site, 121-124: *see* Oxford, Mendicant Orders.
Franciscans: *see* Table of Contents; Franciscan Order.
Custody, 68, 171-2, 180, 238.
Friary, foundation of, 2-3, 178.
— houses, 3, 12, 21-8, 176-7, 295, *seq.*, 318, 320.
— — Vice-chancellor's court at, 95-6, 132.
— Church, 3, 6, 21-6, 39, 46, 49, 104, 105, 106, 117, 123, 124, 177, 180, 182, 251, 273, 299, 318.
— — sermons in, 46, 181, 275, 290.
— — used as a sanctuary, 308.
— — gild in, 24, 110.
— Churchyard, 17, 19, 27, 106, 122, 123, 300, 302.
— Property, held for the friars by the city, 3, 13, 295; by the King, 17, 299; *cf.* 76-7, 322.
— Boteham, 122, 123.
— Paradise : *see* Oxford City.
— garden leased to Richard Leke : *see* Leke.
— Library, Part I, Ch. IV; 195, *n.* 4, 251, 273, 283.
— Schools, Part I, Ch. III; 21, 66, 67, *n.* 2, 177, 186, 189, 246, 251, 278, 284, 329.
— — payments at inceptions, 41, 50-2, 132, 258, 260, 264, 265, 267, 269, 270, 274, 275, 276, 277, 278, 279, 280, 282, 283, 284, 336-8.
— — gratuitous lecturing, 36, 53, 131, 280, 338.
— — foreign friars at, 18, 66, 309, 312 : *see* under names of the various countries.
— — Oxford Franciscans at other Universities, 66-7, 276 : *see* Bologna, Cambridge, Naples, Padua, Paris, Rome, Toulouse.

Friary, Relations to Dominicans : *see* Oxford, Dominicans.
— Number of friars, 43-4, 54.
— Royal grant of 50 marcs, 97-9, 129, 130, 217, 218, 224, 267, *n.* 2, 308, 309, 315.
— wardens, Part II, Ch. I; vice-warden : *see* Bacheler (J.).
— warden at the capture of Tripoli, 8.
— chronicles by Oxford Franciscans : *see* Lanercost, Thomas of Eccleston; *cf.* Bassett (J.), Martin of Alnwick, Oterborne (T.), Somer (J.).
— voyage of an Oxford Franciscan to the North Pole, 245.
— Dissolution, Part I, Ch. VIII; 132, 292, 293, 294.
Sack, Friars of the (or of the Penance of Jesus Christ), settle in Oxford, 17, 300; place bought from Walter Goldsmith, 20.
— property comes into the hands of the Franciscans, 18, 19, 20, 44, *n.* 1, 301-3.
OXFORD CITY :
state of, at time of the Dissolution, 120-1.
citizens subscribe to buy a house for the Grey Friars, 13, 295-6.
the poor of Oxford, 5-6, 307.
Pestilence, 53, 279, 338.
Robbers in the neighbourhood of, 4, 188, 246.
Document dated at, 512.
Government and officers.
Burgesses, 21.
Mayors, 13, 17, 20, *n.* 5, 60, 103, 117, 121, 170, 295, 296, 297, 299, 310.
Aldermen, 106, 110, *n.* 1, 117, 121, 123.
Bailiffs, 5, 69, *n.* 4, 93, 296, 297, 307, 310.
jurisdiction over the friars, 60, 92, 310.
Hustings Court, 92, 101, 310.
sworn inquisitions, 15, *n.* 1, 19, 20, 28, *n.* 2, 303-5.
firma burgi, 5, 69, *n.* 4, 121, 307.
Local Divisions.
Churches and Parishes—
All Saints, 95, 110.
Carfax, proclamation at, 86; records, 124, *n.* 6.
Holywell, 109.
St. Aldate, 14, *n.* 5.
St. Budoc (Bodhoc), 14, 16, 17, 19, 297, 300, 301, 302.
St. Ebbe, parish, 2, 12, 13, 14, 15, 28, 94, 95, 124, 178, 295, 297, 299; alms to friars, 100; church, 23, 26,

OXFORD: CITY—*Churches and Parishes*.
  n. 2, 318; rector, charge of adultery against, 75, *n.* 2; tenement in, 105.
  St. Giles, 124, *n.* 6.
  St. Mary Magdalen, 103, *n.* 6, 107.
  St. Mary the Virgin: *see under* Oxford, University.
  St. Michael, 13, 296.
  St. Peter le Bailey, 74, 124, *n.* 6.
  St. Peter in the East, sermon at, 280, 288.
Streets, &c.—
  Beef Lane, 28.
  Bridge Street, 27.
  Charles Street, 17, *n.* 4, 28.
  Church Place, 23, 28.
  Church Street, *or* Freren Street, 13, 28.
  Grandpont (Folly Bridge), 104.
  Horsemonger Street, 298.
  Littlegate Street, 14, 16, 17, *n.* 4, 28.
  Norfolk Street, 16, *n.* 3.
  Paradise garden, place, and square, 15, *n.* 2, 16, *n.* 3, 19, 23, 122, 123, 124.
  Penson's Gardens, 27.
  Preachers' Bridge, 17, *n.* 4.
  School Street, 37.
  Wheeler's Garden, 23.
  Cherwell, 28.
  Thames, 28; island in the, 16–17, 297.
  Trill Mill Stream, 16, 19, 22, 27, 123, 297, 301.
Buildings and Institutions—
  Bear inn, 95, 285.
  Fleur de Lys, 96.
  Bocardo, 94, 95, 115.
  Castle, 14, 297, 299.
  Eastgate, 12, *n.* 2.
  Hospital of St. John, 12, *n.* 2.
  Littlegate: *see* Watergate.
  Northgate, 16, 296, 298.
  Southgate, 14, *n.* 5, 104.
  Watergate (*or* Littlegate), 14, 17, *n.* 4, 23, 297, 299.
  Westgate, 16, 19, 23, 297, 299.
  Wall, 13, 14, 16, 20, 22, 23, 296, 297, 299, 304.
  — mural mansion, 13, 296.
  Fair at Austin Friars, 121.
  Gild of St. Mary in the Grey Friars Church, 110; *cf.* 24.
  Hospitallers (St. John of Jerusalem), house belonging to, 13, 296.
  — *see* Jews.

OXFORD: UNIVERSITY.
  University: visited by Abp. Arundel, 85, 112: reformed by Cromwell, 116.
  Government and Officers.
  Charter of Hen. III to, 8.
  Chancellor, delegate of the bp. of Lincoln, 8, *n.* 5, 217; election of, 175.
  — court and jurisdiction, 8, 9, 93–7, 101, 130, 155, 268, 274, 276, 286, 310.
  — proclamation against French students, 86.
  — conferment of degrees, 31, *n.* 10, 38, 39, 40, 41, 45, 46, 48, 49, 165, *n.* 7, 253, 265, 274, *cf.* 280, 330–1.
  — relation to the friars, 75, 77.
  — attitude to Wiclif, 84, 85, 251.
  — executor of a will, 102, *n.* 1.
  — seal of, 260.
  — *see* Berton, William; Colman, Robert, Minorite; Eustace of Normaneville, Minorite; Gascoigne, Thomas; Hugh of Willoughby, Minorite; N. de Ewelme; Radulph of Sempringham; Richard Fitzralph; Symon of Ghent.
  Vice-Chancellor, or Commissary, 95, 110, 131, 132, 265, 268, 282, 316–7, 318–9, 338: *see* Chancellor, court.
  Proctors, 38, 40, 41, 45, 84, 107, 130, *n.* 9, 165, *n.* 7, 258, *n.* 7, 260, 267, 336.
  Congregation, 38, 40, 47, 48, 51, 82, 141, 256, 260, 265, 270.
  — exclusion of friars from, 52: *see* Oxford, Mendicant Orders.
  Bedells, 26, 50, 53, 278, 279, 330.
  Faculties; study of Arts before Theology, 37–42, 45, 50, 141, 192, 265.
  Miscellaneous.
  Poem *De laude Univ. Oxon*, 253.
  Lutheran doctrines condemned, 269.
  Secular students; numbers according to Ric. Fitzralph, 79–80; bequests to, 109, 273; gifts to, 280, 338; expenses at inception, 51; murder of a scholar, 17, 297; assault on a scholar, 269, *n.* 4.
  Northerners and Irish students, 142, *n.* 5.
  Local Divisions.—
Colleges and Halls—
  All Souls.
  Balliol, connexion of Franciscans with, 9, 158, 168, 216–217, 260.
  — library, 61, *n.* 7: *see also*, 79, 106.
  Beef Hall, 130.
  Brasenose College and Hall, 107, 191, *n.* 4.

OXFORD: UNIVERSITY—*Colleges and Halls—*
Broadgates Hall, 95, 288.
Christ Church, or Cardinal College, 281.
Corpus Christi, 109.
Durham, 61. *n.* 7; alms to friars, 100; burial at, 269.
Eagle Hall, 105.
Exeter College, 108.
Gloucester : *see* Oxford, Monks.
Lincoln, 59, 61, *n.* 7, 107.
Magdalen, 107, 109, 266, 269, 290; N. de Burgo lectures at, 282.
Merton, founder, 9, 102; warden, 100-1; fellows, 106, 130, *n.* 9, 175, 251, *n.* 2; mentioned, 260; fellows of, become Franciscans, 223, 237, 277.
— Franciscans claimed as Mertonians, 154, *n.* 4, 160, 191, *n.* 4, 214, *n.* 1, 219, *n.* 8.
New, 7, *n.* 3, 58, *n.* 9, 289 : *see* London, J., warden of.
Oriel, 59, *n.* 7, 61, *n.* 7, 104.
Peckwater's Inn, 95.
St. Bernard's College: *see* Oxford Monks.
St. John's, 25, *n.* 9.
Institutions and Buildings—
University Chests, 256, 260.
University Library, exclusion of the friars from, 62; admission to, 62, 270, 275, 277.
—Bodleian, 59, 60.
— MSS. written at Oxford, 166, 208, 225, 268, *cf.* 59, 60, 245, 252.
— Books printed at, 226, 236.
— Booksellers at, 61.
— Archives, Tyssyngton's treatise kept in, 251.
University Church (St. Mary's), 44, 48, 49, 52, 84, 168, 270, 274, 275, 278, 284, 285, 287, 290, 293.
Schools, 31, 37, 41, 45, 46, 47, 261, 262, 274, 275, 279, 336; building of, 41, 265.
Margaret Professor of Divinity, 269.
OXFORD COUNTY, 122, 163.
Sheriff, 5, 14, *n.* 7, 17, 23, *n.* 1, 60, 70, *n.* 3, 297, 298, 309.
— receives land for the use of the Franciscans, 299.
OXFORD DIOCESE, 289.
Archdeacon of: *see* Mepham, Ric., Robert Marsh; 49, *n.* 8, 75, 101, *n.* 5, 102, *n.* 1.
Archdeaconry of, 129 (*see Confessions*).
Oxford, *see* Adam of; John of; Stephen of Ireland.
Owayn, Henry, heirs of, 20.

Owen, Robert : *see* Oen.
Owtred, J.: *see* Ughtred Bolton.
Oyta : *see* Henry of.

P.

P. of Worcester, his bible, 56, *n.* 3, 151.
Padua, 266, 267 : *see* Anthony of, Marsilius of.
Pady, John, mayor of Oxford, 13, 295.
Palestine, 139, *n.* 8, 178 : *see* Saracens, Missionaries, Crusades.
Palmer, Ralph, of Oxford, 296.
Papudo : *see* Anthony.
'Pardoners,' 83.
Parens : *see* John.
Paris, synod at, 194.
— University, 66, *n.* 5, 73, *n.* 1, 231, *n.* 2, 253.
— — teaching of theology, 36-7.
— Carmelites, 103.
— Dominicans at, 36, 39, 43, *n.* 7, 334, *n.* 3.
— Franciscans : general chapters at Paris, 157, 194, 309.
— — at, school for boys, 43.
— — statutes, &c., respecting, 35, 51 : *cf.* 220, 235.
— — English, called to, 67, 137, 189.
— — Oxford Franciscans teach or study at, 139, 142, 143, 154, 162, 166, 167, 182, 187, 192, 193, 213, 214, 215, 220, 222, 223, 224, 238, 242, 243, 244, 249, 283; *cf.* 211, 266, 280.
— — degrees conferred by pope, 244.
— — appointment of lecturers, 220.
— — bequest to, 103.
— — Observant Friars, 88.
— — *see also* 49, *n.* 9, 56, 155, 176.
Paris, Matthew, quoted, 31, 82, *n.* 3, 139, 177, 191.
Parkinson, 124.
Parma : *see* John of.
Parott, John: *see* Porrett.
Passelewe, Rob., justice in Eyre, 23, *n.* 1.
Pastoureaux, 193.
Paston, John, Knt., Sheriff, 99, 130, 315.
Paul, St.: *see* Bible.
Paul, Burgos, 257.
Paulinus, 188.
Payne, Hugh, Observant, 289.
Peasant Revolt, 78, *n.* 4, 84.
Peckham : *see* Gilbert.
— *see* John.
Pecock, Reginald, bp. of St. Asaph and Chichester, 263.
Pekin, Franciscan bishop of, 244.

INDEX

Peldon, 287.
Pembroke, Earl of, 264.
Penerton, James, 94.
Penitence: *see* Sack, friars of the; and Oxford, Mendicant Orders, Friars of the Sack.
Pennard, 158, *n.* 3.
— William, of Oxford, 304.
Pennis: *see* Peter de.
Penreth, John, 60.
Pentecost, bailiff of Oxford, 296.
Péraud: *see* William de.
Percevall, John, provincial minister, biogr. notice, 268.
Pereson, John, bequest, 107.
Perot, William, bequest, 107.
Perpignan, general chapter, 229.
Persole (Pershore): *see* John of.
Person, John, lector at London, 277.
Perugia, general chapter, 166, 167, 224.
Peshall, Sir J., 124.
Pestilence: *see* Oxford, City.
Peter, lecturer to the friars, bp. in Scotland, 30, 31.
— d'Ailly, cardinal, 231.
— of Baldeswell, lector, 163.
— of Gaieta, biogr. notice, 235.
— John Olivi, 144, 157, 164, 214, 215, *n.*
— of Limoges, 151, 226.
— Lombard: *see Sentences*.
— Lusetanus, Minorite, 66, *n.* 9; biogr. notice, 270.
— of Manners, Dominican, 39, 141.
— of Maricourt (Maharncuria), 209.
— Pauli de Nycopia, Oxford friar, 268.
— de Pennis, work on Mahomet, 148.
— Philargus of Candia: *see* Alexander V.
— of Sutton, lector, 165.
— of Tewkesbury, custodian of Oxford and provincial, 11, 68, 187; obtains papal privileges for the Order, 72; minister of Cologne, 188; vicar of Agnellus, 177; mentioned, 1, *n.* 1, 65, *n.* 4, 126, *n.* 3; 139, *n.* 8, 142; biographical notice.
— son of Thorald, Mayor of Oxford, 20, *n.* 5, 296.
— of Todworth, Minorite, 219.
Peterborough, diocese, 289.
Peyntour: *see* John le.
Peyrson, Thomas, Minorite, 277.
Philargus: *see* Alexander V.
Philip the Fair, King of France, 159, 161.
Philip, miller, Oxford, 295.
— of Bergamo, 148, 151.
— of Briddilton, or Bridlington, lector, 163.

Philip of Castello (Arezzo), Minorite, biogr. notice, 243.
— Torrington, bp. of Cashel, biogr. notice, 224.
— Wallensis, lectures at Lyons, 67, *n.* 1.
— Zoriton: *see* Phil. Torrington.
Pico, J., of Mirandola, 159.
Pisa: *see* Agnellus of, Albert of, Bartholomew, Francis de S. Simone.
— council of, 249.
Plummer, William, of Oxford, 110, *n.* 1, 318.
Pokelington; *see* William of.
Poker, John, 95.
Pole, Cardinal, 293.
Polton, Philip, bequest, 106.
Pomay: *see* William.
Pontefract: *see* Thomas of.
Pope, confers degrees, 35, 235, 242, 243-4, 244.
— influence in appointing provincial ministers, 70, 254, 255, 256, 261.
— English tribute, 81, 242.
Porrett, John, Minorite, admitted to University library, 62, *n.* 3; lectures on St. Paul, 113, *n.* 5; biogr. notice, 277.
Porta: *see* James de.
Portu: *see* Maurice de.
Portugal, friars from at Oxford, 66; Observants of, 265: *see* Anthony Papudo, Gonsalvo of Portugal, Peter Lusetanus, Thomas of Portugal.
Poverty: see Evangelical.
Prato: *see* William de.
Prest, wife of, burned, 286.
Preston: *see* Gilbert of, John of.
Prophet, John, dean of Hereford, 313-4.
Pulet, Isaac, Jew, 9.
Puller, Robert, Minorite, 96, *n.* 3, 285, 286, 288, 290.
Pye, Alderman, visits Oxford friaries, 117, lease of the Grey Friars, 121-3.

Q.

Quesuell, Peter, 224, *n.* 1.
Quinton (Quainton?), 25.

R.

R. de Wydeheye, lecturer to the monks at Canterbury, 66.
Radford: *see* Thomas.
Radley, 94.
Radnor, Thomas, provincial, 262; biogr. notice, 260.
Ralph of Colebruge, lector, 34, *n.* 3; biogr. notice, 139.
— of Lockysley, lector, 165.
— of Maidstone, Minorite, bp. of Hereford, helps to build Franciscan Church at Oxford, 3; biogr. notice, 182.

Ralph, of Rheims, 177.
— of Swelm (Ewelme?), Dominican prior at Oxford, 334.
— de Toftis, lector, 157.
Raphoe, bp. of, 267.
Ratforde : *see* John of.
Raxach : *see* Dalmacus de.
Raymund Gaufredi, general minister, 194; work by, 208 ; letter to, 218.
— of Laon, recommends Roger Bacon to pope, 193.
— Lullus : *see* Lully.
— of Pennaforte, 57.
Reading, Grey Friary, 4, *n.* 1, 22, 23, 27, *notes* 3, 5; 235-6, 255, 293.
— — numbers, 44, *n.* 1; in the Oxford custody, 68 ; burial at, 260.
— library, &c., 150, 166, 235-6.
— Adam Marsh called to, 137.
— monk of, 178.
— *see* John of.
Redclive: *see* Robert of.
Rede, William, of Merton, 237, 238.
Redovallensis : *see* John de Ridevaus.
Reformation, 113, 269, 272, 273, 283, 285, 286, 287, 289, 290, 291, 292, 293.
Reginald de sub muro, 19, *n.* 3.
Rense, council, 225.
Repyngdon, Philip, Lollard, 84.
Reresby: *see* Henry of.
Retherfeld (Rotherfield), 20, 305-6.
Rice: *see* Robert ap.
Richard, II, 25; favours Mendicants at Oxford, 41, *cf.* 252; Franciscans loyal to his memory, 86-7; grant to the Franciscans in arrear, 98: *see* 243, 245, 250, 253, 311, 312.
— Earl of Cornwall and King of the Romans, benefactor of the Oxford Franciscans, 25; his heart buried in their church, 25 ; known to Adam Marsh, 137.
— *socius* of W. of Nottingham, dies at Genoa, 184.
— servant of J. de Couton, 92, 310.
— Brynckley: *see* Brinkley.
— de Bury, bp. of Durham, 61.
— of Clare, escheator, 303.
— of Conyngton (Coniton), lector, provincial, 160, *n.* 5, 166; biogr. notice, 164.
— (Rufus) of Cornwall, lector; his secretary, 56, *n.* 5, 187 ; at Paris, 66, *n.* 6, 67: bequest to, 102 ; mentioned, 151, *n.* 3; biogr. notice, 142-3.
— of Cornwall, secular, 142, *n.* 5.
— of Devon, Minorite, 2, 178.
— of Drayton, lector, 168.
— Fitzralph, abp. of Armagh, attack on the Mendicant Orders, 42, 77, 79, 239-240, 248, 255; remarks on friars' libraries, 60-1 ; fellow of Balliol and chancellor, 79, 169.
Richard. of Garaford, bequest, 104.
— of Gravesend, bp. of Lincoln, 300.
— of Heythrop, of Oxford, 304.
— of Ingewrthe, Minorite, 2, 178.
— of Ireland: *see* Lorcan.
— le Lodere, grants land to the Oxford Franciscans, 19, 301.
— Lymynster, wax doctor, 43, 239.
— Malevile: *see* Malevile.
— Marsh, bp. of Durham, leaves library to Adam Marsh, 57, 135.
— Middleton, works in Franciscan library, 58, *n.* 11 ; biogr. notice of, 214.
— the Miller, leases and grants house to Franciscans at Oxford, 3, 12, 13: *see also* 20, *n.* 5, 296.
— Rufus: *see* Richard (Rufus) of Cornwall.
— le Ruys, 142, *n.* 1.
— of Slekeburne, *or* Slikeburne, confessor of Devorguila, 9 ; biogr. notice of, 216.
— of Wallingford, abbat of St. Albans, 251.
— de Wauz, Minorite, 128, *n.* 5.
— de Whitchford, collector of alms, 92, 310.
— de Wiche, bp. of Chichester, 136, 137.
Richeford, Oxford Dominican, 267.
Richmond : *see* Britanny, John of.
— (Yorkshire), Grey Friars of, 274.
Rickes, John : *see* Rycks.
Rigaldus, Minorite, 215.
Rinaldo Conti, protector of the Order, 69, *n.* 7.
Risby, Richard, Observant, 289.
Robert, of Beverley, lector, 164.
— of Bromyard, Dominican provincial, 48.
— of Capell, Minorite, 212, 335.
— of Cowton, presented for license to hear confessions, 64; mentioned, 170 ; biogr. notice, 222.
— Cross, de Cruce, lector and provincial, biogr. notice, 156-7.
— de Sancta Cruce, 156, *n.* 3.
— Eliphat : *see* Eliphat.
— of Flemengville, 9.
— of Fulham, Minorite, lecturer to the monks at Canterbury, 66.
— of Gaddesby, Minorite, 219.
— Grostete : *see* Grostete.
— Halifax: *see* Eliphat.
— of Leicester, lector, proctor of Balliol Coll., 10 ; biogr. notice, 168.

Robert Marsh, archdeacon of Oxford, 135, 136.
— le Mercer, lets house to Franciscans in Oxford, 2, 12, 13, 178: *see also* 20, *n.* 5, 296.
— of Mogynton, Minorite, 219.
— of Newmarket, Dominican, 320, 321, 324, 335.
— of Nottingham, 298.
— of Redclive, lector, 173.
— ap Rice, 272.
— of Thornham, custodian of Cambridge, 65, 139, *n.* 8.
— de Trenge, warden of Merton, 100, 239.
— of Ware, biogr. notice, 211.
— of Watlington, of Oxford, 304.
— de Wysete (Wyshed), provincial, 241.
Roberts, Ric., 96, *n.* 3, 288.
Roby, Minorite at Oxford, 265.
Rochester, bp. of: *see* Merton, Walter de; Fisher, John.
— archdeacon : *see* Browne, Ric.
Rockysley : *see* Ralph Lockysley.
Rodano : *see* Alan of.
Roderham, Ric., proctor of Balliol Coll. 10, 260.
Roderic Witton, Minorite, 271.
Rodnore, Ric., Minorite at Oxford, 265.
Rodromo : *see* Adam Wodham.
Roduricus, Minorite, 271.
Rodyngton : *see* John of.
Roger, king's almoner, 5, 307.
— Dominican, 156.
— Bacon : *see* Bacon.
— de Barton, Minorite, 219.
— Compotista, monk of Bury, 210.
— Conway, provincial, mentioned, 79, 238, 241, 312; biogr. notice, 239.
— Frisby: *see* Frisby.
— de Marston, lector and provincial, mentioned, 159; biogr. notice, 157.
— de Merlawe (Marlow), 165, *n.* 2, 218.
— of Thurkelby, 298.
— of Wendover, 191.
— of Wesham, lecturer to the friars, bp. of Lichfield, 30, 31 and *n.* 5, 168.
Roger, Thomas, warden of Fanciscans, Gloucester, biogr. notice, 268.
Rogers, John, bequest, 108.
Rome; appeals to the pope, 39, 81, 138, 186, 258.
— Lateran Council, 267.
— Franciscans, general chapters, 35, 267; Roman province, 256; Oxford friars at, 127, 180; as ambassadors, 159, 161, 177; as lecturers, 67, 155, 161; deposition of Elias, 69, 181.
— Albert of Pisa buried at, 181.
— mentioned, 313.

Romehale, 178.
Romseye, John, regent master, 252.
Roper, Richard, Minorite, 119, 293.
Rose, Thomas, Minorite, 270.
Roskild, bp. of, 140, *n.* 6.
Rous, John, at Oxford, 25, *n.* 4, 26; quoted, 191, 193, 195.
Rufus, Adam, biogr. notice, 179.
— Richard: *see* Richard (Rufus) of Cornwall.
Rundel, Thomas, lector, biogr. notice, 162.
Rupellis : *see* John de.
Rupescissa : *see* John de.
Russell, John, Minorite, biogr. notice, 218.
— John, bequest, 106.
— Peter, provincial biographical notice, 255.
— Sir Robert, 106.
— William, Warden of Grey Friars, London, heresies of, 85–6; biogr. notice, 257.
Rycks, John, Minorite, reformer, 113, *n.* 5 ; biogr. notice, 286.
Rygbye, Nicholas, 274.
Ryley, Edward, Minorite, 113, *n.* 6; biographical notice, 287.

S.

Sabina, cardinal bp., protector of the Order, 70; *see* Clement IV.
Sack, Friars of the, suppressed, 18 : *see* Oxford, Mendicant Orders.
Saham : *see* Herveius de.
St. Alban's, abbats of, 241, 248 ; document dated at, 297.
S. Amando: *see* Alienora de.
St. Andrew's, Vercelli, 135.
St. Asaph, church of, 274 : *see* Standish, Henry.
St. Crida, parish of (Exeter), 105.
St. Cross : *see* Martin de Sta. Cruce; Robert Cross.
St. David's, bp. of, 30, 31, 136.
St. Dunstan : *see* Thomas of.
St. Edwardstowe, 107.
St. John: *see* John of St. John.
St. John of Jerusalem, brethren of, 13.
St. Simon : *see* Francis de S. Simone.
Salamanca, University, 242.
Salford, Richard, Warden at Oxford, sues for a debt, 99, 315 ; biogr. notice, 130.
Salisbury, 104, 223.
— Grey Friars, martyrology, 138, *n.* 10; Convent, 223.
Sall, Nicholas, Minorite, 286.
Salomon : *see* Solomon.
Sanders, Gilbert, Minorite, 47, 51, *n.* 10, 52; biogr. notice, 275.

INDEX. 365

Sanderson, John, Minorite, 275.
Sanderson, Robert, Minorite, 50, *n.* 1, 52, *n.* 11; biogr. notice, 274.
Sandon, Brian, *syndicus* of the Oxford Minorites, legal business, 93, 94; scandal about, 94: *see also* 96, *n.* 1, 119, 270.
Sanford : *see* John de.
Saracens, 8, 63, 128, 178, 179, 244.
Sauvage : *see* Vincent le.
Savernak forest, 21.
Savona, 266.
Savonarola, 55, *n.* 3.
Saxony, Franciscan province, 181, 257, 237.
Sawnders: *see* Sanders.
Schankton, John, Minorite, bequest to, 104, 251.
Scharshille, William, biogr. notice, 238.
Schaton : *see* Walter de Chatton.
Schism, the great, 249, 250, 252-3.
Schomberg (Scombergt): *see* Nicholas de.
Schyrbourne : *see* William de.
— John, 165, *n.* 8.
Scotland, Minorites in, 66; provincial of, 180.
— parliament in, 238.
— mentioned, 290.
Scotto : *see* Ottaviano.
Scotus : *see* John Duns.
Sebyndon, 105.
Seller, J., warden at London, 269.
Seman, John, bequest, 109.
Sentences of Peter Lombard; study of, 37, 38, 45, 46, 47, 65, *n.* 3, 81, 131, 143, 162, 242, 246, 249, 250, 257, 262, 284, 292, 336–338; works on, 151, 152, 157, 158, 160, 164, 166, 167, 168, 170, 172, 173, 182, 213, 214, 216, 217, 220, 222, 223, *n.* 3, 224, *n.* 5, 227, 235, 238, 242, 249, 254.
Serlo, dean of Exeter, 7, *n.* 5.
Sewal, St., abp. of York, 136.
Sherburn (Durham), master of the hospital, 102.
Shifford, 107.
Shotover, 5.
Shrewsbury, Grey Friars, foundation, 129; burial at, 168.
Sicily, Minorite of, wax doctor, 43, 239.
Simcox, William, of Oxford, 319.
Simeon : *see* Henry Simeonis.
Simon, son of Benedict, 15, 298–9.
— Bruni, Minorite at Toulouse, 311, *n.* 1.
— of Esseby, Minorite, 189.
— minister of Germany, 160, *n.* 9.

Simon, of Ghent, Chancellor of Oxford, 162, *n.* 16, 219, *n.* 4.
— de Montfort : *see* Montfort.
— Tunstede, regent master, provincial, 60, 174; biogr. notice, 241.
Sixtus IV, 266.
Skelton, William, bequest, 105.
Slekeburne, *or* Slikeburne : *see* Richard of.
Smith, Gerard, Minorite, 53, *n.* 2; biogr. notice, 270.
— James, Minorite, 119, 293.
— John, Minorite, 45, 47, 51, *n.* 3, 52; biogr. notice, 274.
— — Minorite, 47, 49, *n.* 4, 51, *n.* 6; biogr. notice, 269.
— — gent., 124.
Smyth : *see* Smith.
Sneyt, 48.
Snotly : *see* Notly.
Solomon, warden of the London Franciscans, 89, *n.* 2.
Solomon of Ingeham, Dominican, accuses Franciscans, 76, 320, 321, 324, 326, 327, 328, 329, 334-5.
Somer, John, Minorite astronomer, 250, *n.* 3, 251, *n.* 1; biogr. notice, 244–6.
Somer, Thomas, of Oxford, 304.
Sorel, Stephen, lector, 172.
Southampton, wine at, 5; chapter of Minorites at, 69.
— *see* Walter de Chatton.
Sowche, John, bequest, 109.
Spain, friars from, at Oxford, 66, 243.
— Peter Russel teaches in, 255.
— Albert of Pisa minister of, 181.
Spellusbury, 109.
Stafford, John, warden at Coventry, 293.
Staffordshire, 238.
— John, Minorite, 119, 293.
Stamford, Grey Friars, in Oxford custody, 68, 172; school at, 25, *n.* 3 (?); burial at, 165; mentioned, 257.
— Carmelites, convocation, 85, 151.
— *see* John of.
Standish (Lancs.), 271, 274.
— E., 101, *n.* 3.
— Henry, Minorite, bp. of S. Asaph, bequests to Grey Friars, Oxford, 24, 61, *n.* 6, 109, 276; opposes new learning, 112; upholds secular power, 114; biogr. notice, 271-4.
Stanle : *see* John de.
Stanschaw, Thomas, lector, biogr. notice, 172.
Stapleton : *see* John de.
Stargil : *see* William de.
Steeple Aston, 109, *n.* 2.

Stephen, St., founder of the Order of Grammont, 185.
— of Ireland, Minorite, 66, *n.* 5; biogr. notice, 213.
— Sorel: *see* Sorel.
— de Wytun, secular master, 332, 334.
Steventon priory, 16, *n.* 2, 20.
Stisted, 287.
Stokes, Peter, Carmelite, 84.
Stokesley, John, bp. of London, 281, *n.* 3.
Ston, John and Agnes, 56, *n.* 6.
Stoughton, Rob., bookseller, 172.
Strasburg (Argentina), province, 66, *n.* 10: *see* 290.
Stratton, Gilbert, 162, *n.* 8.
Straw, Jack, his confession, 78, *n.* 4.
Strensham, Henry, 293, *n.* 3.
Stretsham, Henry, Minorite, 116, *n.* 7, 293.
Strey, Thomas, of Colchester, 282, *n.* 9.
Studeley, Christopher, Minorite, biogr. notice, 269.
Suffolk, 99, 130, 166, 241, 315.
Sunday, John, Minorite, 46, *n.* 1, 10, 336; biogr. notice, 262.
Surrey, 163.
Sussex, 154.
Sutthon: *see* Laurence of.
Sutton, 233: *see* Henry of, Peter of.
— Oliver, bp. of Lincoln, 18.
Swelm (Ewelme?): *see* Ralph of.
Swerford, 109.
Swinfeld, Ric., bp. of Hereford, 168, 169.
Swynshed, 241.
Sylvester, pope, 257, *n.* 3.
Symon, Rob., servant of Dr. Baskerfeld, 132.
Syria, 183: *see* Saracens.

T.

Taillur, Richard, of Oxford, 296.
Talbot, Rob., 236.
Tartars, 128, 244.
Tate, J., will mentioned, 90, *n.* 1.
Taylor, John: *see* Cardmaker.
Taler, Henry le, and Alice his wife, 16, 20, *n.* 5.
Templars: *see* Knights.
Terra Laboris, Franciscan province, 235.
Tewkesbury: *see* John of; Peter of.
Thacker, Cromwell's servant, 117.
Thomas, of Anesti, 138.
— Aquinas, as viewed by Roger Bacon, 42, 73, *n.* 1; his teaching impugned, 73-4, 154; attacked by W. de Mara, 215, 216; works by, 154, 156, 236.
— of Barneby, lector, biogr. notice, 160.

Thomas, de Bek', secular master, 331.
— Bernewell : *see* Bernewell.
— of Bungay, lector and provincial, influenced by Bacon, 195, *n.* 4; biogr. notice of, 153.
— of Cantilupe, St., bp. of Hereford, pupil of Peckham, 154.
— Docking, lector, 36, *n.* 5, 37, *n.* 1; bible assigned to, 56, *n.* 3; takes part in controversy with Dominicans, 324, 325, 326, 335; biogr. notice, 151-2.
— of Eccleston, his chronicle quoted, 1, 6, 11, 30, 65, 70, 71, 72, 126, 128, 129, 134, 135, 143, 177, 178, 180, 181, 182, 184, 185, 189, and notes *passim*; mentioned, 320; student at Oxford, 67; biogr. notice, 189-191.
— of Ireland, doctor of the Sorbonne, 148.
— of Kingsbury (Kyngesbery, &c.), provincial, 60; mentioned, 242, *n.* 5, 245, 251; biogr. notice, 250.
— of London, benefactor of the Oxford friars, 92, 310.
— of Maidstone (Maydenstan), biogr. notice, 186-7.
— of Malmesbury, Dominican, 48.
— Netter of Walden : *see* Netter.
— Oterborne: *see* Oterborne.
— of Pontefract, lector, 164.
— of Portugal, biogr. notice, 242.
— Radford, lector, 174.
— Radnor : *see* Radnor.
— Rundel, lector, 162.
— of St. Dunstan, lector, 168.
— Stanschaw, lector, 272.
— de Valeynes, grants land to the Minorites at Oxford, 15, 21, 298.
— Wallensis, lecturer to the Minorites, bp. of St. David's, 30, 31, 136.
— Wallensis, *or* Walleys, Dominican, 144, *n.* 7, 149, 150, 151, 170.
— of Wycombe : *see* Waldere, Th.
— of Wynchelse, Minorite, 256.
— of York, lector, inception of, 38-9, 128; lectures at Oxford, 65, *n.* 2; mentioned, 143, *n.* 2, 186; biogr. notice, 140-142.
— John, bequest, 105.
— William, obtains part of the Grey Friars' property, 122, 123.
Thorald: *see* Peter, son of.
Thorley, 283.
Thornall, John, Minorite, 44, *n.* 4, 51, *n.* 7; grace to, 338; biogr. notice, 279.
Thornham : *see* Robert of.
Thornton : *see* John of.
Throckmorton, Rob., bequest, 108.
Thüringen, 257.

Thurkelby : see Roger of.
Tinmouth, John, Minorite, bp. of Argos, bequest to Oxford Minorites, 108 ; biogr. notice, 271.
Tithemersch : see William.
Todworth : see Peter of.
Toledo, Minorite of, 209.
Tomsun, John, Minorite, 116, *n.* 7, 288.
Tomsun, Thomas, Minorite, 116, *n.* 7, 290.
Toulouse, Minorite of, 208 ; general chapter, 219, 221.
— University, 242, 311, *n.* 1.
Treners, Ric., Minorite, 262.
Trenge : see Robert de.
Trent (river), 302, 303, 304.
Treviso, Albert of Pisa, minister of, 181 ; see Henry de Ceruise.
Trinitarian Friars, bequest to, 103.
Tripoli, heroism of an Oxford Franciscan at, 8.
Tritheim, 148.
Trivet, Nicholas, Dominican, on J. Peckham, 155.
Tryley : see Ryley.
Tryvytlam (Trevytham), Ric., biogr. notice, 253.
Tuam, abp. of, 267.
Tully, Dionisius, Dominican, heretical teaching in Ireland, 266.
Turco, Robert, 209.
Tunstede : see Simon.
Tuscany, Albert of Pisa, minister of, 181 ; Bernard of Gascony, minister of, 311, *n.* 1.
Tyburn, Franciscans executed at, 87.
Tyeys, Henry, grants land to the Minorites at Oxford, 19, 301.
Tyndale, quoted, 112.
Tyngewick : see Nicholas de.
Tyssyngton, John, Minorite, regent master, 82, *n.* 2, 85 ; biogr. notice, 251.

U.

Ubertino de Casali, Minorite, 215.
Ughtred, Bolton, monk of Durham, 81, *n.* 7, 242, 243, 253, *n.* 5, 254.
Urban V, 311, *n.* 1.
Urban VI, pope, 243 ; oath of obedience to, taken by English Franciscans, 250.

V.

Valeynes : see Thomas de.
Valeys, John, lector, 175.
Valla, Laurence, 171, *n.* 2.
Vallibus : see Anthony de.
Varro : See William of Ware.
Vavasour, William, warden at Oxford, pension to, 119, *n.* 4 ; mentioned, 268, *n.* 2 ; biogr. notice, 130.
Venice, printing press at, 267, *n.* 5.
Ver, G. de : see William of Ware.
Vercelli, abbot of St. Andrew's at, 135.
Vienne, Council of, 163, 164.
Vilers : see Valeys, John.
Vincent Boys : see Boys.
— le Sauvage, Dominican, 321, 323, 324.
Vodromio : see Adam Wodham.
Volterra, J. Gallensis of, 150.

W.

Wakerfeld : see Alan of.
Wakering Parva, 287.
Walden : see Netter, (Thomas) of.
Waldere, Thomas, of Wycombe, bequest, 102.
Wales, 31 ; John Wallensis sent as ambassador to rebel Welsh, 144.
Waleys, Henry, mayor of London, 219.
— Thomas : see Thomas Wallensis.
Walker, William, Minorite, lectures on St. Paul, 113, *n.* 5, 284.
Walle, William, Minorite, 45, *n.* 6, 51, *n.* 8, 52 ; biogr. notice, 277.
Wallensis: see John ; Laurence Briton ; Philip ; Thomas.
Wallingford : see Richard of.
Wallys : see Wellys, Robert.
Walonges : see Thomas de Valeyns.
Walshe, Gilbert, Minorite, 261.
— Nicholas, Minorite, 261.
Walter de Berney, bequest, 104.
— de Bosevile, Minorite, 219.
— Brinkley : see Brinkley.
— de Bukenham, friar of Babwell, 56, *n.* 4.
— of Cantilupe, bp. of Worcester, 137, 308.
— de Chatton, lector, 60, 134 ; biogr. notice, 170.
— canon of Dunstable, becomes Minorite, 180.
— de Foxle, lector, 169.
— of Gloucester, escheator, 303.
— de Knolle, lector, 158.
— de Landen, Minorite, 212, 320.
— de Madele, lecturer in some Franciscan convent, 34 ; biographical notice, 188.
— de Merton, bp. of Rochester, &c., friend of Adam Marsh, and benefactor of the friars, 9, 102, 137, 187.
Waltham : see John of.
Ware (Herts.), Grey Friars of, 91, *n.* 4, 211, 213 ; burial at, 259.
— see John of ; Robert of ; William of.

Warham, William, abp. of Canterbury, 23, 115.
Warin of Dorchester, and Juliana his wife, 16.
Warminster: *see* Adam of.
Warwick, countess of, 300, *n*. 1.
Wastenays, John, Minorite, biogr. notice, 252.
Waterford: *see* William of.
Waterperry, 108.
Waterstoke, 107.
Watlington: *see* Robert of.
Wauz: *see* Richard de.
Waynflete, William, bp. of Winchester, 266.
Wearmouth, Adam Marsh had a living near, 135.
Welle, John, Minorite D.D., his property stolen, 78; 175, 311.
Welleford, 109.
Wells, diocese, 261; canon of, 105; chancellor of, 291.
— John, 175.
Wellys, Robert, provincial, 255.
Welsh: *see* Wales; Wallensis.
Wendover: *see* Roger of.
Went, John, lector and provincial, 174.
Wesham: *see* Roger of.
Westburg: *see* John of.
Westminster, burial at, 25; sermon at, 284; council at, 81, *n*. 7, 242; mentioned, 267, *n*. 2, 298, 300, 301, 302, 306, 308, 310, 312, 315.
Weston: *see* Nicholas de.
— Ric. LL.B., 96, 287.
Westover: *see* John of.
Wetherset, 173, *n*. 6.
Whatele: *see* William of.
Wheathamstede, John, abbat of St. Albans, 248.
Whitchford: *see* Richard de.
Whitehead, David, reformer, 288, *n*. 7.
Whyte, William, heresies, 256.
Whythede, David, Minorite, 288.
Whytheed, John, of Ireland, 255.
Whytwell, John, Minorite, 51, 54, *n*. 3; biogr. notice, 260.
Wiche: *see* Richard de.
Wiclif, quoted, 27, 43, 50, 78, 79; his English prose, 64; on friars' sermons, 64, *n*. 4: his poor priests, 82, *n*. 3; points of agreement with the friars, 81, 114, *n*. 4; attack on the friars, 81, *seq*.; relations to W. Woodford, 81, 246; works written against him, 246, 248, 251; mentioned, 55, 112.
Wileford, William, son of Richard de: *see* William.
Wiley (Essex), 284.
William, warden of the Franciscans at Paris, 220.

William, clerk of Oxford, 296.
— — of Adreston, 304-5.
— — of Auvergne, 192-3, 206.
— de Colvile, Minorite, 179.
— de Conchis, 247, *n*. 7.
— Cornish, 212, 320.
— of Esseby, warden of the Grey Friars, Oxford, 7, *n*. 7, 178, *n*. 2; biogr. notice, 125-6.
— of Euston, of Oxford, 304.
— of Exeter, Minorite, biogr. notice, 217.
— of Gainsborough, lector, lectures at Rome, 68, provincial minister, 157, 158; royal ambassador, 7, *n*. 10, 159; attends general chapter, 159, 218; bp. of Worcester, 162; biographical notice, 160-2.
— of Heddele, lector, accompanies Prince Edward on Crusade, 8; mentioned, 151, *n*. 4, 335; biogr. notice, 153.
— de Hodum, Hozon (Hotham ?), 156; cursory lecturer, 334.
— of Leominster, friar, 134, *n*. 2; biogr. notice, 217.
— lord Lovell: *see* Lovell.
— de Mara, Minorite, influenced by Roger Bacon, 195, *n*. 4; biogr. notice, 215.
— of Constance, 216, *n*. 3.
— de Melton, heresies of, 86; biogr. notice, 251.
— de Menyl, proctor of Balliol College, 10, 158.
— of Middleton, Minorite, 214, *n*. 2.
— of Newport, Minorite.
— of Nottingham, provincial minister, 126, 127, 128, 187; signs Henry III's charter to the University, 8; increase in the friars' property under him, 14; retort to a friar, 28; extends University teaching, 65; friend of Grostete, 69, *n*. 1; popularity, 70; obtains papal privileges for the Order, 72; mentioned, 126, 127, 128, 129, 136, 139, *n*. 8, 141, 155, *n*. 2, 165, 186, 187, 189, 190; biographical notice, 182-185.
— of Nottingham, lector and provincial; copies works of Nicholas Gorham, 57; mentioned, 185, 224, *n*. 7; biogr. notice, 165.
— of Ockham, lectures abroad, 68; followers at Oxford, 77, 173; on evangelical poverty, 77, 164; mentioned, 151, *n*. 7, 166, *n*. 3, 168, 172, *n*. 11, 216, 217, *n*. 3.
— biographical notice, 224; works, 224-234.
— de Péraud, 147.
— of Pokelington, Minorite, biogr. notice, 188.

INDEX. 369

William de la Pomay, secular master, 331.
— de Prato, French Minorite, bp. of Pekin, 66, *n.* 6; biogr. notice, 244.
— of St. Amour, 154.
— of Schyrbourne, lector, biogr. notice, 165.
— of Shareshull, 238.
— de Stargil, Dominican, 324, 325, 326.
— Tithemersch, provincial, biogr. notice, 238.
— of Ware, Minorite, biogr. notice, 213.
— of Waterford, Minorite, 247, 249.
— of Whatele, of Oxford, 304.
— son of Richard de Wileford, of Oxford, his house bought for the Minorites, 13, 90, *n.* 6, 295–6.
— de Wodeford, abbat, 249.
— Woodford (Widford, Wydeforde, &c.), Minorite; on the clothing of the Grey Friars in England, 4, *n.* 1; on the statutes of Benedict XII, 35, *n.* 2; robbed, 5; defends admission of children into the Orders, 80; relations to Wiclif, 81; papal privileges to, 312–3; quoted or mentioned, 42, 167, 170, 195, *n.* 4, 213, 222, 252; biographical notice, 246–9.
— of Worcester, description of the Grey Friars Church, Oxford, 24.
— of Wykeham, 58, *n.* 9.
— of Wykham, Minorite, 212, 323.
— of York, Minorite, 179.
Williams, David, Minorite, 53, *n.* 6; biogr. notice, 278.
— John, Minorite, biogr. notice, 287.
Willoughby: *see* Hugh of.
Wilsnach, miraculous blood of, 257.
Wiltshire, 169.
Winchcombe: *see* Kidderminster (Ric.), abbat of.
Winchelsea: *see* John of; Thomas Wynchelse.
Winchester, Grey Friars at, 4, *n.* 4; numbers, 44, *n.* 1.
— bp. of (Aymer de Lesignan), 136.
— prior and convent of, 136.
Windsor, documents dated at, 297, 298.
Winslow: *see* Wynslo, Richard.
Wisbech, 161.
Witnam, near Oxford, said to be Roger Bacon's birthplace, 191, *n.* 1.
Witton, Roderic, 271.
Wodham: *see* Adam.
Wolsey, Cardinal, 113, 115, 269, 272, 280, 281.
Wood, Anthony, 12, 23, 30, 85, 123, 124, 133, 135, 199.

Woodford: *see* William.
Woodstock, documents dated at, 60, *n.* 2, 307.
Worcester, Grey Friars at, 108, 239; Adam Marsh enters the Order at, 135; burial at, 165.
— bps. of: *see* Walter of Cantilupe, William of Gainsborough.
— *see* P. of, William of.
Wrenche, John son of Walter, bequest, 103.
Writtel, Roger, alms in memory of, 100.
Wrixham, 274.
Wych (Wyth), Laurence, mayor of Oxford, grants land to the friars, 17, 20, 299.
Wychewood forest, 5.
Wycombe: *see* Joanna, wife of Walter of.
— *see* Waldere of.
Wydeheye (*or* Sydeheye): *see* R. de Wydeheye.
Wygmund (Wygerius), German friar, 69, 126, 142.
Wykeham: *see* William of.
Wykham, master John, 185.
Wyllyot, John, fellow of Merton Coll., 175.
Wylton: *see* John of.
Wynchelse: *see* Thomas.
Wynslo, Richard, 96, *n.* 2.
Wyntun: *see* John de.
Wysete (Wyshed): *see* Robert de.
Wystantowe, 103.
Wythman, Thomas, Minorite, 119, 293.
Wytton-Gylbert, 292.
Wytun: *see* Stephen de.
Wyz, John and Emma, grant land to Minorites in Oxford, 19, 301.
Wy3ht, Minorite, 267.

Y.

York, abp. of: *see* Sewal.
— provincial council of, 160, 165.
— canons, &c., of, 102, 105, 165, 166, 235.
— schools and chapter at, 242.
— mystery plays at, 259.
— Grey Friars of, 27, *n.* 9; studium, 35, *n.* 3; burial at, 242.
— — custodians, 127, 129; warden, 130.
— documents dated at, 303, 304.
— *see* Adam of; Thomas of; William of.
Yorkshire, 156, *n.* 2, 188, 222, 242, 261, 274.

Z.

Zoriton: *see* Philip Torrington.
Zortone: *see* John of Thornton.
Zouche, John, provincial, deposed, 70, 253, 254.

FINIS.

www.ingramcontent.com/pod-product-compliance
Lightning Source LLC
Chambersburg PA
CBHW072131220426
43664CB00013B/2208

www.ingramcontent.com/pod-product-compliance
Lightning Source LLC
Chambersburg PA
CBHW062016220426
43662CB00010B/1359